Global Marketing
Fourth Edition

This textbook introduces students to the important concepts of global marketing today, and their managerial implications. Designed to be shorter than many other textbooks, *Global Marketing* focuses on getting to the point faster.

Increasingly, marketing activities must be integrated at a global level. Yet, the enduring influence of culture requires marketers to adapt local strategies in light of cultural differences. *Global Marketing* takes a similar strategic approach, recognizing the need to address both the forces of globalization and those of localization. Other key features include:

- Coverage of often overlooked topics, such as the competitive rise of China's state-owned enterprises; the importance of diasporas as target markets; and the emerging threat to legitimate marketers from transnational criminal organizations.
- A chapter dedicated to understanding global and local competitors, setting the stage for ongoing discussion of both buyers and competitors in an increasingly competitive global marketplace.
- Extensive real-life examples and cases from developed and emerging markets, including insights into the often-overlooked markets of Africa, Latin America, and the Middle East.

Written in a student-friendly style, previous editions have received praise from both students and instructors. This edition continues to build on this strong foundation, making this the book of choice for students of global marketing classes.

Kate Gillespie is Associate Professor of International Business and Marketing at the University of Texas at Austin, USA. She has served as chair of the Global Marketing Special Interest Group of the American Marketing Association, and her research has appeared in top academic journals in the fields of international business, marketing, and area studies.

H. David Hennessey is Professor (Emeritus) of Marketing and International Business at Babson College, USA. He has taught courses on global marketing, marketing strategy, and sales strategy, and has participated in executive education programs around the world.

COMPANION @ WEBSITE www.routledge.com/cw/Gillespie

Global Marketing

Fourth Edition

Kate Gillespie and
H. David Hennessey

Routledge
Taylor & Francis Group

NEW YORK AND LONDON

First published 2016
by Routledge
711 Third Avenue, New York, NY 10017

and by Routledge
2 Park Square, Milton Park, Abingdon, Oxon OX14 4RN

*Routledge is an imprint of the Taylor & Francis Group,
an Informa business*

© 2016 Taylor & Francis

Library of Congress Cataloguing-in-Publication Data
Gillespie, Kate.
    Global marketing / by Kate Gillespie and David Hennessey. —
4th edition.
        pages cm
    Includes bibliographical references and index.
    1. Export marketing.   2. Export marketing—
Management.   I. Hennessey, Hubert D.   II. Title.
    HF1416.G54 2015
    658.8′4—dc23
    2014041447

ISBN: 978-0-7656-4295-0 (hbk)
ISBN: 978-1-315-71688-6 (ebk)

Typeset in Sabon
by Apex CoVantage, LLC

Printed and bound by CPI Group (UK) Ltd, Croydon, CR0 4YY

Brief Contents

Preface   xix
Acknowledgments   xxv

  1   **Introduction to Global Marketing**   1

Part 1
Understanding the Global Marketing Environment   15

  2   **The Global Economy**   17

  3   **Cultural and Social Forces**   55

  4   **Political and Regulatory Climate**   95

Part 2
Analyzing Global Opportunities   133

  5   **Global Markets**   135

  6   **Global Competitors**   167

  7   **Global Marketing Research**   199

Part 3
Developing Global Participation Strategies   239

  8   **Global Market Participation**   241

  9   **Global Market Entry Strategies**   277

Part 4
Designing Global Marketing Programs   309

   10 **Global Product Strategies**   311

   11 **Global Strategies for Services, Brands and Social Marketing**   341

   12 **Pricing for International and Global Markets**   373

   13 **Managing Global Distribution Channels**   409

   14 **Global Promotion Strategies**   443

   15 **Managing Global Advertising**   475

Part 5
Managing the Global Marketing Effort   503

   16 **Organizing for Global Marketing**   505

        Country Market Report   537
        Glossary   545
        Index   559

Detailed Contents

Preface   xix
Acknowledgments   xxv

1 Introduction to Global Marketing   1

The Importance of Global Markets   3
  Why Companies Seek Global Markets   3
The Development of Global Marketing   5
  Domestic Marketing   5
  Export Marketing   6
  International Marketing   6
  Pan-Regional Marketing   8
  Global Marketing   8
Why Study Global Marketing?   9
  A Need for Global Mindsets   9
  Organization of This Book   10

Part 1
Understanding the Global Marketing Environment   15

2 The Global Economy   17

International Trade: An Overview   18
  International Dependence of Nations   19
  The Growth in World Trade   20
The Basic Theories of World Trade: Absolute, Comparative
  and Competitive Advantage   20
  Absolute Advantage   21
  Comparative Advantage   21
  Competitive Advantage   23

Global Outsourcing 24

Balance of Payments 25

Exchange Rates 27

   The Foreign Exchange Market   28

   Causes of Exchange Rate Movements   29

   Managed Currencies   30

   Implications for Global Marketers   32

International Agencies for Promoting Economic and Monetary Stability 36

   International Monetary Fund (IMF)   36

   World Bank   36

   Group of Seven   37

Protectionism and Trade Restrictions 37

   Tariffs   38

   Quotas   38

   Orderly Marketing Arrangements and Voluntary Export Restrictions   39

   Nontariff Trade Barriers   39

   Restrictions on Foreign Exchange   40

   General Agreement on Tariffs and Trade (GATT)   40

   World Trade Organization (WTO)   41

Economic Integration as a Means of Promoting Trade 41

   Free-Trade Areas   42

   Customs Unions   43

   Common Markets   43

   Monetary Unions   43

The Globalization Controversy 44

3 Cultural and Social Forces 55

A Definition of Culture 58

   Cultural Influences on Marketing   58

   Isolating Cultural Influences   59

Religion 59

   Marketing and Western Religions   59

   Marketing and Islam   62

   Marketing and Eastern Religions   64

The Family 65

   Extended Families   67

   Beyond the Family   68

Education 69

Attitudes Toward Time 71

   Monochronic versus Polychronic Cultures and Temporal Orientation   71

   Work and Leisure Time   72

Material Culture and Aesthetics 72

The Hofstede Measures of Culture 73

Power Distance   73
Individualism-Collectivism   76
Masculinity-Femininity   77
Uncertainty Avoidance   77
Uses and Limitations of the Hofstede Measures   78
Cultural Change   79
Language and Communication   81
Forms of Address   81
The Context of Language   82
Body Language   83
Showing Emotion   83
Overcoming the Language Barrier   84
Translating and Translators   84
Translation Problems   85
Which Language to Learn?   85
Adapting to Cultural Differences   86

4 Political and Regulatory Climate   **95**

Host Country Political Climate   97
Political Motivations   97
National Sovereignty and the Goal of Self-Preservation   98
The Need for National Security   99
Fostering National Prosperity   99
Enhancing Prestige   100
Promoting Ideology   101
Protecting Cultural Identity   101
Host Country Pressure Groups   102
Host Government Actions   102
Government Subsidies   102
Ownership Restrictions   103
Operating Conditions   103
Boycotts of Firms   104
Takeovers   105
Home Country Political Forces   105
Home Country Actions   105
Home Country Pressure Groups   107
Legal Environments   108
Common Law   108
Civil Law   108
Islamic Law   109
Socialist Law   109
National Regulatory Environments   110

Legal Evolution   110
Attitudes Toward Rules   112
Regulatory Change   113
Predicting Regulatory Change   113
Managing Regulatory Change   114
Political Risk   116
Political Risk Assessment   117
Risk Reduction Strategies   119
Global Marketing and Terrorism   122

Part 2
Analyzing Global Opportunities   **133**

5 Global Markets   **135**

Understanding Markets and Buyers   136
The Consumer Market   137
Ability to Buy   137
Consumer Needs   139
Consumer Behavior   139
Segmenting Markets   141
Business Markets   148
The Business Buyer's Needs   148
Developing Business Relationships   149
Marketing to Global Buyers   150
Government Markets   151
The Buying Process   151
Government Contracts in Developing Countries   152
Bribery and Government Markets   155

6 Global Competitors   **167**

The Globalization of Competition   169
Global Firm versus Global Firm   169
Global Firm versus Local Firm   171
Strategies for Local Firms   172
Cultural Attitudes Toward Competition   174
Competition in Europe   174
Competition in Japan   175
Competition in Emerging Markets   176
Competitors from Emerging Markets   177
State-Owned Enterprises   178
Business Groups   181
New Global Players   182
Home Country Actions and Global Competitiveness   182

The Country-of-Origin Advantage   183
   Managing Country-of-Origin Perceptions   184
   Beyond Quality   185

7 Global Marketing Research   199

The Scope of Global Marketing Research   200
Challenges in Planning International Research   203
The Research Process   203
   Problem Definition and Development of Research Objectives   203
   Data Collection   204
Utilizing Secondary Data   204
   Sources of Secondary Data   204
   Problems with Secondary Data   205
Analysis by Inference   207
   Related Products   207
   Relative Market Size   207
   Analysis of Demand Patterns   208
Collecting Primary Data   208
   Observation   208
   Focus Groups   209
   Surveys   211
   Social Media and Big Data   214
   Government Regulation of Data Collection   215
   Comparing Studies Across Cultures   216
Studying the Competition   216
Outsourcing Research   219
Developing a Global Information System   220

Part 3
Developing Global Participation Strategies   239

8 Global Market Participation   241

Internationalizing Marketing Operations   243
   Opportunistic Expansion   243
   Pursuing Potential Abroad and Diversifying Risk   243
   Exploiting Different Market Growth Rates   244
   Following Customers Abroad   244
   Globalizing for Defensive Reasons   245
   Born Globals   245
   Is There a First-Mover Advantage?   246
Evaluating National Markets   246
   Standalone Attractive Markets   246
   Globally Strategic Markets   247

Geographic Market Choices   248
   Targeting Developed Economies   249
   Targeting Developing Countries and Emerging Markets   250
   Targeting BRIC and Beyond   253
Country Selection   254
   The Screening Process   254
   Criteria for Selecting Target Countries   255
   Listing Selection Criteria   258
   Psychic Distance   259
   Grouping International Markets   261
In-Country Expansion   262
Limits to Expansion   262
Exit Strategies   263
   Tough Competition   264
   Financial Difficulties   264
   Refocus on the Home Market   264
   Political Considerations   264
Re-entry   265

9 Global Market Entry Strategies   **277**

Exporting as an Entry Strategy   279
   Indirect Exporting   279
   Direct Exporting   281
Foreign Production as an Entry Strategy   284
   Licensing   284
   Franchising   286
   Local Manufacturing   288
Ownership Strategies   290
   Wholly Owned Subsidiaries   290
   Joint Ventures   291
   Strategic Alliances   295
Entering Markets through Mergers and Acquisitions   296

Part 4
Designing Global Marketing Programs   **309**

10 Global Product Strategies   **311**

Product Design in a Global Environment   313
   Benefits of Product Standardization   313
   Benefits of Product Adaptation   314
   Climatic, Infrastructure and Use Conditions   315
   Adapting Products to Cultural Preferences   316
   Product Size and Dimensions   317

Cost and Price Considerations   317
Adapting to Performance and Quality Expectations   318
Global Standards   318
Packaging and Labeling for Global Markets   321
Packaging   321
Labeling   322
Global Warranty and Service Policies   323
Product Warranties   323
Global After-Sales Service   324
Managing a Global Product Line   325
Product-Line Deletions   325
Product-Line Additions   325
Exploiting Product Life Cycles   326
Global Products   327
Modularity   327
Global-Product Development   328
Managing Global Research and Development   328
Centralized Research and Development   328
The Role of Foreign Subsidiaries in Research and Development   329
Outsourcing Options for New Products   331
Acquisitions as a Route to New Products   331
Alliances for New Product Development   331
Introducing New Products to Global Markets   332
Concept Tests   332
Test Marketing   333
Timing of New Product Introductions   333

11   Global Strategies for Services, Brands and Social Marketing   **341**

Marketing Services Globally   342
Business Services   343
Consumer Services   343
Back-Stage versus Front-Stage Standardization   344
Culture and the Service Experience   344
Branding Decisions   347
Selecting Brand Names   347
Selecting a Global Name   348
Changing Brand Names   349
Global Brand Strategies   349
Pan-Regional Branding   352
Global Brands versus Local Brands   353
Private Branding   354
Trademarks and Brand Protection   354
Trademark Preemption   355

Counterfeits and Piracy   357
Fighting Counterfeits   358
Social Marketing in the Global Context   360

12   Pricing for International and Global Markets   373

Profit and Cost Factors That Affect Pricing   375
Fixed and Variable Costs   375
Transportation Costs   377
Tariffs   377
Taxes   378
Local Production Costs   378
Channel Costs   379
Market Factors That Affect Pricing   379
Income Level   379
Culture and Consumer Behavior   381
Buyer Power   381
Competition   382
Environmental Factors That Affect Pricing   383
Exchange Rate Fluctuations   383
Inflation Rates   384
Price Controls   384
Dumping Regulations   385
Credit and Collection Infrastructure   385
Managerial Issues in Global Pricing   386
Managing Export Price Escalation   386
Determining Transfer Prices   387
Quoting Prices in a Foreign Currency   389
Dealing with Parallel Imports or Gray Markets   391
Setting Global Prices   395
Noncash Pricing: Countertrade   396

13   Managing Global Distribution Channels   409

The Structure of the Global Distribution System   411
Foreign-Market Channel Members   411
Import Intermediaries   411
Local Wholesalers or Agents   412
Retailers   412
Business-to-Business Channels   413
Analyzing National Channels   413
Distribution Density   415
Channel Length   415
Channel Alignment   416
Distribution Logistics   417
Factors Influencing the Selection of Channel Members   417

Costs   417
Product and Product Line   418
Control and Coverage   419
Locating and Selecting Channel Partners   419
Managing Global Distribution   420
Motivating Channel Participants   420
Controlling Channel Participants   421
Gaining Access to Distribution Channels   422
The "Locked-Up" Channel   422
Alternative Entry Approaches   423
Global Logistics   424
Logistics Decision Areas   424
Global Supply Chain Management   426
Global Trends in Retailing   427
Larger-Scale Retailers   427
Renewed Interest in Smaller-Scale Retailers   428
International Retailers   428
Direct Marketing   432
Online Retailing   433
Smuggling   434

14 Global Promotion Strategies   443

Global Promotion Strategies   445
Pull Strategies   445
Push Strategies   445
Personal Selling   447
International versus Local Selling   447
International Sales Negotiations   450
Local Selling (Single-Country Sales Force)   451
Global Account Management   454
Identifying Worthwhile Global Accounts   454
Implementing Successful Global Account Programs   455
Selling to Businesses and Governments   456
International Trade Fairs   456
Selling Through a Bidding Process   457
Consortium Selling   458
Other Forms of Promotion   458
Sales Promotion   459
Sports Promotions and Sponsorships   461
Telemarketing, Direct Mail and Spam   462
Product Placement   464
Buzz Marketing: Managing Word of Mouth   464
Public Relations   465
Corporate Social Responsibility   466

15 Managing Global Advertising   **475**

Global versus Local Advertising   477
Developing Global Campaigns   477
    Global Theme Approach   *477*
The Global–Local Decision   479
    Cost Savings   *479*
    Branding   *479*
    Target Market   *479*
    Market Conditions   *480*
    Regulatory Environment   *480*
    Cultural Differences   *481*
Overcoming Language Barriers   483
Global Media Strategy   484
    Global Media   *485*
    Local Media Availability   *485*
    Media Habits   *487*
    Scheduling International Advertising   *490*
Organizing the Global Advertising Effort   491
    Selection of an Advertising Agency   *491*
    Coordinating Global Advertising   *493*

Part 5
Managing the Global Marketing Effort   **503**

16 Organizing for Global Marketing   **505**

Elements That Affect a Global Marketing Organization   507
    Corporate Goals   *507*
    Corporate Worldview   *507*
    Other Internal Forces   *509*
    External Forces   *510*
Types of Organizational Structures   511
    Companies Without International Specialists   *512*
    International Specialists and Export Departments   *512*
    International Divisions   *513*
    Worldwide or Global Organizations   *514*
    Global Mandates   *522*
    Organization of the Born-Global Firm   *522*
Controlling the Global Organization   523
    Elements of a Control Strategy   *523*
    Communication Systems   *524*
    Corporate Culture as Control   *525*

Conflict Between Headquarters and Subsidiaries 525
Considering a Global Marketing Career 527

Country Market Report 537
Glossary 545
Index 559

Preface

Today, virtually every major firm must compete in a global marketplace. Buyers can comprise ordinary consumers or local businesses in international markets, multinational corporations (MNCs) or foreign governments. Competitors can be local firms or global firms. Although some consumer needs and wants may be converging across national markets and multilateral agreements seek to bring order to the international economic and legal environment, global marketers must still navigate among varied cultures where unexpected rules apply. Addressing this varied and increasingly competitive marketplace and developing strategies that are both efficient and effective are the tasks that face the global marketer.

Whether they oversee foreign markets or face international competitors at home, every student who plans to enter marketing as a profession will need to understand and apply the essentials of global marketing. This text prepares them for that challenge.

Why This Book?

There are a number of global marketing texts on the market. Our approach differs from that of other books in several ways.

A Dual Focus: International Buyers and Global Competition. Whereas most texts envisage global marketing as an understanding of international buyers, we envisage it as *competing* for those buyers. Immediately following our chapter on global markets and buyers we present the student with a chapter on global and local competitors. From then on we keep students focused on both buyers and competitors throughout the book.

A Global View Combined with a Strong Appreciation for Cultural Differences. Some global marketing texts downplay culture. Others make cultural differences their focus. Our approach is to recognize that cultural differences do exist and influence global marketing in a plethora of ways. To this end, we introduce the student early on to cultural issues and ways of analyzing culture that are reinforced throughout the book. But we also present students with a global view of managing cultural differences. For example, if you know you are going to sell a new product in 70 countries, why not consider this when you first design the product? What is the best design that will allow for necessary adaptations with the least effort and cost?

Regional Balance. For a text to be a true guide to global marketing, it must present students with a regional balance. Most texts concentrate on the markets of the United States, Europe and China. Our book delivers a balance of developed and developing markets including insights into the often-overlooked markets of Africa, Latin America and the Middle East. We also encourage students to think of competitors as coming from all countries, including emerging markets such as China, India, Korea and Mexico.

Current Coverage Across a Wide Variety of Topics. Our combined research and consulting experience allows us to speak with enthusiasm and conviction across the many areas covered by a global marketing text, including global strategy, cross-cultural consumer behavior and marketing organization as well as the effects government policy can have on international markets and global marketing. Our text combines recent academic research along with in-the-news corporate stories.

Gender Representation. We have taken care to present examples of women as well as men in roles of global marketers. This is apparent in our end-of-chapter cases as well as the many real-life examples in the text.

Recent Technological Advances. Technology continues to impact global marketing. We acknowledge its impact throughout the book from the use of social media in marketing research and promotion to the role of the Intranet in a global marketing organization.

Application Opportunities. To help students better internalize their knowledge of global marketing, this text offers opportunities to apply knowledge of global marketing concepts and skills to business situations. These opportunities include end-of-chapter cases and a *Country Market Report*.

End-of-Chapter Cases. Each chapter concludes with two or three short cases such as:

➤ *ShanghaiCosmopolitan.com.* Young Chinese cosmopolitans love their social networking site, but can the site's owners attract advertising from MNCs without offending the site's users?
➤ *Why Did They Do It?* German automaker Volkswagen AG and Japan's Suzuki form an alliance to help bear the costs of massive investments in new technologies and to better position themselves in emerging markets. But is this alliance doomed from the beginning?
➤ *How Local Should Coke Be?* Coca-Cola has decided to break its European division into several smaller country groupings. But will this reorganization help or hurt its global marketing strategy?
➤ *Fighting AIDS in Asia.* A former global product manager in packaged foods has turned social marketer and must prioritize markets and programs to help alleviate the spread of AIDS in Asia. Can her skills in global marketing be put to use in this new context? And what can she learn from a major donor that entered the market and then quickly exited the market?
➤ *Diaspora Marketing.* World migration has doubled in the past 35 years. How can marketers from both host and home countries help meet the needs of the new diaspora markets?
➤ *Making Products Ethical.* What can global firms do to make their products more socially acceptable? What are the costs and benefits of doing so?

Country Market Report. Included at the end of the book is a *Country Market Report* guide. This guide assists students in assessing whether a firm should enter a foreign market. For example, should Marriott hotels enter Uzbekistan? Should Yoshinoya, a Japanese casual dining chain, enter Brazil? The first half of the *Country Market Report* guide assists students in assessing the economic, cultural, political and regulatory environment of their target country and helps them determine how this environment will impact their company's specific business model. Students are then directed to evaluate current and potential competitors, both local and global. Advice is offered on identifying viable modes of entry and choosing the most appropriate one. The guide then walks students through subsequent marketing mix questions such as what adaptations would a U.S.-based dating service have to make if it were to enter the French market. What pricing, promotion and distribution strategies should it employ?

Content and Organization of the Book

Chapter 1 presents an introduction to global marketing. In this chapter we describe the development of global marketing and the importance of global marketing to both firms and the managers of the future. We explore the need for a global mindset and set forth the structure of the book.

Part 1 is entitled "Understanding the Global Marketing Environment." In this early section we investigate the key ways that the macro environment can affect global marketers. Although the concepts may be macro, we constantly show how they apply to a variety of firms trying to succeed in a vibrant international marketplace. In Chapter 2, "The Global Economy," we present the student with basic theories of trade, explain how exchange rates work and affect marketing decisions, and explore issues of protectionism and trade restrictions as well as economic integration and the challenges of outsourcing. In Chapter 3, "Cultural and Social Forces," we explore the impact on marketing of factors such as religion, family structure, education and attitudes toward time. We describe the Hofstede measures of culture and present ratings for nearly 70 countries—ratings that can be used time and again when analyzing cultural underpinnings of marketing dilemmas later in the book. The chapter continues with a discussion of issues relating to language and communication such as the difference between high- and low-context cultures and the social acceptability (or not) of showing emotion. We explain the dangers of both common and sophisticated stereotyping and conclude with insights into overcoming language barriers and dealing with culture shock. In Chapter 4, "Political and Regulatory Climate," we begin by asking the question, "What do governments want?" We then explore the varied ways that both host and home countries can impact global marketers. We describe how legal systems and attitudes toward rules vary around the world. We continue by explaining the difference to the global marketer between the task of forecasting and managing regulatory change and the task of managing political risk, and we offer concrete ideas on how to do both. The chapter concludes with a discussion of how terrorism can affect global marketing.

Part 2 concentrates on "Analyzing Global Opportunities." Beginning with Chapter 5, "Global Markets," we introduce students to segmentation in international markets and discuss cross-cultural aspects of consumer, business and government markets, including a discussion of bribery and international contracts. Chapter 6, "Global Competitors," introduces students to both issues of global firm versus global firm as well as global firm versus local firm. In particular, we present ways in which one global firm can successfully engage another as well as ways in which a local firm can respond to an encroaching global firm—including going global itself. We then explore cultural attitudes toward competition that can help explain why government regulation of corporate behavior varies around the world and why firms from different countries can be expected to behave differently. We describe how the actions of home countries can affect the global competitiveness of their firms. In addition to discussing firms from the developed world, we devote a separate section to better understanding firms from the emerging markets of the developing world. We conclude by examining the country-of-origin advantage (or sometimes disadvantage) that affects global competition, and we discuss the increasingly visible phenomenon of consumer animosity toward firms from particular countries. In Chapter 7, "Global Marketing Research," we present issues of research design and organization in a global setting and discuss the collection of secondary and primary data across cultures.

Part 3, "Developing Global Participation Strategies," examines the key decisions of determining where and how to compete and how to enter foreign markets. In Chapter 8, "Global Market Participation," we look at traditional patterns of how firms internationalize as well as the more recent phenomenon of born-global firms that enter foreign markets from their inception. We identify the pros and cons of geographic market choices such as targeting developed versus developing economies and explore the concepts of standalone attractive markets and strategically important markets. We then provide a format for country selection. We also discuss when to exit a market and when to re-enter one. In Chapter 9, "Global Market Entry Strategies," we cover the varied options of how to enter a foreign market, including production and ownership decisions, as well as e-business entry options.

Part 4, "Designing Global Marketing Programs," covers the global management of the marketing mix and the cross-cultural challenges involved in decisions concerning products, pricing, distribution and promotion. Chapter 10, "Global Product Strategies," explores necessary and desirable product (including packaging and warranty) adaptations for international markets, and it explains the importance of managing a global product line. We examine a key paradigm—designing a product with multiple national markets in mind. We also explore the decision to design (rather than adapt) a product for an important foreign market. We identify different sources for new products, whether developed in-house or outsourced, and conclude with an examination of global rollouts for new products. In Chapter 11, "Global Strategies for Services, Brands and Social Marketing," we present the particular cross-cultural challenges of services marketing and discuss branding decisions, including issues of brand protection. The chapter concludes with a discussion of the possibilities and challenges of applying global marketing concepts to social marketing internationally. In Chapter 12, "Pricing for International and Global Markets," we examine how cost and market factors as well as environmental factors such as exchange rate movements and inflation can affect pricing in international markets. We then explore managerial issues such as determining transfer prices, quoting prices in foreign currencies, dealing with parallel imports and deciding when and how to participate in countertrade arrangements.

Part 4 continues with Chapter 13, "Managing Global Distribution Channels." This chapter reviews global channels and logistics and introduces the potential differences that exist among local channels, with special emphasis on accessing and managing these channels. Recent trends are examined, including the globalization of retail chains and the growth of direct marketing worldwide, as well as the peculiar challenges of smuggling and the increasing presence of transnational organized crime in the global movement of consumer goods. Chapter 14, "Global Promotion Strategies," begins by exploring global selling and cross-cultural differences in local selling and sales force management. It continues with a discussion of international sports sponsorship and public relations, as well as cross-cultural differences in sales promotions, product placement and managing word of mouth. Part 4 concludes with Chapter 15, "Managing Global Advertising," which explores issues of global versus local advertising as well as global media strategies and agency selection.

Chapter 16, "Organizing for Global Marketing," in Part 5, identifies the elements that will determine the most appropriate organization for a firm's global marketing and outlines the characteristics of various organizational options. The chapter also examines issues of control and discusses the particular problem of conflict between headquarters and national subsidiaries. We conclude with a discussion of global marketing as a career.

Pedagogical Advantages

Our book has incorporated several features to help students learn about global marketing:

- *Chapter-Opening Stories.* Each chapter begins with a short recap of a marketing experience that illustrates key issues from the chapter that follows. This helps students grasp immediately the real-life relevance and importance of issues presented in the chapter.
- *Chapter Outlines and Learning Objectives.* At the beginning of each chapter we present both a chapter outline and a list of clear learning objectives to help focus students on the understanding they can expect to take away from the chapter.
- *"World Beat" Boxed Inserts.* Numerous and timely examples of market challenges from around the world help students further explore international issues.
- *Managerial Takeaways.* Each chapter concludes with a list of key managerial takeaways—advice that students can take to the workplace.
- *Discussion Questions.* We provide discussion questions at the end of each chapter that challenge a student's creativity to stretch beyond the chapter.
- *Short but Evocative End-of-Chapter Cases.* We believe cases can be short but conceptually dense. We have included two or three such cases at the end of each chapter. These cases were written or chosen to work with the chapter content. The end-of-case questions often refer specifically to chapter content in order to test a student's ability to apply the chapter to the case.
- *Country Market Report.* This exercise presents students with an opportunity to apply concepts from the chapters in the book as well as introduces them to Internet sites that are useful to global marketers.
- *Glossary.* The textbook includes a glossary of terms relating to global marketing and its environment.

Complete Teaching Package

A variety of ancillary materials are designed to assist the instructor in the classroom.

- *Online Instructor's Resource Manual.* An instructor's manual provides ideas pertaining to discussion questions and teaching notes for end-of-chapter cases. Suggestions for assigning the Country Market Report are also provided.
- *Test Bank.* The test bank has been completely updated. We provide more than 1,500 questions in the test bank. Approximately 450 are application-oriented questions. The test bank includes true/false, multiple-choice, fill-in-the-blank and essay questions, complete with answers and text-page references. In addition, there are mini-cases with questions. These mini-cases can be used to test a student's ability to apply knowledge to new situations and to think across chapters.
- *Power Points.* Downloadable Power Points for each chapter are also available.

Acknowledgments

We very much appreciate the contributions of cases studies from Anna Andriasova, William Carner, Michael Magers, Liesl Riddle and K.B. Saji. In addition, we are grateful to Harry Briggs of M.E. Sharpe for his insights and guidance and to Sharon Golan and Jabari LeGendre at Routledge for their kind assistance in bringing this fourth edition to fruition.

Chapter 1

Introduction to Global Marketing

THE IMPORTANCE OF GLOBAL MARKETS   3

THE DEVELOPMENT OF GLOBAL MARKETING   5

WHY STUDY GLOBAL MARKETING?   9

When MTV first went international, it aired the same videos it used in the United States. In Europe, this strategy worked well in attracting the top 200 largest pan-European advertisers. But to reach other advertisers, MTV had to adopt a more national approach, tailoring music and programming to local tastes and languages. However, over time the rising costs of production ($200,000–$350,000 per half-hour episode) caused MTV to reevaluate its original strategy. Now local subsidiaries are encouraged to create products that will play across regions or even globally.[1] Thus global firms must constantly balance the unique needs of national markets with global imperatives.

One important job of global marketers is to address the many different cultures of various international markets. For example, Metro, a free newspaper that targets urban commuters, originated in Sweden then spread to 70 cities across Europe, Asia and the United States. It prospered in spite of copycat competitors. However, when a credit crisis hit and advertisers cut back on spending, Metro saw its profits plummet. In response, the company realized that it needed to better adapt its newspapers to the different markets in which they were sold. So Hong Kong readers were provided more business news and Italian readers received more coverage of politics.[2]

Yet, the demands of local consumers are multifaceted and often changing. The Japanese are now eating more sweets than ever. When Krispy Kreme Doughnuts opened its first store in Japan, 10,000 customers arrived in the first three days alone. The Japanese are craving larger portions as well. McDonald's Mega Macs were a great hit, selling 1.7 million in four days.[3] Therefore global marketers must not only understand the current status of international markets; they must be cognizant of key trends in these markets and prepare for the future. This is true despite the fact that no one ever agrees about the future or what to do about it. When Starbucks entered China it decided to emphasize its premium coffee with the goal of changing China's tea-drinking culture. When Dunkin' Donuts entered the market, however, it announced that it would emphasize new tea drinks at first and only later ease into coffee.[4]

Global marketers must also navigate the different political and legal environments overseas and respond to ever-changing regulations that often challenge their operations in international markets. Mexico is the world's tenth largest market for processed pet food and is dominated by multinational corporations (MNCs) such as Mars Inc. and Nestle SA. The Mexican government recently added a substantial new retail tax on pet food as part of a program to extract more taxes from the middle class. As a result, sales of processed pet food in Mexico are expected to decrease, reversing the upward trend that the industry had enjoyed for many years.[5]

Though national markets remain unique, they are increasingly interdependent. Aided by technology, local consumers are more and more aware of products and prices from around the world, and large retailers and MNCs have become powerful global buyers that demand special attention. Competition increasingly occurs across markets, and competitive moves cross national borders at an alarmingly fast rate. In addition, global marketers must also exploit economies of scale in order to deliver quality and value in a competitive global marketplace. Thus a final job of global marketing is to manage these interdependencies across international markets.

This first chapter introduces you to the field of global marketing. Initially, we explore why companies seek global markets and examine the differences among domestic, international, multidomestic and global types of marketing. We then explain why mastering global marketing skills can be valuable to your future career. A conceptual outline of the book concludes the chapter.

> ## Learning Objectives
>
> *After studying this chapter, you should be able to:*
>
> ➤ describe the development of global marketing;
> ➤ explain the importance of global marketing and the need for a global mindset.

The Importance of Global Markets

Global markets are expanding rapidly. The combined value of world merchandise exports has exceeded $18 trillion annually. In addition, exports of commercial services account for over $4 trillion. For many years, international trade has grown faster than domestic economies, further contributing to the ever-increasing pace of globalization.

Furthermore, international trade statistics do not reflect a substantial portion of international marketing operations. In particular, overseas sales of locally manufactured and locally sold products produced by foreign investors are not included in world trade figures. Consequently, the total volume of international marketing far exceeds the volume of total world trade. Sales of overseas subsidiaries for U.S. companies are estimated at three times the value of these companies' exports. Although no detailed statistics are available, this pattern suggests that the overall volume of international marketing amounts to a multiple of the world trade volume.

The scope of global marketing includes many industries and many business activities. Boeing, one of the world's two largest commercial airline manufacturers, engages in global marketing when it sells its aircraft to airlines across the world. Likewise, Ford Motor Company, which operates automobile manufacturing plants in many countries, engages in global marketing, even though a major part of Ford's output is sold in the country where it is manufactured. Large retail chains, such as Wal-Mart, search for new products abroad to sell in the United States. As major global buyers, they too participate in global marketing.

A whole range of service industries are involved in global marketing. Major advertising agencies, banks, investment bankers, accounting firms, consulting companies, hotel chains, airlines and even law firms now market their services worldwide. Many of these multinational services companies enjoy more sales abroad than they do at home. India-based Tata Consultancy Services derives over 50 percent of its sales from North America.[6] Leading orchestras from Vienna, Berlin, New York and Philadelphia command as much as $150,000 per concert. Booking performances all over the world, they compete with new global entrants from St. Petersburg and Moscow.

Why Companies Seek Global Markets

Companies become involved in international markets for a variety of reasons. Some firms simply respond to orders from abroad without making any organized efforts of their own. Some businesses go international almost by accident. A former University of Michigan student from India approached the husband and wife owners of his favorite local brewpub and proposed opening a brewpub in Bangalore. After some initial skepticism, the couple agreed to become part owners in the venture and to receive consulting and licensing fees.[7]

Most companies take a more active role when it comes to entering foreign markets. Many firms enter foreign markets to increase sales and profits. Some companies pursue opportunities abroad when their domestic market has reached maturity. For example, Coca-Cola, the worldwide leader in soft drinks, finds that on a per-capita basis most foreign consumers drink only a fraction of the cola that Americans drink. Consequently, Coca-Cola sees enormous growth potential in international markets.

International markets can also reduce the risk of being overly dependent on the domestic market. When a recession hit the United States, Coca-Cola sales declined 1 percent in its home market. But strong sales in developing countries such as Brazil and India pushed corporate profits up 55 percent—despite the fact that margins tend to be lower in such markets. With nearly 80 percent of corporate sales outside the United States, Coca-Cola was able to weather the storm.[8]

Sometimes a domestic competitive shock provides the impetus to globalize. After Mexico joined the North American Free Trade Association (NAFTA), Mexican companies realized that they would face increased competition from U.S. firms. Bimbo, Mexico's market leader in packaged foods, entered the U.S. market to better understand the competition it would inevitably face back home in Mexico.[9]

Other firms launch their international marketing operations by following customers who move abroad. Major U.S. banks have opened branches in key financial centers around the world to serve their U.S. clients better. Similarly, advertising agencies in the United States have created networks to serve the interests of their multinational clients. When Japanese automobile manufacturers opened plants in the United States, many of their component suppliers followed and built operations nearby. Failing to accommodate these important clients could result in the loss not only of foreign sales but of domestic sales as well.

For some firms, however, the reason to become involved in global marketing has its roots in pure economics. Producers of television shows in Hollywood can spend over $1.5 million to produce a single show for a typical series. Networks in the United States pay only about $1 million to air a single show, and the series producers rely on international markets to cover the difference. Without the opportunity to market globally, they would not even be able to produce the shows for the U.S. market.

Online shopping giant eBay is serious about international market opportunities. Nonetheless, expanding into the important Asian market has not been easy. Tough competition from Yahoo forced eBay to exit the Japanese market. In China, eBay shut down its own website and retreated to owning a minority share in a locally owned site. Despite these setbacks, eBay's global sales are expected to increase to $110 billion by 2015.[10] Like any successful global marketer, eBay must continually rethink its global strategy. Global expansion is not just a decision to venture abroad, it is a commitment to learn from experience.

The Development of Global Marketing

The term *global marketing* has been in use only since the 1980s. Before that decade, *international marketing* was the term used most often to describe marketing activities outside one's domestic market. Global marketing is not just a new label for an old phenomenon, however. Global marketing provides a new vision for international marketing. Before we explain global marketing in detail, let us first look at the historical development of international marketing as a field in order to gain a better understanding of the phases through which it has passed (see Figure 1.1).

Domestic Marketing

Marketing that is aimed at a single market, the firm's domestic market, is known as domestic marketing. In domestic marketing, the firm faces only one set of competitive, economic and market issues. It essentially deals with only one set of national customers, although the company may serve several segments in this one market.

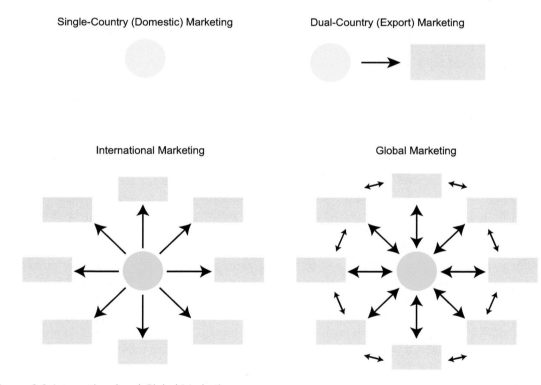

Figure 1.1 International and Global Marketing

Export Marketing

Export marketing covers marketing activities that are involved when a firm sells its products outside its domestic base of operation and when products are physically shipped from one country to another. The major challenges of export marketing are the selection of appropriate markets or countries through marketing research, the determination of appropriate product modifications to meet the demand requirements of export markets and the development of export channels through which the company can market its products abroad. In export marketing, the firm may concentrate mostly on product modifications, running its export operations as a welcome and profitable byproduct of its domestic strategy. Other aspects of marketing strategy, such as pricing, channel management and promotion, may be outsourced either to foreign agents or distributors or to specialist export management companies located in the firm's home country. Although export marketing represents one of the least complicated forms of nondomestic marketing, it remains an important feature for many firms.

International Marketing

A company that practices international marketing goes beyond exporting and becomes much more directly involved in the local marketing environment within a given country. The firm is likely to have its own subsidiaries abroad and will participate in and develop entire marketing strategies for foreign markets. At this point, the necessary adaptations to the firm's domestic marketing strategies become of greater concern. Table 1.1 illustrates typical adaptations in international marketing. Companies need to decide how to adjust an entire marketing strategy, including how they sell, advertise and distribute products, in order to fit new market demands. Understanding different cultural, economic and political environments becomes increasingly necessary for success. Even when companies successfully enter foreign markets, they must constantly reassess the market, focusing both on buyers and competitors. Japan is one of Starbucks' largest and most successful markets. However, increased price competition forced Starbucks Japan to slash prices and cut costs by procuring more ingredients from local suppliers. Demanding consumers forced the company to customize its menu to local tastes.[11]

Typically, much of the field of international marketing has been devoted to making the many national environments understandable and to helping managers navigate these national differences. The need to understand international marketing grew with the expansion of the MNC. These companies, characterized by extensive investments in assets abroad, operate in foreign countries as though they were local companies. Until recently, most MNCs pursued a multidomestic strategy, wherein the MNC competes by applying many different strategies, each one tailored to a particular local market. Often, MNCs would attempt to appear "local" wherever they competed. The major challenge confronting the multidomestic marketer is to find the best possible adaptation of a complete marketing strategy to each individual country. This more extreme approach to international marketing led to a maximum amount of localization and to a large variety of marketing strategies. Ironically, the traditional multidomestic strategies of MNCs failed to take advantage of the global reach of these firms. Lessons learned in one domestic market were often not applied elsewhere.

Table 1.1 Adapting to National Differences

Asia	Ray Ban redesigned its sunglasses to better fit Asian facial characteristics.
Brazil	In Latin America, 25 percent of the population lives on less than $2 a day. Consumers often require smaller packages at lower prices. Sales of Nestlé's Bono cookies increased 40 percent in a single year when the company decreased the package size in Brazil from 200 grams to 149 grams.
China	Cadillacs sold in China provide more legroom for rear-seat passengers, because many wealthy Chinese ride in chauffeur-driven cars.
Finland	Finland wants more Vitamin D added to foods, because Finns are exposed to less sunlight. This is one reason why cereal manufacturer Kellogg has to produce variations of its corn flakes and other cereals for the European market.
France	Apples and pears require different labels across the EU. For example, in France labels on fruit must specify chemical treatments, preservation methods and wax treatments—all in French of course!
India	Disney sells school bags in India that are larger than those sold in the U.S., because Indian schools don't have student lockers.
Japan	The Japanese are said to be in love with the ephemeral. They like products that are here today but gone tomorrow. To tap into this cultural trait, Nestlé offers limited edition candy for each season of the year.
Mexico	To foster loyalty within its distribution system, Coca-Cola has offered life insurance to small retailers in Mexico.
Middle East	When Coty Inc. ran an ad aimed at the Middle East market for its Jennifer Lopez perfume, it placed the ad in the newly launched Middle East edition of Elle. But the ad only showed the singer's face instead of her signature curvy silhouette, which ran in the original ad.
Southeast Asia	Nestlé SA sells its Lipton tea and Nescafé in single-serve sachets to accommodate poorer consumers who view these products as an occasional treat.

Sources: Christina Passariello, "Fitting Shades for Chinese," *Wall Street Journal Online*, April 21, 2011; Merissa Marr, "Small World," *Wall Street Journal*, June 11, 2007, p. A1; Antonio Regalado, "Marketers Pursue the Shallow-Pocketed," *Wall Street Journal*, January 26, 2007, p. B3; Mei Fong, "IKEA Hits Home in China," *Wall Street Journal*, March 2, 2006, p. B1; Christina Passariello, "Chic Under Wraps," *Wall Street Journal*, June 20, 2006, p. B1; Gordon Fairclough, "Chinese Cadillac Offers Glimpse of GM's Future," *Wall Street Journal*, November 17, 2006, p. B1; Kenji Hall, "Fad Marketing's Balancing Act," *Business Week*, August 6, 2007, p. 42; and John Revill, "Food Makers Rethink Europe," *Wall Street Journal*, May 29, 2012.

Good ideas in product development or promotions were not always shared among national subsidiaries. Similarly, MNCs often failed to take advantage of their global size in negotiating with suppliers and distributors.

Pan-Regional Marketing

Given the diseconomies of scale that plague individualized marketing strategies, each tailored to a specific local environment, many companies have begun to emphasize strategies for larger regions. These regional strategies encompass a number of markets, such as pan-European strategies for Europe, and have come about as a result of regional economic and political integration. Such integration is also apparent in North America, where the United States, Canada and Mexico have committed themselves to the far-reaching NAFTA trade pact. Companies considering regional strategies seek synergies in marketing operations in one region with the aim of achieving increased efficiency. Many firms are presently working on such solutions, moving from many multidomestic strategies toward selected pan-regional strategies.

Global Marketing

Over the years, academics and MNCs alike have become aware that opportunities for economies of scale and enhanced competitiveness are greater if firms can manage to integrate and create marketing strategies on a global scale. A multinational or global marketing strategy involves the creation of a single strategy for a product, service or company for the entire global market. It encompasses many countries simultaneously and is aimed at leveraging the commonalities across many markets. Rather than tailoring a strategy perfectly to any individual market, a firm that pursues global marketing settles on a basic strategy that can be applied throughout the world market, all the while maintaining flexibility to adapt to local market requirements where necessary. Such strategies are inspired by the fact that many markets appear increasingly similar in environmental and customer requirements. The management challenges are to design marketing strategies that work well across multiple markets, while remaining alert to the possible adaptations that may be advisable on a market-to-market basis.

Thinking globally has its advantages. As we will see later in this book, global marketers enjoy several benefits beyond those of international marketers. Global marketing can allow firms to offer better products and services at a lower cost, even when adapting for local market conditions. These lower costs can be passed on to customers in the form of lower prices. Alternatively, global marketers can use their increased profits to invest in product development or promotion. Global marketers can often move more quickly than international marketers, introducing new products rapidly into many foreign markets. They are also better armed to engage competition worldwide.

Even though global marketers face the unique challenge of finding marketing strategies that involve many countries at once, the skills and concepts that have been critical since the earliest stages in the history of marketing remain important and continue to be needed. Firms that pursue global strategies must be adept at international marketing as well, because designing a global strategy does not mean ignoring national differences. Instead, a global strategy must reflect a sound understanding of the cultural, economic and political environment of many countries. Few global marketing strategies can exist without local tailoring, which is the hallmark of international marketing and multidomestic strategies. Managing global marketing is the last in a series of skills that managers must acquire to be successful in the global marketplace.

Why Study Global Marketing?

You have probably asked yourself why you should study global marketing. Each year MNCs hire large numbers of marketing professionals. As these firms become increasingly globalized, competence in global marketing will become even more important in the future—and many marketing executives will be pursuing global marketing as a career. Other career opportunities exist with a large number of exporters, where job candidates will require international marketing skills. Even newly formed companies are now entering foreign markets at a young age.

With the service sector becoming increasingly globalized, many graduates joining service industries find themselves confronted with international opportunities at early stages of their careers. Today, consulting engineers, bankers, brokers, public accountants, medical services executives and e-commerce specialists all need global marketing skills to compete in a rapidly changing environment. Consequently, a solid understanding and appreciation of global marketing will benefit the careers of most business students, regardless of the field or industry they choose to enter.

A Need for Global Mindsets

The Swedish firm IKEA is today one of the world's largest furniture retailing chains. IKEA entered the important U.S. market and quickly become a dominant player. IKEA's success was largely attributable to a new concept that it introduced to the United States: setting up large stores where consumers could browse, buy and take furniture home in disassembled form at the end of their visit. IKEA is but one example of an international global competitor entering a previously "safe" market with new ideas, bringing global competition to the doorstep of strictly domestic companies.

Few firms can avoid the impact of global competition today. Foreign competition has made enormous inroads into the manufacture of apparel, textiles, shoes, electronic equipment and steel. Although foreign competition for many consumer goods has been evident for years, inroads by foreign firms into the industrial and capital goods markets have been equally spectacular.

The need to become more competitive in a global economy will force many changes on the typical company. Firms will have to compete in global markets to defend their own domestic markets and to keep up with global competitors based in other countries. These firms will need an increasing cadre of managers who can adopt a global perspective. This requires not only knowledge of other countries, economies and cultures, but also a clear understanding of how the global economy works. Managers with a global perspective will also have to integrate actions taken in one national market with actions in another national market. This means that global marketers will be required to use ideas and experiences from a number of other countries so that the best products can be marketed the most efficiently and effectively. Managers with a global mindset will need to deal with new strategies that were not part of the domestic or older international business scenes.

To compete successfully in today's global marketplace, companies and their management must master certain areas. *Environmental competence* is needed to navigate the global economy. This area of expertise includes knowledge of the dynamics of the world economy, of major national markets and of political, social and cultural environments. *Analytic competence* is necessary to pull together a vast array of information concerning global markets and competitors. *Strategic competence* helps executives focus on the where, why and how of global market participation. A global marketer must also possess *functional competence*, or a thorough background in all areas of marketing such as product development, channel management, pricing and promotion. *Managerial competence* is the ability to implement marketing programs and to organize effectively on a global scale. In addition to these basic competencies, global marketers must attain an overarching global competence or the ability to balance local market needs with the demands of global efficiency and the opportunities of global synergies.

Organization of This Book

This text is structured around the basic requirements for making sound global marketing decisions, as depicted in Table 1.2.

Part 1, Chapters 2 through 4, is concerned with the global marketing environment. Special emphasis is placed on the economic, cultural, political and legal environments that companies must address in order to be successful.

Part 2, Chapters 5 through 7, concentrates on global market opportunity analysis. Chapters in this part discuss global buyers, competitors and the research methods that are necessary to apply in order to understand marketing opportunities globally.

Chapters 8 and 9, which make up Part 3, deal with global market participation. Chapter 8 introduces key issues relating to market choices and Chapter 9 describes the various modes of entry that companies can employ once they decide to enter a foreign market.

Part 4, which comprises Chapters 10 through 15, aims at developing competence in designing global marketing programs consistent with a global strategy. The chapters in this section cover product and service strategies, global branding, social marketing, pricing, channel management, promotion and advertising.

The text concludes with Part 5, which consists of Chapter 16. Here the emphasis is on building managerial competence in a global environment. Chapter 16 discusses how firms organize for effective global marketing and also explores career issues of concern to the global marketer.

At the end of each of Chapters 2 through 16, short cases are included to help you think concretely about global marketing and apply concepts from the chapter. For those of you wishing to put your knowledge to immediate use, you will find at the end of the book a guide to developing a Country Market Report. This guide will help you evaluate a national market for a product or service and determine the best form of market entry. Subsequently, the guide leads you through the steps to determine how your product or service should be adapted for the local market, what location or distribution channel is most appropriate, what price you should charge and what promotional strategy you should pursue.

Table 1.2 Global Marketing Management

Competence Level	Decision Area	
Environmental Competence	**Understanding the Global Marketing Environment**	
	CH 2	The Global Economy
	CH 3	Cultural and Social Forces
	CH 4	Political and Regulatory Climate
Analytic Competence	**Analyzing Global Opportunities**	
	CH 5	Global Markets
	CH 6	Global Competitors
	CH 7	Global Marketing Research
Strategic Competence	**Developing Global Participation Strategies**	
	CH 8	Global Market Participation
	CH 9	Global Market Entry Strategies
Functional Competence	**Designing Global Marketing Programs**	
	CH 10	Global Product Strategies
	CH 11	Global Strategies for Services, Brands and Social Marketing
	CH 12	Pricing for International and Global Markets
	CH 13	Managing Global Distribution Channels
	CH 14	Global Promotion Strategies
	CH 15	Managing Global Advertising
Managerial Competence	**Managing the Global Marketing Effect**	
	CH 16	Organizing for Global Marketing

Conclusion

As a separate activity of business, global marketing is of great importance to nations, individual companies and prospective managers. With markets and industries becoming increasingly globalized, most companies must become active participants in global marketing. The competitive positions of most companies, both abroad and in their domestic markets, rest on their ability to succeed in global markets. At the same time, the economies of entire countries depend on the global marketing skills of managers. The standard of living of many people will be governed by how well local industry performs in the global marketplace. These forces will place a premium on executive talent that is able to direct marketing operations from a global perspective. Clearly, many business professionals will need to understand the global dimension of the marketing function if they are to progress in their careers.

Although the need to develop global competence may be clear, the circumstances that determine successful marketing practices for foreign markets are far less clear. The foreign marketing environment is characterized by a wide range of variables not typically encountered by domestic firms. This continues to make the job of global marketing extremely challenging. Despite the complexities involved, there are concepts and analytic tools that can help global marketers. By learning to use these concepts and tools, you can enhance your own global marketing competence. As a result, you will be able to contribute to the marketing operations of a wide range of firms, both domestic and foreign.

Managerial Takeaways

1. *The global economy is more interconnected than ever before, and the need for marketers to address international opportunities in a proactive manner has never been greater.*
2. *Understanding and adapting to cultural differences will continue to play a major role in successful marketing strategies across the globe, while the need to successfully coordinate strategies across countries will continue to increase.*
3. *Balancing the need to adapt to national differences and the need to gain cost, quality and competitive advantages by coordinating across borders is the major task of global marketing.*

Questions for Discussion

1. How is global marketing as a field related to your future career? How would you expect to come into contact with global marketing activities?
2. What do you think are the essential skills of a successful "global marketer"?
3. Which important skills make up an effective "global mindset"?
4. List ten things that are important to you that you hope to be able to understand or accomplish after studying this book.

Notes

1 Charles Goldsmith, "MTV Seeks Global Appeal," *Wall Street Journal*, July 21, 2003, p. B1.
2 Carol Matlock, "Free Paper, Costly Competition," *Business Week*, November 19, 2007, p. 94.
3 Yuri Kageyama, "Japan Imports American Culture via Calories," *Marketing News*, May 1, 2007, p. 11.
4 Janet Adamy, "Dunkin' Begins New Push into Asia," *Wall Street Journal*, January 17, 2007, p. A4.
5 Amy Guthrie, "Pet Food to be Taxed at 16 Percent in Mexico," *Wall Street Journal*, December 28, 2013, p. B3.
6 Steve Hamm, "IBM vs. Tata: Which is More American?" *Business Week*, May 5, 2008, p. 28.

7   Justin Lahart, "For Small Businesses, the Big World Beckons," *Wall Street Journal*, January 27, 2011, p. B1.
8   Anjali Cordeiro, "Coca-Cola Gets Overseas Lift," *Wall Street Journal*, February 10, 2010, p. B3.
9   David Gregorcyk, "Internationalization of Conglomerates from Emerging Markets," Teresa Lozano Long Institute of Latin American Studies, The University of Texas at Austin, May 2005.
10 Alistair Barr, "EBay Sets Aggressive 2015 Target," Reuters, March 28, 2013.
11 Mariko Sanchanta, "Starbucks Plans Big Expansion in China," *Wall Street Journal*, April 14, 2010, p. B10.

Part 1

Understanding the Global Marketing Environment

2   THE GLOBAL ECONOMY   17

3   CULTURAL AND SOCIAL FORCES   55

4   POLITICAL AND REGULATORY CLIMATE   95

Chapter 2

The Global Economy

INTERNATIONAL TRADE: AN OVERVIEW   18

THE BASIC THEORIES OF WORLD TRADE: ABSOLUTE,
COMPARATIVE AND COMPETITIVE ADVANTAGE   20

GLOBAL OUTSOURCING   24

BALANCE OF PAYMENTS   25

EXCHANGE RATES   27

INTERNATIONAL AGENCIES FOR PROMOTING ECONOMIC
AND MONETARY STABILITY   36

PROTECTIONISM AND TRADE RESTRICTIONS   37

ECONOMIC INTEGRATION AS A MEANS OF PROMOTING TRADE   41

THE GLOBALIZATION CONTROVERSY   44

When EuroDisney opened outside Paris, French attendance at the theme park was disappointing. Some attributed low ticket sales to a cultural snub of this American icon. Others noted a particularly wet and cold season. Still others blamed the strength of the local currency against the U.S. dollar. French consumers could buy—and spend—dollars at bargain prices. If the French wanted Disney, they could catch a plane to Florida's Disney World for not much more than they would pay for a weekend at EuroDisney.

The global economy constantly affects international marketing. Billions of dollars of goods and services are traded among nations each day. Currency exchange rates fluctuate, affecting sales and profits. Businesses establish operations and borrow funds in locations throughout the world. Banks lend and arbitrage currencies worldwide. When these transactions are interrupted or threatened, we can truly appreciate the scope and significance of the international economy.

This chapter introduces the important aspects of world trade and finance and how these affect global marketers. We begin by explaining the concepts of comparative advantage and competitive advantage, the bases for international trade. Then we explain the international system to monitor world trade, particularly the balance-of-payments measurement system. From this base, we describe the workings of the foreign exchange market and the causes of exchange rate movements. We discuss the international agencies that promote economic and monetary stability, as well as the strategies that countries use to protect their own economies. We look at economic integration as a means of promoting trade and conclude with a discussion of the globalization controversy.

Learning Objectives

After studying this chapter, you should be able to:

➤ distinguish among the basic theories of world trade: absolute advantage, comparative advantage and competitive advantage;
➤ discuss the pros and cons of global outsourcing;
➤ list and explain the principal parts of the balance-of-payments statement;
➤ describe how and why exchange rates fluctuate;
➤ list and describe the major agencies that promote world trade, as well as those that promote economic and monetary stability;
➤ describe common trade restrictions and explain their impact on international marketers;
➤ compare the four different forms of economic integration;
➤ explain why globalization is politically controversial.

International Trade: An Overview

Few individuals in the world are totally self-sufficient. Why should they be? Restricting consumption to self-made goods lowers living standards by narrowing the range and reducing the quality of the goods we consume. For this reason, few nations have economies independent from the rest of the world, and it would be difficult to find a national leader willing or able to impose such an economic hardship on a country. This interdependency of global markets is apparent in even the most isolated regions of the world. When a recession in the United States causes consumers to cut back on purchasing cashmere sweaters and coats, nomadic herders in Mongolia who supply cashmere to manufacturers around the world see their earnings plummet.[1]

International Dependence of Nations

Foreign goods are central to the living standards of all nations. But as Table 2.1 shows, countries vary widely in their reliance on foreign trade. Imports are 15 percent of the gross domestic product (GDP) of Japan and 14 percent of the GDP of the United States, whereas Switzerland and Mexico have import-to-GDP ratios of 31 and 32 percent, respectively.

The figures given in Table 2.1 are useful for identifying the international dependence of nations, but they should be viewed as rough indicators only. In any widespread disruption of international

Table 2.1 Imports and Exports as a Percentage of GDP (in billions of dollars)

	GDP*	Imports**	Imports/GDP	Exports**	Exports/GDP
Industrial Countries					
France	2,612	674	26%	569	22%
Germany	3,428	1,167	34%	1,407	41%
Canada	1,821	475	26%	455	25%
Japan	5,960	886	15%	799	13%
Italy	2,014	487	24%	501	25%
Switzerland	631	198	31%	226	35%
United Kingdom	2,471	690	28%	474	19%
United States	16,244	2,336	14%	1,546	10%
Developing Countries					
Argentina	475	69	15%	81	17%
Brazil	2,252	233	10%	245	11%
China	8,227	1,818	22%	2,049	25%
India	1,841	490	27%	294	16%
Mexico	1,178	380	32%	371	31%
Russian Federation	2,014	335	17%	529	26%
South Africa	384	124	32%	87	23%

*Year Reported: 2012
**Adapted from Imports/Exports, World Trade Organization, 2014

Note: Percentages calculated by authors

Source: Adapted from GNP—World Bank 2014, Imports/Exports World Trade Organization

trade, there is little doubt that the United States would be harmed much less than the Netherlands. Yet this is not to say a disruption of trade would not be harmful to countries with large domestic markets such as the United States and Japan, which both depend heavily on world trade for growth. In the United States, $1 billion of exports supports the creation, on average, of about 11,500 jobs.[2]

The Growth in World Trade

After its stock market crash of 1929, the United States turned its back on free trade. Fearing losses of jobs at home, this country tried to assist local industries by sharply increasing taxes on imports from other countries. Unfortunately, other countries retaliated with similar measures. In less than a year, world trade collapsed, sending the world into a global depression. Two hard-hit countries were Germany and Japan. Many believe that this severe economic downturn encouraged the militaristic regimes that precipitated World War II. After the war, the United States and other industrialized nations were eager for world trade to be promoted and to expand.

Their vision has certainly come to pass. World trade has increased over 22-fold since 1950, far outstripping the growth in world GDP. This growth has been fueled by the continued opening of markets around the world. The Bretton Woods conference of world leaders in 1944 led to the establishment of the General Agreement on Tariffs and Trade (GATT), which we will discuss in detail later. GATT, and subsequently the World Trade Organization (WTO), helped to reduce import tariffs from 40 percent in 1947 to an estimated 4 percent today. The principle of free trade has led to the building of market interdependencies. International trade has grown much more rapidly than world GDP output, demonstrating that national economies are becoming much more closely linked and interdependent via their exports and imports. This interdependence has created many opportunities for international marketers but has made world trade more vulnerable to global recessions. The WTO predicted a 9 percent drop in world trade as a result of collapsing global demand in 2009.[3]

Foreign direct investment, another indication of global integration, increased over 100 percent in a single decade, and services are an important and growing part of the world's economy. Industries such as banking, telecommunications, insurance, construction, transportation, tourism and consulting make up over half the national income of many rich economies. A country's invisible exports include services, transfers from workers abroad and income earned on overseas investments.

The Basic Theories of World Trade: Absolute, Comparative and Competitive Advantage

Internationally traded goods and services are important to most countries, as shown in Table 2.1. Because jobs and standard of living seem to be so closely tied to these inflows and outflows, there is much debate about why a particular country finds its comparative advantages in certain goods and services and not in others.

The past 35 years have witnessed not only a dramatic rise in the volume of trade but also numerous changes in its patterns. Countries that once exported vast amounts of steel, such as the United States, are now net importers of the metal. Other nations, such as India, once known for producing inexpensive handicrafts, now compete globally in high-tech products. What caused these changes in trade patterns? Why do countries that are able to produce virtually any product choose to specialize in certain goods? Where do international cost advantages originate? As the twenty-first century continues, will we still think of Indonesia and China as having the greatest advantage in handmade goods, or will they come to be like Japan and Taiwan are today?

The early work of Adam Smith provides the foundation for understanding trade today. Smith saw trade as a way to promote efficiency because it fostered competition, led to specialization and resulted in economies of scale. Specialization supports the concept of absolute advantage—that is, sell to other countries the goods that utilize your special skills and resources, and buy the rest from those who have some other advantage. This theory of selling what you are best at producing is known as *absolute advantage*. But what if you have no advantages? Will all your manufacturers be driven out of business? David Ricardo, in his 1817 work *Principles of Political Economy*, offered his theory of *comparative advantage*. This theory maintains that it is still possible to produce profitably what one is best at producing, even if someone else is better. The following sections further develop the concepts of absolute and comparative advantage, the economic basis of free trade and hence of all global trade.

Absolute Advantage

Although many variables may be listed as the primary determinants of international trade, productivity differences rank high on the list. Take, for example, two countries—Vietnam and Germany. Suppose the average Vietnamese worker can produce either 400 machines or 1,600 tons of tomatoes in one year. Over the same time period, the average German worker can produce either 500 machines or 500 tons of tomatoes (see example 1 in Table 2.2). In this case, German workers can produce more machinery, absolutely, than Vietnamese workers can, whereas Vietnamese workers can produce more tomatoes, absolutely, than can their German counterparts. Given these figures, Vietnam is the obvious low-cost producer of tomatoes and should export them to Germany. Similarly, Germany is the low-cost producer of machines and should export them to Vietnam.

Recently, China began to exploit its absolute advantage in garlic production. Chinese farm labor receives $1 per day versus $5 in Mexico and $8.50 an hour in California. Garlic has a shelf life of up to nine months and can be easily shipped. Not unexpectedly, the California producers have been devastated.[4]

Comparative Advantage

We should not conclude from the previous examples that absolute differences in production capabilities are necessary for trade to occur. Consider the same two countries in the first example—Vietnam and Germany. Now assume that the average Vietnamese worker can produce either 200 machines or 800 tons of tomatoes each year, whereas the average German worker can produce

Table 2.2 Absolute Versus Comparative Advantage: Worker Productivity Examples

	Vietnam	Germany
Example 1		
Yearly output per worker		
Machinery	400	500
Tomatoes	1,600 tons	500 tons
Absolute advantage	Tomatoes	Machinery
Example 2		
Yearly output per worker		
Machinery	200	500
Tomatoes	800 tons	1,000 tons
Opportunity costs of production	1 machine costs	1 machine costs
	4 tons tomatoes *or*	2 tons tomatoes *or*
	1 ton tomatoes costs	1 ton tomatoes costs
	0.25 machine	0.50 machine
Absolute advantage	None	Tomatoes
		Machinery
Comparative advantage	Tomatoes	Machinery

either 500 machines or 1,000 tons of tomatoes (see example 2 in Table 2.2). Germany has an absolute advantage in both goods, and it appears that Vietnam will benefit from trade because it can buy from Germany cheaper goods than Vietnam can make for itself. Even here, however, the basis for mutually advantageous trade is present. The reason lies in the concept of comparative advantage.

Comparative advantage measures a product's cost of production not in monetary terms but in terms of the forgone opportunity to produce something else. It focuses on tradeoffs. To illustrate, the production of machines means that resources cannot be devoted to the production of tomatoes. In Germany, the worker who produces 500 machines will not be able to grow 1,000 tons of tomatoes. The cost can be stated as follows: Each ton of tomatoes costs half a machine, or one machine costs 2 tons of tomatoes. In Vietnam, producing 200 machines forces the sacrifice of 800 tons of tomatoes. Alternatively, this means that 1 ton of tomatoes costs a quarter of a machine, or one machine costs 4 tons of tomatoes.

From this example, we see that even though Vietnam has an absolute disadvantage in both commodities, it still has a comparative advantage in tomatoes. For Vietnam, the cost of producing 1 ton of tomatoes is a quarter of a machine, whereas for Germany the cost is half a machine. Similarly, even though Germany has an absolute advantage in both products, it has a comparative cost advantage only in machines. It costs Germany only 2 tons of tomatoes to produce a single machine, whereas in Vietnam the cost is 4 tons of tomatoes.

Table 2.3 Mutually Advantageous Trading Ratios

Tomatoes	Machines
Germany, 1 ton tomatoes = 0.5 machine	Vietnam, 1 machine = 4 tons tomatoes
Germany, 1 machine = 2 tons tomatoes	Vietnam, 1 ton tomatoes = 0.25 machine

The last step in examining the concept of comparative advantage is to choose a mutually advantageous trading ratio and show how it can benefit both countries. Any trading ratio between one machine = 2 tons of tomatoes (Germany's domestic trading ratio) and one machine = 4 tons of tomatoes (Vietnam's domestic trading ratio) will benefit both nations (see Table 2.3). Suppose we choose one machine = 3 tons of tomatoes. Because Germany will be exporting machinery, it gains by getting 3 tons of tomatoes rather than the 2 tons it would have produced domestically. Likewise, because Vietnam will be exporting tomatoes, it gains because one machine can be imported for the sacrifice of only 3 tons of tomatoes, rather than the 4 tons it would have to sacrifice if it made the machine in Vietnam.

Our discussion of comparative advantage illustrates that relative rather than absolute differences in productivity can form a determining basis for international trade. Although the concept of comparative advantage provides a powerful tool for explaining the rationale for mutually advantageous trade, it gives little insight into the source of the differences in relative productivity. Specifically, why does a country find its comparative advantage in one good or service rather than in another? Is it by chance that the United States is a net exporter of aircraft, machinery and chemicals, but a net importer of steel, textiles and consumer electronic products? Or can we find some systematic explanations for this pattern?

The notion of comparative advantage requires that nations make intensive use of those factors they possess in abundance—in particular, land, labor, natural resources and capital. Thus Hungary, with its low labor cost in manufacturing of US$9 per hour, will export labor-intensive goods such as unsophisticated chest freezers and table linen, whereas Sweden, with its high-quality iron ore deposits, will export high-grade steel.

Competitive Advantage

Michael Porter argues that even though the theory of comparative advantage has appeal, it is limited by its traditional focus on land, labor, natural resources and capital. His study of ten trading nations that account for 50 percent of world exports and 100 industries resulted in a new and expanded theory.[5] This theory postulates that whether a country will have a significant impact on the competitive advantage of an industry depends on the following factors:

- ➤ the elements of production;
- ➤ the nature of domestic demand;
- ➤ the presence of appropriate suppliers or related industries; and
- ➤ the conditions in the country that govern how companies are created, organized and managed, as well as the nature of domestic rivalry.

Porter argues that strong local competition often benefits a national industry in the global marketplace. Firms in a competitive environment are forced to produce quality products efficiently. Demanding consumers in the home market and pressing local needs can also stimulate firms to solve problems and develop proprietary knowledge before foreign competitors do.

A good example of a country that enjoys a competitive advantage in digital products is South Korea. South Koreans are among the most "wired" people on earth. Korea became the first country to achieve 100 percent broadband service, and more than 70 percent of Koreans own smartphones. Seventy percent of share trades in the Korean securities market are done online. Korean companies can use entire urban populations in their home market as test markets for their latest digital ideas. This in turn gives these Korean companies an advantage when they want to export new products or know-how abroad. Similarly, Japan has a competitive advantage in energy conservation. With few domestic sources of energy, Japan has been at the forefront of designing manufacturing processes that consume the least amount of energy. When the price of oil rises, this gives Japan an advantage—especially compared to other Asian countries.

A nation's competitive advantage can change over time. China was once known for ultra-cheap labor and a business environment relatively free of government regulaton. Many believe those days are now over. Manufacturing costs are increasing in China, threatening the country's previously successful export model that was based on low export prices.

Global Outsourcing

For 200 years, most economists have agreed with the theory of comparative advantage: nations gain if they trade with each other and specialize in what they do best. However, advances in telecommunications, such as broadband and the Internet, have created for the first time a global market for skilled workers that threatens traditional ideas of national specialization. According to comparative advantage, India, with its vast numbers of low-paid, low-skilled workers, should specialize in low-wage standardized products. Yet the country competes successfully in a global market for white-collar workers, undercutting the wages of highly skilled Americans and Europeans. Tata Consultancy Services, the largest outsourcing company in India for information technologies, derives the majority of its income from Europe and North America. Increasingly, information technology (IT) jobs and back-office services (such as credit collection, benefits and pension administration, insurance claims processing and tax accounting) are outsourced to cheaper labor in developing countries.

A study published by the McKinsey Global Institute on the national impact of outsourcing back-office services and IT jobs to India reveals that outsourcing need not be a zero-sum game. This is not to say there are not national winners and losers.[6] As depicted in Table 2.4, the United States and India would appear to be net winners, while Germany would be a loser.

Direct benefits of outsourcing are captured by India, such as wages, profits to local firms and taxes collected by the Indian government. Indian workers in the back-office services and IT fields, who are usually college educated and proficient in English, have seen their wages soar in recent years—though not enough to stop the outsourcing to India. However, new revenues and repatriated earnings from multinational corporations (MNCs) selling to firms in India are captured in Germany

Table 2.4 National Net Gains for Each U.S. Dollar in India Outsourcing Back-Office Services and IT Functions

	India	U.S.	Germany
Outsourced wages, profits, taxes	$0.33	—	—
Cost savings	—	$0.58	$0.52
New revenues from India	—	$0.05	$0.03
Repatriated earnings	—	$0.04	—
Redeployment of workers	—	$0.46	$0.25
Total	**$0.33**	**$1.13**	**$0.80**

and the United States. Because U.S. MNCs have a larger presence in the Indian market than do German MNCs, the United States captures more of these particular benefits than does Germany. Cost savings from outsourcing is an important benefit as well. Again, this benefit is lower for Germany than the United States because Indian businesses in these areas operate in English. This raises the relative coordination costs for German companies working with Indian firms. The biggest advantage in realized benefits for the United States over Germany lies in the redeployment of workers (particularly to higher-value-added jobs). Workers in the United States who are displaced by outsourcing are more likely to find new jobs, and find them more quickly, than are similar workers in Germany.

However, even if the United States currently gains as a whole from global outsourcing, the losses and benefits of outsourcing accrue differently to different groups. For this reason, global outsourcing remains very controversial and politically explosive. New revenues from India and repatriated earnings accrue primarily to investors, not workers. How the cost savings from outsourcing are distributed depends on the relative power of the different groups—investors, labor and buyers. As labor in the United States loses its bargaining power in the new global labor market, most of the savings are likely again to accrue to investors, not labor.

If white-collar job losses rise to 6 percent in the United States, the wages for remaining workers could be depressed by 2 to 3 percent. This is similar to the wage-level losses due to earlier outsourcing in manufacturing. Another concern is whether the United States can continue to realize gains from redeployment of labor as the type of job outsourced becomes increasingly sophisticated. Despite the greater worker mobility in the United States, only about 30 percent of laid-off workers earn the same or more after three years. When only manufacturing jobs moved to developing countries, about 25 percent of the U.S. labor force was affected. With the addition of professional jobs at risk to outsourcing, a majority of American workers could lose more from job losses and the depression of wages than they gain from lower prices of goods.[7]

Balance of Payments

Newspapers, magazines and nightly TV news programs are filled with stories related to aspects of international business. Often, media coverage centers on the implications of a nation's trade deficit or surplus or on the economic consequences of an undervalued or overvalued currency. What are

25

trade deficits? What factors will cause a currency's international value to change? The first step in answering these questions is to gain a clear understanding of the contents and meaning of a nation's balance of payments.

The balance of payments (BOP) is an accounting record of the transactions between the residents of one country and the residents of the rest of the world over a given period of time. Transactions in which domestic residents either purchase assets (goods and services) from abroad or reduce foreign liabilities are considered *outflows of funds*, because payments abroad must be made. Similarly, transactions in which domestic residents either sell assets to foreign residents or increase their liabilities to foreigners are *inflows of funds*, because payments from abroad are received.

Listed in Table 2.5 are the principal parts of the balance-of-payments statement: the current account, the capital account and the official transactions account. There are three items under the current account. The goods category states the monetary values of a nation's international transactions in physical goods. The services category shows the values of a wide variety of transactions, such as transportation services, consulting, travel, passenger fares, fees, royalties, rent and investment income. Finally, unilateral transfers include all transactions for which there is no quid pro quo. Private remittances, personal gifts, philanthropic donations, relief and aid are included within this account. Unilateral transfers have less impact on the U.S. market but are important to markets elsewhere. For example, remittances from workers abroad have fueled demand for consumer products in many developing countries such as Egypt, Mexico and the Philippines.

The capital account is divided into two parts on the basis of time. *Short-term transactions* refer to maturities less than or equal to one year, and *long-term transactions* refer to maturities longer than one year. Purchases of Treasury bills, certificates of deposit, foreign exchange and commercial paper are typical short-term investments. Long-term investments are separated further into portfolio investments and direct investments.

Table 2.5 Balance of Payments

	Uses of Funds	Sources of Funds
Current Account		
1. Goods	Imports	Exports
2. Services	Imports	Exports
3. Unilateral transfers	Paid abroad	From abroad
Capital Account		
1. Short-term investment	Made abroad	From abroad
2. Long-term investment	Made abroad	From abroad
a. Portfolio investment		
b. Direct investment		
Official Transactions Account		
Official reserve changes	Gained	Lost

In general, the purchaser of a portfolio investment holds no management control over the foreign investment. Debt securities such as notes and bonds are included under this heading. Foreign direct investments are long-term ownership interests, such as business capital outlays in foreign subsidiaries and branches. Stock purchases are included as well, but only if such ownership entails substantial control over the foreign company. Countries differ in the percentage of total outstanding stock an individual must hold in order for an investment to be considered a direct investment in the balance-of-payment statements. These values range from 10 percent to 25 percent.

Because it is recorded in double-entry bookkeeping form, the BOP as a whole must always have its inflows (sources of funds) equal its outflows (uses of funds). Therefore, the concept of a deficit or surplus refers only to selected parts of the entire statement. A deficit occurs when the particular outflows (uses of funds) exceed the particular inflows (sources of funds). A surplus occurs when the inflows considered exceed the corresponding outflows. In this sense, a nation's surplus or deficit is similar to that of individuals or businesses. If we spend more than we earn, we are in a deficit position. If we earn more than we spend, we are running a surplus.

The most widely used measure of a nation's international payments position is the statement of balance on current account. It shows whether a nation is living within or beyond its means. Because this statement includes unilateral transfers, deficits (in the absence of government intervention) must be financed by international borrowing or by attracting foreign investments. Therefore, the measure is considered to be a reflection of a nation's financial claims on other countries.

Exchange Rates

The purchase of a foreign good or service can be thought of as involving two sequential transactions: the purchase of the foreign currency followed by the purchase of the foreign item itself. If the cost of buying either the foreign currency or the foreign item rises, the price to the importer increases. A ratio that measures the value of one currency in terms of another currency is called an exchange rate. An exchange rate makes it possible to compare domestic and foreign prices.

World Beat 2.1

Devaluation All Over Again

Venezuela devalued its currency twice over a period of three years. Both times the devaluation was large. Prior to the first devaluation, the government tried to support an artificially high exchange rate by enacting currency controls. These controls particularly hurt foreign companies operating in Venezuela. Telefonica, Spain's second largest company, was prevented from repatriating nearly $2 billion in profits. Dollars were available on the black market but were selling for over three times the official rate.

The first devaluation of the Venezuelan bolivar cut the value of the local currency in half from 2.15 bolivars to the dollar to 4.3 bolivars to the dollar. But this action failed to make life any easier for global marketers. A complicated regime of price and currency controls remained. Companies with significant sales in Venezuela such as Avon, Colgate and Clorox saw their reported earnings drop. Many reported millions of dollars in currency losses. Avon reported an expected one-time after-tax loss of $60 million.

The first devaluation temporarily eased the demand for dollars and helped Venezuela's balance of payments, but these advantages were quickly negated. Inflation surged due to the fact that almost all consumer goods sold in-country were imported. Soon Venezuela was nearly out of dollars again, prompting a second devaluation from 4.3 bolivars to the dollar to 8.6 bolivars to the dollar. Still there remained a shortage of dollars to meet local demand, and currency controls remained in place. On the black market, the price for a dollar soared to 18 bolivars, signaling the large gap that remained between the official price and what the market would pay.

Sources: Jason Sinclair and Santiago Perez, "Venezuelan Currency Controls Curb Profit," *Wall Street Journal*, September 15, 2009; "Update 3-Revlon Q4 Profit Rises, Sees Venezuela Hurting 2010," Reuter News, February 25, 2010; Kejal Vyas and David Luhnow, "Venezuela to Devalue Currency," *Wall Street Journal*, December 31, 2010; and Ezequiel Minaya and Kejal Vyas, "Venezuela Slashes Currency Value," *Wall Street Journal Online*, February 9, 2013.

When a currency rises in value against another currency, it is said to appreciate. When it falls in value, it is said to depreciate. Therefore, a change in the value of the U.S. dollar exchange rate from 0.50 British pound to 0.65 British pound is an appreciation of the dollar and a depreciation of the pound. The dollar now buys more pounds, whereas a greater number of pounds must be spent to purchase one dollar.

The Foreign Exchange Market

Foreign exchange transactions are handled on an over-the-counter market, largely by phone or e-mail. Private and commercial customers as well as banks, brokers and central banks conduct millions of transactions on this worldwide market daily.

As Figure 2.1 shows, the foreign exchange market has a hierarchical structure. Private customers deal mainly with banks in the retail market, and banks stand ready either to buy or to sell foreign exchange as long as a free and active market for the currency exists. Banks that have foreign exchange departments trade with private commercial customers on the retail market, but they also deal with other banks (domestic or foreign) and brokers on the wholesale market. Generally, these wholesale transactions are for amounts of US$1 million or more. Not all banks participate directly in the foreign exchange market. Smaller banks may handle customers' business through correspondent banks.

Central banks play a key role in the foreign exchange markets because they are the ultimate controllers of domestic money supplies. When they enter the market to influence the exchange rate directly, they deal mainly with brokers and large money market banks. Their trading is done not to make a profit but to attain some macroeconomic goal, such as altering the exchange rate value, reducing inflation or changing domestic interest rates. In general, even if central banks do not

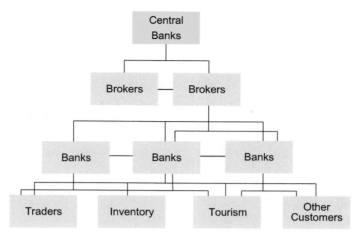

Figure 2.1 Structure of the Foreign Exchange Market

intervene in the foreign exchange markets, their actions influence exchange rate values because large increases in a nation's money supply increase its inflation rate and lower the international value of its currency.

Causes of Exchange Rate Movements

Exchange rates are among the most closely watched and politically sensitive economic variables. Regardless of which way the rates move, some groups are hurt and other groups are helped. When a currency's value rises against other currencies, domestic businesses find it more difficult to compete internationally, and the domestic unemployment rate may rise. When the value of a currency falls, foreign goods become more expensive, the cost of living increases and domestically produced goods can become cheaper to foreign buyers. What are the causes of these exchange rate movements, and to what extent can governments influence them?

Most major currencies are freely floating. Their exchange rates are determined by the forces of supply and demand. Consumers in different countries can affect the supply and demand for these national currencies. An increase in a nation's GDP gives consumers in that country the wherewithal to purchase more goods and services. Because many of the newly purchased goods are likely to be foreign, increases in GDP will raise the demand for foreign products and therefore raise the demand for foreign currencies.

Similarly, a relatively high inflation rate can shift consumer demand and weaken a currency. If the U.S. inflation rate exceeds that of Japan, then U.S. goods will become progressively more expensive than Japanese goods. Consequently, U.S. consumers may begin to demand more Japanese goods, thereby increasing the supply of dollars to the foreign exchange market while increasing the demand for Japanese yen. For the same reason, Japanese consumers will reduce their demand for dollars as they purchase fewer U.S. goods. Therefore, inflation in the United States will cause the international value of the dollar to fall and the value of other currencies to rise.

Supply and demand for currencies are also affected by investors and speculators. If, for example, Japanese interest rates were greater than U.S. interest rates (adjusted for such things as risk, taxes and maturity), then investors would have an incentive to sell dollars and purchase yen in order to place their funds where they earned the highest return—in Japan. Speculators buy and sell currencies in anticipation of changing future values. If there were a widespread expectation that the Japanese yen would rise in value relative to the dollar, speculators would try to purchase yen with dollars in anticipation of that change.

Political risk can also affect exchange rate movements. The Turkish lira twice suffered a significant depreciation as a result of government corruption scandals. The Russian ruble depreciated as a result of large-scale protests following a disputed parliamentary election.[8]

Finally, governments affect foreign exchange markets in a variety of ways. Because governments exercise strong and direct controls over domestic money supplies, their activities affect inflation rates and interest rates, which, in turn, affect the exchange rates of their currencies. Governments also influence exchange rates as major buyers and sellers in foreign exchange markets.

Managed Currencies

The foreign exchange market just described is not applicable to all currencies. Small, less developed countries often have currencies that attract little global demand. No effective international markets develop for these soft currencies. Also, until recently, most foreign exchange rates in developing countries were set by the government. This is still true in many countries today. Managed currencies are usually pegged to the currency of a developed country that is a major trading partner. Many are pegged to the U.S. dollar. Some are pegged to a combination, or basket, of major currencies. The value of the local currency relative to the major currency is sometimes kept stable and other times allowed to fluctuate a few percentage points based on market demand.

Pegged currencies are not immune to the forces of supply and demand. Defending a peg from devaluation requires keeping a relatively strong demand for the local currency in line with the price set by the government. If domestic inflation is higher than that of trading partners, local goods can quickly become too overpriced to sell on export markets. Governments cannot indefinitely prop up currencies if there is little demand for them because of such factors as low levels of export earnings or low levels of inward bound foreign investment. Trying to defend a peg too long can result in sudden large devaluations in developing countries instead of more gradual ones.

World Beat 2.2

The Land of the Rising and Falling Yen

A 34 percent rise in the yen against the dollar over five years should worry Japanese exporters. After all, a strengthening yen makes products made in Japan more expensive when costs accrued in yen are translated into foreign currencies. Some exporters, however, not only survived but expanded under these adverse conditions. One Japanese exporter of gyros and sensors used in hybrid cars and fighter jets discovered that their customers had few if any options to substitute for their products. Their customers had no choice but to accept a higher price for the Japanese imports.

A strong yen also proved beneficial to the many Japanese MNCs that were investing overseas. Whether used to set up production abroad or purchase local companies, a strong yen translates into more local currency and consequently makes the cost of these overseas investments cheaper for a Japanese company. Not surprisingly, Japan became the single largest source of foreign investment in a number of Asian countries.

However, the yen's strong run eventually came to an abrupt halt when the Japanese currency fell over 20 percent against the U.S. dollar in a matter of months. Japanese exporters who had been hurt by the strong yen, such as Nissan Motors, applauded the depreciation, while the CEO of Toyota lamented that the yen needed to fall even further. Toshiba reported mixed reactions. A lower yen helps its semiconductor business that exports from Japan but hurts its television and computer businesses that are highly dependent on imported components.

Sources: Emily Chasan, "US Firms Brace for a Wallop," Dow Jones Top Global Market Stories, March 19, 2013; "China Begins to Lose Edge as World's Factory Floor," *Wall Street Journal Online*, January 16, 2013; Chester Dawson, "Japan Inc. Battles in Yen's Shadow," *Wall Street Journal*, November 24, 2012, p. B1; Daisuke Wakabayasi and Hiroyuki Kachi, "Yen's Tumble Brightens Prospects for Earnings in Japan," *Wall Street Journal Online*, January 30, 2013; and Phred Dvorak, Daisuke Wakabayasi and Yoree Koh, "Weaker Yen a Mixed Blessing for Japanese Businesses," *Wall Street Journal Online*, May 11, 2013.

For example, Venezuela experienced several years of depressed export earnings because of continued low prices on oil, its major export. The Venezuelan bolivar plunged against the U.S. dollar after the Venezuelan government relinquished a six-year-old system to keep the bolivar steady with the dollar. Even with the collapse of the bolivar, Venezuela experienced capital flight as people hurried to exchange bolivars for dollars. Although few currencies today are nonconvertible, Venezuela was forced to establish currency controls to restrict access to foreign exchange. This caused problems for foreign firms in the country such as General Motors, Ford and Procter & Gamble. These firms waited months for the government to approve requests to change local currency into U.S. dollars for purposes of paying foreign suppliers.[9]

In the past, the Chinese yuan was pegged to the U.S. dollar. Neighboring Asian countries sometimes saw their currencies appreciate against a weakening U.S. dollar. When this occurred, manufacturers in Korea, Thailand and Taiwan had to decide whether to raise prices in the United States or cut into their already thin margins at home. This put manufacturers in these countries at a disadvantage compared with manufacturers in China where the yuan remained more aligned to the dollar. However, the Chinese government has slowly responded to international pressure to revalue its currency, and today the Chinese yuan is pegged to a basket of currencies. The appreciation of the Chinese yuan compounded by rising labor costs in China has increased the competitiveness of other countries. Many U.S. companies that moved manufacturing to China for its cost advantage are now relocating to Mexico.[10]

Implications for Global Marketers

Intuitively, citizens may be proud of a strong national currency. A strong currency can, however, present challenges to international marketers and particularly to firms that export products manufactured in their home country. The strengthening of a domestic or home currency against the currency of that country's trading partners can have a negative effect on exporters. On the other hand, weakening currency in its domestic market can be a challenge to a firm that depends on critical imports. An airline in Brazil saw its costs to fuel a Boeing jet with imported fuel priced in U.S. dollars increase by 40 percent when the Brazilian real depreciated against the U.S. dollar.[11] The cost of servicing debt denominated in a foreign currency can also increase when the foreign currency appreciates against a firm's domestic currency.

Currency fluctuations can also affect global marketers in other ways such as the valuation of overseas sales, profits and licensing fees. Currency fluctuations also impact the costs of marketing investments in foreign markets and may serve as the catalyst for a firm to expand operations in a foreign market or even leave a market.

Impact on Export Markets

When the currency of a foreign market depreciates against an exporter's home currency, there are immediate implications for export pricing. The costs of producing the product increase immediately when translated into the foreign currency in which the product is priced and sold. Marketers must decide between two options. They can raise prices in the export market to preserve profit margins, or they can keep prices steady in hopes of sustaining or even increasing market share.

MAINTAINING THE EXPORT PRICE An exporter may decide against raising prices in an export market where currency devaluation has occurred. Choosing this option means that the firm decides to accept lower margins and consequently lower profits on its export sales. Such a decision is not an easy one to make. However there are good reasons to consider this option.

Significant currency devaluation often denotes a period of economic stress. Some necessary goods that are imported, such as energy and food, will increase in price. This leaves local buyers with less discretionary income. Many consumers look for bargains and cut back on non-essential products. Following a major devaluation of the ruble, Russian consumers saw their purchasing power plummet. Consequently sales of Coca-Cola fell 60 percent in Russia.[12] Similarly, business buyers put off capital purchases such as buying new machinery. Raising prices in this environment may result in a significant loss of sales volume. This loss of sales volume may not be offset by the product's increased price.

Another reason to maintain prices is a competitive concern. Some competitors may enjoy a currency advantage as the result of the depreciation in the export market. Local producers in the export market will not immediately experience a rise in costs. Consequently, locally produced products become more competitive compared to imported products. In addition, certain global competitors may also experience a currency advantage if their home currencies do not appreciate as much against the currency of the export market. For example, were the Australian dollar to appreciate more against the euro than the Brazilian real appreciated against the euro, then Brazilian beef exporters would experience a currency advantage over Australian beef exporters when selling to the euro zone. Brazilian suppliers might feel little need to raise prices in the European market thus forcing Australian producers to keep prices down as well. Therefore exporters must not only consider the impact of currency fluctuations on customers. Exporters must monitor their major competitors whose home currencies could provide them with an advantage as a result of currency fluctuation.

Such a competitive currency advantage has helped many non-traditional destinations to increase their share of the American study abroad market. Nearly a quarter of a million U.S. students study abroad every year, and a favorite destination is Europe. However, when the U.S. dollar depreciates too much against the euro, universities seek cheaper overseas opportunities for their students. As a result, African countries such as Ghana, Mali and South Africa have increased their market share of American students studying abroad.[13]

In the case of exporters that compete fully or partially on cost, raising prices can be especially problematic. When India's rupee appreciated against the U.S. dollar it particularly hurt India's IT services industry. While industry costs rose in dollar terms, Indian IT firms did not increase their prices to U.S. customers to fully cover these increased costs. Profitability in the industry fell an estimated 8 percent.[14]

If management decides that prices cannot be increased, they may seek ways to contain costs instead. When the U.S. dollar reached a 16-year high against most foreign currencies, the cost of American-made products (translated into those foreign currencies) soared. This forced U.S. manufacturers to find creative ways to compete overseas as well as to protect their own home market from foreign competitors that enjoyed a cost advantage. Automatic Feed Company of Ohio embarked on its most extensive product redesign in its 52-year history trying to offset the cost advantage of its foreign competitors.[15]

Another way to contain costs is to source the export market from a cheaper location. For many years O.R.T. Technologies resisted moving any operations outside its home base of Israel. However, when the Israeli shekel soared 31 percent against the U.S. dollar, the company was forced to transfer some of its development work to Eastern Europe.[16] Many Canadian exporters are hurt when the Canadian dollar increases in value against the U.S. dollar, especially since over 70 percent of merchandise exports go to the United States. However, some Canadian exporters can better weather the appreciation of the Canadian currency because they have U.S. manufacturing operations as well.

Of course the ability to enact cost containment varies by situation as well as by firm. If the devaluation of a currency in an overseas market is large and swift, this makes adapting to it more difficult than if it is more predictable and gradual. In any case, larger firms usually have more resources to respond with cost-cutting measures than do smaller firms.

RAISING THE EXPORT PRICE Exporters may also decide to raise prices in an export market in response to a depreciating foreign currency. This is an attempt to pass on to buyers some or all of the exporter's increased costs. In order to successfully employ this strategy, a global marketer must answer the following questions:

Can the brand command a higher price? As we will discuss in Chapter 11, the value of a brand is the difference between a price the branded product commands and the price a buyer would pay for the product without a brand. A strong global brand may be able to sustain increased prices without losing as many buyers as would a lesser known brand or a generic product.

Are we selling a prestige product? Some consumer goods and services are bought largely for prestige. In such cases, consumers may be more likely to accept higher prices, since price is not their major purchase criterion. High prices may in fact bestow increased prestige on the product. Hermes, a European firm that sells luxury scarves and ties, marked up its entire U.S. line by 5 percent when the U.S. dollar depreciated against the euro.[17]

Can we deliver more value to the buyer in return for charging a higher price? Marketers should be wary, however, about relying on a product's brand or prestige. During the most recent global downturn, even luxury products with prestigious global brands experienced declines in sales. If companies raise prices in export markets they may need to invest in more salespeople and market research in order to deliver better value to customers. One creative way to offer value to buyers is to mitigate some of their foreign exchange risk. One year when the U.S. dollar was tumbling against the euro, many European hotels offered guaranteed prices in dollars to American tourists seeking to book rooms.[18]

Impact on Import Pricing

Sometimes currency fluctuations impact importers as well, especially when the importer is a retail establishment. When the Japanese yen surged in value against the U.S. dollar and the euro, many Japanese retailers advertised "strong-yen sales" and offered discounts on imported products. Department stores discounted Italian shoes and supermarkets discounted Australian beef and American broccoli.[19] Currency fluctuations can even impact the competitiveness of retailers. Failure to pass on currency savings to customers threatened Australian retailers when the Australian dollar appreciated significantly. Online shopping overseas suddenly increased 74 percent as Australians went to the Internet to spend their valuable currency on products abroad that were denominated in weaker currencies. Many even flew to New York for buying sprees where an iPad cost only AUS\$520 compared to AUS\$630 back home.[20]

Impact on Subsidiary Earnings

Many global marketers own subsidiaries abroad where products sold in that market are produced in that market. In such cases, devaluation of the local currency does not cause an immediate increase in production costs for the local subsidiary of the foreign firm. (If the subsidiary imports a significant portion of their products' inputs, however, production costs will eventually rise as import costs rise.)

Nonetheless, currency fluctuations overseas affect the reporting of earnings in the market where depreciation or appreciation has occurred. In the year following a major devaluation of the Argentine peso, consumer expenditures on leisure and recreation remained steady when measured in pesos. However, these expenditures fell 68 percent when measured in U.S. dollars.[21] A U.S.-based entertainment firm operating in the Argentine market would inevitably report a significant drop in dollar earnings. Alternatively, if the peso appreciates against the U.S. dollar, reported earnings in Argentina rise in dollar terms even when sales in pesos remain the same. Nestlé, the world's largest foods company, posted a 13 percent decrease in sales due to the appreciation of its domestic currency, the Swiss franc. Sales in Nestlé's vast overseas markets actually increased by nearly 80 percent, but those sales were denominated in foreign currencies and consequently translated into less and less Swiss francs.[22]

MNCs tend to think primarily in terms of their own home currencies and sometimes evaluate the attractiveness of a market solely on those terms. However, global marketers should differentiate between market realities and currency fluctuations. The Turkish sales force of a U.S. multinational pharmaceutical firm was congratulated for attaining the highest sales per salesperson of any of the firm's national sales forces. Two weeks later after a major devaluation of the Turkish lira, headquarters told the Turkish sales force that their contribution (measured in U.S. dollars) no longer looked good. Of course the Turkish sales force had no control over the fluctuations of their national currency. Needless to say, headquarters' attitude resulted in a morale crisis at their Turkish subsidiary.

Impact on Licensing and Franchising Fees

Some firms do not directly sell their products or services abroad. Instead they license or franchise them to local companies overseas. (These modes of market entry are discussed in Chapter 9.) MNCs that license or franchise collect fees from their foreign partners. These fees are usually determined as a percentage of local sales denominated in the local currency and are therefore subject to the same translation issues that face subsidiary earnings.

Reevaluating Market Participation

Sometimes a relative change in currencies causes marketers to reevaluate their participation in certain international markets. Some currency fluctuations create new market opportunities. However, currency fluctuations can also cause marketers to leave a foreign market. This can occur if exporters decide that they cannot reasonably raise prices in response to currency devaluation in an export market. However, many MNCs take a longer-term view of the situation. They remain in the market, temporarily accept lower margins and attempt to defend their market share. A local currency devaluation can even make buying assets or purchasing companies cheaper for those holding foreign currency. At the same time that the Indian IT firms faced export difficulties because of a strong rupee, they also took advantage of a strong rupee to purchase U.S. companies. The dollar prices of these companies, translated into rupees, appeared to be real bargains.

An appreciating currency can even motivate some MNCs to rethink the location of their global or regional headquarters. Many firms who located their international or regional headquarters in Switzerland balked at how expensive the country had become after the Swiss franc soared 32 percent against the U.S. dollar and 14 percent against the euro in the space of a year. Despite possible tax savings available in Switzerland, a number of firms considered relocating to other countries in order to capture significant savings on expenses and expatriate pay packages.[23]

International Agencies for Promoting Economic and Monetary Stability

Stability in the international economy is often thought to be a prerequisite for worldwide peace and prosperity. It was for this reason that at the end of World War II, representatives from several countries met at Bretton Woods, New Hampshire, and formed both the International Monetary Fund and the World Bank (the International Bank for Reconstruction and Development). With headquarters in Washington, D.C., these two agencies continue to play major roles on the international scene.

International Monetary Fund (IMF)

The core mission of the International Monetary Fund (IMF) was to help stabilize an increasingly global economy. The IMF's original goals were to promote orderly and stable foreign exchange markets, restore free convertibility among the currencies of member nations, reduce international impediments to trade and provide assistance to countries that experienced temporary BOP deficits.

Over the years, the IMF has shifted its focus from exchange rate relations among industrialized countries to the prevention of economic instability in developing countries. The Mexican economic crisis in 1994 prompted an unprecedented bailout of $47 billion and launched the recent trend of providing rescue packages to major economies in the developing world. In the past several years, the IMF approved a $19 billion rescue package for Turkey and led a $17.2 billion rescue for Thailand, a $42 billion package for Indonesia and a $41.5 billion deal for Brazil. South Korea got a whopping $58.4 billion when it was on the verge of bankruptcy. These rescue packages helped stabilize the respective economies and avoid total economic collapse of the countries involved.

To qualify for assistance, the IMF may require that countries take drastic economic steps, such as reducing tariff barriers, privatizing state-owned enterprises (SOEs), curbing domestic inflation and cutting government expenditures. Although many nations have resented such intervention, banks worldwide have used the IMF as a screening device for their private loans to many developing countries. If countries qualify for IMF loans, they are considered for private credit. A growing world economy in the early twenty-first century resulted in fewer crises for the IMF to manage. Its loan portfolio fell to the lowest level since the 1980s, and its influence over countries and their economies diminished. However, the global downturn in 2009 reversed this trend.

World Bank

The World Bank (International Bank for Reconstruction and Development) acts as an intermediary between the private capital markets and the developing nations. It makes long-term loans (usually 15 or 25 years) carrying rates that reflect prevailing market conditions. By virtue of its AAA credit rating, the bank is able to borrow private funds at relatively low market rates and pass the savings along to the developing nations. However, because it must borrow to obtain capital and is not funded by members' contributions, the World Bank must raise lending rates when its costs (that is, market interest rates) rise.

When private funds were pouring into developing economies, some critics questioned the future role of the World Bank. However, a pan-Asian economic crisis caused the flow of private funds to developing countries to drop by more than $100 billion in 1998. The World Bank has expanded its role from mostly loans to partial guarantees of government bonds for investment projects. In Thailand, the World Bank partially guaranteed the Electricity Generating Authority of Thailand. The guarantee attracted investors and spawned interest in similar programs in South Korea and the Philippines. In addition, the World Bank is encouraging governments to improve financial supervision and reduce red tape.

Group of Seven

The world's leading industrial nations have established a Group of Seven, which meets regularly to discuss the world economy. Finance ministers and central bank governors from the United States, Japan, Germany, France, Britain, Italy and Canada make up this group, which is often referred to as the G7. (When Russia joins the talks, the group calls itself the G8.) The members work together informally to help stabilize the world economy and reduce extreme disruptions. For example, the G7 developed proposals to reduce the debt of 33 impoverished nations, mostly in Africa, by 70 percent. The G8 agreed to help rebuild the Balkans, including Serbia, if it continued to demonstrate a full commitment to economic and democratic reforms.

Protectionism and Trade Restrictions

It is a fact of life that like virtually all changes, free trade creates both beneficiaries and victims. By increasing competition, free trade lowers the price of imported goods and raises the overseas demand for efficiently produced domestic goods. In these newly stimulated export industries, sales will increase, profits will rise and stock prices will climb. Clearly, consumers of the imported good and producers of the exported good benefit from these new conditions. However, it is equally clear that other groups are harmed. Domestic producers of the import-competing goods are one of the most visible of such groups. They experience noticeable declines in market share, falling profits and deteriorating stock prices.

Herein lies the major reason for protectionist legislation. The victims of free trade are highly visible and their losses quantifiable. Governments use protectionism as a means of lessening the harm done to these easily identified groups. Conversely, the individuals who are helped by free trade tend to be dispersed throughout the nation rather than concentrated in a specific region. However, when too many citizens face economic hardship, governments reconsider protectionist measures. Despite an overall trend toward trade liberalization in the past several decades, protectionism rose in 2009 in response to a worldwide economic crisis. Large and small countries alike raised taxes on imports, and national economic stimulus packages unabashedly favored national suppliers.[24]

Protectionist legislation tends to take the form of tariffs, quotas, a variety of non-tariff barriers and restrictions on access to foreign exchange. This section describes these barriers and their economic effects.

Tariffs

Tariffs are taxes on goods moving across an economic or political boundary. They can be imposed on imports, exports or goods in transit through a country on their way to some other destination. In the United States, export tariffs are constitutionally prohibited, but in other parts of the world they are quite common. Export tariffs can provide a source of government funding. Brazil used tariffs on agricultural exports such as soybeans to fund various social programs. However, similar export tariffs in Argentina motivated many farmers to stockpile their grain and refuse to export.

The most common type of tariff is the import tariff. Import tariffs have a dual economic effect. First, they tend to raise the price of imported goods and thereby protect domestic industries from foreign competition. Second, they generate tax revenues for the governments imposing them. Regardless of what the goals are, tariffs may not be the most direct or effective means of attaining them. For example, foreign sellers may lower their prices to offset any tariff increase. The net effect is for the consumer-paid price to differ only slightly, if at all, from the price before the tariff was imposed. Consequently, the nation has greater tariff revenues but little additional protection for the domestic producers.

When tariffs do raise the price of an imported good, consumers are put at a disadvantage, whereas the import-competing industries are helped. However, tariffs can have wider implications. For example, when the U.S. Department of Commerce imposed a high duty on advanced flat screens used on laptop computers, the duty helped some small U.S. screen manufacturers. But it hurt computer companies such as Apple, Compaq and IBM, who argued that the high duty inflated the cost of their products, undermined their ability to compete abroad and would force them to shift production to other countries.

Quotas

Quotas are physical limits on the amount of goods that can be imported into a country. Unlike tariffs, which restrict trade by increasing the cost of importing, quotas directly restrict imports. Once the quota limit has been reached, imports cease to enter the domestic market, regardless of whether foreign exporters lower their prices. For domestic producers, quotas are a much surer means of protection. For exporters, quotas can be disastrous. Complaining that Uzbekistan had failed to adhere to a free trade agreement, Ukraine restricted imports of automobiles from Uzbekistan to only three vehicles a year for a period of three years. This three-car quota severely injured a General Motors joint venture in Uzbekistan that expected Ukraine to be one of its major export markets.[25]

Consumers also lose with the imposition of quotas. Not only are their product choices limited and the prices increased, but the goods that foreign exporters choose to ship often carry the highest profit margins. Restrictions on imported automobiles, for instance, result in the import of more luxury models with high-cost accessories. Foreign producers are restricted in the number of cars they can sell and consequently seek the highest margin per car. Sometimes higher prices create political backlash from consumers that leads to the lifting of import quotas. Indonesia imposed quotas of cattle and frozen beef as part of its goal to foster food self-sufficiency. However, the government retracted the quotas when beef prices soared.[26]

Orderly Marketing Arrangements and Voluntary Export Restrictions

An orderly marketing arrangement or voluntary export restriction (VER) is an agreement between countries to share markets by limiting foreign export sales. Usually, these arrangements have a set duration and provide for some annual increase in foreign sales to the domestic market. The euphemistic terms are intended to give the impression of fairness. After all, who can be against anything that is orderly or voluntary?

Scratch the surface of these so-called negotiated settlements, however, and a different image appears. First, the negotiations are initiated by the importing country with the implicit threat that unless concessions are made, stronger unilateral sanctions will be imposed. They are really neither orderly nor voluntary. They are quotas in the guise of negotiated agreements. For example, the U.S. Commerce Department reached an agreement whereby Russia would voluntarily limit its steel imports into the United States to 750,000 tons per year, compared with 3,500,000 tons in the previous year. If Russia had not agreed to the limits, the Commerce Department was prepared to announce duties of 71 to 218 percent on Russian steel.[27]

At one time there were approximately 300 VERs worldwide, most protecting the United States and Europe. Today signatories to the WTO agree not to enact such agreements. However, exceptions can be granted to protect a single sector of a national economy. For example, solar-panel manufacturers in China told the European Union (EU) that they would be open to voluntary export restrictions as a way to avoid steep tariffs that the EU was proposing to enact in order to protect European solar-panel companies from low-priced imports from China.[28]

Nontariff Trade Barriers

Nontariff barriers include a wide range of charges, requirements and restrictions, such as surcharges at border crossings, licensing regulations, performance requirements, government subsidies, health and safety regulations, packaging and labeling regulations, and size and weight requirements. Not all of these barriers are discriminatory and protectionist. Restrictions dealing with public health and safety are certainly legitimate, but the line between social well-being and protection is a fine one.

At what point do consular fees, import restrictions, packaging regulations, performance requirements, licensing rules and government procurement procedures discriminate against foreign producers? Is a French tax on automobile horsepower targeted against powerful U.S. cars, or is it simply a tax on inefficiency and pollution? Are U.S. automobile safety standards unfair to German, Japanese and other foreign car manufacturers? Does a French ban on advertising bourbon and scotch (but not cognac) serve the public's best interest?

Sometimes, nontariff barriers can have considerable impact on foreign competition. For decades, German authorities forbade the sale of beer in Germany unless it was brewed from barley malt, hops, yeast and water. If any other additives were used—a common practice elsewhere—German authorities denied foreign brewers the right to label their products as beer. The law was eventually struck down by the European Court of Justice.

Nevertheless, many nontariff barriers continue in many creative ways. For example, under China's WTO commitments, quotas for imported cars were to be abolished. However, a Chinese policy paper that outlined China's plan to become a major car manufacturer suggested a number of nontariff ideas to support the local automobile industry, such as restricting the number of ports where foreign imports can be offloaded and requiring Chinese-made and foreign-made automobiles to use different sales outlets. The latter would increase the cost of introducing new brands and effectively slow imports.[29] Similarly, Argentina attempted to support its publishing industry by informing customers of online booksellers such as Amazon that their imported books would be held at airport customs until they personally went there and proved that the ink in the books contained less than 0.06 percent lead.[30]

Restrictions on Foreign Exchange

Restricting access to foreign exchange to pay for imports is another way countries can restrict imports. Such actions can protect local industry, but they are most often employed when a country is running low of foreign reserves. Argentina enacted currency controls that allowed local companies to import products only if those imports were matched by exports. In order for one local manufacturer of plasma-television screens to import needed electronic parts, the company turned to exporting tons of seafood to buyers in Europe, China and Russia.[31]

General Agreement on Tariffs and Trade (GATT)

Because of the harmful effects of protectionism, which were most painfully felt during the Great Depression of the 1930s, 23 nations banded together in 1947 to form the General Agreement on Tariffs and Trade (GATT). Over its life, GATT has been a major forum for the liberalization and promotion of nondiscriminatory international trade between participating nations.

The principles of a world economy embodied in the articles of GATT are reciprocity, nondiscrimination and transparency. The idea of *reciprocity* is simple. If one country lowers its tariffs against another's exports, then it should expect the other country to do the same. *Nondiscrimination* means that one country should not give one member or group of members preferential treatment over other members of the group. This principle is embodied in the most favored nation (MFN) status. MFN does not mean that one country is most favored, but rather that it receives no less favorable treatment than any other. *Transparency* refers to the GATT policy that nations make any trade restrictions overt, such as replacing nontariff barriers with tariffs. Through these principles, many trade restrictions have been effectively reduced.

Although its most notable gains have been in considerably reducing tariff and quota barriers on many goods, GATT has also helped to simplify and homogenize trade documentation procedures, discourage government subsidies and curtail dumping (that is, selling abroad at a cost lower than the cost of production).

The Uruguay Round of GATT talks, which lasted seven years, was finally completed in late 1993. This agreement covered several controversial areas, such as patents and national protection of agriculture and the textile and clothing industry.

World Trade Organization (WTO)

The final act of GATT was to replace itself with the World Trade Organization (WTO) in 1996. The WTO continues to pursue reductions in tariffs on manufactured goods as well as liberalization of trade in agriculture and services. With 159 member countries, the WTO is the global watchdog for free trade. China became part of the WTO in 2001 after 14 years of negotiations concerning its vast semi-planned economy, with its formidable array of import quotas, trade licenses and import inspections. Russia was admitted in 2012. Since its inception the WTO has established an agreement on tariff-free trade in IT among 40 countries, as well as a financial services agreement that covers 95 percent of trade in banking and insurance. An agreement on intellectual property covering patents, trademarks and copyrights has also been negotiated.

A major advantage that the WTO offers over GATT involves the resolution of disputes. Under GATT, any member could veto the outcome of a panel ruling on a dispute. WTO panels are stricter. They must report their decisions in nine months and can be overturned only by consensus. Countries that break the rules must pay compensation, mend their ways or face trade sanctions.

The use of quotas has declined with the strengthening of the WTO and with increased compliance by its member countries. The WTO has also been instrumental in addressing some of the many nontariff barriers global marketers still face. The WTO ruled against the Chinese government's distribution monopoly of imported U.S. films, music, video games and other copyrighted materials. Previously China forced motion picture suppliers to use the state-run China Film Group Corporation whose high fees resulted in thin margins and diminished profits for U.S. studios.[32]

The WTO has not been used by the more powerful countries solely to control the less powerful ones, as some feared. Costa Rica, for example, asked the WTO to rule against American barriers to its export of men's underwear. It won the case, and the United States was forced to change its import rules.

The WTO's current concerns focus on several challenges. First, the WTO continues to push for liberalization of foreign investment. Other challenges comprise the "new issues" of trade policy such as competition policy, labor standards and even censorship. Taiwan, for example, has a strong modern dance culture that is accepting of nudity onstage. Mainland Chinese authorities consider this pornographic. Did joining the WTO mean that China could someday lose its right to ban performing arts from Taiwan that it considered offensive?

Economic Integration as a Means of Promoting Trade

Another important issue facing the WTO is the spread of regional trading agreements. The WTO exempts members of regional trade agreements from the MFN principle. In other words, the United States could extend Israel a lower tariff rate under a free-trade agreement that it would not have to extend to other countries under the MFN principle expected by WTO membership. Recently there has been a significant increase in the number of such agreements. There are nearly 400 active regional agreements between countries granting preferential access to each other's markets. Nearly all members of the WTO belong to at least one regional pact. Table 2.6 lists examples of such agreements.

Although the degree of economic integration can vary considerably from one organization to another, four major types of integration can be identified: free-trade areas, customs unions, common markets and monetary unions.

Table 2.6 Selected Integration Agreements

Agreement	Countries	Founding Date	Agreement Type
NAFTA (North American Free Trade Agreement)	Canada, Mexico, United States	1994	Free-trade area
EU (European Union)	Austria, Belgium, Bulgaria, Croatia, Cyprus, Czech Republic, Denmark, Estonia, Finland, France, Germany, Greece, Hungary, Ireland, Italy, Latvia, Lithuania, Luxembourg, Malta, Netherlands, Poland, Portugal, Romania, Slovak Republic, Slovenia, Spain, Sweden, United Kingdom	1951	Common market
AFTA (ASEAN Free Trade Area)	Brunei Darussalam, Cambodia, Indonesia, Laos, Malaysia, Myanmar, Philippines, Singapore, Thailand, Vietnam	1992	Free-trade area
MERCOSUR (Southern Common Market)	Argentina, Brazil, Paraguay, Uruguay, Venezuela	1991	Customs union
CAN (Andean Community)	Bolivia, Colombia, Ecuador, Peru, Venezuela	1969	Customs union
CIS (Commonwealth of Independent States)	Azerbaijan, Armenia, Belarus, Kazakhstan, Kyrgyz Republic, Moldova, Russian Federation, Tajikistan, Ukraine, Uzbekistan	1999	Free-trade area
GCC (Gulf Cooperation Council)	Bahrain, Kuwait, Oman, Qatar, Saudi Arabia, United Arab Emirates	1981	Customs union (as of 2003)
EFTA (European Free Trade Association)	Iceland, Liechtenstein, Norway, Switzerland	1960	Free-trade area
CACM (Central American Common Market)	Costa Rica, El Salvador, Guatemala, Honduras, Nicaragua	1960	Customs union

Free-Trade Areas

The simplest form of integration is a free-trade area. The most famous is the North American Free Trade Association (NAFTA), which includes the United States, Canada and Mexico. Within a free-trade area, nations agree to drop trade barriers among themselves, but each nation is permitted to maintain independent trade relations with countries outside the group. There is little attempt at this level to coordinate such things as domestic tax rates, environmental regulations and commercial codes. Generally such areas do not permit resources (that is, labor and capital) to flow freely across national borders. Moreover, because each country has autonomy over its money supply, exchange rates can fluctuate relative to both member and nonmember countries.

Despite the apparent simplicity of this form of economic integration, unexpected complications can arise. When NAFTA was being negotiated, U.S. business groups demanded that foreign investors be protected, noting that the Mexican government had a history of nationalizing U.S. assets. Consequently, arbitration procedures established by the World Bank ensure that governments in the United States, Mexico and Canada will pay compensation to any foreign investor whose property is seized. Arbitration panels cannot make new law. However, they can interpret law, and their rulings cannot be appealed. One NAFTA panel issued its own interpretation of the Mexican constitution and awarded $16.7 million to a California waste disposal company after the governor of the state of San Luis Potosi and a town council refused to honor the company's permit to open a toxic-waste site. The idea that NAFTA law may give foreign investors privileges over those enjoyed by local companies has many concerned in all NAFTA countries.[33]

Customs Unions

Customs unions, a more advanced form of economic integration, possess the characteristics of a free-trade area but with the added feature of a common external tariff/trade barrier for the member nations. Individual countries relinquish the right to set trade agreements outside the group independently. Instead, a supranational policymaking committee makes these decisions.

Common Markets

The third level of economic integration is a common market. This arrangement has all the characteristics of a customs union, but the organization also encourages the free flow of resources (labor and capital) among the member nations. For example, if jobs are plentiful in Germany but scarce in Italy, Italian workers can move from Italy to Germany without having to worry about severe immigration restrictions. In a common market, there is usually an attempt to coordinate tax codes, social welfare systems and other legislation that influences resource allocation. The most notable example of a common market is the European Union. The EU has been an active organization for trade liberalization and continues to increase its membership size.

When Vicente Fox was elected president of Mexico, he called for expanding NAFTA into a common market. He admitted, however, that this would be a long-term project that would gradually evolve over 20 to 40 years. As an initial step, however, he wanted the United States to accept more Mexican labor, expanding its temporary-worker program so that 300,000 or more Mexicans a year could be legally employed in the United States.

Monetary Unions

The highest form of economic integration is a monetary union. A monetary union is a common market in which member countries no longer regulate their own currencies. Rather, member-country currencies are replaced by a common currency regulated by a supranational central bank. With the passage of the Maastricht Treaty by EU members, the European Monetary System became the first monetary union in January 1999.

The EU single currency, the euro, has replaced 18 national currencies in Europe. The European Central Bank (ECB) has control over the euro and is obliged to maintain price stability and avoid inflation or deflation. The changeover to the euro was not easy, however. One study showed that a vending machine in France that dispensed coffee for two French francs could not charge the equivalent in euros. The conversion rate turned out to be 0.3049. The coffee could be repriced at 0.30 euro, causing the vendor to lose 1.5 percent of gross revenue. Alternatively, the vending machine could be expensively reconfigured to dribble out slightly less coffee.[34]

Nonetheless, supporters of the euro believed it would reduce transaction costs and foreign exchange risk within Europe and provide a strong viable currency alternative to the dollar. To date, their faith appears to be justified. A report by 11 economists estimates that trade among the euro-zone members increased by 30 percent in the first four years alone. Britain didn't adopt the euro, and UK trade with the euro zone rose by only 13 percent.[35]

The Globalization Controversy

In the wake of the recent serious recession, a *Wall Street Journal*/NBC poll revealed that 53 percent of Americans believed that free-trade agreements hurt the United States. This percentage was up from only 32 percent 11 years earlier.[36]

Some parties believe that the free trade and globalization fostered by the WTO favor developed countries seeking to sell to developing countries and not vice versa. For example, the United States, Japan and Europe maintain some of their highest tariffs on agricultural products, which account for a large portion of exports from the developing world. Agricultural subsidies in the developed world further undermine the ability of developing countries to compete in the global marketplace. Developing countries also claim that food safety standards imposed by developed countries are often discriminatory. Thailand sued Australia for requiring chicken parts to be precooked at such a high temperature that it renders the product inedible.[37]

Other opposition to globalization comes from traditional labor unions in industrialized countries as well as new groups opposed to the outsourcing of professional jobs. Both conservatives and liberals in developed and developing countries are concerned that the WTO usurps sovereignty from governments. For example, the state of Utah outlawed gambling for 110 years, and this prohibition was later extended to Internet gambling. However, the WTO ruled that the Utah law discriminated against foreign providers of "recreational services." Such rulings fuel the fears of those who believe that the WTO is an attempt to impose a one-world government.[38]

Is globalization bad or good? As we saw with the case of global outsourcing, this depends on who you are. The distribution of income in the United States reflects increased inequality over the past 25 years. Geoffrey Garrett argues that this pattern can also be observed at a national level. Twenty years of increased globalization appears to have been more advantageous to industrialized countries and the world's poorest countries. However, countries that comprise the economic middle—many of which are located in Asia and South America—have not fared as well. Real per-capita income (PCI) grew by less than 20 percent in these countries in the last two decades of the twentieth century. This was less than half the growth rate in upper-income countries and less than one-eighth the growth in the low-income countries.[39]

Middle-income countries appear to face the possibility of being squeezed out of the world economy. They do not have the political institutions or as educated a workforce to compete with the upper-income countries, so they are forced to compete with countries such as China and India in the production of more standardized products. However, this may be a losing battle as well, because these low-income countries have considerably lower wage rates.

Thus globalization remains controversial. Even countries such as South Korea that have benefited substantially from trade liberalization can express hostility toward it. South Korea's largest teachers union has urged members to tell students that free trade can increase poverty, hurt the environment and increase inequality. A survey of 8,000 respondents in ten Asian economies revealed South Koreans to be skeptical of globalization. Only 27 percent of Koreans viewed globalization positively compared to the Asian average of 38 percent.[40]

Conclusion

The global economy is in a state of transition from a set of strong national economies to a set of interlinked trading groups. This transition has accelerated over the past decades with the collapse of communism, the coalescing of the European trading nations into a single market and the expansion of membership in the WTO. The investment by Europeans, Japanese and Americans in one another's economies is unprecedented. In much of the developing world, trade and investment liberalization has accelerated as well, and companies from developing countries now invest and compete in developed countries.

There is no doubt that the world has been moving toward a single global economy. IT, telecommunications and the Internet have made worldwide information on prices, products and profits available globally and instantaneously. With markets more transparent, buyers, sellers and investors can access better opportunities, lowering costs and ensuring that resources are allocated to their most efficient use. Past changes have helped some groups and hurt others, and it remains unclear what the future of globalization will be. Successful companies will be able to anticipate trends and respond to them quickly. Less successful companies will miss the changes going on around them and wake up one day to a different marketplace governed by new rules.

Managerial Takeaways

1. *The liberalization of trade barriers due to the WTO and economic integration among and between countries is one of the major contributors to the growth of global marketing.*
2. *Nonetheless, trade barriers—quotas, tariffs and nontariff barriers—remain and can affect the global marketer's ability to compete in foreign markets.*
3. *Containing costs (while assuring quality) is paramount to success in a globally competitive environment. Global marketers increasingly look to a country's competitive advantages when deciding where to source products and services.*
4. *Different national currencies lead to exchange rate fluctuations that add significant risk to global marketing operations. Such fluctuations affect decisions concerning location of activities and pricing and in extreme cases may force a company to withdraw from certain markets.*
5. *Overall, globalization has increased incomes worldwide, and it is unlikely that trade liberalization will be reversed. But the benefits of globalization are not distributed evenly, and this leads to continued debate concerning the costs and benefits surrounding the global integration of markets.*

Questions for Discussion

1. Suppose that Brazil can produce, with an equal amount of resources, either 100 units of steel or ten computers. At the same time, Germany can produce either 150 units of steel or ten computers. Explain which nation has a comparative advantage in the production of computers. Choose a mutually advantageous trading ratio and explain why this ratio increases the welfare of both nations.

2. What problems could export tariffs cause?

3. Do you agree with critics who claim that the WTO has excessive power over national governments? Will free trade widen the gap between rich and poor? Why or why not?

4. Should the WTO have forced Utah to accept gambling?

CASE 2.1 Argentina: Trouble in Mercosur

During its first eight years, Mercosur became Latin America's most successful integration agreement. Among its members were Latin America's largest economy Brazil and its third-largest economy Argentina. From the creation of Mercosur in 1991, trade between Brazil and Argentina had increased 500 percent to reach $15 billion in 1998. However, in 1999, Mercosur's trade volume fell 20 percent. Argentina and Brazil were both experiencing recessions and disagreed on which foreign exchange policy to follow. This disagreement threatened the future of Mercosur.

Currency Challenges

During the 1990s, Argentina's Convertibility Plan pegged its peso to the U.S. dollar and banned the printing of unbacked currency. By restricting its money supply and curbing government spending, Argentina reduced inflation from 5,000 percent in 1989 to 1 percent by the year 2000. Through the early and mid-1990s, Argentina experienced an economic boom attributed to its trade liberalization, monetary and foreign exchange stability and the privatization of previously state-owned companies.

Similarly, Brazil's Real Plan initially pegged the Brazilian real to the U.S. dollar. Inflation fell from 2,500 percent in 1993 to 2.5 percent in 1998. Trade and investment liberalization encouraged investment in Brazil, but pent-up demand for capital and consumer goods caused the country's merchandise balance to drop from a surplus of US$10.5 billion in 1994 to a deficit of US$6.3 billion in 1998. The Asian financial crisis in mid-1997 caused foreign investors to worry about the future of other developing countries. Foreign capital fled Brazil, and the country's BOP deteriorated. A subsequent recession, augmented by the failure of the Brazilian Congress to pass key spending reforms, further eroded investor confidence in the country. Brazil's foreign exchange reserves continued to dwindle. The government responded by announcing a change to the free float of the real. The real plummeted against the dollar and consequently plummeted against the Argentine peso.

Argentina initially refused to consider a devaluation of its peso and even began discussing with the U.S. Treasury the possibility of formally dollarizing its economy. The idea was feasible. Panama had adopted the U.S. dollar as its official currency in 1904. Already over half of the bank deposits and loans in Argentina were in dollars. Automated teller machines dispensed both pesos and dollars. The U.S. Federal Reserve shipped tons of dollar-denominated bills overseas every year. Nearly two-thirds of the almost $500 billion in U.S. currency circulated outside the United States.

Nonetheless, dollarization would be practically irreversible. Argentina would give up control over its money supply to the U.S. Federal Reserve. Critics argued that the U.S. Federal Reserve set policy to assist the U.S. economy, which had little in common with the Argentine economy. Even talking about dollarization would undermine confidence in the peso. Others noted that the alternative of allowing the peso to float freely like the real would erode confidence even more, resulting in a devaluation of the peso.

The Argentine government remained committed to foreign exchange stability, and soon the costs of doing business in Brazil were 30 percent lower than the costs of doing business in Argentina. Argentina saw its trade surplus with Brazil disappear. Many Argentine companies and MNCs, such as Philips Electronics NV and Goodyear Tire and Rubber Company, shifted production from Argentina to Brazil. Argentina claimed to have lost 250,000 jobs since the devaluation in Brazil and responded by placing quotas on certain products imported from Brazil—the first quotas in Mercosur history. Unemployed workers marched with signs saying "Made in Brazil—No!" The state governor of Buenos Aires summed up the anti-Brazilian feeling: "The Brazilians are like bad neighbors that come into our house to steal the furniture."

In December 2001, the Argentine government temporarily set limits on the amount of money that Argentines could withdraw from banks or transfer abroad. In the previous year, 20 percent of bank deposits in the country had been converted by their owners into dollars and moved to overseas accounts. Banks were concerned about how long dollar reserves would last in the country at the rate of 1 peso to 1 dollar. Rumors of a possible devaluation of the peso were rife by early 2002. But devaluation remained problematic. Many debts and contracts in Argentina were denominated in dollars. A devaluation of the peso would increase the cost in pesos of meeting those dollar obligations. This situation in turn could cause a banking crisis.

Nonetheless, a devaluation was inevitable. Argentina allowed the peso to float temporarily, and by early November 2002 it had fallen 70 percent against the U.S. dollar. Unemployment in Argentina climbed to 20 percent, and the country defaulted on $93 billion of external debt. A general economic collapse escalated into violent street demonstrations, and the Argentina government went through five presidents in two weeks.

Rising Protectionism

In the 12 years that followed, Argentina was ruled by left-of-center administrations. The country's debt default and later restructuring still left its government with considerable debt to repay in U.S. dollars along with a restriction on issuing new debt. For a few years after the devaluation of the peso, Argentinian manufacturers regained their international competitiveness. However, beginning in 2005 double-digit inflation increasingly diminished that competitiveness resulting in an erosion of the country's trade balance. As a response, the government enacted new measures to discourage imports and maintain a favorable balance of trade. These included import quotas and an intentionally slow processing of imports through customs. The number of product categories affected by these measures grew to 600. The country blocked the import of books into the country claiming that the ink might not be safe. Imports from Brazil were not exempt from these new restrictions, and Brazil retaliated by slowing the process of moving automobiles and auto parts through customs, some of Argentina's major exports to Brazil.

Ironically, the Argentinian government also moved to restrict or tax a number of the country's key exports. Exported soya was taxed at 35 percent, wheat at 23 percent, maize at 20 percent and scrap metal at 40 percent. Restrictions on beef exports resulted in the raising of fewer cattle and lower leather output. Many foreign leather firms left the country.

Supporters of the new protectionist policies could point to some key successes. In 2002, most of the 30,000 motorcycles sold in the country were imported. By 2013, all 800,000 motorcycles sold were made in Argentina. Of the two million bicycles sold, only 2 percent were imported. The resurgence of the Argentinian bicycle industry was credited with providing 3,000 direct jobs as well as additional jobs in parts production. However, critics pointed to the fact that local production required imports. Motorcycles made in Argentina contained only 30 percent locally produced parts.

Despite Argentina's protectionist measures, imports continued to grow faster than exports. Deficit spending by the government had pushed inflation to 28 percent in 2013 and many expected that rate to grow even higher. Declaring that overseas tourism was a drain on Argentina's foreign currency reserves, the government enacted a tax of 35 percent on overseas travel and purchases abroad. Argentinians who wished to exchange pesos for dollars for other purposes faced currency controls consisting of increased paperwork, required approval from the country's tax agency, and faced unexplained delays. Several foreign retailers responded by exiting the Argentine market.

In early 2014, the government chose to devalue the peso from six pesos to a dollar to eight pesos to a dollar—Argentina's largest devaluation in 12 years. Many retailers responded by immediately raising prices by 30 percent. On the black market, the peso fell to 12.25 per dollar and many predicted another significant devaluation of the peso.

Discussion Questions

1. How might Argentina's devaluation in 2002 and again in 2014 affect a U.S. exporter of heavy machinery? A European exporter of cosmetics? A Brazilian exporter of automobiles? An Argentinian textile exporter with debt denominated in U.S. dollars?
2. Why do you think Argentina enacted certain export taxes while at the same time creating more barriers to imports?
3. What are some unintended consequences of protectionism?
4. What problems related to regional integration agreements are illustrated in this case?

Sources: "Trouble in Mercosur" in Kate Gillespie and H. David Hennessey, *Global Marketing* (Mason, OH: Cengage Learning, 2011), pp. 46–48; "Argentina Regulations: Keep Out," Economist Intelligence Unit, September 24, 2011; Leonie Barrie, "US File WTO Complaint Against Argentina Import Curbs," Just-Style, August 24, 2012; Michael Warren, "Top Designers Abandon Argentina," Associated Press Newswires, October 4, 2012; "Argentina: Trade Regulations," Economist Intelligence Unit, July 1, 2013; Ken Parks, "Argentina Extends Currency Controls on Tourism to Shore Up Reserves," *Wall Street Journal Online*, December 3, 2013; Marcela Valente, "Argentina: Imports Climb Despite State Controls," Inter Press Service, September 18, 2013; Raul Gallegos, "The Price of Argentina's Devaluation," Bloomberg, January 30, 2014; and Jonathan Gilbert, "Argentina: Devaluation Done, Problems Persist," *Financial Times*, February 3, 2014.

CASE 2.2   Textile Trauma

When the GATT was first signed, the textile and apparel industries were too controversial to be included within its scope. Employment in these industries was still high in Europe and the United States, and developed countries feared significant unemployment if protective measures were not continued against new producers from developing economies. As a result, textile trade was negotiated bilaterally and governed for 20 years by the rules of a separate international agreement, the Multifibre Arrangement (MFA), which allowed for the emergence of an international quota system regulating world trade in textiles and clothing.

Despite these protectionist measures, employment in these industries continued to decline in the developed world as manufacturers closed facilities or relocated production in lower-cost countries. And textile and apparel quotas were not immune from politics. After the terrorist attacks of September 11, 2001, on New York and Washington, D.C., Pakistan was recruited to the U.S. war on terror. The country was extended US$143 million in new textile quotas by the United States, and the EU increased Pakistan's quota by 15 percent.

The MFA was later replaced by the WTO Agreement on Textiles and Clothing, which set out a transitional process for the ultimate removal of these quotas by January 1, 2005. Tariffs would remain. These were generally higher in developing countries, ranging from 5 to 30 percent in Malaysia (depending on the category), 13 to 35 percent in Mexico, and up to 44 percent in Turkey. Among developed countries, tariffs were highest in Australia, Canada and the United States, where they ranged between 0 and 15 percent.

The end of quotas was expected to create big winners and losers. For example, sources at the WTO estimated that India's share of U.S. clothing imports would rise from 4 percent before to 15 percent after the lifting of quotas, and China's share of imports would increase from 16 percent before to 50 percent after the lifting of quotas. China was also expected to see a large increase in its position in the EU. Estimates put that share at 29 percent of total imports the first year quotas were lifted, threatening currently strong regional producers such as Turkey.

China's textile and apparel industries had several advantages over those in other developing countries. Chinese labor was often cheaper and usually more productive, which was a particular advantage in the labor-intensive apparel industry. Huge factories attained substantial economies of scale, and China provided a good transportation infrastructure with especially quick turnaround times for ships in Chinese ports. Locally produced inputs such as cotton also helped keep costs low. Productive Chinese textile mills provided cheap cloth to Chinese garment manufacturers. In addition, opponents accused China of unfairly gaining advantage by pegging its currency too low and not allowing it to appreciate based on market demand. China was also notorious for massive software pirating, including software used in the textile and apparel industries, resulting in savings from the avoidance of paying royalties on the intellectual property of others. Critics argued that many Chinese manufacturers were government owned and thereby received unfair subsidization.

However, others were less sure about the ability of China to attain and sustain its projected gains in market share. The Chinese government was allowing its currency to slowly appreciate. In addition, the Chinese economy showed signs of overheating. Consequently, the government might decide to tighten credit to textile mills. As many foreign clothing manufacturers moved production to China, prices for materials and labor could increase. Already, clothing factories in China's more developed coastal cities were experiencing difficulty in recruiting new labor. As China's rural incomes rose, fewer Chinese migrated to its cities. Many international producers—as well as global buyers—were considering the risk (both political and economic) of relying too heavily on a single source such as China. The large increases in market share predicted for China were based on actual experience in Australia, where quotas had been removed several years earlier. But some analysts believed that supplier countries near to major markets could partially defend their positions if they focused on "replenishment" products—fashion-oriented products whose buyers (such as Wal-Mart) were sensitive to a supplier's ability to fill reorders very quickly and reliably.

The lifting of textile and apparel quotas threatened the economies of developing countries more than it did those of the United States or Europe. Cambodia, for example, expected its economic growth rate to be halved by expected losses in its garment sector. A system originally designed to protect jobs in Europe and the United States had become the vehicle by which many countries in the developing world could receive guaranteed, if limited, access to these developed markets. For example, if Wal-Mart sought to source a large amount of T-shirts, its preferred supplier in China might not be able to deliver the full amount due to a U.S. quota on T-shirts from China. Wal-Mart could be forced to seek additional suppliers in other developing countries, even if the output from those manufacturers was more costly and of lower quality than that of the preferred Chinese supplier.

But guaranteed market access for less-efficient developing countries was now disappearing. In response, a coalition consisting of U.S. manufacturers and those from 24 developing countries convened a Summit on Fair Trade in Brussels and issued a communiqué warning the WTO that 30 million jobs were at risk in the developing world with the passing of the Multifibre Arrangement. Not everyone was sympathetic. The executive director of the U.S. Association of Importers of Textiles and Apparel sent a letter to the trade representatives at Brussels scoffing, "There is no 'crisis' other than the one created by those who did not prepare or who are unwilling to compete without the crutch of protection."

One of the early promoters of the summit was Mauritius, a tiny island state located off the coast of East Africa. Its population was largely ethnic Indians, many bilingual in French and English. A stable, business-friendly government had offered tax incentives to export-oriented industries, and large amounts of foreign investment in clothing manufacture had poured into the country. The garment industry grew to employ one in five working Mauritians, producing products for such global brands as Calvin Klein and Gap. As a result, the median household income of the country had doubled in ten years to US$4,560, making it one of the highest-income countries in Africa. However, the entry of China into the world market had already resulted in the closing of garment factories on the island, and unemployment had risen from 3 percent to 10 percent.

Bangladesh, a mostly Muslim country of 140 million, was another case in point. Its garment industry employed half the country's industrial workforce and supplied 80 percent of its hard-currency earnings. Bangladesh was one of the poorest countries in Asia and had once been designated the most corrupt country in the world by watchdog organization Transparency International. Political tension was pervasive, and Muslim fundamentalist parties were expanding their control in parliament. Some rural areas had become essentially ungovernable harbors of militant Islamic extremists who were opposed to the neighboring governments of India and Myanmar.

Bangladesh ranked low in basic infrastructure such as transportation and communications, and delays and strikes at its ports often forced garment exporters to employ expensive air-cargo space in order to meet order deadlines. While its garment workers earned less than half of what Chinese garment workers earned, its garment factories had never attained the economies of scale found in China. Unlike China, its apparel industry had no homegrown source of cotton and remained dependent on imported fabrics. Nonetheless, under the MFA Bangladesh had become a major supplier of apparel to both the United States and Europe.

Now experts estimated that over half of the jobs in the Bangladesh apparel industry would disappear. In addition, 15 million jobs in related industries would be lost as well. As in Mauritius, factory closings had already begun. The burden of this unemployment would fall on both men and women, as over half the workers in the industry were female. An earlier increase in female employment (attributed to the garment industry) had resulted in improvements in women's lives, such as increased enrollments in primary education. Also, studies had linked a decline in domestic violence against women in developing countries with a woman's ability to earn cash outside the home.

By 2012, China had indeed grabbed considerable world market share in both textile exports (33 percent) and clothing exports (38 percent) but had fallen short of the predicted high of 50 percent. An appreciating Chinese currency and rising labor costs had sent some global brands in search of outsourcing contractors in other less developed countries. Some Chinese clothing contractors reported that they were beginning to decline orders from overseas, because the price offered was too low. They calculated that they would lose money at the price offered.

In the meantime, Turkey remained the world's sixth largest clothing exporter and second largest to the important EU market. The importance of this sector was diminished, however, accounting for only 40 percent of Turkey's manufactured exports down from 64 percent in 2000. Significant tariffs on textile imports enacted in 2011 helped some Turkish manufacturers but hurt those clothing manufacturers who depended on textile imports. Mexico saw its position as a clothing exporter decline. Its government responded by filing a complaint against China with the WTO, claiming that the Chinese government had supported its textile and clothing industries by exempting them from key taxes and subsidizing their prices for land, electricity and loans.

In Mauritius, local productions suffered considerably as the result of the end of the MFA. Nonetheless, its clothing and textile industry remained the country's second largest employer and accounted for half the country's exports. The country retained a cost advantage over Asian competitors on shipping costs to Europe. One major company had moved some of its more labor-intensive manufacturing to Madagascar. Bangladesh, on the other hand, increased its market share in clothing exports, and a report on the industry by the McKinsey consulting firm proposed that Bangladesh would someday become the new China.

Discussion Questions

1. What factors contribute to a country's success as an apparel exporter?
2. Which theory best explains a nation's success in this industry post-MFA—the theory of comparative advantage or the theory of competitive advantage? Explain.

3. What actions would you suggest for textile and garment producers in Mexico and Turkey?

4. What advice would you give to clothing manufacturers in Mauritius and Bangladesh?

Sources: "Textile Trauma" in Kate Gillespie and H. David Hennessey, *Global Marketing*, Cengage Learning, 2011, pp. 48–50; Paul Adams, "Consolidation Leaves Sector Stronger," *Financial Times*," September 7, 2012, p. 5: "Mexico Challenges Chinese Textile, Clothing Support," Reuters News, October 15, 2012; Jonathan Dyson, "Mexico Clawing Back Role as Key U.S. Clothing Supplier," just-style.com, May 8, 2012; Daniel Dombey, "Can Istanbul Produce its Own Armani or Versace?" *Financial Times*, October 2, 2012, p. 10; Yan Yiqi and Zhang Jianming, "Winter Blues for China's Textile Industry," *China Daily*, October 27, 2012; China-Measures Relating to the Production and Exportation of Apparel and Textile Products, World Trade Organization, www.wto.org, accessed February 3, 2014.

Notes

1 Gordon Fairclough, "The Global Downturn Lands with a Zud on Mongolia's Nomads," *Wall Street Journal Europe*, April 21, 2009, p. 30.

2 Bob Donath, "Don't Miss Opportunities in Global Market," *Marketing News*, July 21, 2003, p. 7.

3 Frances Williams, "WTO Predicts 9% Fall in World Trade," *Financial Times*, March 24, 2009, p. 8

4 "Garlic Wars," CBSNEWS.com, viewed July 23, 2003.

5 Michael E. Porter, *The Competitive Advantage of Nations* (New York: Macmillan, 1990), pp. 69–175.

6 Diana Farrell, "How Germany Can Win From Outsourcing," *McKinsey Quarterly*, 2004, No. 4.

7 Aaron Bernstein, "Shaking Up Trade Theory," *Business Week*, December 6, 2004, pp. 116–120.

8 Ira Iosebashvili and Erin McCarthy, "Ruble Sweats Amid Russian Turmoil," *Wall Street Journal Online*, January 10, 2012.

9 Marc Lifsher, "Venezuela's Ills Confound Foreigners," *Wall Street Journal*, June 23, 2003, p. A13.

10 David Luhnow, "For Mexico an Edge on China," *Wall Street Journal Online*, September 16, 2012.

11 Paulo Winterstein, "From Brazil to India, Pain From Currencies," *Wall Street Journal*, September18, 2013, p. B10.

12 Betsy McKay, "Coke Bets on Russia," *Wall Street Journal*, January 28, 2009, p. A1.

13 Kelly Evans and Sara Murray, "Weak Dollar Crimps Study Abroad," *Wall Street Journal*, May 14, 2008, p. D1.

14 Manjeet Kripalani and Nandini Lakshman, "Rise of the Rupee," *Business Week*, August 6, 2007, p. 66.

15 Timothy Aeppel, "Survival Tactics," *Wall Street Journal*, January 22, 2002, p. A1.

16 Neal Sandler, "Israel: Attack of the Super-Shekel," *Business Week*, February 25, 2008, p. 38.

17 Katy McLaughlin, "The Rising Cost of Being Fabulous," *Wall Street Journal*, May 13, 2003, p. D1.

18 Darren Everson, "Foreign Travel Deals on a Weak Dollar," *Wall Street Journal*, January 4, 2007, p. B7.

19 Yuka Hayashi and Miho Inada, "Japanese Splurge on Imports, Foreign Deals," *Wall Street Journal*, November 29, 2010, p. A12.

20 James Glynn, "Australian Dollar Weights on Retailers," *Wall Street Journal*, December 2, 2010, p. B8.

21 Consumer Expenditures on Leisure and Recreation, Euromonitor International, 2007.

22 Deborah Ball, "Nestle Takes Currency Hit," *Wall Street Journal Online*, August 11, 2011.

23 Deborah Ball, "As Franc Climbs, Swiss Allure to Companies Goes Downhill," *Wall Street Journal Online*, August 18, 2011.

24 Bob Davis, "Surge in Protectionism Threatens to Deepen World-Wide Crisis," *Wall Street Journal*, January 12, 2009, p. A2.

25 "Uzbekistan's Autos to Lose Out in Trade," Business Monitor Online, November 3, 2011.

26 Andreas Ismar, "Indonesia to Allow More Beef Imports," *Wall Street Journal*, May 29, 2013.

27 Helene Cooper, "Russia Agrees to Limit Steel Shipments," *Wall Street Journal*, February 23, 1999, p. A8.

28 Wayne Ma and Matthew Dalton, "China Solar Firms Seek Truce," *Wall Street Journal*, May 28, 2013.

29 David Murphy, "Car Makers Worry China Is Planning a U-Turn," *Wall Street Journal*, July 31, 2003, p. A14.

30 "No Kindle for Kirchner," Kyodo News, April 4, 2012.

31 Sara Schaefer Munoz, "Companies in Argentina Get Creative," *Wall Street Journal*, December 26, 2012, p. A9.

32 John W. Miller, Peter Fritsch and Lauren A.E. Schuker, "Hollywood Upstages Beijing," *Wall Street Journal*, August 13, 2009, p. A1.

33 Paul Magnusson, "The Highest Court You've Never Heard Of," *Business Week*, April 1, 2002, pp. 76–77.

34 Thomas T. Semon, "Euro Currency's Ripple Effects Are Far, Wide," *Marketing News*, February 18, 2002, p. 7.

35 Marc Champion, "Euro-Zone Debate Keeps Britain Abuzz," *Wall Street Journal*, May 21, 2003, p. A1.

36 Sara Murray and Douglas Belkin, "Americans Sour on Trade—Majority Say Free-Trade Pacts Have Hurt U.S.," *Wall Street Journal*, October 4, 2010, p. A1.

37 William Drozdiak, "Poor Nations May Not Buy Trade Talks," *Washington Post*, May 15, 2001.

38 Paul Magnusson, "States' Rights vs. Free Trade," *Business Week*, March 7, 2005, pp. 102, 104.

39 Geoffrey Garrett, "Globalization's Missing Middle," *Foreign Affairs*, vol. 83, no. 6 (November/December 2004), pp. 84–97.

40 Gordon Fairclough, "Korea Torn Over Open Markets," *Wall Street Journal*, November 18, 2005, p. A14.

Chapter 3

Cultural and Social Forces

A DEFINITION OF CULTURE   58

RELIGION   59

THE FAMILY   65

EDUCATION   69

ATTITUDES TOWARD TIME   71

MATERIAL CULTURE AND AESTHETICS   72

THE HOFSTEDE MEASURES OF CULTURE   73

LANGUAGE AND COMMUNICATION   81

OVERCOMING THE LANGUAGE BARRIER   84

ADAPTING TO CULTURAL DIFFERENCES   86

When Disney, the U.S.-based entertainment giant, decided to open a theme park in Europe, it had almost no direct overseas experience. Tokyo Disneyland had proved successful, but it had been developed and run by a local Japanese partner. When EuroDisney opened in France, management had already incorporated changes in its successful models from California and Florida. To accommodate the cooler, damper climate in France, more indoor attractions were developed and more covered walkways were installed. Multilingual telephone operators and guides were hired to assist visitors from different European countries. Kennels were built for the many French families who would never think of going on vacation without the family dog. Estimates of restaurant traffic took into consideration the fact that Europeans like to linger over their food and are far less tolerant of standing in lines than Americans.

Still, for the first year of operations, EuroDisney refused to sell alcohol on its premises because this practice clashed with its American idea of family entertainment. The management also refused to cut prices during off-season months, despite a time-honored European tradition of doing this at vacation destinations. The first year of operation was disappointing. Disney then bowed to cultural realities and adopted wine, beer and differentiated prices. Adapting to European culture paid off. EuroDisney became Europe's top tourist attraction—even more popular than the Eiffel Tower.[1]

However, when Disney later opened a theme park in Hong Kong, the cultural challenges resumed. Originally Disney planned to serve the Chinese delicacy shark's fin soup—until Chinese conservationists objected. Disney also underestimated visitor demand during mainland China's weeklong Lunar New Year holiday. Hundreds of guests with valid tickets found themselves shut out of the park.[2] Learning from this early misstep, Disney later took advantage of China's special Lunar New Year celebrations to promote its mascot Mickey Mouse during the Chinese Year of the Rat.[3]

Wal-Mart also experienced cultural challenges as it expanded abroad. When the company first entered India, it was not allowed to compete directly with local retailers. Instead it was allowed to act as a supplier to these small businesses. Wal-Mart handed out cards in English explaining that merchants would have to present their business licenses to buy from Wal-Mart. Many merchants, however, did not read English and did not have official business licenses.

Like Disney, Wal-Mart had extensive experience overseas. Navigating cultural differences in marketing activities is a complex and challenging task.[4] In Chapter 1 we noted that the complexities of international marketing are partially caused by societal and cultural forces. In Chapter 3 we describe some of these cultural and societal influences in more detail. However, because it is not possible to list all of them—or even to describe the major cultures of the world—only some of the more critical forces are highlighted. Figure 3.1 shows the components of culture that are described in this chapter. Rather than identifying all the cultural or societal factors that might affect international marketers, we concentrate on analytic processes that marketers can use to identify and monitor any of the numerous cultural influences they will encounter around the globe.

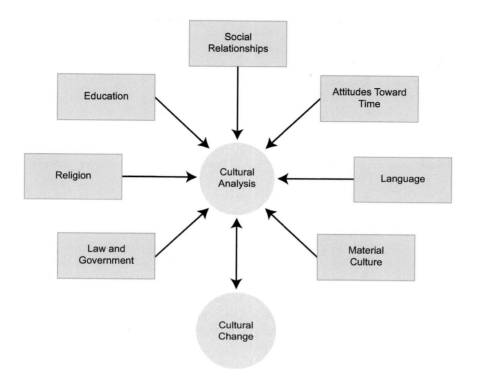

Figure 3.1 Cultural Analysis

Learning Objectives

After studying this chapter, you should be able to:

➤ define what *culture* is and demonstrate how various components of culture affect marketing;
➤ explain how different world religions affect marketing;
➤ describe how family structure can vary and explain its impact on marketing;
➤ illustrate ways in which the educational system of a country can affect marketers;
➤ differentiate between monochronic and polychronic cultures and explain the three temporal orientations;
➤ identify ways in which material culture and aesthetics affect global marketing;
➤ list and describe Hofstede's dimensions of culture;
➤ explain why language can be important in gaining true understanding of a culture;
➤ identify ways of adapting to cultural differences.

A Definition of Culture

Anthropology is the study of human behavior. Cultural anthropology examines all learned human behaviors, including social, linguistic and family behaviors. Culture encompasses the entire heritage of a society transmitted orally, via literature, or in any other form. It includes all traditions, morals, habits, religion, art and language. Children born anywhere in the world have the same essential needs for food, shelter and clothing. But as they mature, children experience desires for non-essential things. *How these wants develop* and *what relative importance the individual assigns to them* are based on messages from families and peers. This socialization process reflects each person's culture.

For example, eating habits and tastes vary greatly around the world, but few of these variations reflect physiological differences among people. Instead, food is extremely culture-bound. One exception relates to milk products. Many people in China lack the enzymes to digest milk products. But like many things Western, milk is becoming increasingly popular in China among a new generation more socialized to Western products. To bridge the gap—in taste and enzymes—many dairy producers in China are selling yogurt-based drinks, which many Chinese find easier to digest.[5]

The role and influence of culture in modern society are evolving as more and more economies become interlinked. Samuel Huntington identifies the cultures of the world as Western (the United States, Western Europe, Australia), Orthodox (the former Soviet republics, Central Europe), Confucian (China, Southeast Asia), Islamic (the Middle East), Buddhist (Thailand), Hindu (India), Latin American, African and Japanese.[6] He argues that conflict in the post-cold-war era will occur between the major cultures of the world rather than between nations. Francis Fukuyama disagrees that cultural differences will necessarily be the source of conflict. Instead, he foresees that increasing interaction between cultures will lead to cross-stimulation and creative change.[7] In any case, better understanding cultural differences can help marketers avoid costly mistakes in the marketplace today.

Cultural Influences on Marketing

The function of marketing is to earn profits from the satisfaction of human wants and needs. To understand and influence consumers' wants and needs, we must understand their culture. Cultural understanding is also necessary when international marketers interact with foreign competitors, distributors, suppliers and government officials.

Figure 3.2 is a diagram of how culture affects human behavior. As the figure shows, culture is embedded in such elements of the society as religion, language, history and education. These aspects

Figure 3.2 Cultural Influences of Buyer Behavior

of the society send direct and indirect messages to consumers regarding the selection of goods and services. The culture we live in answers such questions as the following: Is tea or coffee the preferred drink? Is black or white worn at a funeral? What type of food is eaten for breakfast?

Isolating Cultural Influences

One of the most difficult tasks for global marketers is assessing the cultural influences that affect their operations. In the actual marketplace, several factors are always working simultaneously, and it is extremely difficult to isolate any one factor. Frequently, cultural differences have been held accountable for any noticeable differences among countries. But do these differences result from underlying religious beliefs, from the prevailing social structure, or simply from different sets of laws? In this chapter we will examine the cultural influences of religion, the family, education, attitudes toward time, material culture, social interactions and language. The cultural factors of government and law will be discussed in Chapter 4.

Religion

McDonald's operates in over 100 countries and is the world's largest user of beef. The U.S.-based fast-food chain was drawn to India with its population of over 1.2 billion, even though the majority of Indians were Hindus and did not eat beef. At the McDonald's in Delhi a sign reads, "No beef or beef products sold at this restaurant." Pork is also omitted to avoid offending India's many Muslims.

Religion can have a profound impact on the marketing environment. It helps determine attitudes toward social structure and economic development. Its traditions and rules may dictate what goods and services are purchased, when they are purchased and by whom. For example, the Shinto religion encourages the Japanese people to cultivate a strong patriotic attitude, which may in part account for why Japanese consumers tend to prefer products made in Japan. Alcoholic beverages are banned in Saudi Arabia on religious principles, and Israeli airline El Al does not fly on Saturday, the Jewish Sabbath.

Table 3.1 lists the leading religions for selected countries. It is beyond the scope of this text to provide a complete description of all world religions and their implications for marketing. By briefly examining several of the world's major religions, however, we can illustrate their potential impact.

Marketing and Western Religions

Historically, the religious tradition in the United States, based on Christianity and Judaism, has emphasized hard work, thrift and a simple lifestyle. These religious values have certainly evolved over time; many of our modern marketing activities would not exist if these older values had persisted. Thrift, for instance, presumes that a person will save hard-earned wages and use these savings for purchases later on. Today, Americans take full advantage of the ample credit facilities that are available to them. The credit card is such a vital part of the American lifestyle that saving

Table 3.1 Leading Religions of Selected Countries

Country	Religion		
Africa			
Cameroon	Christian	Muslim	Animist
Congo	Christian	Animist	Muslim
Ethiopia	Orthodox Christian	Muslim	Protestant
Ghana	Christian	Muslim	Animist
Kenya	Protestant	Catholic	Animist
Mauritius	Hindu	Christian	Muslim
Nigeria	Christian	Muslim	Animist
South Africa	Christian	Animist	Secular
Zambia	Christian	Hindu	Muslim
Zimbabwe	Christian	Animist	Secular
Asia			
China	Secular	Buddhist	Taoist
India	Hindu	Muslim	Christian
Indonesia	Muslim	Christian	Hindu
Japan	Buddhist	Shinto	Christian
Malaysia	Muslim	Buddhist	Hindu
Pakistan	Muslim	Christian	Hindu
Philippines	Catholic	Muslim	Other
Singapore	Buddhist	Muslim	Christian
South Korea	Buddhist	Christian	Secular
Thailand	Buddhist	Muslim	Christian
Europe			
Denmark	Catholic	Protestant	Secular
France	Catholic	Secular	Muslim
Germany	Protestant	Catholic	Secular
Italy	Catholic	Secular	Protestant
Netherlands	Secular	Christian	Muslim
Norway	Protestant	Secular	Catholic
Poland	Catholic	Secular	Orthodox Christian
Portugal	Catholic	Secular	Protestant
Russia	Orthodox Christian	Secular	Muslim
Spain	Catholic	Secular	Protestant
Switzerland	Catholic	Protestant	Secular
United Kingdom	Christian	Muslim	Sikh

Country	Religion		
Middle East/Central Asia			
Armenia	Orthodox Christian	Secular	Other
Egypt	Muslim	Christian	Other
Israel	Jewish	Muslim	Secular
Jordan	Muslim	Christian	Secular
Kazakhstan	Muslim	Orthodox Christian	Catholic
Morocco	Muslim	Jewish	Christian
Saudi Arabia	Muslim	—	—
Tunisia	Muslim	Christian	Jewish
Turkey	Muslim	Christian	Jewish
Turkmenistan	Muslim	Orthodox Christian	Secular
North America			
Canada	Catholic	Protestant	Secular
United States	Protestant	Catholic	Secular
Latin America/Caribbean			
Brazil	Catholic	Traditional	Secular
Chile	Catholic	Protestant	Other
Colombia	Catholic	Protestant	Secular
Cuba	Secular	Catholic	Protestant
Jamaica	Protestant	Traditional	Catholic
Mexico	Catholic	Protestant	Secular
Peru	Catholic	Protestant	Traditional
Uruguay	Catholic	Protestant	Secular
Venezuela	Catholic	Secular	Other

Note: In descending order left to right.

Source: Authors' calculations based on data derived from *Cultural Practices and Heritage: Leading Religions*, UNESCO and CIA World Factbook and United States State Department Country Reports.

before buying seems archaic. Most Americans feel no guilt in driving a big SUV or generously heating a large house.

Christmas is one Christian tradition that remains an important event for many consumer goods industries in all Christian countries. Retailers have their largest sales around that time. However, Christmas is a good illustration of the substantial differences that still exist among even predominantly Christian societies. A large U.S.-based retailer of consumer electronics discovered these differences the hard way when it opened its first retail outlet in the Netherlands. The company planned the opening to coincide with the start of the Christmas selling season and bought advertising space accordingly for late November and December, as retailers do in the United States. The results proved less than satisfactory. Major gift giving in Holland takes place not around

December 25, Christmas Day, but on Saint Nicholas Day, December 6. Therefore, the opening of the company's retail operation was late and missed the major buying season.

From a marketing point of view, Christmas has increasingly become a global phenomenon. For many young Chinese, Christmas is not regarded as a religious holiday but simply represents "fun." Fashionable bars charge up to $25 for entrance on Christmas Eve, and hotel restaurants charge $180 for a Christmas Eve function.[8] The week around Christmas is the top grossing week for movie theaters in China, as young Chinese head out to theaters together instead of watching pirated DVDs at home.[9] Santa Claus is increasing in popularity in the predominantly Sunni Muslim country of Turkey. In Istanbul shopping centers, children stand in line to sit on Santa's lap and ask for gifts. Stores sell Santa suits and statues.[10]

Another Christian holiday, Saint Valentine's Day, has become popular in Iran despite disapproval of conservative Muslim clerics who view the holiday dedicated to love as decadent and immoral. Its popularity is spawned by young people who hear about it via satellite television and the Internet and respond by throwing parties and buying Valentine's Day gifts. Stores note sales in the week prior to Valentine's Day are now similar to those before *Norouz*, the traditional Iranian New Year's Day. Valentine paraphernalia is both imported (from China!) and produced locally.[11]

The kosher diets of Orthodox Jews present certain marketers with both challenges and opportunities. For example, eating pork is forbidden, and meat and milk may not be eaten together. Many processed foods containing meat products have come under increased scrutiny. These include cereals, such as Kellogg's Frosted Mini Wheats, that are traditionally eaten with milk.[12]

The rigorously Orthodox make up about 12 percent of Israel's 6 million Jews, but their numbers are growing more rapidly than those of the rest of the population. As a result, many companies are addressing this segment of the market. Israeli food manufacturers have expanded their lines of strictly kosher products and have employed packaging and advertising in keeping with the more traditional sensitivities of Israel's Orthodox communities. Elite, a chocolate manufacturer, ran a contest for Orthodox children in which chocolate wrappers could be exchanged for cards showing prominent rabbis or religious teachers. Coca-Cola ran a separate line of advertisements aimed at Orthodox consumers in Israel. These ads depicted Coke drinkers in conservative dress instead of the scantily clad young people used in advertisements aimed at the Israeli public in general.[13] In addition, a cell phone company in Israel developed phones stripped to basic voice service. This offering was in response to many orthodox Jews who did not want the distractions of the myriad of services and features offered on the typical cell phone.[14]

Marketing and Islam

Islam is the religion of nearly 20 percent of the world's population. It is an important cultural force not only in the Middle East but in Asia and Africa as well. In fact, some of the world's largest Muslim populations live in China, Indonesia and Malaysia.

The prophet Mohammed established Islam in Mecca, located in modern-day Saudi Arabia, in the year 610. By the time of the prophet's death in 632, the holy book of Islam, the Koran, had been completely revealed. Muslims believe it contains God's own words. The Koran was supplemented by

Table 3.2 Marketing and Islamic Culture

Cultural Aspect	Implications for Marketing
Religious requirement to fast during the month of Ramadan as a reminder to be generous to the poor	Advertisements during the month of Ramadan encouraging giving to and empathy for the less fortunate
Prohibition on interest	No-interest financing incorporated into pricing policies/Leasing options
Halal requirements	Certification that foods and other products such as cosmetics adhere to halal standards
Prohibition on personally benefiting from one's charitable acts	Corporate philanthropic giving encouraged but corporate social responsibility (CSR) projects that also benefit the company (such as donations to charity for each product sold) may be unacceptable
Expectation of modest behavior	Both men and women depicted in advertisements should be modestly clothed
	Some Muslim cultures may expect men and women to be separated in certain cases such as eating areas or focus groups

the Hadith and the Sunna, which contain the reported words and actions of the prophet Mohammed. These works are the primary sources of guidance for all Muslims on all aspects of life.

Islam affects marketers in a number of ways (see Table 3.2). For example, Islam prohibits the paying or collecting of interest. In most Muslim countries, commercial banks must compete with Islamic banks, which do not offer savings accounts that pay interest. Although these accounts are not attractive to all, many devout Muslims prefer to keep their money in these banks. Islamic banks have also developed a unique product to compete with interest-bearing accounts at other banks. The profit-loss account allows customers to invest their savings in businesses that the bank pre-selects. Annual profits from the businesses are distributed into the shareholders' accounts.

Greater awareness of Islamic traditions can create new business opportunities. For example, Muslims are also required to pray five times daily in the direction of the holy city of Mecca. Dubai-based Ilkone Mobile Telecommunications launched a phone in the Middle East with an internal compass to identify the direction to Mecca and an alarm for prayer times. A complete version of the Koran in Arabic and English was also included.[15]

Islam also prescribes a number of rules concerning food consumption and personal cleanliness. Products that contain no forbidden ingredients such as pork and alcohol may be certified halal (acceptable under Islamic teaching). Halal not only affects food products but many other products as well such as lipsticks and vaccines. It is estimated that prices for some halal-compliant products are on average 20 to 30 percent higher than for non-halal products. Nonetheless, the global halal market has been growing at 20 percent a year.[16]

In Malaysia, a government agency certifies that products are halal. Products must be free of forbidden foods, and production facilities must meet standards of cleanliness and proper storage. Every product sold by Nestlé Malaysia is certified halal. Even Singapore, where only 14 percent of the

3 million population is Muslim, has established its own halal certification body. Indonesia has a Muslim population of nearly 200 million. In response to consumer demand, the Indonesian government also established halal certification. When it was discovered that the Japanese food company Ajinomoto was using a pork-based enzyme in its halal seasoning products in Indonesia, the company had to pull tons of product off the shelves. The company not only faced possible legal action but also suffered a loss of consumer trust.[17]

The world market for Muslim halal food alone is estimated at $4 trillion. Nestlé is the largest producer of halal foods, which it produces in 75 factories worldwide.[18] Fast-food companies such as McDonald's and Kentucky Fried Chicken have also obtained halal certificates to serve the Muslim market. Even a Brazilian beef processor adapted some of its packing plants to meet halal certification after managers visited Egypt and realized the potential of the halal beef market.[19] In fact, the United Arab Emirates (UAE) imports 80 percent of its halal food from countries such as Brazil and Australia.[20]

In many Muslim countries such as Indonesia, Ramadan (the month in which Muslims fast from dawn to dusk) is the major annual shopping season. Market-research company Nielsen estimates that food and beverage companies in Indonesia make about 45 percent of their annual sales during the Ramadan quarter.[21] Following the evening meal most families watch television with its special Ramadan programming. Because of this, advertising slots in the evening during Ramadan command the highest prices of any time during the year.[22]

Many companies even adopt a religious message in their advertisements at this time. A Coca-Cola commercial, developed by McCann-Erickson Malaysia, featured a small boy and his mother going with gifts to an orphanage, the mother with a rug and basket of food, the boy with his cherished bottle of Coca-Cola. After sunset the little boy leaves his house to go back to the orphanage to break fast and share the Coca-Cola with his new friends. The ad ends with the slogan "Always in good spirit. Always Coca-Cola." It appealed to religious sentiment across national boundaries and was scheduled to air in 20 countries.[23]

Marketing and Eastern Religions

Asia is a major market today for many international firms, and global marketers must take into account the possible impact of the Eastern religious and philosophical traditions of Hinduism, Buddhism, Confucianism and Shintoism. Hinduism and Buddhism are the two largest Eastern religions. Hinduism is professed by about 450 million people, most of whom live in India, where Hindus constitute nearly 85 percent of the population. Hindu theology varies among believers but is generally polytheistic, with different groups showing a preference for one or several gods. In India, October and November are full of traditional holidays. As such, the two months are the Indian equivalent of the Christmas shopping season in Europe and the United States—a time for gift giving and major purchases.[24]

Hinduism includes a doctrine of rebirth into conditions determined by a person's prior life. A person can be reborn as a human, an animal or a celestial being. Hinduism also encompasses a hereditary caste system that requires Hindus to marry within their own caste. Many Hindus are vegetarian, and eating beef is particularly taboo. Buddhism also began in India but rejected many of Hinduism's hierarchical structures. Today it is influential predominantly in East and Southeast Asia.

In India, Hyundai respects local beliefs when it launches new car models on auspicious days selected from the Hindu calendar.[25] A Seattle-based company showed far less sensitivity when it launched a line of toilet seats. The Sacred Seat Collection depicted images of Hindu gods such as Ganesh, the elephant god of learning. Several Indian politicians joined members of the large U.S. Hindu population in condemning the company.[26]

Confucianism is not a religion, but its founder Confucius is regarded as the greatest of China's sages and his impact is still greatly felt. Confucius taught respect for one's parents and for education, values common among Chinese today. Confucius' name has also proved valuable to marketers in China. Kong Demao, one of two surviving members of the 77th generation of the family of Confucius, became the nominal chair of three distillers in the Qufu region of China, the ancestral home of Confucius. When all three distillers took the Confucius family name for their products, sales soared. However, two of the distillers went to court over who really owned the name. Nonetheless, all three distillers decided it would be wise to contact Kong and pay a stipend for the use of her name. She was also named "Lifetime Honorary President" of the Confucius International Travel Agency.[27]

Japan has been heavily influenced both by Buddhism from Korea and by Confucianism from China. In the late nineteenth century, Japan's earlier Shinto religion was revived as the patriotic symbol of Japan, the emperor being exalted as the descendant of the sun goddess. Shinto rituals were performed at state occasions. State Shinto was abolished after World War II, but popular cults persist. When the first Starbucks abroad opened in Tokyo, Shinto priests offered prayers at the opening ceremony.[28] One enterprising tour group brings foreign tourists to Japan to view Shinto processions during October, a festival month in a number of Japanese cities.[29]

Global marketers require a keen awareness of how religion can influence business. They need to search actively for influences that may not be readily apparent. Showing respect for local religious traditions is an important part of cultural sensitivity.

The Family

The role of the family varies greatly among cultures, as do the roles that the various family members play. Across cultures, we find differences in family size, in the employment of women and in many other factors of interest to marketers. Companies familiar with family interactions in Western society cannot assume that they will find the same patterns elsewhere.

In the United States, there has been a trend toward the dissolution of the traditional nuclear family. With people marrying later and divorcing more often, the "typical" family of father, mother and children living in one dwelling has become far less common than in the past. More recently, a similar trend in Western Europe has resulted in an increase in the number of households even in countries where the overall population is decreasing. This outcome has in turn increased demand for many consumer durables, such as washing machines and ovens, whose sales correlate with number of households rather than with population. Also, an increasing number of women are working outside the home (see Table 3.3), a situation that boosts demand for frozen dinners and child-care centers.

Marketers should not expect to find the same type of family structure in all countries. In many societies, particularly in Asia and Latin America, the role of the male as head of the household remains pronounced. Some cultures still encourage the bearing of male rather than female children. In most cultures, 105 boys are born for every 100 girls, but in China the figure for boys is 118.5

Table 3.3 Family Statistics of Selected Countries (in percentages)

Country	Population Growth Rates*	Share of Women in Labor Force**
Australia	1.6	59
Austria	0.5	55
Belgium	0.9	47
Brazil	0.9	60
Canada	1.1	62
Chile	0.9	49
China	0.5	64
Denmark	0.4	59
Egypt	1.7	24
France	0.5	51
Germany	0.1	54
Greece	−0.2	44
Hungary	−0.3	45
India	1.3	27
Indonesia	1.2	51
Italy	0.3	39
Japan	−0.2	48
Malaysia	1.7	44
Mexico	1.2	45
Netherlands	0.4	59
Nigeria	2.8	48
Norway	1.3	62
Pakistan	1.7	24
Russian Federation	0.4	57
Singapore	2.5	59
South Africa	1.2	44
Spain	0.1	53
Sweden	0.7	60
Switzerland	1.1	61
Thailand	0.3	64
Turkey	1.3	29
United Kingdom	0.8	56
United States	0.7	57
Venezuela	1.5	51

* Average annual population growth rate 2012
** 2012

Source: Adapted from World Bank, Population Growth, 2014

and in South Korea, 116. In some areas of South Korea, boy births outnumber girls 125 to 100, indicating that female fetuses may be being aborted.[30] This male dominance coincides with a lower rate of participation by women in the labor force outside the home. This situation results in a lower average family income. The number of children per family also varies substantially by country or culture. In many Eastern European countries and in Germany, one child per family is fast becoming the rule, whereas families in some developing countries are still large by Western standards.

Extended Families

So far we have discussed only the nuclear family. However, for many cultures, the extended family—including grandparents, in-laws, aunts, uncles and so on—is of considerable importance. In the United States, older parents usually live alone, whether in individually owned housing, in multiple housing for the elderly or in nursing homes (for those who can no longer care for themselves). In countries with lower income levels and in rural areas, the extended family still plays a major role, further increasing the size of the average household. In China, 67 percent of parents with grown children live with one of their children, and 80 percent of such parents have contact with their children at least once a week.[31]

Extended families or clans play an important role among overseas Chinese as well. Driven by poverty and political upheaval, waves of families fled China to other countries in Asia during the past 200 years. They developed dense networks of thrifty, self-reliant communities united by their Chinese ethnicity. These Chinese communities have flourished in both commerce and industry. For example, ethnic Chinese make up 1 percent of the population and 20 percent of the economy in Vietnam, 1 percent and 40 percent in the Philippines, 4 percent and 50 percent in Indonesia and 32 percent and 60 percent in Malaysia.[32]

Ironically, the Chinese homeland has followed a one-child policy during the past generation in an attempt to curb its population growth. This policy is having an immediate impact on the younger generation's ability to form the traditional Chinese family business. Young entrepreneurs in China report that they establish business relationships with fellow students from high school or university instead of with siblings and cousins.

World Beat 3.1

A New Japanese Woman?

Some consider Japan's record on gender empowerment to be less than impressive. The country ranks 101 out of 135 countries. Even Bangladesh ranks higher! Some attribute this phenomenon to the persistence of traditional gender roles in Japan despite its high economic development level. Others cite limited child-care options for working women as a key factor keeping mothers at home. Many companies pay men higher salaries if their wives stay home, and 70 percent of working women quit their jobs after having their first child.

67

However, female labor participation increases economic growth, and Japan may need more women in the workforce to support its aging population. The Japanese workforce peaked in 1995 at 87 million and is expected to decrease to 55 million by 2050. Already the mass retirement of Japanese in the baby boom generation is opening new opportunities for Japanese women. Even airlines, that previously only hired male pilots, are beginning to hire women as well.

With these changes come new marketing opportunities in Japan. Traditionally, aging parents were cared for by the wife of the eldest son. Yet senior care company, Home Instead, quickly expanded its franchises into Japan. Changing lifestyles, including many more women working outside the home, create a demand for professional caregivers to come into Japanese homes.

Professional housecleaners are also becoming more common in Japan. For decades, housecleaning was considered the job of the Japanese housewife, and even well-to-do families didn't hire strangers to clean their houses. A recent poll revealed that even today only 20 percent of Japanese women would consider hiring a professional housecleaner. Nonetheless, the housecleaning industry has started to expand in Japan despite a number of challenges—not least of which is the high cost of delivering services in Japan. The country discourages immigration and labor costs remain high.

Still a bias hangs over the industry. Housecleaners have their own section in the yellow pages, but they're listed under the English word *housecleaning*, which is preferred over the Japanese word *soji*. And one company ran a half-price sale on weekdays promoting the idea that guilty housewives could keep their outsourcing secret from their husbands.

Sources: Dan Bauwens, "Japan Values Women Less—As It Needs Them More," Inter Press Service News Agency, January 2013; "Women's Dream of Becoming Airline Pilots No Longer Pie in the Sky," Kyodo News, December 23, 2008; Chad Steinberg, "Can Women Save Japan (and Asia Too)?" *Finance and Development, International Monetary Fund*, vol. 49 no. 3, October 2012; Richard Gibson, "US Franchises Find Opportunity to Grow Abroad," *Wall Street Journal*, August 11, 2009, p. B5; and "A New Growth Industry; Professional Housekeeping," *Japan Today*, December 27, 2013.

Beyond the Family

Most societies appreciate and promote a strong family unit. However, Francis Fukuyama argues that a culture can suffer from too great an emphasis on family values. Some cultures, such as that of southern Italy, emphasize nuclear family relationships to the exclusion of all others. It has been said that adults are not persons in southern Italy; they're only parents. In this low-trust society, trust is extended only to immediate family members.[33]

Yet business relationships depend on trust. Even with contracts and law courts, businesses could not survive if managers spent all their time in litigation. If trust is not extended beyond the family, business dealings must stay within the family. This practice stymies the growth of modern large-scale enterprises and impedes development. For this reason, southern Italy remains one of the poorest regions in Western Europe. Most of the developing world qualifies as relatively low-trust, according to Fukuyama's paradigm. Comparatively few large corporations in the private sector evolved outside North America, Europe and Japan. Those that did retained their family ties much longer than firms in developed countries.

Germany, Japan and the United States are all very different in many aspects of culture. However, Fukuyama notes that these three countries are high-trust societies. They all share a history of voluntary associations—civic, religious and business—that extend beyond the family. This history of associating with nonfamily members to accomplish common goals taught people that they could trust others who were not blood relations. This experience paved the way for large, publicly owned corporations to emerge, because family businesses could feel secure in raising money outside the family, and stockholders could eventually trust their investments in the hands of professional managers. Marketers who compete in high-trust countries usually must contend with these large corporate competitors. However, the history of associations can also be exploited by savvy marketers. Marketers of credit cards in Japan discovered that consumers took quickly to credit cards cobranded with associations and clubs, because the typical Japanese person was proud to belong to civic groups.

Education

Education shapes people's outlooks, desires and motivations. To the extent that educational systems differ among countries, we can expect differences among consumers. However, education not only affects potential consumers; it also shapes potential employees for foreign companies and for the business community at large.

In the United States, compulsory education ends at age 16. Virtually all students who obtain a high school diploma stay in school until age 18. In high school, about 25 percent take vocational training courses. After high school, students either attend college or find a job. About half of all high school graduates go on to some type of college. This pattern is not shared by all countries. Many students in Europe go to school only until age 16. Then they join an apprenticeship program. This is particularly the case in Germany, where formal apprenticeship programs exist for about 450 job categories.

The extent and quality of education in a society affect marketing on two levels: the consumer level and the employee level. In societies where the average level of participation in the educational process is low, one typically finds a low level of literacy. Basic literacy levels can vary widely across countries (see Table 3.4). This variation in reading ability not only affects the earning potential of consumers, and thus the level of consumption, but also determines the communication options for marketing programs, as we will see in Chapters 14 and 15. Another concern is how much young people earn. In countries such as Germany, where many of its youth have considerable earnings by age 20, the value and potential of the youth market is quite different from that in the United States, where a substantial number of young people do not enter the job market until age 21 or 22. Recently, however, high youth unemployment rates in Europe have closed this gap in purchasing power.

The educational system also affects employee skills and executive talent. In the United States, the sales organizations of many large companies are staffed strictly with university graduates. In many other countries, sales as a profession has a lower status and attracts fewer university graduates. The typical career path of an American executive involves a four-year college program and, in many cases, a master's degree in business administration (MBA) program. This format for

Table 3.4 Adult Literacy Rates for Selected Countries (in percentages)

Country	Male	Female
Algeria	81	64
Argentina	98	98
Armenia	100	100
Benin	55	30
Bolivia	96	87
Brazil	90	91
Bulgaria	99	98
Cambodia	83	66
Cameroon	78	65
Chile	99	99
China	98	93
Egypt	82	66
Estonia	100	100
Ghana	78	65
Honduras	80	80
Indonesia	94	87
Iran	89	81
Israel	99	96
Mexico	94	94
Morocco	76	58
Peru	96	89
Qatar	97	95
Russian Federation	100	100
Saudi Arabia	90	81
South Africa	94	92
Thailand	95	91
Turkey	98	92
Vietnam	96	92

Source: Adapted from CIA World Factbook, 2014

executive education is less common in other countries, despite the fact that MBA programs have proliferated around the world in the past 25 years. For example, large corporations in South Korea hire fewer MBAs than their American counterparts, but they import top management educators to teach in their in-house executive programs.

Thus different countries have substantially different ideas about education in general and about management education in particular. Traditional European education emphasizes the mastery of a subject through knowledge acquisition. In contrast, the U.S. approach emphasizes analytic ability and an understanding of concepts. Students passing through the two educational systems probably develop different thinking patterns and attitudes. It requires a considerable amount of cultural sensitivity for an international manager to understand these differences and to make the best use of the human resources that are available.

Attitudes Toward Time

In Poland, decisions are usually made quickly. In Kazakhstan, canceling a meeting at the last minute is common, whereas punctuality is strictly observed in Romania.[34] These are all examples of behaviors that reflect cultural attitudes toward time. In the United States, time is seen as having economic value. It is a commodity to be planned for and used wisely. Schedules are set and appointment times are interpreted precisely. If a meeting is scheduled at 3:00 p.m., participants are expected to arrive at 3:00 p.m. In many other countries, such as Costa Rica and Saudi Arabia, meetings rarely begin on time. An American arriving at a meeting in Saudi Arabia can wait quite a while for others to show up. Faced with this phenomenon, the American is likely to be annoyed. Time is being wasted!

Monochronic versus Polychronic Cultures and Temporal Orientation

The United States is basically a monochronic culture. Activities are undertaken one at a time. People respect schedules and agendas. However, Asian cultures are basically polychronic cultures, and expectations are different.[35] At any one time, a manager is expected to be managing multiple tasks. Schedules and agendas must bend to the needs of people, and interruptions are not the exception but the rule. It is not unusual for a high-ranking Indian manager to stop work to listen to an employee's family problems. Similarly, it would be impolite to abruptly cut off a conversation with one group to attend a prearranged meeting with another group. Salespeople from monochronic cultures who travel to polychronic cultures should expect to be kept waiting and should not interpret their clients' tardiness as lack of interest or disrespect.

Latin culture sometimes appears to be more monochronic and sometimes more polychronic.[36] Managers from South America explain that a monochronic orientation is more appropriate for work situations, but a polychronic orientation is more appropriate for private life and entertaining.

Temporal orientations also vary by culture. Some cultures, such as Mexico and Brazil, are oriented to the present: life is enjoyed for the moment. One Mexican ceramics manufacturer noted that as soon as his employees made enough money for the week, they stopped coming to work. The United States is a future-oriented culture, where efforts are focused more on working to achieve a future goal. European and Middle Eastern cultures are more oriented to the past, placing a greater emphasis on historical achievements and relationships. When Israel and Egypt signed a peace treaty 40 years ago, it ended a war that had been going on for nearly 30 years. The U.S. government, which had assisted in the peace process, expected business relations to blossom between the two countries. Today, Israeli firms have barely begun to penetrate the Egyptian market. Egyptians—consumers, distributors, potential partners and government officials—are still highly aware of the 30 years of war that preceded the peace.

Work and Leisure Time

Different societies have different views about the amounts of time it is appropriate to spend at work and in leisure pursuits. In most economically developed countries, leisure has become a major aspect of life. In such countries, the development of the leisure industries is an indication that play and relaxation can be as intensely consumed as any other products.

Society significantly influences work and leisure through statutory vacation allowances and public holidays. Traditionally, European statutes have required companies to give employees 25–30 days of vacation annually, whereas many workers in the United States, Japan, Mexico and the Philippines enjoy only 5–10 vacation days. These differences result in lower working hours per year in Europe than in the United States, Japan and Mexico.

Increasingly, globalization may force a convergence in work hours. For example, on average, German employees work about 25 percent fewer hours than their counterparts in the United States. For 25 years, German unions successfully pushed for a shorter workweek in the hope of creating more jobs. However, this resulted in German labor costs becoming the highest in the world, and German companies are now shifting jobs out of Germany in order to remain globally competitive. The recent addition of Eastern European countries to the EU is expected to accelerate this trend. Facing the threat of job losses, French workers at a car components factory owned by Bosch voted to work longer hours for the same pay. Some saw this vote as the beginning of a de facto rollback of France's 35-hour legal workweek.[37]

Material Culture and Aesthetics

Material culture is the aggregate of physical objects and technologies used by a society. It includes infrastructure such as transportation and communications systems as well as housing and energy supplies. Many urban Vietnamese prefer motorcycles to cars because traffic is so congested in their major cities. This presents a cultural barrier to entry for foreign automobile companies. On the other hand, cell phones were adopted early in many developing countries. This resulted from limited conventional communications infrastructure in these markets. Many potential customers found themselves waiting years for a landline phone.

Aesthetics is a cultural concept relating to what a society considers to be beautiful or pleasing. Global marketers involved with product or packaging design should be aware of the impact of aesthetics on consumer purchasing decisions. Aesthetic considerations can even affect the music played in the background of commercials.

One example of cross-cultural similarities and differences in this regard involves color preferences. A study of consumers in eight countries revealed that some universal color preferences do exist. Blue was either the first or the second favorite color in every country, and there was no difference in liking in respect to black, green, red or white. However, there were differences in preferences for brown, gold, orange, purple and yellow.[38]

Black and red signify happiness to the Chinese and are commonly chosen for wedding invitations. In India, Hindus consider orange the most sacred color. The color purple is associated with expensive products in Japan, China and South Korea but with inexpensive products in the United States. Red is unlucky in Chad, Nigeria and Germany but lucky in China, Denmark and Argentina. Japanese associate black with fear and Indians associate it with dullness and stupidity. But black is seen as powerful and expensive in China, Japan, South Korea and the United States.[39]

The top global vehicle colors according to DuPont are silver (25 percent), black (23 percent), white (16 percent), gray (13 percent), blue (9 percent) and red (8 percent). But there are regional differences. Black is more popular in Europe than in the United States. And sales of both blue and red cars are much higher in India than the global average.[40]

The Hofstede Measures of Culture

Geert Hofstede developed a four-dimensional framework by which to measure several key attributes of cultures. This framework emerged as a result of his research on International Business Machines Corporation (IBM) employees and has since attracted considerable interest among business scholars.[41] The research involved over 116,000 questionnaires and incorporated 72 different national subsidiaries, 20 languages and 38 occupations. Hofstede's insights can be very useful to international marketers. The four dimensions are power distance, individualism-collectivism, masculinity-femininity and uncertainty avoidance. The scores for selected countries and regions from Hofstede's early work are listed in Table 3.5. For more information concerning these scores, including some updated scores, see the online site for the Hofstede Centre.

Power Distance

Power distance is the extent to which the less powerful members within a society accept that power is distributed unevenly. Geert Hofstede tells the story of a clash of cultures between the high-power-distance culture of France and the low-power-distance culture of Sweden:

> The nobles of Sweden in 1809 deposed King Gustav IV, whom they considered incompetent, and surprisingly invited Jean Baptiste Bernadotte, a French general who had served under their enemy Napoleon, to become King of Sweden. Bernadotte accepted and he became King Charles XVI; his descendents occupy the Swedish throne to this day. When the new king was installed, he addressed the Swedish Parliament in their language. His broken Swedish amused the Swedes, and they roared with laughter. The Frenchman who had become king was so upset that he never tried to speak Swedish again.[42]

As a French general, Bernadotte was used to deference from those below him in the hierarchy. Members of Parliament would never laugh at a king in France or criticize him to his face. Even today, France has a high-power distance score compared with other Western European countries. Nearly all the top jobs in the French public and private sectors are held by graduates of two elite institutions—the École Nationale d'Administration and the École Polytechnique.

Beginning in the family, children in high-power distance cultures are expected to be obedient to their parents. Respect for parents and elders is considered a virtue. In low-power distance

Table 3.5 Values of Hofstede's Cultural Dimensions for 69 Countries or Regions

Country/Region	Power Distance	Individualism	Masculinity	Uncertainty avoidance
Arabic countries[a]	80	38	53	68
Argentina	49	46	56	86
Australia	36	90	61	51
Austria	11	55	79	70
Bangladesh	80	20	55	60
Belgium	65	75	54	94
Brazil	69	38	49	76
Bulgaria	70	30	40	85
Canada	39	80	52	48
Chile	63	23	28	86
China	80	20	66	30
Colombia	67	13	64	80
Costa Rica	35	15	21	86
Czech Republic	57	58	57	74
Denmark	18	74	16	23
East African region[b]	64	27	41	52
Ecuador	78	8	63	67
Estonia	40	60	30	60
Finland	33	63	26	59
France	68	71	43	86
Germany	35	67	66	65
Greece	60	35	57	112
Guatemala	95	6	37	101
Hong Kong	68	25	57	29
Hungary	46	80	88	82
India	77	48	56	40
Indonesia	78	14	46	48
Iran	58	41	43	59
Ireland	28	70	68	35
Israel	13	54	47	81
Italy	50	76	70	75
Jamaica	45	39	68	13
Japan	54	46	95	92
Luxembourg	40	60	50	70
Malaysia	104	26	50	36
Malta	56	59	47	96

Country/Region	Power Distance	Individualism	Masculinity	Uncertainty avoidance
Mexico	81	30	69	82
Morocco	70	46	53	68
Netherlands	38	80	14	53
New Zealand	22	79	58	49
Norway	31	69	8	50
Pakistan	55	14	50	70
Panama	95	11	44	86
Peru	64	16	42	87
Philippines	94	32	64	44
Poland	68	60	64	93
Portugal	63	27	31	104
Romania	90	30	42	90
Russia	93	39	36	95
Salvador	66	19	40	94
Singapore	74	20	48	8
Slovakia	104	52	110	51
South Africa	49	65	63	49
South Korea	60	18	39	85
Spain	57	51	42	86
Surinam	85	47	37	92
Sweden	31	71	5	29
Switzerland	34	68	70	58
Taiwan	58	17	45	69
Thailand	64	20	34	64
Trinidad	47	16	58	55
Turkey	66	37	45	85
United Kingdom	35	89	66	35
United States	40	91	62	46
Uruguay	61	36	38	100
Venezuela	81	12	73	76
Vietnam	70	20	40	30
West African region[c]	77	20	46	54
Yugoslavia	76	27	21	88

[a] Egypt, Iraq, Kuwait, Lebanon, Libya, Saudi Arabia and UAE.
[b] Ethiopia, Kenya, Tanzania and Zambia.
[c] Ghana, Nigeria and Sierra Leone.

Sources: Country scores found in Geert Hofstede, *Cultures and Organizations: Software of the Mind* (New York: McGraw-Hill, 1991), pp. 53, 68, 84, 113; Geert Hofstede, *Culture's Consequences* (Thousand Oaks, CA: Sage, 2001), p. 502.

countries, children learn to say no at a young age and are encouraged to attain personal independence from the family. In these societies, subordinates are less dependent on their bosses and are more comfortable approaching their bosses and contradicting them.

Individualism-Collectivism

Hofstede's second dimension of culture is the individualism-collectivism dimension. The United States rates very high on individualism. However, most of the world is far more collectivist. In collectivist societies, the good of the group prevails over the good of the individual. From birth, individuals are integrated into strong, cohesive groups. They are identified in terms of their group allegiance and their group role.

The collectivist worldview tends to divide people into in-groups and out-groups. In other words, people do not simply choose which in-group to join. Often one has to be born into an in-group, such as a family, an ethnic group or a nationality. Collectivist societies tend to be more suspicious of outsiders, whereas individualistic societies are more welcoming of them. For example, only one of an individual's parents needs to be an American for the individual to qualify as an American citizen. Furthermore, one can be an American citizen simply by virtue of having been born in the United States, even of foreign parents. And if one does not qualify by birth, immigration is a possibility. Each year hundreds of thousands of immigrants request and are granted American citizenship. More collectivist societies, on the other hand, do not bestow citizenship so freely. For one to qualify as an Egyptian citizen, both of one's parents should be Egyptian, and naturalization is virtually unknown in that country.

Individuals in collectivist societies are more dependent on their group and more loyal to it than members of individualistic societies. Group members are expected to take care of one another. In turn, they tend to follow group norms and to avoid deviating from the group in opinions or behavior. This group cohesiveness may transfer to groups joined later in life, such as friends from high school and college or corporate colleagues.

A difference between a collectivist and an individualist market is illustrated by the South Korean social networking site Cyworld. Cyworld differs from U.S. social sites that specializes in bringing strangers together. Cyworld emphasizes strengthening relationships between current friends, co-workers and relatives. It creates a space to keep in contact from high school through parenthood.[43]

George Friedman, founder of Stratfor Global Intelligence, recalled an incident that exemplifies the individualism-collectivism divide:

A Chinese businessman once told me that he thought Americans were vile and immoral because they would hire strangers over family merely because the stranger was better qualified. He argued that valuing merit over blood was the height of immorality. I would not have liked to build my company on his basis, but his comments reminded me that our convictions as to how a society should function are neither universally shared nor admired.[44]

Outsiders may come to be trusted in collectivist societies, but only after they have invested much time and effort. Many firms relate a common experience in Saudi Arabia where a manager is sent to Saudi Arabia to establish business relations. After a long time, the potential Saudi client agrees to do business with the firm, but only if the manager who originally established the relationship stays and manages the relationship. In other words, the trusted outsider must be a person, not a firm.[45]

Masculinity–Femininity

Hofstede's third dimension of culture is masculinity-femininity. This was (not surprisingly) the only dimension identified in the IBM study in which male and female respondents' scores were significantly different. Nonetheless, some countries were rated more masculine overall, including their women, and some more feminine overall, including their men. Masculinity is associated with assertiveness. Femininity is associated with modesty and nurturance. Masculine societies value ambition, competitiveness and high earnings. Feminine societies are concerned with public welfare. For example, the percentage of gross national product (GNP) that a state allocates for aid to poor countries does not correlate with wealth but does correlate with femininity.

In Denmark, a feminine country, students tend to prepare a résumé that underplays their achievements. Interviewers know that they must ask probing questions to elicit an account of these achievements in the interview. Students in more masculine societies, such as the United States, tend to construct their résumés to broadcast any achievements. In this regard, Hofstede noted that Americans look like braggarts to Danes and that Danes look like suckers to Americans.

Uncertainty Avoidance

Uncertainty avoidance is the state of being uneasy or worried about what may happen in the future. It is not the same as being averse to risk. People who are risk-averse are afraid that something specific might happen—for example, that an inflated stock market might crash or that they might fail their final exams because they haven't studied hard. People who are uncertainty-avoidant are *anxious in general*. Exams always make them anxious, even if they have studied hard and have done well in the past. The future is uncertain for all of us. Typical persons from low uncertainty-avoidant societies accept this fact and are confident that they can deal with whatever might arise. In other words, they are comfortable "rolling with the punches." Typical persons from high uncertainty-avoidant societies try to control and minimize future uncertainty. They have a tendency to work hard or at least to feel more comfortable if they are busy doing something.

Uncertainty-avoidant cultures don't like ambiguity. Events should be clearly understandable and as predictable as possible. Teachers in these cultures are expected always to have the answers. In low uncertainty-avoidant cultures, on the other hand, teachers are allowed to say, "I don't know." High uncertainty-avoidant cultures have an emotional need for formal and informal rules. Low uncertainty-avoidant cultures dislike rules. What rules they do employ, however, are generally more respected than are the many rules of uncertainty-avoidant cultures.

High uncertainty-avoidant cultures tend to think that what is different is potentially dangerous. This fear may make such cultures less innovative than low uncertainty-avoidanct cultures, because radically new ideas are suspect to them. However, they can prove outstanding at

77

implementing the ideas of others. As Hofstede noted, Britain (a low uncertainty-avoidant culture) has produced more Nobel Prize winners than Japan (a high uncertainty-avoidant culture), but Japan has brought more new products to the world market.[46]

Uses and Limitations of the Hofstede Measures

The Hofstede measures are an excellent way to identify quickly those areas where significant cultural differences exist. Americans dealing with distributors in Guatemala must remember that their agents come from a very different culture. Guatemala scores much higher on power distance and uncertainty avoidance. It is a very collectivist society, whereas the United States is a very individualistic one. If we send a young American manager to negotiate terms with Guatemalan distributors, our American manager must be careful to show proper respect and deference to any older distributors. Our manager should expect the distributors to ask for clear and detailed contracts. In turn, our manager should take care that the distributors belong to the right in-group. For example, do their group ties allow them to reach the right retailers and to access preferential financing? Have the potential distributors conformed to group norms, and have they established themselves as trustworthy within their group?

We must remember that all these scores are relative. Depending on the reference point, Japan can appear collectivist or individualistic. American culture is more individualistic than Japanese culture, but Japanese culture is more individualistic than South Korean culture. When a multinational corporation (MNC) sends American managers to deal with Japanese customers, these managers must adjust to a more collectivist culture. When the MNC sends South Korean managers to deal with the same Japanese customers, they must adjust to a more individualistic culture.

Hofstede's framework is the culture framework that has received by far the most interest by business researchers.[47] Yet, the framework has a number of limitations. Not all countries were included in the original IBM study. Because IBM had no subsidiaries in Russia or Eastern Europe in the late 1970s, with the exception of Yugoslavia we have no original scores for these markets. For reasons of sample size, some countries in both Africa and the Middle East were grouped together despite probable cultural differences between them. We must also keep in mind that ethnic groups and regional populations within a country can vary significantly from the national average.[48] Luckily, new studies have added to the original list. For example, included on the Hofstede centre site are updated scores for Egypt and Saudi Arabia, two countries that were combined under Arabic countries in the original study. Both countries score 80 on uncertainty avoidance and 20 on individualism. But Saudi Arabia scores higher on power distance—95 versus 70 for Egypt—and masculinity—60 versus 45 for Egypt.

Also, the Hofstede measures should not be used for stereotyping people. They do present us with central tendencies or averages for a culture, but they cannot be used to describe any one person who might come from that culture. Some individual Swedes will behave in a more "masculine" manner than some Japanese, even though Sweden as a whole is a feminine culture and Japan as a whole is a masculine one.

Although the Hofstede measures are useful for identifying cultural differences and suggesting potential cross-cultural problems that international marketers may face, they do not capture or elucidate all aspects of a culture. Britain and the United States appear nearly similar across all the

Hofstede measures. Still, they differ in many aspects of culture. For example, Britain exhibits greater class consciousness than is found in the United States, and the United States scores higher on religiosity, as exhibited, for example, in church attendance. People in the United States are more outgoing in expressing their emotions while the British are more reserved.

In fact, the Hofstede scores sometimes fall prey to cultural paradox. In other words, they appear to argue *against* an observed cultural phenomenon. For example, Japanese score lower than Americans on uncertainty avoidance. Yet they intentionally use ambiguous clauses in business contracts, while Americans incorporate every contingency in their contracts.[49] Of course cultural paradoxes can also be observed for cultural phenomena beyond the Hofstede framework. In China, the term guanxi refers to the system of social networks and influential relationships that facilitate business and other dealings. Guanxi still plays the major role in finding top management jobs. However, employers seeking to fill lower level managerial and technical positions have proven amenable to using online sites, one of which offers 2.5 million job openings.[50]

Finally, the Hofstede measures do not encompass all aspects of culture. One cannot hope to capture a complete culture in four numeric measures. They are a great place to start, but they are only a start.

Cultural Change

How quickly does culture change? Are the Hofstede measures valid after 40 years? Will they be valid 40 years from now? Culture does change, but most writers on culture agree that it changes very slowly. In the 1920s, the Ottoman Empire that ruled Turkey was ousted in a military uprising. A new charismatic leader, Ataturk, attempted in various ways to distance Turkey from its culture of the past and force Turks to adopt more European ways. A major assault was made on collectivism. Voluntary organizations such as political parties and business associations were required by law to be open to all. Ethnic affiliations that had played a major role in the politics of the Ottoman Empire were discouraged under Ataturk. Citizens were socialized to think of themselves simply as Turks. Physical emblems of religious affiliations, such as the veil worn by Muslim women and the fez worn by Muslim men, were outlawed. Ninety years later, much has changed in Turkey, and Ataturk enjoys hero status among nearly all Turks. Yet his attempt to defeat collectivism has failed. Modern Turkey struggles with the Kurdish ethnic question in the east, Islamic political parties win elections and Turkey scores only 37 on Hofstede's individualism-collectivism measure.

World Beat 3.2

Who's the Boss?

In traditionally hierarchal India, bosses are known for their autocratic ways. However, making employees happy has become a new priority for many Indian managers in the technology and call-center sectors, and this means introducing a more democratic workplace.

Rival companies constantly try to poach each other's best workers. At one point employee turnover in the call-center industry hit 50 percent a year. High turnover in the technology sector also makes life particularly difficult for managers in companies that increasing win high-end multiple-year contracts. A first step to making employees happy is increased benefits from training to health benefits for parents of employees. But changes go further than good pay and perks. In India's outsourcing industry it is common for workers to e-mail the company chairman and acceptable to go over the head of one's immediate boss. Employees even put suggestions in the corporate suggestion boxes. And managers take them seriously.

Indian company, HCL Industries, has also introduced a 360-evaluation system that allows bosses, peers and underlings to rate a manager. HCL even posts these reviews online. A number of major companies in the West have visited HCL to learn more about their management style. But most have deemed it too democratic.

One reason for this change in management style may be the fact that more senior managers no longer come from India's traditional elites. Top universities in India are no longer sure bets for heritage students. Children of alumni must compete for entrance slots just like other applicants. Some of India's top management programs have even opened branches in Dubai in order to target the Indian diaspora.

Recent polls appear to reflect the ambiguity that Indian workers may feel toward their bosses. A survey performed by Kenexa Corporation revealed that Indians rated their senior managers higher than any other country in the survey including Germany, Japan and the United States. However in another poll of 2,500 Indian executives, 62 percent reported having an abusive boss.

Sources: Sumant Sinha, "The Indian Way of Management," *Business Today*, October 3, 2010; Jared Sandberg, "'It Says Press Any Key; Where's the Any Key?'—India's Call-Center Workers Get Pounded, Pampered," *Wall Street Journal*, February 20, 2007, p. B1; Joe Light, "Chinese, Indian Workers Give Bosses Top Marks," *Wall Street Journal Online*, November 21, 2010; "Sixty-two Percent of Indian Employees Say They Have Abusive Bosses," *Hindustan Times*, October 12, 2012; and "Overseas Branches of Indian B-Schools Target the Diaspora," *Business Today*, October 28, 2012.

It is true that most developing countries rate high on power distance and collectivism, and the average religiosity of a country's population tends to decline with increased economic development. These observations have led some to conclude that as economies develop, all societies will someday converge in a single, modern culture. Americans in particular tend to believe that this modern culture will resemble American culture. Yet, ironically, the United States remains an outlier regarding the religiosity rule. Despite enjoying one of the highest PCIs in the world, America remains one of the world's most religious societies.[51] Also, Americans rate higher on the traditional value of national pride than do citizens in other developed countries. Based on overall patterns of social development, Sweden and the Netherlands are arguably better examples of modernity than is the United States.[52]

It is important to remember that cultures in the world today vary greatly. With global media, Internet connection and human migration, virtually all cultures are affected by other cultures. All societies are evolving. In 100 years, Indonesia will undergo cultural change, but it won't become America. In 100 years, America will undergo cultural change as well. Marketing managers from all nations will continue to deal with the cultural differences that make all nations unique.

Language and Communication

Knowing the language of a society can become the key to understanding its culture. Language is not merely a collection of words or terms. Language expresses the thinking pattern of a culture—and to some extent even forms the thinking itself. Linguists have found that cultures with more primitive languages or a limited range of expression are more likely to be limited in their thought patterns. Some languages cannot accommodate modern technological or business concepts, forcing the cultural elite to work in a different language.

The French are particularly sensitive about their language as an embodiment of their culture and seek to protect it from outside influence. The French government has proposed legal action to limit further incursions by other languages, especially by English. For example, the official word for *le airbag* is *coussin gonflable de protection* and *fast food* is *restauration rapide*. English words arising from new technologies such as podcasting must receive a certified French equivalent that requires approval from three organizations, a process that can take years. Each year, about 300 new terms complete the process and are officially translated into French.[53]

Table 3.6 lists the official languages of selected countries. Note that some countries have more than one official language. When Disney released its first animated film produced in India it was available in three languages—Hindi, Tamil and Telugu.[54] In fact India has 19 official languages, although the most commonly spoken language is Hindi. South Africa has 11 official languages. Very few countries, such as the United States, do not designate an official language. African countries with diverse tribal languages often adopt a colonial European language as their official language. However, the use of this official language may be restricted to elites. Similarly, Spanish is one of the official languages of Bolivia, but two native Indian languages are also official. Certain languages are associated with certain regions of the world, but key markets in these regions may speak a different language. For example, Arabic is associated with the Middle East, but Persian (Farsi) is spoken in Iran and Turkish in Turkey. Spanish is associated with Latin America, but Portuguese is spoken in Brazil.

Forms of Address

The English language has one form of address: all persons are addressed with the pronoun *you*. This is not the case in many other languages. The Germanic, Romance and Slavic languages always have two forms of address, the personal and the formal. Japanese has three forms. A Japanese person will use a different form of address with a superior, a colleague or a subordinate, and there are different forms for male and female in many expressions. These differences in language represent different ways of interacting. English, particularly as it is spoken in the United States, is much less formal than Japanese. Americans often address their bosses and customers by their first names. In Japan this practice could be considered rude. Consequently, knowing the Japanese language gives a foreigner a better understanding of cultural mores regarding social status and authority.

Table 3.6 Official Languages of Selected Countries

Country	Language(s)	Country	Language(s)	Country	Language(s)
Africa		**Americas**		**Asia**	
Angola	Portuguese	Argentina	Spanish	Japan	Japanese
Cameroon	French, English	Belize	English	Malaysia	Malay
Chad	French, Arabic	Bolivia	Aymara, Quechua, Spanish	Pakistan	Urdu, English
Ethiopia	Amharic			Philippines	Tagalog, English
Kenya	Swahili			Singapore	Chinese, English, Malay, Tamil
Mozambique	Portuguese	Brazil	Portuguese		
Niger	French	Canada	English, French	South Korea	Korean
Nigeria	English	Chile	Spanish	Sri Lanka	English, Sinhala, Tamil
Rwanda	French, Kinyarwanda	Haiti	French, Creole		
		Jamaica	English	Thailand	Thai
Somalia	Somali	Mexico	Spanish		
		Peru	Spanish		
		Venezuela	Spanish		
Europe		**Middle East**			
Belgium	Dutch, French, German	Egypt	Arabic, English, French		
Finland	Finnish, Swedish	Iran	Farsi		
France	French	Iraq	Arabic		
Germany	German	Israel	Hebrew, Arabic		
Italy	Italian	Lebanon	Arabic, French		
Netherlands	Dutch, Frisian	Turkey	Turkish		
Russian Federation	Russian				
Spain	Spanish				
Switzerland	French, German, Italian, Romansh				
United Kingdom	English, Welsh				

Sources: Data derived from *Cultural Practices and Heritage: Leading Languages*, UNESCO Cultural Policy Resources (www.unesco.org), One World Nations Online (www.nationsonline.org) and Access Alliance (http://accessalliance.ca).

The Context of Language

When an American executive says "yes" in a negotiation, this usually means "yes, I accept the terms." However, *yes* in Asian countries can have a variety of meanings. It can mean that your hearers recognize that you are talking to them but not necessarily that they understand what you are saying. It can mean that they understood you but disagree with you. It can mean that they understand your proposal and will consult with others about it. Or, finally, it can indicate total agreement.

The simple term *yes* is a good example of how some languages can be affected by social milieu or context. In low-context cultures such as the United States, communication is explicit and words tend to retain their meaning in all situations. In Asian high-context cultures, meanings are more implicit. The meanings of words change depending on who is speaking to whom, where that person is speaking and under what circumstances. These subtleties make communication all the more difficult for persons who were not born and raised in those cultures.[55] Not surprisingly, collectivist cultures tend to be high-context cultures.

Before beginning a conversation or a negotiation in high-context cultures, the parties involved need to take part in preliminary chats in order to place one another in the correct social context. For example, do both parties come from the same social background, or is one an outsider? Do both negotiators possess the status required to make a final decision on their own, or will they need to consult with others? In high-context cultures, these questions would never be asked or answered directly. Instead, people are socialized to pick up on the right cues, such as where someone went to school or how long that person has been employed with his or her company. "Placing each other" helps negotiators determine how they will interact and interpret each other's statements.

Also, *how* something is said may be considered as important, or even more important, than what is said. When U.S. Secretary of State James Baker told the Iraqis that the United States would attack Iraq if they did not retreat from their occupation of Kuwait, the high-context Iraqis understood that the Americans would not attack them. Baker spoke calmly and did not seem angry. Therefore, the Iraqis concluded that they needn't take the threat seriously.[56] Nonetheless, the United States mobilized its armed forces and drove the Iraqi army from Kuwait in the First Gulf War. Clearly some soft spoken words should be taken seriously.

Body Language

As important as understanding a verbal foreign language is, it is only part of the challenge. The use of nonverbal communications, or body language, is also important. Body language includes such elements as touching, making arm and hand gestures and keeping the proper distance between speakers. Mexicans happily come within 16–18 inches of a stranger for a business discussion. For Latins, Arabs and Africans, proximity is a sign of confidence. Asians, Nordics, Anglo-Saxons and Germanic people consider space within 1 yard or meter as personal space. When a Mexican moves closer than this to an English person, the English person feels invaded and steps back, giving the Mexican the incorrect message that he or she does not want to do business.[57] The appropriateness of eye contact varies with culture as well. Americans consider making eye contact while speaking a sign of trustworthiness. Many Asian cultures, such as that of Korea, can consider it a sign of disrespect.

Showing Emotion

Another way in which cultures vary in their communication style is the degree to which they exhibit emotion. In affective cultures, such as Italy, the United States and Arab countries, speakers are allowed—even expected—to express emotions more than in nonaffective or neutral cultures, such as China, Korea and Japan. If upset or even excited, a speaker is allowed to speak louder and gesticulate. This is not to say that Americans and Italians feel emotions more strongly than Koreans but merely that Koreans are expected not to *show* emotions. Persons from affective cultures can unnerve those from neutral cultures with their displays of emotion. On the other hand, persons from neutral cultures can appear inscrutable to those from affective cultures.

Despite their nonaffective culture, Japanese marketers are reconsidering the power of a smile. Some retail and service businesses are sending employees to newly opened smile schools that consider "importing joviality" to be their corporate mission. Yoshihiko Kadokawa, author of *A Laughing Face*, believes that smiling at customers increases sales and boosts employee morale. However, teachers at Japan's smile schools concede that smiling excessively is still controversial in Japan, where it is thought to reflect suicidal tendencies, especially among males.[58]

Overcoming the Language Barrier

International marketing communications are heavily affected by the existence of different languages. Advertising has to be adjusted to each language, brand names can prove problematic and personal contacts are made difficult by the language barrier.

Even differences among dialects of the same language plague global marketers. For example, the American CEO of RecycleBank was offended when he expanded his company into Britain and the local press referred to his business model—a rewards program for individuals based on how much they recycle—as a "scheme." The word in American English connotes deceit, a connotation absent in British English.[59] Different dialects must be addressed as well. Chinese is especially replete with dialects. Microsoft lengthened its search engine's name from *Bing* which sounded like "illness" or "pancake" in certain Chinese dialects to *you qui bi ying* which translates roughly to *seek and ye shall find*.[60]

To overcome this language barrier, businesspeople all over the world have relied on three approaches: the translation of written material, the use of interpreters and the acquisition of foreign-language skills.

Translating and Translators

Translations are needed for a wide range of documents, including sales literature, catalogues, advertisements and contracts. Some companies send all correspondence through a translation firm. For a company that does not have a local subsidiary in a foreign market, competent translation agencies are available in most countries. The largest translation staff in the world belongs to the EU, which has 1,500 people translating 1.2 million pages of text per year into its three working languages: English, French and German. EU bureaucrats also use machine translation to provide rough translations used for e-mail and other less official communications.

Traveling with executives and attending meetings, personal translators can perform a very useful function when a complete language barrier exists. They are best used for a limited time only. Realistically, they cannot overcome long-term communication problems. When one is traveling in Asia, it is tempting to use senior subsidiary managers, who are usually bilingual, as translators. However, this practice should be avoided. Translators are often considered low-level staff members in Asia, and senior managers employed in this manner would be looked down on.

Translation Problems

Both translation services and translators work by translating one language into another. In certain situations, however, it is almost impossible to translate a given meaning accurately and fully into a second language. When the original idea, or thought, is not part of the second culture, for example, the translation may be meaningless. When China first liberalized its economy after years of strict communism, Chinese translators had difficulty translating basic English business terms such as *profit* and *loss*, because these concepts were unknown in the communist-planned economy.

Translation problems abound with the use of brand names in various markets. Brand names can be particularly affected by language, because they are not normally translated but are merely transliterated. Today, global companies tend to choose brand names carefully and test them in advance to ensure that the meaning in all major languages is neutral and positive. They also make sure that the name can be easily pronounced. Language differences may have caused many blunders, but careful translations have now reduced the number of international marketing mistakes. Still, the language barrier remains, and companies that make a conscientious effort to overcome this barrier frequently achieve better results than those that do not.

Which Language to Learn?

One can draw two major conclusions about the impact of language on global marketing. First, a firm must adjust its communication program and design communications to include the languages used by its customers. Second, the firm must be aware that a foreign language may reflect different thinking patterns or indicate varying motivations on the part of prospective clients and partners. To the extent that such differences occur, the simple mechanical translation of messages will not suffice. MNCs require marketing managers with foreign-language abilities. Still, managers cannot be expected to speak all languages. Global marketers are increasingly united by the use of English as a global business language. Chile inaugurated a nationwide campaign to ensure that all high school students became fluent in English. The objective: to make Chile a world-class exporter.[61]

English has the advantage of being a noncontextual language that many consider relatively easy to learn. Its influence in international commerce was established first by the British Empire and later by the influence of the United States and U.S. MNCs. Today over half the websites on the Internet are in English, despite the growing popularity of other languages.

The widespread use of English has even allowed U.S. firms to outsource customer service tasks to call centers based in India. These centers tap into a large pool of English-speaking labor to answer calls from U.S. consumers concerning anything from late credit card payments to problems with software. Indian service personnel call themselves by American names—Barbara, not Bhavana—and learn to speak with an American accent. Customers on the line have no idea they're talking to someone on the other side of the world.[62]

Many companies are adopting English as their primary language, even companies that operate largely outside the English-speaking world.[63] Rakuten Inc., a major Japanese online retailer, declared that work documents should be written in English. Japanese employees were given two years warning that all would be required to speak with each other in English or be fired if they failed to become proficient in English. Rakuten had recently acquired businesses in Europe and the United States and considered English essential to advancing as a global company.[64]

Although English has become the language of commerce and electronic communications, a marketing manager's personal relationships will often benefit from the manager having achieved language skill in a customer's native tongue. Both Philips Electronics NV, the Dutch consumer giant, and U.S.-based General Electric have adopted English as their corporate language, and managers are not required to speak a local language to run a subsidiary. However, both companies appreciate multilingual managers and consider language skills to be an advantage.[65] In fact, cultural empathy may best be developed by learning a foreign language, and learning any language will help develop cultural sensitivity. By learning even one foreign language, a student can gain a better appreciation of all different cultures.

Adapting to Cultural Differences

Some companies make special efforts to adapt their products or services to various cultural environments. One such celebrated case is McDonald's, the U.S. fast-food franchise operator. Nearly 70 percent of McDonald's sales and all of its top ten restaurants, measured in terms of sales and profits, are now overseas. Still, there are some countries where the standard McDonald's hamburger menu does not do well. In Japan, McDonald's had to substantially adapt its original U.S.-style menu. It introduced McChao, a Chinese fried rice dish. This dish proved to be a good idea in a country where 90 percent of the population eats rice daily. The results were astounding. Sales climbed 30 percent after the McChao was introduced. McDonald's continues to innovate in Japan with the Teriyaki McBurger and Chicken Tatsuta.

Even when a firm tries hard to understand the culture of a new market, it is difficult to foresee every cultural surprise. When Big Boy, a U.S.-based hamburger chain, opened in Bangkok, the franchisee in Thailand also discovered that he needed to make adaptations to the menu to suit Thai tastes. However, those were not the only cultural surprises. Many Thai consumers were at a loss about what to make of the chain's giant statue of a boy in checkered overalls. Some Thais left bowls of rice and incense at the feet of the statue as though it were a religious icon. Other Thais said the statue spooked them.[66]

Cultural adaptation is not limited to better understanding and meeting the needs of consumers. Cultural differences also affect how marketers interact with employees in international markets. Big Boy discovered that its Thai employees would not eat on shifts but insisted on eating together, all at the same time.[67] Interbrew, the Belgian brewing giant, entered the Korean market by purchasing 50 percent of Korea's Oriental Brewing Company. Both sides experienced a high degree of stress when managers from Belgium and the United States arrived in South Korea. The Western managers insisted that the staff speak their minds. The Korean managers, on the other hand, were used to a hierarchical relationship based on respect and unswerving loyalty to the boss. Still, after a bumpy start, the blend of two cultures turned out to be a good thing for the company.[68]

Marketing managers who enter different cultures must learn to cope with a vast array of new cultural cues and expectations as well as to identify which old ones no longer work. Often they experience stress and tension as a result. This effect is commonly called culture shock. The authors of *Managing Cultural Differences* offer the following ten tips to deflate the stress and tension of cultural shock:

- ➤ Be culturally prepared.
- ➤ Be aware of local communication complexities.
- ➤ Mix with the host nationals.
- ➤ Be creative and experimental.
- ➤ Be culturally sensitive.
- ➤ Recognize complexities in host cultures.
- ➤ See yourself as a culture bearer.
- ➤ Be patient, understanding, and accepting of yourself and your hosts.
- ➤ Be realistic in your expectations.
- ➤ Accept the challenge of intercultural experiences.[69]

Conclusion

In this chapter, we explored a small sample of the wide variety of cultural and social influences that can affect international marketing operations.

It is essential for international marketers to avoid cultural bias in dealing with business operations in more than one culture. As the president of a large industrial company in Osaka, Japan, once noted, our cultures are 80 percent identical and 20 percent different. The successful businessperson is the one who can identify the differences and deal with them. Of course, this is a very difficult task, and few executives ever reach the stage where they can claim to be completely sensitive to cultural differences.

Managerial Takeaways

1. *Despite increasing contact among nations worldwide, the influence of culture on global marketing remains impressive.*
2. *Culture significantly impacts not only the relationship between global marketers and their customers but also the relationships between them and their employees, competitors, local partners and government officials.*
3. *Fully predicting how culture might affect a particular marketing decision is difficult due to the breadth and complexity of culture. And cultural paradoxes abound.*
4. *Studying culture helps global marketers avoid missteps abroad. But missteps inevitably occur. The best global marketers make mistakes but learn from those mistakes.*

Questions for Discussion

1. How might the educational systems of the United States and Germany affect the marketing of banking services to young adults aged 16 to 22?

2. You have been asked to attend a meeting with Belgian, Turkish and Japanese colleagues to develop a global plan for a new aftershave. Using the Hofstede scores for these countries, discuss the challenges you would face in the meeting. Assume your native culture.

3. What effects might the Internet have on cultural differences?

4. Why do you think food is such a culturally sensitive product?

5. When a firm enters a new market, how can managers "learn" the culture?

CASE 3.1 Banning Barbie

The Institute for Intellectual Development of Children and Young Adults has declared Barbie a cultural threat to Iran. The tall, blond, blue-eyed doll represents the American woman who never wants to get old or pregnant. She wears makeup and indecent clothes. She drinks champagne in the company of boyfriend doll Ken. To replace Barbie, the Institute designed Sara. Sara has darker skin and black hair, and she wears the traditional floor-length chador. Sara has no boyfriend doll. The idea of having a boyfriend is a concept not acceptable to most Middle Eastern families. Sara's brother, Dara, is dressed in the coat and turban of a Muslim cleric or mullah.

Since its Islamic Revolution over 30 years ago, the Iranian government has been particularly wary of Western influences. A Coca-Cola factory was shut down for promoting American culture. A call to ban Barbie is not popular with all Iranians, however. Some toy-store owners think Barbie is about business, not culture, and many moderate Iranians oppose attempts to protect national culture by force and prohibitions. While some Iranians agree that Barbie is "more harmful than an American missile," others declare her competition Sara to be "fat and ugly."

Barbie's continued popularity with some segments of Iran's population has resulted in the doll being smuggled into Iran. A government crackdown in 2002 on retailers selling contraband Barbies was soon abandoned, suggesting that the government may have had little will to stop the traffic in illicit dolls. However, a new crackdown in 2012 resulted in the closing of stores that were still exhibiting the Western doll in their shop windows. Barbies are now sold under the counter.

For many years, Barbie remained the most popular doll among affluent consumers in the neighboring Arab world. In an attempt to give Arab girls a feeling of pride in belonging to their own culture, the Arab League sponsored feasibility studies to interest private-sector investors in producing the Leila doll. Leila was envisioned to look about ten years old with black eyes and hair. Her wardrobe options would include Western outfits as well as traditional dresses from the various Arab regions, such as Egypt, Syria and the Gulf states. Similar to Sara, Leila would enjoy government subsidies and sell at about $10 whereas Barbie can sell for between $30 and $150 in various capitals of the Middle East. Nonetheless, Leila was never launched.

In the United States, competition to Barbie has also emerged. A manufacturer in Livonia, Michigan, introduced a Razanne doll for Muslim Americans. The doll's creator claimed that the main message of the doll was that what matters is what's inside you, not how you look. Razanne has the body of a pre-teen and comes in three types: fair-skinned blond, olive-skinned with black hair and black skin with black hair. Her clothing is modest but her aspirations are those of "a modern Muslim woman." For example, there is a Girl Scout Razanne and a Teacher Razanne.

However, it would be a doll designed and sold by NewBoy Studios from the Arab private sector that would finally dethrone Barbie among Muslim consumers in Arab countries. Brown-haired Fulla has a beautiful face and is shaped similarly to Barbie but with a more modest bosom. Her outside wear keeps her fully covered. The skirts of her inside clothes fall just below her knee. Similar to Sara, Fulla doesn't have a boyfriend. Though more expensive than Sara, Fulla sells for half the price of Barbie. Fulla is supported by television commercials that show her praying, reading a book and baking a cake for a friend. In addition, the remarkably successful doll has dozens of related products such as bicycles, cereal, chewing gum and stationery.

As Fulla prepared to make her Western debut at the Toy Fair in New York, one NewBoy manager declared Fulla to be a global doll, not a Muslim doll. He noted that Fulla is sold in India wearing the traditional sari. Everyone doesn't agree, however. There have been calls to ban Fulla in France where some see Fulla as an Islamist plot to reach children in their homes and divide the nation between a majority who play with Barbie and a Muslim minority who play with Fulla.

Discussion Questions

1. Why was Barbie popular in both France and the Middle East?
2. Should Muslim countries ban Barbie? Should France ban Fulla? Why or why not?
3. Why do you think Fulla was far more successful than Sara or Razanne?

Sources: Elizabeth Flock, "Iran Removes Barbie Doll from Shelves," *Washington Post*, January 17, 2012; "Banning Barbie" in Kate Gillespie and H. David Hennessey, *Global Marketing* (Mason, OH: Cengage Learning, 2011), pp. 85–86; Catherine Poe, "Iran Declares War on Barbie," *The Washington Times*, January 21, 2012; "Iran Attacks an Old Enemy: Barbie," Associated Press, January 21, 2012.

CASE 3.2 Work versus Leisure

Unlike their counterparts in many countries, employers in the United States are not required by law to provide paid vacations for their employees. In fact, American culture in general appears suspicious of leisure. Some attribute this to the Protestant work ethic. Many Americans fill their free time with intellectually or physically demanding hobbies or *volunteer work*. Even on vacation, Americans stay in touch with the workplace via their iPhones and laptop computers.

Europeans, on the other hand, hold leisure in high regard. By law France has the shortest workweek in Europe. Most workers must be paid overtime for working over 35 hours a week. In addition, the French spend the most time sleeping of all industrial nations. They also spend over two hours a day eating, twice the time Americans spend eating. Americans enjoy a disposable income that is 34 percent higher than the French, but the French are generally conceded to enjoy a better balance between work and leisure.

In Germany, however, longer workweeks may soon be the norm. To Germans, prosperity once meant less work and more leisure time. However, a low birthrate has resulted in fewer workers supporting more and more retired Germans in the generous state pension system. Germans in the workforce may soon have to work longer hours to support the retirees.

The restful German Sunday has also come under attack. Sunday is designated "a day for spiritual reflection" in the German constitution. This custom results in a ban on Sunday shopping. Since the reunification of Germany, former East Germans who grew up in a largely atheistic society have waged war on Sunday closings. East German cities routinely exploit loopholes in the law to allow stores to stay open; one loophole that is commonly invoked allows sales to tourists. Department stores in Berlin now welcome tens of thousands of Sunday shoppers, using the argument that their products could be of interest to tourists. Union leaders, bent on protecting leisure time for their members, have joined churches in denouncing this trend.

If Germans may soon work longer hours, Japanese are considering working less. Japanese workers take an average of only nine vacation days a year. However, many have been reconsidering the value of leisure since their prime minister suffered a stroke brought on by overwork. Japan has seen a sharp increase in suicides and *karoshi*, or death caused by overwork. Japan has also introduced "Happy Mondays," creating longer weekends by switching certain public holidays from Saturdays to Mondays. The government hopes that more holidays will deliver the added bonus of encouraging Japanese to spend more money in pursuit of leisure and thus boost the economy.

Overall, working hours have decreased considerably over the past 50 years in developed countries. This trend can be attributed to increased productivity—not increased laziness. As many Asian countries have become more prosperous, employees now work less for the same salaries. As a result, the five-day workweek is becoming the norm across much of Asia—with controversial results. South Koreans currently work on average 2,193 hours a year versus 1,700 hours for the Japanese and 1,408 for the Germans. However, with work hours expected to fall in the future, The Korean Culture and Tourism Policy Institute provides leisure counselors to help workers learn how to adapt to time off, since many Koreans don't know what to do with their extra time. Other Koreans are finding that fewer hours at work add stress to the family as housewives complain that their husbands are around at home too much. Still others have discovered that leisure can be expensive. Visits to museums, meals at restaurants and sports lessons all add up. A survey of Koreans revealed that 63 percent of respondents worried about the economic burden resulting from their leisure time spending.

Differences within countries as to work versus leisure also exist. Over a decade after France passed its law limiting workweeks to only 35 hours, the French were working nearly as many hours as the Germans. Workers in the country's public sector largely kept to the 35-hour week, but workers and entrepreneurs in the private sector work longer hours.

Discussion Questions

1.   What cultural factors influence a society's attitudes toward work and leisure?
2.   How can different attitudes toward leisure affect the marketing of products?

Sources: Catherine Bremmer, "Many French Can Only Dream of 35-Hour Work Week," Reuters, July 31, 2013; Hugh Carnegy, "France's 35-Hour Working Week is Spared," *Financial Times*, November 1, 2012; "Work versus Leisure" in Kate Gillespie and H. David Hennessey, *Global Marketing* (Mason, OH: Cengage Learning, 2011), pp. 86–87; Wesley Stephenson, "Who Works the Longest Hours," *BBC News Magazine*, May 23, 2012; Alexander Stille, "Why the French are Fighting Over Work Hours," *The New Yorker* (online), October 3, 2013.

CASE 3.3   Cultural Norm or Cultural Paradox?

Which of the cultural insights below describe a cultural norm? Which present cultural paradoxes? Explain your answers.

1. In Brazil, nepotism is not only an acceptable practice, many consider it a good thing. Hiring a relative assures you have an employee you can trust. Brazil's individualism score is 38.
2. In Egypt, business leaders often distance themselves from lower-level employees and often make all the decisions themselves. Titles are very important. Egypt's power distance score is 63.
3. In Indonesia, senior managers are expected to make all major decisions. However, they often encourage discussion from employees and seek consensus. Indonesia's power distance score is 72.
4. The majority of people working in Dubai (UAE) are foreigners. Foreigners are allowed to drink alcohol in this Muslim country in certain places such as hotels. The individualism score for UAE is 22 and its uncertainty avoidance score is 69.
5. In China, managers may sacrifice family time and leisure for work. Many workers leave their families to seek better employment opportunities elsewhere. China's individualism score is 16. Its uncertainty avoidance score is 21, and its masculinity score is 68.
6. Mexico is generally considered a polychronic country. Managers will likely show up late for a meeting. However, foreign managers are expected to be on time.
7. Russians are tough negotiators. Their aim is to gain the greatest advantage by wearing down the other side. If you concede anything too easily, they will interpret this as a sign of weakness. Russia's masculinity score is 34.
8. Senior managers in Sweden are addressed by their first names and their dress is not ostentatious. Sweden's power distance score is 22. Its masculinity score is 5.
9. Nigerians are generally friendly and outgoing. At an initial business meeting, you should expect to devote at least two hours to getting to know your Nigerian colleagues before getting down to business. Nigeria's individualism score is 28.
10. In the Philippines, initial greetings are formal. The eldest or most senior manager is greeted first. Many Filipinos are motivated by the concept of saving face. If they do not live up to accepted norms, they will not only bring shame upon themselves but on their families as well. The power distance score for the Philippines is 81. Its individualism score is 31.

Notes

1   Paula Prada and Bruce Orwall, "A Certain 'Je Ne Sais Quoi' at Disney's New Park," *Wall Street Journal*, March 12, 2002, p. B1.
2   Geoffrey A. Fowler and Merissa Marr, "Disney and the Great Wall," *Wall Street Journal*, February 9, 2006, p. B1.
3   Jonathan Cheng, "Hong Kong Disneyland Gets New Manager," *Wall Street Journal*, August 15, 2008, p. B4.
4   Eric Bellman, "Wal-Mart Exports Big-Box Concept to India," *Wall Street Journal Online*, May 28, 2009.
5   "Give Me a Big Mac But Hold the Beef," *The Guardian*, December 28, 2000, p. 4.
6   "Cultural Explanations: The Man in the Baghdad Café," *The Economist*, November 9, 1996, pp. 23–26.
7   Francis Fukuyama, *Trust: The Social Virtues and the Creation of Prosperity* (New York: Free Press, 1996), p. 6.
8   David Murphy, "Selling Christmas in China," *Wall Street Journal*, December 24, 2002, p. B1.
9   Geoffrey A. Fowler, "China's Yuletide Revolution," *Wall Street Journal*, December 22, 2005, p. B1.
10 Hugh Pope, "A New Holiday Hit in Muslim Turkey," *Wall Street Journal*, December 24, 2003, p. A1.
11 Farnaz Fassihi, "As Authorities Frown, Valentine's Day Finds Place in Iran's Heart," *Wall Street Journal*, February 12, 2004, p. A1.
12 Ibid.
13 Joel Greenberg, "Who in Israel Loves the Orthodox? Their Grocers," *New York Times*, October 17, 1997, p. 4.
14 Sarmad Ali, "New Cellphone Services Put God on the Line," *Wall Street Journal*, March 27, 2006, p. B1.
15 Ibid.
16 "Connecting Islamic Liquidity with Halal Opportunity," *Islamic Business and Finance*, September 12, 2013.
17 Shahidan Shafie and Osman Mohamed, "'Halal'—The Case of the Malaysian Muslim Consumers' Quest for Peace of Mind," *Proceedings of the American Marketing Association* (Winter 2002), p. 118.
18 Ibid.
19 Lauren Etter and John Lyons, "Brazilian Beef Clan Goes Global as Troubles Hit Market," *Wall Street Journal*, August 1, 2008, p. A1.
20 "Halal Growth Means Big Things for the UAE," *Al-Bawaba News*, October 9, 2007.
21 Ben Bland, "Ramadan Gives Fast Profits in Indonesia," *Financial Times*, August 5, 2015, p. 4.
22 Yasmine El-Rashidi, "Ramadan Turns into Big Business," *Wall Street Journal*, October 6, 2006, p. B3.
23 Kang Siew Li, "Coca-Cola's Global Ramadhan Commercial," *Business Times*, *The New York Straits Times Press*, January 14, 1998, p. 17.
24 Anna Slater, "Indian Monsoon Drenches the Land; Marketers Drench the Consumer," *Wall Street Journal*, July 24, 2003, p. A12.
25 Henry Sender, "Foreign Car Makers Make Mark in India," *Asian Wall Street Journal*, August 22, 2000, p. 1.
26 "U.S. Company Criticized for Misusing Images of Indian Hindu Deities," *BBC Monitoring*, November 18, 2000.
27 John Pomfret, "80-Year-Old Cashes In on Famous Name," *Seattle Times*, August 25, 1998, p. A13.
28 "Trouble Brewing," *Newsweek*, July 19, 1999, p. 40.
29 Karin Esterhammer, "Fall Festivals Fill Japan's Streets with Pageantry," *Los Angeles Times*, June 10, 2001, p. L6.
30 Sheryl Wu Dunn, "Korean Women Still Feel Demands to Bear a Son," *New York Times International*, January 14, 1997, p. A3.
31 Fuq-in Bian, John R. Logan and Yanjie Bian, "Intergenerational Relations in Urban China," *Demography*, vol. 35, no. 1 (February 1998), pp. 119–122.
32 Simon Saulkin, "Chinese Walls," *Management Today* (September 1996), pp. 62–68.
33 Fukuyama, *Trust*, pp. 62, 98.
34 Scheherazade Daneshkhu, "Poor Communication and Bureaucracy Make Eastern Europe Frustrating," *Financial Times*, September 9, 1996, p. 12.

35 Glen H. Brodowsky, Beverlee B. Anderson, Camille P. Schuster, Ofer Meilich and M. Ven Venkatesan, "If Time is Money is It a Common Currency? Time in Anglo, Asian and Latin Cultures," *Journal of Global Marketing*, vol. 21, no. 4 (2008), pp. 245–257.

36 Ibid.

37 Jo Johnson and Ralph Atkins, "Workers at French Plant Vote for a Longer Week," *Financial Times*, July 20, 2004, p. 1.

38 Thomas J. Madden, Kelly Hewlett and Martin S. Roth, "Managing Images in Different Cultures: A Cross-National Study of Color Meaning and Preferences," *Journal of International Marketing*, vol. 8, no. 4 (2000), pp. 90–107.

39 Mubeen M. Aslam, "Are You Selling the Right Colour? A Cross-Cultural Review of Colour as Marketing Cue," *Journal of Marketing Communications*, vol. 12, no. 1 (2006), pp. 15–30.

40 Dupont News, www2.dupont.com, accessed December 20, 2010.

41 K. Sivakumar and Cheryl Nakata, "The Stampede Towards Hofstede's Framework: Avoiding the Sample Design Pit in Cross-Cultural Research," *Journal of International Business Studies*, vol. 32, no. 3 (2001), p. 555.

42 Geert Hofstede, *Culture and Organizations: Software of the Mind* (New York: McGraw-Hill, 1991), p. 23.

43 "Move Over, Myspace; Korean Social Site Targets U.S. Teenagers," *Marketing News*, September 15, 2006, pp. 52–53.

44 George Friedman, "Geopolitical Journey: Azerbaijan and America," Stratfor Global Intelligence, June 11, 2013.

45 Hofstede, *Culture and Organizations*, p. 50.

46 Ibid., p. 123.

47 K. Sivakumar and Cheryl Nakata, "The Stampede Toward Hofstede's Framework: Avoiding the Sample Design Pit in Cross-Cultural Research," *Journal of International Business Studies*, vol. 32, no. 3 (2001), pp. 555–574.

48 Tomasz Lenartowicz, James P. Johnson and Carolyn T. White, "The Neglect of Intracountry Cultural Variation in International Management Research," *Journal of Business Research*, vol. 56, no. 12 (2003), pp. 999–1008.

49 Joyce S. Osland and Allan Bird, "Beyond Sophisticated Stereotyping: Cultural Sensemaking in Context," *Academy of Management Executive*, vol. 14, no. 1 (2000), pp. 65–79.

50 Tom Orlik, "Boss Talk: Chinese Job Site Offers 2.5 Million Openings," *Wall Street Journal*, August 14, 2013.

51 Samuel P. Huntington, *Who Are We?: The Challenges to America's National Identity* (New York: Simon and Schuster, 2004), pp. 365–366.

52 Ronald Inglehart and Wayne E. Baker, "Modernization, Culture Change, and the Persistence of Traditional Values," *American Sociological Review*, vol. 65 (February 2000), p. 31.

53 Max Colchester, "The French Get Lost in the Clouds over a New Term in the Internet Age," *Wall Street Journal*, October 14, 2009, p. A1.

54 Merissa Marr, "Small World," *Wall Street Journal*, June 11, 2007, p. A1.

55 Jean-Claude Usunier, *Marketing Across Cultures* (New York: Prentice-Hall, 2000), pp. 416–420.

56 Harry C. Triandis, "The Many Dimensions of Culture," *Academy of Management Executive*, vol. 18, no. 1 (2004), p. 90.

57 Judith Bowman, "Before Going Overseas, Be Ready: Know the Protocol," *Mass High Tech*, April 26, 1999, p. 31.

58 Valerie Reitman, "Japanese Workers Take Classes on the Grim Art of Grinning," *Los Angeles Times*, April 8, 1999, p. E4.

59 Emily Maltby, "Expanding Abroad? Avoid Cultural Gaffes," *Wall Street Journal*, January 19, 2010, p. B5.

60 James Hookway, "IKEAs Products Make Shoppers Blush in Thailand," *Wall Street Journal*, June 5, 2012.

61 "Se Habla Ingles," *Wall Street Journal*, December 30, 2004, p. A8.

62 "It's Barbara Calling," *The Economist*, April 29, 2000.

63 Phred Dvorak, "Plain English Gets Harder in Global Era," *Wall Street Journal*, November 5, 2007, p. B1.

64   Daisuke Wakabayashi, "English Gets the Last Word in Japan," *Wall Street Journal*, August 6, 2010, p. B2.

65   Kathryn Kranhold, Dan Bilefsky, Matthew Karnitschnig and Ginny Parker, "Lost in Translation?" *Wall Street Journal*, May 18, 2004, p. B1.

66   Robert Frank, "Big Boy's Adventures in Thailand," *Wall Street Journal*, April 12, 2000, p. B1.

67   Ibid.

68   Michael Schuman, "Foreign Flavor," *Wall Street Journal*, July 24, 2000, p. A1.

69   Philip R. Harris and Robert T. Moran, *Managing Cultural Differences*, 4th ed. (Houston, TX: Gulf, 1996), pp. 218–223.

Chapter 4

Political and Regulatory Climate

HOST COUNTRY POLITICAL CLIMATE   97

HOST GOVERNMENT ACTIONS   102

HOME COUNTRY POLITICAL FORCES   105

LEGAL ENVIRONMENTS   108

NATIONAL REGULATORY ENVIRONMENTS   110

REGULATORY CHANGE   113

POLITICAL RISK   116

GLOBAL MARKETING AND TERRORISM   122

Oil-rich Venezuela was once considered an attractive Latin American market. However, when Venezuelans elected Lieutenant Colonel Hugo Chavez president, he threatened to default on Venezuela's foreign debt and to reassert government control over much of the economy. The new president overhauled the country's constitution and judiciary, centralizing more power in the presidency. The response of foreign businesses was immediate. The next year foreign investment fell 40 percent. Eli Lilly and Honda were among the multinational corporations (MNCs) that closed operations in Venezuela.[1] Conditions did not improve for companies that stayed. Several years later Venezuela announced that cement companies were to be nationalized. Mexican-based Cemex, the world's largest cement company, rejected a government offer of $500 million for its Venezuelan assets. Venezuela eventually paid Cemex $600 million in compensation for its expropriated assets. After Hugo Chavez died, Cemex's chairman announced that Cemex would consider a return to Venezuela, but only if there was a change in government.[2]

This chapter identifies the political forces that influence global marketing operations. These forces include both the host and home governments of MNCs. Governments both support and restrict business as they seek to achieve a variety of goals from self-preservation to protecting their nation's cultural identity. International marketers must also be aware of special-interest groups that exert pressure on governments with respect to an increasing number of issues from environmental concerns to human rights.

Dealing simultaneously with several political and regulatory systems makes the job of the global marketing executive a complex one. These factors often precipitate problems that increase the level of risk in the international marketplace. Global companies have learned to cope with such complexities by developing strategies that address the more predictable regulatory changes and the less predictable political risks. These strategies are explained at the end of the chapter.

Learning Objectives

After studying this chapter, you should be able to:

➤ list and explain the political motivations behind government actions that promote or restrict global marketing;

➤ identify pressure groups that affect global marketing;

➤ discuss specific government actions salient to global marketing, such as boycotts and takeovers;

➤ list and compare the four basic legal traditions that marketers encounter worldwide;

➤ cite examples illustrating how national laws can vary and change;

➤ differentiate between the steps involved in managing political risk and those involved in planning for regulatory change.

Host Country Political Climate

The rapidly changing nature of the international political scene is evident to anyone who regularly reads, listens to or watches the various news media. Political upheavals and changes in government policy occur daily and can have an enormous impact on international business. For the executive, this means constant adjustments to exploit new opportunities and minimize losses.

Besides the international company, the principal players in the political arena are the host country governments and the home country governments. Sometimes transnational bodies or agencies such as the EU or the WTO can be involved. Within a national market, the interactions of all these groups result in a political climate that may positively or negatively affect the operations of an international business. The difficulty for the global company stems from the firm being subject to all these forces at the same time. The situation is further complicated by the fact that companies maintain operations in many countries and hence must simultaneously manage many sets of political relationships.

In this section of the chapter, we discuss the political climate of host countries. Any country that contains an operational unit (marketing, sales, manufacturing, finance or research and development) of an international company can be defined as a host country. International companies deal with many different host countries, each with its own political climate. These political climates are largely determined by the motivations and actions of host country governments and local interest groups.

Political Motivations

Businesses operate in a country at the discretion of its government, which can encourage or discourage foreign businesses through a variety of measures. The host government plays the principal role in host countries in initiating and implementing policies regarding the operation, conduct and ownership of businesses. Today more than 193 nations have been accepted as members of the United Nations, a figure that gives some indication of the large number of independent countries that exist at this time. Although each government may give the impression of acting as a single and homogeneous force, governments in most countries represent a collection of various, and at times conflicting, interests. Governments are sharply influenced by the prevailing political philosophy, local pressure groups and the government's own self-interest. All of these factors lead to government actions that MNCs must recognize and actively incorporate into their marketing strategies. Of prime importance is the marketer's ability to understand the rationale behind government actions.

As many political scientists have pointed out, government actions usually arise from the government's interpretation of its own self-interest. This self-interest, often called national interest, may be expected to differ from nation to nation, but it typically includes the following goals:

- ➤ *Self-preservation.* This is the primary goal of any entity, including states and governments.
- ➤ *Security.* To the greatest extent possible, each government seeks to maximize its opportunity for continued existence and to minimize threats from the outside.

➤ *Prosperity.* Improved living conditions for the country's citizens are an important and constant concern for any government. Even dictatorships base their claim to legitimacy in part on their ability to deliver enhanced prosperity.

➤ *Prestige.* Most governments or countries seek this either as an end in itself or as a means of reaching other objectives.

➤ *Ideology.* Governments frequently protect or promote an ideology in combination with other goals.

➤ *Cultural identity.* Governments often intervene to protect the country's cultural identity.[3]

The goals just cited are frequently the source of government actions either encouraging or limiting the business activities of MNCs (see Table 4.1). Many executives erroneously believe that such limiting actions occur largely in developing countries or emerging markets. On the contrary, there are many examples of restrictive government actions in the most developed countries. Such restrictive behavior most often occurs when a government perceives the attainment of its own goals to be threatened by the activities or existence of a body beyond its total control, namely the foreign subsidiary of a MNC.

National Sovereignty and the Goal of Self-Preservation

A country's self-preservation is most threatened when its national sovereignty is at stake. Sovereignty is the complete control exercised within a given geographic area, including the ability to pass laws and regulations and the power to enforce them. Governments or countries frequently view the existence of sovereignty as critical to achieving the goal of self-preservation. Although sovereignty may be threatened by a number of factors, it is the relationship between a government's attempt to protect its sovereignty and a company's efforts to achieve its own goals that is of primary interest to us.

Table 4.1 Host Government Goals and Policy Actions

Action	Goal					
	Self-Preservation	Security	Prosperity	Prestige	Ideology	Cultural Identity
"Buy local"	X	X	X			
Nontariff barriers	X		X			
Subsidies	X		X	X		
Operating restrictions	X	X				X
Local content			X			
Ownership conditions		X			X	X
Boycotts					X	
Takeovers	X	X	X		X	

X = Likelihood of using given action to accomplish that goal.

Subsidiaries or branch offices of MNCs can be controlled or influenced by decisions made at headquarters, beyond the physical or legal control of the host government. Therefore, foreign companies are frequently viewed as a threat to the host country's national sovereignty. (It is important to recognize in this context that *perceptions* on the part of host countries are typically more important than actual facts.)

Many attempts at restricting foreign firms are now discouraged under agreements established by the WTO. Still, these agreements exclude a number of sensitive areas. Countries often limit foreign ownership of newspapers, television and radio stations for reasons of preserving national sovereignty. They fear that if a foreign company controlled these media, it could influence public opinion and limit national sovereignty. Internet businesses can be especially vulnerable to government censorship. Google's YouTube has been banned or temporarily blocked in China, Turkey and Thailand in response to postings deemed insulting or threatening by the national governments of those countries. Google concedes that balancing free expression and local laws is a delicate task.[4]

The Need for National Security

It is natural for a government to try to protect its country's borders from outside forces. The military typically becomes a country's principal tool to prevent outside interference. Consequently, many concerns about national security involve a country's armed forces or related agencies. Other areas sensitive to national security are aspects of a country's infrastructure, its essential resources, utilities and the supply of crucial raw materials, particularly oil. To ensure their security, some host governments strive for greater control of these sensitive areas and resist any influence that foreign firms may gain over such industries.

A Chinese bid for a U.S. oil company was abandoned due to security concerns and political opposition in the United States. Soon thereafter, Dubai Ports World, a company owned by the government of Dubai, acquired a British company with shipping terminal operations at five U.S. ports. Faced with an almost certain veto from the U.S. congress, Dubai Ports World agreed to shed the U.S. port operations of the purchased company.

However, the protection of national security interests through regulations requiring local sourcing is experiencing an overall decline in the defense and telecommunications industries. This trend has been influenced by two factors. First, it is not economical for each country to have its own defense and telecommunications industry. Second, the high cost of research and development means that in many cases the small local defense supplier will have inferior technologies.

Fostering National Prosperity

Another key goal for governments is to ensure the material prosperity of their citizens. Prosperity is usually expressed in national income or GNP, and comparisons between countries are frequently made in terms of per-capita income or GNP per capita. (Comparisons are also made on the basis of GNP adjusted by purchasing-power parity to reflect comparable standards of living.)

However prosperity is measured, most governments strive to provide full employment and an increasing standard of living. Part of this goal is to enact an economic policy that will stimulate the economic output of businesses active within their borders. International companies that set up production facilities in a host country can assume an important role, because they can add to a host country's GNP and thus enhance its income. Cognizant of this, Japanese auto company Toyota pledged to produce in North America at least two-thirds of the vehicles it sold in that region as a form of political insurance.

Many host governments also try to improve the nation's prosperity by increasing its exports. Particularly in Europe, heads of governments often engage in state visits to encourage major export transactions. Political observers often note that both the French president and the German chancellor spend a substantial amount of their state visits on business and trade affairs, more so than is typically the case for the president of the United States. Attracting international companies with a high export potential to set up operations in their countries is of critical interest to host governments. Frequently, such companies can expect special treatment or subsidies, especially from governments in developing countries. For example, Egypt offered attractive tax holidays to foreign investors who undertook export-oriented projects, and Mexico exempted foreign investors from local-partner requirements if their projects were totally for export.

However, the pursuit of national prosperity goals can sometimes discourage global marketers from investing in a country. Wal-Mart delayed entering the Indian retail market when India required all foreign retailers to source at least 30 percent of their products and services from local small businesses.[5]

Fostering national prosperity can also involve goals other than supporting economic development and employment. New legislation involving health issues is increasingly common worldwide. Ecuador bans packaged foods producers from using images of animal characters, cartoon personalities or celebrities to promote products high in salt, sugar or fat. The Mexican congress recently enacted a new beverage tax to curb sugary-drinks intake in Mexico, Coca-Cola's second largest market.[6]

Enhancing Prestige

When Olusegun Obasanjo was elected president of Nigeria, he inherited a decision to host the next All-Africa Games. Nigeria had recently rescheduled its foreign debt. By hosting the games, the Nigerian government had accrued building costs for a new stadium that exceeded $340 million, twice what the government planned to spend on health care for one year.[7]

The pursuit of prestige has many faces. Whereas the governments of some countries choose to support team sports or host international events to enhance national prestige, other governments choose to influence the business climate for the same reason. Having a national airline may give rise to national prestige for a developing country. Other countries may support industries that achieve leadership in certain technologies, such as telecommunications, electronics, robotics or aerospace.

Promoting Ideology

For nearly 70 years North and South Korea have been technically at war. In the 1950s, North Korea was the richer and more industrialized of the two Koreas. North Korea pursued the ideology of *juche*, or self-reliance. Today it is South Korea that is by far the wealthier and more industrialized country.

Governments often attempt to promote ideology. In doing so, they affect business in a variety of ways. Throughout most of the twentieth century, communist governments disallowed private enterprise. Trade with noncommunist Western countries was strongly discouraged. Like North Korea, the Soviet Union paid a high price for its desire to be free of the capitalist world. Rather than taking advantage of licensing technology that was developed in the West, the Soviets followed the more expensive route of attempting to develop their own parallel technologies.

The role that ideology plays in communist China seems ambiguous from the point of view of foreign firms doing business there today. China reopened trade and investment relations with the West in the early 1970s. Since then the country has undergone significant market liberalization. General Motors and Starbucks operate with and alongside China's traditional state-owned industries. Some SOEs have been privatized. In other words, they have been sold, wholly or in part, to private owners. Chinese firms must now generate profits or face the specter of new bankruptcy laws. Still the Chinese government insists that these changes do not compromise communist ideology.

Protecting Cultural Identity

With the global village becoming a reality, one of the major effects on countries is in the area of culture. Governments can sometimes resist what they believe to be a foreign assault on their culture. For example, both Iran and Venezuela have at one time attempted to outlaw foreign brand names, requiring global marketers to establish names for their products in Persian and Spanish, respectively.

Whereas most countries once were able to determine broadcast policy on their own, control over broadcasting, and therefore culture, is now perceived to be in the hands of a few large, mostly U.S. firms. These firms are most visible in entertainment, the production and distribution of movies, TV programs, videos and music recordings. Even more important have been the roles of TV companies through the use of satellite transmission. As we saw in Chapter 3, this massive invasion of foreign cultural products has prompted a negative reaction among certain European governments. France launched a campaign against Google's alleged encroachment on French culture when Google announced a plan to scan millions of books in the English language from libraries in Britain and the United States. The president of France's national library warned that English-language sources and the American view of history would dominate the Internet.[8] Led by France, several European countries established a counteroffensive—a book-scanning project dubbed the European Digital Library.[9]

Host Country Pressure Groups

Host country governments are not the only forces able to influence the political climate and affect the operations of foreign companies. Other groups have a stake in the treatment of companies and in political and economic decisions that indirectly affect foreign businesses. In most instances, they cannot act unilaterally. Thus they try to pressure either the host government or the foreign businesses to conform to their views. Such pressure groups exist in most countries and may be made up of either ad hoc groups or established associations. For example, the Beijing-based non-profit Institute of Public and Environment Affairs has released names of 70 MNCs (and thousands of Chinese companies) that it alleges have violated China's environmental laws. MNCs include DuPont, Nestlé, PepsiCo and Suzuki Motor Corporation. The institute's Green Choice initiative collects and posts environmental records on a publicly accessible online database. Some companies have since cleared their names or addressed the issues raised by the institute.[10]

Some of the most potent pressure groups are found within the local business community itself. These include local industry associations and occasionally local unions. When local companies are threatened by foreign competition, they frequently petition the government to help by placing restrictions on the foreign competitors. When Pakistan became a potentially critical U.S. ally in the Afghan war, the Pakistani government asked the United States to reduce tariffs on textiles from Pakistan. However, officials at the American Textile Manufacturing Institute moved immediately to stop any possible cuts in tariffs that could hurt U.S. textile firms.[11]

Blogging is an increasingly important tool for grassroots protests. China alone has over 20 million bloggers who could possibly target a MNC. In one case, a 29-year-old TV news anchor in Hong Kong posted on his blog a condemnation of Starbucks opening a store in Beijing's Forbidden City (the former residence of the country's emperors), stating that it marked an erosion of Chinese culture. Within a week the posting was viewed half a million times.[12]

Host Government Actions

Governments promulgate laws and take actions in a variety of ways to advance their agendas. In Chapter 2 we reviewed a number of government actions that affect a firm's ability to transfer products across borders. Many government actions, such as those affecting exchange rates, can indirectly affect international markets. Other actions can have a more direct impact on a firm's ability to access a foreign market and operate successfully. Some of these actions are discussed next.

Government Subsidies

Government subsidies represent free gifts that host governments dispense in the hope that the overall benefits to the economy will far exceed such grants. They are popular instruments used to attract foreign investment. Governments are especially inclined to use direct or indirect subsidies to encourage firms that will be major exporters. Exporters bring multiple benefits, providing employment and increasing national revenue through export sales.

An example of a direct subsidy is a government's paying $1 for each pair of shoes to help a local producer compete more effectively in foreign markets. An indirect subsidy is the result of a subsidy on a component of the exported product. For example, a government may provide a subsidy on the electricity used to manufacture tents that are then exported. Or it might subsidize research in the pharmaceutical industry. WTO agreements outlaw direct export subsidies. Indirect subsidies are usually not prohibited. However, they remain a contentious issue between trading nations.

Ownership Restrictions

Host governments sometimes pursue the policy of requiring that local nationals become part owners of foreign subsidiaries operating within their borders. These governments believe that this guarantees that MNCs will contribute to the local economy. Restrictions can range from an outright prohibition of full foreign ownership to selective policies aimed at key industries.

India has used ownership conditions extensively. India's Foreign Exchange Regulation Act of 1973 stipulated that foreign ownership could not exceed 40 percent. IBM decided to leave rather than give up majority control over its subsidiary. Coca-Cola also decided to leave rather than share its secret formula with Indian partners. However, when changes in the government brought a softening of India's stance, the country tentatively began to court foreign firms. Today both IBM and Coca-Cola are active again in the Indian market.

In many ways, the Indian case reflects the patterns of many countries. The 1960s and 1970s saw a tightening of the control over foreign ownership. By the 1980s the trend shifted toward investment liberalization. Most countries now recognize that foreign investment provides significant benefits to the nation, such as employment, technology and marketing know-how. This new trend has brought the elimination of many prior restrictions, such as those related to ownership.

Nonetheless, ownership restriction persists in some markets. In the wake of U.S. occupation, many Iraqi businesses feared that large corporate investors from abroad would take over whole sectors of the economy and crowd out local competition. Consequently, they called for investment rules similar to those in the UAE, which require that domestic ventures be at least 51 percent locally owned.[13] SABMiller PLC, a major global beer company, announced that it would offer 10 percent of its South African business to black investors to comply with a government policy. The government mandate also requires companies operating in South Africa to change procurement and hiring practices to incorporate more South African blacks.[14]

Operating Conditions

Governments establish and enforce many regulations that affect the environment in which businesses operate. Host countries control firms in the areas of product design and packaging, pricing, advertising, sales promotion and distribution. Some of these restrictions, and strategies to deal with them, are included in later chapters that deal directly with the marketing mix. Where such operating restrictions apply to all firms, domestic and international, the competitive threat is lessened.

Companies may still find restrictions a problem when the way they have to operate varies from that to which they are accustomed. Furthermore, local restrictions may sometimes be peculiar to a certain market and thus hard to predict. For example, the province of Buenos Aires in Argentina passed a law requiring shops targeting female adolescents to stock clothing in sizes equivalent to size 6–16 in the United States. Brazilian shops usually cater only to the very thin. Officials believe this has contributed to Argentina experiencing one of the world's highest rates of anorexia and bulimia.[15]

Where operating restrictions apply to foreign or international firms only, the result will be a lessening of competitiveness, and companies should seriously consider these constraints before entering a market. One such restriction involves work permits or visas for foreign managers or technicians whom MNCs may wish to employ in their various national subsidiaries. Any citizen of an EU country is free to work in any other EU country, but visa constraints remain an operational hindrance in most of the world.

Local restrictions may also pose a problem to global marketers when they become unusually burdensome in certain markets. Signing up to be an Avon sales representative takes only minutes unless you are in China. There it takes two weeks and potential saleswomen must take a written test and listen to a lecture on China's latest sales regulations. Although China lifted a prior ban on direct sales, the industry remains tightly regulated. The government caps sales commissions at 30 percent and sales representatives can only make money by selling the products and not by recruiting other sales representatives.[16]

Sometimes operating conditions are affected by what governments fail to do, such as failing to enforce the law. For several years, Mexico City became particularly notorious for kidnappings by criminal gangs, and foreign companies found it difficult to recruit expatriate managers for their operations there. In any case, operating costs may increase in these countries as a result of the need to provide employees with heightened security.

Boycotts of Firms

Government boycotts can be directed at companies of certain origin or companies that have engaged in transactions with political enemies. Boycotts tend to shut some companies completely out of a given market. For example, the United States imposed a two-year ban on imports from Norinco, a major Chinese defense and industrial manufacturer, because of the company's alleged sale of ballistic-missile technology to Iran. The Norinco boycott made it illegal for U.S. companies to purchase products from the company or any of its many subsidiaries.[17]

One of the most publicized boycott campaigns was the 50-year boycott waged by Arab countries against firms that engaged in business activity with Israel. The boycott was administered by the Arab League. Ford Motor Company was one U.S. company placed on the Arab boycott list when it supplied an Israeli car assembler with flat-packed cars for local assembly. Xerox was placed on the list after financing a documentary on Israel, and the Coca-Cola Company was added to the boycott list for having licensed an Israeli bottler.

The Arab boycott became less relevant with the changing political situation in the Middle East. The last major fighting between Israel and the Arab states took place in 1973, and since then Egypt has signed a peace treaty with Israel. By the 1990s, many Arab countries only selectively enforced the boycott. After the Iraq conflict and Desert Storm, many more countries abandoned it. Coca-Cola returned to the Arab soft-drinks market and Coca-Cola quickly attained a large share of the market.

Takeovers

Though relatively rare, no action a host government can take is more dramatic than a takeover. Broadly defined, takeovers are any host-government-initiated actions that result in a loss of ownership or direct control by the foreign company. There are several types of takeovers. Expropriation is a formal, or legal, seizure of an operation with or without the payment of compensation. Even when compensation is paid, there are often concerns about the adequacy of the amount, the timeliness of the payment and the form of payment. Confiscation is expropriation without any compensation. The term domestication is used to describe the limiting of certain economic activities to local citizens. This can involve a takeover by compensated expropriation, confiscation or forced sale. Governments may also domesticate an industry by merely requiring the transfer of partial ownership to nationals or by requiring that nationals be promoted to higher levels of management. If an international company cannot or will not meet these requirements, however, it may be forced to sell its operations in that country.

Today expropriations have virtually ceased. In fact, a reverse trend has emerged. In renewed attempts to encourage foreign investment, countries such as Algeria, Egypt and Tanzania have considered returning companies to prior foreign owners, or at least allowing these former owners to repurchase them. The British bank Barclays International returned to Egypt, where it had been expropriated 15 years earlier. Like many oil-exporting countries, Saudi Arabia nationalized its energy sector in the 1970s. However, the Saudi government began to reopen the sector in the twenty-first century when it named Exxon, the world's largest publicly owned oil company, as operator of a major natural-gas project requiring an investment of $15 billion.[18]

Home Country Political Forces

Managers of international companies need to be concerned not only about political developments abroad; many developments that take place at home also have a great impact on what a company can do internationally. Political developments in a company's home country tend to affect either the role of the company in general or, more often, some particular aspects of its operations abroad. Consequently, restrictions can be placed on companies not only by host countries but by home countries as well. Therefore, an astute international marketer must be able to monitor political developments both at home and abroad. This section of the chapter explores home country policies and actions directed at international companies.

Home Country Actions

Home countries are essentially guided by the same six interests described earlier in this chapter: self-preservation, national security, prosperity, prestige, ideology and cultural identity. For example, subsidies, offered by host governments to foreign investors, may also be offered by home governments. In general, a home government wishes to have its country's international companies accept its national priorities. As a result, home governments at times look toward international companies to help them achieve political goals.

In the past, home country governments have tried to prevent companies from doing business overseas on ideological, political or national security grounds. In the extreme, this can result in an embargo on trade with a certain country. One long-running trade embargo imposed by the U.S. government involved Vietnam. Imposed in 1975, this embargo was lifted in 1994. More recently, the United States banned the sale of luxury goods including iPods and plasma televisions to North Korea in what was called a novel effort to undermine the lavish lifestyle of that country's eccentric president and his political elite. Organizations fined for allegedly breaking a U.S. embargo include Chevron Texaco, for trading with Iraq (fined $14,071); Wal-Mart and the New York Yankees, for trading with Cuba (fined $50,000 and $75,000, respectively); Exxon Mobil, for trading with Sudan (fined $50,000); and Fleet Bank, for trading with Iran (fined $41,000).[19] On the other hand, the United States, an ally of Israel, passed legislation forbidding U.S. firms from complying with the Arab boycott of Israel. The U.S. government did not want U.S.-based MNCs to comply with someone else's embargo.

World Beat 4.1

Caught in the Middle

For nearly 40 years, Iran has been the target of on-again off-again sanctions, sometimes from the United States and sometimes from a broader community of countries. In 2014, a tentative rapprochement between Iran and the United States raised hopes in the international business community that a once vibrant economy might reopen to them.

Companies are often caught in the middle when their home countries agree to sanctions on a foreign market. In 2010, the United Nations imposed new and stricter sanctions against Iran aimed at crippling the country's nuclear program by cutting off international suppliers to Iran's critical oil and gas sector. The United States declared its own additional sanctions.

Responses by foreign companies varied. U.S.-based General Electric had already announced that it would cease business in Iran except for the sale of authorized humanitarian goods. Dublin-based Ingersoll-Rand PLC decided to cease doing business with Iran, a market that represented less than 0.1 percent of the company's revenue. Similarly, Toyota Motor Corporation stopped car exports to Iran. However, the year before Toyota had only shipped 220 cars to the now-sanctioned nation. The United States, in contrast, remained Toyota's largest market.

For German engineering firm Siemens AG, the decision proved more complicated. Siemens announced that it would not pursue future contracts in Iran, but decided to honor the ones currently in force. Corporate lawyers were alleged to have determined that breaking current contracts would cost the company €4 billion if tried before a Swiss arbitration court as many contracts specified. Lobbyists explained the issue to U.S. authorities who reportedly agreed that fulfilling the contracts was preferable to paying Iran so much money.

Sources: Kris Maher and Jay Solomon, "Ingersoll Bars Units From Sales to Iran," *Wall Street Journal Online*, March 10, 2010; Kazuhiro Shimamura, "Sanctions Lead Toyota to Halt Iran Exports," *Wall Street Journal*, August 12, 2010, p. A10; David Crawford and Vanessa Fuhrmans, "Siemens Business Surges in Iran," *Wall Street Journal Online*, April 5, 2011; Mia Wasikowska, "Iran Says Nuclear Equipment was Sabotaged," *The New York Times*, September 22, 2012; and "Iran-US Rapprochement: Historic Opportunities Beckon," *Business Monitor*, January 7, 2014.

Unilateral restrictions, those imposed by one country only, put businesses from that country at a competitive disadvantage and are often fought by business interests. Because of this risk to the competitiveness of their businesses, governments prefer to take multilateral actions together with many other countries. Such actions may arise from a group of nations or, increasingly, from the United Nations. The trade embargo by the international community against South Africa was one of the first such actions. As a result of consumer group pressures, many companies had already left South Africa to protest its apartheid regime. However, the embargo affected a wider group of firms in the late 1980s when it was imposed by most countries. When the political situation in South Africa changed and apartheid was abolished, the United States, together with other nations, lifted the embargo. The United States has since been the largest foreign investor in South Africa, some of the largest firms being Dow Chemical, Ford, General Motors, Coca-Cola and Hyatt.

Home Country Pressure Groups

The kinds of pressures that international companies are subject to in their home countries are frequently different from the types of pressures brought to bear on them abroad. International companies have had to deal with special-interest groups abroad for a long time. The types of special-interest groups found domestically have come into existence only recently. Such groups are usually well organized and tend to get extensive media coverage. They have succeeded in catching many companies unprepared. These groups aim to garner support in order to pressure home governments to sponsor regulations favorable to their point of view. They also have managed to place companies directly in the line of fire.

International companies come under attack for two major reasons: (1) for their choice of markets and (2) for their methods of doing business. A constant source of controversy involves international companies' business practices in three areas: product strategies, promotion practices and pricing policies. Product strategies include, for example, the decision to market potentially unsafe products such as pesticides. Promotional practices include the way products are advertised or pushed through distribution channels. Pricing policies include the possible charging of higher prices in one market than in another.

The infant formula controversy of the early 1980s involved participants from many countries and still serves as one of the best examples of the type of pressure that international companies face from consumer boycotts. Infant formula was being sold all over the world as a substitute for or supplement to breast-feeding. Although even the producers of infant formula agreed that breast-feeding was superior to bottle-feeding, changes that had started to take place in Western society decades before had caused infant breast-feeding to decline. Following World War II, several companies had expanded their infant formula production into developing countries, where birthrates were much higher than in the West. Companies that had intended their products to be helpful found themselves embroiled in controversy. Critics blasted the product as unsafe under Third World conditions. Because the formula had to be mixed with water, they maintained poor sanitary conditions and contaminated water in developing countries led to many infant deaths. Poor mothers could also water down the formula to such an extent that babies were malnourished. As a result, these critics urged an immediate stop to all promotional activities related to infant formula, such as the distribution of free samples.

The Nestlé Company, as one of the leading infant formula manufacturers, became the target of a boycott by consumer action groups in the United States and elsewhere. Under the leadership of INFACT, the Infant Formula Action Coalition, a consumer boycott of all Nestlé products was organized to force the company to change its marketing practices. Constant public pressure resulted in the development of a code sponsored by WHO that primarily covers the methods used to market infant formula. Under the code, producers and distributors may not give away any free samples. They must avoid contact with consumers and are forbidden to do any promotion geared toward the general public. The code is subject to voluntary participation by WHO member governments.

Boycotts have even been attempted at the state level in the United States. Massachusetts passed a state law denying state contracts to companies that did business in Myanmar because of that country's brutal dictatorship. Apple, Motorola and Hewlett-Packard all cited the Massachusetts law when pulling out of Myanmar. A U.S. District Court judge subsequently ruled that the Massachusetts law interferes with the federal government's right to set foreign policy.[20] Despite this setback, global firms must contend with the growing influence of home country pressure groups.

Legal Environments

In many ways, the legal framework of a nation reflects a particular political philosophy or ideology. Just as each country has its own political climate, so the legal system changes from country to country. Internationally active companies must understand and operate within these various legal systems. Most legal systems of the world are based on one of four traditions: common law, civil law, Islamic law or socialist law.

Common Law

Common law is derived from English law found in the United Kingdom, the United States, Canada and other countries previously part of the British Commonwealth. Common law acknowledges the preeminence of social norms. Law arises from what society acknowledges as right and from what has commonly been done and accepted. Laws passed in such countries are frequently interpreted in the courtroom, where a jury consisting of citizens often determines the outcome of a case. Lawyers in these countries are as likely to look to prior case decisions as to the law itself in order to argue their own cases.

Civil Law

Civil, or code, law is based on the Roman tradition of the preeminence of written laws. It is found in most European countries and in countries influenced by European colonialism, such as countries in Latin America. In these countries, laws may be more encompassing as well as precise. Judges play a far more important role in the civil-law system than under common law, whereas juries usually play a lesser role. A traditional difference between civil-law countries and common-law countries has been the way they have viewed trademark protection. The first to officially register a trademark in civil-law countries owned the trademark. However, in common-law countries, someone who actually used the trademark before another registered it could successfully challenge the registration.

Islamic Law

Islamic law is derived from the Koran as well as from other Islamic traditions. Islamic law dominates family law in most Muslim countries, but its application to business situations varies greatly from country to country. To begin with, there are four major schools of Islamic law, and countries differ as to which they follow. Furthermore, not all Muslim countries apply Islamic law to commercial transactions. Some do, of course. Saudi Arabia forbids the collection of interest on loans. An importer cannot go to a bank and pay interest to borrow money to import automobiles from overseas. However, an importer can borrow money and pay interest in many Muslim countries. In fact, during the nineteenth and twentieth centuries, most Muslim countries adopted their commercial laws from one or more European countries. Because of this, business law in the Middle East often falls under the civil-law tradition.

Socialist Law

Socialist law arose from the Marxist ideological system established in China, Russia and other former Eastern bloc countries during the twentieth century. Under Marxist rule, economic power was often centralized, and market economies were virtually unknown. Business laws as we know them were absent or underdeveloped. For example, Chinese citizens have only recently been allowed to bring lawsuits against foreign companies or Chinese government ministries.

As many socialist countries liberalize their economies, they are often forced to look outside for quick fixes for their lack of legal sophistication. For example, Russia turned to the United States and law professors in Houston to help develop laws pertaining to petroleum. When Russia joined the WTO, it agreed to adopt new laws concerning trademarks and patents. Unfortunately, many observers note that Russia today has difficulty enforcing these laws effectively. Even the judges have little experience with the new legislation.

China faces similar problems. The Chinese legal system has inspired little confidence from foreign investors. However, when China joined the WTO, the government began training judges to administer the new trade regulations. Legal teams were organized to ensure that city and provincial governments adhered to the new policies.[21] Still, China's current legal system is based on a very limited statutory code. In addition, it also lacks a recognized body of precedent case law.[22]

109

National Regulatory Environments

Regulatory environments also vary among countries. Businesses face greater regulatory burdens in developing countries than they do in developed countries. It takes 18 steps to register a commercial property in Nigeria compared with only three steps in Finland. The World Bank estimates that the least regulated countries from a business point of view are Singapore, Hong Kong, New Zealand and the United States.

Some sectors of the economy, such as banking, insurance and natural resources, tend to be more regulated than others. In India, steel, power and telecommunications are more regulated than other industries.[23] Regulations can also be regional and may even vary by city. Beijing announced new regulations aimed at curtailing car traffic in China's capital city, including limiting the number of license plates available for new cars.[24]

Japan has had the most regulated business environment among the developed countries. Twenty years after Temple University established its Tokyo campus, it is the only U.S. university offering full-degree courses. Forty other U.S. universities pulled out of Japan due to a plethora of regulations. For example, to qualify as an official Japanese university, universities must own their own buildings, have their own sports field and gym, operate on less than a 25 percent debt-equity ratio and get government approval for new programs. Even Temple doesn't meet all these criteria but operates as a designated foreign university. Some believe this status puts Temple at a competitive disadvantage when trying to recruit students.

In recent years, however, Japan has experienced a trend toward deregulation and market liberalization. As a result of this shift, conflict has increased and corporate lawsuits are becoming more common. Japan now needs more lawyers as Japanese increasingly shun mediation and the number of court cases soars. Japan estimates that it will need to more than double its number of lawyers by 2018. In one year alone, nearly 70 new law schools opened within Japanese universities.[25]

Japan is not the only country where international marketers face an ambiguous or evolving regulatory environment. In addition to dealing with many different legal systems' national laws, managers must constantly contend with changes. As the global marketplace becomes ever more interconnected, regulatory changes appear all the more regularly.

Legal Evolution

One area of law that has seen considerable evolution worldwide is product liability law. Regulations concerning product liability were first introduced in the United States. If a product is sold in a defective condition such that it becomes unreasonably dangerous to use, then both the manufacturer and the distributor can be held accountable under U.S. law. For a long time, product liability laws in Europe were lax by U.S. standards, but they have been expanded in the past 20 years. Still there are differences that result from the different legal and social systems. In the EU, trials are decided by judges, not common jurors, and the extensive welfare system automatically absorbs many of the medical costs that are subject to litigation in the

United States. Traditionally, product liability suits seldom posed problems for international marketers in developing countries. However, when accidents attributable to Firestone tires on Ford Explorers occurred, plaintiffs appeared in Saudi Arabia and Venezuela as well as in the United States. Today, global publicity surrounding product crises no doubt prompts more consumers in more countries to seek redress for problems.

A second area of law that varies from country to country involves bankruptcy. In the United Kingdom, Canada and France, the laws governing bankruptcy favor creditors. When a firm enters bankruptcy, an administrator is appointed. The administrator's job is to recover the creditors' money. In Germany and Japan, on the other hand, bankruptcies are often handled by banks behind closed doors. The emphasis is on protecting the company and helping it reestablish itself. In the United States, bankruptcy law also tends to protect the company. Management prepares a reorganization plan that is voted on by the creditors. Creditor preference varies by country as well. For example, Swiss law gives preference to Swiss creditors.

As with product liability, attitudes toward bankruptcy and regulations pertaining to it have not remained static. In China, bankruptcies were unheard of under the communist system until China drafted its first bankruptcy code in 1988. One proponent of the new law noted that nobody understood it and everybody was scared of it. A major case involving a trust and investment corporation revealed that many vagaries in the law still existed. Creditors settled out of court and experienced huge losses. Nonetheless, the number of bankruptcies in China has soared since 2000.[26]

Today the regulation of transactions in cyberspace is critical to the future of electronic commerce. WTO members have made a political commitment to maintain a duty-free cyberspace. However, many other issues concerning the governance of the Internet have not been resolved, and it even remains unclear which country can claim territorial jurisdiction in this inherently international medium. What will be the future of Internet taxation, privacy safeguards and censorship? The complexity of the technology, as well as its rapid change, challenges traditional ideas of regulation.

In the following chapters, we will be discussing other national and international laws that affect the management of products, pricing, distribution and promotion. In many cases these laws are also evolving. Regional associations, especially the EU, are increasingly setting supranational laws that affect marketing within their member states. Attempts are also under way to set global standards of legal protection, such as in the area of patents and trademarks. In the future, this may help simplify the job of the global marketer.

Some moves to internationalize laws, however, are opposed by MNCs. The Hague Conference on International Private Law has considered a global treaty for enforcement of legal judgments. This agreement would require U.S. courts to enforce judgments by foreign courts in exchange for similar treatment abroad for U.S. judgments. Internet providers were among the many U.S. firms that opposed the treaty. E-commerce businesses were especially concerned that the treaty would subject them to a plethora of lawsuits by allowing consumers to sue businesses under local law wherever their websites were accessible. For the time being, however, national laws still prevail in the vast majority of cases, and even global standards, when established, will be administered through local legal systems.

Attitudes Toward Rules

Egypt experiences 44 traffic deaths per 100 million kilometers of driving. This compares with 20 deaths in Turkey and only 1.1 in the United States. To try to decrease traffic fatalities, the Egyptian government began the new millennium by instituting tough new speeding and seat belt laws, complete with hefty fines. Seat belt sales soared at first and then precipitously declined. One auto parts dealer who once sold 250 seat belts a day saw his sales fall to only two or three a day. A year later, Egypt's fatality statistics remained the same. Many Egyptians had chosen to buy cheap seat belts that could fool the police but didn't really work. Furthermore, the police were deluged with complaints when they gave out tickets. Because the seat belts didn't work, why should the driver be fined for not buckling up? One Egyptian summed up the public's skepticism, "I think those laws are just so the government can make our lives more miserable than they already are. They want to imitate the West in everything."[27]

Jean-Claude Usunier notes that rules and laws can be established that are respected and implemented quite explicitly. On the other hand, there may be a discrepancy between rules and what people actually do. He suggests that attitudes toward rules are affected by two basic criteria—the level of power distance in a society and whether a society has a positive or a negative human nature orientation (HNO). HNO-positive societies assume people can be trusted to obey the rules, whereas HNO-negative societies assume just the opposite. The United States is an HNO-positive society with low power distance. This results in pragmatic rules that most people respect and obey. In countries such as Italy and France, HNO is also positive but power distance is high. Ordinary people view themselves as being better than their rulers. As a result, many feel that laws can be challenged to a certain degree. In Germany and Switzerland, power distance is low but HNO is negative. Laws are made democratically, but society still does not trust people to obey them. To ensure compliance, rules must be applied strictly and with very explicit sanctions. In many developing countries, power distance is high and HNO is negative. Rules may often be strict, formal and even unrealistic. In this atmosphere there is often a high discrepancy between the law and what people actually do or what is even enforced by the authorities.[28] Societies such as these can be especially confusing to global marketers who come from countries such as the United States.

Harry Triandis explains differences in attitudes toward rules by categorizing cultures as either tight or loose. In tight cultures, there are many rules, norms and standards for correct behavior. In loose cultures, such rules are few. Tight cultures criticize and punish rule breakers more severely. Triandis proposes that tight cultures are likely to be more isolated and less influenced by other cultures, since agreement on norms is important. Afghanistan under the Taliban would be an extreme example of a tight culture. High population density may also contribute to tight cultures, since people might need tightness to interact more smoothly under close conditions.[29]

However, sometimes a national attitude toward rules is best explained by historical experience. Many Israelis believe that rules are made to be broken. They point to the fact that Jews obeyed laws in Europe and still experienced the Holocaust. This gave rise to the belief that those who adhere to the rules are *freiers* or suckers.[30]

Regulatory Change

Global marketers must understand the different political and regulatory climates in which they operate. This is a challenging job in itself because of the many national markets involved. They must also be prepared to deal with changes in those environments. These changes can be moderate or drastic, and they can be more or less predictable. The more moderate and predictable changes we call regulatory change. The more drastic and unpredictable changes we call political risk, which we discuss in the next section. Regulatory change encompasses many government actions, such as changes in tax rates, the introduction of price controls and the revision of labeling requirements. Although less dramatic than the upheavals associated with political risk, regulatory changes are very common. International marketers lose far more money to regulatory change than to political risk.

Predicting Regulatory Change

Whatever strategy a firm chooses to employ in the face of regulatory change, it is useful to be able to predict whether and when such change will occur. Nothing is certain, but most regulatory change affecting international marketers should not come as a total surprise. Many government actions have economic bases. By understanding the issues covered in Chapter 2, an international marketer can identify probable government responses to prevailing conditions. For example, if export earnings are depressed in a developing country and if foreign investment is low, the government may be forced to devalue the currency. No one may be able to predict what day this will occur, but contingency plans should be in place for when it does occur.

It is also very important that the international marketer listens for signals from the government or influential parties. For months before Egypt disallowed additional foreign investment in packaged foods, local business leaders could be heard in the local media calling for such restrictions. When foreign investors first returned to China, the Chinese government warned them concerning repatriation of profits. They were told that their ability to remove profits from China would be somehow contingent on their export sales. Many firms paid no attention to this warning and later discovered that they did not qualify to repatriate profits. Some even admitted that they thought China had been joking about the possible restriction.

World Beat 4.2

Pork Politics

The U.S. has a strategic oil reserve, but China has a strategic pork reserve. With pork the favorite meat for most consumers in China, the Chinese government maintains a strategic frozen pork and live pig reserve to guard against severe shortages. Furthermore, in Chinese culture pigs are associated with prosperity and good fortune. Many prospective parents try to time the birth of a child to fall within the year of the pig to assure their child has a lucky life.

However, the importance of pork in the Chinese diet and culture does not make pigs immune from politics. Shortly before China entered the last year of the pig, China Central Television banned all images or spoken references to pigs in advertisements. The reason: respect for Muslims who consider pigs unclean. Muslims constitute about 2 percent of the Chinese population. Some believed the ban was an attempt to ease ethnic tensions arising from an incident in which Chinese security forces killed 18 suspected Muslim terrorists. Others attributed the ban to the fact that China imports vast quantities of oil from Muslim countries.

Many foreign companies, including Nestlé and Disney, had already developed advertising campaigns featuring pigs to coincide with China's year of the pig. However, advertising agencies in China confessed that they were used to such surprise legislation. Despite the advertising ban on pigs, the Chinese post office launched a series of special issue stamps featuring Disney's cartoon pig, Piglet, to celebrate the new year.

Back in the United States, pork politics threatened to stop the sale of Smithfield, America's largest pork producer, to a rival Chinese firm. Members of the U.S. Senate argued that the sale would adversely affect U.S. food safety and threaten national security. Despite these fears, the acquisition was eventually approved.

Sources: Ted Kemp, "Hog Stock: Inside China's Strategic Pork Reserve," *CNBC Online*, June 6, 2013; Gordon Fairclough and Geoffrey A. Fowler, "Pigs Get the Ax in China TV Ads," *Wall Street Journal*, January 25, 2007, p. A1; Tim Devaney, "Smithfield CEO Defends Sale of Pork Producer to Chinese Firm," *Washington Times*, July 10, 2013.

Firms can find themselves caught in embarrassing situations if they fail to heed signals. On the other hand, if they take signals seriously, they can formulate plans for different contingencies. How should the firm respond to a currency devaluation, an increased tax or new restrictions on advertising? Contingency planning enables marketing managers to avoid crises and to make deliberate and careful decisions about what strategy will be appropriate to employ in the face of regulatory change.

Managing Regulatory Change

James Austin suggests four strategic options for a company to consider when faced with regulatory change:

➤ *Alter.* The company can bargain to get the government to alter its policy or actions.
➤ *Avoid.* The company can make strategic moves that bypass the impact of a government's action.
➤ *Accede.* The company can adjust its operations to comply with a government requirement.
➤ *Ally.* The company can attempt to avoid some risks of government actions by seeking strategic alliances.[31]

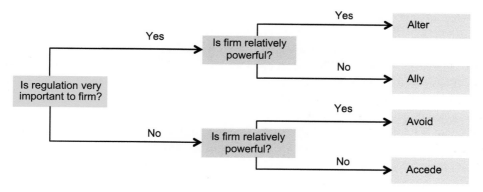

Figure 4.1 Strategic Responses to Regulatory Change

Before deciding to try to alter a new regulation, the company should assess its bargaining power vis-à-vis the government. As depicted in Figure 4.1, a company is more likely to try to alter a new regulation when the regulation significantly affects its operations and the firm's bargaining power is high. If the firm's bargaining power is low, it will be more successful by seeking an appropriate ally or allies. If a policy is not very threatening and the firm's power is relatively low, the firm may be best served by acceding. After all, the firm should pick its battles with a government. It is too expensive and exhausting to fight every new regulation.

A firm's bargaining power is enhanced by its ability to pay taxes, employ citizens and deliver exports to assist the national trade balance. During diplomatic tensions between the United States and France prior to the Iraq War, the South Carolina state legislature took up a resolution calling for a boycott of French products. The resolution passed the state House, 90–9. But suddenly the bill died and wasn't taken up by the state Senate. As it turned out, most of the tires sold in the United States by the French group Michelin were made in factories located in South Carolina.[32]

To bargain more successfully, a company should utilize political mapping of a government.[33] Political mapping consists of identifying all individuals involved in a regulatory decision—politicians, bureaucrats, pressure groups—and understanding their various points of view. This allows the firm to better address their concerns. However, it is not always easy to do this. Chinese companies estimated that billions of dollars in Chinese–Iraqi contracts were left in limbo after the United States invaded Iraq. They were particularly concerned because China did not support the U.S. invasion. Even more daunting was identifying who in Iraq could make a decision about the many contracts.[34] Similarly, MNCs have noted that shifting power among bureaucrats in China makes it difficult to do political mapping in that country.

Ravi Ramamurti argues that increasingly a company's bargaining power lies not in itself alone but in the motivation and power of its home government to influence the firm's host government.[35] For example, Motorola discovered after it had designed and test-marketed a new pager in Japan that the pager did not meet new industry standards. These standards were developed by Motorola's Japanese competitors and enforced by the Japanese government. Instead of redesigning its pager, Motorola first attempted to convince the Japanese government to alter its policy and allow the Motorola design to go to market. Redesigning the pager would prove costly,

115

and Motorola believed its bargaining power was high, especially if the U.S. government would back it in its appeal.[36]

If a firm believes its bargaining power is relatively weak, an ally strategy may be employed. During the Firestone tires/Ford Explorer product-harm crisis, the government of Saudi Arabia impounded the affected vehicles as they arrived on the shipping dock. However, Saudi Ford dealers were able to help rescind this order by convincing the government that they were the ones being hurt and not the MNCs.[37] Pepsi tried unsuccessfully for several years to enter the Indian market as a wholly owned subsidiary. Finally, the company found a powerful local partner in the Indian beverage industry with whom to enter into a joint venture. The joint venture was quickly approved.

Pepsi also employed the other strategy associated with low bargaining power—accede—when negotiating to enter the Indian market. At the time, India had strict foreign exchange regulations that would stop Pepsi from taking profits out of the country. Pepsi believed that any attempt to convince the Indian government to alter this policy on its behalf would prove futile. The firm also expected to reinvest all Indian profits in the local market for the foreseeable future. Therefore, Pepsi acceded to the government policy. This accession allowed the firm to save time on lengthy negotiations and enter a potentially lucrative market sooner.

Other companies find that they can avoid regulations by making relatively minor changes in their marketing mix. For example, Clearasil could sell its product in Japanese supermarkets if it did not explicitly promote the product as an acne medicine. Otherwise, it was restricted to selling through pharmacies. For years Brazil's price control board allowed firms to set any price they wanted on newly introduced products. Current products or improved versions of current products, however, were subjected to a tedious and unpredictable appeal process before any increase in price was authorized. As a result, companies such as Gillette were inclined to introduce an improved product, such as a better razor blade, as a totally new product rather than as an improved version of an existing line. However, the avoid option may not always work. Because of this, it is best employed when a regulatory change has a relatively minor impact on a company.

Political Risk

Drug-related violence cost Mexico 31,000 lives over four years and an estimated $4 billion in foreign direct investment in one year alone. Japanese car manufacturer Toyota chose to build a plant deep in Mexico's interior to avoid the particularly violent border region to the country's north. But violence continued to expand to sections of the country once considered safe. A director at an executive-recruitment firm reported difficulty filling a position for a pharmaceutical company seeking a top executive in Mexico City. Two appliance makers, Electrolux AB and Whirlpool Corporation, chose production sites in Tennessee over ones in Mexico despite the latter's lower labor costs.[38]

The presence of political risk means that a foreign company can lose part or all of its investment, market or earnings in another country as a result of political actions on the part of a host government, the firm's home government or pressure groups. As we have noted, the political climate of a country is hardly ever static. Sometimes, a firm is faced with sudden and radical changes in the political climate of a host country.

Political risk is the possibility that an unexpected and drastic change due to political forces will result in adverse circumstances for business operations. Sudden changes of power, especially when the new leadership is committed to a leftist economic and political philosophy, have led to hostile political climates and takeovers. Such changes in government can happen as a result of unexpected coups d'état or revolutions. However, as occurred in Venezuela, it can sometimes result from a democratic election.

All political instability may not pose the possibility of negative consequences to every firm. Many businesses in the tiny emirate of Kuwait viewed the Iraq war and the toppling of the regime of Saddam Hussein as presenting potential business opportunities in the neighboring country of 20 million people.[39] The security industry is booming in Central America where gang-related crime is a serious problem. Guatemala's business community alone pays $335 million for protection from 250 licensed security firms. Who has the biggest market share in the region? Wackenhut, a Miami-based security firm, acquired by Denmark's Group 4 Flack.[40]

The fall of the Iranian shah in 1979 is a vivid example of a sudden change that caught many companies by surprise and did adversely impact their business interests. Unlike communist revolutions earlier in the century, Iran's revolution was centered on Islam. Still, anti-American sentiment resulted in the taking of U.S. hostages at the American Embassy in Tehran. President Jimmy Carter retaliated by seizing Iranian assets under U.S. jurisdiction and ordered all U.S. companies to cease doing business with Iran. The impact on U.S. business alone involved around 4,000 firms whose claims against Iran were eventually settled by the International Tribunal at the Hague. One of the largest settlements outside the petroleum industry was paid to the tobacco company R.J. Reynolds.[41] And not only U.S. companies sustained damage. Many companies operating from Europe and Japan were forced, as a result of the revolution, to shut down either all or parts of their operations. The subsequent war between Iran and Iraq further limited the attractiveness of the Iranian market and inflicted additional losses on remaining foreign investors.

The Iranian experience taught international marketers an important lesson pertaining to political risk. For many years, firms believed political risk applied only to capital investments in foreign countries. After all, expensive manufacturing plants could be seized. Surprisingly, the Reynolds case involved damage not to brick-and-mortar facilities but rather to unpaid accounts receivable for cigarettes exported to Iran. In fact, many companies that were simply exporting to Iran found themselves the victims of political risk, as did firms that were licensing their technology or brand names to local Iranian manufacturers. In many cases, the new government forbade importers and licensees from making payments to foreign businesses. However a firm chooses to enter a market, political risk may be a concern.

What can companies do? Internationally active companies have reacted on two fronts. First, they have started to perfect their own intelligence systems to avoid being caught unaware when changes disrupt operations. Second, they have developed several risk-reducing strategies that help limit their exposure, or the losses they would sustain, should a sudden change occur. The following sections will concentrate on these two solutions.

Political Risk Assessment

The business disruption in Iran inspired many companies to establish systems to systematically analyze political risk. To establish an effective political risk assessment (PRA) system, a company has to decide first on the objectives of the system. Another aspect concerns the internal organization, or the assignment of responsibility within the company. Finally, some agreement has to be reached on how the analysis is to be done.

Objectives of Political Risk Assessment

Companies everywhere would like to know about impending government instabilities in order to avoid making new investments in those countries. Even more important is the monitoring of existing operations and their political environment. Particularly with existing operations, knowing in advance about potential changes in the political climate is of little value unless such advance knowledge can also be used for future action. As a result, PRA is slowly moving from predicting events to developing strategies that help companies cope with changes. But first, PRA has to deal with the potential political changes. Many questions must be answered: Should we enter a particular country? Should we stay in a particular country? What can we do with our operations in market X, given that development Y can occur? In undertaking PRA, companies are well advised to look for answers to six key questions:

- ➤ How stable is the host country's political system?
- ➤ How strong is the host government's commitment to specific rules of the game, such as ownership or contractual rights, given its ideology and power position?
- ➤ How long is the government likely to remain in power?
- ➤ If the present government is succeeded by another, how will the specific rules of the game change?
- ➤ What would be the effects on our business of any expected changes in the specific rules of the game?
- ➤ In light of those effects, what decisions and actions should we take now?

Organization and Analysis

One survey of large U.S.-based international firms found that over half the firms had internal groups reviewing the political climate of both newly proposed and current operations. In companies that did not have formalized systems for PRA, top executives tended to obtain firsthand information through foreign travel and talking with other businesspeople.[42]

Rather than rely on a centralized corporate staff, some companies prefer to delegate PRA responsibility to executives or analysts located in a particular geographic region. Some use their subsidiary and regional managers as a major source of information. Other firms employ distinguished foreign-policy advisers or maintain outside advisory panels.

Several public or semipublic sources exist that regularly monitor political risk. The Economist Intelligence Unit (EIU), a sister company of *The Economist*, monitors some 80 countries on the basis of a variety of economic and political factors. These factors include debt, current account position, economic policy and political stability. Business Monitor International publishes country risk ratings and differentiates between short- and long-term political risk. Table 4.2 briefly summarizes some of Business Monitor's conclusions about political risk in Mexico, South Africa, Russia and Vietnam.[43] Like many emerging markets, these four countries are more politically risky than developed economies. However, as the table reveals, the reasons for their political risk vary. This illustrates that knowing the reasons behind political risk scores is important, because different sources of risk impact global marketers in different ways.

Table 4.2 What Makes a Country Politically Risky?

Country	Short-Term Political Stability Rating	Source of Risk	Long-Term Political Stability Rating	Source of Risk
Mexico	63.3	A continuing but not escalating war against powerful drug cartels	67.1	Endemic corruption despite relatively stable government and developed institutions
South Africa	67.3	A high degree of unionization increases the threat of industrial action and economic disruption. Union influence also poses a risk to government policy continuity	68.8	High levels of poverty and inequality persist despite the general affluence of this emerging market
Russia	71.0	Recent indications that government is becoming more inhospitable to foreign companies and agencies	57.4	High degree of authority in the executive branch could stymie institutional development in legislative and judicial branches
Vietnam	79.0	Communist party enjoys monopoly of power, but slower growth and inflation may pose challenges in the short term	57.7	One-party rule is likely unsustainable in the longer term

Usually firms use several approaches and sources to assess political risk. What companies do with their assessment depends on the data they collect. Political risk assessment can help the firms stay out of risky countries. However, go/no-go decisions can be difficult to make. Risk analysis is not fortunetelling. No one can predict with certainty when the next revolution or war will take place. Some politically risky countries may possess very attractive markets. Therefore, political risk analysis is only one of the activities that must be undertaken in the course of deciding whether or not to enter or stay in a foreign market. Many companies integrate their political assessments into their overall financial assessments of projects. In cases where the firm expects higher political risk, the company may add anywhere from 1 percent to 5 percent to its required return on investment. In this manner the company balances political risk against market attractiveness.

Risk Reduction Strategies

Political risk assessment not only aids firms in market entry and exit decisions but can also alert them to the necessity of risk-reducing strategies. Such strategies can enable companies to enter or stay in riskier markets. A classic way to deal with politically risky countries is to seek higher and faster returns on investment. The average return on foreign direct investment in Africa is often higher than that for any other region of the world, according to a United Nations Conference on Trade and Development (UNCTAD) study. This is partially because firms invested in projects that promised quick returns.[44] Many companies have also experimented with different ownership and financing arrangements. Others utilize political risk insurance to reduce potential losses.

Local Partners

Relying on local partners who have excellent contacts among the host country's governing elite is a strategy that has been used effectively by many companies. This may range from placing local nationals on the boards of foreign subsidiaries to accepting a substantial capital participation from local investors. For example, General Motors joined forces with Shanghai Automotive Industry Corporation, a SOE, in a 50–50 joint venture to make Buicks, mini-vans and compact cars in China.

However, the use of local partners may not decrease the chance of expropriation, and such partners can become liabilities if governments change. General Motors (GM) entered into a joint venture in Iran with a partner closely connected with the shah. After the revolution ousted the shah, GM's partner's shares were expropriated. GM then found itself in partnership with the new Islamic government.

Minimizing Assets at Risk

If a market is politically risky, international marketers may try to minimize assets that are at risk. For example, R.J. Reynolds could have refused to extend credit to its cigarette importer in Iran. Instead of accumulating accounts receivable that were at risk, the firm could have demanded payment before shipment. However, as we have mentioned before, some politically risky countries can be attractive markets. This was the case in Iran in the mid-1970s, when many foreign firms were vying for Iranian markets. In light of such intense competition, few companies could afford to be heavy-handed with their Iranian customers.

Another way to minimize assets at risk is to borrow locally. Financing local operations from indigenous banks and maintaining a high level of local accounts payable minimize assets at risk. These actions also maximize the negative effect on the local economy if adverse political actions are taken. Typically, host governments are reluctant to cause problems for their local financial institutions. Local borrowing is not always possible because restrictions may be imposed on foreign companies that might otherwise crowd local companies out of the credit markets. However, projects located in developing countries can sometimes qualify for loans from the World Bank. Pioneer, a major global firm in hybrid seeds, was offered such financing when it considered investing in Ethiopia. These arrangements not only reduce the capital at risk but also lend multilateral support for the venture.

Finally, larger MNCs may attempt to diversify their assets and markets across many countries as a way to manage political risk. If losses are realized in one market, their impact does not prove devastating to the company as a whole. Of course, this is more difficult to do if a company is small. Several smaller U.S. firms faced bankruptcy as a result of losses ensuing from the Iranian revolution.

Political Risk Insurance

As a final recourse, international companies can often purchase insurance to cover their political risk. With the political developments in Iran and Nicaragua occurring in rapid succession and the assassinations of President Park of South Korea and President Sadat of Egypt all taking place between 1979 and 1981, many companies began to change their attitudes on risk insurance. One of the ongoing difficulties involving political risk insurance is convincing some MNCs that they need the insurance before it is too late. Even in the wake of the Arab Spring in which several supposedly stable Arab governments fell to popular democratic movements, many firms fail to see the advantage in buying coverage for seemingly stable authoritarian regimes.[45] Political risk insurance can be costly but can offset large potential losses. For example, as a result of the UN Security Council's worldwide embargo on Iraq, companies stood to collect $100–$200 million from private insurers and billions from government-owned insurers.[46]

Companies based in the United States can utilize the Overseas Private Investment Corporation (OPIC). OPIC was formed by the U.S. government to facilitate the participation of private U.S. firms in the development of less developed countries. Since the Islamic revolution in Iran, OPIC has covered exporters as well as foreign investors. OPIC offers project financing and political risk insurance in 100 developing countries. The agency covers losses caused by currency inconvertibility, expropriation and bellicose actions such as war and revolution. Selected OPIC services are listed in Table 4.3. But even OPIC faces challenges from special-interest groups. A lawsuit was brought

Table 4.3 Selected OPIC Offerings for Political Risk Losses

Currency Inconvertibility
- Increased foreign exchange regulations
- Failure to access hard currency
- Unlawful blocking of funds for repatriation

Expropriation and Unlawful Government Interference
- Repudiation of government contracts
- Confiscation of funds or tangible assets
- Imposition of confiscatory taxes
- Nationalization of projects or businesses

Regulatory Risk
- Critical changes to taxes
- Critical changes to other regulations affecting operations
- Revocation of licenses needed for operation

Political Violence
- Evacuation expenses
- Temporary losses due to evacuation
- Damage to tangible assets
- Income losses due to damage to tangible assets

against OPIC by Friends of the Earth, Greenpeace and others. They accused the agency of failing to conduct environmental reviews before financing projects that contributed to global warming.[47]

Global Marketing and Terrorism

The Overseas Security Advisory Council is a public–private partnership that seeks to provide early warning of bombings or other attacks to corporate offices worldwide as terrorists look increasingly toward "soft targets." The council is overseen by the U.S. State Department and advises international companies such as Citigroup, Boeing, Dupont and McDonald's. Its site gets about 1.8 million visits a month, and the council distributes about 10,000 e-mails daily. Jennifer Harris, 23, handled a call from a company whose CEO was planning to meet with a regional governor in India. Ms. Harris's research revealed that there had been seven attempts on the governor's life in the past year. The CEO decided to telephone instead.[48]

The rise of international terrorism has affected global marketers in different ways, both directly and indirectly. Direct effects include disruption of power, communication and transport systems as well as physical damage to facilities and loss of life. Indirect effects of terrorism include increased costs to supply chains and increased regulations imposed by governments.[49] Some firms choose to avoid or leave certain markets because the local government has alleged ties to terrorists. General Electric was one of several companies that chose to stop seeking contracts in Iran when the company was criticized by a U.S. senator for taking "blood money" from a state that supported terrorists.[50] Other companies have found their marketing strategies affected by terrorism. Coca-Cola and Proctor & Gamble once advertised on Al-Manar Television, a satellite news channel run by the militant Shiite group Hezbollah. However, the U.S. Treasury designated Al-Manar a terrorist entity, making it illegal for U.S. firms to continue to advertise on the channel.[51]

MNCs must consider a possible terrorist threat to their own operations. Businesses are the most common target of terrorist attacks, and bombings are the most common terrorist events.[52] Faced with the possibility of such an attack, Starbucks pulled out of Israel.[53] Terrorists have also been known to extort payments from MNCs. However, such payments may be deemed illegal by home governments. Chiquita pleaded guilty to breaking U.S. law and agreed to $25 million in fines for paying a terrorist group in Colombia to assure the safety of its employees there.[54]

Whole industries have also been affected by the rise in terrorism. One of the immediate industries to feel the impact of global terrorism was tourism. With a high risk of terrorism, Americans spent more tourism dollars in Mexico instead of taking trans-Atlantic flights to Europe.[55] Tourists from the Middle East began to shun the United States where they faced new border checks and suspicion, favoring a new destination—Malaysia.

Another industry directly affected by global terrorism is international education. Tightened security in the United States has made acquiring student visas more difficult for foreign students planning to study there. Consequently, a battle for global market share of international students has emerged. Among the most aggressive countries are Malaysia, India, China, Sweden and the Netherlands. Two other proactive competitors are the Middle East kingdom of Dubai and Singapore. Dubai particularly targets students from the Middle East who face difficulties in obtaining U.S. visas. Both Dubai and Singapore follow the model of partnering with high-quality foreign universities to set up local programs. Among such universities participating in Dubai are the University of Southern Queensland, India's Mahatma Gandhi University and Dublin Business School. Singapore has attracted Stanford and Cornell from the United States, French business school INSEAD and the German Institute of Science and Technology. Singapore's goal is to attract 150,000 foreign students, resulting in a contribution of 5 percent to the national economy.[56]

Global terrorists may particularly target infrastructure such as ports, airlines and other transportation and communication systems.[57] Such attacks threaten to wreak havoc as companies try to supply international buyers. Dow Corning makes over 10,000 deliveries a month to 20,000 customers in 50 countries. Its products are used in the manufacture of products from shampoos to textiles. September 11 and other terrorist attacks can disrupt the firm's ability to deliver products to customers. For example, Dow Corning's team of planners met for months to discuss backup plans if the war in Iraq were to upset their global logistics. During the Gulf War, one product destined for a cosmetics company in France ended up in Saudi Arabia. This held up production for two weeks and upset the French customer.

Similar to Dow, a number of large companies already had systems in place to respond to disruptions caused by situations other than terrorism. For example, DaimlerChrysler had control centers to deal with disruptions from hurricanes to industrial disputes.[58] However, Dow Corning's chief logistics officer for China estimates that most big companies could be better prepared with scenario planning. They would probably only have to invest $1.5 million in contingency plans.[59]

Corporate security has been heightened in a number of companies. PepsiCo, with over $500 billion in sales and over 143,000 employees worldwide, responded to the terrorist threat by creating a new position—vice president of global security. At Oracle, a corporate steering committee coordinates a number of departments, including security, IT, product development and human resources. At Marriott, crisis management has been centralized to ensure consistency across its different businesses. Seventy percent of respondents to a survey administered by the U.S. Chamber of Commerce reported that their firms had reviewed their security policies in light of a terrorist threat, and 53 percent had acted on recommendations arising from those reviews.[60]

The U.S. government has made certain precautions mandatory by law. Companies that export agricultural products or processed foods to the United States must register with the U.S. Department of Agriculture and submit to increased scrutiny. The Treasury Department maintains a list of individuals and organizations believed to be linked with terrorism. To do business with anyone or any company on that list is a criminal offense for U.S. citizens or companies. Needless to say, these new regulations have vastly increased demand by companies for preemployment screening as well as background checks on clients, vendors, distributors and business partners.[61]

The direct and indirect costs associated with terrorism for the S&P 500 companies alone are estimated to be over $100 billion a year. This number includes insurance, redundant capacity and lost revenues due to decreased purchases from fearful consumers.[62] Nonetheless, 90 percent of the respondents in the Chamber of Commerce survey reported that they did not believe their company would be a target for terrorists.[63] As the immediate threat fades, many midsize companies, in particular, may regard the expense of planning for terrorist attacks as too costly. In another survey, conducted by the Conference Board, 40 percent of top executives of midsize companies agreed that "security is an expense that ought to be minimized."[64] It is further estimated that 40 percent of very large U.S. companies do not have terrorism insurance.[65]

Conclusion

In this chapter, we have outlined major political and regulatory issues facing MNCs. Our approach was not to identify and list all possible government actions that may have an impact on international marketing. Instead, we have provided a background to make it easier to understand these actions and the motivations behind them. It is up to executives with international responsibility to devise strategies and systems for dealing with these challenges posed by governments.

What is important is to recognize that companies can—to a degree—forecast and manage regulatory change. They can also adopt risk reduction strategies to compensate for some of the more unpredictable political risks. For effective global marketing management, executives must be forward looking, must anticipate potentially adverse or even positive changes in the environment and must not merely wait until changes occur. To accomplish this, systematic monitoring procedures that encompass both political and regulatory developments must be implemented.

The past several years have brought enormous political changes to the world, changes that are affecting global marketing operations of international firms. On the one hand, these changes have resulted in the opening of many previously closed markets. On the other hand, global terrorism has emerged, presenting its own challenges. Regulatory change and political risk will continue to play a large role in global marketing. Firms must learn how to avoid disasters as well as how to identify and take advantage of opportunities.

Managerial Takeaways

1. *Governments—both host and home—provide global marketers with both predictable and unpredictable business environments. Governments determine the rules of legal behavior within a market.*
2. *Governments can significantly change the competitive dynamics of markets through such actions as subsidies, ownership restrictions, expropriations, trade restrictions, embargoes and rules concerning local operating conditions.*
3. *Legal environments, like any cultural institution, vary across cultures. They usually change slowly, but they do change. Legal variation combined with legal evolution requires global marketers to be especially sensitive to the various legal environments in which they operate.*
4. *Political risk can affect the decision to enter a market, expand in a market or even leave a market. While it may be easy to determine that a market is politically risky, global marketers often find it very difficult to determine exactly when or how a politically motivated action will affect their operations.*
5. *If a market is attractive despite political risk, global marketers should examine how best to manage their risk rather than trying to predict the future.*
6. *Regulatory changes happen continuously while major political disruptions are rare. Global marketers lose far more money from tax increases than from business losses due to revolutions.*
7. *Regulations and regulatory change reflect a variety of sometimes contradictory political motivations. Understanding these motivations can help global marketers predict future government actions and prepares them to better negotiate with governments.*

Questions for Discussion

1. The construction industry in Japan has traditionally been dominated by its domestic suppliers. Few foreign construction companies have won projects in Japan. What aspects of Japan's political forces may have influenced this local control over the Japanese construction market? What political or regulatory forces may lead to the opening of this market for foreign firms?

2. Do ownership restrictions such as local-partner requirements always ensure that MNCs will contribute more to the local economy than they would otherwise?

3. What are the different methods a company can use to obtain and/or develop political risk assessment information? What do you think are the strengths and weaknesses of each?

4. John Deere has decided to enter the tractor market in Central America. What strategies could it use to reduce the possible effects of political risk?

5. Choose a cause promoted by Public Citizen's Global Trade Watch. Do you agree with the cause? Why or why not? What firms are or could be involved in the controversy?

6. How is global terrorism similar to and different from prior political risk faced by global marketers?

CASE 4.1 Cuba: Reentering the World

Enacted in 1960, the U.S. embargo of Cuba became the longest embargo in history. Over half a century later, the United States was still debating whether to finally lift sanctions against Cuba. A recent survey revealed that the majority of Americans supported changing U.S. policy toward Cuba. The major reason was the cost of the embargo. One study suggested that lifting the embargo would create 6,000 new jobs in the United States and increase U.S. exports by $365 million a year.

In the 1950s, the economy of Cuba was dominated by Spanish landowning families and U.S. corporations. A communist revolution led by Fidel Castro resulted in thousands of confiscations of foreign and local properties. These confiscations included factories, plantations, mines and real estate. The U.S. government responded to the confiscations by placing an embargo on Cuba in 1960. The embargo disallowed U.S. exports to or imports from Cuba. In addition, U.S. foreign investment in Cuba was forbidden. Castro originally offered to pay claimants with money from sugar sales to the United States, but the U.S. government refused to negotiate with the dictator. At one time the United States recognized nearly 6,000 claims against Cuba, totaling nearly $7 billion.

For years Cuba remained a satellite of the Soviet Union. Virtually all its trade was with Russia or the Soviet bloc. With the dissolution of the Soviet Union, Cuba was left one of the few remaining communist states in the world. It lost its traditional trading partners and found itself financially destitute. Though wary of capitalism, the island nation began tentatively to encourage foreign investment in the mid-1990s. Investments, primarily from Canada and the EU, quickly grew to several hundred in number.

The United States, never having lifted its embargo on Cuba, was quick to respond. The Helms-Burton law was passed allowing U.S. citizens to sue foreign companies that used property that had been previously confiscated by the Cuban government. In addition, the U.S. government would deny visas to corporate officers of such companies. Some foreign companies quickly complied by checking for claims against their new Cuban investments. Many more ignored the U.S. threat. President Clinton eventually waived the right to sue under the Helms-Burton law in response to an EU initiative to ask for a WTO ruling against the American law.

Then, after nearly 40 years, the United States partially lifted its embargo against Cuba. The embargo had failed in its primary mission to remove Fidel Castro. Supported by a politically powerful farm lobby, the embargo was amended to allow sales of agricultural products and medicine to Cuba. Still the Cuban government remains wary of closer economic ties with the United States. Although the Cuban economy has improved somewhat, the country remains a tightly controlled society with 11 million people living at subsistence level.

Cuba has suggested that it is ready to meet its claims obligations under international law, but it is unclear where Cuba would find the money. Cuba has stated that it plans to seek redress from the United States for the economic cost inflicted by the U.S. embargo, a cost estimated at over $60 billion. Another option could be the sale of government-owned properties. Some suggest that the U.S. government should offer Cuba a bailout plan to welcome the nation back into the fold. Others note that renewed economic ties between Europe and Cuba have done nothing to improve Cuba's poor human rights record. In the meantime, a Miami financier proposed pooling corporate and personal claims against Cuba into a fund that would issue shares to claim holders. These shares would then be speculatively bought and sold.

Discussion Questions

1. List the various issues covered in Chapter 4 that are illustrated by this case.
2. Should claim holders be compensated? If so, *who* should pay? Why?
3. If you were considering investing in the proposed claims fund, what discount rate would you apply? In other words, how many cents on the dollar do you think these claims are worth? Why?

Sources: "Cuba Re-enters the World" in Kate Gillespie and H. David Hennessey, *Global Marketing* (Mason, OH: Cengage, 2011), p. 119; Elizabeth Flock, "Cuba Trade Embargo Turns 50," *Washington Post* (Online), February 7, 2012; Daniel Hanson, Dayne Batten and Harrison Ealey, "It's Time for the U.S. to End Its Senseless Embargo of Cuba," *Forbes* (Online), January 16, 2013; Jaime Suchlicki, "Why Sanctions on Cuba Must Remain," *New York Times* (Online), November 20, 2013; and Rick Gladstone, "Majority of Americans Favor Ties With Cuba, Poll Finds," *New York Times* (Online), February 10, 2014.

CASE 4.2   Coke Under Fire

Coca-Cola may be one of the world's most recognized brands, but the company's relationships with governments across the world have often been contentious.

For over two years, Coca-Cola struggled to acquire the soda brands of Cadbury Schweppes, which included Dr Pepper and 7-Up. The proposed purchase originally encompassed all of Cadbury Schweppes's international markets except those in the United States, France and South Africa. A successful purchase would increase Coca-Cola's market share in soda in over 150 countries. For example, Coca-Cola's share in Canada was expected to rise from 39.4 percent to 49.1 percent. In Mexico, its share would rise from 68.4 percent to 72.6 percent.

Not everyone was pleased with the proposed purchase. Pepsi, Coke's major rival, sent letters to legislators in Canada asking the Canadian government to disallow the purchase of the Canadian operations, maintaining that it would result in weaker competition, higher prices and the loss of 300 jobs in Pepsi's Canadian operations. Smaller independent bottlers joined Pepsi in opposition. Canada's Federal Competition Bureau agreed to undertake a costly investigation that resulted in Coke canceling its plans in Canada. In the meantime, Australia, Belgium and Mexico rejected the purchase. A number of European countries and the Chilean government also put it under review. As a result, Coke scaled back on its attempts to buy the brands in Europe. Instead, South Africa was added to the deal.

The Cadbury Schweppes purchase is not the only encounter Coke has had with competition regulators in Europe and elsewhere. The offices of Coca-Cola Enterprises were raided in London and Brussels. EU regulators were seeking incriminating documents related to Coke's allegedly having given German, Austrian and Danish supermarkets illegal incentives to stock fewer rival products. A similar investigation the year before in Italy had resulted in a $16 million fine being levied on the company.

The new head of Coca-Cola had visited Europe and personally met with top antitrust officials at the EU and various European countries. He wanted to present Coke's case personally and to achieve a better understanding of the concerns of the officials. He stated that Coke was committed to playing by the house rules wherever they did business. However, what Coke called aggressive yet honest competition, Europe viewed as abrasive, domineering and unacceptable American behavior.

Problems had cropped up in Latin America as well. In Mexico, Pepsi had accused Coca-Cola of forbidding its many small shopkeepers to sell rival soft drinks. After battling these allegations in the Mexican courts for several years, Coke lost the first of 70 similar cases brought against it for anticompetitive actions. Mexican antitrust authorities also rejected the plans for Coca-Cola and its Mexican bottler to purchase Mexico's second largest juice company.

In addition, about 9 percent of Mexico's population had diabetes. Seven out of ten Mexicans over the age of 20 were either obese or overweight. A government campaign against soda consumption had begun. Billboard ads asked: "Would you eat 12 spoonfuls of sugar? Why do you drink soda?" The government had even announced a new 1-peso tax on each bottle of soda, a move that would raise the cost to consumers by about 10 percent.

In China, Coca-Cola had for years used hand-held global positioning system (GPS) devices to collect information in order to improve customer service and improve fuel efficiency within its logistics system. The company was therefore alarmed when the Chinese government accused its employees of illegally using GPS to gather confidential information. Companies providing online map and location services must seek approval by the government, and such approval was typically restricted to Chinese companies. In fact market research in general was very regulated in China. One American was sentenced to eight years in prison for trying to purchase information about the Chinese oil industry.

Discussion Questions

1. Why do you think some countries disallowed the Cadbury Schweppes acquisition whereas others did not?

2. Given Coca-Cola's position that the company is committed to playing by the rules, why was the firm in trouble in so many countries?

3. What are the government motivations behind Coca-Cola's problems concerning the new soda tax in Mexico and China's reaction to the company's use of GPS?

4. What advice would you give Coca-Cola concerning its handling of government relations?

Sources: "Coke Under Fire" in Kate Gillespie and H. David Hennessey, *Global Marketing* (Mason, OH: Cengage, 2011), p. 120; Laurie Burkitt, "China Accuses Coca-Cola of Illegally Using GPS," *Wall Street Journal Online*, March 13, 2013; Edward Wong, "Coca-Cola Cooperating with Chinese GPS Investigation," *New York Times*, March 14, 2013; and Amy Guthrie, "Mexico Finds a New Target: Soft Drinks," *Wall Street Journal*, August 29, 2013, p. B1.

CASE 4.3   Evaluating National Regulatory Environments

Go to the website for Doing Business at www.doingbusiness.org/rankings and contrast the four proposed markets below:

Argentina, Saudi Arabia, South Africa and Vietnam

1. First note how difficult it is to do business *overall* in each of these countries. Order the countries from easiest to work in to hardest to work in.

2. Now dig deeper. For each of these countries, identify which categories of *doing business* are more challenging or less challenging than the country's average score would suggest. (For example, starting a business, protecting investors, enforcing contracts, trading across borders.)

3. For *each of the three companies* below, identify which categories are most relevant to the company's business model. Which factors are irrelevant or of lesser importance? Why?

   a. **Happy-Mart** is a large retailer of packaged food and household products. It is looking to expand into emerging markets. It plans to enter markets alone without seeking local partners. It will buy land and build its own stores. It will buy most of its food and other products locally but will import some of its household items from China.

   b. **Knuckle-Tech** makes artificial knuckles for replacement surgery. It plans to export knuckles made in America to emerging markets. However, in order to sell in each emerging market, Knuckle-Tech will have to receive approval for its products from each national government. The company will also need to find qualified local distributors to market their artificial knuckles to doctors and hospitals. Knuckle-Tech also worries that local manufacturers might ignore its patents, reverse-engineer its artificial knuckles and start selling a competing product.

c.   **Tarrytown Toys** is seeking a new location for producing its toys for export to the United States and Europe. However, the company fears that poor regulatory environments might offset any savings from lower labor costs. To offset what the company considers more risky business environments, Tarrytown Toys will be seeking local joint-venture partners who already operate manufacturing plants in their emerging market.

4.   Based on your analysis for question 3, order the four countries from easiest to work in to hardest to work in *from the point of view of each of the three businesses above.*

5.   Compare your country rankings for Happy-Mart, Knuckle-Tech and Tarrytown Toys to your overall country rankings from question 1.

6.   What can you learn from this exercise?

Notes

1   Kerry A. Dolan, "Dancing with Chavez," *Forbes*, November 13, 2000, p. 72.
2   Anthony Harrup, "Cemex Chief Wouldn't Rule Out Return to Venezuela," *Wall Street Journal* (Online), March 21, 2013.
3   Vern Terpstra and Kenneth David, *The Cultural Environment of International Business*, 3rd ed. (Cincinnati: Southwestern, 1992), p. 203.
4   "YouTube Confronts Censors Overseas," Dow Jones Chinese Financial Wire, March 21, 2008.
5   Shelly Banjo and R. Jai Krishna, "Wal-Mart Curbs Ambitions in India," *Wall Street Journal*, October 10, 2013.
6   Amy Guthrie, "Latin America's Public Enemy #1," *Wall Street Journal Asia*, December 30, 2013.
7   "Bill, Borrow, and Embezzle," *The Economist*, February 17, 2001.
8   Kevin J. Delaney and Andres Cala, "France Mobilizes, Seeks European Allies to Fend Off Google," *Wall Street Journal*, May 12, 2005, p. B1.
9   Stephen Castle, "Europe Puts Its Culture Online from Books to Art," *International Herald Tribune*, November 20, 2008, p. 4.
10 Jane Spencer, "Chinese Activists Launch Drive to Shame Polluters," *Wall Street Journal*, March 28, 2007, p. B3A.
11 Helene Cooper, "Looming Battle," *Wall Street Journal*, October 29, 2001, p. A1.
12 Geoffrey A. Fowler, "It's Called the Forbidden City for a Reason," *Wall Street Journal*, January 19, 2007, p. B1.
13 Neil King Jr., "Iraq's Business Elite Gropes in Dark," *Wall Street Journal*, June 25, 2003, p. A4.
14 Robb M. Stewart and Kathy Sandler, "Sale in Unit," *Wall Street Journal*, July 2, 2009, p. B3.
15 Matt Moffett, "In Argentine Province, Fashion Police Say Small Isn't Beautiful," *Wall Street Journal*, November 26, 2005, p. A1.
16 Mei Fong, "Avon's Calling," *Wall Street Journal*, February 26, 2007, p. B1.
17 "Chinese Defense Firm Banned for Selling Tech to Iran," *Dow Jones Business News*, May 22, 2003.
18 Bhushan Bahree, "Exxon, Shell Poised to Win Saudi Deals," *Wall Street Journal*, June 1, 2001, p. A11.
19 "Wal-Mart, NY Yankees, Others Settle Charges of Illegal Trading," CNN.com, April 14, 2003.
20 "U.S. Court Hears Appeal of Massachusetts' Burma Law," *Dow Jones News Service*, May 4, 1999.
21 Peter Wonacott, "As WTO Entry Looms, China Rushes to Adjust Legal System," *Wall Street Journal*, November 9, 2001, p. A13.
22 David Ahlstrom, Michael N. Young and Anil Nair, "Deceptive Managerial Practices in China: Strategies for Foreign Firms," *Business Horizons* (November–December, 2002), pp. 49–59.

23 Amol Sharma, "India's Tata Finds Home Hostile," *Wall Street Journal Asia*, April 14, 2011, p. 14.

24 Aaron Back, "Beijing Cracks Down on Car Buyers," *Wall Street Journal*, December 24, 2010, p. A6.

25 Ichiko Fuyuno, "Japan Grooms New Lawyers," *Wall Street Journal,* April 3, 2004, p. A18.

26 "Of Laws and Men," *The Economist*, April 7, 2001.

27 Susan Postlewaite, "A Crackdown on Madcap Drivers," *Business Week International Editions*, April 30, 2001, p. 5.

28 Jean-Claude Usunier, *Marketing Across Cultures* (New York: Prentice-Hall, 2000), pp. 83–85.

29 Harry C. Triandis, "The Many Dimensions of Culture," *Academy of Management Executive*, vol. 18, no. 1 (2004), p. 92.

30 Shahar Ilan, "Thou Shalt Not Be a Freier," Haaretz.com, January 28, 2007.

31 James E. Austin, *Managing in Developing Countries* (New York: The Free Press, 1990), p. 166.

32 Glenn R. Simpson, "Multinational Firms Take Steps to Avert Boycotts Over War," *Wall Street Journal*, April 4, 2003, p. A1.

33 Austin, *Managing in Developing Countries*, pp. 148–153.

34 Peter Wonacott, "Chinese Firms Find Their Iraq Projects in Limbo," *Wall Street Journal*, July 10, 2003, p. A8.

35 Ravi Ramamurti, "The Obsolescing 'Bargaining Model'? MNC-Host Developing Country Relations Revisited," *Journal of International Business Studies*, vol. 21, no. 1 (2001), pp. 23–39.

36 David B. Yoffie and John J. Coleman, "Motorola and Japan," Harvard Business School Case # 9-388-056.

37 Orit Gadiesh and Jean-Marie Pean, "Manager's Journal: Think Globally, Market Locally," *Wall Street Journal*, September 9, 2003, p. B2.

38 Nicholas Casey and James R. Hagerty, "Companies Shun Violent Mexico," *Wall Street Journal Online*, December 17, 2010.

39 Chip Cummins, "Business Mobilizes for Iraq," *Wall Street Journal*, March 24, 2003, p. B1.

40 Joel Millman, "Gangs Plague Central America," *Wall Street Journal*, December 11, 2003, p. A14.

41 "Slow Progress on Iran Claims," *New York Times*, November 14, 1984, pp. D1, D5.

42 Stephen J. Kobrin et al., "The Assessment and Evaluation of Noneconomic Environments by American Firms: A Preliminary Report," *Journal of International Business Studies*, vol. 11 (Spring–Summer, 1980), pp. 32–47.

43 Business Monitor International, Risk Summaries for Mexico (January 24, 2014), South Africa (January 24, 2014), Russia (February 10, 2014) and Vietnam (February 7, 2014).

44 "Business in Difficult Places," *The Economist*, May 20, 2000.

45 Paul Barbour, Persephone Economou, Nathan Jensen and Daniel Villar, "The Arab Spring: How Soon Will Investors Return?" Columbia FDI Perspectives, No. 67, May 7, 2012.

46 "Political Risk Insurers Fear Crisis Escalation," *Business Insurance*, vol. 24, no. 33a (1990), p. 1.

47 Vanessa Houlder, "Climate Change Could Be Next Legal Battlefield," *Financial Times*, July 14, 2003, p. 10.

48 Gary Fields, "Protecting 'Soft Targets'," *Wall Street Journal*, November 26, 2003, p. A4.

49 Gabriele Suder and Michael Czinkota, "Terrorism Studies in International Business," *Academy of International Business Insights*, vol. 12, no, 4 (2013), p. 4.

50 Kathryn Kranhold and Carla Anne Robbins, "GE to Stop Seeking Business in Iran," *Wall Street Journal*, February 3, 2005, p. A3.

51 Jay Soloman and Mariam Fam, "Air Battle," *Wall Street Journal*, July 28, 2006, p. A1.

52 Michael R. Czinkota, Gary A. Knight, Peter W. Liesch and John Steen, "Positioning Terrorism in Management and Marketing: Research Propositions," *Journal of International Management*, vol. 11 (2005), pp. 581–604.

53 "Starbucks Plots Global Conquests," *Kitchener-Waterloo Record*, April 16, 2003, p. E4.

54 Laurie P. Cohen, "Chiquita Under the Gun," *Wall Street Journal*, August 2, 2007, p. A1.

55 John Lyons, "Mexico's Safety Wins Tourists," *Wall Street Journal*, April 28, 2004, p. A15.

56 "Fight for Global Education Pie Gets Fiercer," *Straits Times*, February 14, 2005.

57 Thomas Mucha, "10 Ways to Protect Your Business from Terror," *Business 3*, no. 1 (January 2002), pp. 50–51.

58 Michael Czinkota and Gary Knight, "Managing the Terrorism Threat," *European Business Forum*, no. 20 (Winter 2005), p. 45.

59 Gabriel Kahn, "A Case Study of How One Company Prepared for War," *Wall Street Journal*, March 25, 2003, p. A14.

60 Sherry L. Harowitz, "The New Centurions," *Security Management*, January 1, 2003, p. 50.

61 Howard Winn, "Risk Management: The Quest for Quality," *Far Eastern Economic Review*, October 21, 2004, p. 46.

62 Nanette Byrnes, "The High Cost of Fear," *Business Week*, November 6, 2006, p. 16.

63 Ibid.

64 Paul Magnusson, "What Companies Need to Do," *Business Week*, August 16, 2004, p. 26.

65 "Terrorism Insurance Deemed Reasonable But Many Firms Don't Have It," *Security Director's Report*, December 2008, p. 9.

Part 2

Analyzing Global Opportunities

5   GLOBAL MARKETS   135

6   GLOBAL COMPETITORS   167

7   GLOBAL MARKETING RESEARCH   199

Chapter 5

Global Markets

UNDERSTANDING MARKETS AND BUYERS   136

THE CONSUMER MARKET   137

BUSINESS MARKETS   148

GOVERNMENT MARKETS   151

Since the signing of NAFTA many U.S.-based companies have eyed Mexico's market with great interest. Thanks in part to the rising purchasing power of women, Mary Kay, a Dallas-based manufacturer of cosmetics, has watched Mexico become one of its top foreign markets. Wal-Mart has become Mexico's number one retailer. But for latecomer Starbucks, Mexico presented an enigma. Mexico was the fifth largest producer of coffee in the world, yet Mexicans rarely drank coffee. The average Mexican consumed less than two pounds of coffee a year, compared with the ten pounds consumed by the average American and the 26 pounds consumed by the average Swede. Could Starbucks create a greater demand for coffee among Mexican consumers? Could its upscale coffee shop format offer a product that was attractive to customers in a developing country?[1]

To begin to develop an effective strategy for global markets, a firm must first consider the type of market in which it competes. Markets can comprise consumers, businesses or governments.

In this chapter we explore issues that arise when targeting these different categories of markets in global markets. We address factors that make each category similar—and yet different—across cultures. Consumer markets may exhibit global segments whose needs and behaviors are relatively uniform across cultures. Business-to-business markets can produce global buyers with unique demands. Government buyers often have multiple agendas. Still, national differences affect all these markets, making the job of addressing their wants and needs all the more challenging for the global marketer.

Learning Objectives

After studying this chapter, you should be able to:

➤ list the factors that influence consumers' abilities to buy and explain how these affect various national markets;

➤ describe Maslow's hierarchy-of-needs model and apply it to consumers in different cultures;

➤ give examples of how consumer behavior is similar across cultures and examples of how it may differ from one culture to another;

➤ describe segmentation options for consumer markets abroad;

➤ explain why business-to-business markets vary in buyer needs and behavior from one country to another;

➤ list the special qualities of national and multinational global buyers;

➤ describe the five "screens" a foreign firm must pass through to win a government contract;

➤ explain the role of bribery in international contracts.

Understanding Markets and Buyers

In every marketing situation, it is important to understand potential buyers and the process they use to select one product over another. In the case of each type of buyer—consumer, business and government—global marketers must be able to identify who the buyers are and how they make a purchase decision.

When launching disposable diapers worldwide, Procter & Gamble established a global marketing team in Cincinnati, believing that babies' diaper needs would be the same around the globe. They later found out that whereas mothers in most countries are concerned about keeping their babies' bottoms dry, Japanese mothers are not. In Japan, babies are changed so frequently that thick, ultra-absorbent diapers were not necessary and could be replaced by thin diapers that take up less space in the small Japanese home.[2] Similarly, many business-to-business (B2B) marketers have discovered that CEOs in developing countries make purchase decisions that are usually delegated to purchasing managers in developed countries.

The Consumer Market

Consumers around the world have many similar needs. There is even some evidence that global consumption patterns are converging. The traditionally wine-drinking French are drinking more beer, and beer-drinking Germans are drinking more wine. Japan, traditionally a fish-eating country, is consuming more beef, and many Swiss now prefer French cheese to their traditional Swiss varieties. However, to assume that buyers in different countries engage in exactly the same buying processes and apply exactly the same selection criteria can be disastrous. Buyers can differ in terms of who decides to buy, what they buy, why they buy, how they buy, when they buy and where they buy.

All people must eat, drink and be sheltered from the elements. Once these basic needs are met, consumers then seek to improve their standard of living with a more comfortable environment, more leisure time and increased social status. Still, consumption patterns vary greatly from one country to another, because consumers vary widely in their ability and motivation to buy. For example, consumption patterns for wine vary tremendously from country to country. In France, the average annual consumption is 15.6 liters (4.12 gallons) per person, compared with 7.2 liters in the United States, 1.2 liters in Japan and only 0.2 liters in Turkey. Consumption patterns of contact lenses vary by country as well. Japanese per capita purchase nearly twice as many contact lenses as Americans purchase. Mexicans per capita purchase ten times as many contact lenses as the Chinese purchase.[3]

Basic needs and the desire for an improved standard of living are universal throughout the world, but unfortunately, not everyone can achieve these objectives. The economic, political and social structure of the country in which consumers live affects their ability to fulfill their needs and the methods they use to do so. To understand a consumer market, we must examine the following three aspects:

➤ The consumer's ability to buy
➤ Consumer needs
➤ Consumer behavior

Ability to Buy

To purchase a product or service, consumers must have the ability to buy. The ability to buy may be affected by the amount of wealth a country possesses. A very important indicator of total market potential is GNP because it reflects the generation of wealth in a country, which is an indicator of overall market size.

A country's GNP divided by its population results in its per-capita income (PCI), a crude indicator of market potential per consumer. PCI can vary significantly from country to country. With a PCI of $47,880 in Japan and $55,970 in Sweden, one can expect the demand for automobiles to be greater in those countries than in Kenya or Nepal, each with a PCI below $1,000. One of the main reasons why Starbucks was attracted to Mexico was its increasing PCI. Despite some cultural differences among markets, Starbucks noticed a strong correlation between PCI and coffee consumption.

It is important to note, however, that PCI statistics have an inherent flaw that can undermine their comparability across all markets. The International Monetary Fund (IMF) recognizes that converting income denominated in local currencies into U.S. dollars at market rates can underestimate the true purchasing power of consumers in poor countries relative to those in rich countries. Because of this, the IMF suggests using statistics pertaining to purchasing-power parity, which take into account national differences in product prices. For example, assessed in terms of purchasing-power parity, Egypt's buying power increases from $2,980 (PCI) to $6,450. Table 5.1 shows purchasing-power parity for selected developed and developing countries.

Distribution of wealth also has implications for market potential. Income distribution across the population of a country can distort the market potential in a country. For example, over 68 percent of India's population and nearly 29 percent of China's population live on less than $2 a day. If a few

Table 5.1 Per-Capita Gross National Income at Market Exchange Rates and Purchasing-Power Parity in Selected Countries

Country	Market Exchange Rates	Purchasing Power Parity	Country	Market Exchange Rates	Purchasing Power Parity
Australia	59,360	43,300	Korea	22,670	30,970
Brazil	11,630	11,530	Mexico	9,640	16,450
Chile	14,310	21,310	Paraguay	3,400	5,720
Egypt	2,980	6,450	Philippines	2,500	4,380
Ethiopia	380	1,110	Poland	12,660	21,170
Germany	44,260	42,230	Romania	8,820	16,860
Hungary	12,380	20,710	Russia	12,700	22,720
India	1,580	3,910	Sweden	55,970	43,980
Indonesia	3,420	4,730	Switzerland	80,970	55,090
Iraq	5,870	4,230	Turkey	10,830	18,190
Japan	47,880	36,300	UAE	35,770	41,550
Kazakhstan	9,780	11,780	United States	52,340	52,610
Kenya	860	1,730	Vietnam	1,550	3,620

Source: Adapted from "1.1 World Development Indicators, Size of Economy 2013 World View," World Bank. This is an adaptation on an original work by the World Bank. Responsibility for the views and opinions expressed in the adaptation rests solely with the authors of the adaptation and are not endorsed by the World Bank.

people possess nearly all the wealth and the remainder are poor, there will be few people in the middle. As a result, many products that depend on a middle-class market may fare poorly.

The Gini Index measures the degree of income inequality in a country. Inequality is greater in developing countries, although there are significant differences among these. China, for example, possesses more income equality than Brazil, Russia or South Africa. Still, Chinese in urban areas on average earn three times what rural Chinese do.[4]

Consumer Needs

Products and services are purchased to fulfill basic human needs. Abraham Maslow's hierarchy of needs divides human needs into five levels and proposes that humans will satisfy lower-level needs before seeking to satisfy higher-level needs. The lowest level of needs is physiological needs. These include the need for food, water and sleep. The second level relates to the need for safety—security of body, employment, resources, family, health and property. The third encompasses the social needs of friendship and love. The fourth level consists of the need to receive respect from others, and the highest level of needs is related to self-actualization or developing one's personality. The structure of consumption for each country varies depending on the PCI. A developing country, such as China, may spend over 50 percent of the national income on food, whereas consumers in developed countries, such as France and the United States, spend less than 20 percent on food.

Although it is possible to generalize about the order of consumer purchases on the basis of Maslow's hierarchy of needs, there is some debate about its cross-cultural applicability. Hindu cultures emphasize self-actualization before materialism. In developing countries, consumers may deprive themselves of food in order to buy refrigerators to establish their social status and fulfill their need for esteem.[5] Asian consumers often purchase luxury goods to enhance or maintain face even when their income is relatively low. Such consumers may be thrifty in everyday life yet splurge on luxury consumption.[6] Consumers from more individualistic countries such as the United States may attach less importance to purchases related to belonging to a group or enhancing face and more importance to hobby-related products that may enhance self-actualization. In Japan, on the other hand, great attention and expense are devoted to ritual gift-giving even among business associates, and Japanese children are socially obliged to hold lavish funerals for their parents.

Consumer Behavior

The ability to buy is influenced by a variety of economic elements, which are much easier to identify and quantify than elements related to consumers' motivations to buy. As we noted earlier, all consumers exhibit some similarities as members of the human race. However, buyer behavior is not uniform among all humans. Buyer behavior is learned, primarily from the culture, and so it differs from one culture to another. Throughout this book many cultural differences in consumer behavior will be addressed.

To begin with, culture can directly affect product usage. For example, selling insurance in Muslim countries may prove more difficult because some religious leaders consider buying insurance gambling, which is prohibited under Islam. However, marketers of luxury goods find the Japanese to be excellent customers. Cramped living conditions in Japan combined with a heritage of aesthetic sensibility result in a desire for luxury designer items. A Japanese preoccupation with travel has helped promote a preference for foreign luxury brands in particular.[7]

The structure of the family and the roles assigned to each member also play an important part in determining what products are purchased and how the decision to purchase is made. Table 5.2 depicts the decision-making roles of husbands and wives in product purchases in five countries and suggests that there are similarities and differences across countries. Therefore, international marketers should be aware that variations in family purchasing roles may exist in foreign markets as a result of social and cultural differences. Marketing strategy may need to change to take into account the respective roles of family members. In Saudi Arabia, housewives primarily make decisions as to what packaged foods to buy even if a male servant or member of the family does the actual shopping.

Table 5.2 Summary of Cross-Culture Buying Decision According to Purchase Categories and Country

Buying Decision	Country	Vacation	Food	Appliances	Savings	Furniture	Auto
		Decision-Makers					
What	Turkey	J	W	W	J	J	H
	Guatemala	J	W	W	J	J	H
	Vietnam	J	W	W	J	J	H
	U.S.A.	J	W	J	J	J	H
	Canada	J	W	W	J	J	H
When	Turkey	H	W	W	J	J	H
	Guatemala	H	W	W	J	J	H
	Vietnam	H	W	W	J	J	H
	U.S.A.	H	W	J	J	J	J
	Canada	H	W	J	J	J	J
Where	Turkey	J	W	W	J	J	H
	Guatemala	J	W	W	J	J	H
	Vietnam	J	W	W	J	J	H
	U.S.A.	J	W	J	J	J	H
	Canada	J	W	J	J	J	H
How	Turkey	J	W	J	J	J	H
	Guatemala	J	W	J	J	J	H
	Vietnam	J	W	J	J	J	H
	U.S.A.	J	W	J	J	J	J
	Canada	J	W	J	J	J	H

Decision-Makers' Key: Joint = **J**, Wife = **W**, Husband = **H**

Source: Talhar Harcar, John E. Spillan and Orsay Kucukemiroglo, "A Multi-National Study of Family Decision Making," *The Multinational Business Review*, vol. 13, no. 2 (2007), p. 17.

Segmenting Markets

Once global marketers identify possible national markets to enter, they must remember that further market segmentation is important for three reasons:

➤ All residents of a country are not alike. Consequently, marketers cannot develop one marketing strategy that will adequately address the needs of everyone in a country. UPS discovered this when it surveyed Chinese consumers. Its research concluded that China could not be viewed as a single market, because Chinese consumers had "countless personal preferences."[8]

➤ You do not need every consumer in a country to buy your product in order to be successful in that market—you just need a large enough segment of the market to be willing and able to buy your product.

➤ How—and how much—you adapt your marketing mix (product, price, distribution, promotion) in a national market will depend on the segment you target in that market.

Most segmentation is done within country. Should a Japanese cosmetics firm target French housewives or French working women? Should a U.S. soft-drinks company develop a different marketing mix for Brazilian teens than the one it developed for Brazilian adults? Should a Bolivian furniture company enter the U.S. market by targeting the East Coast or the West Coast?

Segmenting by Region

There are several reasons why global firms may decide to target a geographical region within a national market. In Chapter 3 we noted that some countries have multiple cultures that can vary by region. Regions may also vary by their acceptance of foreign products. For many years, Midwesterners in the United States resisted imported beer. More recently, imports have been making inroads there—but sales are still lower than along the coasts.[9] Some firms even choose to target by municipality: the Belgium beer Stella Artois entered the U.S. market by targeting key trend-setter cities.

Certain regions within a national market may be richer or poorer than others. This can be particularly evident when comparing urban and rural populations in developing countries. Economists at the World Bank were startled to discover that the average family of four living in Hanoi, the capital of Vietnam, spent the equivalent of $20,000 when calculated as purchasing-power parity even though Vietnam is considered one of the poorest countries in the world.[10]

Furthermore, urban populations in emerging markets have long been thought to be more accessible (physically and psychologically) than rural populations. Table 5.3 depicts the urban–rural distribution of population across selected countries. Nonetheless, many companies are beginning to target rural populations. Consumers in rural China have lower incomes and are less knowledgeable about products. Distribution is difficult due to long distances between cities and poor roads. Nonetheless, rural China has emerged as a market of interest to computer firms. Chinese computer giant Lenovo targets rural customers with cheaper computers and markets them as high-status betrothal gifts which are traditionally high-ticket items in this market.[11] Foreign competition is also

141

Table 5.3 Urban/Rural Population Distribution (%)

Country	Urban	Rural	Country	Urban	Rural
Afghanistan	24	76	India	32	68
Bahamas	84	16	Japan	92	8
Bolivia	67	33	Mexico	78	22
Brazil	85	15	Nigeria	50	50
Burundi	11	89	Poland	61	39
Chile	89	11	Russian Federation	74	26
China	52	48	Saudi Arabia	82	18
Egypt	44	56	South Korea	83	17
France	86	14	Spain	78	22
Germany	74	26	Turkey	72	28
Greece	62	38	United States	83	17

Source: Copyright 2013 The World Bank. This is an adaptation on an original work by the World Bank. Responsibility for the views and opinions expressed in the adaptation rests solely with the authors of the adaptation and are not endorsed by the World Bank.

interested in this market. When demand for personal computers slowed across the globe, Hewlett-Packard targeted rural China, a growing and largely untapped market.[12]

In order to successfully target these rural markets, simplifying products and lowering prices may not be enough. Understanding the unique needs of rural consumers helps marketers design new products and services particularly for this segment. In doing so, they create markets that didn't exist before. For example, India's 750,000 villages remain largely isolated. However, extensive cell phone reception across the country allows providers to offer unique services. Tata Teleservices offers a service that allows farmers to use cell phones to control water pumps for their crops. Rural customers of Reliance can listen to live cricket matches by phone, and Bharti Airtel introduced a service allowing users to hear live prayers from popular temples and mosques.[13]

Segmenting by Demographics

Although we often think of culture as a geographic phenomenon, culture can vary to a certain degree by class and generation as well. Men and women are often socialized differently, resulting in certain cultural differences between the genders. Therefore, segmentation by demographics such as income, gender or age is common domestically and useful in international markets as well. Often marketers segment by more than one demographic variable such as age and gender. Table 5.4 presents a segmentation scheme for Chinese women of different ages.

Targeting a market segment determined by the right combination of demographic considerations can result in an attractive marketing strategy. In India, young people, especially women, make up a small segment of the competitive automobile market. But with a growing middle class and rising salaries for young people, Suzuki successfully designed an attractive car for young, middle-class women—the Zen Estilo. Buyers could choose between eight fashion colors including purple fusion and virgin blue, and the price was less than $8,000. When the car was first launched, consumers faced a six-week wait to purchase one in Mumbai.[14]

Table 5.4 Three Female Consumer Groups in Mainland China

Ideologues Born before or during the founding of New China (1949)	Traditionalists Born during the Cultural Revolution (1966–76)	Moderns Born after the open-door policy (1978)
Focus: • Communist philosophy • Democratic family system	**Focus:** • Family-oriented • Confucianistic	**Focus:** • Self-indulgent • Self-oriented
Values: • Serving country, promoting national welfare • Patriotic, societal, and instrumental • Devoted to community activities	**Values:** • Devoted to traditional family values • Family responsibility • Belief in "face" and "reciprocity" • Concern with loyalty and harmony	**Values:** • Social and economic independence • Materialism; modernism • Belief in Western ideas
Consumer behavior: • Active participation in environmental protection and political affairs; loyalty to indigenous and green products • Prefer local products to promote the nation's economy and employment	**Consumer behavior:** • Influenced by family members and friends • Planned consumption • Aroused to buy by gift-giving situations • Concerned with saving; price sensitivity	**Consumer behavior:** • Concerned with self-giving • Favor beauty and health products • Overriding authority over allocation of household expenses • Favor foreign brands • Brand and quality key factors in purchase decisions • Less time to shop • Impulse buying • Get information through reading
Marketing strategies: • Promote national loyalty by forming JVs with local companies to localize product image • Get support from socially respected individuals or government figures • Promotion should emphasize societal rather than individual values	**Marketing strategies:** • Emphasize family values • Promote occasions or events to stimulate gift buying • Promote sales through discounts and coupons • Encourage repeat buying by promoting brand loyalty • Design ads with light-hearted, humorous themes	**Marketing strategies** • Create brand names for quick reference • Make buying and consumption more convenient • Design sales effort to stimulate impulsive buying • Consider using in-store stimuli (attractive packaging, point-of-purchase) • Use magazine and direct-mail ads

Source: Lee, Jenny (S.Y.) et al., "Changing Roles and Values of Female Consumers in China," *Business Horizons*, vol. 47, no. 3 (May–June 2004), p. 18.

TARGETING ELITES Segmenting by income is common and particularly salient in developing countries. Some companies target wealthy elites. A Dior phone priced from $5,000 was created in response to the new luxury markets in China and Russia.[15] Italian jeweler Bulgari and sport-car maker Maserati originally entered the Chinese market targeting wealthy males. More recently both companies have joined other luxury brands in targeting wealthy women who are self-made entrepreneurs.[16]

Many believe that buyers of luxury products are relatively similar across national markets. However, regional differences can arise even among luxury buyers. Lexus sedans became the luxury-class market leader in the United States in just ten years, but their sales remained stymied in Europe. Europeans associated luxury with brand heritage and attention to detail, while Americans focused on comfort, size and dependability. The biggest selling point of the Lexus in the U.S. market was its reliability; it didn't break down. For Europeans, that just wasn't enough from a luxury car.[17]

TARGETING THE MIDDLE CLASS Perhaps the most interesting income segment to the global marketer is the emerging middle class. The World Bank has classified 430 million people worldwide as middle class, but this number can be expected to grow to 1.5 billion by 2030. Middle class is defined as having enough money to spend on non-necessities.[18] This definition is particularly appropriate for global marketers. In China, a household with an annual income of more than $8,800 can afford a basic car.[19] If one assumes that a household with a disposable income of over $10,000 would qualify as middle class, we still see vast differences in the size of the middle class across countries. The percentage of middle-class households ranges from 4.8 percent of households in Kenya to 99.5 percent of households in the UAE.[20]

Middle-class individuals often adopt values of ambition and self-improvement. Middle-class consumers in emerging markets may seek out aspirational goods and often exhibit a preference for imported goods because they are perceived as being higher quality.[21] These qualities make middle classes all the more attractive to global marketers.

TARGETING THE POOR Surprisingly, lower-income segments of the population can be attractive markets for consumer goods. In many developing countries, the buying power of the poor may be underrepresented in official statistics. Much of the income earned by the poor in these countries is never reported to the authorities. Thus they are said to participate in the informal economy. Informal economies can be very large. More than 200 million people in the Middle East and North Africa depend on income from the informal economy.[22] In Mexico, 60 percent of the labor force is estimated to be in the informal sector.[23] However, this number is dwarfed by India's informal economy where more than 90 percent of the country's 487 million workers are employed in the informal sector. In addition, the relatively high cost of real estate in urban centers keeps many of the poor locked in slums. Any increase in their disposable income is spent not on relocating but on purchasing more upscale consumer products. For example, mothers in poor neighborhoods of Calcutta, India, often buy the most expensive brand of milk for their children.

Still, the market potential of the very poor in developing countries, or bottom of the pyramid (BOP), is hotly debated. C.K. Prahalad proposed that marketing to the very poor in developing countries could earn profits for companies while also alleviating poverty. He encouraged firms to rethink a potential market of consumers who earned less than $2 a day.[24] By providing poor consumers with quality products at low prices, companies could help developing countries and build brand loyalty among consumers who would eventually earn more money. This proposal has garnered much attention from multinational corporations (MNCs). However, evidence suggests that BOP marketing is not an easy proposition to put into practice.

Prahalad's original estimate of 4 billion consumers at the bottom of the pyramid (BOP) has been challenged by many who think the number may be as low as 600 million worldwide.[25] Others have noted that many BOP consumers live in rural areas that are hard to reach, causing distribution costs to eliminate possible profits. The characteristics of BOP markets can also vary greatly across cultures, limiting a firm's ability to transfer marketing know-how from one country to another. Furthermore, a number of BOP marketing initiatives, including ones undertaken by Nestlé and Unilever, have been eliminated or scaled back.[26]

Nonetheless, the interest in poor consumers in developing countries continues to grow despite these obstacles. In Indonesia, many MNCs discovered that poorer consumers can make more reliable customers during economic downturns. Unlike middle-class consumers who tend to cut back on discretionary spending on fashion or gadgets, poorer consumers are likely to continue spending on necessities such as food and soap.[27] However, the definition of this segment varies. Definitions can range from consumers who make less than $6,000 a year to those who make less than $2 a day.[28] Therefore marketers must be clear as to what income level they are actually envisaging when they target this segment.

TARGETING BOTH RICH AND POOR Choosing between rich and poor is not always necessary. Many companies target both richer and poorer segments in the same market, adapting their marketing strategies accordingly. L'Oreal sells its global brand Excellence Cream hair color in India for $11 a bottle. It has also introduced another hair dye priced below $3 targeted at the lower-income Indian consumer.[29] Similarly, Wal-Mart in Mexico targets different income segments with different store chains. Its flagship Wal-Mart Supercenter chain targets Mexicans ranging from the lower middle class to the elite, while its Sam's Club chain targets the upper middle class and elites only, and its Bodega Aurrera chain targets lower-income Mexicans.[30]

Segmenting by Psychographics

Psychographics is the classification of people according to their attitudes, aspirations, worldviews or other psychological criteria. When Starbucks planned its expansion into Colombia they considered the attitudes of possible customers. Many Colombian coffee drinkers were very concerned that much of the coffee available in Colombia came from neighboring countries, since Colombia exported most of the coffee it grew. Starbucks realized that this psychographic segment overlapped with its demographic segment of middle-class urban Colombians. In response, Starbucks decided to offer their Colombian customers coffee that was both grown and roasted in Colombia. To assure its local supply of coffee, the company partnered with U.S. AID to supply local farmers with technical support.[31]

COSMOPOLITANS One psychographic segment that has long been of interest to global marketers is the cosmopolitan segment. Within any country there may be segments that are more open to the idea of buying foreign products as well as possessing the means to do so. Certain segments within a national market may be inclined to purchase global brands because they enhance their self-image of being cosmopolitan, sophisticated and modern.[32] Such cosmopolitans arguably make easier targets for global marketers. Cosmopolitans have often been associated with a younger, urban demographic segment.

Global Segments

The cosmopolitan phenomenon has motivated some global marketers to think in terms of global segments, transnational consumer segments based on age, social class and lifestyle rather than on national culture. Market researcher Euromonitor International undertook a global survey of 16,000 online consumers. The survey included questions relating to personality traits, shopping preferences, green attitudes, technology usage, healthy living habits and eating and drinking behavior. Based on this data, Euromonitor proposed four global segments. The *Undaunted Striver* is trendy, optimistic, empowered and outgoing. The *Savvy Maximizer* is family-oriented, confident, practical and a bargain hunter. The *Content Streamer* is media savvy, price conscious, still forming opinions and a spectator. *Secure Traditionalists* are settled in their ways, comfortable, independent and savers.

The Undaunted Striver may be particularly interesting to global marketers of consumer products because individuals in this segment consider outward appearance to be extremely important and are attracted to brand names and new products. Undaunted Strivers tend to be young, married, working full-time and living in emerging markets such as Brazil, China and India. Thirty-three percent of Brazilian respondents, 41 percent of Chinese respondents and 49 percent of Indian respondents were Undaunted Strivers. This compares to only 4 percent in France and Germany, 13 percent in the United States and only 2 percent in Japan.[33]

Marketing to global segments may still require national adaptions. A study of MBA students representing 38 nationalities revealed cross-cultural similarities in how these students evaluated product quality. The students were young, affluent, mobile, well-educated and fluent in English. Across nationalities and cultural groups, all rated brand names the highest as a cue to product quality. Similarly, all rated retailer reputation the lowest and placed price between the other two cues. The importance of physical appearance of the product did vary among cultures, however.[34] Similarly, a study of American, European and Korean women relating to fashion consumption identified four lifestyle segments across cultures—information seekers, sensation seekers, utilitarian consumers and conspicuous consumers—but cautioned that minor adaptations to marketing strategy would still be necessary across national markets.[35] As these studies show, some—but not all—aspects of buyer behavior may converge across cultures when examining a possible global segment.

World Beat 5.1

Segmenting China

With the Chinese market appearing ever more attractive, global firms are seeking to expand their presence in the country. But a question remains: Which China to target? China is an amalgam of many cultures and different buying behaviors.

In big cities, shoppers are increasingly frequenting global retailers such as Wal-Mart and Carrefour. In villages, consumers shop at small mom-and-pop stores. Many urban Chinese are sophisticated and experienced shoppers while many villagers are still first-time buyers of many products. There are differences across regions and ethnic groups as well. Chinese in the south value personal recognition more than consumers in the north and are less likely to be satisfied with products and services. Compared with the Han majority, Chinese Uyghurs pay more attention to personal recognition and less to quality expectations.

China's luxury segment is of particular interest to many MNCs. China's luxury car market is expected to grow at a rate of 12 percent and soon overtake the United States as the largest luxury car market. But the road to success in China's luxury market can sometimes be bumpy. Swiss makers of luxury watches experienced a downturn in sales when the Chinese government cracked down on illegitimate gift-giving to government officials. Some luxury brands are cautious about sales forecasts concerned that it has become less acceptable for Chinese to display wealth. Other luxury brands face the challenge of becoming passé. One wealthy customer no longer buys Louis Vuitton or Gucci because the brands have become too commonplace.

Sources: Björn Frank, Gulimire Abulaiti and Takao Enkawa, "Regional Differences in Consumer Preference Structures Within China," *Journal of Retailing and Consumer Services*, vol. 21 (2014), pp. 201–210; Melanie Lee, "Super-Rich Turning Away from 'Common' Luxury Labels," *The Vancouver Sun*, June 11, 2012; "Swatch Data to Tick Better in 2014," *The Irish Times*, January 11, 2014, p. 20; and Michael Harvey, "Is the Luxury Car Market Runing Out of Gas?" *The Telegraph*, January 17, 2014.

Just-Like-Us Segmentation

Of course, some marketers simply decide that they will position their product in international markets exactly as it is positioned in the home market. Such a strategy appears easy. Marketers simply sell their product to anyone overseas who wants to buy it as is. They bet on attracting only customers in foreign markets who are the same as those they already serve domestically.

However, targeting the just-like-us segment overseas is likely to result in sales to fewer consumers worldwide and limits a firm's global profit potential. In addition, such a strategy blinds marketers to unique national opportunities. For example, toy stores in China discovered that some of their biggest buyers were adults shopping for themselves. The same proved true for comic books. For some adults it was an excuse to enjoy a childhood they missed first time around when China was much poorer and consumer products were practically nonexistent in the marketplace. For others, it was a way to escape and relax in the very competitive climate of reform-era China.[36] If global toy companies simply targeted children like they would in their home markets, they could miss the adult-market opportunity in China.

DIASPORA MARKETS One phenomenon that supports a just-like-us strategy is the increase in world migration and the size of diasporas. A diaspora is a group of people who live outside their ancestral homeland but who retain a psychological tie to that homeland. Diasporas are larger than ever before. There are 215 million first-generation migrants in the world today. More Chinese people live outside mainland China than French people live in France.[37] Affordable air travel, inexpensive telecommunications and satellite television enable migrants to better stay in touch with their homeland. This opens opportunities for companies in the homelands to target these diasporas. For example, India's Reliance MediaWorks targets Indian immigrants in the United States who regularly watch Bollywood movies.

While overseas, these mobile consumers can be good target markets for products from their homelands. When migrants return to their homelands, they can also be good target markets for products from former host countries. Market researchers note that Central American consumers are faithful purchasers of American products. A large percentage of the population of Central America has lived in the United States at one time, thus increasing their familiarity with American brands.[38]

However, marketers should be wary of treating diasporas simply as just-like-us segments. Some adaptations in pricing, promotion and distribution may be necessary for these markets. Tecate, a Mexican beer brand, targeted first-generation Mexican Americans but adapted its marketing communications to better address the migrant experience, extolling the virtues of blue-collar work and immigrant perseverance.[39]

Business Markets

It is commonly said that business buyers around the world are much more predictable and similar than consumers in their purchasing behavior. They are thought to be more influenced by the economic considerations of cost and product performance and less affected by social and cultural factors. After all, purchasing agents in Japan who are buying specialty steel for their companies will attempt to get the best possible products at the lowest cost, which is similar to how purchasing agents in the United States or Germany would act.

In fact, B2B marketing in the global arena is considerably influenced by variations across cultures. Take, for instance, the offer of a personal gift to a prospective buyer. In Latin America, Europe and the Arab world, offering a gift at first meeting is usually considered inappropriate and may even be construed as a bribe. However, small gifts are often given at first meetings in Japan. In China a carefully chosen gift is interpreted as a sign that the giver values a business relationship.[40]

A number of cross-cultural differences can be observed in buyer motivation and behavior. Because business markets often encompass longer-term relationships between customer and supplier, cultural attitudes toward social relationships are especially important. Sales are often subject to negotiations, and negotiating encompasses many aspects of culture. In addition to dealing with cross-cultural differences, international marketers increasingly find themselves selling to MNCs, whose buyer behavior presents its own set of challenges.

The Business Buyer's Needs

Industrial products, such as machinery, intermediate goods and raw materials, are sold to businesses for use in a manufacturing process to produce other goods. If the objective of the manufacturer is to maximize profits, the critical buying criterion will reflect the performance of the product purchased relative to its cost. This cost–performance criterion is a key consideration for industrial buyers, along with such other buying criteria as the service and dependability of the selling company.

Similar considerations arise in other B2B transactions. A study of how MNCs chose foreign exchange suppliers revealed that price was an important factor in both the selection of a supplier and the volume of business allotted to a supplier. Also, large suppliers were generally preferred over smaller suppliers. Nonetheless, account management and service quality could outweigh price, and customers favored suppliers from their home markets.[41]

Because the cost–performance criterion is often critical, the economic development level of the purchasing country may affect the decision process. This is particularly true for the purchase of new machinery. When buying machinery, a firm must weigh the advantages of adopting a capital-intensive technology against those of adopting a labor-intensive technology. Labor costs can be quite low in developing countries. Therefore, firms in these countries will likely choose the labor-intensive option.

Of course, there are exceptions to this rule. When international banks expanded into the U.A.E they were faced with a decision concerning the level of technology for teller services. In other developing countries, the banks employed older, labor-intensive technology. However, labor in the U.A.E was scarce and expensive as a consequence of the region's sudden oil wealth and its small population. In light of this, many banks chose to purchase the latest technology available from the United States.

The newly industrialized countries of Asia, such as South Korea, Taiwan and Singapore, are becoming increasingly important markets for industrial products. For example, during the 1990s, Asia-Pacific overtook both North America and Europe as the major market for new elevator sales. Still, some differences can be observed in buyer needs and wants in these markets. Business buyers look for long-term commitment from their suppliers. They expect to see foreign firms adapt products to local needs and commit themselves to frequent contact with the buyer. A global competitor should expect to keep a well-stocked warehouse and to locate a technical staff and sales office in the local market. Because many of the industrial buyers in this region are medium-sized firms, they might expect more regular training to be provided over the life of the business relationship. Price can be a critical factor in the sales as well, because many of these businesses work on tight margins. Similarly, special product features that might appeal to buyers in more industrially developed markets are less important in these markets.[42]

Developing Business Relationships

B2B sales usually involve ongoing relationships. The seller and buyer communicate more directly and establish a relationship that continues over time. For example, sales may involve the design and delivery of customized products, or after-sale service may be an important component of the product. These business relationships are based on mutual understanding, past experiences and expectations for the future.

Building such a relationship involves a social exchange process. One firm (usually, but not always, the supplier) takes the initiative and suggests that the two firms do business. If the other firm responds, commitments gradually are made. The parties determine how to coordinate their activities, trust is established and a commitment to a continued relationship arises. The firms may become increasingly interdependent, such as by agreeing to develop a new product together.[43] Because of this close working relationship, cultural sensitivity will be necessary in cases in which seller and buyer come from different cultures.

Although these business relationships have an overall informal character, specific transactions, many of which can be unique to the relationship, will need to be formalized. Because of this, negotiations are often involved in B2B sales. Negotiations encompass not only specifics concerning price and financing terms but also such issues as product design, training and after-sale service.

Cross-cultural negotiations are a particular challenge to global marketers. To begin with, marketers may face the translation problems that we discussed in Chapter 3. Furthermore, whereas some cultures enter negotiations with a win-win attitude, other cultures envisage negotiations as a zero-sum game wherein one side is pitted against the other. Americans can be especially nonplussed when they find themselves negotiating with Russians. Russian negotiators often begin with unreasonable requests in order to test their American counterparts and see how tough they really are. Russian negotiators can surprise Americans with emotional outbursts and anti-Western tirades. Russians also take advantage of Americans' sense of urgency and desire to use time effectively. They may ask the same question repeatedly, feign boredom and even appear to fall asleep during negotiations![44]

Perhaps some of the toughest cross-cultural negotiations took place after China reopened to world trade. Many foreign firms were interested in the potential of the Chinese market. Americans wanted to negotiate clear, legal contracts with Chinese clients and partners. The Chinese, on the other hand, interpreted this approach as betraying a lack of trust on the part of Americans. They sought to establish close relationships with foreign firms based on mutual loyalty. To them a contract was far less important than these relationships. For their part, Americans found the Chinese as irreverent of time as the Russians. Unlike the Russians, the Chinese appeared passive in their demeanor. Any display of anger, frustration or aggression on the part of American negotiators was likely to backfire, and mock tantrums were definitely taboo.[45] Furthermore, many Chinese would appear at the negotiating table, and American negotiators found it difficult to figure out who had real authority to agree to terms. Cross-cultural negotiations frustrated many Americans and discouraged, or at least delayed, their entry into this huge market. In the meantime, competitors from Japan and Asia's overseas Chinese community found the negotiations less culturally harrowing. As a result, many entered the Chinese market more rapidly.

Because negotiations involve many aspects of culture—social relationships, attitudes toward power, perceptions of time and of course language—they must be undertaken with the greatest cultural sensitivity. In most B2B sales, negotiations do not end with the first purchase decision. They permeate the continuing relationship between global marketer and buyer. For this reason, global marketers must never assume that B2B marketing remains the same worldwide.

Marketing to Global Buyers

Global buyers present marketers with new challenges. There are two kinds of global buyers: national global buyers and multinational global buyers.[46] National global buyers search the world for products that are used in a single country or market. Their job has been far easier since the introduction of the Internet. Multinational global buyers similarly search the world for products but use those products throughout their global operations. Such buyers are commonly MNCs, but they also include organizations such as the WHO. Because both national and multinational global buyers are relatively sophisticated about suppliers and prices, competition for their business tends to be intense.

Multinational global buyers in particular may represent large accounts. They use their market power to command better service and even lower prices. Finding cost-effective inputs is increasingly crucial for most MNCs, because they too are often under pressure to deliver good products at a low price. Centralized purchasing is one way in which MNCs attempt to keep costs down. For example, General Motors and three Japanese automakers—Fuji Heavy Industries, Isuzu Motors and Suzuki Motor—announced that they had unified their purchasing organizations for selected parts, components and services in order to reduce costs. GM held equity stakes in the three Japanese firms.[47]

Many Fortune 500 companies have recognized this strategic importance of purchasing and have elevated purchasing managers to the vice-president level within their organizations. Firms that sell to multinational global buyers often give them special attention. Practicing what is called global account management, they assign special account executives and service teams to these valuable but demanding global buyers. We will discuss this further in Chapter 14.

Government Markets

A large number of international business transactions involve governments. Selling to governments can be both time-consuming and frustrating. However, governments are large purchasers, and selling to them can yield enormous returns.

The Buying Process

Governmental buying processes tend to be highly bureaucratic. To sell to the U.S. Department of Defense, for example, a firm has to get on a bidding list for each branch of the armed forces. These bidding lists are issued on an annual basis. A firm that is unable to get on the list must wait a full year to try again. Similarly, negotiating with other governments can be a very long and formal process. The WTO has attempted to make government contracts more transparent and open to foreign bidders. However, only 42 countries are party to this agreement, and the agreement only covers larger government contracts.

As we saw in Chapter 4, governments pursue several different agendas, which often complicate government purchasing. For example, a government might wish to promote its local industry as well as decrease its trade deficit. For these reasons, governments often discriminate against foreign suppliers and give preference to local suppliers. In some sophisticated industries such as aerospace, there may be no viable local competitor in many countries. Then the government might ask potential foreign suppliers to subcontract simpler project inputs to local firms. Alternatively, Saudi Arabia asks major foreign government contractors to invest some of their profits in local Saudi industries.

Global marketers pursuing government sales in high-tech fields may also run afoul of the national agendas of their home countries. The threat of compromising national security has prompted governments, especially that of the United States, to institute restrictions on the overseas sale of certain technologies, such as nuclear plants, computers, telecommunications and military weapons.

Government procurement processes vary from country to country. Here are some strategies global firms might have to consider when bidding on a government contract overseas:

➤ *Source the proposed project with local manufacturing.* As noted above, many countries such as Russia and the UAE still give preference to local suppliers if other things are equal. Governments rarely expect all sourcing to be local, but they can require or prefer that some is. Multinational contractors do not have to establish their own manufacturing facilities in-country if there are competent local suppliers from which to source.

➤ *Partner with a respected local firm or individual.* Even when local agents are not required to bid on a government contract, an esteemed local business partner may help a foreign firm maneuver through the local bureaucracy.

➤ *Commit to training locals.* Companies may be favored if they will employ and train local citizens.

➤ *Be flexible as to pricing.* Governments often appreciate favorable financing terms. Countertrade arrangements, in which a foreign supplier agrees to take partial payment in local goods or services, may be required for some contracts.

➤ *Use the appropriate language.* Although English is sometimes acceptable in bids, the local language may be required or preferred.

➤ *Be patient.* Many different decision-makers may be involved in granting a government contract. This can slow the process.

Government Contracts in Developing Countries

While the procedure for winning a major government contract can be lengthy, it can be particularly so in developing countries. There are five "screens" that global marketers must pass through to secure large government contracts in developing countries.[48]

Eligibility Screen

A foreign firm must first address the eligibility screen. To make the bidding process efficient and manageable, governments seek to weed out firms that are not serious or are too small to handle the contract. For example, Saudi Arabia may ask bidders on a contract to submit a $100,000 fee with their bid or to provide a bond for 1 percent of the tender value, and the Malaysian government expects top management to be actively involved in the process as a sign of the firm's long-term commitment to the market.[49] Alternatively, governments may simply restrict the bidding to several well-known international firms that are invited to bid on a particular project. This approach is common in the defense and civil aviation industries.

If the project is complicated or represents a new task for the purchasing government, outside consultants may be employed to design the project and oversee its implementation. For example,

Bechtel, a large U.S. engineering firm, could be hired as a consultant for complex construction projects. As a result, Bechtel's designs are more likely to follow U.S. industry standards, and this gives U.S. firms a competitive advantage when bidding on the contract.

Political considerations can play a role at this stage as well. For example, China is now the world's largest arms importer, ahead of India, Turkey, Taiwan and Saudi Arabia. Ninety percent of Chinese arms imports are from Russia.[50] Russian armament firms are considered by the Chinese to be more reliable than American ones, because U.S. firms could at any time be forbidden by the U.S. government to enter into or fulfill a contract with China.

Procedural Screen

After passing the eligibility screen, the foreign firm encounters the procedural screen. The procedural screen encompasses bureaucratic procedures that must be followed and numerous forms that need to be properly filled out. This can be all the more difficult because the process may not be overt. In Mexico, bids may be disqualified if they fail to address minute technical details.[51] It is suggested that firms seeking government contracts in Brazil be patient, establish significant in-country presence and budget considerable financial resources in order to respond to legal challenges and bureaucratic delays.[52] The firm may need to take special care to discover who is actually in charge and to understand exactly what needs to be done. Laws and procedures can and often do change. Hiring local consultants who have had experience with the process is often a good idea.

Linkage Screen

The firm must then negotiate the linkage screen. It must address and implement the various government requirements related to assisting local businesses. This can include finding a local partner with whom to establish a joint venture. Alternatively, it might involve finding local suppliers to outsource a portion of the contract. For example, Abu Dhabi and Dubai, two oil-rich Arab states, have asked Airbus and Boeing for commitments to outsource some of their parts production to local firms in return for billions of dollars' worth of jetliner sales.[53]

Competitive Screen

After passing through these three screens, the firm must still face the competitive screen. Passing this screen involves bidding a competitive price. In most cases, competitive bids will be determined not only by the profit each firm seeks to capture but the different product-service offerings proposed by each competitor. In some cases, governments will pay more for higher quality and elite features. In other cases, governments may focus more on low price. For example, the U.S. Commercial Service alerts U.S. firms that government employees in Egypt are judged on their ability to squeeze the final penny from the lowest bidder.[54] In addition to price, the firm's reputation, its past experience in developing countries and its cultural sensitivity are also important. Because large projects can take several years to negotiate and many years to implement, the firm must exhibit an ability to be flexible as situations evolve and change.

World Beat 5.2

Avon Bribing

Nine years after an internal audit at Avon suggested that questionable payments had been made in its Chinese subsidiary, the direct-sales cosmetics company had incurred $340 million in legal and other expenses related to its ongoing bribery investigation. In addition, the company was facing an estimated $132 million fine for U.S. Foreign Corrupt Practices Act (FCPA) infractions. The company's first offer to settle for $12 million was rejected as being far too low.

The investigation was instigated by an employee who wrote to the company's CEO, Andrea Jung, alleging improper conduct. Several years later, Avon disclosed to the Security Exchange Commission (SEC) that it had fired its head of global internal audit and security along with three top Chinese executives because of bribes that included improper travel and entertainment expenses. It also expanded internal investigation to other regions including Latin America where the company garnered its greatest sales and profits.

Concerns about Avon's behavior in emerging markets were reflected in the price of Avon stock. Its value had declined by over 50 percent. More Avon executives lost their jobs. The company's directors debated whether to fire Ms. Jung. The bribery probe was making her marketing background look more like a liability than an asset. They eventually decided to remove her as CEO but to retain her as chairman, stating that she had become the well-known face of the company.

Sources: Ellen Byron, "Avon Bribe Investigation Widens," *Wall Street Journal Online*, May 5, 2011; Lauren Coleman-Lochner, "Avon's Andrea Jung Exit Marks End of Era at Cosmetics Retailer," *Bloomberg*, October 5, 2012; Joe Palazzolo and Joann S. Lubin, "Avon Fires Vice Chairman," *Wall Street Journal Online*, January 31, 2012; and Joann S. Lubin, Joe Palazzolo and Serena Ng, "Avon Near Settling U.S. Probe of Bribery," *Wall Street Journal*, February 13, 2014, p. B1.

Firms may even be asked to help finance the project they bid on. One Indian state sought highway contractors that would agree to operate the roads as private concerns before turning them over to the state. In lieu of direct payment from the government for building the highways, the contractors could collect tolls for ten years.[55]

Influence Screen

The final hurdle, the influence screen, requires a firm to identify the different decision-makers and to be sure it meets the needs of each. This involves political mapping that we discussed in Chapter 4. For example, selling radar to the Taiwanese may involve high officers in the air force who are pursuing a defense agenda. However, the ministry of industry may be involved as well. It may be pursuing an agenda of technology transfer and local outsourcing. The firm must be sure to address all these concerns. Managing this process is challenging for global marketers, but winning a large and attractive contract can make it all worthwhile.

Bribery and Government Markets

Pfizer, the world's leading pharmaceutical company by sales, was accused of bribing doctors, hospital administrators and regulators in several countries in Europe and Asia to prescribe Pfizer drugs. The company agreed to pay $60.2 million to settle a U.S. federal investigation into its overseas bribery.[56] German multinational Siemens agreed to pay a record $1.6 billion to U.S. and European authorities to settle bribery cases involving government infrastructure contracts worldwide.[57] Since the bribery allegations involved some projects financed by the World Bank, Siemens also settled with that institution by recusing themselves from bidding on any World Bank project for two years and agreeing to pay an additional $100 million to assist in anti-bribery efforts.[58]

Bribery is the giving of something of value to an individual in a position of trust to influence their judgment or behavior. Bribes can be offered to purchasing agents or other decision-makers within private-sector companies to induce them to favor one supplier over another. Most bribery scandals in global marketing, however, involve government contracts. Government employees are in a particular position of trust because they are hired to work for the public good. If a government is awarding an aerospace contract, the government employees responsible for choosing the supplier should consider the value of the supplier to the country as a whole. If a key decision-maker influences the decision for his or her personal gain, then public trust is betrayed. Bribes offered to win contracts are most common in industries where contracts are large and where few public employees are involved in the award decision.

Bribery is more endemic in less developed countries. One study confirmed that a country's PCI is the best barometer of the level of government bribery (corruption) in that country. The same study also showed that bribery is more prevalent in countries that score higher on the Hofstede power-distance dimension.[59] Table 5.5 lists ratings by country on an index of perceived corruption with Denmark (#1) ranking the least corrupt and Somalia (#175) ranking the most corrupt.

Although most developing countries seek foreign investment for economic growth, several studies have found that governmental corruption is a serious obstacle to foreign investment in a country. The difference in corruption levels between host and home countries affects investment as well: corruption significantly reduces investment from less corrupt countries.[60] Another study found that foreign entrants into national markets chose joint ventures more often than wholly owned subsidiaries as the level of corruption increased.[61]

U.S. Foreign Corrupt Practices Act

All countries outlaw the bribing of their own government officials. In the late 1970s, the United States went a step further and outlawed the bribing of foreign officials. Until then, American firms that bribed foreign officials were not prosecuted under U.S. law, even though U.S. law disallowed claiming foreign bribes as tax deductions. This resulted in many MNCs keeping records of these bribes for their tax accountants. When government investigators were searching for illegal contributions to President Nixon's reelection fund, they discovered many such entries in company books.

The American public was dismayed. Despite heavy business lobbying against its passage, the U.S. Foreign Corrupt Practices Act (FCPA) was passed in 1977. This law forbids U.S. citizens to bribe foreign government employees and politicians. U.S. citizens are also forbidden to pay money to agents or other individuals who in turn pass money on to government employees. In short,

Table 5.5 Corruption Perception Index (CPI)

Rank	Country/Territory	Score	Rank	Country/Territory	Score	Rank	Country/Territory	Score
1	Denmark	91	45	Malta	56	83	Trinidad and Tobago	38
2	New Zealand	91	46	Korea (South)	55	83	Zambia	38
3	Finland	89	47	Hungary	54	91	Malawi	37
3	Sweden	89	47	Seychelles	54	91	Morocco	37
5	Norway	86	49	Costa Rica	53	91	Sri Lanka	37
5	Singapore	86	49	Latvia	53	94	Algeria	36
7	Switzerland	85	49	Rwanda	53	94	Armenia	36
8	Netherlands	83	52	Mauritius	52	94	Benin	36
9	Australia	81	53	Malaysia	50	94	Colombia	36
9	Canada	81	53	Turkey	50	94	Djibouti	36
11	Luxembourg	80	55	Georgia	49	94	India	36
12	Germany	78	55	Lesotho	49	94	Philippines	36
12	Iceland	78	57	Bahrain	48	94	Suriname	36
14	United Kingdom	76	57	Croatia	48	102	Ecuador	35
15	Barbados	75	57	Czech Republic	48	102	Moldova	35
15	Belgium	75	57	Namibia	48	102	Panama	35
15	Hong Kong	75	61	Oman	47	102	Thailand	35
18	Japan	74	61	Slovakia	47	106	Argentina	34
19	United States	73	63	Cuba	46	106	Bolivia	34
19	Uruguay	73	63	Ghana	46	106	Gabon	34
21	Ireland	72	63	Saudi Arabia	46	106	Mexico	34
22	Bahamas	71	66	Jordan	45	106	Niger	34
22	Chile	71	67	Macedonia (FYR)	44	111	Ethiopia	33
22	France	71	67	Montenegro	44	111	Kosovo	33
22	Saint Lucia	71	69	Italy	43	111	Tanzania	33
26	Austria	69	69	Kuwait	43	114	Egypt	32
26	United Arab Emirates	69	69	Romania	43	114	Indonesia	32
28	Estonia	68	72	Bosnia and Herzegovina	42	116	Albania	31
28	Qatar	68	72	Brazil	42	116	Nepal	31
30	Botswana	64	72	Sao Tome and Principe	42	116	Vietnam	31
31	Bhutan	63	72	Serbia	42	119	Mauritania	30
31	Cyprus	63	72	South Africa	42	119	Mozambique	30
33	Portugal	62	77	Bulgaria	41	119	Sierra Leone	30
33	Puerto Rico	62	77	Senegal	41	119	Timor-Leste	30
33	Saint Vincent	62	77	Tunisia	41	123	Belarus	29
36	Israel	61	80	China	40	123	Dominican Republic	29
36	Taiwan	61	80	Greece	40	123	Guatemala	29
38	Brunei	60	82	Swaziland	39	123	Togo	29
38	Poland	60	83	Burkina Faso	38	127	Azerbaijan	28
40	Spain	59	83	El Salvador	38	127	Comoros	28
41	Cape Verde	58	83	Jamaica	38	127	Gambia	28
41	Dominica	58	83	Liberia	38	127	Lebanon	28
43	Lithuania	57	83	Mongolia	38	127	Madagascar	28
43	Slovenia	57	83	Peru	38	127	Mali	28

Rank	Country/Territory	Score	Rank	Country/Territory	Score	Rank	Country/Territory	Score
127	Nicaragua	28	144	Papua New Guinea	25	163	Chad	19
127	Pakistan	28	144	Ukraine	25	163	Equatorial Guinea	19
127	Russia	28	150	Guinea	24	163	Guinea-Bissau	19
136	Bangladesh	27	150	Kyrgyzstan	24	163	Haiti	19
136	Cote d'Ivoire	27	150	Paraguay	24	167	Yemen	18
136	Guyana	27	153	Angola	23	168	Syria	17
136	Kenya	27	154	Congo Republic	22	168	Turkmenistan	17
140	Honduras	26	154	Dem. Rep. of the Congo	22	168	Uzbekistan	17
140	Kazakhstan	26	154	Tajikistan	22	171	Iraq	16
140	Laos	26	157	Burundi	21	172	Libya	15
140	Uganda	26	157	Myanmar	21	173	South Sudan	14
144	Cameroon	25	157	Zimbabwe	21	174	Sudan	11
144	Central African Republic	25	160	Cambodia	20	175	Afghanistan	8
144	Iran	25	160	Eritrea	20	175	Korea (North)	8
144	Nigeria	25	160	Venezuela	20	175	Somalia	8

Source: 2013, Transparency International. © Transparency International. All Rights Reserved. For more information, visit www.transparency.org.

American companies are held accountable for agents that bribe. Titan corporation paid $28.5 million in fines for failing to properly supervise and control 120 agents working in 60 countries.[62] In addition, U.S. citizens are required to report any bribery occurring within their organizations and must not cover it up. The firm itself is required to keep good records. If audited, it must be able to account for all payments overseas. Fines are assessed for noncompliance.

Furthermore, managers can face jail sentences. A former chairman of Kellogg, Brown & Root received a seven-year prison sentence.[63] Although originally envisaged as a deterrent to U.S. citizens, the FCPA has been increasingly interpreted in such a way as to prosecute non-U.S. citizens as well. For example, a Swiss lawyer was indicted in the United States for conspiring to bribe foreign officials in connection with a failed $450 million Caspian Sea oil deal.[64]

U.S. firms are allowed to make expediting payments under the FCPA, however. Expediting, or facilitating, payments are small sums paid to civil servants to do their jobs. For example, if office computers were sitting at customs and not being processed, an expediting payment might speed up the paperwork. Some firms have refused to participate in facilitating payments. Procter & Gamble refused to do so when entering Brazil, despite the prevalence of such payments there. One P&G manager recalls that government employees soon learned not even to ask the firm for such payments. But many others accept facilitating payments as part of doing business abroad. Two MNCs, Unilever and BP Amoco, admitted in parliamentary hearings in London that their managers made facilitating payments in developing countries. The counsel for Unilever said that these payments were not encouraged, but they were tolerated as long as they were small and were used to expedite something that would have happened eventually. The general auditor of BP Amoco said the payments were made to avoid delays and not to gain an unfair advantage over competitors.[65]

Despite the acceptance of expediting payments under the FCPA, some firms can and have been prosecuted under the law because of them. This may occur if such payments are unusually high or are used to gain a competitive advantage.[66] Wal-Mart came under scrutiny when an internal audit revealed that the company's expediting payments in Mexico totaled $24 million over several years. Wal-Mart Mexico paid $156,000 to facilitate building permissions from the Urban Development Ministry and $273,000 in bribes to local officials and managers of a power company to expedite construction projects. In addition, the company paid more than $117,000 to an energy company to jump ahead of other customers to get power for a distribution center outside Mexico City.[67] Similarly, Ralph Lauren Corporation agreed to pay $1.6 million in fines under the FCPA for bribing Argentine customs officials with dresses, perfume and cash to expedite the passage of its merchandise through customs. Some of the items were valued as high as $22,500.

Many U.S. businesses feared that the FCPA would put them at a competitive disadvantage overseas, especially in emerging markets, because other competitor nations had not adopted a similar law. The law no doubt has been a handicap in some cases, but overall it does not appear to have undermined U.S. exports to bribe-prone countries. The law may have helped U.S. managers in one respect: it has kept them out of jail overseas. A study of bribery scandals in the Middle East over a period of nearly 20 years revealed no American having been imprisoned for bribing a government official. This was in contrast to the experiences of Asians and Europeans.[68]

The Travel Act

The Travel Act is a U.S. federal law that has recently been used as a complementary statute in prosecuting companies under the FCPA. Broadly interpreted, this law criminalizes acts overseas that are illegal in the United States as long as travel or telecommunications are employed in any way. California-based Control Component Inc. pleaded guilty of bribing not only government officials abroad but of also bribing individuals in private-sector companies abroad. Bribing private-sector actors did not fall under the jurisdiction of the FCPA but did fall under the jurisdiction of the Travel Act because private-sector bribery is outlawed under California law.[69]

Other Anti-Bribery Conventions and Laws

In 1997, 34 nations signed an anti-bribery pact. Under the agreement, the member countries agreed to propose to their parliaments national laws designed to combat overseas bribery. Fifteen years later, 40 countries had ratified or acceded to the convention. Similarly, the United Nations Convention against Corruption was signed in December 2003. Signatories include most member countries of the United Nations. The convention aims at encouraging the recovery of funds moved overseas by corrupt officials and was prompted by developing countries anxious to recover such funds.[70]

The efficacy of these multilateral agreements has been controversial. Germany embarked on a number of major overseas bribery investigations of its MNCs. However, watchdog organization Transparency International published a report concluding that only one-third of OECD (Organization for Economic Co-operation and Development) member states had taken significant action to enforce anti-bribery laws. It identified Britain, Canada, Italy, Japan and the Netherlands as falling particularly short.[71] Some non-U.S. executives have complained that they are now targeted in FCPA investigations because Washington believes that their home countries are not seriously combating corruption despite the new anti-bribery conventions.[72]

However, the British Bribery Act of 2010 (referred to by some as the FCPA on steroids) actually surpasses the FCPA for restrictions on overseas bribery. The Bribery Act covers any company that conducts business in Britain irrespective of where the company is based or where the bribery takes place. In addition to outlawing bribes to government officials, the Bribery Act outlaws bribes that occur between private-sector actors.[73] It also forbids expediting payments that are often acceptable under the FCPA.[74]

Table 5.6 ranks 28 leading exporting countries based on the perceptions of business executives as to the propensity of firms from those countries to engage in bribery, with zero representing the

Table 5.6 Bribe Payers Index

Rank	Country/Territory	BPI 2011 Score
1	Netherlands	8.8
1	Switzerland	8.8
3	Belgium	8.7
4	Germany	8.6
4	Japan	8.6
6	Australia	8.5
6	Canada	8.5
8	Singapore	8.3
8	UK	8.3
10	USA	8.1
11	France	8.0
11	Spain	8.0
13	South Korea	7.9
14	Brazil	7.7
15	Hong Kong	7.6
15	Italy	7.6
15	Malaysia	7.6
15	South Africa	7.6
19	Taiwan	7.5
19	India	7.5
19	Turkey	7.5
22	Saudi Arabia	7.4
23	Argentina	7.3
23	UAE	7.3
25	Indonesia	7.1
26	Mexico	7.0
27	China	6.5
28	Russia	6.1
	Average	7.8

Source: 2012, Transparency International. © Transparency International. All Rights Reserved. For more information, visit www.transparency.org.

worst bribery and ten representing no bribery. Overall, firms from developed countries are perceived as being less prone to bribery than those from developing countries. In some cases, however, the difference is arguably small.

Conclusion

In this chapter we introduced some basic issues of buyer behavior across cultures. We showed that buyers in various national markets can exhibit similar needs, wants and even behaviors. In many ways, however, buyers differ from one culture to another. This is true whether the buyer is a consumer, a business or a government. The challenge to the global marketer is to understand when it is possible to exploit similar needs and behaviors and when it is important to adapt to different buyer conditions. In addition, we observed that many buyers increasingly search the world for products. This intensifies competition and makes it all the more imperative that global marketers understand their markets and address the needs of their buyers.

Managerial Takeaways

1. *A whole national market rarely matters to a global marketer. What matters is an attractive segment of that market.*
2. *Global segments sometimes exist but vary in size from country to country. And some national adaptations are still necessary to reach these segments.*
3. *MNCs operating in developing countries no longer rely on only elites as customers. Rising incomes worldwide have created new opportunities for targeting middle classes and the poor. But different marketing strategies are necessary for reaching these different segments.*
4. *Culture affects B2B marketing as well as consumer marketing. Global marketers must remember that selling to businesses requires cross-cultural negotiations and relationship building as well as knowledge of how decisions are made within companies overseas.*
5. *Government markets, particularly those in developing countries, may be subject to various government agendas. A global marketer seeking a government contract must be adept at addressing these agendas.*
6. *Bribery is a bad idea. Most bribes hurt innocent people, and the costs of bribery can be astronomical to a MNC. If you bribe, your chances of getting caught have never been higher and the jail sentences have never been longer.*

Questions for Discussion

1. What critical factors influence a consumer's ability to purchase a product such as a stereo system?
2. How might segmenting by country be useful to global marketers of cosmetics? What could limit the usefulness of such segmentation?

3. As noted in the chapter, there are significant country differences as to the size of Euromonitor's *Undaunted Striver* global segment. What could explain these national differences?

4. Will the buying process be more similar from country to country for deodorant or delivery vans? Why?

5. If you were selling a product that is purchased mostly by governments, such as a nuclear power plant, how would you prepare to sell to Belgium, Egypt and Mexico? What means would you use to understand the government buying process in each of these countries?

6. Why do you think that the U.S. Foreign Corrupt Practices Act allows expediting payments? Why are these payments seen as less reprehensible than other forms of bribery?

CASE 5.1   Diaspora Marketing

Globalization has given rise not only to an accelerated flow of goods and services around the world, but it has also fostered dramatic increases in the movements of people across borders. A diaspora is defined as any body of people living outside their traditional homeland. Thus a diaspora is comprised of migrants and their descendants who maintain a relationship to their country of origin. This broader definition reflects the changing magnitude and nature of global migration. Since 1975, world migration has more than doubled. Many migrants have emigrated from a developing country to a developed country. One in ten persons living in a developed country today is a migrant.

Diasporans, individuals living in the diaspora, are able to remain connected to their countries of origin more easily and cheaply than ever before, reinforcing and strengthening their group identity. Innovations in transportation and communication technologies now allow migrants to psychologically and physically connect with their countries of origin in ways that were virtually unimaginable in the past. Declining costs in air and other transportation modes make it easier for immigrants and their descendants to visit their countries of origin. Global media provide immigrants with a constant stream of information about their origin countries. Ethnic bulletin boards, cyber communities and e-commerce sites on the Internet offer immigrants an opportunity to socially connect not just with each other but also with family, friends and other individuals in their country of origin.

Savvy global marketers are beginning to recognize and unlock the marketing potential of diasporas in several different ways. For example, many diasporans long for the products or services produced in their home countries. On Tulumba's online marketplace (www.tulumba.com), Turkish diasporans can satisfy their craving for Turkish food products, like *simit* and *mantı*, purchase Turkish books, music and movies, and even acquire Evil Eye jewelry. Fast-food giant, Jollibee, often actively selects its overseas locations near high concentrations of Filipino migrants. The company website (www.jollibee.com.ph/) describes the importance of Jollibee for overseas Filipinos as "more than home for them. It is a stronghold of heritage and a monument of Filipino victory."

Thamel.com's web portal (www.Thamel.com) allows Nepalese diasporans to purchase goods and services online from Nepalese suppliers and have them delivered to the homes of friends and family living in Nepal. After a huge success selling more traditional items, such as flowers, cakes and CDs, the company has expanded its product line to enable Nepalese diasporans to purchase health insurance, arrange for limousine service, finance automobiles and household durables or pay tuition, utility or other bills for friends and family in Nepal.

Diasporans often visit friends or family back in their countries of origin or simply travel to learn about their cultural heritage. Wizz Air (http://wizzair.com/) is a low-cost travel airline targeting the nearly 1 million Eastern Europeans who have moved to Western European nations since the 2004 EU expansion. Many travel agencies are offering "cultural heritage tours" to diaspora groups. For example, the African-American Travel Agency (www.africanamericantravelagency.com/) offers educational tours for African Americans who want to "learn about the African presence in Brazil."

Diasporans are important for nongovernmental organizations (NGOs) and government marketing efforts too. To raise resources for relief efforts following an Asian tsunami, NGOs actively targeted the Indian, Thai, Indonesian and Sri Lankan diasporas. And the Armenian government partnered with Armenian diaspora groups around the world. Coptic Orphans (www.copticorphans.org/) is an example of an NGO fully supported by a diaspora community. Through its fundraising efforts among Egyptians living in the U.S. of the Coptic Christian faith, Coptic Orphans provides tuition, tutoring and other services to Coptic children in Egypt. Numerous governments and diaspora organizations have put on investment-promotion events for diaspora communities living abroad to encourage them to invest in existing companies or start new businesses in their country of origin.

Discussion Questions

1. How and why might diasporans' ability to buy differ from individuals of a similar age who remained in their country of origin or homeland?
2. Referring to Maslow's hierarchy of needs, identify and describe the level of needs that the companies featured in this case (e.g. Tulumba, Jollibee, Thamel.com, Wizz Air, the African American Travel Agency and Coptic Orphans) fill for the diasporans who purchase products and services from them.
3. Are the companies featured in this case (e.g. Tulumba, Jollibee, Thamel.com, Wizz Air, the African American Travel Agency and Coptic Orphans) targeting a *global segment* when they target their diaspora communities? Why or why not?

Source: Prepared by Liesl Riddle. Used by permission.

CASE 5.2   Questionable Payments

Scenario 1: Thomas Karel is a Swiss national who works as the export manager for a major U.S. producer of machinery and software systems for petroleum exploration. His company is bidding on a $50 million contract that could produce $10 million in profit for his firm. The potential customer is the state-owned oil company in a Latin American country. Thomas has recently heard from his company's agent in that country. The agent suggests that he can assure the contract if Thomas will give him $2 million to pass on to an influential cabinet member in charge of awarding the contract. The competition, a French MNC, is also bidding on the contract. *What should Thomas do?*

Scenario 2: David Yang has been sent to a country in Southeast Asia to negotiate the possible sale of a large-scale traffic control system to be adopted across the country. The contract involves not only traffic lights but also their installation and servicing, as well as computer software to monitor traffic flows. Another American in the country has suggested to David that he retain the public relations firm owned by the wife of the country's prime minister. The prime minister is not directly involved with the negotiations for the traffic control system. *What should David do?*

Scenario 3: Michael Avila is the general manager of a subsidiary of an American shipping company in the Middle East. His company specializes in moving the household belongings of expatriates working for MNCs. Michael is about to authorize the monthly slush fund for payments to customs officials to expedite the movement of his clients' goods through customs when he catches sight of an article in the local newspaper. The government has announced a crackdown on corruption. *What should Michael do?*

Scenario 4: Ana Weiss is the new general manager of DeluxDye in Taiwan. DeluxDye produces high-quality industrial paints and dyes that are used in the manufacture of such products as toys and housewares. Compared to competitors' products, DeluxDye products are relatively expensive to purchase. However, they save costs over the long run. Their higher quality ensures more consistent color and performance and less manufacturing downtime. The money customers save can more than make up for the higher initial price of the product.

Corporate guidelines, established in the United States, forbid the paying of any bribes, however small. In Taiwan, Ana's sales force is complaining that their inability to offer "tea money" is discouraging sales growth in the market. Tea money consists of small cash payments or gifts, such as tickets to rock concerts or sports events. These payments are often given to lower-level employees who act as gatekeepers to the higher-level manager—often the head of one of Taiwan's many family-owned manufacturing firms—who in turn makes the buying decision. DeluxDye believes its products are superior to those of its competitors and insists that its sales forces around the world promote the product on its merits alone. Bribery is immoral, and it casts doubts on the integrity of the briber. *What should Ana do?*

Discussion Questions

1. Explain and defend a course of action for each of the managers above.
2. When considering questionable payments, should marketers emphasize ethical concerns, legal considerations or making the sale? Explain your answer.

Notes

1 Brendan M. Case, "Latin Flavor Brewing," *Dallas Morning News*, March 26, 2002, p. 1D.
2 Brian Dumaine, "P&G Rewrites the Rules of Marketing," *Fortune*, November 6, 1989, p. 48.
3 Euromonitor Passport accessed April 4, 2014 and CIA Factbook accessed April 16, 2014.
4 Andrew Batson, "China Narrows Inequality Between the Rich and Poor," *Wall Street Journal*, February 3, 2010, p. A13.
5 Jean-Claude Usunier, *Marketing Across Cultures* (New York: Prentice-Hall, 2000), p. 104.

6   Julie, J. Li and Chenting Su, "How Face Influences Consumption," *International Journal of Market Research*, vol. 49, no. 2 (2007), pp. 237–256.

7   David McHardy Reid, "Consumer Change in Japan: A Longitudinal Study," *Thunderbird International Business Review*, vol. 49, no. 1 (2007), pp. 77–101.

8   Michael Fielding, "Special Delivery: UPS Conducts Surveys to Help Customers Export to China," *Marketing News*, February 1, 2007, pp. 14–15.

9   Joseph T. Hallinan, "Imported Beers Win Converts in the Heartland," *Wall Street Journal*, July 25, 2006, p. B1.

10 Margot Cohen, "Urban Vietnamese Get Rich Quick," *Wall Street Journal*, October 26, 2004, p. A22.

11 Loretta Chao, "PC Makers Cultivate Buyers in Rural China," Dow Jones Chinese Financial Wire, September 23, 2009.

12 Ibid.

13 Eric Bellman, "Cellphone Entertainment Takes Off in Rural India," *Wall Street Journal*, November 23, 2009, p. B1

14 Eric Bellman, "Suzuki's Stylish Compacts Captivate India's Women," *Wall Street Journal*, May 11, 2007, p. B1.

15 Christina Passariello, "Dior to Unveil Line of Mobile Phones," *Wall Street Journal*, May 21, 2008, p. B9.

16 "In China, Women Begin Splurging," Dow Jones Chinese Financial Wire, June 12, 2011.

17 Gail Edmondson, Paulo Prada and Karen Nickel Anhalt, "Lexus: Still Looking for Traction in Europe," *Business Week*, November 17, 2003, p. 122.

18 David Brooks, "Ben Franklin's Nation," *New York Times Online*, December 13, 2010.

19 Norihiko Shirouzu, "Sweet Spot for Car Firms in China," *Wall Street Journal*, May 10, 2010, p. B1.

20 Sarah Boumphrey and Eileen Bevis, "Reaching the Emerging Middle Classes Beyond BRIC," Euromonitor International, 2013, p. 11.

21 Lois Rene Berman and Sakina Balde, "Business Opportunities and Challenges in Africa," Euromonitor International, 2013, p. 2

22 Hernando de Soto, "The Secret to Reviving the Arab Spring's Promises," *Wall Street Journal*, February 27, 2013, p. A13.

23 Krista Hughes, "Mexico Aims to Bring Shadow Economy into Light," Reuters, June 6, 2013.

24 C.K. Prahalad, *The Fortune at the Bottom of the Pyramid: Eradicating Poverty through Profits* (Upper Saddle River, NJ: Wharton School Publishing, 2004).

25 Van R. Wood, Dennis A. Pitta and Frank F. Franzak, "Successful Marketing by Multinational Firms to the Bottom of the Pyramid: Connecting Share of Heart, Global 'Umbrella Brands', and Responsible Marketing," *Journal of Consumer Marketing*, vol. 25, no. 7 (2008), p. 421.

26 John Ireland, "Lessons for Successful BOP Marketing from Caracas' Slums," *Journal of Consumer Marketing*, vol. 25, no. 7 (2008), pp. 430–438.

27 Eric Bellman, "Multinationals Market to the Poor," *Wall Street Journal*, July 24, 2012.

28 Annel Karnani, "The Mirage of the Bottom of the Pyramid: How the Private Sector Can Help Alleviate Poverty," *California Business Review*, vol. 49, no. 4 (Summer 2007); and C.K. Prahalad and Allen Hammond, "Selling to the Poor," *Foreign Policy* (May/June 2004).

29 Christina Passariello, "Beauty Fix," *Wall Street Journal*, July 13, 2007, p. A1.

30 Wal-Mart de Mexico Social Responsibility and Sustainable Development, 2007 Annual Report, p. 9.

31 Julie Jargon, "Starbucks to Serve Locally Grown Coffee in Colombia," *Wall Street Journal Online*, August 26, 2013.

32 Jan-Benedict E.M. Steenkamp, Rajeev Batra and Dana L. Alden, "How Perceived Brand Globalness Creates Brand Value," *Journal of International Business Studies*, vol. 34, no. 1 (2003), pp. 53–65.

33 Eileen Bevis and Lisa Holmes, "Four Consumer Types to Optimize Marketing Strategy," Euromonitor International, 2014.

34 Niraj Dawar and Philip Parker, "Marketing Universals: Consumers' Use of Brand Name, Price, Physical Appearance, and Retailer Reputation as Signals of Product Quality," *Journal of Marketing*, vol. 58, no. 2 (April 1994), pp. 81–95.

35 Eunji Ko, Eunyoung Kim, Charles R. Taylor, Kyung Hoon Kim and Ie Jeong Knag, "Cross-National Market Segmentation in the Fashion Industry," *International Marketing Review*, vol. 24, no. 5 (2007), pp. 629–651.

36 Leslie Chang, "In China, Adults Find Comfort as Toys Become More Available," *Wall Street Journal*, September 12, 2002, p. A13.

37 "Weaving the World Together," *The Economist*, November 19, 2011.

38 Michael Fielding, "Explore New Territory," *Marketing News*, March 1, 2007, p. 26.

39 Nirmalya Kumar and Jan-Benedict E.M. Steenkamp, "Diaspora Marketing," *Harvard Business Review*, October 2013, pp. 127–131.

40 Allen K.K. Chan, Luther Denton and Alex S.L. Tsang, "The Art of Gift Giving in China," *Business Horizons* (July–August, 2003), pp. 47–52.

41 Douglas Bowman, John U. Farley and David C. Schmittlein, "Cross-National Empirical Generalization in Business Services Buyer Behavior," *Journal of International Business Studies*, vol. 31, no. 4 (2000), pp. 667–685.

42 Lawrence H. Wortzel, "Marketing to Firms in Developing Asian Countries," *Industrial Marketing Management*, vol. 12 (1983), pp. 113–123.

43 Desirée Blankenburg Holm, Kent Eriksson and Jan Johanson, "Business Networks and Cooperation in International Business Relationships," *Journal of International Business Studies*, vol. 27 (1996), pp. 1033–1053.

44 James K. Sebenius, Rebecca Green and Randall Fine, "Doing Business in Russia: Negotiating in the Wild East," Harvard Business School, Note #9–899–048 1999, pp. 6–7.

45 John L. Graham and N. Mark Lam, "The Chinese Negotiation," *Harvard Business Review*, October 2003, pp. 82–91.

46 George S. Yip, *Total Global Strategy II* (Englewood Cliffs, NJ: Prentice-Hall, 2003), pp. 36–39.

47 "GM Network Unifies Auto Parts Buys," Dow Jones Newswire, June 11, 2002.

48 Mushtaq Luqmani, Ghazi M. Habib and Sami Kassem, "Marketing to LDC Governments," *International Marketing Review*, vol. 5, no.1 (Spring 1988), pp. 56–67.

49 U.S. Commercial Service, Malaysia Country Commercial Guide, 2009.

50 David Lague and Susan V. Lawrence, "China's Russian-Arms Spree," *Wall Street Journal*, December 10, 2002, p. A15.

51 U.S. Commercial Service, Mexico Country Commercial Guide, 2013.

52 U.S. Commercial Service, Brazil Country Commercial Guide, 2013.

53 Stefania Bianchi, "Mideast Widens Aircraft Ventures," *Wall Street Journal*, July 30, 2008, p. B2.

54 U.S. Commercial Service, Egypt Country Commercial Guide, 2012.

55 Daniel Pearl, "In India, Roads Become All the Rage," *Wall Street Journal*, January 3, 2001, p. A10.

56 Jonathan D. Rockoff and Christopher M. Matthews, "Pfizer Settles Federal Bribery Investigation," *Wall Street Journal Online*, August 7, 2012.

57 Bruce Watson, "Siemens and the Battle Against Bribery and Corruption," *The Guardian*, September 18, 2013.

58 Vanessa Fuhrmans, "Siemens Settles with World Bank on Bribes," *Wall Street Journal*, July 3, 2009, p. B1.

59 Bryan W. Husted, "Wealth, Culture, and Corruption," *Journal of International Business Studies*, vol. 30, no. 2 (1999), pp. 339–359.

60 Mohsin Habib and Leon Zurawicki, "Corruption and Foreign Direct Investment," *Journal of International Business Studies*, vol. 33, no. 2 (2002), pp. 291–307.

61 Jonathan P. Doh, Peter Rodriguez, Klaus Uhlenbruck, Jamie Collins and Lorraine Eden, "Coping with Corruption in Foreign Markets," *Academy of Management Executive*, vol. 17, no. 3 (2003), pp. 114–127.

62 Benjamin Norris, "Don't Ignore the FCPA," *Journal of Commerce*, February 27, 2006.

63 Russell Gold and David Crawford, "U.S., Other Nations Step Up Bribery Battle," *Wall Street Journal*, September 12, 2008, p. B1.

64 Kara Scannell, "Swiss Lawyer Faces Charges in Bribery Case," *Wall Street Journal*, September 15, 2003, p. A16.

65   "Two Companies Admit Payments to Officials," *New York Times,* January 11, 2001, p. CP10.

66   Peter Lattman, "Ralph Lauren Pays 41.6 Million to Resolve Bribery Case," *New York Times*, April 22, 2013.

67   Jef Feeley, "Wal-Mart Accused of Using Mexican Governor to Push Bribes," Bloomberg, January 29, 2013.

68   Kate Gillespie, "Middle East Response to the U.S. Foreign Corrupt Practices Act," *California Management Review*, vol. 29, no. 4 (1987), pp. 9–30.

69   "United States vs. Control Component Inc.," 2014 SEC Whistleblower Act Disclosure, www.secwhistle blowwerprogram.org, accessed December 11, 2014.

70   Associated Press, "U.N. Anticorruption Treaty Aims to Ease Retrieval of Dirty Money," *Wall Street Journal*, December 9, 2003, p. A10.

71   Michael Peel, "Hurdles in Countering Cross-Border Corruption," *Financial Times*, August 14, 2006, p. 10.

72   Ibid.

73   Dionne Searcey, "U.K. Law on Bribes Has Firms in a Sweat," *Wall Street Journal Online*, December 28, 2010.

74   David Wighton, "If China is Curbing Corruption, Why Can't We?" *The Times*, February 7, 2011.

Chapter 6

Global Competitors

THE GLOBALIZATION OF COMPETITION 169

CULTURAL ATTITUDES TOWARD COMPETITION 174

COMPETITORS FROM EMERGING MARKETS 177

HOME COUNTRY ACTIONS AND GLOBAL COMPETITIVENESS 182

THE COUNTRY-OF-ORIGIN ADVANTAGE 183

Procter & Gamble largely created the market for shampoo in China. Previously, many Chinese still washed their hair with bar soap. Slick Western-style commercials launched P&G's Head and Shoulders brand, and its success encouraged other multinational corporations (MNCs) to develop the Chinese market further. These MNCs included Japan's Kao Corporation, France's L'Oreal and Anglo-Dutch Unilever, as well as U.S.-based Colgate-Palmolive and Bristol-Myers Squibb. For ten years, big global brands such as Coca-Cola and Head and Shoulders killed local brands in China. Then things changed. Chinese brands recaptured two-thirds of the shampoo market and strongly reasserted themselves in other consumer nondurables such as soap, laundry detergent and skin moisturizer. A state-owned company even produced one of China's largest-selling brands of toothpaste.

Local brands competed first on price but were learning to develop other selling points as well. One Chinese shampoo, Olive, successfully advertised that it made black hair glossier, an attribute that appealed to local consumers. P&G took note and introduced a new shampoo that included traditional medicinal elements to add sheen to black hair. The general manager of P&G's shampoo business summed up the new environment: "These days new local brands are always coming at you. And we take them very seriously."[1]

MNCs who entered the Chinese market later often found tough local competitors had upgraded their products and services in order to preempt any new foreign competitors. When Disney opened a theme park in Hong Kong, many visitors from the Chinese provinces complained that it was smaller than their locally owned theme parks. Groupon closed its business in China after investing nearly $9 million and struggling to establish market share. Hundreds of Chinese companies were offering online buying services in China by the time Groupon entered the market.[2]

In addition, Chinese firms are no longer satisfied to stay in China.[3] A survey of the top 100 Chinese companies revealed that 70 percent had already entered foreign markets and most others were considering doing so.[4]

To begin to develop an effective strategy for global markets, a firm must consider not only buyers but competitors as well. Understanding global buyers is only half the job. Global marketers must compete for those buyers. Potential competitors include both global competitors and local competitors. Each presents unique challenges. Furthermore, the national origin and cultural heritage of firms can determine their organization, their sources of competitive advantage and the tactics they employ to compete.

In this chapter we address issues of global competition. We begin by noting ways in which competitors can engage each other globally—global firm versus global firm and local firm versus global firm. We explore why cultures developed different attitudes toward competition and look at differences among competitors from different parts of the world. The chapter concludes by examining how buyers respond to firms from different countries.

Learning Objectives

After studying this chapter, you should be able to:

➤ describe ways in which one global competitor can address another;
➤ list and explain four basic strategic options that local firms can employ in the face of competition from MNCs;

➤ explain how attitudes toward competition have evolved differently in different cultures, and cite examples from both developed and developing countries;

➤ note examples of how home governments can still support the global competitiveness of their firms despite the trend toward trade liberalization;

➤ discuss the major competitors from developing countries—SOEs and business groups—and explain how they differ from MNCs;

➤ describe how a firm's country of origin can help or hurt it in the global marketplace.

The Globalization of Competition

To be successful in global markets, firms must not only understand their potential buyers but also learn to compete effectively against other firms from many different countries. International firms have both advantages and disadvantages when they encounter local competition in foreign markets. MNCs may be larger than local firms and may have better access to sources of finance. They may enjoy greater experience worldwide in product development and marketing. This experience can be brought to play in the new market. However, local competitors may better understand the local culture and therefore operate more effectively not only in addressing consumer needs but in dealing with local distributors and governments as well. Today many local competitors, even those in less developed markets, have built up popular brands that a foreign newcomer can find difficult to dislodge.

Global Firm versus Global Firm

Some industries are becoming increasingly global. In these industries, the same global competitors hold significant global market share and face each other in virtually every key market. Major global competitors consider each other carefully on a worldwide basis. They watch each other's moves in various markets around the world in order to respond to, or even preempt, any actions that will give the competitor a market advantage. Unilever, a European-based firm, and Procter & Gamble, of the United States, clash in many markets, particularly in laundry products. The two firms compete with each other in most world markets, and action in one market easily spills over into others. The same phenomenon occurs in the aerospace industry. Buyers are global, and research and development (R&D) costs are high. Competitors are few, and they keep close tabs on one another. In fact, the industry is largely defined by just two firms—Airbus and Boeing.

George Yip suggests several ways in which one global competitor can address another.[5]

➤ **Cross-country subsidization.** Using profits from one country in which a business operates to subsidize competitive actions in another country. Bic was one of the first companies to do this effectively. Bic used profits made in France to attack competitor Scripto's pen business in Britain. Then Bic used profits made in Europe to attack Scripto in its U.S. home market. Because

Scripto's national subsidiaries were largely independent of each other, the firm didn't see Bic coming.

➤ **Counterparry.** Defending against a competitive attack in one country by counterattacking in another country. Fuji successfully entered the United States and gained 25 percent of the film market. Kodak counterattacked in Japan, exerting great efforts to strike back at Fuji in its home market.

➤ **Globally coordinated moves.** Mounting a coordinated assault in which competitive moves are made in different countries. For example, some MNCs now choose global rollouts for products. By introducing new products in all major national markets simultaneously, a firm ensures that its global competitors have no time to learn from one market in order to respond in another.

➤ **Targeting of global competitors.** Identifying actual and potential global competitors and selecting an overall posture—attack, avoidance, cooperation or acquisition. We will have more to say about cooperating with potential competitors in Chapter 9.

One of the longest-running battles in global competition has been the fight for market dominance between Coca-Cola and PepsiCo, the world's largest soft drink companies. Traditionally, the two firms have been relatively close in the U.S. market, but Coca-Cola has long been the leader in international markets. In terms of worldwide market share, Coke leads Pepsi by better than a two-to-one margin. However, the battle for global market share is an ongoing one that erupts simultaneously on several fronts. Key battleground markets are the emerging markets of Russia, China and India.

Despite entering the Russian market over 30 years after Pepsi did, Coke was able to pull ahead of its global rival in that market.[6] However, the market shares of the two brands are very close in China. In an attempt to overtake Pepsi, Coke paid $80 million for four-year sponsorship rights for the Beijing Olympics. While Pepsi was not an actual sponsor, some Chinese bottlers handed out Pepsi shirts to onlookers along the Olympic torch route. As a result, 10 percent of Chinese consumers thought Pepsi was an Olympics sponsor.[7]

In India, Coca-Cola had previously relinquished its market position when the Indian government passed a law that would require the company to share its secret cola formula with local partners. Although the law was later repealed, Coke delayed returning to India while rival Pepsi made India a priority market. When Coke finally returned, it found Pepsi well established in the market. To catch up quickly, Coca-Cola purchased a local company with substantial market share in carbonated drinks.[8] The Coke brand still trails Pepsi, but the competition between the two brands is fierce. Pepsi accused Coke of hoarding over 5 million returnable Pepsi bottles collected from recyclers in order to disrupt Pepsi production. Pepsi called the police, and a court ordered Coke to return the bottles. The two companies subsequently agreed to a regular exchange of bottles.[9] Mirroring the Pepsi–Coke rivalry for India, global competitors Dunkin' Donuts and Starbucks both announced that they would enter India within months of each other.[10]

As can be expected in true global competition, Coke and Pepsi square off in all-important markets. Both firms coordinate their strategies across markets, leverage knowledge and experience gained in many national markets, and employ vast global resources as they battle for global market share.

World Beat 6.1

Cooperate, Compete and Don't Forget the Dirty Tricks

For many years Coca-Cola distributed rival Danone's Evian mineral water in the United States. The two MNCs were also founding members, along with the World Wildlife Fund (WWF), of Bioplastic Feedstock Alliance, an organization to promote the development of plant-based plastics.

However, the two packaged-foods giants do not always cooperate. When Coca-Cola attempted to launch Dasani in the British market, calcium chloride was added to the water in order to adhere to U.K. regulations. This resulted in increasing the level of bromate in the water that could increase the risk of cancer. A public outcry arose, and Dasani was withdrawn from the market. Coca-Cola claimed that two months after launching its flagship bottled water brand Dasani in Argentina, Danone in partnership with its advertising agency sent anonymous e-mails to journalists and NGOs accusing Coca-Cola of exploiting weaker regulations in Latin America in order to sell its "cancer water" there.

It took Coca-Cola two years to trace the "cancer water" e-mails back to Danone's Argentinian subsidiary. In the meantime, Coca-Cola Argentina researched the effect the e-mails had on consumers. Thirty percent of consumers surveyed reported that they were aware of the rumor that Dasani caused cancer. Sixty percent of that group believed the rumor. Furthermore, the rumor was not contained to Argentina. Consumers across Latin America had heard it as well.

Coca-Cola concluded that sales of Dasani in Argentina were only half what market research had predicted and consequently brought a lawsuit against Danone for spreading the cancer rumor and damaging the Dasani brand. An Argentine judge acknowledged Danone's complicity in spreading the rumor but dismissed the suit nonetheless. The reason: since Dasani had barely entered the Argentine market at the time of the rumor attack, the rumor could not have influenced many consumers. Coke appealed the ruling and subsequently won the lawsuit.

Sources: Billy Kenber and Murad Ahmed, "Multinationals with Something to Hide," *The Times*, November 17, 2012; Jonathan Prynn, "Coca-Cola Tries to Tap into the Bottled Water Market Again," *London Lite*, May 22, 2008, p. 21; "Coca-Cola Company Goes for Dasani Fizz," *Just-Drinks*, November 7, 2013; and "Major Brands Form Bioplastic Alliance," European Plastics News, November 20, 2013.

Global Firm versus Local Firm

Local firms can often compete effectively against much larger international companies if they act wisely. Although Chile is one of the smallest of the South American markets, its retail sector is one of the most advanced and per-capita purchasing power in the country is high by regional standards. Local competitors have fiercely defended their home market, while foreign entrants such as Home Depot, J.C. Penney and Sears have lost money and left. Grocery retailing in Chile has long been dominated by two strong local competitors: Cencosud and D&S. These two grocery chains successfully drove global competitors Carrefour and Ahold out of the Chilean market. D&S hired a former manager of Carrefour Spain and studied Carrefour operations in Argentina to better understand its multinational rival. It solidified its market position by promoting everyday low prices, accepting lower margins and cutting expenses in logistics and inventory handling.[11]

Strategies for Local Firms

Although global firms may have superior resources, they often become inflexible after several successful market entries and tend to stay with standard approaches when flexibility is needed. Often the global firm's strongest local competitors are those who watch global firms carefully and learn from their moves in other countries. Several top Indian retailers decided to invest over $1 billion each to upgrade their operations to world-class standards before global competitors like Wal-Mart enter the Indian market.[12] These local competitors don't simply respond to the entry of global competitors into their markets. They prepare for it.

Niraj Dawar and Tony Frost suggest four successful strategies for smaller local firms that suddenly find themselves competing with more powerful MNCs. Depending on the type of industry they are in, local firms can choose to be defenders, extenders, contenders or dodgers. In industries where customization to local markets remains a competitive asset, defender and extender strategies can be successful. Other industries, such as telecommunications and automobiles, are by nature more global—buyer needs vary relatively little from one market to another, and both economies of scale in production and high R&D costs favor enterprises with global reach and vast resources. In such global industries, local firms must consider contender or dodger strategies.[13]

Defender Strategy

A defender strategy focuses on leveraging local assets in market segments where MNCs may be weak. Local assets often include knowledge of local tastes and customs, as well as good relationships with local distributors and suppliers. A good example of a defender strategy is the trend in Turkey for restaurants to bring back regional cuisines to compete with multinational fast-food chains. Ibrahim Tatlises, a Turkish pop music and television star, successfully created a fast-food chain based on lahmacun, a thin pizzalike dough with meat and spices.[14] Similarly, Chinese competitors in Internet businesses have proven very competitive against invading MNCs by being market savvy. Dangdang, China's largest online retailer, allows consumers to pay with postal money orders or cash-on-delivery since credit cards are not commonly used in China.[15] Despite their local assets, local firms may need to seek out new efficiencies to defend their home markets. Chilean banks chose to outsource check processing to a single service supplier in order for all to achieve the necessary economies of scale to compete with the MNCs.[16]

Extender Strategy

Sometimes local firms find that the assets that worked well for a defender strategy can also work in certain foreign markets. Extenders focus on expanding into foreign markets similar to their own, using successful practices and competencies that they have already developed in their home market. SAB's (South African Breweries, now SABMiller PLC) earlier experience in African countries with primitive distribution channels and antiquated production facilities proved useful when the company entered Eastern Europe.[17] Televisa, Mexico's largest media company, has extended to become one of the world's largest producers of Spanish-language soap operas.[18] Its impact is felt in the United States as well as in Latin America. In some local markets, such as Los Angeles and Houston, Spanish-language Univision is the most-watched network.[19] However, when Mexican packaged-foods giant Bimbo moved into the United States, it faced more difficulties. Like Televisa, Bimbo knew the Mexican consumer and was well poised to target the Mexican market in the United States. However, like SAB, one of Bimbo's key competencies—the ability to deal with small mom-and-pop stores—did not extend well into the U.S. market.[20]

Contender Strategy

Competing in more global industries can be difficult for smaller local firms faced with established global competitors. Yet some have succeeded by upgrading their capabilities to take on the MNCs. This usually means expanding their resources to invest in the necessary R&D expenditures and larger-scale production that these industries can demand. Many privately held local companies find that they need to go public to raise more money through a stock offering. Because their resources may still be limited compared to those of entrenched MNCs, contenders may seek out niches—at least at first—that are underserved by their competitors. Arçelik is a top competitor in the Turkish market for appliances such as refrigerators, washing machines and dishwashers. At home Arçelik enjoys a renowned brand name and vast distribution. It first entered the British market by targeting consumers who wanted small, tabletop refrigerators, a segment that U.S. and European competitors ignored. However, Arçelik moved beyond its initial niche by investing heavily in R&D. The Japan Institute of Product Maintenance chose Arçelik's washing-machine factory in Turkey for the first award for excellence given any such plant outside Japan.[21]

Dodger Strategy

If local firms in more global industries lack the resources or managerial vision to become contenders, they can find themselves edged out even in their home market by MNCs offering better and cheaper products. To survive, a local firm can avoid, or dodge, competition by finding a way to cooperate with its more powerful competitors. It can focus on being a locally oriented link in the value chain, becoming, for instance, a contract manufacturer or local distributor for a MNC. Many dodgers just sell out to a multinational firm that wishes to acquire them. Many such acquisitions have occurred in Europe and the United States as well as in developing countries.

When a MNC buys a local competitor, it can change the competitive dynamics of a market practically overnight. For many years, Heinz in Indonesia faced little competition to its ABC brand from local soy sauce manufacturers. Then global rival Unilever bought the local Bango brand and added it to its extensive distribution system. Bango's market share tripled while Heinz's ABC brand fell 20 percent in only four years. Heinz was forced to re-formulate the ABC recipe, since many Indonesians said they preferred the less salty taste of Bango. It also introduced the first package upgrade in 15 years.[22]

Cultural Attitudes Toward Competition

Not surprisingly, understanding and responding appropriately to competitors is much more difficult if competitors come from different countries and cultures. Cultures vary in their attitudes toward competition and in their histories of industrial development. These attitudes affect the rules of the competitive game—both written and unwritten—in societies. Understanding these attitudes and histories can help marketers better understand both local competitors in host markets and global competitors that come from different home markets.

Is competition good or bad? Most Americans would agree that competition is good. It encourages new ideas and keeps prices down. However, this is not a universal attitude. In the late nineteenth and early twentieth centuries, the United States established antitrust laws to discourage monopolies and encourage competition. Shortly before, Americans watched powerful firms cut prices to drive competitors out of the market. Afterward, these firms or trusts took advantage of their monopolist positions to raise prices to consumers. Newspapers roused citizens across the country, and the U.S. government received a mandate to trust-bust. Even years later, General Motors was forced to operate divisions as separate firms to help dissipate its strong market power in the United States. Other countries have experienced different histories relating to competition and have therefore developed different attitudes toward it.

Competition in Europe

Europe, like the United States, is a major source of MNCs. However, industry structure and attitudes toward competition have traditionally differed between these two regions. In most European countries, family-owned businesses play a greater role in the economy than they do in the United States. In Germany, family-owned businesses employing fewer than 500 persons account for almost 80 percent of all employment. Even among publicly traded companies, it is not uncommon to find the board dominated by the founding family and their friends. Many Europeans remain suspicious of the pressures caused by stock markets, believing they force management toward short-term goals to the detriment of longer-term goals. Some also believe that the corporate governance associated with publicly traded companies is a burden that is more about policing than adding value.[23]

For many years, European governments allowed their firms to engage in cartel behavior that was outlawed in the United States. Even as late as the 1970s, European airlines met openly to discuss and later establish the mutual dropping of first-class services on trans-European flights. In fact, Europe rarely enforced antitrust laws until the 1980s. However, the EU has surprised many with a new vigilance in enforcing antitrust laws.

Although Europe imported much of its antitrust law from the United States, it has evolved differently. In the United States, the laws aim to protect consumers from monopolists. In the EU, they exist to guarantee fairness among competitors in the unified market. For example, Microsoft was fined over $2 billion for "abusing its near-monopoly position" in the EU. Microsoft had been found guilty of illegally bundling Windows Microsoft Player inside its Windows operating system thereby hurting independent producers of media-player software. The director of the U.S. Department of

Justice disagreed with this ruling, noting that Europe's stance would harm consumers by discouraging corporate innovation.[24]

Furthermore, under U.S. law, if a merger helps enable two companies to offer a broad portfolio of related products, this is seen as creating efficiencies that could in turn benefit consumers. In the EU, however, this would be seen as having the potential of blocking competitors out of the market. Consequently, the EU objected to a merger between two EU firms, Grand Metropolitan and Guinness, that would have created the world's largest liquor company. The EU feared that the new firm, by combining their portfolios of products from champagne to whiskey, could pressure distributors to shut out competitors. The EU also blocked a merger under their jurisdiction of General Electric and Honeywell International, two U.S.-based MNCs in the aerospace industry, despite the fact that the United States had approved the merger. This decision prompted allegations that European takeover rulings were biased against U.S. firms. However, an independent inquiry found no evidence of systematic bias.[25]

Historically, European governments have intervened more than the U.S. government to save their failing companies. Recently this may be changing. After September 11 devastated the airlines industry, the U.S. government offered its airlines a $5 billion bailout with an additional $10 billion in loan guarantees. But European antitrust legislation refused to allow European governments to bail out airlines. European carriers had to respond immediately—cutting costs and reducing debts. This has left them leaner and meaner than U.S. rivals.[26] Similarly, during the global economic downturn of 2009, European governments were more reluctant to interfere to save failing companies than was the U.S. government.

Competition in Japan

In the last three decades, Japanese markets have experienced more intense competition than markets in the United States and Europe. Whereas IBM enjoyed dominance in the computer mainframe market in the United States, four major competitors—Fujitsu, Hitachi, NEC and IBM Japan—fought for market share in Japan. In fact, four to eight strong contenders can be found in virtually every industry. Japanese firms are rarely seen to leave mature industries through acquisition, bankruptcy or voluntary exit.

Largely contributing to this phenomenon are the horizontal keiretsus. *Keiretsu* means "order or system." In Japan, six large industrial groups, or keiretsus, have evolved, and each keiretsu is involved in nearly all major industries. Group companies are technically independent and publicly owned. However, they are loosely coordinated by minority cross-shareholdings and personal relationships. A major player in these groups is the keiretsu bank. Group companies and especially the group bank will help members out in times of trouble. When Mazda faced bankruptcy, the Sumitomo Bank provided the car company with generous financing and encouraged employees of group companies to buy Mazdas. Banks retain shares of group companies despite low returns and have been effective in preventing takeovers by competitors.[27]

For decades, Japanese managers never worried about stock prices, and postwar Japan never experienced a hostile takeover of a major business. Despite increased competition, weak companies were not forced out of the Japanese market. However, the poor economic environment in Japan during the late 1990s began to show cracks in the system. The Japanese government made it clear that it would allow banks to fail, which caused Japanese banks to be more wary about propping up group companies. In fact, Japan is experiencing one of the biggest transfers of corporate ownership in 50 years, with many U.S. companies now buying into Japanese firms. Despite these recent trends, a study of Japanese keiretsus revealed that the system appeared to be very much intact.[28]

Competition in Emerging Markets

Developing countries have traditionally been wary of competition. In the mid-twentieth century, many of these countries were still dependent on commodities and were attempting to industrialize rapidly. However, the moneyed segments of society preferred to keep to the businesses they knew best—agriculture, commerce and the military. The few who ventured into industry and were successful discovered that others quickly followed them into the same business. Soon there were far too many competitors vying for market share in a small market. New ventures failed. As a consequence, potential industrialists became even harder to find. To encourage local investment in industry and the building of factories, governments often limited foreign competition by raising tariffs or imposing quotas on imports. In addition, many governments licensed local production. For example, the Iranian government refused to issue further licenses for new factories once producers could establish that they were capable of supplying the entire Iranian market.

More recently, most developing countries, as well as the transitional economies of the former Soviet bloc, have embraced market liberalization. Market liberalization is the encouraging of competition where prior monopolies or strict entry controls previously existed. It takes a variety of forms. Production licensing is often relinquished and import controls relaxed. Host governments may invoke further competition by encouraging MNCs to invest in their markets. India liberalized its market and encouraged foreign investment by granting MNCs freer access to foreign exchange, the right to hold majority equity stakes in their Indian investments and permission to use foreign brand names where these were previously not permitted. Other countries, such as Egypt, courted foreign investors with tax holidays for up to ten years.

There are several reasons for this change in attitude toward competition in emerging markets. Some of the pressure to liberalize markets has been external. Most countries in the emerging world have now joined the WTO. Consequently they needed to remove barriers to imports in order to comply with WTO regulations. For example, India dismantled the last of its major import quotas in response to a ruling from the WTO. Until then, manufacturers of consumer goods faced virtually no import competition in India. Other countries are under pressure to liberalize from bilateral partners such as the United States.

Much of the pressure to liberalize is internal, however. After 50 years of protection, local competitors have often failed to deliver quality products for reasonable prices. Part of this failure is due to conditions outside their control, such as limited financing available for businesses in developing countries. Still, consumers in emerging markets, along with their governments, have begun to think that protecting infant industries contributes to their failure to ever grow up. A study of 3,000 Indian firms revealed that productivity grew more slowly in the 1990s than in the 1980s.[29]

Furthermore, many governments are setting their sights on competing in export markets. Allowing more competition in the national market forces local companies to be more globally competitive. MNCs in particular—with their higher technology, more extensive financial resources and global market know-how—are expected to help fuel export expansion.

As developing countries liberalize their markets, governments are also cracking down on what they deem to be improper competitive behavior. Many actions that have been accepted for many years are now outlawed. In Mexico, a new antitrust commission acts as both judge and jury on complaints of anticompetitive behavior brought against firms. The commission has the authority to investigate allegations and impose fines. It can block any corporate acquisition in Mexico and can prevent the creation of a private monopoly in cases where the government decides to sell prior state-owned monopolies to the private sector.

Mexico's antitrust commission found Coca-Cola and its bottlers guilty of abusing their dominant position in Coke's largest market outside the United States. Needless to say, Pepsi initiated the investigation. Coke holds the dominant share of the Mexican carbonated soft drinks market and most of its sales came from small mom-and-pop stores located across the country. Coke was ordered by the commission to stop using its exclusivity agreements that forbade the small retailers from carrying competitors' products. Pepsi has similar agreements with its retailers in Mexico. But the ruling didn't apply to Pepsi, because Pepsi didn't occupy the dominant position in the market.[30]

Sometimes antitrust rulings appear to target MNCs more than local firms, but local players are not immune to antitrust actions. When China fined six dairy companies over $100 million for anticompetitive and monopolistic practices, most of the companies were foreign MNCs.[31] However, Mexico's supreme court ruled against Carlos Slim, a Mexican citizen and the world's richest man, declaring that his cell phone company could not block competitors by using court injunctions (a common tactic in Mexico) to undermine Mexico's attempt to liberalize the industry.[32]

Competitors from Emerging Markets

Until recently, most global strategists focused on the MNCs from the United States, Europe and Japan. But as we saw in the cases of Procter & Gamble in China and Arçelik in Britain, MNCs now find themselves competing with firms from emerging markets.

Increasingly, competitors from emerging markets are entering international markets. A South Korean-led consortium won a contract valued at over $20 billion to build four nuclear reactors in the UAE. Their bid was chosen over bids from France and the United States. Both price and a record of on-time delivery helped them secure the contract.[33] Of course, many firms from emerging markets possess certain disadvantages compared to MNCs from developed countries. Many lack cutting-edge technologies, global brands, global scale and international experience. However, they may possess certain competitive advantages such as ultra low-cost production, frugal innovation and the ability to develop new products quickly and cheaply. They also have experience working successfully in adverse conditions.[34]

Major firms in emerging markets are usually quite different from MNCs from the United States. Large firms that have evolved locally in emerging markets are usually one of two types—SOEs and

Table 6.1 The World's Large Competitors

	Strengths	Weaknesses
MNCs	• Global brands • Strong R&D • High technology • International experience • Significant financial resources	• Less local knowledge abroad • Difficulty extending business model to many different markets
Business Groups	• Strong local brands • Improving technologies • Low-cost manufacturing • Experience in difficult markets	• Less international experience • Less financial resources • Commitments to weaker group companies may hinder growth opportunities
State-Owned Enterprises (SOEs)	• Local market protection • Government financing and subsidies	• Less international experience • Non-commercial agendas set by governments

business groups (see Table 6.1). With the trend toward market liberalization, both face strong challenges at home from foreign MNCs. Nonetheless, these local firms can still prove quite competitive both in their own national markets and, increasingly, in global markets. Furthermore, new entrepreneurial ventures in developing countries are evolving and targeting overseas markets.

State-Owned Enterprises

State-owned enterprises (SOEs) sometimes appear in the developed world, but their scope and impact have been significantly greater in developing countries. In the second half of the twentieth century, many governments in developing countries were trying to end their dependence on commodity exports by rapidly industrializing their economies. Often the private sector failed to meet government expectations in this regard. Most shied away from investing in factories and production, areas they knew little about. To meet their goals, governments increasingly fell back on doing the job themselves and established SOEs that operated not only in the manufacturing sector but sometimes in wholesaling and retailing as well. For example, SOEs in Egypt came to account for 25 percent of nonagricultural employment in the country.

Being state owned can provide firms certain competitive advantages over firms in the private sector, but some disadvantages are also involved. SOEs may receive priority access to financing that is scarce in developing countries. They may be protected from bankruptcy and may be granted monopoly positions in their home markets. They may even derive trade protection by virtue of their government ownership. Some believe that Chinese petroleum SOEs may be immune from U.S. sanctions for cooperating with countries the United States considers to be supporters of terrorism, because such actions could be interpreted as direct economic warfare against the Chinese government.[35]

However, these advantages may be offset by the many ancillary agendas SOEs are forced to accept. For example, Sri Lanka's state-owned timber company was expected to sell timber below market prices to subsidize housing in the country. Egyptian college graduates were guaranteed jobs in SOEs, and the Venezuelan government could commandeer the earnings of its state-owned oil company to help with a fiscal shortfall. Furthermore, the U.S. Committee on Foreign Investment undertakes an investigation whenever an SOE wishes to undertake a merger or acquisition in the United States due to the concern that SOEs may pursue objectives other than commercial interests.[36]

In the 1980s and 1990s, many SOEs in developing countries, as well as those in the former Soviet Union and Eastern Europe, underwent privatization. Privatization occurs when SOEs or their assets are sold to private firms or individuals. Rather than investing the money necessary to revamp these enterprises, governments chose to sell them. Part of the impetus to do so involved a change in ideology. Many governments lost faith in continued government-led industrialization. Privatizations swept through more than 100 countries and involved over 75,000 SOEs. In many cases, MNCs purchased these firms. For example, Philip Morris, the U.S.-based food and tobacco company, was able to acquire a stake in Czechia's Tabak, previously the Czech monopolist in tobacco.

However, the global impact of SOEs in the oil industry continues despite the trend toward privatization. The state-owned oil companies of Kuwait and Venezuela have ventured out of their countries and have invested in Europe and the United States. The Kuwaiti company purchased refinery capacity in Europe as well as an extensive network of retail outlets from former Gulf Oil. Both of these SOEs are considered serious global competitors. In Russia, a major source of future oil supplies, the state has moved to increase its ownership in the previously privatized sectors of oil and natural gas.

World Beat 6.2

Multinational Corporation or Agent of the State?

China-based Huawei is the largest networking and telecommunications company in the world with nearly 75 percent of its business located overseas. *But what is it really*—a MNC or a Trojan horse for Chinese spying?

The company was founded in 1987 by a former Chinese military officer and was established as a private company owned by its employees. However, the company is thought to be primarily owned by the founder and a smaller group of managers. A U.S. Congress House Intelligence Committee report alleged the Communist Party committee within the company provides the Chinese government with a shadow source of power and influence. Huawei denied the allegations.

Huawei's attempt to enter the U.S. market has been stymied by the U.S. Congress which has warned domestic telecommunications companies against doing business with the Chinese MNC. American officials have long considered Huawei to be a security threat, noting that its equipment could allow the Chinese government to steal corporate and government secrets. The seriousness of their concern was made all the more evident when former contractor Edward J. Snowden leaked classified documents from the U.S. National Security Agency (NSA) revealing that the NSA was itself spying on Huawei.

The U.S. government was somewhat successful in curtailing Huawei's advancement into the South Korean market as well. U.S. officials complained that allowing Huawei to develop South Korea's advanced wireless network would run the risk that Huawei equipment could be used to spy on U.S.–Korean communications. The Korean government responded with changes that assured sensitive communications between the two countries would not travel through Huawei's equipment.

Despite these challenges, Huawei has not given up on the important U.S. market. Instead it switched its objectives to targeting the consumer smartphone market.

Sources: Siobhan Gorman, "China Tech Giant Under Fire," *Wall Street Journal Online*, October 8, 2012; "Huawei's Ally: IBM," Dow Jones Chinese Financial Wire, October 10, 2012; Adam Entous, "U.S.-South Korea Communications Won't Use Huawei Gear," *Wall Street Journal Online*, February 13, 2014; "Huawei Target U.S. Smartphone Market," Dow Jones Top North American Equities Stories, February 27, 2014; and David E. Sanger and Nicole Perlroth, "N.S.A. Breached Chinese Servers Seen as Security Threat," *New York Times*, March 22, 2014.

Although the era of SOEs is waning, their importance in the Chinese market is still largely intact. For example, private express shipping companies, including U.S.-based FedEx, UPS and DHL, were directed not to deliver letters or packages under 1.1 pounds and not to charge prices below those of the China Post. In addition, they could not deliver any mail to private homes or to offices of the Chinese government. The industry estimated that the new restrictions could amount to a loss of 60 percent of the Chinese market just as business was soaring. Industry executives claimed that the order violated commitments China made when it entered the WTO. However, the Chinese government maintained the action was legal and noted that China Post had to deliver mail to all locations in China, including places where it could not make a profit. Private companies were under no such obligation. China also invoked an antiterrorism rationale for the move. The government needed to ensure that all deliveries were subjected to screening for anthrax and other poisons.[37]

Chinese SOEs or hybrids dominate many sectors of the Chinese economy. (Hybrids are firms in which governments hold a partial, though usually significant, equity position.) Incidents such as the one involving the express shipping carriers have led to concerns that China's new antitrust laws—based on European laws—may target foreign MNCs while sidestepping reforms to China's powerful SOEs. The Chinese government is also encouraging SOEs, such as those in the auto industry, to combine forces to become bigger and stronger global competitors.[38] Chinese hybrid and computer giant, Lenovo, even acquired the personal computer business of U.S.-based IBM. While Chinese SOEs are proving worthy adversaries to foreign firms, they are increasingly open to hiring foreign managers, particularly in middle management positions. Lenovo hired an American as its CEO.[39] But Chinese SOEs have recently become controversial at home where critics claim they pay their workers too little while enriching management.[40]

Business Groups

In the private sector of most developing countries, business groups emerged as the major competitors. Business groups differ from large corporations in developed countries in several key ways. Business groups have been exclusively or almost exclusively concentrated in their home markets. But most striking is their diversity. Business groups participate in many industries. It would not be uncommon to find a business group involved in steel, insurance, packaged goods, automobile distribution and textiles. For example, Arçelik is part of the larger Koç Group in Turkey. This group participates in industries as diverse as consumer goods, energy, mining, finance and construction. Starbucks entered India by joint venturing with Indian business group Tata. Tata Coffee is Asia's largest coffee-plantation company, but the Tata Group also has extensive hotel and retail operations that can serve as sites for the new coffee shops.

Group businesses are often interlinked, with group companies owning partial shares of each other. The true bond, however, is not one of equity ownership but is a fiduciary bond or bond of trust. It is the culture of businesses in the group to work for the good of the whole. Managers often move between these companies, and personal bonds are forged. In the difficult business environments of developing countries, all eventually benefit from mutual aid.[41]

Similar to Japanese keiretsus, most groups have a financial core—a business with access to cash to finance the other businesses. This is commonly a bank or an insurance company. In the case of Arab Contractors in Egypt, it was the parent company's own extensive retirement fund. This financial core proved a key competitive advantage in an environment where financing was scarce. Because these groups evolved in highly controlled economies, another competitive advantage was their adroit handling of government relations. For example, the Tata Group established India's first steel mill and attempted to seriously address the industrial policy goals of India. Dynastic marriages between business group families and politically connected families were not uncommon. For example, the son of the head of Arab Contractors married the daughter of Egyptian president Anwar Sadat.

Like virtually all firms in developing countries, business groups began as family-owned enterprises, and today the original families still play an important role in most cases. However, as these firms expanded, more professional management was introduced. Other changes have swept through business groups as well. Perhaps the most important of these has been the new competition that business groups face from MNCs. Many more MNCs have entered emerging markets in the wake of trade and investment liberalization. With the lifting of protectionist policies that once protected local firms by excluding imports and even discouraging foreign investment, MNCs now threaten business groups with new technology, quality products at competitive prices, global brands and strong financial resources. They also compete for the best management talent in the country, something that was once the domain of the business groups. Also, as governments loosen their hold over their economies, the groups' competitive advantage in managing government relations has become less important.

In response to these new threats, many business groups are rethinking the strategies that have served them well in the past. Some experts argue that the diversity of the past should be abandoned. Instead, the firm should restructure itself around its strongest business or businesses and expand these into foreign markets. In other words, business groups should consider becoming more like MNCs. Tata, India's largest business group, refocused itself at home by cutting back participation in low-margin businesses. Still the group remained in such varied industries as tea, cars, power and phone networks. With global ambitions, it purchased Britain's Tetley Tea, as well as automakers Jaguar and Land Rover, to gain immediate access to global brands.

Even so, some experts argue that it is premature to expect that business groups will disband in developing countries. The political and economic environments in these countries remain tumultuous, and the strategic value of rendering mutual assistance and forming strong government ties is as real today as before. In fact, many SOEs in Vietnam are themselves aligning into business groups.[42] This suggests that the benefits of business groups may not be restricted to the private sector. Whatever their future, business groups currently represent the strongest local competition in many developing countries.

New Global Players

Recently, firms from developing countries have appeared as major regional and even global competitors in a number of industries. These firms increasingly challenge the established positions of MNCs from the United States, Europe and Japan. Some, like Arçelik, are outstanding units of older, restructuring business groups. Others are firms that have been established more recently. For example, Acer, the Taiwanese computer giant, rose to a strong position in the Asian consumer PC market.[43] Hikma Pharmaceuticals was established in Jordan and carved out a niche for itself as a respected producer of generic drugs with operations in the United States, Europe and several developing countries. A number of firms, such as Mexico's Cemex and SAB, have used a strong cash flow from their dominant position in one of the larger emerging markets to fund the purchase of established companies abroad. This has helped catapult such companies into positions among the top-ranked global competitors of their industries. The success of companies from newly emerging markets requires a rethinking of the impact that competitors from the emerging world may have on global markets in the future.

Home Country Actions and Global Competitiveness

In Chapter 4, we discussed how the home governments of firms can affect these firms' global marketing—in particular, how home governments might possibly harm their firms and in so doing create political risk. However, most home governments are eager for their firms to prove competitive in the global marketplace, and many seek out specific ways to improve the competitiveness of their firms. The WTO discourages direct government subsidies to firms and restricts, in most cases, the ability of member states to protect home markets with quotas and high tariffs.

Still, many other government policies exist that can affect global competitiveness. Governments can offer export assistance in the form of export promotion organizations that help educate local firms about foreign markets. Home governments may also assist in negotiations for major contracts with foreign governments. The competition between aerospace giants Airbus and Boeing also involves government assistance for R&D. Furthermore, some analysts judge the competition between the two companies to be so intense that no new player could enter the market without significant government support. However, both the Chinese and Russian governments have signaled that they are ready to supply such support to ensure a national presence in this industry.

Governments can also pursue economic and competition policies at home that enhance the ability of their firms to compete in foreign markets. These policies can include tax rates, labor laws and the extent to which home governments tolerate monopolistic or oligopolistic behavior in the home market. The heads of state of the EU met in Barcelona and determined that Europe should try to become the world's most competitive economy. The Barcelona summit resolved to liberalize labor markets by lowering labor taxes and reducing benefits to the unemployed. It also took steps to deregulate energy markets, giving businesses the freedom to choose their gas and electricity suppliers. It was hoped that these measures would decrease the costs of European-based businesses, allowing them to compete more effectively internationally.[44]

Many assert that China's earlier market liberalization has been replaced by more active government involvement in the economy.[45] For example, China has supported both SOEs and other national champions in order to help the nation obtain advanced technology. The technology for its high-speed trains was based on technology introduced to China by German, French and Japanese competitors. Major Western competitors such as Siemens AG have complained to the Chinese government over its attempts to compel foreign companies to transfer key intellectual property in order to access the Chinese market. Beijing has focused recently on creating national champions in telecommunications and technology.[46] In addition, the Chinese government has offered low-cost capital to domestic industries. Some argue that such "state capitalism" could erode the global competitiveness of U.S. and other non-Chinese firms.

One ongoing controversy concerning home-government policy and competitiveness involves the cement industry. Mexico's Cemex grew from a regional player to the world's third largest cement supplier and the leading brand in the United States. U.S. rivals accused Cemex of using its dominance in Mexico to finance its expansion overseas unfairly and to cut prices in the U.S. market. Cemex's position in the Mexican market, where it held a 60 percent share of the market, allowed it to charge unusually high prices. Profits in Mexico were an extraordinary 46 percent before taxes—nearly double what they were in the more competitive U.S. market. Such profits at home enabled Cemex to buy competitors abroad as well as to decrease prices in foreign markets. An investigation by Mexico's competition commission found Cemex innocent of monopolistic behavior. Unsatisfied with the commission's decision, the U.S. government decided to impose antidumping duties on cement imported from Mexico. In some years, these amounted to more than 100 percent for Cemex.[47]

The Country-of-Origin Advantage

Does an international company enjoy a market advantage—or disadvantage—because of the reputation of its home market? When Arçelik entered the European market, the firm was concerned that its home country, Turkey, would diminish its brand in the eyes of European consumers. Consumer response to the country of origin of products has been studied for 30 years. The findings are mixed, but certain trends can be observed. Although certain biases persist, consumers seem to change their minds over time, reflecting a dynamic environment for global competition.

Country of origin denotes the country with which a firm is associated—typically its home country. For example, IBM is associated with the United States and Sony with Japan. Several studies have concluded that consumers usually favor products from developed countries over those from less developed countries. The reputation of some countries appears to enhance the credibility of competitors in product groups for which the country is well known, such as wines and perfumes for France, video recorders for South Korea and Persian carpets for Iran. A positive or negative effect of country of origin can sometimes be product-specific. Russian automobiles may evoke a negative image in the minds of consumers, but Russian vodka may evoke a positive response.[48] In a few cases, country of origin can connote more general product attributes. Germany is known for engineering quality and Italy for design quality.

Nonetheless, country of origin can be confusing. A study of American college students found that they associated famous brands with Germany, Japan or the United States. The vast majority of student respondents (over 90 percent) failed to associate Nokia with Finland, Lego with Denmark or Samsung with South Korea. Over half of respondents thought Nokia was Japanese, Lego was American and Ericsson was German.[49]

A country-of-origin bias is not limited to products or to consumer markets. Country-of-origin biases toward services appear to be similar to those toward products.[50] These biases have been observed among industrial buyers as well. Buyers of industrial products in South Korea rated Japanese, German and American suppliers higher than suppliers from their own country.[51] Another study revealed that U.S. buyers were more willing to purchase from established industrialized countries than from newly industrialized ones, with the exception of Mexico.[52]

The issue of country of origin is increasingly complicated by the fact that MNCs produce products in various countries. Which matters most to consumers—the home country associated with the brand or the country where the product is actually manufactured or assembled? Research on this question is inconclusive. A strong global brand may sometimes offset a negative country of manufacture. However, this is not always the case. For example, a study of Nigerian consumers of high-tech products revealed that where a product was produced was considered more important than the company name or brand of the product.[53] Globalization has also resulted in products whose inputs come from a number of countries. One study confirmed that country of parts affected perceptions of both manufacturing quality and overall quality of products.[54]

Managing Country-of-Origin Perceptions

Buyer attitudes toward certain countries can change, and this has important implications for global competitors. Both Japan and South Korea saw their products rise in esteem over a relatively short period of time.[55] Japanese products have scored higher than U.S. or German products in some countries, including China and Saudi Arabia.[56] In recent years, a number of countries, including Portugal, Estonia and Poland, have employed branding experts to help them project a better image. Finland even undertook a campaign to enhance its image as a center of high-tech innovation, hoping that a better national image would help its high-tech companies in the U.S. market. But countries must realize that branding is more than hype; it must be backed by reality. Consequently, major changes in country brand image can take 20 years to achieve.[57]

Firms that suffer from a negative country of origin commonly settle for lower prices to offset perceptions of lower quality. However, there are a number of strategies that can improve buyer perception of the quality of products that suffer from a negative country-of-origin effect:

➤ Production may be moved to a country with a positive country-of-origin effect. If this is too difficult, key parts can be sourced from such countries. Kia's Sorento is assembled in South Korea but relies on high-profile brand-name components from European and U.S. suppliers to boost its image overseas.[58]

➤ A negative country-of-origin bias may be offset by using a channel that distributes already accepted complementary products. A study determined that consumers dining in a Mexican-theme restaurant were significantly more likely to buy Mexican wine than were consumers in other restaurants.[59]

➤ Communication and persistence can eventually pay off. When Arçelik attempted to introduce its Beko brand washing machines to the French furniture chain Conforama, the French sales staff objected to displaying the Turkish product. Then Valerie Lubineau, Beko's head of marketing in France, revealed that the firm had been manufacturing Conforama's respected in-house brand for years. Eight months later, the new Beko machines were outselling their European rivals.[60] Firms that consistently provide good products and service can even change buyers' attitudes toward their country of origin. A study showed industrial buyers who were experienced with suppliers from Latin America rated these countries higher than buyers who had had no such business dealings.[61]

Of course some country-of-manufacture preferences expressed by consumers reflect reality, not bias. The physical attributes of Cadbury chocolates can vary by country reflecting different national tastes. Similarly, many consumers in the United States prefer Coca-Cola produced in Mexico whose ingredients differ from the American version.[62]

Beyond Quality

Up until now we have been discussing how country of origin can affect perceptions of quality. However, country of origin can affect purchase behavior in other ways. These include consumer ethnocentrism and consumer animosity.

Consumer Ethnocentrism

Some consumers are disinclined to purchase foreign products altogether. They believe that buying imported products results in job loss, and consequently hardship, at home. This phenomenon is called consumer ethnocentrism. Russian consumers often rate high on ethnocentrism despite their belief that imported products surpass the quality of domestic goods.[63] Within a national population, some segments will exhibit higher levels of consumer ethnocentrism than others. Research has not revealed consistent results as to who is more likely to be ethnocentric. However, several studies suggest that women and older consumers may be more ethnocentric. During economic downturns when unemployment rises, consumer ethnocentrism is likely to rise as well.

Some retailers may respond to ethnocentrism by stocking more domestically produced items. Wal-Mart recently announced that it would stock more U.S.-made goods in order to create more than 1,200 jobs in the United States. Still, the amount of goods sourced in the United States will only represent about 2 percent of Wal-Mart's merchandise.[64] Given the interdependency of the world economy, responses to ethnocentrism are likely to be limited.

Consumer Animosity

Other buyers harbor political objections to purchasing products from a specific foreign country. This phenomenon is called consumer animosity. During a territorial dispute between China and Japan, which strained diplomatic relationships, Chinese mobs attacked Toyota cars. Toyota responded with programs to compensate customers for damage they sustained in anti-Japanese violence.[65]

Consumer animosity can be stable or situational. Stable animosity arises from difficult historical relations between two countries.[66] For example, Chinese rate Japanese products high in quality. However, many Chinese harbor animosity toward the Japanese because of Japan's occupation of China during World War II. This animosity can negatively affect purchase of Japanese products independent of judgments concerning product quality.[67]

Situational animosity is a response to a current economic or political event.[68] Such animosity surfaced in response to the Iraq War, particularly pitting Britain and the United States against Canada, France and Germany. Activist websites in Germany urged consumers not to purchase 250 British and American products and suggested local alternatives.[69] But it was the U.S. consumer population that exhibited the greatest consumer animosity. An American backlash against French products arose when France objected to America's invasion of Iraq. Exports of French wine to the United States dropped nearly 18 percent, and overall French exports decreased by over 17 percent, suggesting that Americans responded to calls to boycott French products.[70] Even some U.S.-based firms were vulnerable. A poll determined that many Americans thought U.S. firms Grey Poupon and Yoplait were French.[71]

French businesses became very concerned about consumer animosity in the United States. France's principal employer's association called upon U.S. consumers not to take out their antagonism on French businesses, but to send telegrams to the French embassy.[72] Similarly, the president of Canada's Automotive Parts Manufacturers Association reported that members had noticed a chilly response from purchasing agents for U.S. automakers. Although most Canadians agreed with their government's refusal to join the U.S.-led war in Iraq, Canadian business leaders also worried that deteriorating relations with the United States could imperil the $1 billion in daily trade between the neighboring countries.[73]

Social media can further contribute to situational animosity. Organizers of consumer boycotts, such as ones brought against American products in the Arab world, increasingly turn to the Internet to communicate. The sales of Americana Foods—an Arab company that owns franchises for Pizza Hut, KFC, Baskin-Robbins, Hardee's, TGI Friday's and Subway in several Middle East countries— plunged 30 percent during one such consumer boycott.[74]

Sometimes situational consumer animosity proves short-lived. Once besieged by angry farmers who believed their livelihoods were threatened by the American fast-food chain, KFC retreated to a single store in India. However, three years later the company had expanded to 30 stores.[75] McDonald's responded to a consumer boycott in Egypt with leaflets stressing its local Egyptian ownership of outlets and its employment of 2,000 Egyptians. Sales soon recovered.

However, the disruptions caused from consumer animosity can linger. Many Americans upon abandoning French wine discovered that they preferred wine from America, Australia and Chile. Arla Foods, along with all Danish firms, experienced consumer animosity in the Arab world when a Danish newspaper published cartoons of the prophet Mohammed. Some Muslim consumers believed the insult to their religion was so great that it could never be forgiven.[76] Arla also experienced difficulty returning to the limited space available on grocery store shelves in Saudi Arabia after competition had replaced Arla during the height of the consumer boycott against the firm.

Conclusion

This chapter has introduced some basic issues of global competition. We have explored ways by which global competitors engage each other and strategies that local firms employ to survive in an increasingly global marketplace.

We also saw that the cultural challenge in the global marketplace is not limited to buyers. The rules of the competitive game will vary from country to country. Both local and global competitors may possess strengths and weaknesses that reflect to some extent the environment and history of their home countries. Strategic global marketers must not only target appropriate buyers worldwide but also understand and successfully engage the competition that exists for those buyers.

Managerial Takeaways

1. *Not only must global marketers understand current and potential buyers, they must compete for them.*
2. *Some competition is global. Global competitors should and do target each other.*
3. *However, much competition is local. Local competitors can be surprisingly tough, sophisticated and nimble.*
4. *Global marketers must play by different rules of the game in different countries. And these rules are constantly evolving.*
5. *Competitors from different cultures—MNCs, SOEs and business groups—increasingly engage each other in the global marketplace adding complexity to strategic decisions.*
6. *Some companies may enjoy a country-of-origin advantage. Others must contend with a country-of-origin disadvantage. But these advantages aren't carved in stone. And even firms that enjoy a quality perception advantage may fall victim to ethnocentrism and consumer animosity.*

Questions for Discussion

1. What advantages might a Japanese competitor have in the Japanese market over an American firm attempting to enter that market?

2. What do you think governments should be allowed to do to help their home firms be more globally competitive? What do you think constitutes unfair assistance?

3. Are business groups doomed?

4. Nearly all studies of the country-of-origin effect focus on how buyers evaluate products and on their intention to purchase products. How might the country-of-origin effect manifest itself in other situations?

CASE 6.1   Jollibee Goes Global

Jollibee is the dominant fast-food restaurant chain in the Philippines, with over 60 percent share of the market. The company aims to be a global player by 2020 with half its sales abroad. A survey revealed that 69 percent of Filipino respondents visited Jollibee most often, compared with only 16 percent for McDonald's. Jollibee's founder, Tony Tan, is ethnically Chinese. His family emigrated from China, and his father worked as a cook in a Chinese temple. Mr. Tan was just getting started with Jollibee when McDonald's entered the market in 1981. His friends suggested that he apply for a McDonald's franchise. Mr. Tan declined.

Instead, Mr. Tan went on to develop his own chain that offers unique Filipino food, such as spaghetti with meat sauce topped with smoked fish, deep-fried pork skin, bean curd, sliced boiled eggs and spring onions. In keeping with local tastes that appreciate food with lots of sugar and salt, Jollibee hamburgers are especially sweet. Beef is served with honey and rice, and of course there are mango shakes. Jollibee is recognized by its bee icon, which symbolizes the Filipino spirit of lightheartedness and happiness as well as representing a busy worker. Besides its flagship Jollibee restaurants, Jollibee Foods Corporation (JFC) also owns a chain of Chinese restaurants, Chowking, in the Philippines. But the importance of this chain is relatively low compared to JFC. Only 2 percent of Filipino respondents in a poll replied that Chowking was their most-visited restaurant.

Over 25 years after Mr. Tan declined to become a franchisee of McDonald's, Jollibee operated 1,400 restaurants in the Philippines compared to 280 run by McDonald's. During that time, the Philippines emerged as a major outsourcing destination for 24-hour call centers serving the U.S. market. Jollibee was quick to tap into this trend. It built restaurants near the call centers and kept them open day and night.

Many surveys of Asian businesses rank Jollibee high. A poll of Asian business leaders conducted by *Asian Business Magazine* rated Jollibee number one in Asia in terms of growth potential and contribution to society, number two in honesty and ethics, number three in long-term vision and number four in financial soundness. In total, Jollibee received the highest ranking of all firms in the consumer category—ahead of major MNCs such as Coca-Cola, Nestlé and Procter & Gamble. Another poll, this one conducted by *Far Eastern Economic Review*, ranked Jollibee the highest on its leading-companies indicator, ahead of Toyota Motor of Japan and Singapore Airlines.

Like most other fast-food chains in the Philippines, Jollibee buys most of its food inputs from overseas. Imports tend to be cheaper and of better quality than food products available locally. The company decided that it would build a $32 million food-processing plant and logistics and distribution center in the Philippines with the incentive of a four-year tax holiday from the government of the Philippines. The center would serve both local and international operations. Keeping costs low is essential to a company already working on low margins. With the country in recession, Jollibee refused to raise prices in the Philippines, opting instead to try to increase revenues through expansion. Mr. Tan announced that he would like to see JFC open at least 15 stores in every major market around the world. To finance expansion, the company went public, raising money by selling shares on the stock market.

Jollibee began its overseas expansion in 1987 with a restaurant in Brunei, a small, oil-rich country with a relatively large Filipino migrant worker population. JFC moved on to enter other Asian and Middle East markets such as Indonesia, Doha, Kuwait, Guam, Malaysia and New Guinea. In 1998, the company opened its first restaurant in the United States in a location near San Francisco. Soon more locations were opened in California, in areas with high Filipino populations where brand awareness of Jollibee was already high. For example, the clientele at the restaurant in the San Francisco Bay area is about evenly split between ethnic Filipinos and others. All the California restaurants exceeded expectations, and new restaurants were opened in several other states.

However, an earlier attempt to open a Jollibee restaurant in China proved less successful. The restaurant was eventually closed. When Jollibee re-entered the Chinese market several years later, it changed its entry strategy. Instead of promoting its brand from the Philippines, the company purchased three Chinese brands that were already popular in the market.

With further internationalization a priority at Jollibee, expansion in the Middle East looked particularly interesting. There were only two Jollibee restaurants in Doha, despite the presence of 200,000 Filipino expatriates in that city. And nearly 300,000 Filipinos lived and worked in Dubai.

Discussion Questions

1. What strategies did Jollibee follow—or consider following—during its evolution: dodger, defender, extender and/or contender? Explain your answer.
2. Which strategy do you think is most appropriate for Jollibee? Why?
3. Why do you think Jollibee was originally successful in the United States but not in China?
4. Do you think Jollibee's second attempt to enter the Chinese market might be more successful than the first? Why or why not?

Sources: "Jollibee Goes Global" in Kate Gillespie and H. David Hennessey, *Global Marketing* (Mason, OH: Cengage, 2011), pp. 185–186; Doris C. Dumlao, "Jollibee to Put Up 100 New Stores in China," *Philippine Daily Inquirer*, August 31, 2012; "Billionaire Tony Tan Caktiong Takes Jollibee Foods Global," *Forbes Asia*, February 11, 2013; and www.jollibeeusa.com (accessed March 11, 2014).

CASE 6.2 Arming the Middle East

At a time when many defense-industry executives predicted a market contraction, the Middle East countries remained a golden opportunity for arms sales due to high oil prices and concerns over Iran's regional ambitions. But selling to Arab governments presented its own challenges as U.S.-based Lockheed Martin Corporation discovered when it pursued a major contract with the United Arab Emirates (UAE).

Lockheed Martin's UAE Contract

When the UAE first considered major defense purchases, it invited companies from France, Sweden, Russia and the United States to bid on an order of expensive advanced fighter planes. Six years later, the competitors were narrowed down to Lockheed and France's Dassault Aviation S.A. In an attempt to remain in the bidding, another U.S. firm, McDonnell Douglas, had offered steep price cuts but to no avail. Two years later, the UAE announced its final decision in favor of Lockheed. Still, details of the contract remained unresolved, and negotiations began that lasted two more years. At one time, Lockheed became so discouraged that its negotiators were called home. The U.S. government intervened and brought the two sides back together.

Like virtually all defense firms worldwide, Lockheed needed permission from its home government to make sales to foreign governments. Accordingly, the U.S. government closely monitored and even joined in the sales negotiations. U.S. firms could not sell to embargoed countries. Certain technologies could not even be sold to friendly countries. Yet the U.S. government played a proactive role in assisting U.S. defense firms to win contracts abroad. Both the president and vice president became personally involved in promoting the Lockheed sale.

The UAE finally agreed to purchase Lockheed's Desert Falcon planes. To clinch the deal, Lockheed made concessions that would have seemed outlandish 20 years earlier. The company agreed to supply state-of-the-art technology and to put up a $2 billion bond to safeguard against technological failure. It also signed on to an "offset" agreement of $160 million to help the UAE expand its state-owned petroleum sector. Offset agreements had increasingly become a part of arms deals. Defense contractors found themselves agreeing to reinvest part of their earnings in the client country, participating in projects such as building hotels and factories or, in the case of Korea, helping to upgrade the electronics industry.

It would be nearly ten years between the signing of the first contract between Lockheed and the UAE and the delivery of all the ordered Desert Falcons. During this period the UAE emerged as an even more important defense market. In one day alone, the UAE presented two U.S. firms—Lockheed and Boeing—with orders totaling $2.8 billion.

The emirate of Abu Dhabi, in particular, increasingly utilized its position as a major buyer to enlarge its own participation in the aerospace industry. Boeing based one of its subsidiaries, Integrated Defense Systems (IDS), in Abu Dhabi. Lockheed signed a Memorandum of Understanding with Mubadal Development Company to collaborate on various aerospace projects. Mubadal was wholly owned by the Abu Dhabi government.

A Resurgent Russia

As Lockheed relaxed with its Desert Falcon contract in hand, across the globe the Russian government hosted Ural Expo Arms. Fifty foreign delegations were in attendance to view its 800 exhibits. The Expo was designed to highlight Russian defense suppliers and to help increase overseas sales. At that time, Russia's market share of global exports was fluctuating between 2 and 4 percent, and the Russian government was eager to increase exports to generate foreign exchange. Longtime clients such as India and China appeared to show some preference for the Russians. Potential clients agreed that Russian products possessed certain advantages, such as simplicity of use, reliability and low cost. However, Russian servicing was unreliable, and spare parts could be hard to get. The Russian bureaucracy moved very slowly in approving export licenses, and Russian firms rarely became involved in offset agreements. Furthermore, there were so many intermediaries involved in Russian defense sales that the Russian companies themselves saw only a fraction of the profits. Still, the Russian government vowed to increase armament purchases at home and to support Russia's defense industry abroad.

By the time Lockheed concluded the UAE contract, the Russian defense industry had significantly strengthened its global position. During a decade when European countries were decreasing defense spending, Russia increased defense spending by 79 percent. Over the same time frame, India, China and Pakistan became the top importers of defense equipment. The United States remained the largest exporter with 29 percent of global arms exports and 42 percent of total arms supplied to the Middle East. However, Russia's market share of global exports had risen to 27 percent.

Some industry experts believed that the Russian defense industry was still hampered by corruption and outdated equipment. Nonetheless, at a recent Dubai Air Show a Russian MiG-29 fighter plane performed a stunt that impressed the crowd below, and a high-level delegation from Russia headed to Egypt to try to negotiate a $2 billion defense contract. As U.S. political influence in the Arab world appeared to be waning, Russia's prestige was headed for a 20-year high.

Discussion Questions

1. How is the global arms market similar to other government markets? How does it differ?
2. How can home governments help and hurt firms competing in this market?
3. Do you foresee any advantages or disadvantages to Lockheed partnering with an SOE?
4. What qualities are necessary for a firm to compete in this market? Why are Russian defense companies still viable global competitors? Might they successfully compete for sales to Middle East countries? Why or why not?

Sources: Thom Shanker, "U.S. Arms Deal with Israel and Two Arab Nations is Near," *New York Times*, April 18, 2013; Gopal Ratman, "U.S. Seeks 10.8 Billion Weapons Sale to U.A.E., Saudis," *Bloomberg*, October 15, 2013; "Arming the Gulf" in Kate Gillespie and H. David Hennessey, *Global Marketing* (Mason, OH: Cengage, 2011), pp. 186–187; John Dowdy and Melanie Taylor, "Defense Outlook 2015," *McKinsey Reports*, April, 2013. Gerard O'Dwyer, "Russia Surges in Global Arms Sales," defensenews.com, January 31, 2014; Thalif Deen, "Gulf and 'Eldorado' for Arms Sales," *Asia Times*, March 19, 2014; and "NATO's Military Decline," *Wall Street Journal*, March 25, 2014, p. A14.

CASE 6.3 The New Cola Wars

For many years, the battle between Coke and Pepsi dominated the world stage. Private labels began to make inroads supported by powerful retailers, but no national or global brands arose to threaten the cola duopoly. More recently, however, newcomers with unique histories and international ambitions have emerged to challenge the status quo.

Europe and the Middle East

Mecca Cola was launched in France and the Middle East by a Tunisian-born businessman who had moved to France over 20 years earlier. His goal was to make the new product the cola of choice for Muslims worldwide and to combat America's imperialism by providing a substitute for American products. The company pledged 20 percent of its profits to Palestinian and Muslim charities and had a bottling plant in Gaza. Despite its desire to distance itself from competitors such as Coca-Cola, Mecca Cola's packaging was surprisingly similar to that of Coke's—white script on red cans.

Mecca Cola dubbed itself the sponsor of the 1-million-strong peace march in London that demonstrated against U.S. involvement in Iraq. The company handed out 36,000 bottles of cola and 10,000 T-shirts bearing the messages "Stop the war" and "Not in my name." On the heels of this publicity, Mecca Cola entered the U.K. market with the stated goal of capturing 5 percent of the world's tenth largest cola market. Distribution of Mecca Cola in Britain was primarily through small shops in communities where Britain's 1.5 million Muslims were concentrated. But succeeding in the U.K. market would not be easy. Sales of carbonated drinks had stabilized. The market was saturated with soda brands, and mineral waters and fruit juices were attacking cola's traditional position.

Qibla Cola was launched in Britain shortly before Mecca Cola entered the market. Its slogan: Qibla Cola, liberate your taste. (Qibla means "direction" in Arabic.) The Qibla Cola Company also called for a boycott of all American brands to protest the U.S.-led war in Iraq and proclaimed that people should switch to brands that were independent of governments and their unjust policies. Management was planning to target students and young people and claimed that through its branding and distribution it would position itself as a global rather than a Middle Eastern or ethnic brand. Qibla's early distribution was through an informal network of independent retailers, but it aspired to enter supermarkets. The company vowed to give 10 percent of profits to humanitarian causes around the world.

In the Middle East itself, Coca-Cola had already encountered a competitor that positioned itself as an Islamic alternative to Coke: Zam Zam cola from Iran. But as Zam Zam was expanding into Middle Eastern markets such as Saudi Arabia, Coke was returning to shelves in Iran. The United States still imposed trade sanctions on Iran but had exempted foodstuffs. Elsewhere in the Middle East, the Coca-Cola Company signed a franchise with the National Beverage Company (NBC) to bottle and distribute Coke products throughout the West Bank and Gaza Strip. Arguably, the benefits of direct and indirect jobs created for Palestinians by this project far outweighed the charitable contributions that Palestinians would receive from Mecca Cola.

Back in Europe, Coca-Cola announced that it would take a minority stake in smoothie maker Innocent. Based in London, Innocent had become one of Britain's top brands as a result of its social commitment and ethical marketing. Innocent dedicated 10 percent of its profits to charity and utilized recycled bottles. Coke's investment in the company would help Innocent expand throughout Europe.

Latin America

Half a world away, Coca-Cola faced a different kind of challenge in Latin America, where Kola Real was emerging as a multinational threat. Kola Real had been established by a family who had seen their farm in southern Peru destroyed by the Shining Path terrorist group. Eduardo and Mirtha Aranos decided to turn disaster into opportunity. Rebels routinely hijacked Coca-Cola trucks, so the couple, along with their five sons, decided to make their own cola and sell it locally. By cutting costs such as advertising, the Ajegroup's new cola sold at an extremely low price compared to Pepsi and Coke. Kola Real captured 22 percent of the Peruvian market. Kola Real then moved into neighboring Ecuador and Venezuela. The new cola captured 16 percent of the market in Ecuador and 17 percent of the market in Venezuela and forced Coke to cut prices in those markets.

But it was the subsequent entry into Mexico by the Ajegroup that truly threatened the global market leader. Eleven percent of Coca-Cola's global profits came from Mexico, where Mexicans drank more Coke per capita than any other nation. A former head of Coca-Cola's Mexican operations, Vincente Fox, had even become president of Mexico. When the Ajegroup entered the market with cola prices set at 20 to 50 percent below those of competition, Pepsi experienced a rapid 5 percent drop in sales and Coca-Cola saw sales growth disappear. Still, Coke was reluctant to lower prices. Regional newcomers had previously entered the soft-drink market in Brazil and eventually captured 30 percent of the market. As a result, Brazilian profit margins decreased for Coke and Pepsi. The possibility of the same thing happening in Mexico was a real threat.

Furthermore, most newcomers in Latin America had distributed through supermarkets, which were growing in strength but still held smaller market shares of the retail market than did the many small mom-and-pop stores throughout Latin America. Newcomers did price lower than the multinational brands but did not compete aggressively on price. The Ajegroup, however, introduced big bottles at very low prices (the brand was even called Big Cola in Mexico) and relied on hundreds of salespeople to reach the smaller stores that in Mexico accounted for 75 percent of cola sales. In a short time, they succeeded in gaining distribution in 25 percent of such outlets in Mexico City.

Some distributors declined the new cola, citing threats from the Coca-Cola Company to pull Coke products in retaliation (an allegation Coke denied). An earlier ruling by Mexico's antitrust board had ordered Coke to stop abusing its market power over distributors. As a result of this ruling, many distributors first became aware that they had a choice about what they sold. Still, Coke could buy loyalty by offering free refrigerators to chill Cokes and buying its small retailers life-insurance policies. Coca-Cola also offered free cases of Coke, and Coke employees were constantly visiting stores to help with stocking and display. The Ajegroup, on the other hand, kept an eye on costs. Even distribution was outsourced to third parties who often delivered in rundown trucks.

Just three years after entering the Mexican market, Big Cola had grabbed 7 percent market share with a stated goal of increasing market share to 10 percent. Long the largest international market for Coke and Pepsi, Mexico had come to represent 45 percent of Ajegroup's consolidated sales. Consequently, it decided to move its international headquarters to Mexico.

After successfully entering several Central American markets, the Ajegroup decided to take Big Cola to Asia. The company first entered Thailand followed by Vietnam, Indonesia and India. Compared to Mexico, consumption of soft drinks in India was very low. Upon entering that market, Big Cola was sold as a non-caffeine beverage in three flavors—cola, orange and lime. It was only available in larger retail outlets. Coca-Cola and Pepsi retained strong control over the smaller retail outlets. Nonetheless, some at the Ajegroup envisaged that Asia would one day surpass Latin America sales of Big Cola.

Discussion Questions

1. What are the strengths and weaknesses of Qibla and Mecca Cola compared to Coca-Cola?
2. Why has the new cola launched by the Ajegroup been so successful?
3. Evaluate Coca-Cola's response to Ajegroup. What suggestions would you give Coca-Cola?
4. Do you think Big Cola can be as successful in Asia as it has been in Latin America? Why or why not?

Sources: "The New Cola Wars," in Kate Gillespie and H. David Hennessey, *Global Marketing* (Mason, OH: Cengage, 2011), pp. 188–189; Ethan Bronner, "Gaza Mends," *New York Times*, December 17, 2010, p, 6; "Big Cola Moves Marketing Arm to Bangkok," *The Nation*, August 10, 2011; "Can Big Cola Live Up to Its Name?" *Business Standard*, July 23, 2012; "Ajegroup to Launch Big Cola in India," India Retail News, June 15, 2012; and Jim Edwards, "Thailand Cola Conflict Leaves Pepsi Out in the Cold," *Global Post*, March 11, 2013.

Notes

1 Michael Flagg, "Enjoy Shinier Hair! Chinese Brands Arrive," *Wall Street Journal*, May 24, 2001, p. A17.
2 Loretta Chao, "Groupon Stumbles in China," *Wall Street Journal*, August 24, 2011, p. B1.
3 Merissa Marr and Geoffrey A. Fowler, "Chinese Lessons for Disney," *Wall Street Journal*, June 12, 2006, p. B1.
4 Shaun Rein, "Lessons for Chinese Companies as They Go Global," *Business Week Online*, December 2, 2008.
5 George S. Yip, *Total Global Strategy* (New York: Prentice-Hall, 2002), pp. 171–175.
6 Betsy McCay, "Pepsi Uncaps Russian Juice Deal," *Wall Street Journal*, March 21, 2008, p. B4.
7 Geoffrey A. Fowler and Betsy McKay, "Coke Pins China Hopes on Blitz in Beijing," *Wall Street Journal*, August 19, 2008, p. A1.
8 Nikhil Gulati and Rumman Ahmed, "India Has 1.2 Billion People But Not Enough Drink Coke," *Wall Street Journal Online*, July 13, 2013.
9 Manjeet Kripalani and Mark L. Clifford, "Finally Coke Gets It Right," *Business Week*, February 10, 2003, p. 18.
10 Rumman Ahmed, "Dunkin, Starbucks to Duke It Out in India," *Wall Street Journal Online*, February 22, 2012.
11 Constanza C. Bianchi and Carolina Reyes, "Defensive Strategies of Local Companies Against Foreign Multinationals: Evidence from Chilean Retailers," *Latin American Business Review*, vol. 6, no. 2 (2005), pp. 67–85.
12 Eric Bellman, "Why Indian Retailers May Thrive Alongside Many Big New Rivals," *Wall Street Journal*, December 13, 2006.
13 Niraj Dawar and Tony Frost, "Competing with Giants," *Harvard Business Review*, vol. 77 (March–April 1999), pp. 119–129.

14 Guliz Ger, "Localizing in the Global Village: Local Firms Competing in Global Markets," *California Management Review*, vol. 41, no. 4 (Summer 1999), pp. 64–83.

15 Jason Dean, "China's Web Retailers Beat U.S. Rivals at Their Own Game," *Wall Street Journal*, August 22, 2006, p. B1.

16 Tomas Elewaut, Patricia Lindenboim and Damian L. Scokin, "Chile's Lesson in Lean Banking," *McKinsey Quarterly*, no. 3 (2003).

17 Jack Ewing and Joseph Weber, "The Beer Wars Come to a Head," *Business Week*, May 24, 2004, p. 68.

18 Dawar and Frost, "Competing with Giants," p. 124.

19 Jaime Mejia and Gabriel Sama, "Media Players Say 'Si' to Latino Magazines," *Wall Street Journal*, May 15, 2002, p. B4.

20 David C. Gregorcyk, *Internationalization of Conglomerates from Emerging Markets: Success Stories from Mexico*. Unpublished honors thesis, Teresa Lozano Long Institute of Latin American Studies, The University of Texas at Austin, 2005.

21 Hugh Pope, "Turkish Surprise," *Wall Street Journal*, September 7, 2004, p. A1.

22 Steven Gray, "In Indonesia, a Fight for the Soy-Sauce Crown," *Wall Street Journal*, April 20, 2007, p. B3.

23 Marcus Walker and Martin Gelnar, "Europe's Dysfunctional Family Businesses," *Wall Street Journal*, December 22, 2003, p. A13.

24 Charles Forelle, "Microsoft Loss in Europe Raises American Fears," *Wall Street Journal*, September 18, 2007, p. A1.

25 Nikki Tait, "European Takeover Rulings Have Not Been 'Biased'," *Financial Times*, July 14, 2003, p. 10.

26 Carol Matlack, Joseph Weber and Wendy Zellner, "In Fighting Trim," *Business Week*, April 28, 2003, p. 26.

27 Ibid.

28 J. McGuire and S. Dow, "The Persistence and Implications of Japanese Keiretsu Organization," *Journal of International Business Studies*, vol. 34 (2003), pp. 374–388.

29 Ibid.

30 Betsy McKay and David Luhnow, "Mexico Finds Coke and Its Bottlers Guilty of Abusing Dominant Position in Market," *Wall Street Journal*, March 8, 2002, p. B3.

31 Xiaoqing Pi, "China Fines Six Dairy Companies," *Wall Street Journal*, August 8, 2013, p. B3.

32 David Luhnow and Anthony Harrup, "Court Slams Carlos Slim," *Wall Street Journal*, May 4, 2011, p. B1

33 Margaret Coker, "Korean Team to Build U.A.E. Nuclear Plants," *Wall Street Journal*, December 28, 2009, p. B3.

34 Ravi Ramamurti, "Competing with Emerging Market Multinational," *Business Horizons*, vol. 55 (2012), pp. 241–249.

35 Ilan Berman, "A Dangerous Partnership," *Wall Street Journal*, February 22, 2007, p. A14.

36 Karl P. Sauvant and Jonathan Strauss, "State-Controlled Entities Control Nearly US$ 2 trillion in Foreign Assets," *Columbia FDI Perspectives*, April 2, 2012.

37 Josh Gerstein, "Chinese Law Delivers Shipping Controversy," *USA Today*, April 5, 2002, p. B8.

38 Joe McDonald, "Chinese Auto Makers Announce Mergers," Associated Press, December 27, 2007.

39 Jane Spencer, "Why Lenovo Can't Tame U.S.," *Wall Street Journal*, February 2, 2007, p. A14.

40 Bob Davis, "China Tries to Shut the Rising Income Gap," *Wall Street Journal Online*, December 10, 2012.

41 James E. Austin, *Managing in Developing Countries* (New York: The Free Press, 1990), pp. 127–129.

42 James Hookway, "Vietnam Pushes State-Owned Firms to Diversity," *Wall Street Journal*, December 19, 2007, p. A11.

43 Tim Culpan, "Acer Net Misses Estimates on Dropping Sales," Blumberg.com, October 22, 2012.

44 Gary S. Becker, "Is Europe Starting to Play by U.S. Rules?" *Business Week*, April 22, 2002, p. 24.

45 Jason Dean, Andrew Browne and Shal Oster, "China's 'State Capitalism' Sparks a Global Backlash," *Wall Street Journal*, November 16, 2010, p. A1.

46 John Bussey, "In Huawei's Bid to Crack Market, U.S. Sees a Threat from China Inc.," *Wall Street Journal Online*, February 28, 2011.

47 Peter Fritsch, "Hard Profits," *Wall Street Journal*, April 22, 2002, p. A1.

48 Eugene D. Jaffe and Israel D. Nebenzahl, *National Image and Competitive Advantage* (Copenhagen: Copenhagen Business School Press, 2001), p. 53.

49 Elizabeth Woyke, "Flunking Brand Geography," *Business Week*, June 18, 2007, p. 14.

50 Rajshekhar G. Javalgi, Bob D. Cultler, and William A. Winans, "At Your Service! Does Country of Origin Research Apply to Services?" *Journal of Services Marketing*, vol. 15, no. 6/7 (2001), pp. 565–582.

51 Dae Ryun Chang and Ik-Tae Rim, "A Study on the Rating of Import Sources for Industrial Products in a Newly Industrialized Country: The Case of South Korea," *Journal of Business Research*, 32 (1995), pp. 31–39.

52 Hans B. Thorelli and Aleksandra Glowaka, "Willingness of American Industrial Buyers to Source Internationally," *Journal of Business Research*, vol. 32 (1995), pp. 21–30.

53 Chike Okechuku and Vincent Oneyemah, "Nigerian Consumer Attitudes Toward Foreign and Domestic Products," *Journal of International Business Studies*, vol. 30, no. 3 (1999), pp. 611–622.

54 Gary S. Inch and J. Brad McBride, "The Impact of Country-of-Origin Cues on Consumer Perceptions of Product Quality: A Binational Test of the Decomposed Country-of-Origin Construct," *Journal of Business Research*, vol. 57 (2004), pp. 256–265.

55 Michael A. Kamins and Akira Nagashima, "Perceptions of Products Made in Japan versus Those Made in the United States Among Japanese and American Executives: A Longitudinal Perspective," *Asia Pacific Journal of Management*, vol. 12, no. 1 (1995), pp. 49–68; and Inder Khera, "A Broadening Base of U.S. Consumer Acceptance of Korean Products" in Kenneth D. Bahn and M. Joseph Sirsy (eds.), *World Marketing Congress* (Blacksburg, VA: Academy of Marketing Science, 1986), pp. 136–141.

56 Owen Brown, "China Consumers Rate Japan Cars, Electronics Tops," *Wall Street Journal*, June 7, 2004, p. A17.

57 Jim Rendon, "When Nations Need a Little Marketing," *New York Times*, November 23, 2003, p. 5.

58 Sarah McBride, "Kia's Audacious Sorento Plan," *Wall Street Journal*, April 8, 2002, p. A12.

59 Janeen E. Olsen, Linda Nowak and T. K. Clarke, "Country of Origin Effects and Complimentary Marketing Channels: Is Mexican Wine More Enjoyable When Served with Mexican Food?" *International Journal of Wine Marketing*, vol. 14, no. 1 (2002), pp. 23–34.

60 Hugh Pope, "Turkish Delight," *Wall Street Journal*, September 7, 2004, p. A1.

61 Massoud M. Saghafi, Fanis Varvoglis and Tomas Vega, "Why U.S. Firms Don't Buy from Latin American Companies," *Industrial Marketing Management*, vol. 20 (1991), pp. 207–213.

62 Joe Barrett and Timothy W. Martin, "What's in a Name? Not Much for These Fans of Imported Cadbury," *Wall Street Journal*, September 14, 2009, p. A1.

63 Shawn Thelen, John B. Ford and Earl D. Honeycutt Jr., "Assessing Russian Imported Versus Domestic Product Bias," *Thunderbird International Business Review*, vol. 48, no. 5 (2006), pp. 687–704.

64 James R. Hagerty, "Pitching to Wal-Mart," *Wall Street Journal*, October 7, 2013, p. B1.

65 Colum Murphy, "Interior China Stills Balks at Japanese Cars," Dow Jones Top Global Market Stories, September 11, 2013.

66 Lyn S. Amine, Mike C.H. Chao and Mark J. Arnold, "Exploring the Practical Effects of Country of Origin, Animosity, and Price-Quality Issues," *Journal of International Marketing*, vol. 113, no. 2 (2005), pp. 114–150.

67 Jill G. Klein, Richard Ettenson and Marlene D. Morris, "The Animosity Model of Foreign Product Purchase: An Empirical Test in the People's Republic of China," *Journal of Marketing*, vol. 62 (1998), pp. 89–100.

68 Ibid.

69 John Quelch, "The Return of the Global Brand," *Harvard Business Review*, vol. 81 (August 2003), pp. 22–23.

70 John Carreyrou and Jenny E. Heller, "U.S. Rift Hits Bottom Line," *Wall Street Journal*, June 16, 2003, p. A13.

71 Salah AlShebil, Abdul A. Rasheed and Hussam Al-Shammari, "Battling Boycotts," *Wall Street Journal*, April 28, 2007, p. R6.

72 Carreyrou and Heller, "U.S. Rift Hits Bottom Line."

73 Tamsin Carlisle and Joel Baglole, "Canadian Businesses Fear Fallout of Iraq Stance," *Wall Street Journal*, March 28, 2003, p. A11.

74 James Cox, "Firms Say Arab Boycott Sinking," *USA Today*, June 4, 2001.

75 Peter Wonacotte and Chad Terhune, "Path to India's Market Dotted with Potholes," *Wall Street Journal*, September 12, 2006, p. A6.

76 T. Kenn Gaither and Patricia A. Curtin, "Examining the Heuristic Value of Models of International Public Relations Practice: A Case Study of the Arla Foods Crisis," *Journal of Public Relations Research*, vol. 20 (2008), pp. 115–137.

Chapter 7

Global Marketing
Research

THE SCOPE OF GLOBAL MARKETING RESEARCH 200

CHALLENGES IN PLANNING INTERNATIONAL RESEARCH 203

THE RESEARCH PROCESS 203

UTILIZING SECONDARY DATA 204

ANALYSIS BY INFERENCE 207

COLLECTING PRIMARY DATA 208

STUDYING THE COMPETITION 216

OUTSOURCING RESEARCH 219

DEVELOPING A GLOBAL INFORMATION SYSTEM 220

Spanish retailer Zara believes that speed and responsiveness are more important than cost.[1] The company takes only four or five weeks to design a new fashion collection, compared with the six months it takes its major competitors. Zara's designers frequent fashion shows and talk to customers. One designer remarks, "We're like sponges. We soak up information about fashion trends from all over the world." The firm sent out new skirts during the night to some of its 1,770 stores worldwide. From their desks at headquarters, Zara managers can check real-time sales on computers to see where the skirts are selling. They keep in constant contact with store managers in order to spot and react to trends quickly.[2] Understanding the market allows Zara to thrive even during global recessions.[3] Zara competitor, Princess Polly, targets women aged 16 to 26. The fast-fashion company finds social media to be an excellent market research tool and a way to get rapid consumer feedback on new products.[4]

Our purpose in this chapter is to explore methods for collecting appropriate data to better understand potential markets. Our emphasis is managerial rather than technical. Throughout the chapter, we focus on how companies can obtain useful and accurate information that will help them make more informed strategic decisions, such as decisions related to market choice and to the marketing mix that will be discussed in later chapters. This chapter begins by examining the scope and challenges of international research. We then describe the research process, with particular emphasis on data collection. The chapter concludes with a discussion of global information systems.

Learning Objectives

After studying this chapter, you should be able to:

➤ list and describe the four steps involved in the research process;
➤ differentiate between the challenges posed by secondary data collection and those posed by primary data collection;
➤ note cultural differences in marketing research and explain ways in which market researchers can adjust to them;
➤ describe problems related to comparability of studies undertaken in different national markets;
➤ explain the value of analysis by inference to global marketers;
➤ note ways to monitor global competitors;
➤ explain the requirements for a global marketing information system.

The Scope of Global Marketing Research

Global marketing research is meant to provide adequate data and cogent analysis for effective decision-making on a global scale. The analytic research techniques practiced by domestic businesses can be applied to international marketing projects. The key difference is in the complexity of assignments because of the additional variables that international researchers must take into account.

Global marketers have to judge the comparability of their data across a number of markets and are frequently faced with making decisions based on the basis of limited data. Because of this, the researcher must approach the research task with flexibility, resourcefulness and ingenuity.

Traditionally, marketing research has been charged with the following three broad areas of responsibility:

➤ *Environmental studies*. Given the added environmental complexity of global marketing, managers need timely input on various national environments.
➤ *Market studies*. One of the tasks that researchers most frequently face is to determine the size of a market and the needs of potential customers.
➤ *Competitive studies*. Another important task for the global marketing researcher is to provide insights about competitors, both domestic and foreign.

In earlier chapters we have covered many issues involved in an environmental study. Of particular interest are the economic, physical, sociocultural and political environments of a market. Studies focusing on a national market are frequently undertaken when a major decision regarding that market has to be made. This could include a move to enter the country or an effort to significantly increase the firm's presence in that market through large new investments. As a company gains experience in any given country, its staff and local organization accumulate considerable data on the social and cultural situation, and this store of information can be tapped whenever needed. Therefore, a full study of these environmental variables is most useful when the company does not already have a base in that country and its relevant experience is limited.

Nonetheless, managers should carefully monitor changes in their markets. They may also find it useful to keep informed about the latest regulations governing their industry in other countries, even if they do not conduct any business there. Policies in one country often spread to others. This is particularly true within regional blocs. And on an even larger scale, the trade and investment policies of a country have been shown to be influenced by the country's trading partners.[5]

Global marketing research is also used to make both strategic and tactical decisions. Strategic decisions include deciding what markets to enter, how to enter them (exporting, licensing, joint venture), where to locate production facilities and how to position products vis-à-vis competitors. Tactical decisions are decisions about the specific marketing mix to be used in a country and are made on an ongoing basis. Decisions about advertising, sales promotions and sales forces all require data derived from testing in the local market. The type of information required is often the same as that required in domestic marketing research, but the process is made more complex by the variety of cultures and environments. Table 7.1 shows the various types of tactical marketing decisions needed and the kinds of research used to collect the necessary data.

The complexity of the international marketplace, the significant differences that exist from country to country and the company's frequent lack of familiarity with foreign markets accentuate the importance of international marketing research. Before making market entry, product positioning or marketing mix decisions, a marketer must have accurate information about the market size, customer needs, competition and relevant government regulations.

Table 7.1 International Marketing Decisions Requiring Market Research

Marketing Mix Decision	Type of Research
Product policy decisions	Focus groups and qualitative research to generate ideas for new products Survey research to evaluate new product ideas Concept testing, test marketing Product benefit and attitude research Product formulation and feature testing
Pricing decisions	Price sensitivity studies
Distribution decisions	Survey of shopping patterns and behavior Consumer attitudes toward different store types Survey of distributor attitudes and policies
Advertising decisions	Advertising pretesting Advertising post-testing/recall scores Surveys of media habits
Sales promotion decisions	Surveys of response to alternative types of promotion
Sales force decisions	Tests of alternative sales presentations

Source: C. Samuel Craig and Susan P. Douglas, *International Marketing Research*, © 2005, p. 35. Reprinted by permission of John Wiley & Sons, Ltd., Chichester, West Sussex, U.K.

The lack of proper marketing research can sabotage product development for a foreign market. On the strength of a research study conducted in the United States, one U.S. firm introduced a new cake mix in England. Believing that homemakers wanted to feel that they participated in the preparation of the cake, the U.S. marketers devised a mix that required homemakers to add an egg. Given its success in the U.S. market, the marketers confidently introduced the product in England. The product failed, however, because the British did not like fancy American cakes. They preferred cakes that were tough and spongy and could accompany afternoon tea. The ploy of having homemakers add an egg to the mix did not eliminate basic differences in taste and style.[6]

On the other hand, well-conceived market research can provide insights that promote success. To better fine-tune their services at Hong Kong Disneyland, Disney employed researchers with stopwatches to time how long Chinese guests took to eat. They discovered that the Chinese took an average of ten minutes longer than Americans. As a result, Disney added 700 extra seats to the park's dining areas.[7] Based on research from questionnaires filled out by clients, matchmaking firm eHarmony changed its matching algorithm for couples in different countries. For example, the firm discovered that romantic closeness was more important for marital success in Britain than it was in the United States, and anger management was more important for successful marriages in Britain and the United States than it was in Brazil.[8]

Challenges in Planning International Research

After determining what key variables to investigate, international marketers still face a number of challenges. Whereas domestic research is limited to one country, international research includes many. The global market researcher must choose which countries and market segments to investigate. For many countries, secondary information may be limited or expensive. Primary research can prove culturally challenging. In addition, the comparison of research results from one national study to another is hindered by the general difficulty of establishing comparability and equivalence among various research data. Definitions of socioeconomic status, income and education can vary widely among countries, which makes even the simplest demographic comparisons between markets challenging.

The Research Process

Although conducting marketing research internationally adds to the complexity of the research task, the basic approach remains the same for domestic and international assignments. Either type of research is a four-step process:

1. Problem definition and development of research objectives.
2. Determination of the sources of information.
3. Collection and analysis of the data from primary and secondary sources.
4. Analysis of the data.

These four steps may be the same for both international and domestic research, but problems in implementation may occur because of cultural and economic differences from country to country.

Problem Definition and Development of Research Objectives

In any market research project, the most important tasks are to define the problem and, subsequently, to determine what information is needed. This process can take weeks or months. It eventually determines the choice of methodologies, the types of people to survey and the appropriate time frame in which to conduct the research.

In determining the research question, managers must decide on an etic or an emic approach. The etic approach assumes that a research question developed in one culture can be more or less translated for use in another cultural context. Etic research is useful in that it allows comparisons across countries but can miss important differences between countries. In contrast to the etic approach, the emic approach focuses on understanding each local context from its own cultural frame of reference. The emic approach assumes that cultures are so different that mere translation of a concept across cultures is dangerous to truly insightful research. For example, bicycles in a developed country may be competing with other recreational goods, such as skis, baseball gloves and exercise equipment. In a developing country, however, they provide basic transportation and hence compete with small cars, mopeds and scooters. A global firm could fail to understand why growth in bicycles was declining in Malaysia if it asked questions only about the consumer's purchase and use of other recreational products.

Data Collection

For each assignment, researchers may choose to base their analyses on primary data (data collected specifically for this assignment), secondary data (previously collected and available data) or a combination of both secondary and primary sources. Because costs tend to be higher for research based on primary data, researchers usually exhaust secondary data first. Often called desk research or library research, this approach depends on the availability and reliability of material. Secondary sources may include government publications, trade journals and data from international agencies or service establishments such as banks, ad agencies and marketing research companies.

Utilizing Secondary Data

For any marketing research project, the location and analysis of secondary data should be a first step. Although secondary data are not available for all variables, data can often be obtained from public and private sources at a fraction of the cost of obtaining primary data. Increasingly, these sources are disseminating or selling their data over the Internet.

Sources of Secondary Data

A good approach to locating secondary sources is to ask yourself who would know about most sources of information on a specific market. For example, if you wanted to locate secondary information on fibers used for tires in Europe, you might consider asking the editor of a trade magazine on the tire industry or the executive director of the tire manufacturing association or the company librarian for Akzo Nobel, a Dutch company that manufactures fibers.

Sources of secondary data for international markets include web search engines, banks, consulates, embassies, foreign chambers of commerce, libraries with foreign information sections, foreign magazines, public accounting firms, security brokers and state development offices in foreign countries. Marketers can also "eavesdrop" on the Internet. Every day customers comment online concerning products and services. By monitoring chatrooms, newsgroups, listservs and social media, marketers can analyze comments to learn what their customers and their competitors are thinking. For-pay subscription sources for secondary research, such a Factiva or Euromonitor, can often be accessed via a university or corporate library.

Many governments collect and disseminate information concerning foreign markets to encourage their national firms to export. To make access to information easier and more streamlined, the U.S. government combined the foreign market research of its various embassies, departments and bureaus into a single export portal located at www.export.gov. Although designed for exporters, the site is useful to foreign investors as well.

Problems with Secondary Data

There are problems associated with the use of secondary data. They include: (1) the fact that not all the necessary data may be available; (2) uncertainty about the accuracy of the data; (3) the lack of comparability of the data and (4) the questionable timeliness of some data. In some cases, no data have been collected. For example, many countries have little data on the number of retailers, wholesalers and distributors. In Ethiopia and Chad, population statistics were unavailable for many years.

The quality of government statistics is definitely variable. For example, Germany reported that industrial production was up by 0.5 percent in one month but later revised this figure, reporting that production actually declined by 0.5 percent, an error of 100 percent in the opposite direction. An *Economist* survey of 20 international statisticians rated the quality of statistics from 13 developed countries on the criteria of objectivity, reliability, methodology and timeliness. The leading countries were Canada, Australia, Holland and France; the worst were Belgium, Spain and Italy.[9]

Although a substantial body of data exists from the most advanced industrial nations, secondary data are less likely to be available for developing countries. Not every country publishes a census, and some published data are not considered reliable. In Nigeria, for example, population size is of such political sensitivity that published census data are generally believed to be highly suspect. A study by the International Labor Organization found actual unemployment to be 10.4 million people in Russia, compared with the official figure of 1.7 million people unemployed![10] However, income remains the most problematic demographic category of all state statistics in developing countries. For example, in Central Asia a significant share of family income comes from the informal economy such as black markets, street vending and bribery. Since respondents won't admit these sources of income, Central Asian governments estimate incomes based on questions relating to household expenditures.[11]

According to a report by the U.S. Foreign Commercial Service in Beijing, Chinese government statistics are often riddled with *shuifen* or "water content." China has begun to crack down on fraudulent statistics, however, using new laws to discipline local officials who exaggerate their successes. Still, data reliability remains a problem in many developing countries. For this reason, companies sometimes have to proceed with the collection of primary data in developing countries at a much earlier stage than in the most industrialized nations.

World Beat 7.1

Argentina's Inflation is Off Limits to Researchers

When the Argentine government didn't like the country's inflation numbers, it simply changed the inflation measures. The new numbers showed lower inflation resulting in lower interest payments on the government's inflation-linked bonds. Subsequently, the Argentine president replaced independent civil servants at the national statistics agency with her own political appointees.

According to official statistics, inflation in Argentina fell below 10 percent. However, almost all independent economists disagreed. They put the figure above 20 percent. In one year alone, the government fined nine economic research firms $122,000 dollars each for failing to agree with the government. The Argentine government charged MyS Consultores with "publishing false information about inflation data" and claimed the economic consultants were attempting to benefit themselves and their clients by spurring speculation in the bond market. MyS denied the charges.

Independent economists continued to estimate Argentina's inflation rate despite the threat of retaliation from the government. Consensus reached 28 percent shortly before the government resorted to a devaluation of the peso. After Argentina devalued its currency by 15 percent, inflation worsened. Local prices soared as many importers passed on the costs of devaluation to Argentine customers. A home appliance salesman declared that raising prices was the only alternative to losing money. And the owner of a Hyundai dealership in Buenos Aires opined that being used to inflation didn't make it any easier to deal with its challenges.

Sources: Michael. J. Boskin, "Don't Like the Numbers? Change 'Em," *Wall Street Journal*, January 14, 2010, p. A19: Taos Turner, "Argentina Charges Economists," *Wall Street Journal Online*, July 9, 2012; and Taos Turner, Juan Forero and John Lyons, "Inflation Fuels Crises in Two Latin Nations," *Wall Street Journal*, February 6, 2014.

The entry of private-sector data collectors into major emerging markets may help ameliorate the shortcomings of government statistics. Since the late 1990s, the Gallup Organization has collected data on the Chinese. Gallup interviewers poll 4,000 randomly selected respondents from both rural and urban China. Questions cover a wide range of topics: How much money do you make? What do you buy? What are your dreams? The results of these surveys are compiled in Gallup publications of consumer attitudes and lifestyles in modern China.[12]

Another problem is that secondary data may not be directly comparable from country to country. France surveys a sample of its population every year, but the population statistics in the United States are collected every ten years and Germany waited over 20 years between its last two censuses.[13] Similarly, population statistics in Bolivia are collected every 25 years. Also, countries may calculate the same statistic but do so in different ways. GDP is the value of all goods and services produced in a country and is often used in place of GNP. GDP per capita is a common measure of market size, suggesting the economic wealth of a country per person. As we noted in Chapter 5, the IMF has decided that the normal practice of converting expressions of GDP in local currencies into dollars at market exchange rates understates the true size of developing economies relative to rich ones. Therefore, the IMF has decided to use purchasing-power parity, which takes into account differences in prices among nations.

Finally, age of the data is a constant problem. With different markets exhibiting different growth rates, it may be unwise to use older data to make decisions among markets. Market surveys previously undertaken by governments or private research firms are seldom as timely as a marketing manager truly needs.

Analysis by Inference

Data available from secondary sources are frequently of an aggregate nature and fail to satisfy the specific information needs of a firm. A company must often assess market size on the basis of very limited data on foreign markets. In such cases, market assessment by inference is a possibility. This technique uses available facts about related products or other foreign markets as a basis for inferring the necessary information for the market under analysis. When shipments of Apple smartphones more than doubled in a single quarter mainly due to sales in Europe and Asia, developers of iPhone applications took note. Tapulous International, a producer of music games, experienced similar growth the next year.[14]

Market assessment by inference is a low-cost activity that should take place before a company engages in the collection of any primary data, which can be quite costly. Inferences can be made on the basis of related products, relative market size and analysis of demand patterns.

Related Products

Few products are consumed or used "in a vacuum"—that is, without any ties to prior purchases or to products in use. If actual consumption statistics are not available for a product category, proxies can prove useful. A proxy is a related product that indicates demand for the product under study. Relationships exist, for example, between replacement tires and automobiles on the road and between electricity consumption and the use of appliances. In some situations, it may be possible to obtain data on related products and their uses as a basis for inferring usage of the product to be marketed. From experience in other, similar markets, the analyst is able to apply usage ratios that can provide for low-cost estimates. For example, the analyst can determine the number of replacement tires needed by looking at the number of automobiles on the road. Radio audiences also tend to increase with the number of automobiles in a country. This was observed in China, prompting more interest in radio advertising among firms operating there.[15]

Relative Market Size

Quite frequently, if data on market size are available for other countries, this information can be used to derive estimates for the particular country under investigation. For example, say that market size is known for the United States and that estimates are required for Canada, a country with a reasonably comparable economic system and consumption patterns. Statistics for the United States can be scaled down, by the relative size of GNP, population or other factors, to about one-tenth of U.S. figures. Similar relationships exist in Europe, where the known market size of one country can provide a basis for inferences about a related country. Of course, the results are not exact, but they provide a basis for further analysis.

Analysis of Demand Patterns

By analyzing industrial growth patterns for various countries, researchers can gain insights into the relationship of consumption patterns to industrial growth. Relationships can be plotted between GDP per capita and the percentage of total manufacturing production accounted for by major industries.

During earlier growth stages with corresponding low PCIs, manufacturing tends to center on necessities such as food, beverages, textiles and light manufacturing. With growing incomes, the role of these industries tends to decline, and heavy industry assumes greater importance. By analyzing such manufacturing patterns, it is possible to make forecasts for various product groups for countries at lower income levels, because they often repeat the growth patterns of more developed economies.

Similar trends can be observed for a country's import composition. With increasing industrialization, countries develop similar patterns modified only by each country's natural resources. Energy-poor countries must import increasing quantities of energy as industrialization proceeds, whereas energy-rich countries can embark on an industrialization path without significant energy imports. Industrialized countries import relatively more food products and industrial materials than manufactured goods, which are more important for the less-industrialized countries. Understanding these relationships can help the analyst determine future trends for a country's economy and may help determine future market potential and sales prospects.

Collecting Primary Data

Often, in addition to secondary data or when secondary data are not available or usable, the marketer will need to collect primary data. Researchers can design studies to collect primary data that will meet the information requirements for making a specific marketing decision. Primary sources frequently reveal data that are simply not available from secondary sources. For example, Siar Research International undertook a survey on shaving habits in Central Asia and discovered that over 50 percent of Kazakhstan men shaved every day, whereas most Azerbaijan men shaved only once a week.[16]

For the global marketer, collecting primary data involves observation, focus groups, Surveys and analyzing the new big data.

Observation

Observation is a valued methodology in international market research and increasingly attracts top management participation. For example, the new head of Wal-Mart International spent a few days in India in order to better understand Indian consumers. He looked in kitchens and bathrooms and noted that one family had three televisions but no refrigerator.[17] Similarly, the new chief marketing and corporate-affairs officer for McDonald's in China began his job with a ten-day trip, living with families across China, in order to become familiar with their eating and spending habits.[18]

Observation is particularly useful for revealing new ideas about consumer behavior that are free from the biases that researchers may bring to a study. Thus it lends itself well to the emic approach. Observation can be a powerful research tool in developing countries where other techniques may be taboo or difficult to administer. In Cuba, where administering questionnaires on the street is strictly forbidden, foreign marketers can explore how Cubans behave by unobtrusively watching them shop. However, this approach should be used with caution. Unless a researcher is very familiar with the culture, observations can prove difficult to interpret and can lead to wrong research conclusions.[19]

Carefully crafted observational studies designed to understand subtle nuances in consumer behavior are sometimes referred to as consumer ethnographies and can prove useful in an increasingly complex global marketplace. Often these studies are administered by trained anthropologists. Visual cues are used to supplement field notes. Such cues are collected via photographs or videotape (when culturally acceptable) and capture elements of décor, design aesthetics, color, fashion, architecture and icons.[20]

A European furniture manufacturer commissioned a visual survey that created a database of nearly 13,000 photos from 30 countries. The visual survey revealed that Indians liked products that were both simple and practical. There was little decoration or storage space in the Indian kitchen. Windows rarely had curtains or blinds. In Sweden, however, the kitchen was the heart of the home. Utensils were prominently displayed, and small plants and candles were commonly used to give kitchens a cozy feel.[21]

To better understand consumers overseas, P&G has introduced videotaping to learn about the lifestyles and local habits of consumers in different countries. Videotaping one household in Thailand revealed that a mother engaged in multiple tasks, from watching television to cooking a meal, while feeding her baby. P&G believes that the behaviors that consumers don't talk about—such as multitasking while feeding a baby—could inspire product and package design in ways that could give the company a competitive edge over its rivals.[22]

Focus Groups

Another technique that can be used for collecting marketing research data is focus groups. The focus group can be particularly useful at an early stage in the development of a new product concept to gain valuable insights from potential consumers. The researcher assembles a small group of carefully selected respondents to discuss a product. The number may vary by culture. The norm is seven in Europe and eight to ten in the United States. A focus group of six or less may be more appropriate in Asia, where respondents may have more difficulty opening up in front of others.[23] The research company assembles the participants and leads the discussion; this avoids the bias that the active presence of a company representative might introduce. Of course, the discussion leader must speak in the mother tongue of the participants. Representatives of the company can observe the focus group via audiotaping or videotaping, through a one-way mirror, or by sitting in the room.

Focus groups may face government regulation in certain countries. Communist Vietnam has only recently opened to Western businesses, yet marketing researchers find that the Vietnamese are enthusiastic about joining focus groups. Participation rates can range between 35 and 50 percent.

But similar to China, the government of Vietnam restricts what can be asked in these groups and bans topics it considers too sensitive.[24]

Focus groups are also subject to a number of cross-cultural challenges:

➤ In certain Central Asian countries such as Kazakhstan, Turkmenistan and Uzbekistan, men and women should not be present in the same focus group.[25] In some Muslim countries, it can even be difficult to find women who will agree to participate at all.

➤ In other countries, such as Japan, it may be difficult to get participants to criticize a potential product due to courtesy bias.

➤ Expect participants in polychronic cultures, such as Thailand, Malaysia and Indonesia, to show up late—or not at all—for the focus group. Plan on inviting a few extra participants to be sure you have enough for your group to continue.[26]

➤ In high-power-distance countries (most developing countries) young participants may not contradict older ones.

➤ A focus group in Brazil consisting of eight women can take an hour longer than a similar focus group in the United States due to the considerable time participants invest up front getting to know one another.[27] After all, introductory chats are the norm in high-context cultures.

Given these many cultural challenges, focus group leaders must be resourceful at using a questioning technique—and even interpreting body language—to get full value from this research approach.

World Beat 7.2

Middle East Research

The size of the global marketing research market is estimated at nearly $35 billion. But the Middle East and North Africa has the smallest slice of the pie at only $600 million. Government restrictions abound in this part of the world. Governments retain the right to censor all questionnaires, although market research is less scrutinized than political polling. This has led some political pollsters to slip in controversial questions into predominately nonpolitical surveys.

Culture also impacts how research can be conducted. For example, mixed-gender focus groups may be unacceptable unless they solely consist of close family members. In conservative Saudi Arabia, where strict interpretation of Islam demands segregation of the sexes, mixed-gender focus groups are prohibited. Even in more liberal Muslim nations such as Egypt, mixed-gender groups are usually not recommended. Muslim women often defer to men, letting males dominate the conversation, which skews the results of a focus group. Segregation is still the best way to get Muslim women to speak up. Researchers note, however, that focus groups of Arab women should be restricted in size due to the fact that the women tend to speak at the same time and hold side conversations.

Participation in surveys in the Middle East is generally high, but most surveys have to be conducted in person causing them to be time-consuming and costly. Many experienced researchers avoid surveying during the month of Ramadan when participation tends to be unusually low. No matter what time of the year the research is undertaken, experts warn marketers to expect a research project in the Middle East to take at least twice as long as it would in Europe or the United States.

Sources: Carl Bialik, "Pollsters Struggle for Accurate Picture of Middle East," *Wall Street Journal*, February 26, 2011, p. A2: Wendy Wilkins Winslow, Gladys Honein and Margaret Ann Elzubeir, "Seeking Emirati Women's Voices: The Use of Focus Groups With an Arab Population," *Qualitative Health Research*, vol. 12, no. 4 (April 2002); and "MENA Research Market Worth $600 Million," *Mist News*, March 10, 2013.

Surveys

Survey research is extensively used in international marketing research. It lends itself to the etic approach but is also useful for testing emic insights developed via observation or focus groups. Survey research involves developing a research instrument, determining a sampling methodology and then collecting the data. Each of these tasks is more complex in the global context.

Developing a Research Instrument

The process of developing a research instrument such as a survey questionnaire must often be done with multiple markets in mind, and every effort should be made to capture the appropriate environmental variables. Even research aimed at a single market might be compared, at a later date, with the results of research in another country. Nonetheless, translation of a questionnaire is prone to difficulties. For instance, a surprising problem arises when translating questionnaires from English (an alphabetic-based language) into Japanese (a character-based language): they become longer! Since most respondents around the world prefer shorter questionnaires to longer ones, this presents market researchers with yet another cross-cultural obstacle.[28]

Indeed, a major challenge of instrument design involves translation from one language to another. Accurate translation equivalence is important, first to ensure that the respondents understand the question and second to ensure that the researcher understands the response. Back translation is commonly used. That is, first the questionnaire is translated from the home language into the language of the country where it will be used; this is done by a bilingual speaker who is a native speaker of the foreign country. Next a bilingual person who is a native speaker of the home language translates this version back into the home language. This translation is then compared to the original wording. Another translation technique is parallel translation, in which two or more translators translate the questionnaire. The results are compared and any differences are discussed and resolved.

Even when back translation or parallel translation techniques are employed, translation problems can still occur. For example, the concept of *bitterness* when used in the context of food has different meanings in different cultures. In Turkey it is associated with a pungent, spicy taste. In Japan it is associated with poison.[29]

Furthermore, idiomatic expressions and colloquialisms are often translated incorrectly. One international market research firm discovered this when working with a camera manufacturer. The client proposed to use in an advertisement a direct translation into Spanish of the English sentence "I get a good shot every time I use it." Unfortunately, this translated into "I get a good *gunshot* every time."[30] To avoid these translation errors, experts suggest the technique of back translation be used even in the local dialect, so that *ji xuan ji*, which means "computers" to Chinese speakers in China and Taiwan, does not become "calculators" to Chinese speakers in Singapore.[31] Similarly, the translation of "retail outlet" works in Mexican Spanish but not in Venezuelan Spanish. Venezuelans could interpret the translation to mean "electrical outlet".[32] Even within the same city, differences in social class can result in different idioms. In one study of the adoption of new products, interviewers in Mexico City were selected from among the same social class as respondents.[33]

Translation problems also arise with measurement scales. U.S. respondents may readily recognize and understand the "school-grade" scale of A–F. However, such a scale would be meaningless elsewhere.[34] Similarly, researchers who employ scales with concepts such as "satisfied," "happy" and "delighted" may discover that some cultures fail to determine sufficient differences between such terms. In general, unless a researcher is very familiar with a culture, it is best to employ a numeric, or Likert, scale.

Finally, even with the best of translations, research can suffer if a concept is not readily understood. For example, Western researchers discovered that the Vietnamese tend to be very literal in their understanding of ideas. If a company asks for an opinion on a new package design concept, Vietnamese consumers may say they never saw it before, so it can't be done. Researchers must instead explain that the new packaging is available in other countries and then ask what consumers think of it.[35]

Selecting a Sample

After developing the instrument and translating it into the appropriate language, the researcher must determine the appropriate sample design. What population is under investigation? Is it housewives between 20 and 40 years old or manufacturing directors at textile plants? When investigating buyer behavior, researchers must remember that the purchase decision-maker can vary by country. For example, the key decision-maker for purchasing diagnostic equipment in the United States is often a laboratory director. In Europe, where medical testing is more decentralized, the decision-maker could be a department director or nurse manager.[36] The international market researcher must adjust the target population accordingly.

Researchers prefer using a probability sample in order to have greater assurance that sample results can be extrapolated to the population under investigation. To have a probability sample, potential respondents must be randomly selected from frames, or lists, of the population. In many developing countries such lists are difficult to find.[37] Instead probability samples may need to be derived from neighborhood maps. In Saudi Arabia, researchers commonly construct sampling frames based on residences located by city blocks in major cities.[38] Even where sampling frames are available, they are often out-of-date. Some market researchers use telephone directories. However, in Mexico, for example, the telephone directory may not correspond with those who currently possess the phone numbers. Further difficulties arise from inadequate transportation, which may prevent fieldworkers from reaching selected census tracts in some areas of the country.

Nonprobabilistic sampling assumes no prior list of names (or residences) and may be employed when sampling frames are unavailable. Nonprobabilistic sampling includes convenience, judgment, snowball and quota sampling. Convenience sampling includes any respondent who is easily available. Judgment sampling chooses available respondents who are better informed or particularly appropriate for the study. When developing a light sport-utility vehicle for the Brazilian youth market, Ford polled young upper-class Brazilians at trendy nightclubs.[39] Snowball sampling asks initial respondents to identify other respondents who are appropriate for the study. Quota sampling specifies a certain number of respondents from each of several different demographic categories. Quota sampling is particularly appropriate in countries where populations are not homogeneous. This is less of a problem in countries like Japan or South Korea. However, Hong Kong and Indonesia have culturally diverse populations. Population migration also poses a challenge. Approximately two-fifths of the residents of the Arab Emirates are expatriate males who are temporarily working in the region.[40] Quota sampling is also appropriate when consumer behavior is known or suspected to differ greatly between groups. For example, in the U.A.E there are significant differences by nationality and income with regards to brand preferences and loyalty for cigarettes.[41]

Collecting Data

The next task of the international market researcher is to collect the data. An immediate problem may involve finding the right people to undertake the data collection. Finding the proper personnel in developing countries can be particularly challenging since most people may not even understand the concept of marketing research. To overcome this problem in South Africa, the managing director of one research firm guest lectures at tecknicons (schools where students who do not attend universities go to earn diplomas) in order to generate interest in marketing research. She reports that interest in this new profession is high, and she encourages students to volunteer at market research firms in order to gain experience.[42]

Another problem in developing countries can be the fact that many data collectors are poorly paid and are often paid by the response. This can lead to collectors simply filling out questionnaires themselves. Some of the safeguards against this in developed countries cannot be easily replicated in developing ones. To ensure quality, supervisors can call back respondents on a random basis to confirm their responses. Alternatively, supervisors can randomly listen in on telephone interviews. However, phone interviews are rare in developing countries, and collectors must often intercept respondents on the streets. This can make it more difficult for supervisors to check responses.

Firms often depend on channel members to help them collect data but cannot always expect the same cooperation across different markets. Amassing so-called big data allows companies to investigate shopping patterns. In the United States, many marketers of consumer products depend on scanner data collected by retailers to develop this data and run their models. However, retailers in China have been far less cooperative in supplying such data. This has forced firms to return to directly surveying consumers.[43]

COLLECTION METHODS Data can be collected by mail, by telephone, electronically or face-to-face. In developed countries, telephone interviews have often been the method of choice. However, as noted, interviews by telephone are more difficult in developing countries where landline phones have less penetration and (as also noted earlier) telephone directories may be nonexistent or woefully out-of-date.

Face-to-face interviews may be necessary in developing countries, but researchers may encounter challenges in approaching respondents in these traditional collectivist societies. Face-to-face interviews are decreasing in most developed countries and being replaced by more Internet-based research. While developing countries lag behind developed ones in Internet access, market researchers are planning for the future. The number of consumers with Internet connection is rising in developing countries, where access is increasingly possible via mobile phones as well as via computers.

PARTICIPATION AND RESPONSE A major issue in primary research, of course, is the willingness of the potential respondent to participate in the study. For example, in many cultures a man will consider it inappropriate to discuss his shaving habits with anyone, especially with a female interviewer. Respondents in the Netherlands or Germany are notoriously reluctant to divulge information about their personal financial habits. The Dutch are more willing to discuss sex than money.[44]

Respondents in developing countries may be particularly wary of sharing information for fear of how it may be used against them. During China's latest economic census, millions of surveyors questioned business owners about production, sales and profits. The government sought to better understand its own economy and to improve the dismal reputation of Chinese statistics. With hopes of eliciting better responses, the government went to great lengths to assure respondents that they would not use any information from the census to pursue tax evaders.[45] In the sub-Saharan country of Liberia, respondents are also wary of the census, believing it is undertaken for the purpose of tax collection. Some even worry that it could be part of a military recruitment drive. In recent memory, boys as young as five have been conscripted to fight. To address these concerns, the Liberian government employed a pop star to write an upbeat song about the census. Translated into the country's 16 languages, the song played daily on the radio.[46]

Developing countries can present additional problems to market researchers, including poor infrastructure, lower literacy levels and disinclination to share information with strangers. In Mexico, unreliable mail service makes mail surveys impractical.[47] Mexican respondents prefer shorter questionnaires administered face-to-face but may be less forthcoming if interviewed at home than they would be if intercepted on the street. This is particularly true regarding information about personal income, because respondents may believe that the researchers are the tax authorities in disguise.[48] Convincing business buyers to participate in research studies is also difficult in many developing countries. Potential respondents are often concerned that the information they provide will be released to competitors or to the authorities.

Social Media and Big Data

With the growth of social media, marketers have the ability to collect and subsequently analyze a huge amount of information relating to online activity in order to better understand both customers and competitors. Big data is a term referring to the technologies used to collect, store, process and analyze massive volumes of data including text, documents, pictures and videos. Utilizing data from social media for marketing research can be extremely cost efficient compared to focus groups or surveys. While more traditional ways of market research can take months to administer, social media research may only take minutes or hours.[49]

An estimated 80 percent of consumers with Internet access use social media. Social media platforms such as Twitter or Facebook provide marketers with ways to analyze trends and conduct market research. Market researchers might also search the latest posts or popular terms.[50] They could then trace trends as they emerge in real time and address opportunities as well as potential problems with targeted responses. Or a potential buyer of a smartphone seeking information online can be tracked by a potential seller who will immediately send out a personalized advertisement to the potential buyer.[51] The Chief Marketing Officer at Dell recounted a story of how her company traced social media to assist in B2B marketing. When Dell analysts noticed a competitor's customer posting a remark that he was upset with the competitor's customer service, Dell sent out their own representative to solve the problem. As a result, Dell won a new business customer.[52]

The use of big data is not limited to developed markets in advanced economies. In Africa, ownership of smartphones is expected to rise from 67 million to 360 million by 2025. A survey of businesses in Kenya and Nigeria revealed that 64 percent of companies were planning or implementing a project utilizing big data.[53] In China, both multinational corporations (MNCs) and state-owned companies utilize big data to better understand their customers. U.S.-based budget hotel operator Super 8 Worldwide utilizes big data to better understand the rapidly growing market for budget hotels in China.[54]

Government Regulation of Data Collection

Survey design, sampling and data collection can all be affected by national legislation. For example, market researchers in the United States, where telephone interviews are common, now face state and national no-call lists that restrict their access to potential respondents. In Germany, street and mall interviews have become less common because researchers must have a license from local authorities to approach respondents.[55] Opinion polls in China are subject to government screening. In addition, questions about politics and sex are often disallowed.[56]

Data collection and privacy concerns being raised in the EU may affect marketing research globally. The EU Data Privacy Directive requires unambiguous consent from a person for each use of his or her personal data.[57] This limits both the use of telephone interviews and how data over the Internet is collected and used. All EU nations have data privacy legislation and a government privacy commission to enforce the EU policy. This legislation stipulates that data cannot be sent to a country that is not a member of the EU unless that country has an adequate level of privacy protection. The U.S. Department of Commerce has worked with EU officials to develop the Safe Harbor Framework. This framework provides a streamlined way for individual U.S. firms to comply with the European standards and thus continue to receive data from Europe. More recently, Japan has exhibited concerns about privacy similar to those in the EU and passed legislation forbidding market research companies from using secondhand lists to contact individuals without first acquiring the consent of those individuals.[58]

Issues of customer privacy have increased with the use of big data, and evolving laws in different countries have complicated its storage and use by MNCs. The EU is particularly concerned that customers be given more determination over how their information is used including the right to have their online information erased from databases. The EU proposes to fine companies up to

2 to 5 percent of their global sales for the abuse of customer data. Microsoft became the first company to comply with the EU's most recent changes in privacy regulations, which limits the sharing of information between operations in Europe and the United States. Microsoft operates big data centers in Amsterdam and Dublin that allow European customers of cloud-based products to store their data locally. In the Asia-Pacific region, data is stored in Singapore or Hong Kong.[59]

Comparing Studies Across Cultures

A researcher must deal with problems of comparability when research is undertaken in more than one country to compare buyer attitudes or behavior in different markets. Were the samples similar in all markets? A study comparing software adoption among small-business owners in Brazil with that among managers in large U.S. corporations may identify differences based more on firm size than on nationality. Are measures comparable cross-culturally? For example, measures of affluence such as size of residence or number of vacations may prove problematic because Europeans live in smaller homes and receive more vacation days than Americans do.[60] Needless to say, issues of comparability should be addressed at the beginning—not the end—of the research process.

Another issue of comparability that arises concerns the response to scales commonly used in survey research. Some cultures express themselves comfortably in extremes, whereas responses in other cultures hover more centrally, making it difficult to determine whether consumers in that country are indeed more neutral about products or whether these tepid responses are an artifact of culture. When interpreting surveys in particular, researchers should be concerned with scalar equivalence. What does it mean to rate a product "seven" or "eight" on a ten-point scale? In Latin America, an "eight" would indicate lack of enthusiasm, whereas in Asia it would be a very good score.[61] One study of respondents in Australia, France, Singapore and the United States suggests that the use of a five- or seven-point scale (as opposed to a ten-point scale) minimizes such cross-cultural differences without sacrificing much research insight.[62]

Another issue that affects comparability is courtesy bias. Courtesy bias arises when respondents attempt to guess what answer the interviewer wants to hear and reply accordingly. For example, a taste test could result in respondents saying they liked the product even if they didn't. The level of courtesy bias varies among cultures. It can be a particular problem in Mexico as well as in many Middle Eastern and Asian countries. AlertDriving, a company that provides online driving training courses for companies with vehicle fleets, expanded into 20 countries before it realized that its product needed cultural adaptation. For example, the course told drivers that the inside lane was the safest on a multi-lane highway, but in Dubai that lane is used exclusively for passing. It took years to realize that its foreign clients were dissatisfied. This was largely due to the fact that in many markets customers were reluctant to provide negative feedback, because voicing criticism is considered disrespectful.[63]

Studying the Competition

Results in the marketplace do not depend solely on researching buyer characteristics and meeting buyer needs. To a considerable extent, success in the marketplace is influenced by a firm's understanding of and response to its competition. Firms may investigate competitors in order to benchmark.

Benchmarking involves identifying best practices in an industry in order to copy those practices and achieve greater efficiency. For example, when the pharmaceutical firm Merck decided to rejuvenate its subsidiary (Merck Banyu) in the important Japanese market, it looked into what competitors, including world leader Pfizer, were doing. As a result, Banyu salespersons were told to focus on a smaller number of drugs in order to achieve increased efficiencies.[64]

Keeping track of a firm's competitors is also an important strategic function. Kodak learned through competitive intelligence that Fuji was planning a new camera for the U.S. market. Kodak launched a competing model just one day before Fuji. Motorola discovered through one of its intelligence staff members, who was fluent in Japanese, that the Japanese electronics firms planned to build new semiconductor plants in Europe. Motorola changed its strategy to build market share in Europe before the new capacity was built. This type of strategic intelligence can be critical to a firm.[65]

To undertake effective research about its competition, a company must first determine who its competitors are. The domestic market will certainly provide some input here. However, it is important to include any foreign company that either currently is a competitor or may become one in the future. The monitoring should not be restricted to activity in the competitors' domestic market but, rather, should include competitors' moves anywhere in the world. Many foreign firms first innovate in their home markets, expanding abroad only when the initial debugging of the product has been completed. Therefore, a U.S. firm would lose valuable time if it began monitoring a Japanese competitor's activities only upon that competitor's entry into the U.S. market. Any monitoring system needs to be structured in such a way as to ensure that competitors' actions will be spotted wherever they occur first. Komatsu, Caterpillar's major competitor worldwide in the earth-moving industry, subscribed to the *Journal Star*, the major daily newspaper in Caterpillar's hometown, Peoria, Illinois. Also important are the actions taken by competitors in their foreign subsidiaries. These actions may signal future moves elsewhere in a company's global network of subsidiaries.

Table 7.2 lists the types of information a company may wish to collect on its competitors. Aside from general business statistics, a competitor's profitability may shed some light on its capacity to pursue new business in the future. Learning about others' marketing operations may enable a company to assess, among other things, the market share to be gained in any given market. Whenever major actions are planned, it is extremely helpful to anticipate the reactions of competitive firms and include them in the company's contingency planning. Of course, monitoring a competitor's new products or expansion programs may give early hints of future competitive threats.

There are numerous ways to monitor competitors' activities. Thorough study of trade or industry journals is a starting point. Also, frequent visits can be made to major trade fairs where competitors exhibit their products. At one such fair in Texas, Caterpillar engineers were seen measuring Komatsu equipment.[66] In fact, the high level of competitive espionage that goes on at trade fairs can sometimes discourage participation. When one manufacturer exhibited a new toy at the famous Hong Kong Toy Fair, within three days retailers were being offered a duplicate toy. Some toy makers like Mattel stopped exhibiting at the show. Instead, they decided to invite prospective buyers to their own in-house presentations.[67]

Important information can also be gathered from foreign subsidiaries located in the home markets of major competitors. The Italian office equipment manufacturer Olivetti assigned a major intelligence function to its U.S. subsidiary because of that unit's direct access to competitive products in the U.S. marketplace. A different approach was adopted by the Japanese pharmaceutical company

Table 7.2 Monitoring Competition: Facts to be Collected

Overall Company Statistics

Sales, market share and profits

Balance sheet

Capital expenditures

Number of employees

Production capacity

Research and development capability

Marketing Operations

Types of products (quality, performance, features)

Service and/or warranty granted

Prices and pricing strategy

Advertising strategy and budgets

Size and type of sales force

Distribution system (includes entry strategy)

Delivery schedules (also spare parts)

Sales territory (geographic)

Future Intentions

New product developments

Current test markets

Scheduled plant capacity expansions

Planned capital expenditures

Planned entry into new markets/countries

Competitive Behavior

Pricing behavior

Reaction to competitive moves, past and expected

Esei, which opened a liaison office in Switzerland, home base to several of the world's leading pharmaceutical companies.

Governments may also develop market reports (see, for example, the U.S. Export Portal). Some of these reports are free and others are provided for a fee. Private research organizations, such as PriceWaterhouseCoopers Industry Reports and Hoover's Online, also provide reports on particular companies or industries. These reports are easier to find on developed countries but are increasingly available for developing countries as well. In some cases, however, there may be no research report covering a specific country or product category. And be aware that reports from private sources can sell for hundreds or even thousands of dollars.

Outsourcing Research

The global firm can either attempt to collect and analyze all data itself or outsource some of its marketing research by utilizing marketing research companies. Today all major national markets have local marketing research firms that can assist the international marketer. The early marketing research industry in China was strongly supported by Procter & Gamble—in fact, some believe that it wouldn't have survived without P&G.[68]

The development of an independent marketing research industry in some countries is constrained by culture and economic conditions. In much of Latin America, market volatility leads many local firms to believe they do not have the resources to pay for outside research. Poor enforcement of intellectual property laws makes market research firms wary of developing then trying to sell secondary research. A customer could legally buy a copy of the report then illegally sell it to others.[69] Nonetheless, the demand for quality multi-country research has spurred the marketing research industry to expand beyond traditional national boundaries and become increasingly global. Table 7.3 lists the world's top research companies.

Table 7.3 2013 Top 25 Global Research Organizations

2012	Organization	Country	Website	No. of Countries with Subsidiaries/ Branch Offices	Global Research Revenue (US$ millions)	Percent of Global Revenue from Outside Home Country
1	Nielson Holdings	U.S.	Nielsen.com	100	$5,429.0	51.2%
2	Kantar	U.K.	Kantar.com	80	$3,338.6	72.2%
3	Ipsos SA	France	Ipsos.com	85	$2,301.1	93.2%
4	GfK SE	Germany	GfK.com	68	$1,947.8	70.0%
5	IMS Health Inc.	U.S.	IMSHealth.com	74	$775.0	65.0%
6	Information Resources Inc.	U.S.	IRIworldwide.com	8	$763.8	37.3%
7	INTAGE Inc.	Japan	Intage.co.jp	7	$500.3	2.6%
8	Westat Inc.	U.S.	Westat.com	8	$495.9	1.0%
9	Arbitron Inc.	U.S.	Arbitron.com	3	$449.9	1.3%
10	The NPD Group	U.S.	NPD.com	13	$272.0	29.5%
11	comScore Inc.	U.S.	comScore.com	22	$255.2	28.1%
12	Video Research	Japan	VideoR.co.jp	2	$250.2	
13	IBOPE Group	Brazil	IBOPE.com.br	14	$246.8	23.1%
14	ICF International	U.S.	ICFI.com	6	$239.7	20.2%

(Continued)

Table 7.3 (*continued*)

2012	Organization	Country	Website	No. of Countries with Subsidiaries/ Branch Offices	Global Research Revenue (US$ millions)	Percent of Global Revenue from Outside Home Country
15	J.D. Power & Asso.	U.S.	JDPA.com	8	$234.4	33.4%
16	Macromill Inc.	Japan	Macromill.com	3	$197.8	7.9%
17	Maritz Research	U.S.	MaritzResearch.com	5	$188.4	18.3%
18	Abt SRBI Inc.	U.S.	AbtAssociates.com	36	$175.6	10.4%
19	Symphony Health Solutions	U.S.	SymphonyHealth.com	2	$153.5	
20	Harris Interactive	U.S.	HarrisInteractive.com	5	$140.7	39.4%
21	Lieberman Research	U.S.	LRWonline.com	3	$101.8	28.4%
22	Médiamétrie	France	Mediametrie.com	1	$100.4	12.0%
23	Nikkei Research	Japan	Nikkei-r.co.jp	2	$97.5	
24	ORC International	U.S.	ORCInternational.com	6	$95.9	41.2%
25	YouGov plc	U.K.	YouGov.com	10	$91.9	73.0%
			TOTAL		**$18,843.2**	**53.7%**

Source: Adapted with permission from Marketing News, published by The American Marketing Association, "Top 25 Global Research Organizations," August 2013

Developing a Global Information System

Companies that already have become global marketers, as well as those that plan to do so, must look at the world marketplace to identify global opportunities. The forces that affect an industry must also be analyzed to determine the firm's competitiveness. To evaluate the full range of opportunities requires a global perspective for market research. Researchers must provide more than data on strictly local factors within each country. All firms that market their products in overseas markets require information that makes it possible to perform analysis across several countries or markets. However, leaving each local subsidiary or market to develop its own database will not result in an integrated marketing information system (MIS). Instead, authority to develop a centrally managed MIS must be assigned to a central location, and market reports need to be sent directly to the firm's chief international marketing officer.

A principal requirement for a worldwide MIS is a standardized set of data collected from each market or country. The actual data collection can be left to a firm's local units, but they must proceed according to central and uniform specifications. By assessing buyer needs on a worldwide basis, the company ensures that products and services are designed with the global marketplace in mind.

Increasingly global marketers also share information with key suppliers making them a part of their integrated MISs. For example, Wal-Mart has pioneered an MIS that opens its computer system to its suppliers across the globe. Suppliers can track how well their products are selling worldwide or at one particular store.[70]

Conclusion

In this chapter we discussed some major challenges and difficulties that companies encounter in securing data necessary for international marketing. Major difficulties include the lack of basic data on many markets and the likelihood that research methods will have to be adapted to local environments. A final goal of global marketing research is to provide managers with a uniform database covering all the firm's present and potential markets. This will allow for cross-country comparisons and analysis, as well as the incorporation of worldwide consumer needs into the initial product design process.

Still, the world has changed greatly in the past 25 years. Previously, market information around the world was sparse and unreliable, especially in developing and undeveloped countries. Now, through the efforts of governments, transnational organizations and global marketing research companies, information is available for virtually every market in the world from Canada and Mexico to Uzbekistan and Mongolia. As a revolutionary communications tool, the Internet continues to push research horizons. Today global marketers can use more widely available information to make better market decisions and devise more effective marketing strategies.

Managerial Takeaways

1. *Greater knowledge of international markets allows global marketers to better succeed overseas and avoid costly errors.*
2. *An emic approach to research provides deeper understanding of a particular market. It better captures what you don't know you don't know. But an etic approach allows cross-national comparisons.*
3. *Secondary research is the best place to start. It is faster, easier and cheaper than primary research. But primary research can provide the best market insights.*
4. *Managers must consider how culture affects global marketing research from the definition of the research question through the analysis of the collected data.*
5. *What is legal for market researchers to do in one country may be illegal in another.*
6. *Market research in the global context demands cultural knowledge and sensitivity, resourcefulness and tenacity.*

Questions for Discussion

1. Why is it so difficult to do marketing research in multicountry settings?
2. What are the challenges of using a marketing research questionnaire that is developed in the United States but will be used in Japan and Mexico as well?
3. If you were estimating the demand for vacuum cleaners, what type of inference analysis would you use? Give a specific example.
4. Note various ways in which the Internet could assist global marketing researchers.
5. List ways in which Pepsi might monitor Coca-Cola. Why is such surveillance important?

CASE 7.1 Surveying the Turkish Clothing Industry

Gretchen Renner had escaped to the serenity of a small tea garden overlooking the Bosporus Sea, which separates the European and Asian sides of Istanbul. As she sipped a glass of strong tea, she fought the urge to abandon her thesis research project and return to the United States.

Before arriving in Istanbul, Gretchen had been excited about the project. She had designed a survey to measure Turkish clothing firm owners' use and satisfaction with the services offered by the Textile Association of Istanbul (TAI). This association offers marketing, export counseling and educational services designed to encourage producers to pursue export opportunities.

Two months before Gretchen had come to Turkey, a Turkish friend had told her that she must apply for a research visa from the Turkish government. Foreigners planning to conduct research projects in Turkey must possess a government-approved research visa to display to government officials and potential research participants. Foreigners conducting research projects without a research visa in Turkey risk arrest and deportation. Gretchen was surprised that the research visa application had to be completed prior to her arrival in Turkey. She waited four months to receive the visa, inconveniently postponing her trip.

Once in Turkey, Gretchen sought a list of Turkish clothing firm owners from which she could draw a representative sample for her survey. Although TAI was supportive of Gretchen's project, it hesitated to share its membership list. Gretchen spent months developing relationships with key officials at TAI, conducting interviews and collecting information. TAI officials readily shared information about the organization's history, structure and services. Yet each time she asked about the list, she was denied access. Some of Gretchen's contacts claimed that releasing such information compromised the firms' privacy. Others maintained that no precedent existed for releasing the list to a non-TAI employee. Additionally, several of her close contacts explained to her that she could not have the list because she was not Turkish. Finally, with no explanation, TAI supplied the list of names.

Problems then emerged during survey pretesting. The questionnaire was administered via telephone by interviewers employed by *İtimat*, a well-known Istanbul market research firm. During this pretesting, Gretchen and her interviewers discovered that it was difficult to circumvent gatekeepers, such as secretaries and receptionists, to interview Turkish clothing firm owners.

Hoping to increase response rates, Gretchen sent potential respondents a presurvey fax introducing herself, explaining the survey's objectives and noting the involvement of *İtimat*. But respondents voiced concerns about the fax. Most complained that no high-level *İtimat* executive had signed the fax; it had been signed only by Gretchen and an *İtimat* interview supervisor. Others were suspicious of Gretchen's authenticity. They remembered Turkish media reports that several Europeans recently had posed as academic researchers to expose child labor practices in Turkish clothing factories. Because of Gretchen's German name and the unfamiliar name of her university, many suspected that Gretchen was actually an industrial spy.

Even when Gretchen or the interviewers gained access to firm owners, few agreed to participate in the survey. One scoffed, "If you really valued my opinion, you would make an appointment and discuss this with me in person. I am a very busy person. I don't have time to talk on the phone about such things."

Face-to-face interviews, however, would be more time-consuming than telephone interviews. First, it would take time to get past the gatekeepers to make appointments with potential respondents. Second, because the firms were widely dispersed and Istanbul is a very large and traffic-congested city, Gretchen and her team of four *İtimat* interviewers could complete only ten surveys a day. Gretchen needed to complete 300 surveys. Gretchen's research funding was dwindling, and she had to return home in six weeks.

Looking toward the Asian side of Istanbul, Gretchen wondered how she could successfully complete her research project in the remaining time.

Discussion Questions

1. What cultural factors might contribute to the obstacles Gretchen encountered while attempting to execute the survey? How might Hofstede's dimensions of culture explain Gretchen's difficulties?
2. Why do you think Gretchen finally received the list of Turkish clothing exporters from TAI? If TAI had not supplied the list, where else could Gretchen have looked to find a suitable list?
3. How should Gretchen proceed with the survey? Do you think the benefits of the face-to-face option outweigh the costs? Or could changes be made to the telephone survey to increase response rates? Are there other research options that Gretchen should consider instead?

Source: Prepared by Liesl Riddle. Used by permission.

CASE 7.2   Selector's European Dilemma

Ken Barbarino, CEO of Selector Inc., was ecstatic. The president of Big Burger, one of Selector's largest clients, had arranged for Ken to meet with the vice president of Big Burger's European operations. "Selector is going global," Ken smiled to himself.

Selector was a market research firm that provided market analyses to restaurant and retail chains. Selector's products helped clients select optimal geographic locations for successful chain expansion.

Although Big Burger was an international restaurant chain, currently Big Burger utilized Selector's services only for its U.S. operations. Specifically, Selector provided Big Burger's real estate team with trade-area profiles for prospective Big Burger locations. Because Big Burger was a quick-service hamburger restaurant, most of its customers were drawn from the homes and businesses within a two-mile radius around each location. Selector's trade-area profiles provided Big Burger with an overview of the individuals, households and businesses within a potential location's trade area.

By purchasing and amalgamating databases from a large number of data vendors, Selector had amassed a broad warehouse of U.S. demographic, business and consumer behavior data, and the reports were extremely detailed. For example, Selector's trade-area profile described proximal households according to their composition, annual income, type of residence and commute time to work. It also reported the number of area households that dined at a quick-serve hamburger restaurant last year as well as the total dollars these households spent at quick-serve hamburger restaurants during that year. Selector's trade-area profiles also included a count of the total number of businesses and employees in the two-mile radius, as well as the percentage of businesses and employees within each two-digit standard industry code (SIC) and a list of all quick-serve hamburger restaurants within a five-mile radius and their gross unit sales. These trade-area profiles enabled Big Burger's real estate team to determine whether there was enough demand in the trade area to support a successful Big Burger location.

Ken waltzed into the office of Selector's research director, Katrina Walsh. "Guess what? Big Burger is sending us overseas!" he exclaimed. Ken told Katrina that the president of Big Burger had asked Selector to provide trade-area profiles for their prospective European locations. The president had arranged for Ken to meet with Big Burger's vice president of European operations in two weeks to demonstrate the trade-area profiles that could be used to assess potential European Big Burger locations. Big Burger had provided Ken with the addresses of seven potential sites (two in London, one in Madrid and four in Berlin) so that Selector could create examples of their trade-area profiles for these sites. Katrina was excited about the international project and assured Ken she would acquire the European data that was needed to generate the trade-area profiles.

Katrina contacted Selector's data vendors—the companies that sold the various databases that Selector had compiled in its broad data warehouse—and inquired about purchasing European demographic, business and consumer behavior data. She quickly learned that acquiring the data at a small, precise level of geography would be a greater challenge than she had anticipated.

In the United States, the U.S. Census Bureau aggregates the data it collects into a set of standard hierarchical geographic units (see Table 7.4). To protect individual privacy, data are released at the Zip+4 level and higher. The standardization of the Census Bureau's geographic order and the degree of detail within the Zip+4 level enable companies like Selector to extract precise data for a geographic area, such

Table 7.4 U.S. Statistical Territorial Units: Lowest Five Geographies Available From the U.S. Census

Statistical Unit	Total Number	Approximate Number of Households
Metropolitan standard unit	316	30,245
Zip code	41,940	3,167
Census tract	62,276	1,551
Block group	229,466	420
Zip+4	28,000,000	10

as a two-mile radius around a particular location, because the Census Bureau units are typically small enough to fit within that area.

However, as Katrina learned from her data vendors, European countries were geographically organized in a different way. All members of the EU were organized according to the Nomenclature of Territorial Units for Statistics (NUTS) devised by the Statistical Office of the European Communities (Eurostat) in 1988.

There were several design challenges associated with the NUTS program because the countries possessed divergent geographic organizational systems and were reluctant to abandon their existing geographic hierarchies. Five NUTS levels were created. The geographic data of most EU countries are divided into NUTS Levels 1–3. Some countries further divide their geographic data into NUTS Levels 4 and 5.

Ideally, Eurostat would have liked to standardize units by either territorial size or population size. It proved difficult to do either. For example, the largest geographic unit, NUTS Level 1, includes British government office regions, German *länder* and Finnish *ahvenanmaa*. But the southeast government office region of England possesses over 17 million inhabitants, whereas the Finnish *ahvenanmaa*, Åhland, includes only 25,000 people. These disparities also exist at lower levels of geography. Greater London, Berlin and the Spanish provinces of Madrid and Barcelona—all NUTS Level 3 geographies—comprise populations exceeding 3 million people, whereas several NUTS Level 3 regions in Germany, Belgium, Austria, Finland and Greece include fewer than 50,000 people. The NUTS levels also differed greatly in territorial size. For example, some Level 5 geographies could be as small as 50 square meters, and others could comprise an entire town.

Katrina also discovered that it would be challenging to acquire data for a two-mile radius around a specific address in Europe. NUTS data—even those at Levels 4 and 5—were for areas much larger than the two-mile radius that Big Burger was interested in. Even a simple analysis of the NUTS level that a prospective site resided in would not be comparable across national boundaries within the EU. Furthermore, although she could identify data vendors that could provide demographic and "firmographic" data, such as the total population, the number of households, household composition, marital status, the sex and age distribution of the population and the number of businesses and employees, she could not locate a data vendor that offered the more important consumer behavior data. Estimating quick-serve hamburger dollar demand would be extremely difficult—if not impossible—without a measure of the total dollars spent on quick-serve hamburger restaurants and the number of households dining at quick-serve hamburger restaurants last year. It was also unclear whether Katrina would be able to acquire a reliable database of quick-serve restaurant competitors and their unit sales, because most of the existing European restaurant databases were old and out-of-date.

With ten days left to go before Ken's meeting with Big Burger, Katrina wondered how she would generate trade-area profiles for Big Burger's seven European prospective locations.

Discussion Questions

1. What assumptions have Ken and Katrina made in their response to Big Burger's request for European trade-area data?
2. How—if at all—can Katrina utilize the available European data?
3. What should be included on the trade-area profiles for Big Burger's seven European locations?

Source: Prepared by Liesl Riddle. Used with permission.

CASE 7.3   AGT, Inc.

AGT, Inc. is a marketing research company located in the city of Karachi, Pakistan. Jeff Sons Trading Company (JST) has approached it to look at the potential market for an amusement park in Karachi. Because the city is crowded and real estate costs are high, it will be difficult to find a large enough piece of land on which to locate such a facility. Even if land is available, it will be expensive and that will have a detrimental effect on the overall costs of the project. JST needs to know the potential of this type of investment. They want the market research to identify if a need for the amusement park exists and, if it does, what the public's attitude toward that type of recreational facility might be. If a need is found and support is sufficient, then they want to know the type of amusement park required by potential customers. JST will make its investment decision based on the results of this study.

Background

Pakistan is a typical less developed country (LDC) of the Third World faced with the usual problems of rapidly increasing population, sizable government deficit and heavy dependence on foreign aid. The country's economy has grown rapidly in the last decade, with GDP expanding at 6.7 percent annually, more than twice the population growth. Like any other LDC, it displays dualism in its economic system: the cities have modern facilities, the smaller towns have some or none. The same holds true for income distribution patterns. Real per-capita GDP is Rupees 10,000, or US$400 annually. There is a small wealthy class (1 to 3 percent), a middle class consisting of another 20 percent, and the remainder of the population is poor. Half of the population lives below the poverty line. Most of the middle class is an urban working class.

Karachi, as the country's largest city and boasting a dense population of over 6 million, has been chosen as the site of the first large-scale amusement park in Pakistan. Current recreational facilities in Karachi, including a poorly maintained zoo, are modest, and people with families avoid visiting most facilities because of the crowds. There are other small parks, but they are not sufficient to cater to such a large population. The main place people go for recreation is the beach. The beaches near Karachi are not well developed and are regularly polluted by oil slicks from the port.

Our working hypothesis is that Karachi citizens have a growing need to spend their leisure time in recreational activities. (Indeed, many middle class and wealthy citizens already take vacations with their families and spend money on recreational activities abroad.) To determine whether there is a true need for this type of recreational facility, we propose to conduct a market research feasibility study.

Potential problems facing the construction of an amusement park in Karachi include the facts that:

- the communications infrastructure is poor;
- only a small percentage of the people own their own transportation;
- public and private transportation systems are not efficient;
- maintaining law and order is a problem, said to be similar in scope to the crime problem in Los Angeles.

Research Objectives

To make an investment decision, JST outlined the research objectives necessary to design a marketing strategy that would accomplish the desired return on investment goals. These objectives were the following:

1. identify the potential demand for this project;
2. identify the primary target market and what they expect of an amusement park.

Information Needs

To fulfill their objectives, JST determined that they would need the following information:

Market

a. Is there a need for this project in this market?
b. How large is the potential market?
c. Is this market large enough to be profitable?

Consumers

a. Are the potential customers satisfied with the existing facilities in the city?
b. Will these potential consumers utilize an amusement park?
c. Which segment of the population is most interested in this type of facility?
d. Is the population ready to support this type of project?
e. What media could be used to promote the park successfully to potential customers?

Location

a. Where should this project be built to attract the most visitors?
b. How will consumers' existing attitudes on location influence the viability and cost of this project?
c. Will the company have to arrange for transportation to and from the facility if it is located outside the city area?
d. Is security a factor in determining the location of the facility?

Recreation Facilities

a. What type of attractions should the company provide at the park to attract customers?
b. Should there be overnight accommodations within the park?
c. Should the facility be available only to certain segments of the population or should it be open to all?

Proposal

With the objectives just outlined in mind, AGT, Inc. presented the following proposal:

The city of Karachi's population has its different economic clusters scattered haphazardly throughout the city. To conduct market research under these conditions and obtain accurate results will consequently be difficult. We recommend an extensive study to make sure we have an adequate sampling of opinion from the target market. Given these parameters, we recommend that the target market be defined as follows:

Desired Respondent Characteristics

*   Upper Class: 1 percent (around 60,000)
*   Middle Class: 15 to 20 percent (around 900,000 to 1,200,000)
*   Male and female
*   Age: 15 to 50 years (for survey; market includes all age groups)
*   Income level: Rs 25,000 and above per year (Rs 2,000 per month)
*   Household size: families will be better for the purposes of the sample
*   Involved in entertainment activities
*   Involved in recreational activities
*   Actively participates in social activities
*   Member of different clubs
*   Involved in outdoor activities

To obtain accurate information regarding respondents' characteristics, we have to approach the market very carefully because of prevailing circumstances and existing cultural practices. People have little or no knowledge of market surveys. Obtaining their cooperation, even without cultural barriers, via a phone or mail survey will be difficult. In the following paragraphs we will discuss the negative and positive points of all types of surveys and select the appropriate form for our study.

The first, and possibly best, method for conducting the survey under these circumstances will be through the mail, which will not only be cheaper than other methods but can also cover all the population clusters easily. We cannot rely on a mail survey alone, however, because the mail system in Pakistan is unreliable and inefficient. We can go through courier services or registered mail, but doing so will cause the cost to skyrocket.

The other option is to conduct a survey by telephone. In this city of 6 million there are about 200,000 working telephones (one per 152 persons). Most of the telephones are in businesses or government offices. The problem is not that the citizens of Karachi cannot afford a telephone, but that they cannot get one because of the short supply. Another problem with a telephone survey is cultural; it is not considered polite in Pakistani society to call a stranger and start asking questions. It would be even more of a breach of etiquette if a male survey member were to reach a female household member. Because people are not familiar with marketing surveys, they would not be willing to volunteer the information we require on the telephone. The positive feature of a telephone survey is that most upper-class women do not work and can be reached easily. To contact them, however, we would need to use a survey staff composed of females only. Overall, the chances of cooperation with a telephone survey are very low.

A mall/bazaar intercept could also be used. Again, however, we will face some cultural problems. It's not considered ethical for a male to approach a female in the mall. The only people willing to talk in public are likely to be men and we will thus miss female opinion.

To gather respondent data by survey in a country such as Pakistan, we will have to tailor our existing data collecting methods and make them fit the circumstances and cultural practices of that marketplace. As a company based in Pakistan with experience in living under these cultural practices, we propose the following design for the study and the questionnaire.

Design of the Study

Our study will contain a mixture of three types of survey, with each survey making use of a different method. We recommend the following types of surveys, tailored to fit the prevailing circumstances:

1. Mail Survey

We plan to modify this type of survey to fit the existing situation and to be maximally efficient. Specific changes have been made to counter the inefficient postal system and to generate a better percentage of response. We plan to deliver the surveys to respondents by the newspaper deliverymen rather than by mail. The average circulation of the various newspapers in Karachi ranges from 50,000 to 200,000 per day. The two dailies chosen have the largest circulation in the city.

A questionnaire will be placed in each newspaper delivered to respondents. This questionnaire will introduce us to the respondent and will ask for his cooperation, and it will include return postage and the firm's address. Identification of the firm will give respondents some confidence that they are not volunteering information to unknown parties. A small promotional gift will be promised for returning the completed survey. Since respondents who intend to claim the gift will give us their address, this will help us maintain a list of respondents for future surveys. Delivery with the daily newspaper will also allow us to focus easily on specific clusters.

We expect some loss in return mail because there is no acceptable way to get the questionnaires back except through the government postal system. Accordingly, we plan to deliver 5,000 questionnaires to counter the anticipated loss in return mail. The cost of this survey will be less than it would be if we mailed the questionnaires. Because this will be the first exposure for many respondents that allows them to give their views about an as yet nonexistent product, we do not have any return percentage on which to base our survey response expectations. In fact, this information may well provide the basis for future studies.

2. Door-to-Door Interviews

We will have to tailor the mall/bazaar intercept, as we did the mail survey, to get the highest possible response percentage. Instead of intercepting at malls, we believe it will be better to send surveyors door to door. This method can generate a better percentage of responses and also allows us to identify the respondents accurately. To conduct this survey, we will solicit the cooperation of the local business schools in providing us with students who will act as our surveyors. By using these young students we stand a better chance of generating a higher response than we would using older staff. We also plan to hire some additional personnel, mostly females, and train them to conduct this survey.

3. Additional Mail Survey

We plan to conduct this part of the survey to identify different groups of people already involved in similar types of recreational activity. There are eight to ten exclusive clubs in the city of Karachi. A few focus solely on some outdoor activity such as yachting and boating, golf and the like. Their membership numbers vary from 3,000 to 5,000. The high cost of membership and monthly fees have restricted these clubs to the upper middle class and the wealthy. We can safely say that the people using these clubs belong to the 90th percentile of income level.

We propose to visit these clubs and personally ask for members' cooperation in participating in our survey. We also plan to obtain the clubs' membership list and have the questionnaire delivered to them. They will be asked to return the completed questionnaire to the club office or to mail it in the postage-paid reply envelope. We believe that this group will cooperate and give us high-quality feedback.

The second delivered survey will be to local schools. With the schools' cooperation, we will ask that the questionnaires are delivered by pupils to their parents. The cover letter will ask parents to fill out the questionnaire and return it to the school. This survey will provide a good sample of people who want outdoor activities for their children. We hope to generate a substantial response through this method.

Questionnaire Design

The type of questions asked should help our client make the decision about whether to invest in the project. (See proposed questionnaire.) Through the survey questionnaires we should be able to answer the question "Is the population ready for this project and are they willing to support it?" The questionnaire, a mixture of open-ended and close-ended questions, should also help to answer the following questions:

- Is there a market for this type of project?
- Is the market substantial?
- Is the market profitable?

- Will this project fill a real need?
- Will this project be only a momentary fad?
- Is the market evenly distributed in all segments/clusters, or is there a high demand in some segments?
- Is the population geared toward and willing to spend money on this type of entertainment facility? If so, how much?
- What is the best location for this project?
- Are people willing to travel some distance to reach this type of facility? Or do they want it within city limits?
- What types of entertainment/rides do people want in an amusement park?
- Through what type of media or promotion can prospective customers best be reached?

Discussion Questions

1. What are the objectives of the research project? Does the survey satisfy these objectives?
2. How do elements of culture affect the research design, collection of data and analysis? Contrast this case with the design, collection of data and analysis of a similar survey project in a more developed country such as the United States.
3. What alternative data collection methods might be useful to pursue? What are the strengths and weaknesses of these alternative methods?

Source: Prepared by William J. Carner. Used by permission.

Questionnaire

1. Are there adequate recreational facilities in the city?

    Yes ☐
    No ☐

2. How satisfied are you with the present recreational facilities?
    (Please rate from 0–10 degrees)

    0–1—2–3—4–5—6–7—8–9—10
    Poor   Excellent

3. How often do you visit the present recreational facilities? (Please check)

    Weekly ☐
    Fortnightly ☐
    Monthly ☐
    Once in two months ☐
    Yearly ☐
    More (indicate number)_____ ☐
    Not at all ☐

4. Do you visit recreational areas with your family?

Yes ☐
No ☐
If no, why not?
Security ☐
Distance ☐
Expense ☐
Crowd (not family oriented) ☐
Poor service ☐
Other (Please specify) _____ ☐

4a. Do you stay overnight?

Yes ☐
No ☐
If yes, how long? _____
(Please indicate number of days)

4b. If no, would you have stayed if provided the right circumstances or facilities?

Yes ☐
No ☐

5. Have you ever visited an amusement park?

(Here in Pakistan ☐ Abroad ☐)
Yes ☐ (Please go to question 5b)
No ☐ (Please go to question 5a)

5a. If no, why not?

Security ☐
Distance ☐
Expense ☐
Crowd (not family oriented) ☐
Poor service ☐
Other (Please specify) _____ ☐

5b. If yes, when did you last visit an amusement park?

Last month ☐
Last six months ☐
Within a year ☐
More (specify number) _____ ☐
Where? _____

6. What did you enjoy most in that park?

Roller coasters ☐
Water slides ☐
Children's play areas ☐
Shows ☐
Games ☐
Simulators ☐
Other _____ ☐

6a. How much did you spend in that park (approximately)?

Rs 50 or less ☐
51 to 100 ☐
101 to 150 ☐
151 to 200 ☐
More than 200 ☐
Where? _____

6b. How would you rate the value received?

(Please rate from 0–10 degrees)

0–1—2–3—4–5—6–7—8–9—10
Poor   Excellent

7. Would you utilize an amusement park if one were built locally?

Yes ☐
No ☐

8. What would you like to see in an amusement park?

(Please give us your six best choices)

a. _____
b. _____
c. _____
d. _____
e. _____
f. _____

9. Where would you like its location to be?

Within city area ☐
Beach area ☐

Suburbs ☐
Outskirts of city ☐
Indifferent ☐

10. How many kilometers will you be willing to travel to the park?

Under 10 ☐
11 to 20 ☐
21 to 35 ☐
36 to 55 ☐
56 to 65 ☐
More than 65 ☐

11. How often do you take vacations for recreational purposes?

Never ☐
Once a year ☐
Twice a year ☐
More (please specify) _____ ☐

Please Tell Us About Yourself:

12. Please indicate your age.

Under 15 ☐
16 to 21 ☐
22 to 29 ☐
30 to 49 ☐
50 to 60 ☐
Over 60 ☐

13. Please indicate your gender:

Male ☐
Female ☐

14. Are you married?

Yes ☐
No ☐

15. How many children do you have? Please indicate number _____

16. Please indicate your total family income.

(Yearly)
Under 12,000 ☐
Between 12,000 and 15,000 ☐
Between 15,000 and 20,000 ☐
Between 20,000 and 25,000 ☐

Between 25,000 and 40,000 ☐
Between 40,000 and 60,000 ☐
Between 60,000 and 80,000 ☐
Over 80,000 ☐

17. Do you own your own means of transport?

Yes ☐

No ☐

18. Any other comments?

(If you need more space, please attach an additional sheet)

_____
_____
_____
_____
_____
_____

Thank you, we appreciate your time!

Important:

If you want us to contact you again in the later stages of this project, or if you are interested in its results, give us your name and address and we will be glad to keep you informed. Thank you.

Notes

1   Susan Berfield and Manuel Baigorri, "Zara's Fast-Fashion Edge," *Business Week*, November 13, 2013.
2   Carlta Vitzthum, "Just-in-Time Fashion," *Wall Street Journal*, May 23, 2001, p. B1.
3   Cecile Rohwedder, "Zara Grows as Retail Rivals Struggle," *Wall Street Journal*, March 26, 2009, p. B1.
4   James Thompson, "How Social Media Helped Us Build a $10 Million Fashion Business," BRW, December 6, 2013.
5   Balaji R. Koka, John E. Prescott and Ravindranath Madhavan, "Contagion Influence on Trade and Investment Policy: A Network Perspective," *Journal of International Business Studies*, vol. 30, no. 1 (1999), pp. 127–148.
6   David A. Ricks, *Blunders in International Business*, 3rd ed. (New York: Blackwell, 1999), pp. 130–136.
7   Merissa Marr and Geoffrey A. Fowler, "Chinese Lessons for Disney," *Wall Street Journal*, June 12, 2006, p. B1.
8   Joe Light, "Greg Waldorf," *Wall Street Journal*, November 22, 2010, p. B10.
9   C. Samuel Craig and Susan P. Douglas, *International Marketing Research: Concepts and Methods* (New York: Wiley, 1999), pp. 16–19.
10 "Russia's Unemployment Rate Rises Year-on-Year," *Interfax News Agency*, June 21, 1999, p. 1.
11 Leonard Gurevich, "Focus on Central Asia: Conducting Research in the Post-Soviet Era," *Quirk's Marketing Research Review*, no. 1048 (November 2002).
12 Brian Palmer, "What the Chinese Want," *Fortune*, October 11, 1999.
13 Vanessa Fuhrmans, "Germans Tally Their Concerns Over Census," *Wall Street Journal*, July 29, 2011, p. A9.

14 Yukari Iwatani Kane and Ben Worhten, "As iPhone Goes Global, App Makers Follow," *Wall Street Journal*, April 30, 2010, p. B5.

15 Geoffrey A. Fowler, "China Radio is Wave of Future for Advertising," *Wall Street Journal*, April 28, 2004, p. A6.

16 "Sharp as a Razor in Central Asia," *The Economist*, June 5, 1993, p. 36.

17 Geraldo Samor, Cecille Rohwedder and Ann Zimmerman, "Innocents Abroad?" *Wall Street Journal*, May 16, 2006, p. B1.

18 Gordon Fairclough, "McDonald's Marketing Chief in China Preaches On-the-Ground Experience," *Wall Street Journal*, May 7, 2007, p. B4.

19 Elizabeth Robles, "In Cuba, the Usual MR Methods Don't Work," *Marketing News*, June 10, 2002, p. 12.

20 Tim Plowman, Adrien Lanusse and Astrid Cruz, "Observing the World," *Quirk's Marketing Research Review*, no. 1171 (November 2003).

21 Michael Fielding, "In One's Element," *Marketing News*, February 1, 2006. pp. 15–20.

22 Emily Nelson, "P&G Checks Out Real Life," *Wall Street Journal*, May 17, 2001, p. B1.

23 Michael Fielding, "Shift the Focus," *Marketing News*, September 1, 2006, p. 18.

24 Dana James, "Back to Vietnam," *Marketing News*, May 13, 2002, p. 1.

25 Gurevich, "Focus on Central Asia."

26 Rod Davies, "Focus Groups in Asia." Posted on *Orient Pacific Century*, 2005, www.orientpacific.com (accessed June 1, 2005).

27 Sharon Seidler, "Qualitatively Speaking: Conducting Qualitative Research on a Global Scale," *Quirk's Marketing Research Review*, no. 1182 (December 2003).

28 Lyn Montgomery, "Simplifying Research in Japan," *Quirk's Marketing Research Review*, no. 729 (November 2001).

29 Jean-Claude Usunier and Stephanie Sbizzera, "Comparative Thick Description: Articulating Similarities and Differences in Local Consumer Experience," *International Marketing Review*, vol. 30, no. 1 (2013), pp. 42–55.

30 Eileen Moran, "Managing the Minefields of Global Product Development," *Quirk's Marketing Research Review*, no. 625 (November 2000).

31 Kevin Reagan, "In Asia, Think Globally, Communicate Locally," *Marketing News*, July 19, 1999, pp. 12–14.

32 Robert B. Young and Rajshekhar G. Javalgi, "International Marketing Research: A Global Project Management Perspective," *Business Horizons*, vol. 50 (2007), p. 118.

33 J. Brad McBride and Kate Gillespie, "Consumer Innovativeness Among Street Vendors in Mexico City," *Latin American Business Review*, vol. 1, no. 3 (2000), pp. 71–94.

34 Moran, "Managing the Minefields."

35 Dana James, "Back to Vietnam," *Marketing News*, May 13, 2002, pp. 1, 13–14.

36 Moran, "Managing the Minefields."

37 See, for example, N.L. Reynolds, A.C. Simintiras and A. Diamantopoulos, "Sampling Choices in International Marketing: Key Issues and Guidelines for Research," *Journal of International Business Studies*, vol. 34 (2003), p. 81.

38 Craig and Douglas, *International Marketing Research*, p. 282.

39 Geraldo Samor, "In Brazil, Ford Has Discovered the Way Forward," *Wall Street Journal*, July 10, 2006, p. B1.

40 Tim R. Davis and Robert B. Young, "International Marketing Research: A Management Briefing," *Business Horizons*, March–April 2002, p. 33.

41 Craig and Douglas, *International Marketing Research*, p. 286.

42 Arundhati Parmar, "South African Research," *Marketing News*, September 15, 2003, p. 19.

43 Don E. Shultz, "Bad Data, Bad Models, or Bad Managers?" *Marketing News*, April 30, 2012, pp. 13–14.

44 Robin Cobb, "Marketing Shares," *Marketing*, February 22, 1990, p. 44.

45 Brian Bremner and Dexter Roberts, "Fuzzy Numbers No More?" *Business Week*, February 14, 2005, p. 7.

46 Rukmini Callimachi, "Wary Liberians a Challenge for Census-Takers," Associated Press, March 21, 2008.

47 Gary S. Insch and Stewart R. Miller, "Perception of Foreignness: Benefit or Liability?" *Journal of Managerial Issues*, vol. 17, no. 4, pp. 423–438.

48   McBride and Gillespie, "Consumer Innovativeness," p. 80.

49   Ray Nelson, "How to Use Social Media for Market Research," *Social Media Today*, March 19, 2013.

50   Ibid.

51   "When Big Data Can Lead to Big Profits," Industry Updates BDU, China Daily Information Company, April 21, 2014.

52   Karen Quintos, Public Lecture, University of Austin, May 1, 2014.

53   Kamau Mbote, "Disruptive Technologies to Continue Offering Business Competitive Advantage," *All Africa*, February 28, 2014.

54   "When Big Data Can Lead to Big Profits," Industry Updates BDU, China Daily Information Company, April 21, 2014.

55   "Research in Denmark, Germany and the Netherlands," *Quirk's Marketing Research Review*, no. 731 (November 2001).

56   Gabriel Kahn, "Chinese Puzzle: Spotty Consumer Data," *Wall Street Journal*, October 15, 2003, p. B1.

57   James Heckman, "Marketers Waiting, Will See on EU Privacy," *Marketing News*, June 7, 1999, p. 4.

58   "Japan-Market Research-Competitive Landscape," *Data-Monitor Market Research Profiles*, November 1, 2004.

59   Mark Scott, "Data Privacy as Selling Point in Europe," *International New York Times*, April 11, 2014, p. 11.

60   J.M. Batista-Foguet, J. Fortiana, C. Currie and J.R. Villalba, "Socio-Economic Indexes in Surveys for Comparisons Between Countries," *Social Indicators Research*, vol. 67 (2004), p. 328.

61   Jennifer Mitchell, "Reaching Across Borders," *Marketing News*, May 10, 1999, p. 19.

62   Irvine Clarke III, "Global Marketing Research: Is Extreme Response Style Influencing Your Results?" *Journal of International Consumer Marketing*, vol. 12, no. 4 (2000), pp. 91–111.

63   Emily Maltby, "Expanding Abroad? Avoid Cultural Gaffes," *Wall Street Journal*, January 19, 2010, p. B5.

64   Peter Landers, "Merck, Pfizer in Japan," *Wall Street Journal*, October 2, 2003, p. B4.

65   "High Price of Industrial Espionage," *Times of London*, June 5, 1999, p. 31.

66   Ibid.

67   Geoffrey A. Fowler, "Copies 'R' Us," *Wall Street Journal*, January 31, 2003, p. B1.

68   Barton Lee, Soumya Saklini and David Tatterson, "Research: Growing in Guangzhou," *Marketing News*, June 10, 2002, pp. 12–13.

69   Thomas Rideg, "Traditional Survey Instruments Encounter Difficulties When Applied to LatAm," Infoamericas, December 7, 2004.

70   Gabriel Kahn, "Made to Measure," *Wall Street Journal*, September 11, 2003, p. A1.

Part 3

Developing Global Participation Strategies

8   GLOBAL MARKET PARTICIPATION   241

9   GLOBAL MARKET ENTRY STRATEGIES   277

Chapter 8

Global Market Participation

INTERNATIONALIZING MARKETING OPERATIONS 243

EVALUATING NATIONAL MARKETS 246

GEOGRAPHIC MARKET CHOICES 248

COUNTRY SELECTION 254

IN-COUNTRY EXPANSION 262

LIMITS TO EXPANSION 262

EXIT STRATEGIES 263

RE-ENTRY 265

Kraft was the largest packaged-foods company in North America. In the United States, it dominated grocery store shelves for years, with such famous brands as Jell-O, Kool-Aid, Life Savers, Oreo cookies and Philadelphia Cream Cheese. However, Kraft found itself stuck in a slow-growth industry in the United States. Despite careful cost cutting and imaginative marketing, sales dropped 16 percent over a seven-year period. Furthermore, Kraft's strongest overseas market was Western Europe, a market that was nearly saturated as well. As a result, Kraft decided to expand into emerging markets. The company identified China, Russia, Brazil and Southeast Asia as the growth engines of the international market.[1]

Unfortunately, Kraft's strongest products—convenience foods such as Kraft Macaroni & Cheese—don't sell as well in developing countries where consumers have less disposable income. To better address this issue, the company decided to split in two. Kraft would retain the slow-growth but profitable North American convenience-foods business. The new spin-off company, Mondelez, received the company's snack brands.

At the time Mondelez was created, the fast-growing emerging markets accounted for 80 percent of sales for snack brands at Kraft.[2] However, two years later the economies of key emerging markets were in trouble. Mondelez's operating income from these markets declined 22 to 26 percent. Nonetheless, the company responded by increasing their investments in these volatile markets, convinced they were the future of the company.[3]

In this chapter, we introduce key issues that companies face as they pursue global market participation. Historically, internationalization patterns of firms range from opportunistic, or unplanned, responses to overseas opportunities to carefully constructed expansion. Increasingly, firms must determine whether going international is merely an option or a necessity for survival in the global marketplace. Firms must be more proactive in selecting an appropriate course for market expansion. Entering new foreign markets can be expensive and can place heavy demands on management time. Firms must decide which regions and specifically which foreign markets will receive priority.

Learning Objectives

After studying this chapter, you should be able to:

➤ list and describe five reasons why firms internationalize;
➤ differentiate between born-global firms and other companies;
➤ explain the difference between a standalone attractive market and a globally strategic one;
➤ cite the advantages and disadvantages of targeting developed countries, developing countries or transitional economies;
➤ list and describe the filters used for screening national markets;
➤ cite the pros and cons of choosing markets on the basis of market similarity;
➤ differentiate between in-country expansion and new market entry;
➤ understand the possible drawbacks and limitations of international growth;
➤ explain why market exit—and possibly re-entry—strategies might be necessary.

Internationalizing Marketing Operations

Internationalization is the term we use for a firm's expansion from its domestic market into foreign markets. Whether to internationalize is a strategic decision that will fundamentally affect any firm, including its operations and its management. Today, most large companies operate outside their home markets. Nonetheless, it is still useful for these companies to consider their motivations for continued international expansion. For many smaller or newer companies, the decision to internationalize remains an important and difficult one. There can be several possible motives behind a company's decision to begin to compete in foreign markets. These motives range from the opportunistic to the strategic.

Opportunistic Expansion

Many companies promote their products on the Internet or in trade journals to their domestic customers. These media may be read by foreign business executives or distributors who subsequently place orders that are initially unsolicited. Such foreign transactions are usually more complicated and more involved than a routine shipment to a domestic customer. Therefore, the firm must decide whether to respond to these unsolicited orders. Some companies adopt an aggressive policy and begin to pursue these foreign customers actively. Many have built sizable foreign businesses by first responding to orders and then adopting a more proactive approach later. Most large, internationally active companies began their internationalization in this opportunistic manner.

Social networking site Friendster.com exemplifies opportunistic internationalization. Among the first to launch during America's social networking phenomenon, technical difficulties on Friendster eventually caused most domestic users to switch to competitors. Luckily Friendster had a strong customer base among Asian-Americans with family in Asia, and the site caught on and managed to survive on the other side of the globe. Eventually 90 percent of Friendster daily traffic occurred in Asia.[4]

Pursuing Potential Abroad and Diversifying Risk

Perhaps the most common reason for a company to expand internationally is the lure of increasing sales and profits from entering new markets. Expanding a firm's product lines abroad can be an attractive alternative to launching new products. For example, Coca-Cola's push to develop new products, such as bottled water, only came after the company had taken its original cola into virtually every country in the world.

Sometimes tough competition at home makes the overseas sales appear all the more alluring. This is one reason why Ford, then number two in the U.S. car market, internationalized faster than then-dominant General Motors. More recently, a survey of Chinese firms—both state-owned and private—discovered that a growing number of Chinese companies are seeking to market abroad in order to escape the intense competition that now exists in the Chinese market.[5]

Another major reason to internationalize is the possibility of avoiding risks inherent to operating in only one market. Having alternative sources of sales can also offset negative results from political risk or economic downturns in the domestic market. A year into a major U.S. recession which devastated sales in its home market, Starbucks' corporate earnings were bolstered by growing overseas sales. Diminishing the impact of macroeconomic risk at home has also been forwarded as a major reason why Latin American firms seek foreign markets.

Exploiting Different Market Growth Rates

Companies seeking growth abroad often pay particular attention to market growth rates, which are subject to wide variations among countries. A company based in a low-growth country may wish to expand into faster-growing countries to take advantage of growth opportunities. Table 8.1 demonstrates how the growth rates of soft drinks vary by region. Some beverages, such as carbonated drinks and juices, are in the decline stage of the product life cycle in North America but still experience strong growth elsewhere. On the other hand, North America is one of the best growth markets for bottled water.

When the domestic market for a firm's product becomes mature, a company can open new opportunities by entering foreign markets where the product may not be very well known. Companies often target markets where the per-capita consumption of their products is still relatively low. With economic expansion and the resulting improvement in personal incomes in these new markets, these companies can experience substantial growth over time—even though operations in the United States and Europe show little growth. After consumption of Budweiser fell 24 years in a row in the U.S. home market, AB InBev launched the beer in the growing beer markets of Brazil, China, Russia and Ukraine.[6]

Following Customers Abroad

For other companies, the decision to internationalize may occur when one of its key customers moves abroad to pursue international opportunities. Global hoteliers such as Marriott International Inc. and Hilton Worldwide have recently added Africa to their global expansion plans, because

Table 8.1 Exploiting Different Market Growth Rates; Percentage Growth in Soft-Drink Sales by Region 2013–2018

Region	Carbonates	Fruit/Vegetable Juice	Bottled Water
World	7.70%	21.14%	29.67%
Asia Pacific	16.21%	41.70%	45.33%
Australasia	–2.80%	–6.58%	10.02%
Eastern Europe	7.24%	5.65%	13.89%
Latin America	9.24%	26.70%	22.64%
Middle East and Africa	31.43%	27.72%	50.52%
North America	–7.85%	–7.82%	11.12%
Western Europe	–0.57%	1.41%	6.31%

Source: Adapted from Soft Drinks: Euromonitor trade sources/national statistics

business travelers have begun to flock to the continent in response to opportunities in minerals, oil and natural gas.[7]

The establishment of international networks of major professional accounting and consulting firms was motivated by a desire to service domestic clients overseas. Similarly, express shipper DHL probably became the first Western firm to re-enter war-torn Afghanistan. Its rationale: the U.S. military was one of its biggest customers.[8] Sometimes a customer will specifically request that a supplier follow them to an international market. Gruma, Mexico's largest flour producer, has been a major supplier of tortillas to KFC's Taco Bell for years. At KFC's request, Gruma expanded into China.[9]

Following current customers into foreign countries can help to minimize the risk associated with entering a new market. Foods firm McCormick & Company entered China by supplying McDonald's and other Western fast-food chains that it first supplied in the United States. This allowed the company to establish a solid base in China from which to pursue new Chinese restaurant customers and retail chains.[10]

Globalizing for Defensive Reasons

Sometimes companies are not particularly interested in pursuing new growth or potential abroad but decide to enter the international business arena for purely defensive reasons. When a domestic company sees its markets invaded by foreign firms, that company may react by entering the foreign competitor's home market in return. As a result, the company can learn valuable information about the competitor that will help in its operations at home. The company can also slow down a competitor by denying it some of the cash flow from its profitable domestic operation—cash that could otherwise be invested in expansion abroad.

Many U.S. companies opened operations in Japan to be closer to their most important competitors. Major companies such as Xerox and IBM use their local subsidiaries in Japan to learn new ways to compete with the major Japanese firms in their field. Similarly, Kao, the Japanese packaged-goods giant, opened an office in Cincinnati to be close to the headquarters of Procter & Gamble.

Cemex is the largest cement producer in the Western Hemisphere. The Mexican company began its drive to internationalize by expanding across its border into the United States. Cemex then acquired two large cement plants in Spain, taking the company into Europe. Cemex's entry into international markets occurred partly in response to the invasion of its market by Holderbank, a Swiss-based company and the world's largest cement producer. Cemex has since expanded its international operations into over 50 countries.

Born Globals

Most large global corporations have followed a similar sequence of internationalization. Typically, these companies develop their domestic markets and then tentatively enter international markets, usually by exporting. As their international sales grow, these companies gradually establish marketing and production operations in many foreign markets. This traditional pattern seems to be followed by most firms. However, some newer firms are abandoning this gradual approach and are jumping into global markets. Such firms are termed born global.

Born-global firms recognize from the beginning that their customers and competition are international. This is particularly true of many high-tech startup companies. Logitech, the maker of computer input devices, is one such company. Logitech's market coverage and its marketing strategy were global virtually from its inception. The company not only opened sales offices rapidly throughout the world but also established factories in China, Taiwan, the United States, Switzerland and Ireland. Sometimes born globals target overseas markets even before their own home markets. India's Tata Consultancy first established itself as a provider of high-end services to multinational clients in Europe and the United States before turning its sights to companies in India.[11]

Is There a First-Mover Advantage?

Even when a new company isn't technically born global, most firms today begin internationalizing earlier and faster than they did in the past. This is due in part to the advantages of internationalization discussed earlier in this chapter. However, a fast move overseas can be taxing even for the most successful domestic companies, since developing each new national market can entail significant startup costs. Starbucks is a case in point. Starbucks only projected to see its first profit for its international business five years after it began its overseas expansion.[12]

One reason to internationalize quickly and to enter foreign markets early may be a desire to capture a first-mover advantage. Volkswagen and General Motors forecasted slowing growth in their home markets and were among the first foreign automobile manufacturers to enter China. The two companies have been rewarded for their foresight with significantly stronger brand recognition in one of the fastest growing auto markets.[13] However, a first-mover advantage is not guaranteed to all early entrants. An analysis of 4,500 foreign investors in China revealed that market pioneers enjoyed a small advantage in market share but not in profitability. Also, large firms in high-growth industries appeared to be best positioned to realize a first-mover advantage.

Evaluating National Markets

Whether a domestic firm is first internationalizing or an established multinational is looking to extend its global reach, deciding which markets to enter, and prioritizing those markets, is a major requirement for successful global marketing strategy. The most common way to assess a national market is to evaluate its standalone attractiveness. However, George Yip suggests that global marketers should further assess national markets on global strategic importance as well.[14] (See Table 8.2.)

Standalone Attractive Markets

A national market can appear attractive in a number of ways. First, the potential primary market needs to be assessed. Two key considerations are the size of market and its growth rate. Then the firm must consider its possible competitive position. What share of market could it reasonably

Table 8.2 Evaluating National Markets

Standalone Attractive Markets	Globally Strategic Markets
Large markets	Potential source of major profits
Significant potential for growth	Important foreign market for key competitors
Less competitive market	Home market of major customers
Government incentives	Lead market

attain? The less competitive a national market, the better chance to attain a larger market share. A government may also increase the standalone attractiveness of its national market by offering potential market entrants a variety of incentives. A low level of taxation and regulation will increase market attractiveness.

Governments can also grant tax or other incentives to individual firms that choose to invest in their country. Such incentives are not as common as they once were. However, they still play a role in certain countries and in certain industries. Singapore, for example, has offered elite foreign universities incentives to open branches and offer degrees in Singapore. The incentives include preferential real-estate terms and tax-free status. The University of Chicago and French business school INSEAD have each opened small campuses while other schools, including Cornell's School of Hotel Administration, have set up joint ventures with local academic institutions. Singapore hopes these incentives will eventually attract 150,000 foreign students a year. And Singapore is not alone. The emirates of the UAE are attempting to attract private investment in higher education and offering incentives to overseas institutions. South Korea has adopted Singapore's model and opened an Economic Free Zone to attract branches of foreign universities.[15]

Globally Strategic Markets

Some standalone attractive markets are also globally strategic markets. However, certain standalone *unattractive* markets might also be judged to be globally strategic. Globally strategic markets are the current and future battlegrounds where global competitors engage one another.

Must-Win Markets

As global marketers eye the array of countries available, they soon become aware that not all countries are of equal importance on the path to global leadership. Markets that are defined as crucial to global market leadership, markets that can determine the global winners among all competitors, markets that companies can ill afford to avoid or neglect—such markets are must-win markets. Typically, these markets show potential for major profits. A market that delivers large profits can subsidize competitive battles elsewhere in the world.

In the past, the United States has been the largest single market for many industries, making it globally strategic to many firms. Similarly, the larger developed countries often qualify as must-win markets because of their relative wealth and purchasing power. More recently, China has

247

emerged as another country that many global firms consider to be a must-win market. China is a very competitive market, and for many foreign companies, current profits in this market are dismal. However, many firms are afraid to leave this potentially large market for their competitors to exploit unchallenged. For Caterpillar, a U.S.-based construction machinery company, China is a must-win market. The company concluded that China's market is so huge that Caterpillar could not be the global industry leader if it didn't perform well there.[16]

Home Markets of Global Customers

Other globally strategic markets are the home countries of global customers. As multinational business buyers become more centralized in their purchasing decision-making, having a presence close to their headquarters can give a global supplier an advantage. Many multinational corporations (MNCs) also have major sales in their home markets and consequently want global suppliers to understand—and supply—their needs in those markets.

Home Markets of Global Competitors

The home markets and important foreign markets of global competitors are also globally strategic markets. This is where innovations are likely to first appear. As noted in Chapter 6, a presence in such markets allows a firm to undertake counterparries against its global competitors in markets where such actions will deliver the most harm. The home markets of major global competitors in an industry are usually lead markets as well.

Lead Markets

Lead markets include major research and development sites and vary by industry. Such markets are characterized as having demanding customers who push for quality and innovation. For example, Japan is a lead country for many industries, but Toray Industries, a major Japanese company in a number of plastic and textile industries, chose to run its artificial-leather affiliate, Alcantara, from Italy. Alcantara's success can be attributed largely to the design of its leather products. Toray's management considered Italy the world leader in design, and Italy is a recognized lead market for high-end textiles and clothing.[17]

Lead markets may also be global or regional trend-setters. Cold Stone Creamery, an ice cream company based in Arizona, entered the Asian market with the strategy of targeting sophisticated urbanites. Japan was chosen as the first country to enter because of its role as lead fashion and fad market of Asia. What becomes cool in Japan often spreads to Korea, China and other Asian countries.[18]

Geographic Market Choices

While evaluating national markets one by one has its advantages, at any one time a company may decide to target the developed nations of Europe, Japan and North America. Alternatively, it may prefer to pursue emerging markets—less developed and newly industrialized countries in Africa, Asia and Latin America and the transitional economies of the former Soviet bloc. Each of these options presents its own challenges and opportunities as depicted in Table 8.3.

Table 8.3 Marketing Attractiveness by Country Category

Developed Countries	Developing Countries	Transitional Economies
Richest markets	Poorer markets	Many close to Western Europe
Potential sources of major profits	Great variation in size of national markets	Some members of EU Educated population
Lead markets	Generally higher growth potential	
Major markets of key competitors	Poorer markets are usually less competitive	Cultural distance from West varies across countries
Home markets of many global customers	Cultural distance is higher for triad firms but lower for regional competitors	High growth potential
Lower political risk	Government incentives may be available for less-attractive markets	Less developed legal infrastructure relating to business and marketing
	Higher political risk	Higher political risk
	Some developing countries emerging as lead markets and home markets of global competitors	

Targeting Developed Economies

Developed economies account for a disproportionately large share of world GNP and thus tend to attract many companies. As a result, companies that see themselves as world-class marketers cannot afford to neglect these pivotal markets. Firms with technology-intensive products have especially concentrated their activities in the developed world. Although competition from both international firms and local companies is usually more intense in these markets, developed countries are often deemed to be more standalone attractive than are most developing countries. This is primarily because the business environment is more predictable and the trade and investment climate is more favorable. Also, developed countries are usually more globally strategic as they are most often the home countries or major markets of global competitors as well as lead research markets.

Developed countries are located in North America (the United States and Canada), Western Europe and Asia (Japan, Australia and New Zealand). Although some global firms such as IBM[19] operate in all of these countries, others may be represented in only one or two areas. U.S. MNCs established strong business bases in Europe very early in their development but only more recently in Japan. Not surprisingly, Europe accounts for about 20 to 25 percent of sales for large U.S. companies. On the other hand, Japanese firms tend to start their overseas operations in the United States and Canada and then move to Europe.

Kenichi Ohmae first articulated the importance of developing a competitive position in the major developed markets. Ohmae maintained that for most industries, it was important to compete effectively in all three parts of the triad—United States, Europe and Japan. In some cases, the position of competitors in triad markets can determine the outcome of the global competitive battle. Companies need to be strong in at least two areas and at least to be represented in the third. Real global competitors are advised to have strong positions in all three areas.[20]

Despite their attractiveness, developed countries do present some problems to global marketers. Competition can be tough and costs, including marketing costs, can be high. High operating costs were a major reason why Starbucks long ignored Nordic countries despite their high coffee consumption. Personnel costs account for about 30 percent of Starbucks' revenue in Sweden compared to 23 percent in other European markets.[21]

Though the more mature markets of developed countries are arguably more difficult to enter, these markets may still hold potential for a late entrant who is determined and creative—as Toyota discovered. While the European auto market shrank in the mid-2000s, Toyota's European sales soared. What contributed to this surge in sales? A design studio in France that turned out models that looked distinctively Mediterranean. Products were well received and deemed to match the avant-garde styling of the Europeans while ranking first in quality surveys across Europe.[22]

Targeting Developing Countries and Emerging Markets

Developing countries differ substantially from developed countries in terms of both geographic region and level of economic development. Markets in Latin America, Africa, the Middle East and some parts of Asia are characterized by a higher degree of risk than markets in developed countries. The past experience of international firms doing business in developing countries has not always been positive. Trade restrictions often forced companies to build local factories in order to access the local market. Many firms believed that such an investment was not justified, given the market size and the perceived risk of the venture. However, with the present trend toward global trade liberalization, many formerly closed countries have opened their borders to imports. Global marketers have come to consider many developing countries that have undergone market liberalization and have experienced growing PCI to be emerging markets worthy of serious interest. However, political and economic risks are still higher in these countries than in the triad.

Because of the less stable economic climates in those areas, a company's operation can be expected to be subject to greater uncertainty and fluctuation. Furthermore, the frequently changing political situations in developing countries often affect operating results negatively. As a result, some markets that have experienced high growth for some years may suddenly experience drastic reductions in growth. For example, Whirlpool's sales in Brazil, measured in U.S. dollars, declined by $200 million as a result of a devaluation of the Brazilian currency.[23] And Exxon, the world's largest publicly traded company, stood virtually helpless when Hugo Chavez's Venezuelan government expropriated significant company assets present in the country. Despite the difficulties associated with operating in these emerging markets, the average market value of MNCs with operations in developing countries has been shown to be significantly higher than that of MNCs that are not present in such countries.[24]

Developing countries may appear to be attractive markets for several reasons. Market growth in developing countries can sometimes be higher than in the triad, often as a result of higher population growth. Middle-class consumers are appearing in markets once seen as consisting of a small elite and a large impoverished underclass. India now boasts the world's largest middle-class market in absolute numbers. In very poor developing countries, governments may still offer MNCs government incentives such as tax breaks for bringing manufacturing jobs to the country.

With a substantial increase in global migration, remittances sent home from emigrant workers overseas have significantly increased the buying power in many developing countries—including

Turkey, Pakistan and the Philippines. In Latin America, Mexico receives over $10 billion annually in remittances, and Brazil receives over $4.5 billion. Even smaller countries like Colombia, El Salvador and the Dominican Republic each receive over $2 billion in remittances. While many of the overseas workers who send remittances home work in the United States, this is in no way the sole destination of workers. At least 500,000 Latin Americans work in Spain, and Brazil receives half its remittances from Brazilians of Japanese descent who work in Japan.[25]

World Beat 8.1

Africa Rising?

Long ignored by global marketers, Africa is now garnering more attention. The middle class in Africa grew 60 percent in the first decade of the twenty-first century and is estimated at about 21 percent of the population. These new consumers spend between $4 and $20 a day. And Internet access is growing in Africa as well. This enticed Google to enter the market, operating offices in Ghana, Kenya, Nigeria, Senegal, South Africa and Uganda. One of its first initiatives was to provide Google maps for 51 African countries.

Nonetheless, Africa still presents challenges. Some argue that a more realistic operationalization of the middle class would cause the size of Africa's estimated middle class to fall from an overly optimistic 120 million to only 32 million. Poverty still abounds. In Ethiopia, half the population lives on only $1.25 a day despite the fact that PCI nearly doubled in a decade.

In addition, global marketers face an array of problems related to poor infrastructure and weak institutions. When SABMiller began production of soft drinks in Ethiopia it was plagued by electrical blackouts and restrictive currency laws that impeded the importation of factory equipment. One manager used to working in emerging markets noted that Africa was more complicated than Asia. There are 54 countries, and governments are unstable. Getting a visa to go into an African country can take up to three weeks, and flying from South Africa to North Africa often requires changing planes in Europe.

Despite these challenges, global competition is already making an impact on daily life across the continent. In Kenya, competition between Britain's Vodafone Group and India's Bharti Airtel drove the cost of a text message to only one cent. But unlike European, Chinese and Indian investors, U.S. MNCs have been relatively timid about entering the continent. One exception is Coca-Cola. Coca-Cola has been operating in Africa since 1929, and coke is sold in every country in Africa. Today the soft-drinks company is the largest single employer on the continent, and the company plans to spend $12 billion over ten years to improve its production and sales network across the continent.

Sources: Andrew Meldrum, "Can Walmart and Coca-Cola Make Profits in Africa?" *GlobalPost*, November 8, 2010; Peter Wonacott, "Africa Rising: A Continent of New Consumers Beckons," *Wall Street Journal*, January 13, 2011, p. B1; Peter Wonacott, "SABMiller Taps Ethiopia's 'Holy Water'," *Wall Street Journal*, January 13, 2011, p. B1; Peter Wonacott, "Africa Rising: A New Class of Consumers Grows in Africa," *Wall Street Journal*, May 2, 2011, p. A8; Will Connors, "In Africa, Google Sows Seeds for Future Growth," *Wall Street Journal*, May 18, 2010, p. B1; James R. Hagerty and Will Connors, "U.S. Companies Race to Catch Up in Africa," *Wall Street Journal*, June 6, 2011, p. A1; and Andrew Cave, "Glaxo and Unilever Take Note: How General Electric and Coca-Cola Are Winning in Africa," *Forbes*, April 2, 2014.

In many situations, the higher risks in these markets are compensated for by higher returns, because competition can be less intense in developing markets. Hyundai, the largest of South Korea's major car manufacturers, has expanded by acquiring or building car plants in Turkey, India, Egypt, Botswana and Eastern Europe. Hyundai was particularly attracted to these markets by the lack of intense competition there.[26] However, not all developing countries exhibit low levels of competition. As noted earlier, China is one of the most competitive markets in the world.

When evaluating developing countries, most firms focus on standalone attractiveness. However, some developing countries are becoming increasingly globally strategic. The growth potential of markets in China and India put them into this category. As the second largest beer market in the world, China attracted as many as 60 foreign brewers. Carlsberg of Denmark, a brewer with a large international business, predicted that China would become the world's largest beer market in the near future, usurping that distinction from the United States. Today China has achieved that status.[27] Coke considered India a problematic market and had withdrawn from India, but as soon as Pepsi invested there, Coke committed itself to re-entering India. At the time, Coke still considered India to be unattractive on a standalone basis but was afraid it could lose its permanent global position to Pepsi if Pepsi captured the Indian market unopposed.

Thus firms should watch for rapidly changing competitive situations in major emerging markets and adapt accordingly. Citibank had long been a favorite bank among the Brazilian elite. However, it became distracted by a merger with Travelers Group and failed to pursue the Brazilian market aggressively just as other foreign banks were rapidly making headway through acquisitions. Because of this, Citibank dropped to 14th place in the market.[28] In addition, as we saw in Chapter 6, competitors from certain emerging markets such as China, India, Mexico and South Korea are now global contenders. MNCs may need to establish a presence in the home countries of key competitors from the emerging markets just as they have done in the home markets of their more traditional triad competition.

Table 8.4 lists the largest emerging markets. While most of these are traditional developing countries, three—Russia, Poland and the Czech Republic—are transitional economies from the former Soviet bloc. The recent economic performance of these transitional economies has varied. Many Eastern European states have joined the EU, but they remain among the poorest members. Nonetheless, the countries of Eastern Europe enjoy the location advantage of being next to the triad region of Western Europe. And as more firms enter these markets, other firms appear to follow. One reason for this phenomenon is the fear of losing a new market to a competitor. However, another reason is that presence in these markets of more and more international players reassures other firms and lowers the perceived uncertainty associated with Eastern Europe. French retailer Auchon cited the presence of rivals Leclerc and Casino as a key driver behind their decision to enter the Polish market.[29]

The Russian market has proved to be more problematic than most markets in Eastern Europe and is sometimes viewed by firms as less attractive on a standalone basis. Liberalization has been slower, and the market has often been plagued by currency volatility. The year after Cadbury opened its first chocolate plant in Russia, the Russian ruble underwent a significant devaluation. Cadbury's Russian operation took years to recover from that shock. Organized crime has also been cited by global marketers as an impediment to doing business in Russia. Nonetheless, because of its size and abundant natural resources, Russia has the most potential to become a globally strategic market among the transitional economies.

Table 8.4 Largest Emerging Markets

Country	Market Rank	Market Size	Market Growth Rate
China	1	100	100
India	2	37	74
Russia	3	19	45
Brazil	4	18	36
Indonesia	5	10	68
South Korea	6	9	40
Mexico	7	9	31
Turkey	8	6	73
Pakistan	9	5	37
South Africa	10	5	29
Argentina	11	4	68
Saudi Arabia	12	4	68
Egypt	13	4	33
Philippines	14	4	24
Poland	15	3	33
Malaysia	16	3	60
Thailand	17	3	19
Colombia	18	3	44
Venezuela	19	3	40
Peru	20	2	76
Singapore	21	1	86
Hong Kong	22	1	44
Israel	23	1	39
Czech Republic	24	1	11
Chile	25	1	40
Hungary	26	1	1

Source: Adapted from Market Potential Index for Emerging Markets 2013, global EDGE, Michigan State University www.globallogicmsu.ed

Copyright 2014 by Michigan State University, All Rights Reserved. Reprinted with Permission.

Targeting BRIC and Beyond

The term BRIC designates Brazil, Russia, India and China. These four countries represent very large emerging markets. Because of this, some firms believe that these countries represent the strategic growth markets of the near future. (Some add South Africa or BRICS and others add South Korea or BRICK.) While these markets are indeed large, they are dissimilar in many ways. For example, Russia has a smaller and more literate population and possesses a much higher PCI than other BRIC countries. However, it lacks diversified exports and faces a declining and aging population.[30]

253

Given the large number of emerging markets—both developing countries and transitional economies—focusing on four or five countries reduces the complexity of market entry choices. However, firms should be cautious of oversimplification and ignoring opportunities in other national markets. Despite the attention given to BRIC, H.J. Heinz Company found that sales in Indonesia were growing at a faster rate than either India or China.[31] Mexico, Poland, South Korea and the Philippines grew more slowly than the BRIC countries after the global economic downturn in 2009, but they also failed to incur the large trade deficits and debts of the BRIC countries. When BRIC economies began to sputter, these other countries became more attractive. Mexico especially suffered when the United States went into deep recession, but during the lean years that ensued, the Mexican government revamped the country's labor laws, education and telecommunications systems and improved the country's financial and energy sectors.[32] These policies proved successful in attracting new foreign investment to Mexico.

Today other market acronyms compete with BRIC. CIVETS—Colombia, Indonesia, Vietnam, Egypt, Turkey and South Africa—are deemed by some to be the next group of emerging markets to experience exciting growth.[33] Even Goldman Sachs economist, Jim O'Neill, who first proposed the idea of BRIC, now promotes MINT instead—Mexico, Indonesia, Nigeria and Turkey.[34]

Country Selection

After determining what type of foreign markets it wishes to pursue, the firm must choose which countries in particular to target. There are more than 200 countries and territories, but very few firms compete in all of these. Adding another country to a company's portfolio requires additional investment in management time and effort, as well as in capital. Each additional country also represents a new business risk. It takes time to build up business in a country where the firm has not previously been represented, and profits may not be realized until much later on. Consequently, companies need to perform a careful analysis before they decide to move ahead.

The Screening Process

The assessment of country markets usually begins with gathering relevant information on each country and screening out the less desirable countries. The overwhelming number of market opportunities makes it necessary to break the selection process down into a series of steps. Although a firm does not want to miss a potential opportunity, it cannot conduct extensive marketing research studies in every country of the world. The screening process is used to identify good prospects. Two common errors that companies make in screening countries are: (1) ignoring countries that offer good potential for the company's products and (2) spending too much time investigating countries that are poor prospects.

The first stage of the selection process is to use macroindicators to discriminate between countries that represent basic opportunities and those that either offer little or no opportunity or involve excessive risk. Macroindicators describe the total market in terms of economic, social, geographic and political information. (See Table 8.5.) The variables that are included reflect the potential market size and the market's acceptance of the product or similar products. The second stage of

Table 8.5 Macroindicators of Market Size

Geographic Indicators

Size of country, in terms of geographic area

Climatic conditions

Topographical characteristics

Demographic Characteristics

Total population

Population growth rate

Age distribution of the population

Degree of population density

Economic Characteristics

Total GNP

PCI

Income growth rate

Personal or household disposable income

Income distribution

the screening process focuses on microlevel considerations such as competitors, ease of entry, cost of entry and profit potential. The focus of the screening process switches from total market size to profitability. The final stage of the screening process is an evaluation and rank-ordering of the potential target countries on the basis of corporate resources, objectives and strategies. Lead markets and must-win markets receive extra consideration.

Criteria for Selecting Target Countries

The process of selecting target countries through the screening process requires that the companies decide what criteria to use to differentiate desirable countries from less desirable countries. In this section, we explain several key factors and their uses in the market selection process.

Macroindicators of Market Size and Growth

The greater the potential demand for a product in a country, the more attractive that market will be to a company. On a macro basis, it may be determined that the country needs a minimum set of potential resources to be worth further consideration. The macroindicators of market potential and growth are generally used in the first stage of the screening process, because the data are readily available and can be used to quickly eliminate those countries with little or no potential demand. Table 8.5 summarizes the potential macroindicators of market size.

A variety of readily available statistics can serve as macroindicators of market size. A company that sells microwave ovens may decide not to consider any country with a personal disposable income per household of less than $10,000 a year. The rationale for this criterion is that if the average household has less than $10,000, the potential market for a luxury item such as a microwave oven will not be great. However, a single statistic can sometimes be deceptive. For example, a country may have an average household income of $8,000, but there may still be a million households with an income of over $10,000. These million households will be potential buyers of microwave ovens.

Political Conditions as Macroindicators

The importance of the host country's political environment was described in detail in Chapter 4. Although political risk tends to be more subjective than the quantitative indicators of market size, it is equally important. Any company can be hurt by political risk, which can result in anything from limitations on the number of foreign company officials and on the amount of profits paid to the parent company, to refusal to issue a business license. Though less radical than invasions, industrial disputes such as strikes can be a major disruption to business. Table 8.6 shows some indicators of political risk that may be used in country selection.

Microindicators of Market Size and Growth

Because the macroindicators of market size are general and crude, they do not necessarily indicate a perceived need for the product. For example, a country such as Iran may have the population and income to suggest a large potential market for razors, but the male consumers, many of whom are Muslims and wear beards, may not feel a need for the product. In the next stage of the screening process, it is recommended that microindicators of market potential be used. Microindicators usually indicate actual consumption of a company's product or a similar product, therefore signaling a perceived need. Table 8.7 lists several examples of microindicators of market size.

These microindicators can be used to estimate market size further. The number of households with televisions indicates the potential market size for televisions if every household purchased a new television. Depending on the life of the average television in use, one can estimate the annual demand. As we noted in Chapter 7, consumption figures for similar or substitute products can be used as proxies if actual consumption statistics are not available for a certain product category. For

Table 8.6 Indicators of Political Risk

Probability of nationalization	Percentage of voters who are Communist
Bureaucratic delays	Restrictions on capital movement
Number of expropriations	Government intervention
Number of riots or assassinations	Limits on foreign ownership
Political executions	Soldier/civilian ratio
Number of Socialist seats in the legislature	

Table 8.7 Microindicators of Market Size

Radios	Hotel beds
Televisions	Telephones
Cinema seats	Tourist arrivals
Scientists and engineers	Passenger cars
Hospitals	Civil airline passengers
Hospital beds	Steel production
Physicians	Rice production
Alcohol consumption	Number of farms
Coffee consumption	Land under cultivation
Gasoline consumption	Electricity consumption

example, if Apple Inc. is trying to measure the potential market size and receptivity for its iPhone, it might choose as a proxy the number of personal computers per person or cellular telephone usage. Similarly, in determining the market size for surgical sutures, marketers might use the number of hospital beds or the number of doctors as a proxy. The number of farms might indicate the potential demand for tractors, just as the number of cars is likely to indicate the number of tires needed.

Competition as Microindicator

In general, it is more difficult to determine the competitive structure of foreign countries than to determine the market size or political risk. Because of the difficulty of obtaining information, competitive analysis is usually done in the last stages of the screening process, when a small number of countries are being considered. However, when firms seek to identify globally strategic markets (as opposed to simply standalone attractive markets) competitive analysis will be undertaken earlier in the screening process.

As noted in Chapter 7, there are various sources of information on competition, though availability varies widely, depending on the size of the country and the product. Many of the larger countries have chambers of commerce or other in-country organizations that may be able to assist potential investors. For example, if a firm is investigating the Japanese market for electronic measuring devices, the following groups could help it determine the competitive structure of the market in Japan:

- ➤ U.S. Chamber of Commerce in Japan
- ➤ Japan External Trade Organization (JETRO)
- ➤ American Electronics Association in Japan
- ➤ Japan Electronic Industry Development Association
- ➤ Electronic Industries Association of Japan
- ➤ Japan Electronic Measuring Instrument Manufacturers Association

Listing Selection Criteria

A good way to screen countries is to develop a set of criteria that serve as minimum standards that a country must meet in order to move through the stages of the screening process. The minimum cutoff number for each criterion will be established by management. As one moves through the screening process, the selection criteria become more specific. The screening process that could be used by a manufacturer of kidney dialysis equipment is depicted in Table 8.8.

The analysis begins by looking at GNPs. Introduction of dialysis equipment in a new market requires a significant support function, including salespeople, service people, replacement parts inventory and an ensured continuous supply of dialysate fluid, needles, tubing and so on. Some countries lack the technical infrastructure to support such high-level technology. Therefore, management may decide to consider only countries that have a minimum size of $25 billion GNP, a criterion that excludes many of the developing economies of the world from consideration.

The selection process continues by examining the concentration of medical services in the remaining countries. Hemodialysis is a sophisticated procedure that requires medical personnel with advanced training. For a country to support advanced medical equipment, it requires a high level of medical specialization. Higher levels of medical concentration allow doctors the luxury of specializing in a field such as nephrology (the study of kidneys). Management may determine that a population of less than 1,000 per doctor and a population of less than 200 per hospital bed indicate that medical personnel will be able to achieve the level of specialization needed to support a hemodialysis program.

Public health expenditures reflect the government's contribution to the medical care of its citizens—a factor of obvious importance with respect to hemodialysis. Management may believe that countries that do not invest substantially in the health care of their populations generally are not interested in making an even more substantial investment in a hemodialysis program. Thus,

Table 8.8 Screening Process Example: Targeting Countries for Kidney Dialysis Equipment

Filter Number	Type of Screening	Specific Criteria
1	Macrolevel research	GNP over $25 billion
		GNP per capita over $1,500
2	General market factors related to the product	Fewer than 200 people per hospital bed Fewer than 1,000 people per doctor
		Government expenditures over $200 million for health care
		Government expenditures over $40 per capita for health care
3	Microlevel factors specific to the product	Kidney-related deaths over 1,000 Patient use of dialysis equipment—over 40 percent annual growth in treated population
4	Final screening of target markets	Numbers of competitors Political stability

countries that do not have a minimum of $40 in public health expenditure per capita or $200 million in total expenditures for health care would be eliminated from consideration.

Then management may decide that there are two microlevel factors to consider: the number of kidney-related deaths and the growth rate of the treated patient population. The number of deaths due to kidney failure is a good indicator of the number of people in each country who could have used dialysis equipment. The company will be interested only in countries with a minimum of 1,000 deaths per year due to kidney-related causes. Analysis of the growth rate of the population requiring kidney treatment demonstrates a growth in potential demand.

Finally, management must consider political risk and competition. Emerging markets with the greatest growth potential may be the best targets for a new supplier of dialysis equipment, because competition is not so entrenched as it would be in a mature market. Alternatively, management may decide to enter a lead market where a major competitor is strong in order to monitor technology development and possibly block that competitor. The weighting of these microlevel factors will determine the primary target market.

Psychic Distance

Strong evidence exists that market similarity can be used for country selection. A study of 954 product introductions by 57 U.S. MNCs found a significant correlation between market selection and market similarity.[35] Born-global firms also exhibit a propensity to first enter national markets that are more similar to their home markets.[36] As shown in Table 8.9, the selection of foreign markets by Australian exporters correlates closely with psychic distance. Of the ten major markets closest to Australia in psychic distance, only one is not among the country's top ten export destinations.

The concept of market similarity is simple. Managers believe that their success in the home market is more easily transferable to markets similar to the one in which they already compete. This idea is called psychic distance. Therefore, when a company decides to enter foreign markets, it will first tend to enter markets that are psychically close or most similar to its home market. A typical U.S. firm usually enters Canada, Australia and the United Kingdom before entering less similar markets such as Egypt, South Korea and India.

The premise behind the selection of similar markets is the desire of a company to minimize risk in the face of uncertainty. Entering a market that has the same language, a similar distribution system and similar customers is less difficult than entering a market in which all these variables are different. During the recent recession, some U.S. retailers such as J. Crew Group Inc. and Victoria's Secret looked to enter Canada as a source of growth that was relatively risk-free compared to more culturally distant markets in Europe or Asia.[37]

The unforeseen dangers of entering psychically distant markets can be illustrated by the recent push of international liquor companies into Muslim Turkey. Many liquor companies were lured by Turkey's expanding economy and the fact that younger Turks possessed growing disposable income. But Turkey proved a psychically distant market for most of these companies. First, the new market entrants had to deal with legal differences relating to their promotion strategies. Television advertising of liquor is forbidden in Turkey, making it difficult to educate new consumers on how to use or mix drinks. Then the Turkish government introduced an additional 30 percent tax on alcohol companies in addition to already high consumption taxes. Finally, there was the

Table 8.9 Impact of Psychic Distance on Export Markets of Australian Exporters

Country	Psychic Distance Rank	Exporter Rank
United Kingdom	1	4
New Zealand	2	1
United States	3	2
Singapore	4	3
Hong Kong	5	5
Japan	6	6
Canada	7	16
Papua New Guinea	8	8
Fiji	9	10
Malaysia	10	7
South Africa	11	17
India	12	19
Italy	13	21
Indonesia	14	11
Philippines	15	18
Sweden	16	19
Germany	17	13
China	18	9
Chile	19	23
Taiwan	20	12
United Arab Emirates	21	20
Kuwait	22	24
Kenya	23	25
Thailand	24	15
South Korea	25	14

Source: Adapted from Paul Brewer, "Operationalizing Psychic Distance: A Revised Approach," *Journal of International Marketing*, vol. 15, no. 2 (2007), pp. 44–66.

Note: Psychic distance calculated from 15 variables including culture, immigration, trade agreements, language, colonial ties and development level.

issue of religion. During the Islamic holy month of Ramadan, Pernod's Turkish operations experienced a 30 percent decline in sales.[38] No wonder market dissimilarity breeds risk!

Although it is intuitive to choose markets that are psychically close to the home market, there are dangers of choosing markets on the basis of similarity. The benefits of similarity need to be balanced against the market size. Australia may be similar to the United States but may have relatively little demand compared with China or Indonesia. Air France flies to more African cities than any other non-African airline. France's colonial history arguably gives Air France (and other French companies) a competitive advantage in its former African empire, which includes Cameroon, Chad, Gabon, Guinea, Ivory Coast, Mali, Senegal and other countries, due to linguistic, economic and cultural ties.[39] However, some have argued that French firms have lost out on bigger growth markets in the Pacific Rim because of their emphasis on markets in Africa.

Psychic-Distance Paradox

Another problem associated with selecting national markets based on perceived similarity is the fact that firms can overestimate the degree of similarity between markets. When Starbucks internationalized, it discovered that just because foreign consumers spoke English didn't mean that the markets operated the same. For example, in the United States, the firm's strategy was to find the best corners in the best markets to locate its stores. That approach proved too expensive in Britain where real estate prices were higher.[40] When Canadian retail chains entered the United States, managers assumed that the United States was just like Canada only bigger. They believed that the retail concepts that worked in Canada would work in the United States. Instead, U.S. consumers proved very different from Canadian consumers. They demanded more service, shopped harder for bargains and were far less loyal to national chains than were their Canadian counterparts. In addition, competition proved far more intense in the United States. As a result, familiarity bred carelessness, and the chains struggled to survive in what proved to be a very alien market.[41]

This culture shock experienced by managers entering foreign markets that they had perceived to be similar to their own is sometimes called the psychic-distance paradox. A study of firms from Denmark, Sweden and New Zealand suggests that this shock effect may be more common among producers of customized products than among producers of more standardized products.[42]

Grouping International Markets

A final consideration in selecting national markets is the option of entering a group of countries in a single geographic region, be they the developed countries of Western Europe or the less developed countries in South America or the Middle East. It is often necessary to group countries together so that they can be considered as a single market or as a group of similar markets. Two principles that often drive the need for larger market groupings are critical mass and economies of scale. Critical mass, a term used in physics and military strategy, embodies the idea that a certain minimum amount of effort is necessary before any impact will be achieved. Economies of scale is a phrase used in production situations; it means that greater levels of production result in lower costs per unit, which obviously increases profitability.

The costs of marketing products within a group of countries are lower than the costs of marketing products to the same number of disparate countries for four reasons. First, the potential volume to be sold in a group of countries is sufficient to support a full marketing effort. Second, geographic proximity makes it easy to travel from one country to another, often in two hours or less. Third, the barriers to entry are frequently the same in countries within an economic group—for example, the EU. Finally, in pursuing countries with similar markets, a company gains leverage with marketing programs.

There is some debate over the long-term role of market groups. The EU has become a strong group with a single currency, but many economic groups may become subordinate to the role of the WTO. Also, given the broad membership of the WTO and its strong enforcement powers, the regional market group will generally need to conform to the rules and practices of the WTO when dealing with all other WTO countries.

It is also important to remember that just being neighbors isn't enough to make countries into a viable market group. Take, for example, the countries in the Caucasus region. Armenia and Azerbaijan are technically at war. Turkey sometimes blockades Armenia in sympathy with Azerbaijan. Relations between Georgia and Armenia remain strained, as do relations between Iran and Azerbaijan. Travel and shipping among the countries are poor as well. Roads are bad, and the easiest flight connections in the region are all via Moscow or Istanbul.[43] Clearly these countries do not present themselves as a likely group to the global marketer.

Nor does geographic distance necessarily preclude countries from being grouped together. For example, the so-called Anglo cluster consisting of Australia, Canada, England, Ireland, New Zealand, South Africa and the United States, is a collection of countries that were once a part of the British Empire and are today relatively wealthy. In addition, most of their populations speak English and have many cultural values in common.[44] For some firms, it makes sense to target part or all of the Anglo cluster when considering market entry. For example, when Australian winemaker BRL Hardy launched their Banrock Station brand they chose Australia, New Zealand, the United Kingdom and the United States as their key markets.

In-Country Expansion

Global marketers not only make decisions as to which new markets to enter, they also decide which markets deserve expansion. Coca-Cola and its bottling partners decided to invest another $5 billion in India.[45] McDonald's announced it would open 200 new stores in a single year to expand its presence in China.[46] In-country expansion options often compete with new market opportunities for management time and limited capital investment. The decision process for in-country expansion may be similar to that of new market entry. However, in-country experience often helps allay perceptions of risk in a market where a MNC is already present.

Limits to Expansion

Some industries demand a large global footprint. Industries that have high research and development costs must market worldwide in order to recoup their investments. Those that experience large economies of scale in manufacturing must also market worldwide in order to capture those cost advantages in manufacturing. *But are there limits to expansion?*

Arguably, a MNC may run out of good markets to enter. After that, new markets may return less on investment. The larger the number of international markets, the harder it can be to manage them all. U.K. grocery retailer Tesco PLC decided to retreat from global expansion. The company held 31 percent of the U.K. market and had grown to become the third largest retailer in the world after Wal-Mart and Carrefour SA. However, management concluded that overseas expansion had distracted them from their home market resulting in customer defections to competitors. To better focus on its home market, Tesco exited Japan, stopped store expansion in China and postponed entering the Indian market.[47]

Vermeulen and Barkema propose that entering new markets is complex and challenging. The MNC needs time to learn about new local environments, adapt products and services and establish good working relationships with new local managers and employees. Therefore, entering too many markets too fast may have its costs. Management may not be able to absorb all the new knowledge and overall performance of the MNC may suffer.[48]

World Beat 8.2

Say Goodbye to the World's Best Market

For most global competitors, a presence in the U.S. market would seem like a no-brainer. But some companies disagree.

The new president of Japanese car manufacturer Mitsubishi Motors traveled to Detroit to begin talks with potential buyers of Mitsubishi's U.S. operations. Weak sales by the U.S. subsidiary were compounded by losses due to extending credit to young car buyers, many of whom had poor credit ratings and later defaulted on their loans. The company had sustained losses in the United States for the past three years. Losses in the last year totaled $2 billion. Several years later another Japanese car company, Suzuki, exited the U.S. market. Despite their success in the growing emerging markets of Asia, the company's compact cars failed in the United States.

British retailer Tesco PLC also announced that it would leave the U.S. market after five unprofitable years. The company failed to capture American consumers who were unaccustomed to its British-style ready meals, self-service cash registers and store layouts. American shoppers proved more brand-conscious as well and failed to appreciate Tesco's large investment in store brands. Tesco realized too late that Americans expected bakeries in their grocery stores and wanted the flower department to be prominently placed. And these missteps occurred despite substantial market research undertaken by the company prior to entering the market!

Even a company that doesn't leave the U.S. market altogether may decide to shut down some of its business lines. U.S.-based Procter & Gamble decided to remove Max Factor cosmetics from the United States after its attempts to prop up the brand proved disappointing. The iconic line, named after the pioneer Hollywood makeup artist, is still sold abroad and ranks among the top brands in other markets that P&G deems strategically important such as Russia and the United Kingdom.

Sources: Amy Chozick, "A CEO's Personal Touch Revs Up Mitsubishi in the U.S.," *Wall Street Journal*, July 10, 2007, p. B1; Ellen Byron, "Max Factor," *Wall Street Journal*, June 5, 2009, p. B1; Hiroko Tabuchi, "Suzuki's Small Cars Were Wrong Fit in U.S.," *New York Times*, November 6, 2012; Paul Sonne and Peter Evans, "Five Years, $1.6 Billion Later, Tesco Decides to Quit U.S.," *Wall Street Journal*, December 6, 2012, p. B1; and "Tesco Hands Over Fresh & Easy Stores to U.S. Billionaire," *Reuters*, September 10, 2013.

Exit Strategies

As noted above, sometimes a MNC decides to abandon a foreign market. This is not an easy decision. Not only is a market lost, the firm may lose credibility in other markets. Closing operations is often costly as well. The Brink's Company, a U.S.-based armored-truck service, saw its cash-delivery business in Belgium lose $10 million in one year. When workers then went on strike, the company decided to have its subsidiary declare bankruptcy rather than negotiate. Brink's then found itself in a lengthy court battle facing multiple lawsuits over its handling of the closure including its decision not to offer its workers severance pay.[49]

Even if a company can sell its operations, the sale is sometimes to a global competitor and often at a relatively low price. A market exit can often strengthen a global competitor. When French retail giant Carrefour exited Thailand, it sold its stores to Big C, the local subsidiary to global rival Casino Guichard-Perrachon SA.[50]

Nonetheless, there are several reasons why a global marketer might exit a market: tough competition, financial difficulties, the need to refocus on the home market, and political protest.

Tough Competition

Market exit can be an option if a firm fails to establish itself in a particularly competitive market. European retailer Carrefour left the Mexican market in the face of strong local competition.[51] Similarly French cosmetics maker L'Oreal announced that it was pulling its Garnier brand from the Chinese market due to slow sales and tough competition.[52]

Financial Difficulties

Market exit often occurs when a MNC acquires more debt than it can handle. To service the debt, poorly performing markets must be abandoned. Even successful operations may be sold to raise cash. Avon Products sold 60 percent of its successful Japanese company for about $400 million to reduce Avon's debt in the United States. Dutch retailing giant Ahold had to exit the Latin American market when an accounting scandal back home in Europe prompted creditors to call in the company's €11 billion debt.[53] Mexican-based Cemex acquired Australian operations but two years later was hit by the global downturn of the construction industry. Faced with renegotiating $14.5 billion in debt the company agreed to sell its Australian operations to Swiss cement maker Holcim Ltd.[54]

Refocus on the Home Market

Some companies will retreat from foreign markets when their home markets require additional attention. Carrefour left Thailand to refocus on its home market of France, and Lloyds Banking Group announced that it would pull out of half of the 30 countries where it had operations in order to refocus on its home market of Britain.[55]

Political Considerations

Changing government regulations can at times pose problems that induce some companies to leave a country. Political risk can also motivate firms to leave a market. Sainsbury is a U.K.-based supermarket chain that employs 100,000 people worldwide. It entered the Egyptian market by purchasing

80 percent interest in a state-owned retailer. The subsidiary posted a significant loss the next year, partly as a result of problems with goods clearing customs and difficulty in obtaining building permits. These losses were exacerbated by an organized campaign against the company orchestrated by anti-Israel protesters who targeted Western companies operating in Egypt.[56] Three years after entering the market, Sainsbury announced that it would pull out of Egypt, selling its stake to its Egyptian partner and incurring a loss of $140–175 million.[57]

Re-entry

Sometimes companies reverse their exit decision and enter markets a second time. This can occur due to improvements in the political, economic or market environment. Burger King left the Japanese market after a price war with McDonald's. However, six years later after the Japanese began eating more U.S. fast food, Burger King re-entered the market.[58] Similarly, Taco Bell opened stores in Britain in the late 1980s but retreated from the market by the mid-1990s. Fifteen years later, it announced it would re-enter the market. More Mexican food was being sold in the U.K. both at restaurants and in grocery stores and research confirmed that Britons were developing a taste for Mexican food.[59]

Because many companies exit markets under financial duress, some choose to re-enter markets when their financial condition improves. Anheuser-Busch InBev NV sold its South Korean Oriental Brewery when the company needed to shed debt after a series of huge acquisitions. Six years later when the company found itself cash rich again it bought back Oriental Brewery for nearly three times the price for which it had been previously sold.[60]

Sometimes firms simply realize that their first attempt at market entry was ill conceived. Dunkin' Donuts exited the Chinese market after only a few years. Its sweets were too sweet for Chinese tastes. It underestimated the difficulty of selling coffee to a nation of tea drinkers, and it partnered, oddly and unsuccessfully, with an aerospace company. Ten years after leaving the Chinese market, Dunkin' was ready to try again. Success in other Asian markets including Taiwan had given the company more confidence. This time Dunkin' partnered with a Chinese company that specialized in operating shopping centers and restaurants. Dunkin' performed extensive local testing of its products and lowered the level of sugar in its pastries. The company also invested in finding prime real estate for its locations. Even the choice of the company's local Chinese name, "everybody is happy," was only determined after months of debate.[61] China, a market once abandoned, had clearly become a new priority.

Dunkin' Donuts also chose to re-enter Russia. The company exited the Russian market after a disappointing experience with a franchisee who sold liquor along with Dunkin's traditional line of pastries and coffee. Eleven years later, Dunkin' Donuts returned to Moscow to join the rivalry among growing coffee-shop chains. Starbucks' recent success largely inspired the move, and Dunkin's new partner was a real estate developer with a record of developing retail opportunities.[62]

Conclusion

Any company that wishes to engage in global marketing must make a number of very important strategic decisions concerning global market participation. At the outset, the company must commit itself to some level of internationalization. Increasingly, firms are finding that an international presence must be pursued for competitive reasons. It is a necessity, not simply an option. Once committed, the company needs to decide where to go, both in terms of geographic regions and specific countries. Firms must determine what participation they want and need in developed economies and emerging markets. Being in the right international markets establishes the groundwork for the firm's global marketing strategy.

Managerial Takeaways

1. *Expanding into international markets helps global marketers manage risk, exploit growth opportunities and defend against competition.*
2. *Entering new markets often requires significant resources, both financial and managerial. Therefore, deciding which market to enter next is an important decision.*
3. *The country selection process can be a costly task. A serious screening process helps to identify key markets for further investigation.*
4. *Developed markets and emerging markets present unique opportunities and challenges. Global marketers should consider both when planning their market participation strategies.*
5. *Standalone attractive markets must be balanced with markets of global strategic importance.*
6. *Targeting culturally similar markets first makes sense. But don't forget the psychic-distance paradox!*
7. *Sometimes expanding within current markets may be more attractive than entering a new national market.*
8. *Global marketers sometimes exit markets for a variety of reasons—some good and some bad. But re-entry remains an option when circumstances change.*

Questions for Discussion

1. Why might a firm in packaged goods choose to enter a globally strategic market rather than a market that is more standalone attractive? In what way would your answer differ for a firm manufacturing and marketing medical diagnostic equipment?
2. What advantages might a Korean-based company such as Hyundai have entering markets in developing countries?
3. Discuss the pros and cons of packaged-goods manufacturers targeting Eastern Europe and Russia.
4. What could be the advantages and disadvantages of being a born-global firm?
5. Unlike firms early in their internationalization, MNCs do not appear to favor entering new markets that are similar to their home markets over entering those that are dissimilar. Why do you think that is?
6. If a company exits a market and then wishes to return ten years later, what peculiar challenges might it face?

CASE 8.1 Indian Food Goes Global

Mr. R. Krishnan, president of South Indian Foods Limited (SIFL), was deep in thought in his office at corporate headquarters in Coimbatore, India. Eleven years earlier he had founded SIFL with the help of his wife, Maya. Now, after returning from a weeklong business trip to the United States, Mr. Krishnan was pondering the future of his company. Should SIFL enter foreign markets? If so, which ones?

SIFL began as a company selling only three items but had quickly expanded to a dozen products. It produced and marketed batters, pastes and flours that formed the ingredients of traditional South Indian cooking. For example, its Maami's Tamarind Mix consisted of mustard, ground nuts, asafetida, curry leaves, coriander powder and dried chilies fried in oil and then combined with tamarind extract, salt, turmeric and vinegar. The mix was next bottled and vacuum-sealed to preserve the traditional homemade flavor and aroma of tamarind mix.

The company began to market its products in and around Coimbatore. Soon, however, new production units were established in Bangalore and Madras to serve the whole South Indian market. Then three more manufacturing units were established in the states of Maharashtra, Andhra Pradesh and West Bengal. SIFL estimated that its share of market varied between 19 and 27 percent across its product categories in the territories where it competed. Recently, new competitors had entered the market. Their market shares were slightly lower than those of SIFL. In response to increased competition, however, SIFL attempted to avoid adding new product lines that might have to compete head-on with aggressive competitors.

SIFL attributed part of its success to its promotional efforts. It used advertising campaigns in local radio and newspapers. Handbills, printed in the local language of the different Indian states, were distributed in newspapers in selected cities. The company also offered sample packets of its batter products. All these efforts had helped make Maami's a household name in South India.

When Mr. Krishnan raised the question of international expansion at an emergency board meeting, there was great enthusiasm but little agreement. Some of the managers' comments were as follows:

KRISHNAN: Why can't we think of going international? Our strategy did very well in the Indian market. With our state-of-the-art production facilities and marketing expertise, I believe we could easily create a niche overseas.

SUNDER: We have to be optimistic about the U.S. market. As you know, the Indian population there is large enough to absorb our product. Our market research also reveals that our dishes are even favored by native Americans.

SHANKAR: I accept your views, but we are forgetting the fact that in the U.S. market we have to compete with powerful packaged-food companies.

KRISHNAN: What about Asia? In South Asia, the raw materials necessary for making our products are readily available.

MAYA: I do not think targeting all of Asia is a viable option. Although the Chinese and Japanese are accustomed to rice, most of these Asian countries are culturally different from India. Why not the United Kingdom? It has a considerable South Indian population.

DINAKAR: Why not set up production facilities in the United States or the United Kingdom? I believe production overseas would be a better choice than exporting to these markets.

267

Discussion Questions

1. What are SIFL's motivations for expanding abroad?
2. What are the advantages of targeting Indian populations residing in foreign countries? What problems might arise?
3. What are the pros and cons of entering the United States first? The United Kingdom? Neighboring Asian markets?
4. Is there any advantage or disadvantage to this product being "Made in India"?
5. SIFL will face competitors such as Kraft in the United States. What overall posture should SIFL adopt in relation to these strong competitors—attack, avoid or cooperate? How might U.S. competitors respond to SIFL's entry into the market?
6. To investigate the competitive environment for these products in your country, visit a local grocery store or supermarket. What Indian foods or food products are sold there? Do they appear to be targeted at ethnic communities or at a wider segment? What firms make these products? What insights could your visit give SIFL?

Source: Case prepared by Saji, K.B., Professor of Marketing, Indian Institute of Management, Lucknow, India. Used by permission.

CASE 8.2 Targeting Emerging Markets

At the beginning of the millennium, Procter & Gamble was the world's largest consumer goods company, specializing in household products and personal care. Among its well-known brands are Tide detergent, Crest toothpaste, Olay skin care, Pantene shampoo and Pampers disposable diapers. However, with 6 billion consumers worldwide, the company was focused only on the richest 1 billion. Less than a quarter of company sales came from emerging markets, and those sales were mainly to the wealthier segments of those societies.

All that changed when a new CEO decided that P&G would seriously target developing countries and transitional economies. After all, it was estimated that each week 40,000 Asians used a washing machine for the first time. Long known for its product innovation in the United States, P&G designated 30 percent of its research and development funds to the needs of these lower-income markets. Its engineers sought new ways to make products more cheaply, and P&G researchers visited homes in developing countries to better understand consumer needs. P&G's acquisition of the Gillette Company was also seen as a way to expand more quickly into emerging markets. The acquisition was P&G's largest to date. After just six years, company sales in emerging markets reached 50 percent of total sales.

China was a market of particular interest to P&G. In just 20 years the company had established an extensive distribution system and had seen sales rise to $2.5 billion. China had become P&G's second largest market, and P&G had become China's largest consumer goods company. With a wide variety of brands and products, the company aimed at various target markets across different price ranges. Still, China often appeared to be two very distinct markets—urban China and rural China. Urban Chinese would pay $1 for toothpaste in exotic flavors. Rural Chinese might prefer to pay half as much and want salt added because they believed salt whitened teeth.

Despite its success in the Chinese market, P&G experienced a major product crisis there involving P&G's elite SK-II line of skin care products. Chinese authorities announced that banned chemicals were found in the products sold in China. P&G denied the allegation. Almost immediately articles concerning the safety of SK-II appeared on thousands of Chinese websites. Many experts believed that the banned chemicals were safe in small amounts and pointed out that these chemicals were not banned in the European market or Japan. Instead, they noted that SK-II products sold in China were imported from Japan and the Chinese government could be retaliating for Japan's recent adoption of stricter standards for Chinese agricultural imports.

When P&G voluntarily offered refunds to consumers for SK-II products, a number of problems arose. Some consumers tried to return counterfeit products. In some cases violence broke out. Salesclerks were attacked and sales counters robbed. Later the Chinese authorities announced that the banned substances did not pose a health hazard. However, the loss in sales and consumer trust was especially painful to P&G since beauty products accounted for 60–70 percent of the company's sales in China.

One of Gillette's major markets was Russia, another market of particular interest to P&G. However, this market had proven problematic. When a financial crisis caused the Russian ruble to plummet, Russian wholesalers could not afford to buy Gillette products. These products disappeared from retail stores, and Gillette's Russian sales plummeted 80 percent in a single month. Gillette found it could not meet its projected global profit growth of 15–20 percent that year. To save money, Gillette planned to close 14 factories and lay off 10 percent of its workforce worldwide.

Despite the setback in Russia, P&G believed that Gillette's brands, including its line of razors, would benefit from P&G's distribution throughout the developing world. However, in certain countries such as India, Gillette's distribution was already very strong, and when the two companies merged there was considerable overlap. Therefore in the years following the merger, P&G had to restructure distribution in developing countries leading to many distributors being abandoned. This resulted in a disruption of sales.

Unilever, with a much longer history of marketing in developing countries, was a formidable challenger to P&G's aspirations in emerging markets. Sixty percent of Unliver sales were attributed to emerging markets and half its products competed against those of P&G. The other half of its product lines were in packaged foods where Unilever competed against major multinational packaged-food companies such as Kraft and Nestlé. With sales stalling in its home market, Unilever announced that it would shift even more resources to the developing world and would consider selling off some of its current brands to support this move.

One of Unilever's traditional strengths was its positioning strategy of offering different brands at different price points, successfully targeting both the poor and the rich in emerging markets. In India, Unilever had access to many small villages where most MNCs had no distribution. The company worked with a consortium of industry, academics and NGOs to better understand the needs of low-income consumers. However, the company was also focused on expanding its position among the wealthier segments of developing countries, including offering more convenience foods.

Both P&G and Unilever enjoyed years of sustained growth in emerging markets, but then they hit a bump in the road. The economies of several key markets stalled. Issues of inflation and currency devaluations, largely absent for years, returned to hurt the companies' bottom lines and lowered profit projections. P&G responded by announcing that it would raise prices in countries experiencing significant inflation or currency devaluation in order to preserve margins. But both companies remained committed to emerging markets. Unilever noted that growth in these markets remained considerably higher than growth in Europe or North America, and management at P&G asserted that emerging markets were definitely the future for the company.

Discussion Questions

1. Why do companies such as P&G target emerging markets? Do you agree with this strategy?
2. What are the dangers of targeting emerging markets?
3. What advice would you give P&G for engaging competitor Unilever? What advice would you give Unilever?

Sources: "Procter & Gamble Targets Emerging Markets," in Kate Gillespie and H. David Hennessey, *Global Marketing* (Mason, OH: Cengage, 2011), pp. 243–244; "Procter & Gamble Says It Won't Accelerate Emerging-Markets Expansion," Associated Press, May 23, 2012; Peter Evans, "Unilever Sales Growth Slows," *Wall Street Journal Online*, January 21, 2014; Phil Wahba, "Emerging Markets Lift P&G Second-Quarter Sales," Reuters, January 24, 2014; "Procter & Gamble Lowers Profit Outlook," Associated Press Newswires, February 11, 2014; Landon Thomas, Jr., "Once a Golden Goose, Emerging Markets Drag for Some Multinationals," *International New York Times*, March 5, 2014, p. 19; Barney Jopson, "P&G to Raise Prices in Emerging Markets," *Financial Times*, April 23, 2014; and Andy Sharman, "Unilever to Hold Course in Emerging Markets," *Financial Times*, April 24, 2014.

CASE 8.3   The Global Baby Bust

Most people think that the world faces an overpopulation problem. But Phillip Longman argues otherwise in his book *The Empty Cradle*. He warns instead of a global baby bust. World population growth has fallen 40 percent since the late 1960s. The human population is expected to peak at 9 billion by 2070, and many countries will see their population shrink long before that.

Falling birthrates mainly account for these declines (see Table 8.10). Already more than half the world's population lives in aging countries where the fertility rate is less than 2.1 children per woman, the rate necessary to replace both parents once infant mortality is taken into account. And 97 percent of the world lives in countries where the fertility rate is falling.

Several factors contribute to the falling birthrates. Around the world, more women are entering the workforce, and young people delay raising a family in order to attain the higher levels of education needed to compete in a global marketplace. However, a major reason for falling birthrates is the high cost of raising a middle-class child in an industrialized country—a cost estimated at more than $200,000 (exclusive of college) in the United States.

Table 8.10 Birthrates for Selected Countries, 2000 and 2025

Country	Births per 1,000 Population, 2000	Annual Rate of Growth (%) 2000	Births per 1,000 Population, 2025	Annual Rate of Growth (%) 2025
Algeria	20	1.5	13	0.8
Argentina	18	1.1	13	0.5
Brazil	19	1.3	13	0.5
China	14	0.7	11	0.2
Czech Republic	9	−0.1	7	−0.4
Egypt	26	2.0	17	1.1
Ethiopia	42	2.5	27	1.5
France	13	0.5	10	0.1
Ghana	29	1.7	18	0.8
Greece	10	0.2	8	−0.2
Hungary	10	−0.3	8	−0.4
India	25	1.6	17	0.9
Indonesia	23	1.6	15	0.8
Iran	18	1.2	13	0.7
Italy	9	0.3	7	−0.3
Japan	10	0.2	8	−0.6
Kenya	37	2.1	19	1.2
Mexico	23	1.4	16	0.8
Poland	10	0.0	9	−0.3
Russia	9	−0.4	8	−0.6
Saudi Arabia	30	2.9	22	1.3
South Africa	22	0.6	15	−0.7
South Korea	13	0.8	9	−0.1
Spain	10	0.2	7	−0.3
Sweden	10	0.0	10	−0.1
Switzerland	11	0.5	9	0.0
Thailand	17	1.1	12	0.3
Turkey	19	1.3	12	0.6
Ukraine	9	−0.7	9	−0.5
United Kingdom	11	0.4	10	0.2
United States	14	1.0	14	0.8

Source: Adapted from data available at U.S. Census Bureau (www.census.gov).

Among developed countries, the baby bust first appeared in Japan. In the 1980s, Japan was considered to be a surging economy. Then its demographic structure crumbled. Japan's population peaked in 2008. At the current fertility rate of only 1.3, Japan's population will decrease by half by 2100. By 2060, 40 percent of the Japanese population will be 65 years of age or older. Japan is projected to have 49 retirees per 100 workers as early as 2025.

The baby bust is apparent in Europe as well. Germany has a fertility rate of only 1.36, nearly as low as Japan's. By 2050, people 65 and older will account for one-third of the populations in Greece, Portugal and Spain. The baby bust is also affecting the United States. America's fertility rate is 1.93 per woman. If one disregards the higher fertility rate of immigrants, America's fertility rate drops to 1.5 percent—similar to that of Europe.

As developing countries become more industrialized and urban, they too face a high cost of raising children. Thailand's fertility rate fell from seven children per woman in the 1970s to 1.6 today. In Mexico, where fertility rates have declined precipitously, the population is aging five times faster than it is in the United States. By 2050, Algeria could well see its average age increase from 21.7 to 40.

One of the greatest declines in population growth is occurring in China, where government policy has long supported one child per family. Some demographers expect China's population to peak at less than 1.4 billion in 2026. The number of old people for every hundred working-age members of the population will rise from 11 in 2010 to 42 in 2050. Currently many of China's elderly are poor, sick and depressed according to China's first large-scale survey of citizens over 60 years of age. Fear of being old and poor encourages Chinese to save and stymies the Chinese government's attempts to spur the economy through greater domestic consumption.

Already China's reserve of working-age people has declined. China's labor supply has been integral to its substantial growth for three decades, but the United Nations estimates that China's labor force will lose 67 million workers from 2010–2030. Furthermore, the proportion of males to females in the age group under age 14 is 120 to 100, and by 2020 there are projected to be 24 million young Chinese males in the new generation with no prospects of marrying and having children of their own.

In 2013, China amended its one-child policy. Couples are now allowed to have two children as long as one of the parents is an only child. But even if the new policy helps reverse demographic implosion in China, it will have no effect on the working–age population for 20 years.

A nation may experience a "demographic dividend" when birthrates first fall. More working-age citizens support fewer children, freeing up money for consumption and investment. Many attribute the recent boom markets in Asia, such as China and South Korea, to this demographic dividend. However, as population growth continues to slow, the nation faces the problem of supporting older populations. For example, by 2040, Germany's public spending on pensions will exceed 15 percent of GNP. Even China will have 30 retirees for every 100 persons in the workforce by 2025. The level of entrepreneurship in a nation also declines as its population ages. Japan and France, with their already high ratios of retirees to workers, rate among the lowest countries for entrepreneurship. On a more positive note, a decline in terrorism is associated with an aging population. Longman points to the fact that Europe's Red Guard, a terrorist organization active in the 1970s, is now defunct.

Is immigration the answer for industrialized countries? To sustain its current ratio of workers to retirees over time, the United States would need to absorb almost 11 million immigrants a year. Such an influx would require building the equivalent of another New York City every ten months. By 2050, 73 percent of the U.S. population would be immigrants or descendants of immigrants who arrived since 1995. Before this occurs, a potential political backlash against immigrants could materialize. Supply is a problem as well. Puerto Rico—once a major source of immigration to the United States—no longer provides a net flow of immigrants to the United States despite its lower standard of living and free access to the United States. In addition, the United States may have to compete with Europe for immigrants from the developing world.

Several countries have attempted to create more baby-friendly policies in hopes of reversing declining birthrates. Russia's population is expected to decline from 143 million to 107 million by 2050. The government has responded with new incentives for having more children. Families with more than three children receive housing priorities and a special allowance of about $250 a month for each child. The government is also hoping to lure Russian speakers from former Soviet countries and the Russian diaspora to return home. Japan's leaders have proposed offering new parents $3,300 a year for every new child until the child reaches the age of 15. Other suggestions include more state-supported day care and tuition waivers. But the success of throwing money at the problem may be limited. Many believe that cultural acceptance of working mothers and corporate support for them has proven far more successful for increasing the number of children in a country.

Discussion Questions

1. What are the implications of the global baby bust for marketers of consumer goods?
2. What are the implications of the global baby bust for marketers who sell to governments?
3. Why do you think entrepreneurship in a nation declines as its population ages? How could this impact global marketing?
4. How does the global baby bust affect the relative attractiveness of different national markets?

Sources: "Procter & Gamble Targets Emerging Markets," in Kate Gillespie and H. David Hennessey, *Global Marketing* (Mason, OH: Cengage, 2011), pp. 244–246; Phillip Longman, "The Global Baby Bust," *Foreign Affairs*, May/June 2004, pp. 64–79; Daisuke Wakabayashi and Miho Inada, "Baby Bundle: Japan's Cash Incentive for Parenthood," *Wall Street Journal*, October 9, 2009, p. A16; Charles Wolf Jr., "The Facts about American 'Decline'," *Wall Street Journal Europe*, April 14, 2011, p. 13; Jeremy Page, "China's One-Child Plan Faces New Fire," *Wall Street Journal Online*, April 29, 2011; Patricia Kowsmann, "Slowing Birthrates Weigh on Europe's Weak Economies," *Wall Street Journal Online*, January 7, 2013; Jonathan V. Last, "America's Baby Bust," *Wall Street Journal Online*, February 2, 2013; Fred Weir, "Putin Vows to Halt Russia's Population Plunge with Babies, Immigrants," *Christian Science Monitor*, February 15, 2012; Kate Connolly, "Germany's Birthrate is the Lowest in Europe," *The Guardian*, September 21, 2012; Tom Orlik, "Aging Chinese Face a Bleak Future," *Wall Street Journal Online*, May 30, 2013; Bob Davis, "China's Lighter Rules on Births Will First Drain Its Workforce," *Wall Street Journal*, November 22, 2013, p. A9; and James Hookway, "Baby Bust Spreads to Developing World," *Wall Street Journal*, March 20, 2014.

Notes

1   "Kraft to Focus on Ten Brands Overseas," Reuters News, September 3, 2008.
2   Stephanie Strom, "For Oreo, Cadbury and Ritz, a New Parent Company," *New York Times*, May 23, 2012.
3   Lorene Yue, "Mondelez Gets a Lesson in Global Economics," *Chicago Business*, February 17, 2014.
4   Marissa Chew and Yun-Hee Kim, "Friendster Sells Itself to Malaysian Partner," *Wall Street Journal*, November 16, 2010, p. B4.
5   "Chinese Firms Seek to Expand Overseas," Dow Jones Commodities Service, April 4, 2006.
6   Mike Esterl, "'King of Beers' Fizzling in U.S., Sets Goal of World Domination," *Wall Street Journal*, July 27, 2013, p. A1.
7   Patrick Mc Groarty and Alexandra Berzon, "Hoteliers Fill a Gap in Africa," *Wall Street Journal*, September 19, 2012, p. B1.
8   Michael Zielenziger, "DHL Worldwide Express Starts Service in Kabul, Afghanistan," *San Jose Mercury News*, April 6, 2002.
9   Geri Smith and Michael Arndt, "Wrapping the Globe in Tortillas," *Business Week*, February 26, 2007, p. 54.
10 Anil K. Gupta and Haiyan Wang, "How to Get China and India Right," *Wall Street Journal*, April 28, 2007, p. R4.
11 Megha Bahree, "Tata Targets Smaller Clients," *Wall Street Journal Online*, February 22, 2011.
12 "Boss Talk: It's a Grande-Latte World," *Wall Street Journal*, December 15, 2003, p. B1.
13 Amy Chozick, "Japan's Auto Giants Steer Toward China," *Wall Street Journal*, May 16, 2007, p. A12.
14 George S. Yip, *Total Global Strategy II* (Upper Saddle River, NJ: Prentice-Hall, 2003), p. 76.
15 Yojana Sharma, "Branch Campus Growth Has Moved to Asia," *University World News*, January 13, 2012.
16 James R. Hagerty, "Caterpillar Stumbles in China," *Wall Street Journal Europe*, July 20, 2011.
17 "Manager's Hands-Off Tactics Right Touch for Italian Unit," *Nikkei Weekly*, February 3, 1997, p. 17.
18 Amy Chozick, "Cold Stone Aims to be Hip in Japan," *Wall Street Journal*, December 14, 2006, p. B10.
19 Scott Thum and Joseph B. White, "For U.S. Firms, Europe Brings Tears," *Wall Street Journal*, October 25, 2012, p. B1.
20 Kenichi Ohmae, *Triad Power: The Coming Shape of Global Competition* (New York: Free Press, 1985).
21 John D. Stoll, "Starbucks Aims to Invade Nordic Region," *Wall Street Journal Online*, September 27, 2012.
22 Gail Edmondson and Adeline Bonnet, "Toyota's New Traction in Europe," *Business Week*, June 7, 2004, p. 64.
23 "Whirlpool Says Net Fell by 65 Percent on Impact of Brazil Devaluation," *Wall Street Journal*, April 16, 1999, p. B2.
24 Christos Pantzalis, "Does Location Matter? An Empirical Analysis of Geographic Scope and MNC Market Valuation," *Journal of International Business Studies*, vol. 32, no. 1 (2001), pp. 133–155.
25 Joel Millman, "Latin Americans Boost Home Coffers," *Wall Street Journal*, March 17, 2003, p. A2.
26 "Fast Drive Out of the Shadows," *Financial Times*, June 17, 1996, p. 17.
27 "Premium Labels Take Beer in China Beyond the Working Man," *China Economic Review*, December 5, 2013.
28 Pamela Druckerman, "As Brazil Booms, Citibank Is Racing to Catch Up," *Wall Street Journal*, September 11, 2000, p. A30.
29 Katrijn Gielens and Marnik G. DeKimpe, "The Entry Strategy of Retail Firms into Transition Economies," *Journal of Marketing*, vol. 71 (2007), pp. 196–212.
30 Joseph S. Nye, Jr., "Another Overhyped Challenge to U.S. Power," *Wall Street Journal Online*, July 20, 2011.
31 Patrick Barta, "Brands Bet on Indonesia as Spending Booms," *Wall Street Journal*, April 8, 2010, p. B1.
32 Thomas Catan, "Economic Tide Reverses in Latin America," Dow Jones Top North American Equities Stories, September 10, 2013.
33 John Greenwood, "After BRICs, CIVETS?" *Wall Street Journal*, September 19, 2011, p. R10.
34 Laura Baverman, "From Retirement, Famed Goldman Sachs Economist Says MINT is New BRIC," *Upstart Business Journal Online*, January 8, 2014.

35 William H. Davidson, "Market Similarity and Market Selection: Implications for International Market Strategy," *Journal of Business Research*, vol. 11, no. 4 (1983), p. 446.

36 Sylvie Chetty and Colin Campbell-Hunt, "A Strategic Approach to Internationalization: A Traditional Versus a 'Born-Global' Approach," *Journal of International Marketing*, vol. 12, no. 1 (2004), pp. 57–81.

37 Elizabeth Holmes, "U.S. Apparel Retailers Map an Expansion to the North," *Wall Street Journal*, March 29, 2010, p. B4.

38 Dana Mattioli, "Liquor Makers Eye Turkey," *Wall Street Journal*, November 29, 2010, p. B8.

39 Daniel Michaels, "Landing Rights," *Wall Street Journal*, April 30, 2002, p. A1.

40 "Boss Talk: It's a Grande-Latte World," *Wall Street Journal*, December 15, 2003, p. B1.

41 Shawna O'Grady and Henry L. Lane, "The Psychic Distance Paradox," *Journal of International Business Studies*, vol. 27, no. 2 (1996), pp. 319, 324–325.

42 Torben Pedersen and Bent Petersen, "Learning about Foreign Markets: Are Entrant Firms Exposed to a 'Shock Effect'?" *Journal of International Marketing*, vol. 12, no. 1 (2004), pp. 103–123.

43 "The Caucasus, a Region Where Worlds Collide," *The Economist*, August 19, 2000.

44 Neal M. Ashkanasy, Edwin Trevor-Roberts and Louise Earnshaw, "The Anglo Cluster: Legacy of the British Empire," *Journal of World Business*, vol. 37, no. 28–39 (2002).

45 Nikhil Gulati and Rumman Ahmed, "India Has 1.2 Billion People But Not Enough Drink Coke," *Wall Street Journal*, June 27, 2012, p. B1.

46 Laurie Burkitt, "McDonald's Joins the Line Looking to Expand in China," *Wall Street Journal Online*, December 16, 2010.

47 Paul Sonne, "Tesco Loses Its Appetite for Growth," *Wall Street Journal*, November 10, 2012, p. B3.

48 Freek Vermeulen and Harry Barkema, "Pace, Rhythm, and Scope: Process Dependence in Building a Profitable Multinational Corporation," *Strategic Management Review*, vol. 23 (2002), pp. 627–653.

49 John W. Miller, "Brink's Retreat in Belgium Backfires," *Wall Street Journal Europe*, December 22, 2010.

50 Mimosa Spencer, "Carrefour Sells 42 Thai Stores to French Rival," *Wall Street Journal*, November 16, 2010, p. B4.

51 Evette Treewater, "Global Retailers Refocus on Latin America," Infoamericas, November 16, 2007.

52 Nadya Masidlover and Laurie Burkitt, "L'Oreal Pulls Its Garnier Brand From China," *Wall Street Journal*, January 9, 2014, p. B8.

53 Andrea Welsh and Ann Zimmerman, "Wal-Mart Snaps Up Brazilian Chain," *Wall Street Journal*, March 2, 2004, p. B3.

54 Martin Gelnar, "Swiss Cement Maker to Expand," *Wall Street Journal*, June 16, 2009, p. B2.

55 David Enrich and Sara Schaefer Munoz, "Lloyds Joins Retreat of U.K. Banks," *Wall Street Journal*, July 1, 2011, p. C1.

56 William A. Orme, "A Grocer Amid Mideast Outrage," *New York Times*, January 25, 2001, p. C1.

57 "Sainsbury's to Pull Out of Egypt," *Jerusalem Post Daily*, April 10, 2001, p. 10.

58 Yuri Kageyama, "Japan Imports American Culture via Calories," *Marketing News*, May 1, 2007, p. 11.

59 Peter Stiff, "Taco Bell Takes a Second Look at Britain," *The Times*, June 28, 2010.

60 Matthew Dalton, "AB InBev Returns to South Korea," *Wall Street Journal*, January 21, 2014, p. B3.

61 Jenn Abelson, "In 2nd Crack at China Market, Dunkin' Donuts Alters Recipe," *Boston Globe*, November 21, 2008, p. A1.

62 Kevin Helliker, "Dunkin' Donuts Returns to Russia," *Wall Street Journal Europe*, April 29, 2010, p. 22.

Chapter 9

Global Market
Entry Strategies

EXPORTING AS AN ENTRY STRATEGY   279

FOREIGN PRODUCTION AS AN ENTRY STRATEGY   284

OWNERSHIP STRATEGIES   290

ENTERING MARKETS THROUGH MERGERS AND ACQUISITIONS   296

Even the Arts are going global. Russia's Bolshoi Ballet has actively sought overseas expansion since the collapse of the Soviet Union left the world-famous dance troupe strapped for funds. The Guggenheim art museum in New York, concerned with its limited endowment, has also expanded into foreign markets. But what is the best way for ballet companies and art museums to enter foreign markets? Traditionally, they exported their product by taking their dancers or art exhibits on tour. Today other market entry options are being employed. The Bolshoi has licensed its name to schools in Brazil and Japan. The Guggenheim has established subsidiary branches in Bilbao, Venice and Berlin. Even the Vatican is considering ways to enter world markets by licensing the images from its repository of manuscripts, prints, coins and artwork to interested companies in the fields of collectibles, giftware, apparel and décor.

Any enterprise, whether a for-profit company or a not-for-profit museum, that pursues a global strategy must determine the type of presence it expects to maintain in every market where it competes. A company may choose to export to the new market, or it may decide to produce locally. It may prefer full ownership of a local operation or it may seek partners. Once a commitment has been made, changes can be difficult and costly. Therefore, it is important to approach these decisions with the utmost care. Not only is the financial return to the company at stake, but the extent to which the company can implement its global marketing strategy also depends on these decisions. In this chapter, we concentrate on the major entry strategies by explaining each alternative in detail and citing relevant company experiences. An overview of possible entry strategies appears in Figure 9.1.

Learning Objectives

After studying this chapter, you should be able to:

➤ differentiate among market entry options—indirect exporting, direct exporting, licensing, franchising, contract manufacturing, assembly and full-scale integrated manufacturing—and note the conditions under which each is an appropriate strategy;

➤ explain the role of export management companies, export agents and export consortiums;

➤ note the ways in which the Internet has affected the international entry strategies employed by firms;

➤ list the pros and cons of establishing wholly owned subsidiaries and the pros and cons of establishing joint ventures;

➤ compare and contrast technology-based, production-based and distribution-based strategic alliances;

➤ explain when entering a market by acquisition is desirable.

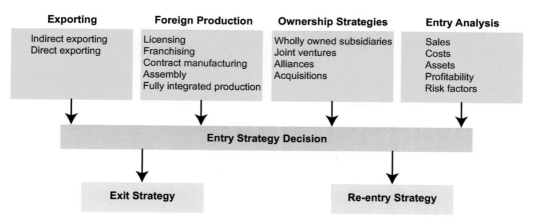

Figure 9.1 Market Entry Strategies

Exporting as an Entry Strategy

Exporting to a foreign market is a strategy that many companies follow for at least some of their markets. Few countries offer a large enough market to justify local production. Exporting allows a company to manufacture its products for several markets centrally and thus achieve economies of scale. When this occurs, a firm can realize more profits, lower its prices or sometimes do both. In addition, both transportation costs and government tariffs have fallen considerably in the past 25 years. These conditions make exporting all the more cost-effective. Therefore, many firms use exporting as a way to grow their business while limiting risk and avoiding large investments.

Home governments often assist firms by providing information concerning export opportunities. As a result there is a great deal of information available on export markets. Much is available online. For example, Table 9.1 lists a number of services offered by the U.S. Export Portal.

However, a study of 992 export decision-makers from the United Kingdom, Austria, Germany, New Zealand and the United States found that firms serving a few countries used less information than firms serving many countries. The study also identified that the sheer volume of export information could be a problem for both large and small exporters without sufficient staff to understand and interpret the available information.[1]

A firm has two basic options for carrying out its export operations. Markets can be contacted through an intermediary located in the exporter's home country—an approach called indirect exporting. Alternatively, markets can be reached directly or through an intermediary located in the foreign market—an approach called direct exporting.

Indirect Exporting

Several types of intermediaries located in the home market are ready to assist a manufacturer in contacting overseas buyers. A major advantage of using a domestic intermediary lies in its

Table 9.1 Typical Services Provided by the U.S. Export Portal

- Basic guide to exporting
- Country market reports
- Industry-specific trade data and analysis
- Trade lead database
- Information on trade fair and other promotional events
- Foreign standards and certification information
- Assistance with export financing
- Information on economic sanctions and export licenses
- Advocacy and dispute resolution
- Assistance finding freight forwarders
- Best methods for handling orders and shipments
- Assistance locating foreign agents and distributors
- Advice on pricing and methods of payment
- Personalized counseling
- Online course for exporters

Source: www.export.gov

knowledge of foreign market conditions. Particularly for companies with little or no experience in exporting, the use of a domestic intermediary provides the exporter with readily available expertise.

Export Management Company

An export management company (EMC) is a firm that handles all aspects of export operations under a contractual agreement. The EMC normally takes responsibility for the marketing research, patent protection, channel credit and shipping and logistics, as well as for the actual marketing of products in a foreign market or markets. An EMC can operate either as a merchant that takes title to the products or as an agent that does not take title but provides services for a fee or commission. Arrangements between an EMC and a manufacturer will vary, depending on the services offered and the volume expected. The advantages of an EMC include the following: (1) little or no investment is required to enter the international marketplace, (2) no in-house personnel are required and (3) the EMC offers an established network of sales offices as well as international marketing and distribution knowledge. The main disadvantage is that the manufacturer gives up direct control of the international sales and marketing effort.

Export Agents

Export agents are individuals or firms that also assist manufacturers in exporting goods. They are similar to EMCs, except that they tend to provide more limited services and to focus on one country or one part of the world. Export agents understand all the requirements for moving goods through international channels, but they do not provide all the services that an EMC provides. These agents focus more on the sale and handling of goods. The advantage of using an export agent is that the manufacturer does not need to have an export manager to handle all the documentation and shipping tasks. The main disadvantage is the export agent's limited market coverage. To cover different parts of the world, a firm would need the services of numerous export agents.

Direct Exporting

A company engages in direct exporting when it exports directly to customers or solely through intermediaries located in foreign markets. In other words, no domestic intermediary is involved. In direct exporting, an exporter must deal with a large number of foreign contacts, possibly one or more for each country the company enters. A direct exporting operation requires more expertise, management time and financial resources than does indirect exporting, but it gives the company a greater degree of control over its distribution channels. Most firms interested in exporting can seek assistance online from home governments for basic training and advice.

Independent Distributor versus Marketing Subsidiary

To handle the marketing of its products within its target market, the company must choose between relying solely on local independent distributors and establishing its own marketing subsidiary. In making this choice, the company must consider costs, control and legal restrictions.

An independent distributor earns a margin on the selling price of the products. Although using an independent distributor entails no direct cost to the exporter, the margin the distributor earns represents an opportunity that is lost to the exporter. By switching to a marketing subsidiary to carry out the distributor's tasks, the exporter can keep the margin previously paid to the distributor. For example, say a manufacturer of electronic machinery exports products priced at $7,500 each (at the factory in Boston), with airfreight, tariffs and taxes added, the product's landed costs amount to $9,000. An independent distributor will have to price the products at $13,500 to earn a desired gross margin of 33.33 percent, or $4,500 per machine.

Alternatively, the exporter can set up a wholly owned marketing subsidiary, in this case consisting of a manager, a sales manager, several sales agents, clerical staff, a warehousing operation and the rental of both an office and a warehouse location. If the total estimated cost of these arrangements is $450,000 annually, the firm can break even at sales of 100 machines.

With increasing volume, the incentive to start a marketing subsidiary grows. On the other hand, if the anticipated sales volume is small, using the independent distributor will be more efficient because sales are channeled through a distributor who is maintaining the necessary staff for several product lines.

Firms marketing products that require the development of special skills or special working relationships with customers tend to have their own marketing subsidiaries. This way the company may better control the delivery of after-sales service. If the firm has definite ideas about the correct way to price and promote its products, it may wish to establish a marketing subsidiary as well. The subsidiary could then implement the full strategy for the marketing mix, such as setting prices, developing advertising programs and choosing media.

Still, a commitment to a marketing subsidiary should not be made without careful evaluation of all the costs involved. The operation of a subsidiary adds a new dimension to a company's international marketing operation. It requires a financial commitment in a foreign country, primarily for the financing of accounts receivable and inventory. Also, the operation of a marketing subsidiary entails a number of general administrative expenses that are essentially fixed in nature. The size of the available market in a country will often determine the appropriate market entry strategy. For example, Duckworth and Kent, the world's leading manufacturer of titanium ophthalmic surgery instruments, located in the United Kingdom, has a marketing subsidiary in the United States, its largest market, but uses distributors in most other markets.[2]

Firms may also face government restrictions on the use of wholly owned marketing subsidiaries. Although these constraints are declining with trade liberalization, they persist in some emerging markets such as Saudi Arabia. Exporters to Saudi Arabia have traditionally been required to use Saudi agents or establish a marketing subsidiary with a Saudi partner.

Cooperating for Export

Companies that compete against each other in their domestic market may sometimes unite to address export markets. Brazil's Ministry of Development, Industry and Foreign Trade promotes such export consortiums wherein companies unite to share the logistical and promotion costs of entering foreign markets. Brazil's two largest frozen meat processors formed a consortium to target Russia and selected countries in Africa, the Middle East and the Caribbean. It is very unlikely that Brazilian antitrust laws would allow such cooperation in the domestic market, but governments often encourage it in export markets.

Export cooperation can also occur among small and medium-sized enterprises (SMEs). One study of exporter SMEs in the Jutland peninsula of Denmark revealed that 83 percent cooperated with other firms in the same industrial sector. For example, a manufacturer of windmills exported to California purchased the motors from another local SME. Firms in the textile and clothing sector mounted mutual exhibits at trade fairs. Manufacturers of wooden furniture might contribute different products—a desk, chair or bookshelf—to a commonly marketed export suite. The success of these smaller ventures in competitive export markets can be attributed in part to this sort of cooperation.[3]

Exporting and the Internet

The Internet has greatly increased the ability of firms to export directly. A company that establishes a server on the Internet and opens up a website can be contacted from anywhere in the world. Consumers and industrial buyers who use modern Internet browsers can search for products, services or companies and, in many instances, can make purchases online. Table 9.2 lists the websites of the top 25 global brands.

The impact of the Internet has been felt by SMEs as well as larger multinational corporations (MNCs). Prior to the Internet, SMEs accounted for about one-quarter of total U.S. exports. With the advent of the Internet, this figure rose quickly to about one-third. SMEs can take advantage of virtual trade missions, videoconferencing and online ordering. They can reach markets with daily

Table 9.2 Websites of Global Brands

Brand	Website
American Express	www.americanexpress.com
BMW	www.bmw.com
Cisco	www.cisco.com
Citi	www.Citibank.com
Coca-Cola	www.coca-cola.com
Disney	www.disneygo.com
GE	www.ge.com
Gillette	www.gillette.com
Google	www.google.com
Honda	www.honda.com
HP	www.hp.com
HSBC	www.hsbc.com
IBM	www.ibm.com
Intel	www.intel.com
Louis Vuitton	www.louisvuitton.com
Marlboro	www.marlboro.com
McDonald's	www.mcdonalds.com
Merrill Lynch	www.ml.com
Mercedes-Benz	www.mercedes.com
Microsoft	www.microsoft.com
Nescafé	www.Nescafe.com
Nokia	www.nokia.com
Samsung	www.samsung.com
Sony	www.sony.com
Toyota	www.toyota.com

communication and advertising without the need to send full-time salespeople into the field or to employ traditional export management companies. In fact, web-based startups in Europe often plan globally from their inception.[4]

Exporters using the Internet as an entry option do face several challenges. They may need to communicate in different languages, conform to different privacy regulations and adapt to different cultures. Cultural factors such as the need to touch and see products (common in Egypt and Mexico) can inhibit consumer purchasing online.[5] Also Internet penetration varies greatly from 78.6 percent in North America to under 15.6 percent in Africa.[6]

Internet exporters must also overcome a number of fulfillment challenges. These challenges include cross-border issues involved with completing a sale, such as shipping the product, paying tariffs, collecting funds and providing after-sale service to customers all over the world. Export management consultants have arisen to help with a number of these problems. One such company, Next Linx, was founded by Rajiv Uppal, an Indian-born engineer working in the United States. Uppal realized that new e-exporters still needed to know that their product could be hit with an education tax in Pakistan or that the same product could be subject to state tariffs as well as a national tariff in Brazil. And exporters of wine to the European Union would need to navigate the EU's 132 different categories of wine, each with its own tariff schedule.[7] Clearly, online exporters must stay alert to the constant regulatory and logistics changes that affect their businesses.

Foreign Production as an Entry Strategy

Licensing

With licensing, a company assigns the right to a copyright or patent (which protects a product, technology or process) and/or a trademark (which protects a product name) to another company for a fee and/or royalty. Royalties are usually based on the licensee's sales of the products utilizing the copyright or patent. Proprietary information, or trade secrets not protected by patents, can also be licensed. The foreign company, or licensee, gains the right to exploit the patent or trademark commercially on either an exclusive (the sole right to sell in a certain geographic region) or a nonexclusive basis.

Licenses are signed for a variety of time periods. Depending on the investment needed to enter the market, the foreign licensee may insist on a longer licensing period to recover the initial investment. Typically, the licensee makes all the necessary capital investments (machinery, inventory, etc.) and markets the products in the assigned sales territories, which may consist of one or several countries. Licensing agreements are subject to negotiation and tend to vary considerably from company to company and from industry to industry.

Reasons for Licensing

Companies use licensing for many reasons. A company may not have the knowledge or the time to engage more actively in international marketing. If so, it can still realize income from foreign markets by using licensees. Licensing may also be employed for less attractive foreign markets, allowing the firm's scarce managerial resources to be concentrated on more lucrative markets. The market potential of the target country may be too small to support a new manufacturing or marketing operation. A licensee may have the option of adding the licensed product to an ongoing operation, thereby reducing the need for a large investment in new fixed assets. Finally, a company may not have sufficient capital to be able to expand into multiple markets. Using licensing as a method of market entry, a company can gain market presence without making an equity investment.

In some countries where the political or economic situation appears uncertain, a licensing agreement may avoid the potential risk associated with investing in fixed facilities. Commercial and political risks are absorbed by the licensee. In other countries, governments favor the granting of licenses to independent local manufacturers as a means of building up a local industry. In such cases, a foreign manufacturer may prefer to team up with a capable licensee despite a large market size, because other forms of entry may not be possible.

Licensing can also help global firms enter difficult markets. Roche continues to expand in the Japanese pharmaceutical market through licensing its products with Chugai Pharmaceuticals. The Japanese market is difficult to penetrate without knowledge of the drug approval process and access to the distribution channels. Chugai Pharmaceuticals has licensed two cancer drugs and a hepatitis drug from Roche. The licensing approach for Roche also speeds up the market entry process, giving them fast access to the second largest pharmaceutical market in the world.[8]

Disadvantages of Licensing

A major disadvantage of licensing is the company's substantial dependence on the local licensee to produce revenues and thus royalties. Royalties are usually paid based on a percentage of sales volume. Once a license is granted, royalties are paid only if the licensee is capable of performing an effective marketing job. Because the local company's marketing skills may be less developed, revenues from licensing may suffer accordingly. Although there is a great variation from one industry to another, licensing fees in general are substantially lower than the profits that can be made through exporting or local manufacturing. Depending on the product, licensing fees may range anywhere between 1 percent and 20 percent of sales, 3 to 5 percent being more typical for industrial products.

Ironically, if a local licensee is too successful, an international firm may reconsider the wisdom of licensing. More direct participation in a successful market can reap higher rewards in profits than mere licensing fees. Some licensing contracts even include provisions for the licensor to increase its participation if it eventually wishes to do so.

Another potential disadvantage of licensing is the uncertainty of product quality. A foreign company's image may suffer if a local licensee markets a product of substandard quality. For this reason, firms often seek licensees based on their production knowledge and reputation for quality. New Zealand-based Fonterra Co-Operative Group signed a licensing agreement with Arab Dairy to produce and sell Fonterra's products in Egypt and other Middle East countries. The two companies had worked on a project before, and Fonterra was convinced of the quality standards of its new licensee. Fonterra had a partner in China, however, who went bankrupt as the result of producing and selling melamine-tainted infant products. These products may have been responsible for several deaths and the hospitalization of thousands of babies.[9] Even when a quality licensee is located, however, ensuring uniform quality requires the licensor to provide additional resources that may reduce the profitability of the licensing activity.

Licensing will also require a certain commitment of management time and resources. Licensees may need to be trained. Appropriate records must be kept, and licensor audits must be conducted. Serious consideration must be given to problems that could arise. In case of disagreements between licensor and licensee, there must be provisions for dispute resolution. In the context of which national law will the contract be interpreted? How and in which country will arbitration take place? What are the conditions for termination of the licensing contract?

The possibility of nurturing a potential competitor is viewed by many companies as a final disadvantage of licensing. Licenses are usually limited to a specific time period. Licensees can use similar technology independently after the license has expired and can, therefore, turn into a competitor. This is less of a concern if the licensed technology changes quickly or if a valuable brand name is involved. Of course, firms must be careful that they—and not their licensee—hold the trademark to their brand in each national market.

Franchising

Franchising is a special form of licensing in which the franchisor makes a total marketing program available, including the brand name, logo, products and method of operation. Usually, the franchise agreement is more comprehensive than a regular licensing agreement, inasmuch as the total operation of the franchisee is prescribed.

Numerous companies that successfully exploited franchising in their home markets are exploiting opportunities abroad. Among these companies are McDonald's, Kentucky Fried Chicken (KFC), Burger King and other U.S. fast-food chains with operations in Latin America, Asia, Europe and the Middle East. Starbucks long avoided franchising due to its wish to keep control over its brand. However, after struggling in Europe, the company opened its first franchisee-owned stores in Great Britain in 2013 with plans to roll out the new franchising strategy in other European markets.[10] Service companies such as Holiday Inn, Hertz and Manpower have also successfully used franchising to enter foreign markets.

The United States is home to the greatest number of franchisors. However, franchising is increasingly important in many non-U.S. markets where growth potential is higher than in the more mature U.S. market. For example, Mexico is the world's fifth largest franchise market with about 1,300 different franchises operating in 70 different industries. Franchising has grown consistently in Mexico at a rate of 14–17 percent annually and now accounts for 6.2 percent of GDP.[11]

U.S.-based franchisors dominate among foreign franchisors in Mexico. In Morocco, however, French franchisors are more common.[12] In fact, franchisors of many national origins have entered international markets. Singapore-based Informatics Holdings Inc. franchises computer training schools in Asia. Interbrew franchises its Belgium Beer Café. The Japanese company Yohinoy D&C has opened 91 stores in California that sell *gydun*, a seasoned beef and rice dish. Even an Egyptian college student who began exporting hookahs, Egypt's traditional water pipes, to the United States branched into franchising, supplying 50 accounts with a complete hookah system for a water pipe café, including equipment, staff training and management advice.[13]

Finding the right franchisee is critical for successful franchising. The U.S. Commercial Service offers an array of services to help U.S. franchisors identify qualified franchisees. Its 125 overseas offices provide trade specialists to help screen potential franchisees, network with local franchise associations and arrange meetings for U.S. franchising executives.

With its rapid global growth, however, the franchising industry has been hit with numerous complaints and has even been plagued by fraud in the past few years. One individual on the Internet actually claimed his government had privatized its Consumer Protection Agency, for which he was selling local franchises.[14] As a result of the surge in complaints, many countries are tightening their franchising laws to help protect franchisees. Chinese law requires that franchisors own at least two directly operated outlets somewhere in the world before being allowed to operate a franchise model in China. But industry experts recommend that companies interested in franchising in China first establish company-owned stores in China to solidify their brands and show potential franchisees that their business concepts can be successful in China.[15]

Master Franchisees

While many franchisees worldwide are individual entrepreneurs, in some countries, companies or wealthy individuals buy master franchises that give them exclusive rights to a whole city, a whole country or even a whole region of the world. Master franchisees have traditionally been sophisticated partners of established multinational franchise chains. Curves, a women's fitness-center chain, successfully entered the Japanese market with the help of an enthusiastic master franchisee who soon opened 149 locations across Japan.[16] The Cheesecake Factory entered into an exclusive franchising agreement with Kuwait-based Alshaya Group to build and operate The Cheesecake Factory restaurants across the Middle East.[17] In the Central Asia state of Kazakhstan, most franchising operations are supervised by master franchisees operating out of Turkey or Russia.[18]

World Beat 9.1

The Middle East Franchise

The Middle East and North Africa (MENA) Franchise Association estimates that the franchise industry in its region is worth $30 billion—and growing at 30 percent annually! When Payless, a U.S.-based discount shoe retailer, set its sights on the Middle East, it entered the market via a multi-country master franchisee. Later when Payless decided to enter India, it followed the same master franchisee strategy it adopted for the Middle East and offered an exclusive pan-India franchise to Reliance Retail Limited.

The use of Middle East franchisees with regional reach is not uncommon. The master licensee of Uno Chicago Grill has locations in Kuwait, Saudi Arabia and the UAE. Big Apple Bagels signed a master franchise agreement with Dubai-based Mont Royal General Trading LLC. The agreement allows Mont Royal to develop operations in ten countries in return for a franchise fee of at least 3 percent of sales.

Franchising is booming across the Arab world. Australian-owned Ecowash offers a waterless car washing franchise and identifies the Middle East as its fastest growing market. Local franchisors are as enthusiastic as foreign firms. However, franchising can have its surprises. Grand Hyatt Hotel in Cairo was banned from selling alcohol by the hotel chain's franchisee in Egypt, a pious Saudi sheikh. The Hyatt parent company objected. Despite Islamic conservatism in Egypt, the Egyptian government had not banned alcohol for fear of hurting its important tourist industry. An agreement was struck between franchisor and franchisee: alcohol could be sold in one restaurant within the hotel.

Sources: "Big Apple Heading to Middle East," Fastcasual.com, May 2, 2014; David Twiddy, "Payless ShoeSource Opens in Middle East," Associated Press Newswires, March 31, 2009; "Payless ShoeSource Continues Global Expansion with Franchise Deals for Stores in India," PRNewswire, November 13, 2013; "Uno Pizzeria & Grill Locations," www.unos. com, March 10, 2014; "Cairo's Grand Hyatt Bring Back Booze after Compromise with Saudi Owner over Alcohol Ban," Associated Press Newswire, August 26, 2008; and MENA Franchise Association website, www.menafranchise association.org, accessed May 19, 2014.

Local Manufacturing

Another widely practiced form of market entry is the local manufacturing of a company's products. Many companies find it advantageous to manufacture in the host market instead of supplying that market with products made elsewhere. Sometimes local production represents a greater commitment to a market. Numerous factors, such as local costs, market size, tariffs, labor laws and political considerations, may affect a choice to manufacture locally. The actual type of local production depends on the arrangements made. It may be contract manufacturing, assembly or fully integrated production.

Contract Manufacturing

Under contract manufacturing, a company arranges to have its products manufactured by an independent local company on a contractual basis. The local manufacturer's responsibility is restricted to production. The local producer manufactures in accordance with orders from the international firm. The products are then turned over to the international company, which assumes the marketing responsibility for sales, promotion and distribution. In a way, the international company "rents" the production capacity of the local firm to avoid establishing its own plant and to circumvent barriers that prevent the import of its products. For example, Finnish tire manufacturer Nokian Tyres contracted with Matador AS of Slovakia to produce up to 500,000 tires a year, tires that Nokian would in turn sell to the European car market.[19]

Sometimes contract manufacturing is chosen for countries with a low-volume market potential combined with high tariff protection. In such situations, local production appears advantageous to avoid high tariffs, but the local market does not support the volume necessary to justify the building of a new plant. These conditions tend to exist in the smaller countries of Central America, Africa and Asia. Contract manufacturing is also employed where the production technology involved is widely available. Otherwise, contract manufacturers would not have the necessary know-how. If research and development and/or marketing are of crucial importance in the success of the product, then contract manufacturing can be an attractive option, especially when excess capacity in an industry makes manufacturing the least profitable part of the product's value chain. However, contract manufacturing is viable only when an appropriate local manufacturer can be located.

Assembly

In choosing an assembly operation, a MNC locates a portion of its manufacturing process in the foreign country. Typically, assembly consists only of the last stages of manufacturing and depends on a ready supply of components or manufactured parts to be shipped in from another country. (In the chemical and pharmaceutical industry, this latter stage is referred to as compounding.) Assembly usually involves the heavy use of labor rather than extensive investment in capital outlays or equipment. Sometimes host governments force firms to establish assembly operations either by banning the import of fully assembled products or by charging excessive tariffs on them.

Motor vehicle manufacturers have made extensive use of assembly operations in numerous countries. General Motors has maintained major integrated production units only in major markets.

In many other countries, disassembled vehicles arrive at assembly operations that produce the final product on the spot. BMW operates assembly plants in Indonesia, Malaysia, Thailand, the Philippines and Vietnam. BMW reports that a demand of 1,500 cars per year can justify the cost of a local assembly plant. Local assembly plants let BMW test the waters and expand into markets where tariffs and other local hurdles cannot be overcome with an export strategy of shipping completed cars to these markets.[20]

Full-Scale Integrated Production

Establishing a fully integrated local production unit is a greater commitment to manufacturing in a foreign market. Companies may decide on this mode of entry if local demand is substantial or if the country involved can also serve as a desirable location for exporting to other markets.

Although most manufacturing tends to shift from developed to developing countries, Mexican firms are moving production to the United States. The DuPont Company sold three plants to Alfa SA. Alfa is refitting the former textile plants to produce plastics used in beverage containers and frozen-food trays. The Alfa case illustrates reasons why U.S. manufacturing looks good to Mexican firms:

➤ Though production costs are higher in the United States, production in Mexico would result in longer delivery times to the U.S. market.
➤ The plants were available relatively cheap as U.S. firms withdrew from older, lower technology industries.
➤ Local governments offered tax and job-creation credits—in this case, $1 million.
➤ Alfa was able to renegotiate contracts with the workforce, decreasing wages by up to 25 percent in some cases.[21]

Establishing Local Operations to Gain or Defend Market Position

Some companies build a plant to gain new business and customers. Local production can represent a strong commitment to a market and is often the only way to convince clients to switch suppliers. This is of particular importance in industrial markets, where service and reliability of supply are main factors in the choice of product or supplier. In some developing countries, establishing local operations may be the only legal way to enter a local market, although this requirement is becoming rarer with the spread of trade liberalization and the impact of the WTO. At other times, companies establish production abroad to protect markets already built through exporting. Such markets can be threatened by new protectionist government policies or by relative changes in currency exchange rates.

Shifting Production Abroad to Save Costs

Firms may also shift production abroad to save costs and remain competitive. In order to continue to compete with American and Japanese carmakers in the important U.S. market, German-based Mercedes-Benz opened a factory in the United States, where total labor, components and shipping costs were among the lowest in the developed world.

289

Some products may be too costly to transport long distances, and this makes them poor candidates for export. Fresh orange juice is one such product. Brazil is currently the top producer of orange juice in the world, whereas the United States consumes 40 percent of all orange juice. The U.S. market has a strong demand for fresh, not-from-concentrate orange juice that sells for higher prices. This fresh product is particularly costly to ship because it consists mainly of water.[22] Brazilian orange juice firms bought land to develop orange groves in Florida and MNCs with Brazilian ties soon accounted for about half of Florida's orange juice industry.[23]

Sometimes, international firms with plants in Taiwan, Malaysia, Thailand and other foreign countries may have little intention of penetrating these markets with the help of their new factories. Instead, they locate abroad to take advantage of favorable conditions that reduce the manufacturing costs of products that are sold elsewhere. This strategy has been employed by many U.S. companies and has more recently been adopted by Japanese and European firms as well. Morinaga, Japan's leading dairy company, built a new powdered-milk plant in China not so much to enter the Chinese market as to establish a low-cost base from which to capture share in other Asian markets. Such decisions of a sourcing or production nature are not necessarily tied to a company's market entry strategy but may have important implications for its global competitiveness.

Manufacturing and Intrafirm Licensing

Although international licensing arrangements were originally designed as an alternative for firms manufacturing abroad, today they are sometimes used in conjunction with a firm's own manufacturing operations. A firm may license its trademark or technology to its own manufacturing subsidiary if taxes on royalties are less than taxes on repatriated profits. Such an arrangement might also be employed when a subsidiary is not wholly owned but, rather, shared with a local partner. A licensing contract with its own joint venture can give an international firm a greater and more guaranteed payback on its contribution to the venture.

Ownership Strategies

As we have noted, companies investing in foreign markets also face ownership decisions. Do they want to establish a wholly owned subsidiary or a joint venture? Alternatively, they may decide to explore longer-term contractual relationships, or alliances. There are advantages and disadvantages to each of these options. For this reason, most firms employ a combination of ownership strategies. For example, the Strauss Group, based in Israel, has ambitions to become a major player in the global coffee market. Its first venture overseas was to Brazil, where it acquired 50 percent ownership in a leading coffee producer. However, in Eastern Europe Strauss chose to establish its own coffee processing and marketing facilities.[24]

Wholly Owned Subsidiaries

Wholly owned subsidiaries are operations in a host country that are fully owned by a foreign parent firm. They can involve marketing, assembly or full-scale integrated production operations. Firms must have the necessary capital investment to undertake this ownership option. There are, of course, advantages to wholly owned subsidiaries. The firm has a free hand to establish the strategy for the subsidiary. It is also able to keep all the profits of the subsidiary and need not share them with partners. For these reasons, national markets that are more strategically important may be good candidates for a wholly owned subsidiary. Such a subsidiary can also be more easily integrated into a global network. For example, a parent can allot the U.S. export market to its wholly owned subsidiary in Taiwan. If relative production and transportation costs change, however, the firm can take the U.S. market away from the Taiwanese subsidiary and give that market to its wholly owned Mexican subsidiary. There would be no local Taiwanese partner to oppose this move.

Nonetheless, global marketers should be wary of equating ownership of a foreign subsidiary with control of that subsidiary. A study of firms that had shut down wholly owned subsidiaries overseas revealed that local management at these subsidiaries often became involved in activities that undermined the marketing strategy of the MNC. These activities included stealing cash, equipment and inventory, misusing expense accounts, registering brand names to third parties and even selling proprietary information to the competition.[25] Wholly owned subsidiaries are only controlled by headquarters when headquarters exerts the effort and oversight necessary to establish such control. Therefore, in addition to committing greater financial resources to wholly owned subsidiaries, firms must also commit to devoting the considerable management time necessary to establish and run a successful overseas operation.

Joint Ventures

If firms do not have the resources to invest in a wholly owned subsidiary, or if host government restrictions disallow them, companies can consider entering a market with a joint venture partner. Under a joint venture arrangement, the foreign company invites an outside partner to share stock ownership in the new unit. Traditionally, the other partner has been a local firm or individual located in the host market. The particular equity participation of the partners may vary, with some companies accepting either a minority or a majority position. In addition, management contracts can designate which partner has management control of the venture. In such cases, management control may not correlate with equity participation.

One study of MNCs revealed that respondent firms had no fewer than four joint ventures in foreign markets and one firm was involved in 385 international joint ventures. Some partners are so pleased with their experience in one market that they join forces to enter a second market. General Motors entered a second joint venture with its Chinese partner SAIC to produce cars in India. The new joint venture introduced the Chevrolet Sail compact sedan and hatchback to the Indian market, a car developed jointly by GM and SAIC for the Chinese market.[26]

However, joint ventures may not be as popular as they once were.[27] Joint ventures once represented 29 percent of U.S. overseas investments. Evidence suggests that this percentage has now declined to 20 percent.[28] Even in developing countries where joint ventures once accounted for 60 percent of foreign investments, the number of new joint ventures has dropped significantly and many current joint ventures are being terminated.[29]

There are several reasons why joint ventures have fallen from favor. International firms often prefer wholly owned subsidiaries for reasons of control; once a joint venture partner secures part

291

of the operation, the international firm can no longer function independently. This sometimes leads to inefficiencies and disputes over responsibility for the venture. If an international firm has strictly defined operating procedures for budgeting, planning, manufacturing and marketing, getting the joint venture to accept the same methods of operation may be difficult. Problems may also arise when the partner wants to maximize dividend payout instead of reinvestment, or when the capital of the venture has to be increased and one side is unable to raise the required funds.

Even when partners are in agreement, joint ventures can prove problematic. Johns Hopkins Medicine International formed a joint venture with Anadolu, a Turkish charitable foundation, to build and operate a state-of-the art medical facility in Istanbul. However, Turkish law forbids foreigners from running hospitals. As a result, Johns Hopkins lost management control and the venture was plagued with quality problems. The local partner eventually allowed Johns Hopkins to place their own manager in the number two position and then dissolved the top position, solving the management problem while technically staying within the requirements of the law.[30]

There has also been a disturbing trend toward local partners competing with their foreign partner. This can occur because technology transfer to a joint venture can easily be adopted by the local parent firm and used in other businesses outside the joint venture. General Motors formed a 50–50 joint venture with Shanghai Automotive Industry Corporation to produce Buicks, Cadillacs and Chevrolets for the Chinese market. The joint venture has been highly successful. However, Shanghai Automotive is increasingly competing with GM as it introduces its own lines after benefiting from GM technology.[31]

Another cause for concern is the phenomenon of parallel firms. Parallel firms are established independently by local partners or managers of a joint venture for the purpose of using the foreign firm's technology, market information, even its brand name. Such firms are theoretically illegal but often compete effectively against the joint venture because of lax enforcement of laws. For example, one well-known producer of condiments discovered that a manager in its Chinese joint venture was using bottles and labels of its brand to sell his own product manufactured in a separate factory. The company tried to shut down the parallel firm through legal means but failed. It had to resort to making a deal with the manager to stop production.[32]

Reasons for Entering into Joint Ventures

Despite the potential for problems, joint ventures can offer important advantages to the foreign firm. In markets where host governments disallow wholly owned investments, joint ventures with a local partner may be the only alternative. When China first opened to foreign investment, the Chinese government required foreigners to partner with local companies, usually SOEs. More recently, the Vietnamese government has steered a number of MNCs into joint ventures with local partners, many of whom do not provide capital contributions equal to their equity shares in these ventures.[33] Legislation that requires foreign investors to enter into joint ventures with local concerns has decreased worldwide but is still in force in many countries. In 2012, India still limited foreign ownership in airlines to 49 percent and limited foreign investments in many retailing ventures to 51 percent.[34]

If a firm is trying to enter many foreign markets quickly, joint ventures may help leverage scarce capital and managerial resources. In some cases, the partner may provide local manufacturing or excellent government or distribution contacts. By bringing in a partner, the company can share the business and political risks for a new venture. Furthermore, the partner may have important skills or market knowledge of value to the international firm. This is particularly important in difficult markets. Virtually every Internet company that attempted to enter the Chinese market faced significant regulatory and competitive challenges. Both Yahoo and eBay finally resorted to joint venturing in this important market.

Of course, to enter into a joint venture, an international firm must find an available partner. Table 9.3 gives some indication of why local partners seek to establish joint ventures with international firms. A survey of Mexican companies identified access to technology and association with recognized international brands as the two most often cited reasons why local firms sought U.S. partners. In certain instances, local firms seek international ties to become more competitive and thus block new competitors from entering their home markets. Others go so far as to try to co-opt potential competitors by directly partnering with them.

Table 9.3 What Motivates Mexican Firms to Seek U.S. Partners?

Motivation	Percentage of Respondents
Access to technology	71
Access to recognized brand	56
Product/service knowledge of partner	47
Access to products and services	40
Supplier access	33
Access to new products/market areas	27
Short-term credit	24
Access to raw materials	22
Customer access	22
Reduce costs	22
Block competitors	20
Capital access	18
Access to marketing infrastructure	16
Geographic market access	16
Reduce risks	13
Co-opt competitor	13
Geographic market knowledge of partner	13
Access to long-term credit	11

Source: Reprinted from Kate Gillespie and Hildy J. Teegen, "Market Liberalization and International Alliance Formation: The Mexican Paradigm," *The Columbia Journal of World Business*, Winter 1995, p. 63. Copyright © 1995, with permission from Elsevier.

Joint Venture Divorce: A Constant Danger

Not all joint ventures are successful or fulfill their partners' expectations. Clothing retailer J. Crew Group Inc. closed 70 failed stores in Japan where it had entered with a joint venture partner. After that experience, the retailer was more inclined to enter new markets alone.[35] Danone took a hands-off approach to its Wahaha joint venture in China until it was too late. Local management refused Danone's attempts to regain control and this led to a very public and acrimonious breakup.[36]

Various studies have placed the failure rates of joint ventures at between 25 and 75 percent depending on the sample of companies in the study and the study's definition of "failure." There are a number of reasons for ending a joint venture. Sometimes the regulations that force foreign firms to take local partners are rescinded. This occurred in China. As a result, joint ventures are no longer the most common mode of entry into China, and many foreign partners who entered China early now seek exclusive ownership of their Chinese joint ventures. Unilever gradually bought out its partners in all of its original 14 joint ventures in China. Similarly, Procter & Gamble has also bought out partners in many of their Chinese ventures. Starbucks also began to buy back the equity of local Chinese partners as soon as China revoked its joint venture requirement.

When joint ventures are used to enter many international markets relatively cheaply and quickly, a parent firm may wish later to increase its stake in the venture or even reclaim full control when financial resources are more readily available. Starbucks undertook rapid international expansion, establishing almost 5,000 coffeehouses overseas in just 12 years. In some international markets, Starbucks stores operate under joint venture agreements. However, the company has increased its stake in some of its joint ventures.

Sometimes the choice of partner turns out to be less than ideal. Cristal, a U.K.-based food hygiene consultancy, advises hotels, food processing plants and restaurants around the world. Joint ventures have played an important part in the firm's international expansion. In Egypt, however, Cristal chose a well-established partner with expertise in engineering rather than in tourism. Trying to learn the tourism industry and the food hygiene industry in a short time proved overwhelming. Cristal had to buy back shares from the partner and take over management of the venture.[37]

At times, problems can arise between parents over the strategic direction of the joint venture. Brasil Telecom is a joint venture between Telecom Italia and Opportunity, a local Brazilian investment company. Despite being one of Brazil's largest fixed-line telecommunications companies, Brasil Telecom found itself headed for arbitration in London when its two parents became deadlocked over expansion options. The Italian parent wanted to move quickly into mobile telephone operations. Opportunity wanted the joint venture to pursue what it thought were more profitable businesses, such as acting as an Internet service provider. The relationship between the parent companies became increasingly hostile, and both wished to take full control of the joint venture.[38]

In some cases, however, joint venture divorce can be amiable. Teijin of Japan dissolved its joint venture with U.S.-based Molecular Simulations (MSI), a major global player in computerized chemistry. The negotiated settlement specified that Teijin would receive $10 million from Pharmacopeia, the company that had since acquired MSI. Teijin was willing to sell its share in the joint venture because it had already accomplished its objective—gaining adequate expertise in computerized chemistry through the venture.[39] Still, buying out partners can be expensive and is further complicated if the two partners vary greatly on their assessment of a venture's worth.

294

It is always wise to have a "prenuptial agreement" that designates under what conditions a joint venture can be dissolved and how the dissolution will proceed. Yet a surprising number of joint venture agreements fail to acknowledge the possibility of joint venture dissolution. AT&T and British Telecom formed a joint venture, Concert, to serve large multinational business customers. A former AT&T executive involved in the negotiations claims that the absence of an exit agreement was deliberate. It was intended to make sure both companies remained committed to the partnership. Two years later, however, the venture was losing $210 million a quarter and was judged a failure by both parents. Without an exit agreement, there was no simple way to determine how Concert's assets—including 75,000 kilometers of fiber optic cable—would be divided.[40]

Strategic Alliances

A more recent phenomenon is the development of a range of strategic alliances. Alliances encompass any relationship between firms that exceeds a simple sales transaction but stops short of a full-scale merger. Thus, the traditional joint venture between a MNC and a local company is a form of alliance, as is a contract manufacturing or licensing agreement. However, the term strategic alliance is commonly used to denote an alliance involving two or more firms in which each partner brings a particular skill or resource—usually they are complementary. By joining forces, each firm expects to profit from the other's experience. Typically, strategic alliances involve the technology development, production or distribution. The number of strategic alliances has been driven by the increased globalization of firms. As firms internationalize more rapidly, they often use strategic alliances to speed up entry into multiple markets as well as to gain access to assets and technologies that may be specific to certain countries.[41]

Technology-Based Alliances

Many alliances are focused on technology and the sharing of research and development expertise and findings. The most commonly cited reasons for entering these technology-based alliances are access to markets, exploitation of complementary technology and a need to reduce the time it takes to bring an innovation to market.

One of the companies most experienced with technological alliances is Toshiba, a major Japanese electronics company. The company's first technological tie-ups go back to the beginning of this century, when it contracted to make lightbulb filaments for U.S.-based General Electric. The company has since engaged in alliances with many leading international companies, many of which are competitors. For example, IBM, Sony and Toshiba joined forces to create the Cell Alliance, which created the Cell chip to compete with chips by Intel. The chip could be used by Sony in its PlayStation, by Toshiba in its digital television sets and by IBM in its computer servers and workstations.[42]

Production-Based Alliances

A large number of production-based alliances have been formed, particularly in the automobile industry where firms seek increased efficiency through component linkages. A production-based alliance also made sense for coffee retailer Starbucks. Starbucks joint ventured with Pepsi to produce bottled frappuccino for sale in the United States and China.[43] Even service providers may reap advantages from production-based alliances. International alliances focused on operations allow airlines to offer fuller services and more extensive routes, as well as providing cost savings to the participating firms.

Distribution-Based Alliances

Alliances with a special emphasis on distribution are becoming increasingly common. General Mills, a U.S.-based company marketing breakfast cereals, had long been number two in the United States, with some 27 percent market share, compared to Kellogg's 40 to 45 percent share. With no effective position outside the United States, the company entered into a global alliance with Nestlé of Switzerland. Forming Cereal Partners Worldwide (CPW), owned equally by the two companies, General Mills gained access to the local distribution and marketing skills of Nestlé in Europe, the Far East and Latin America. In return, General Mills provided product technology and the experience it had acquired competing against Kellogg's. CPW was formed as a full business unit with responsibility for the entire world except the United States. Today CPW has sales of over $1 billion and operates in over 130 countries.[44]

The Future of Alliances

Although many alliances have been forged in a large number of industries worldwide, it is not yet clear whether these alliances will actually become successful business ventures. Experience suggests that alliances with two equal partners are more difficult to manage than those with a dominant partner. Furthermore, many observers question the value of entering alliances with technological competitors. The challenge in making an alliance work lies in the creation of multiple layers of connections, or webs, that reach across the partner organizations.

Many strategic alliances fail. Perhaps more surprisingly, strategic alliances may continue in effect for years even after they have proven unviable. For example, Deutsche Telekom, France Telecom and Sprint created a three-way alliance, Global One. Only after six years of higher than expected losses and internal conflicts did the partners dissolve the alliance. Research indicates that the high cost of terminating an alliance, high sunk costs and high alliance visibility all contribute to a delay in dissolving failing alliances.[45]

Entering Markets through Mergers and Acquisitions

International firms have always made acquisitions. However, the need to enter markets more quickly has made the acquisition route extremely attractive. This trend has probably been aided by the opening of many financial markets, making the acquisition of publicly traded companies much easier. Even unfriendly takeovers in foreign markets are now becoming increasingly common.

By purchasing an established business, the firm eliminates the need to build manufacturing and distribution capabilities from scratch. Buying an established brand gives the firm immediate market presence and market share. South Africa Breweries (SAB) purchased Miller Beer from Philip Morris for $3.4 billion. The acquisition gave SAB instant access to the U.S. market as well as the well-known brands of Miller Lite, Miller High Life, Miller Genuine Draft and Milwaukee's Best.

Acquisition is also an attractive strategy when a market is already dominated by established brands and saturated with competitors. New entrants would find such a market difficult to break into, and the addition of a totally new player might make the market even more competitive and unprofitable for all. eBay has spent more than $1.6 billion on acquisitions, including $150 million to take full control of Eachnet in China.[46] In some extreme cases, the government might allow entry only by acquisition in order to protect a depressed industry from new entrants. Such was once the case with the Egyptian banking industry. At one time the government would only allow international banks to buy existing Egyptian banks and refused to grant them licenses to start new businesses.[47]

Acquisitions can also involve partial purchases of companies abroad. LivingSocial is a deals site that sells deeply discounted services at local businesses such as restaurants. The company purchased a majority interest in Spain's Let's Bonus SL. This partial acquisition gave the U.S.-based company an immediate presence not only in Spain but in Italy, Portugal, Argentina and Mexico as well.[48]

Because they are often late movers into international markets, firms from developing countries frequently opt for acquisitions as a route to enter markets, including more mature markets such as the United States. For example, Brazil's 3G Capital acquired Burger King for $3.3 billion.[49] Mexico's Bimbo is a bakery with a virtual monopoly at home. It expanded into the United States with the purchase of Texas-based Mrs. Baird's Bakeries for $300 million. Later purchases of several other bakeries in Canada and the United States elevated Bimbo to third largest bakery in the world. A number of Indian companies—in industries as diverse as telecommunications, auto parts and pharmaceuticals—are also entering developed countries via acquisition. In fact, after India removed government regulations limiting access to foreign capital, Indian companies spent $3.7 billion on foreign acquisitions in a single year.[50]

Despite their advantages, overseas acquisitions can pose challenges to global marketers. Businesses for sale often have big problems. As late movers to international markets, a number of Chinese firms chose to acquire companies overseas, especially in the competitive markets of the developed world. Chinese computer manufacturer Lenovo bought the PC division of IBM for $1.25 billion, but only after that division had accumulated losses of nearly $1 billion for the four years prior to the sale. China's largest auto-parts manufacturer acquired a 21 percent share in a U.S. company that went bankrupt a year later, and Chinese consumer-electronics maker TCL Corporation bought the RCA and Thomson brands only to discover that the prior owner had failed to keep up with technological changes in the market. Three years after the unfortunate purchase, TCL stock prices had fallen 75 percent.[51]

And increasingly, as companies try to grab market share abroad via acquisitions, competitors are trying to block them from employing this market entry strategy. U.S. white goods company Whirlpool Corporation agreed to pay the high price of $2.8 billion for U.S. competitor Maytag Corporation in order to assure that China's Haier would not acquire Maytag and thus gain an immediate advantage in the U.S. market.[52]

World Beat 9.2

MetLife Expands in Asia

MetLife Inc., the largest life insurer in the United States, was founded in 1868. It currently holds top market shares in the United States, Japan, Latin America, Asia, Europe and the Middle East, and it plans to soon achieve 20 percent of its earnings from emerging markets. The company has been in Asia for over 60 years but is currently seeking to expand its footprint in the region. The region boasts an expanding population, a growing middle class and a relatively young insurance market. Its life insurance sector has been growing at 14 percent a year. To expand in the growing Asian market, MetLife has chosen different modes of entry for different markets.

Malaysia is an attractive insurance market not only for its robust growth rate but because insurers enjoy strong margins. Government licenses to sell insurance are difficult to attain for new entrants to the market making acquisitions or partial acquisitions an attractive option for market entry. In Malaysia, MetLife agreed to acquire 51 percent of AmLife Insurance Bhd., the insurance arm of Malaysia's AMMB Holdings Bhd. MetLife also signed an exclusive 20-year agreement to sell insurance products through AMMB's banking network as part of the acquisition arrangement.

In Vietnam, MetLife signed a joint venture agreement with The Bank for Investment & Development of Vietnam (BIDV) to establish a life insurance business in Vietnam. Only 5 percent of Vietnamese have life insurance, but Vietnam has one of the fastest growing life insurance markets in Asia. The potential market has already attracted 29 non-life insurers, 14 life insurers, 12 insurance brokerage firms, two re-insurance companies and 32 representative offices of foreign insurance companies.

Despite its political risk, Myanmar is also attracting foreign insurers. McKinsey & Company estimates that its economy could quadruple in size to more than $200 billion by 2030. Its market for life insurance premiums is expected to expand from about $1 million in 2012 to nearly $1 billion by 2028. The country was a military dictatorship until recently and its new civilian leaders are currently liberalizing the country's economy. MetLife has won a license to establish a representative office in Myanmar. As a pioneer in this new market, MetLife will have the opportunity to work with government regulators to help shape an industry that is currently in its infancy.

Sources: Enda Curran and P.R. Venkat, "MetLife Sets Up Joint Venture in Vietnam," *Wall Street Journal Online*, September 27, 2013; "MetLife, BIDV to Form Life Insurance JV," Vietnam News Brief Service, July 27, 2013; "BIDV, MetLife to Open $47.6M Life Insurance JV in Vietnam in 2014," Vietnam News Brief Service, October 1, 2013; Cynthia Koons, "MetLife Gets a Green Light in Myanmar," *Wall Street Journal Asia*, October 17, 2013; and Cynthia Koons, "MetLife to Pay $256 Million for AmLife Stake; Southeast Asia's Growing Market Lures Insurers," *Wall Street Journal Online*, December 19, 2013.

Conclusion

This chapter has explained the various entry strategies available to international and global firms. Sometimes companies may even employ more than one entry mode per country. A company may open up a subsidiary that produces some products locally and imports others to round out its product line. A number of variables influence the choice of entry strategy. A meta-analysis of more than 600 articles found that the mode of entry chosen by a firm was significantly influenced by country risk, cultural distance, company assets, international experience and even advertising intensity in the potential country.[53]

Market entry strategies can have a profound impact on a firm's global strategy. They determine the number of foreign markets a firm can enter and the speed at which a firm can internationalize. They affect the profits the firm will make in each national market and the risk it will assume. They can even obligate a firm to local partners, thereby constraining its power to act solely in its global self-interest. Despite the importance of the market entry decision, surprisingly few MNCs appear to recognize its strategic significance. A study of 105 firms in four European countries found that only 36 percent of managers even reviewed alternative entry options.[54] Choosing the best entry strategy is complex and involves many considerations. The relative importance of these considerations varies by industry and by the strategic goals of each firm. It also varies according to the strategic importance of each national market. Table 9.4 presents some key considerations and their impact on the potential appropriateness of different entry options. Clearly, no one option is ideal under all conditions.

Table 9.4 Appropriateness of Market Entry Strategies

Mode of Entry

Strategic Consideration	Indirect Exporting	Direct Exporting– Marketing Subsidiary	Licensing	Wholly Owned Production	Joint Venture	Acquisition
Speed of entry	High	High	High	Low	Low	High
Ease of exit	High	Moderate	Moderate	Low	Low	Low
Rapidly changing technologies	Low	High	High	Moderate	Moderate	Moderate
Resource demands	Low	Moderate	Moderate	High	High	High
Profit potential	Low	High	Low	High	Moderate	Moderate
Competitive intensity of market	Low	Moderate	Moderate	Moderate	Moderate	High
Integration into global network	Low	High	Low	High	Low	Moderate
Strategically important country	Low	High	Low	High	Moderate	Moderate
Unimportant market	High	Low	Moderate	Low	Low	Low
Cultural distance	High	Low	Moderate	Low	Moderate	Low
Congruence with host government's goals	Low	Low	Moderate	High	High	Moderate

For example, speed of market entry may be an important consideration in some cases. If a firm is in an industry where products face high development costs, it will want to sell in many countries. If it is not already present in many markets, it will need to expand rapidly to keep up with global competitors. This is all the more true if products have a short life cycle, as is the case with many high-tech products. Often the need to be in many markets quickly requires a firm to take partners, because it simply doesn't have enough money or managerial depth to take on the task itself. Licensing, joint venturing or entering distribution alliances becomes attractive.

In all cases, managers must decide how many resources they can and want to commit to a market. Resources include investments necessary for increasing or relocating manufacturing as well as investments related to product research and development and to the implementation of marketing strategy. Exporting or licensing might require no new capital investment or very little incremental investment to increase current production. Wholly owned manufacturing facilities require significant capital investments. Joint ventures and other alliances can cut capital costs in research and development, manufacturing and distribution. Another important resource is management time. Direct exporting may not require additional capital investment but will require a greater commitment of management time than indirect exporting. Joint ventures and alliances can help ease the demands on this critical resource.

Other concerns include profitability and flexibility. Will exporting to a market produce higher returns than producing there? Economies of scale in global or regional production may or may not offset the costs of transportation and tariffs. Licensing and joint ventures require that profits be shared. If the political environment or the business prospects of a country are uncertain, the flexibility involved with an entry strategy becomes a consideration. How quickly and at what cost can the firm expand in the market or retreat from it? Redirecting exports is easier than closing an overseas plant. Partnerships or licensing agreements can limit future actions both within the market and globally.

Managerial Takeaways

1. *There is no one ideal mode of entry.*
2. *Global marketers must weigh different considerations—speed of entry, resource demands, profitability and flexibility—in order to decide the best mode of entry for each foreign market.*
3. *Firms must balance the advantages and disadvantages of different entry strategies. Even when a firm is clear about its strategic goals, rarely does an entry option present no drawbacks whatsoever.*
4. *The most managerial effort and the greatest resources should be allotted to the most strategic global markets.*
5. *Managers should always consider how an entry strategy will later affect their ability to integrate operations in that country into the global company.*
6. *Over time, changes to modes of entry may become desirable. These changes may be possible but are likely to be costly. It always pays to think ahead.*

Questions for Discussion

1. Why might entry strategies differ for companies entering the United States, those entering China and those entering Costa Rica?

2. How might the entry strategy of a born-global firm (see Chapter 8) differ from that of a mature MNC?

3. Why would licensing sometimes be appropriate—and sometimes inappropriate—for a strategically important country?

4. Is there such a thing as a "no-fault" joint venture divorce? Or is joint venture dissolution always the result of some sort of failure?

CASE 9.1 Unhappy Marriage

In 2013, Anheuser-Busch InBev received permission from the U.S. government to proceed with their proposed purchase of the remaining equity in their Grupo Modelo joint venture in Mexico. The permission came with strings attached. Due to antitrust concerns, Anheuser-Busch InBev was required to sell the rights to market Modelo's beer brands in the United States to an independent company. Nonetheless, the sale would bring an end to a rocky 20 years that had ensued between the two joint venture partners.

Anheuser-Busch had originally purchased 17.7 percent of Grupo Modelo for $477 million in in 1993, with an option of increasing its shares to 50.2 percent. At the time of the purchase, Anheuser held 45 percent of the U.S. beer market. Modelo was the world's tenth largest beer producer. It held 50 percent of the Mexican beer market and exported to 124 countries in every continent of the world. However, with the passing of NAFTA (North American Free Trade Agreement), Mexico's 20 percent tariffs on imported beer were to be phased out. Modelo feared that U.S. breweries would invade its market. Anheuser viewed its stake in Modelo as a profitable acquisition of brands such as Corona, as well as a way to increase Anheuser's distribution network in Mexico quickly.

Anheuser told its U.S. distributors that they would soon have access to a major imported beer. Distributors assumed this meant Corona, which was fast growing in popularity in the United States. However, in late 1996, management at Modelo renewed the firm's ten-year contract with its existing U.S. distributors, dashing Anheuser's hopes of gaining Modelo brands for its own U.S. distribution system. In December 1996, Anheuser announced that it would exercise its option to increase its stake in Modelo.

A six-month dispute over price ensued, and the parties settled for $605 million. Then in June 1997, Anheuser opted to further increase its stake, this time to the full 50.2 percent allowed under the joint venture contract. Discussions became so contentious that the two parties went into international arbitration, and the price was eventually set at $556 million. By 1998, the price of Anheuser's stake in Modelo, as valued on the Mexican stock exchange, was twice what it had paid for the stock. However, its

50.2 percent stake in Modelo did not give Anheuser a controlling share of board votes. It held only ten of the 21 seats on the board of directors.

Despite trade liberalization, Modelo's brands soon increased their share of the Mexican market to 55 percent. In the United States, where beer imports accounted for 14 percent of the market, Corona had pulled ahead of Heineken to become the best-selling import. Corona was enjoying 40 percent growth per year in the United States and had already become the tenth-best-selling beer in that market. It was particularly successful among college students and consumers in their twenties. Anheuser's major brand, Budweiser, found itself competing against Corona. Anheuser began a campaign to disparage the freshness of Corona. It distributed display cards to thousands of bars and restaurants, noting that Corona didn't put the manufacturing date on its bottles. Anheuser also introduced three Corona clones—Azteca, Tequiza and Rio Cristal—all produced in the United States.

The relationship between Anheuser-Busch and its Corona joint venture became more confused in 2008 when Belgium-based InBev SA announced that it had arranged to acquire Anheuser-Busch. Anheuser had originally resisted the unsolicited acquisition even attempting to convince Modelo to sell them their remaining share in the Mexican joint venture. With the Modelo share, some analysts believed that Anheuser would become too expensive for InBev to purchase. However, when the acquisition proceeded, Grupo Modelo claimed that they could choose to opt out. The Group asserted that under Mexican law a carefully crafted clause in the original joint venture agreement permitted the company to buy back the Anheuser share should the acquisition take place. Then the company could operate independently or seek a new international partner such as InBev's archrival SABMiller.

The InBev acquisition of Anheuser went through in 2009. The next year Modelo lost its case in arbitration including its request to be paid $2.5 billion for not being consulted on the merger. Still Modelo continued to be uncooperative. When Anheuser-Busch InBev, as market leader in the United States, attempted to signal competitors to keep beer prices high in the U.S. market and avoid a price war, Modelo lowered prices on its exported beers. Nonetheless, industry experts predicted that their two-year battle with Anheuser-Busch InBev had left Modelo shareholders ready to deal. They were right. In 2012, Modelo, now boasting over 60 percent of the Mexican beer market, agreed to sell its outstanding stock to its global partner.

Discussion Questions

1. Why did Anheuser purchase its stake in Grupo Modelo?
2. Why was Grupo Modelo willing to sell the stake?
3. What went wrong? Why?
4. What lessons about choosing international partners can be learned from this case?

Sources: "Unhappy Marriage," in Kate Gillespie and H. David Hennessey, *Global Marketing* (Mason, OH: Cengage, 2011), pp. 188–189; Mike Esterl and Dana Cimilluca, "Divestitures Likely in Modelo Deal," *Wall Street Journal Online*, June 25, 2012; Philip Blenkinsop, "AB InBev Buys Out Corona Maker Modelo for $20 Billion," Reuters, June 29, 2012; Nathaniel Parish Flannery, "Anheuser-Busch InBev Buys Corona," *Forbes*, June 30, 2012; and Celeste Perri, "AB InBev Will Sell Corona Unit to Salvage Modelo Takeover," *Bloomberg*, February 14, 2013.

CASE 9.2   Why Did They Do It?

In January 2010, German automaker Volkswagen AG (VW) purchased 19.8 percent of Japan's fourth largest auto company Suzuki for $2.9 billion. Suzuki in turn used half of the income from the sale to purchase 1.49 percent of VW. The Volkswagen-Suzuki alliance coincided with one of the industry's worst global downturns. Many car companies were seeking new alliances to help bear the costs of massive investments in electric and other clean technologies and to better position themselves in emerging markets.

VW was the second largest automaker in the world. Three of its cars had attained the status of all-time best sellers, and the company's array of global brands was considered to be one of its strengths. VW was particularly interested in the growing Asian markets and the global market for small, fuel-efficient cars. However, VW had little experience forming alliances with other independent auto companies.

Suzuki was the tenth largest automaker in the world. Suzuki had significant experience with international alliances despite the fact that one industry expert opined that Suzuki was a notoriously independent company with a chairman who would not bend over backwards to cooperate. Suzuki had already formed an alliance with Fiat to produce diesel engines in Asia. Suzuki's equity alliance with General Motors (GM) lasted 27 years and encompassed joint product development and global purchasing. However, when GM faced bankruptcy in 2008, the U.S. company sold its holdings in Suzuki back to the Japanese company in order to raise much-needed cash. The timing of the sale was particularly painful for GM since Suzuki stock had declined 50 percent in price from two years earlier.

VW's stated goal for its venture with Suzuki was to better enter the Indian budget car market. Suzuki, via a majority-owned joint venture, held the dominant position in India. But competition was heating up. Car sales in India were increasing rapidly, and many global companies had announced plans to enter or expand in what had become one of the world's most exciting car markets. VW aspired to become the largest car company in the world, surpassing GM and Toyota Motors by 2018, and looked to India as a source of substantial growth. However, in 2010 the company had only sold 53,300 cars in India, far short of the 1.13 million cars sold by Suzuki in the Indian market.

From Suzuki's point of view, VW offered technologies including diesel technology and its electronics capability. VW also enjoyed a much stronger position in Europe and was dominant in China where Suzuki had only a modest presence. According to Osamu Suzuki, Suzuki's chairman, the auto industry was in the midst of significant changes and it would be difficult for Suzuki to adapt to these changes on its own.

The two companies declared that they would now cooperate on technology, including technology of hybrids and electric cars, and expansion in emerging markets. At a news conference in Tokyo, executives from both companies pointed out that the alliance would be wide-ranging including sharing car components and jointly developing hybrid and electric cars to sell under both companies' brands. Suzuki also announced that it would hitherto buy diesel engines from VW and would be ending joint development projects with GM in the fields of hybrid cars and fuel-cell technologies.

At first, groups from both companies met regularly for several months in order to identify potential areas of collaboration. Each partner set up offices at the other's headquarters. However, one VW executive soon noted that Suzuki managers had begun to withdraw and were constantly asserting that all the collaboration proposals forwarded by VW presented problems.

In May 2011, VW's CEO announced that his company planned to target the small-car segment in India as a potential joint project with Suzuki and that the two companies would be cooperating on parts procurement and the development of alternative-drive technologies. However, the next month VW accused Suzuki of breach of contract for purchasing diesel engines from Italy's Fiat SpA for cars Suzuki was building in Hungary and gave Suzuki "a few weeks to fix the problem." Chairman Osamu Suzuki responded that he was unable to find any VW technologies that he wanted to use after an extensive review of what VW had to offer. Consequently, he decided to purchase diesel engines from Fiat because VW's diesel engines were too big to install in some Suzuki cars. Chairman Suzuki claimed to have explained this to VW's CEO in January 2011 and followed up a few days later with an official document to that effect. He stated that the Fiat order didn't violate the alliance agreement with VW. Suzuki also announced that it was open to alliances with other auto firms.

In September 2011, another problem arose when management at Suzuki took offense at certain wording in VW's annual report. The report described Suzuki as an "associate" and reported that VW could "significantly influence financial and operating policy decisions" at the Japanese company. Sources within Suzuki retorted that a successful relationship depended on an understanding that the two companies are equal partners.

Shortly thereafter, Suzuki declared that the cross-sharing must be dissolved immediately so that both companies could return to their fully independent status. Suzuki wanted to buy back VW's stake and had the cash to do so. Since the formation of the alliance, VW shares had increased in value by 64 percent. Suzuki shares had dropped in value by 37 percent. Suzuki claimed that VW had denied it access to its core technologies and that the two companies had different understandings of "independence."

Chairman Suzuki remarked, "The relationship is like a marriage and a divorce. We should just have a simple breakup with a smile and say we weren't meant for each other." He went on to say that he didn't see why VW should be upset about the purchase of diesel engines from Fiat and that he didn't expect to have to pay any fines as a result of the proposed breakup.

VW replied that they were disappointed with the Suzuki stance but they were under no legal obligation to surrender their shares and had no intention to do so. VW's coordinator for international projects provided the press with this e-mailed statement, "VW and Suzuki still are, and will continue to be, two independent companies with different business models from different cultural environments. The cooperation is marked by highest respect and acceptance."

Suzuki announced that it was proceeding to international courts with arbitration proceedings against VW in order to regain its company shares from its alliance partner. However, management at VW asserted that Suzuki had more to lose from the breakup than they did. VW could always seek another partner or start again on their own in Japan and India despite the fact that such a new start would be expensive. VW had already been setting up dealerships across India and had opened a plant in Pune. But VW's sales of under 33,000 cars were a fraction of the Indian car market that had grown to two million vehicles a year. The company was talking with its South American subsidiaries about developing an appropriate car for India. Nonetheless, going it alone in the Indian market would be difficult for VW because Indian consumers didn't readily purchase cars sold overseas but instead preferred cars designed specifically for the Indian market.

In November 2012, Suzuki Motor announced that it was pulling out of the U.S. auto market after nearly 30 years. In 2013, the company withdrew from the Canadian car market as well. Suzuki had sold too few cars in the North American market, and new U.S. greenhouse gas regulations disproportionately penalized Suzuki as a low-volume manufacturer of small automobiles. Some industry experts believed that the withdrawal from the U.S. market would allow Suzuki to focus on the Indian and Southeast Asian markets. Sales in India had risen to an estimated 40 percent of Suzuki's global sales. The same month, Suzuki announced that it was developing a new range of turbo diesel engines. The new engines were expected to be ready for its Indian operations by 2015. Prior to that, Suzuki would rely on buying Fiat engines.

Discussion Questions

1. Why do you think VW entered into this alliance? Why do you think Suzuki entered into this alliance? What could be motivations beyond the ones that the companies stated publicly?
2. Why do you think Suzuki now wants out? What could be the reasons besides the issue of diesel technology?
3. Could it be true that a German–Japanese culture clash could be adding to the acrimony? Explain your answer.
4. What lessons does this case raise in respect to global alliances?

Sources: Vanessa Fuhrmans, "Volkswagen, Suzuki For Alliance on Emerging Markets, Small Cars," *Wall Street Journal*, December 10, 2009, p. B1; Makiko Kitamura, Yuri Hagiwara and Andreas Cremer, "Volkswagen-Suzuki Alliance Unraveling Over Control of Driver's Seat," *Bloomberg*, September 5, 2011; Ian Rowley, "GM to Sell the Rest of its Suzuki Stake," *Bloomberg Business Week*, November 16, 2008; Anna Mukai, Yuki Hagiwara and Makiko Kitamura, "Suzuki Seeks 'Divorce' From Volkswagen as Their 20-Month Alliance Crumbles," *Bloomberg*, September 12, 2011; Hiroko Tabichi and Jack Ewing, "Suzuki Seeks to Dissolve Volkswagen Partnership," *New York Times*, September 12, 2011; Chester Dawson, Yoshio Takahashi and Vanessa Fuhrmans, "Suzuki Requests a Divorce From VW," *Wall Street Journal Online*, September 12, 2011; Mihnea Radu, "Suzuki Launches Arbitration to Terminate VW Alliance," *Autoevolution*, November 24, 2011; Ma Jie and Yuki Hagiwara, "Suzuki to Exit U.S. Car Market After Almost Three Decades," *Bloomberg*, November 6, 2012; "Volkswagen, Suzuki Resume Alliance Talks," Reuters, July 29, 2013; Andrew Ganz, "Suzuki: VW Alliance Not Back On," *Left Lane News*, August 1, 2013; and "Maruti Suzuki to Import 1.6 Liter Fiat Multijet Diesel Motor?" Team-BHP, www.team-bhp.com, November 5, 2013.

Notes

1   Anne L. Souchon, Adamantios Diamantopoulos, Hartman H. Holzmuller, Catherine N. Axinn, James M. Sinkula, Heike Simmet and Geoffrey R. Durden, "Export Information Use: A Five-Country Investigation of Key Determinants," *Journal of International Marketing*, vol. 11, no. 3 (2003), pp. 106–127.
2   "Eye Surgery the Material Difference," *Metalworking Production*, March 15, 2004, p. 13.
3   Niles Hansen, Kate Gillespie and Esra Gencturk, "SMEs and Export Involvement: Market Responsiveness, Technology and Alliances," *Journal of Global Marketing*, vol. 7, no. 4 (1994), pp. 7–27.
4   Steve Hamm, "Children of the Web," *Business Week*, July 2, 2007, p. 54.
5   Edward G. Thomas, "Internet Marketing in the International Arena: A Cross-Cultural Comparison," *International Journal of Business Strategy*, vol. 8, no. 3 (2008), pp. 84–98.

6 Internet Eorld Stats, www.internetworldstats.com, accessed May 2, 2014.

7 Chandrani Ghosh, "E-Trade Routes Planning to Do Global Business on the Web? Next Linx Will Ease the Way," *Forbes*, August 7, 2000, p. 108.

8 "Roche Grows Position in Japan," *Chemical Market Reporter*, December 22–29, 2003, p. 10.

9 "NZ Fonterra Signs Deal with Egypt's Arab Dairy," Dow Jones International News, April 7, 2009,

10 Julie Jargon, "Starbucks Shifts in Europe," *Wall Street Journal*, November 30, 2013, p. B3.

11 "Franchising: A Top Prospect for Mexico," U.S. Commercial Service, September 2013.

12 "Doing Business in Morocco: 2012 Country Commercial Guide," U.S. Commercial Service.

13 "Happy Hookahs," *The Economist*, May 5, 2001.

14 Judith Rehak, "Franchising the World: Services and Internet Fuel Global Boom," *International Herald Tribune*, October 14, 2000, p. 20.

15 *Doing Business in China: 2012 Country Commercial Guide*, U.S. Commercial Service, Department of Commerce.

16 Richard Gibson, "U.S. Franchises Find Opportunity to Grow Abroad," *Wall Street Journal*, August 11, 2009, p. B5.

17 "The Cheesecake Factory Announces International Expansion," The Cheesecake Factory Incorporated Press Release, *Business Wire*, January 24, 2011.

18 Oxana Parshina, "Franchising in Kazakhstan," U.S. Commercial Service, April 2009.

19 "Nokian Tyres Expands Contract Manufacturing in Slovakia," *Nordic Business Report*, November 8, 2004, p. 1.

20 "BMW Testing the Water for Local Facilities," *Businessline* (Islamabad), May 17, 2002.

21 Joel Millman, "Go North," *Wall Street Journal*, May 10, 2004, p. A1.

22 Doreen Hemlock, "Florida, Brazil Compete in Citrus Industry," Knight Ridder Tribune Business News, July 11, 2001.

23 Andrew Meadows, "Florida Citrus Processors Concentrate on Brazilian Juice Invasion," Knight Ridder Tribune Business News, June 9, 2001.

24 Neal Sandler, "An Israeli Coffee Outfit Goes Global," *Business Week*, August 14, 2008.

25 Claude Obadia and Irena Vida, "Endogenous Opportunism in Small and Medium-Sized Enterprises' Foreign Subsidiaries: Classification and Research Propositions," *Journal of International Marketing*, vol. 14, no. 4 (2006), pp. 57–86.

26 Chris Ecclestone, "General Motors Rumored to Be Considering Chinese Partner for India Operations," GM Authority, January 17, 2014.

27 Anthony Goerzen, "Managing Alliance Networks: Emerging Practices of Multinational Corporations," *Academy of Management Executive*, vol. 19, no. 2 (2005), pp. 94–107.

28 Margaret Popper, "Flying Solo Overseas," *Business Week*, May 20, 2002, p. 28.

29 Prashant Kale and Jaideep Anand, "The Decline of Emerging Economy Joint Ventures," *California Management Review*, vol. 49. no. 3 (2006), pp. 62–68.

30 Steven J. Thompson, "The Perils of Partnering in Developing Markets," *Harvard Business Review*, June 2012, pp. 1–4.

31 Gordon Fairclough, "Passing Lane," *Wall Street Journal*, April 20, 2007, p. A1.

32 David Ahlstrom, Michael N. Young and Anil Nair, "Deceptive Managerial Practices in China: Strategies for Foreign Firms," *Business Horizons*, November–December 2002, pp. 49–59.

33 Dana James, "Back to Vietnam," *Marketing News*, May 13, 2002, p. 13.

34 Amol Sharma, Rajesh Roy and Shefali Anand, "India Revives Plan to Let In Retailers," *Wall Street Journal Online*, September 14, 2012.

35 Dana Mattioli, "J. Crew Suits Up for Overseas," *Wall Street Journal*, March 22, 2012, p. B8.

36 James T. Areddy, "Danone Pulls Out of Disputed China Venture," *Wall Street Journal Online*, October 1, 2009.

37 "The Advantages of Marrying Local," *Financial Times*, December 21, 2000, p. 16.

38 Janine Brewis, "Brasil Telecom Fears Takeover Bid," *Financial Times*, November 16, 2003, p. 1.

39 Aimin Yan and Yadong Luo, *International Joint Ventures* (Armonk, NY: M.E. Sharpe, 2002), p. 223.

40 "Alliance Tips for a Beautiful Relationship," *Financial Times-FT.com*, accessed July 11, 2001.

41 Rajneesh Narula, "Globalisation and Trends in International R&D Alliances," MERIT-Infonomics Research Memorandum Series, 2003, pp. 2–7.

42 Dean Takahashi, "New Chip Called a Threat to Intel," Knight Ridder Tribune Business News (Washington), February 8, 2005, p. 1.

43 "Starbucks Starts Sales of Bottled Coffee in China," China Knowledge Press, November 2, 2007.

44 General Mills Corporate Website, www.generalmills.com, viewed May 2, 2014.

45 Andrew Delios, Andrew C. Inkpen and Jerry Ross, "Escalation in International Strategic Alliances," *Management International Review*, vol. 44, no. 4 (2004), p. 457.

46 Chris Nuttall, "EBay Backs Its $100 million Outlay in China," *Financial Times*, February 11, 2005, p. 19

47 Mahmoud Kassem, "Banks Seek Takeover Targets in Egypt," *Wall Street Journal Europe*, July 11, 2001.

48 Geoffrey A. Fowler, "LivingSocial Adds Deals of the Day Overseas," *Wall Street Journal*, January 13, 2011, p. B6.

49 Gina Chon, Anupeeta Das, Ilan Brat and Joann Lublin, "Sara Lee Weighs foreign Takeover," *Wall Street Journal Online*, December 8, 2010.

50 Peter Wonacott and Henny Sender, "Indian Firms See Acquisition as Path to World-Wide Growth," *Wall Street Journal*, May 1, 2006, p. A6.

51 Gary McWilliams and Evan Ramstad, "China's Aggressive Buyers Suffer Setbacks on Some Overseas Deals," *Wall Street Journal*, August 22, 2006, p. A1.

52 Pete Engardio, "Emerging Giants," *Business Week*, July 31, 2006, p. 49.

53 Hongxin Zhao, Yadong Luo and Taewon Suh, "Transaction Cost Determinants and Ownership-Based Entry Mode Choice: A Meta-Analytical Review," *Journal of International Business Studies*, vol. 35, no. 6 (2004), pp. 524–544.

54 Frank Bradley and Michael Gannon, "Does the Firm's Technology and Marketing Profile Affect Foreign Market Entry?" *Journal of International Marketing*, vol. 8, no. 4 (2000), pp. 12–36.

Part 4

Designing Global Marketing Programs

10 GLOBAL PRODUCT STRATEGIES 311

11 GLOBAL STRATEGIES FOR SERVICES, BRANDS
   AND SOCIAL MARKETING 341

12 PRICING FOR INTERNATIONAL AND GLOBAL MARKETS 373

13 MANAGING GLOBAL DISTRIBUTION CHANNELS 409

14 GLOBAL PROMOTION STRATEGIES 443

15 MANAGING GLOBAL ADVERTISING 475

Chapter 10

Global Product Strategies

PRODUCT DESIGN IN A GLOBAL ENVIRONMENT	313
PACKAGING AND LABELING FOR GLOBAL MARKETS	321
GLOBAL WARRANTY AND SERVICE POLICIES	323
MANAGING A GLOBAL PRODUCT LINE	325
GLOBAL PRODUCTS	327
GLOBAL-PRODUCT DEVELOPMENT	328
MANAGING GLOBAL RESEARCH AND DEVELOPMENT	328
INTRODUCING NEW PRODUCTS TO GLOBAL MARKETS	332

Once a Hollywood blockbuster movie could take seven months to arrive in some countries. Now this time is cut to 60 days or less. The Internet is one reason for this new speed. Foreign consumers are using online retailers such as Amazon.com to buy films on DVD as soon as they are available in the United States. In many cases, these films have not yet opened in all national markets. Furthermore, movie fans around the world can access movie promotions on the Internet. These promotions appear even before the domestic launch. Waiting months to see these movies frustrates foreign consumers.

Today foreign ticket sales for Hollywood movies account for over two-thirds of total sales. As a result, Hollywoods had made changes in the development of its films. More foreign actors are included in blockbuster movies. Fewer romantic comedies are under development because foreign audiences don't understand American humor.[1] Similarly, in France local television producers look to international markets to break even. Recently several French series have been filmed in English for markets abroad. Street signs in Paris are changed to English and the actors speak with the standard mid-Atlantic accent common on American television. The series are then dubbed into French for the home market.[2]

This chapter examines issues pertaining to the adaptation of products to global markets and the creation of global products. In this chapter we begin by exploring the many environmental factors that can prevent the marketing of uniform or standardized products across a multitude of markets. Subsequent sections focus on packaging and labeling, product warranties and product-line management across countries. The chapter concludes with a discussion of global product development.

Learning Objectives

After studying this chapter, you should be able to:

➤ list the advantages of product standardization and product adaptation;

➤ differentiate between mandatory and discretionary product adaptations;

➤ explain the concepts of global product standards and generic management system standards;

➤ explain why product lines can vary from country to country;

➤ define modularity and explain its impact on global product development;

➤ compare and contrast the product development roles played by a multinational corporation's headquarters and the roles played by its subsidiaries;

➤ explain the importance of lead markets and note their importance to product development;

➤ describe how companies may access new products or technologies by licensing or by importing products from other firms;

➤ discuss the use of acquisitions and alliances for the purpose of product development;

➤ explain the process of introducing new products to global markets, including concept testing, test marketing and the timing of new product introduction.

Product Design in a Global Environment

One of the principal questions in global marketing is whether a firm's products can be sold in their present form or whether they need to be adapted to foreign market requirements. The benefits of adaptation are compared with those of standardization in Table 10.1. Standardizing products across markets has certain advantages. Standardization can help firms realize economies of scale and increases speed to market. In some cases standardization even serves to better satisfy global customers. Adapting products, on the other hand, can better address buyer needs and may even be necessary to legally sell a product in certain national markets.

Benefits of Product Standardization

If a standardized product can be sold in many countries, economies of scale in manufacturing may be realized. Economies of scale vary by industry, but to the extent they exist they allow products to be produced more cheaply. As a result, a firm can sell their product at a cheaper price, likely increasing its share of the market. Alternatively, a firm can keep the price the same but realize a greater profit margin, which in turn can support higher investment in promotion or research and development (R&D).

If a product requires high development costs but has a short product life cycle, as is the case for many high-tech products, it may need to enter global markets very rapidly. In other words, firms must sell high volumes in many markets to recoup their investment before the product becomes obsolete. Adapting such a product to different national markets may simply take too long.

Table 10.1 Benefits of Production Standardization and of Product Adaptation

Benefits of Standardization

Lower costs of manufacturing may be achieved through economies of scale.

Lower input costs may be achieved through volume purchasing.

Cost savings may be achieved by eliminating efforts—market research, design and engineering—to adapt products.

Fast global product rollouts are possible because no time is needed to make product adaptations.

International customers may prefer the same product to be available worldwide.

Standardized products may enhance consumer perceptions of a global brand.

Benefits of Adaptation

Mandatory adaptations allow products to be sold in otherwise closed markets.

Products can be sold for use in different climates and with different infrastructures.

Modified products may perform better under different use conditions.

Product costs may be decreased by varying local inputs.

Product costs may be decreased by eliminating unnecessary product features.

Greater sales may be attained by better meeting industry norms or cultural preferences.

Furthermore, if buyers themselves are multinational corporations (MNCs), they may prefer a standardized product that is available worldwide. This preference for a standardized product is sometimes observed in consumer markets as well. When an Arabized version of the television series *The Simpsons* debuted on Arab television, Homer (or Omar) still worked at the nuclear power plant in Springfield where he lived with his dysfunctional family including his disrespectful son. However, Omar did not hang out at bars or eat bacon, and he drank soft drinks instead of beer. Despite the cultural sensitivity of these adaptations, some Arabs who had watched *The Simpsons* in the United States thought the various cultural adaptations ruined the show.[3] Similarly, when Cold Stone Creamery entered Japan it eschewed culturally sensitive adaptations such as offering green tea ice cream. Instead it kept to American iconic flavors such as cotton candy and cake batter in order to stand out from the local competition.[4]

Benefits of Product Adaptation

Despite the advantages of standardization, many products need to be adapted for different national markets. Even marketers who have long resisted product adaptation now acknowledge its necessity. After years of insisting that foreign buyers adapt to the taste of French wine, wine growers in France's Bordeaux region abandoned tradition and began to develop wines that the global consumer preferred—lighter and more fruity. The strategy reversed a five-year decline in sales, and wine exports from the region increased 26 percent in a single year.[5]

The need for adaptation is true even for Internet firms that only virtually enter international markets. Simply translating the text of a website may not be enough. Do people read from right to left or from left to right, from top to bottom or from bottom to top? What colors and shapes do they like? The answers to these questions will strongly influence the graphical layouts of the site and its use of icons.[6] What standards—governmental or societal—could affect the content of the site? U.S. Internet firms routinely alter the content of their sites in Asia, self-censoring to avoid offending local governments, especially those in China, Singapore and Malaysia.

Many adaptations are discretionary; that is, firms may choose to make certain adaptations or not to do so. In some cases, however, adaptations are mandatory. They are necessary for the product to be sold in a local market. Some mandatory adaptations are responses to differing physical realities. For example, consumer electronics must be adapted to work with different voltages, alternating currents and electric plug designs, each of which varies from country to country.

Most mandatory adaptations, however, are made to adhere to national legal requirements. For example, a French court required Yahoo to block French users from accessing Nazi memorabilia on its U.S.-based website, thereby setting a precedent and suggesting that companies operating on the global Internet could be required to conform to standards of individual countries.

Sometimes discretionary adaptations can become mandatory. Originally, Microsoft declined to translate its software into Icelandic, a language spoken by only 270,000 people. Customers in Iceland were apparently able to manage without it. However, when Iceland's government demanded that Microsoft translate its program, the firm agreed rather than face leaving the market.[7]

Selecting the most desirable product features for each market is an involved decision for global marketers. The approach taken should include a thorough review of a number of factors that could determine both mandatory and discretionary adaptations. These include climatic, infrastructure and use conditions; cultural preferences; size and cost considerations; and performance and quality standards.

Climate, Infrastructure and Use Conditions

Global marketers often adapt products to conform to physical realities such as regional variations in climate, infrastructure and use conditions.

Climate

Climatic differences often call for product adaptations. Air conditioners in Saudi Arabia must be able to operate under conditions that are hotter and dustier than those in most U.S. locations. Paint must be adapted to various climatic conditions, such as heat, cold, moisture and wind. Most chocolate is easily damaged if not kept cool. When Cadbury introduced Cadbury Dairy Milk shots to the Indian market the small chocolate balls were designed with a sugar shell to protect the chocolate from the heat.[8]

Climate may even explain some cultural differences in food preferences. After surveying 4,500 meat recipes from 36 countries, biologists at Cornell University discovered that cultures in hotter climates overwhelmingly favored recipes with higher concentrations of anti-microbial spices such as garlic, cumin and pepper.[9] Therefore it's not surprising that Pringles discovered that its Hot and Spicy potato chips sold especially well in the Middle East.[10]

Infrastructure

Differences in infrastructure matter as well. Automobile manufacturers must consider which side of the street cars are driven on—the left or the right—and adjust the steering wheel accordingly. For instance, drivers in Britain and Japan drive on the left. Marketers of packaged foods must consider the distribution infrastructure of the country. How long will the product be in the distribution channels? Are warehouses air-conditioned and trucks refrigerated? One worldwide manufacturer of industrial abrasives even had to adjust products to differing availability of raw materials. The firm responded by varying the raw-materials input from one country to another, while maintaining exacting performance standards.

Use Conditions

Products may also need to be adapted to different use conditions in various markets. Procter & Gamble was forced to adapt the formulation of its Cheer laundry detergent to accommodate different use conditions in Japan. The Japanese liked to add fabric softeners that decreased the suds produced by detergent. Therefore, Procter & Gamble reformulated Cheer to work more effectively with fabric softeners.

In some local markets, customers may even expect a product to perform a function different from the one for which it was originally intended. One U.S. exporter of gardening tools found that its battery-operated trimmers were used by the Japanese as lawn mowers on their small lawns. As a result, the batteries and motors did not last as long as they would have under the intended use. Because of the different function desired by Japanese customers, a design change was eventually required.

Adapting Products to Cultural Preferences

AB InBev adapts its beer to reflect cultural preferences. The company sells an apple-flavored alcohol-free version of its Budweiser beer in the Middle East to adapt to the region's Islamic culture and preference for apple drinks. In China, the company sells Budweiser with a lower percentage of alcohol to adapt to the Chinese tradition of making many toasts.[11]

Cultural adaptations are usually discretionary adaptations. Yet understanding cultural preferences and adapting products accordingly can be extremely important to success in local markets. To the extent that fashion and tastes differ by country, companies often change their styling. Color, for example, should reflect the aesthetic values of each country. For Japan, red and white have happy associations, whereas black and white indicate mourning. Green is an unpopular color in Malaysia, where it is associated with the jungle and illness. Textile manufacturers in the United States who have started to expand their export businesses have consciously chosen colors to suit local tastes. For example, the Lowenstein Corporation has successfully used brighter colors for fabrics exported to Africa.

The scent and sounds of a product may also have to be changed from one country to another. Strawberry-scented shampoo failed to sell in China, where consumers shun nonedible items that smell like foods.[12] Software engineers had to change programs destined for Japan that "pinged" when users tried to do something that was not possible. Japanese office workers complained that they were mortified that co-workers could hear when they made mistakes. The "ping" was deleted.[13]

As we saw in Chapter 3, food is one of the most culturally distinct product areas. In China, Nestlé snack wafers are sold in flavors such as sesame and red bean to appeal to local tastes.[14] Nestlé's popular instant coffee, Nescafé, is produced in more than 200 variations—more variations than the number of countries where it is sold. Product adaptations are even necessary within some national markets. In Switzerland, the French-speaking Swiss like strong, black coffee. The German-speaking Swiss prefer light coffee with milk.[15]

Cultural differences relating to food can extend beyond mere taste. As we discussed in Chapter 3, religion can dictate what people will and will not eat. Other traditional beliefs may require product adaptations as well. Frito-Lay wondered why its potato chips didn't sell in China in the summertime. Research revealed that Chinese consumers associated fried foods like potato chips with *yang*, which according to Chinese traditional medicine generates body heat and should be avoided in hot weather. The company then introduced a "cool lemon" variety packaged in pastel shades. The new lemon chips became Frito-Lay's best-selling item in China.[16] In general, a branded food product in the United States is likely to be considerably higher in fat, sodium and added sweeteners than the same branded product sold in the Chinese, Japanese and European markets.[17]

Product Size and Dimensions

When other design features require no modification, product size and dimensions may need adaptation.

Adapting to Material Culture

Product size can be affected by physical surroundings and available space. In many countries, limited living space necessitates home appliances and furniture be substantially smaller than those found in a country such as the United States, where people live in larger dwellings. Within three years of entering the U.S. market, IKEA, the Swedish furniture and household products company, decided to abandon its smaller European sizes in furniture and bed linens and developed bigger sizes for the new market. American homes are 1,800 square feet on average—twice the size of the average European home. Larger furniture just looked better in American homes. Even drinking glasses had to be made bigger to accommodate ice, which is rarely used in Europe.[18]

Physical Characteristics of Consumers

The different physical characteristics of consumers can also influence product design. Swiss watch manufacturers learned over the years to adapt their watchbands to different wrist sizes. For example, Japanese have smaller wrists than Americans. A leading Italian shoe manufacturer had a similar experience exporting shoes to the United States. The company learned that Americans have thicker ankles and narrower, flatter feet. To produce a properly fitting shoe, the Italian company decided to make appropriate changes in its design to achieve the necessary comfort for U.S. customers.

Metric versus Non-Metric

Another important decision, particularly for U.S. firms, is whether to select a metric or a nonmetric scale for the sale of their products abroad. With most of the world operating on the metric standard, the United States is one of the few remaining major nonmetric markets. The firm must often go beyond a single translation of nonmetric into metric sizes (or vice versa) to help consumers understand the design of its products. In some cases, companies may be required to change the physical sizes of their products to conform to legal standards based on the metric scale.

Cost and Price Considerations

In markets where many potential consumers have little disposable income, packaged-goods manufacturers often determine that smaller sizes are necessary to offer the customer a lower-priced, accessible product. In Latin America, where 25 percent of the population lives on less than $2 a day, sales of Nestlé Brazil's Bono cookies jumped 40 percent in a single year when the company decreased the package size from 200 grams to 149 grams.[19] In India, Hindustan Lever Ltd., a subsidiary of Unilever, sells Sunsilk shampoo in bottles for the upper classes and in sachets, good for one use, to consumers who cannot afford to buy a bottle.[20] Similarly, Unilever introduced a mini-deodorant stick in several Asian countries, because many consumers in developing countries can afford deodorant only for special occasions.[21]

To keep prices low, companies can also adapt the physical qualities of the product as well as the size. Procter & Gamble considers what price consumers can afford to pay in developing countries. Then they design products to meet these price targets. To keep costs down for its Ace hand-washing detergent, P&G omitted enzymes from its formula.[22] However, global marketers should be aware that consumers in developing countries may demand bigger and better products as their incomes increase. In China, the world's second largest automobile market, consumers are increasingly purchasing more up-scale models.[23]

Adapting to Performance and Quality Expectations

Manufacturers typically design products to meet domestic performance expectations. Such expectations do not always apply in other countries, and product changes are required in some circumstances. Some companies go to great lengths to meet different quality standards in foreign markets. German automaker BMW found that its customers in Japan expected the very finest quality. Typically, cars shipped to Japan had to be completely repainted. Even very small mistakes were not tolerated by customers. When service was required, the car was picked up at the customer's home and returned when the work was completed.

The necessity to increase product quality or performance for a foreign market tends, if the need exists, to be readily apparent. Opportunities for product simplification are frequently less obvious to the firm. Products designed in highly developed countries often exceed the performance needed in developing countries. Customers in these markets may prefer products of greater simplicity, not only to save costs but also to ensure better service over the products' lifetime. Companies have been criticized for selling excess performance where simpler products will do. Some MNCs are addressing this issue. For example, when Philips created a product line for consumers in rural India, it focused on scaling back features in order to deliver inexpensive products such as a wind-up radio and a back-to-basics television set.[24] Also ready to fill this market gap are companies from less developed countries whose present levels of technology are more in line with consumer needs. For example, local Egyptian firms that produce consumer products invest very little in elaborate features or attractive packaging in order to deliver products at very low prices.

Of course, manufacturers from developing countries can face the opposite challenge when attempting to sell overseas. They must increase the performance of their products to meet the standards of industrialized countries. Producing quality products that are competitive on export markets has become something of a national obsession in Mexico. Major companies such as the Alfa business group and Cemex have joined forces with universities to establish programs to supply Mexican industry with top-flight engineers. And the effort has paid off. Fifteen years later Mexico's exports had more than doubled.[25]

Global Standards

Incompatible national standards both help and hinder global competitors. Credit cards in the United States use magnetic strips while most of the rest of the world use the more sophisticated chip and

PIN technology. Ticket kiosks at train stations in Europe will only accept chip and PIN cards. However, the sheer size of the U.S. credit card market, and the consequent cost to switch technologies, has been a deterrent to change.

A lack of international standards also impacts the movie industry. The ultragrisly movie *Hannibal* grossed more than $230 million worldwide, but its scenes of cannibalism and dismemberment caused an outcry in Italy, where its rating suggested it was appropriate for all audiences. In the United States, no one under 17 was supposed to be admitted without an adult, but children as young as eight were seen entering with their parents. In Western Europe, viewers had to be at least 15—with or without accompanying adults. But in Portugal and Uruguay, they only had to be 12 years old.[26]

Voluntary Standards

Many countries have organizations that set voluntary standards for products and business practices. Groups such as the Canadian Standards Association and the British Standards Institute (BSI) formulate standards for product design and testing. If producers adhere to these standards, buyers are assured of the stated level of product quality.

The unification of Europe has forced Europeans to recognize the need for multicountry standards. In areas where a European standard has been developed, manufacturers who meet the standard are allowed to include the European Union (EU) Certification Symbol, CE. Firms both in and out of the EU are eligible to use the CE symbol, but they must be able to demonstrate their compliance with the standards.

The U.S. standard-setting process is much more fragmented than Europe's. In the United States, there are over 450 different standard-setting groups, loosely coordinated by the American National Standards Institute (ANSI). After a standard is set by one of the 450 groups, ANSI certifies that it is an "American National Standard," of which there are over 11,000 on the books.

International Standards Organization

Given the growth in international commerce, there are benefits to having international standards for items such as credit cards, screw threads, car tires, paper sizes and speed codes for 35 mm film. And country-to-country differences become immediately obvious when you try to plug in your hair dryer in various countries. Although national standards institutes ensure consistency within countries, an international agency is necessary to coordinate across countries.

The International Standards Organization (ISO), located in Geneva, was founded in 1947 to coordinate the setting of global standards. The ISO is a NGO, a federation of national standards bodies from some 140 countries. Each member of the ISO is the firm "most representative of standardization in its country"; only one such member is allowed per country. Most standards set by the ISO are highly specific, such as standards for film speed codes or formats for telephone and banking cards. ISO standards for components of freight containers have made it possible for shipping costs around the world to be lowered substantially.[27]

To set an international standard, representatives from various countries meet and attempt to agree on a common standard. Sometimes they adopt the standard set by a particular country. For example, the British standard for quality assurance (BS5750) was adopted internationally as ISO

9000 in 1987. This standard was revolutionary in that it was a generic management system standard. As the first such international standard, ISO 9000 ensured that an organization could consistently deliver a product or service that satisfied the customer's requirements because the company followed a state-of-the-art management system. In other words, the company possessed quality management. ISO 9000 can be applied to any organization, large or small, whatever its product or service. ISO 14000 is a similar generic management system standard that is primarily concerned with environmental management. Companies that meet this standard must show that they do minimal damage to the environment.

Mandatory Standards

Sometimes product standards are not voluntary but regulated by law. In these cases, adaptation is mandatory, not discretionary, for market entry. Most often these mandatory standards involve product quality and safety, hygiene and environmental concerns. Meeting these standards can add costs to the product, but failing to comply may keep a firm out of an important market. For example, Kinder eggs, made by Italian candy giant Ferrero SpA, are popular in 100 countries and are ranked on the ACNielsen list of top global brands. But they were illegal in the United States for many years. Wrapped in orange and white foil, the hollow chocolate eggs contained intricate plastic or wooden toy prizes. These represented a choking hazard according to the U.S. Consumer Product Safety Commission. The company eventually designed an egg cleared to sell in the United States. The egg was larger, and the toy was encased in a yellow capsule between two halves of the chocolate.

World Beat 10.1

Rolling Over

Europeans have long built car roofs to withstand being dropped upside down or flipped off a moving dolly. Saab has tested vehicles by ramming them into a bundle of electrical cable to simulate hitting a moose. For many years, U.S. car companies employed a less rigorous safety test. U.S. automakers claimed their roofs matched the Europeans' in safety. However, the U.S. National Highway Traffic Safety Administration (NHTSA) test, developed by General Motors in the late 1960s, called for vehicles to be tested with their windshields intact. In a rollover, the windshield frequently breaks when the roof first hits the ground, and vehicle roofs lose between 10 percent and 40 percent of their structural strength without the windshield. While rollovers are rare, they account for 30 percent of deaths involving passenger vehicles in the United States.

Over the course of 20 years, the number of German traffic deaths dropped 70 percent. Traffic deaths in the United States only decreased 20 percent. The European experience may have inspired the NHTSA to enact its first changes in roof safety regulations in 38 years. The U.S. code now requires roofs to be at least three times more rigid. Beginning in 2017, roofs on new vehicles are required to comply with this new standard which adds to the weight of vehicles. Ironically, the added weight will make it more difficult for automobile manufacturers to comply with fuel economy standards also set by the U.S. government.

U.S. and European automakers are now working together to harmonize safety standards. Auto manufacturers report it would save considerable expense if safety requirements were standardized so cars wouldn't need to be reengineered for each national market.

Sources: "Automakers Seek Common Ground in Europe, U.S. on Safety Regulations," Car and Driver Blog, December 23, 2013; Aaron Bragman, "U.S. NHTSA Roof Crash Standards Improvement to Cost US$1.4 Billion Annually," Global Insight Dairly Analysis, May 5, 2009; "U.S. Will Require Stronger Roofs," Bloomberg Business News, Tom Murphy, "A-Pillar Conflict: Visibility vs. Roof Crush," WardsAuto, January 8, 2011; Grabe Nelson, "Automakers Call for Backup in Quest to Align EU, U.S. Safety Standards," *Automotive News Europe*, December 18, 2013; and "Rollover 101," *Consumer Reports*, April 2014.

Many believe that Europe has come to dominate the creation of international standards through its influence at the ISO and its proactive stance toward setting mandatory standards. Already the standards established by the European Commission have become effective standards for firms in Asia and Latin America that aspire to export to Europe. EU standards concerning consumer safety are generally tougher than their U.S. counterparts—forcing U.S. companies to take note and conform. For example, the EU ordered manufacturers to eliminate or drastically curtail six toxic substances (such as lead and mercury) or face fines, prison and a ban on their products. One company, Coherent Inc., estimated that changes to comply with the new code would cost the company $10 million.

Despite attempts to make product standards uniform across Europe, many mandatory product standards remain far from standardized. For example, size requirements for license-plate holders on the backs of vehicles vary by country, sometimes only by a few centimeters.

Packaging and Labeling for Global Markets

Differences in the marketing environment may require special adaptations in product packaging and labeling.

Packaging

Different climatic conditions often demand a change in the package to ensure sufficient protection or shelf life. Culture may play a role as well. The Dutch beer brand, Heineken, introduced a longer-neck bottle to 170 countries worldwide except in the United States where beer drinkers preferred a shorter-neck bottle.[28]

Specific packaging decisions that may be affected include size, shape, materials, color and text. Size may differ by custom or in terms of existing standards, such as metric and nonmetric requirements. As noted earlier, higher-income countries tend to require larger unit sizes; these populations shop less frequently and can afford to buy larger quantities each time.

Packages can assume almost any shape, largely depending on the customs and traditions prevailing in each market. Materials used for packaging can also differ widely. Whereas Americans prefer to buy mayonnaise and mustard in clear plastic containers, consumers in Germany and Switzerland buy these same products in tubes. Cans are the customary material in which to package beer in the United States, whereas most European consumers prefer glass bottles.

The package color and text have to be integrated into a company's promotional strategy and therefore may be subject to specific tailoring that differs from one country to another. The promotional effect is of great importance for consumer goods and has led some companies to attempt to standardize their packaging in color and layout. In areas such as Europe and Latin America, where consumers frequently travel to other countries, standardized colors help them identify a product quickly. This strategy depends on devising a set of colors or a layout with an appeal beyond one single culture or market. An example of a product with a standardized package color is Procter & Gamble's leading detergent, Tide. The orange and white box familiar to millions of U.S. consumers can be found in many foreign markets, even though the package text may appear in the language of the given country.

Packaging adaptations may also reflect a country's retailing structure. In countries with a substantial degree of self-service merchandising, firms should choose a package with strong promotional appeal for consumer products. In addition, distribution handling requirements are not identical the world over. In the high-wage countries of the developed world, products tend to be packaged in such a way as to reduce further handling by retail employees. For consumer products, all mass merchandisers have to do is place the products on shelves. In countries with lower wages and less elaborate retailing structures, individual orders may be filled from larger packaged units, a process that entails extra labor on the part of the retailer.

Packaging can even face legal restrictions. A British law cut the number of pills that could be sold in packages of aspirin and acetaminophen to reduce overdoses leading to death and liver failure caused by impulsive self-poisoning. Tablets were also required to be blister-wrapped to make swallowing large quantities impulsively even more difficult. Three years later, deaths by overdoses of these pills had decreased dramatically in the United Kingdom.[29]

Labeling

Labeling is another concern for international marketers. Labeling helps consumers better understand the products they are buying and can convey rudimentary instructions for their use. What languages must the labels be written in? What government requirements are involved?

Cultural implications of labeling can sometimes create problems in unexpected ways. One exporter of software to Saudi Arabia identified its CD-ROMs for the Saudi market by putting the Saudi flag on the box. The flag bears the word *Allah*, the Arabic word for "God." For many devout Muslims, to discard the box would imply disrespect for God. As a result, the local distributor was left with lots of boxes that both customers and employees declined to throw away.[30]

Increasingly, MNCs must adhere to government requirements concerning labeling, but many other products are affected as well. The Chinese government detained 37 employees of Wal-Mart who were arrested for mislabeling pork as organic.[31] Similarly, Chinese manufacturers have fallen afoul of labeling laws in the United States. When China began exporting cashmere sweaters and other garments, many manufacturers exaggerated the amount of cashmere in their products. This brought them into collision with the United States' 60-year-old Wool Products Labeling Act, which requires that fabrics and garments made out of wool and other fine animal hairs be accurately labeled to reflect their true content. The Federal Trade Commission can seek penalties in federal court as high as $11,000 for each violation.[32]

Global Warranty and Service Policies

Buyers around the world purchase products with certain performance expectations and further expect companies to back their promises concerning product performance. A survey of 2,000 consumers in Turkey and 1,100 consumers in Egypt revealed that the acceptance of returned items was considered the highest determinant of ethical business behavior.[33]

Thus, a comprehensive warranty and service policy can become a very important marketing tool for MNCs. In Asia, customers are not used to returning merchandise. Costco in Taiwan decided that a no-questions-asked return policy could be another way in which to differentiate itself in the market. The head of Costco in Taiwan described the policy:

> People return half a watermelon because it's not sweet enough. We say we are happy to do it. We make that return so pleasurable that you are going to tell your family and friends. That's something money can't buy. We consider that part of our advertising.[34]

Product Warranties

A company must address its warranty policy for international markets either by declaring its domestic warranty valid worldwide or by tailoring warranties to specific countries or markets. Although declaring a worldwide warranty with uniform performance standards would be administratively simple, local market conditions often dictate a differentiated approach. In the United States, many computers are sold with a 90-day warranty, whereas 12 months is more typical in Europe and Japan.

Companies are well advised to consider actual product use. If buyers in a foreign market subject the product to more stress or abuse, some shortening of the warranty period may become necessary. In developing countries, where technical sophistication is below North American and European standards, maintenance may not be adequate, causing more frequent equipment breakdowns. Another important factor is local competition. Because an attractive warranty policy can be helpful in obtaining sales, a firm's warranty policy should be at least in line with those of other firms competing in the local market.

In our more connected world, however, it may be increasingly difficult to offer a warranty policy in one country that is less attractive than policies available elsewhere. Apple Inc. came under attack in China by the state-run media that accused Apple of skirting the warranty period, and adopting customer-service policies that discriminated against Chinese customers. The company announced that it would more clearly post its warranty policy on its website, streamline customer feedback and provide further training to its authorized dealers concerning the company's warranty policy.[35]

Global After-Sales Service

For some products, no warranty will be believable unless backed with an effective after-sales service organization. Although service is important to the consumer, it is even more crucial to the industrial buyer, because any breakdown of equipment or product is apt to cause substantial economic loss. This risk has led industrial buyers to be conservative in their choice of products, always carefully analyzing the supplier's ability to provide service in the event of need.

To provide the required level of service outside the company's home base poses special problems for global marketers. The selection of an organization to perform the service is an important decision. Ideally, company personnel are preferable because they tend to be better trained. However, this approach can be organized economically only if the installed base of the market is large enough to justify such an investment. In cases where a company does not maintain its own marketing subsidiary, it is generally more efficient to turn to an independent service company or a local distributor. To provide adequate service via independent distributors requires extra training for the service technicians, usually at the manufacturer's expense. In any case, the selection of an appropriate service organization should be made in such a way that fully trained service personnel are readily available within the customary time frame for the particular market.

Closely related to any satisfactory service policy is an adequate inventory for spare parts. Because service often means replacing some parts, the company must store sufficient inventory of spare parts within reach of its markets. Whether this inventory is maintained in regional warehouses or through sales subsidiaries and distributors depends on the volume and the required reaction time for service calls. Industrial buyers will generally want to know, before placing substantial orders, how the manufacturer plans to organize service.

Firms that demonstrate serious interest in a market by committing themselves to setting up their own marketing subsidiaries are often at an advantage over firms that use distributors. One German truck manufacturer that entered the U.S. market advertised the fact that "97 percent of all spare parts are kept in local inventory," thus assuring prospective buyers that they could get spares readily. Difficulty in establishing service outlets may even influence a company's market entry strategy. This was the case with Fujitsu, a Japanese manufacturer of electronic office equipment. By combining forces with TRW, a U.S.-based company, Fujitsu was able to sell its office equipment in the U.S. market backed by the extensive service organization of TRW.

Because the guarantee of reliable and efficient service can be such an important aspect of a firm's entire product strategy, investment in service centers sometimes must be made before any sales can take place. In this case, service costs must be viewed as an investment in future volume rather than merely as a recurring expense.

Managing a Global Product Line

In early sections of this chapter, we discussed issues concerning individual products. Most companies, however, manufacture or sell a multitude of products. Starbucks doesn't vary its product formulations from country to country, but the product line can vary. For example, local product development produced a Strawberries and Cream Frappuccino specifically for the British market. Green tea Frappuccino was the largest-selling Frappuccino in Taiwan and Japan before the product was offered elsewhere. Pronto Cafes, one of Starbucks' competitor chains in Japan, sold coffee by day and liquor at night. So a Starbucks outlet in the Japanese city of Kobe quietly began selling beer and wine. Selling alcohol in Starbucks USA would be far more difficult because of the stricter alcohol licensing laws in the United States. As with each individual product decision, the firm can either offer exactly the same line in its home market and abroad or, if circumstances demand, make appropriate changes.

Product-Line Deletions

Product lines abroad are frequently narrower than in a company's domestic market. The circumstances that can lead to deletions from product lines vary, but some reasons dominate.

Companies with their home base in large markets such as the United States, Japan or Germany will find sufficient demand in their home markets for even the smallest market segments, justifying additional product variations and greater depth in their lines. Abroad, some segments may be too small to warrant commercial exploitation. Lack of market sophistication is another factor in product-line variation. Poorer developing countries may not demand some of the most advanced items in a product line. Finally, some product lines struggle to find a place in competitive foreign markets. French cosmetics maker L'Oreal announced that it was pulling its Garnier brand from the Chinese market due to slow sales and tough competition. The brand was caught in the middle between cheap cosmetics that were sold online and higher-priced elite brands.[36]

Product-Line Additions

Sometimes global marketers add product lines abroad. Market conditions sometimes lead to product lines overseas that may be broader than those at home. When discount shoe retailer Payless entered the Middle East market, it extended its line of men's sandals by 100 percent.[37] Tupperware Brands Corporation is known in the United States as a maker of plastic food containers. However, the company discovered that consumers in Latin America spend 20 times as much on beauty products as on containers for leftovers. The company bought six beauty brands and now the beauty products category accounts for about half of Tupperware's sales in Latin America.[38]

Firms confronted with deletions in their product lines may develop country-specific offerings to fill the gap in the line. Three months after removing its Garnier line from China, L'Oreal announced a new Chinese brand of cosmetic facial masks designed specifically for the Chinese market. The company's executive vice president of the Asia Pacific region believed that a beauty company in China had to have a Chinese skincare brand.[39]

When considering country-specific product lines, global marketers consider the market potential of the country, its competitive environment and whether the country-specific line can be extended into similar markets. In addition, the firm must commit to adequate R&D resources for the project. This might include developing R&D facilities in its various subsidiaries.

Of course, global marketers often combine local offerings with foreign offerings. Global retailers who sell groceries need to adapt to local tastes. However, foreign product lines can be used to enhance their competitive advantage. The Costco Wholesale Corp. in Taiwan wanted to differentiate itself as a store that carried U.S. brands. Consequently, at Costco stores in Taiwan about two-fifths of the merchandise comes from the United States.[40]

Exploiting Product Life Cycles

Experience has shown that products do not always occupy the same position on the product life cycle curve in different countries. As Figure 10.1 shows, it is possible for a product to be in different stages of the product life cycle in different countries. A firm can extend product growth by expanding into new markets to compensate for declining growth rates in mature markets. On the other hand, a company can enter new national markets too rapidly, before the local market is ready to absorb the new product. To avoid such pitfalls and to take advantage of long-term opportunities, international companies may pursue the following strategies.

During the introductory phase in a product's life cycle, the product may have to be debugged and refined. This job can best be handled in the original market or in a country close to company R&D centers. Also, the marketing approach will have to be refined. At this stage, even the market in the more advanced countries is relatively small, and demand in countries with lower levels of economic development will hardly be commercially exploitable. Therefore, the introductory stage is usually limited to the advanced markets, often the company's domestic market.

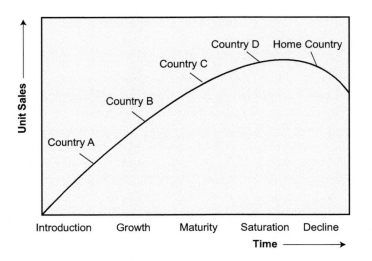

Figure 10.1 Possible Product Life Cycle for a Product in Different Countries

326

When a product faces life cycle maturity or decline in one market, it may still be marketed successfully in others. It should be remembered, however, that for some high-tech products, life cycles are very short. In these cases, products are likely to be sold worldwide—or at least in all viable markets—soon after their introduction in the domestic market.

Global Products

Firms increasingly experience pressure for cost reduction in order to remain competitive. Yet there are relatively few opportunities for producing completely standardized products. As a result, many firms now employ a new strategy: global product development. In global products, a portion of the final design is standardized. However, the design retains some flexibility so that the end product can be tailored to the needs of individual markets. This represents a move to standardize as much as possible those areas involving common components or parts.

Modularity

One of the most significant changes in product development strategy is the move toward modularity. This process involves the development of standard components that can easily be connected with other standard components to increase the variety of products. By doing this, global firms can realize significant cost savings from standardization while providing some customization for different markets.

This modularized approach has come to be especially important in the automobile industry, in which both U.S. and European manufacturers are increasingly creating world components to combat growing Japanese competitiveness. For example, General Motors has established a modular product architecture for all its global automobile projects. Future GM cars will be designed using combinations of components from 70 different body modules and about 100 major mechanical components such as engines, power trains and suspension systems. GM aims to save 40 percent in radio costs alone by reducing the 270 types of car radios it uses worldwide to only 50.[41]

The challenge faced by GM and other automobile manufacturers is similar to that faced by manufacturers and marketers of both industrial and consumer products all over the world. Cost pressures force them to standardize, while market pressures require more customization of products. Conceptually, these companies can gain from increasing the standardized components in their products while maintaining the ability to customize the product "at the end" for each market segment.

Most international firms must take advantage of economies of scale on the standardized portion, or core, of their products. Different firms achieve different levels of standardization, but rarely is a firm able to standardize its product 100 percent. For one company, even moving from a global core representing 15 percent of the total product to 20 percent of the total product may result in a considerable cost improvement and represent the maximum level of standardization desirable. For another firm, the core may have to represent 80 percent of the total product to achieve the same effect. These levels depend on the characteristics of the market that the company or industry faces.

Global-Product Development

Many firms now develop new products with global markets in mind. This shift from domestic to global development requires that the company consider the unique or special concerns for the major markets from the outset, rather than later attempting to make various adaptations to an initial model or prototype.

A global product is not a standardized product. Instead, a global product is designed from the outset to include some standardization but to assure as well that necessary local adaptations can be made quickly and with a minimum of additional costs. Universal's film *How the Grinch Stole Christmas* is an example of global product development. When Universal developed the film, it realized prior to production that the movie would be translated into 30 languages. However, Dr. Seuss presents peculiar problems because of the tricky language that makes it difficult to translate. Local writers were given leeway during the filming of the movie to adjust the translated verse if they thought it didn't make sense. Furthermore, the translation problem was diminished by a decision to modify the original English-speaking version of the movie. The Seussian metered narration was left out of long stretches of the movie and replaced by new dialogue.[42] In short, the product design and development process was altered to make it easier and faster to adapt the product across different national markets.

Managing Global Research and Development

Global marketers must also decide how to manage and organize R&D. This involves deciding where to locate R&D and whether to develop new products and services in-house or whether to seek outside sources from which to purchase or license products and technologies. It may also include the establishment of R&D alliances with other firms.

Centralized Research and Development

Most companies that currently engage in R&D on a global scale originally conducted their development efforts strictly in centralized facilities in the firm's domestic market. Even today, the largest portion of R&D monies spent by international firms goes to support efforts in domestically located facilities. As a result, most new product ideas are first developed in the context of the domestic market. Initial introduction at home is followed by a phase-in introduction to the company's foreign markets.

There are several reasons for this traditional approach. First, R&D must be integrated into a firm's overall marketing strategy. This requires frequent contacts and interfacing between R&D facilities and the company's main offices. Such contacts are maintained more easily with close proximity. Many companies centralize R&D because they are concerned that duplication of efforts will result if this responsibility is spread over several subsidiaries. Centralized R&D is thought to maximize results from scarce research funds. A final important reason for centralization is the company's experience in its domestic market. Typically, the domestic market is very important to the company, and in the case of international companies based in the United States, Germany and Japan, it is often the largest market as well. As a result, new products are developed with special emphasis on the domestic market, and R&D facilities, therefore, should be close by.

Centralized but Global

There are many good reasons for centralizing product development at the company's head office, but it remains a challenge for a centralized engineering and development staff of the firm to keep all relevant product modifications in mind before the design is frozen. Experience shows that later changes or modifications can be expensive. To keep a product acceptable in many or all relevant markets from the outset requires the product development staff to become globalized early in the creation process. Only a "globally thinking" product development staff will ensure the global acceptability of a product by incorporating the maximum possible number of variations in the original product.

The Role of Foreign Subsidiaries in Research and Development

Foreign subsidiaries may assume certain R&D functions if products require some adaptation to the local market. In larger markets, subsidiaries may even be responsible for developing products specifically for local consumption. Disney committed to shooting Russian-language films in Russia after box office sales soared in that country.[43]

As noted above, MNCs utilize their subsidiaries to develop products not only for a single market but for other markets as well. McDonald's in Egypt first introduced delivery in 1994 and delivered sales grew to 30 percent of total sales. The idea quickly spread to other Middle Eastern countries where the concept of restaurant delivery was common. Indian dishes developed for the Indian market have been successfully introduced in the Middle East where a large Indian diaspora resides.[44] U.S.-based bakery chain Cinnabon Inc. developed products for its Central and South American markets that were later introduced in the United States due to a larger Hispanic population in its home market.[45]

Subsidiaries often assume a more global role when they are located in a lead market. As we noted in Chapter 8, participation in lead markets can be an important part of global strategy. In general, a lead market is a market whose level of development exceeds that of the markets in other countries worldwide and whose developments tend to set a pattern for other countries. A subsidiary located in a lead market is usually in a better position to observe developments and to accommodate new demands. Consequently, international firms with subsidiaries in lead markets have an opportunity to turn such units into effective "listening posts."

lead markets ↓

World Beat 10.2

Colombia: Lead Market for Body Armor

The latest innovations sometimes come from emerging markets. After 50 years combating left-wing guerrillas, Colombians have attained a certain expertise in security services and the production of body armor. Not only is Colombian body armor respected for its technological advances, but it is renowned for its fashion as well.

The company of Miguel Caballero produces personal ballistic protection products. The company began exporting its bulletproof clothing to government officials in India and Nigeria and then opened a store in Mexico. Today the company's products are sold in about 20 foreign markets, and 98 percent of the company's sales are overseas. Known as the "Armani of armor," the company has even sold bullet-proof tank-tops and T-shirts to Harrods department store in London.

The company's product line is perfect for the security conscious who also wish to make a fashion statement. Some of its best-selling items include a three-button blazer, a V-neck wool sweater and a polo shirt. But prices are high. A Caballero polo shirt can sell for about $876 in the United States. Caballero invested considerable effort and money to develop a light-weight and flexible armor. Luckily, the company is able to pass on those costs to consumers who are concerned more with personal safety and good looks than with price.

After the Newtown massacre in which 20 students and six teachers were killed at an elementary school in Connecticut, orders for child-sized Caballero armor soared. The products are designed for children ages eight to 16 and include protective undershirts and backpacks with ballistic protection. They sell for $150–$600 but only weigh between two and four pounds.

Sources: David Owen, "Survival of the Fitted," *The New Yorker*, September 26, 2011; Cesar Garcia, "Orders Flooding in for Child-Sized Body Armour in Wake of Newtown Massacre," Associated Press, January 4, 2013; Steve Raabe, "High-Fashion Body Armor is Specialty of New Denver Firm," *Denver Post*, March 7, 2013; and Andres Schipani, "Colombian Security Industry Exports its Expertise," *Financial Times*, June 3, 2013.

Increasingly, MNCs are investing in research facilities abroad in order to obtain input from key markets. Each year General Motors gives what it calls Kettering Awards to employees whose ideas help GM retain technology leadership, improve customer service or save production time and costs. Kettering Awards have recognized researchers and engineers not only from the United States, Canada and Germany but from Brazil and India as well.

China has overtaken the United States in patent applications.[46] And many Western firms have opened development facilities there. Among those firms are Intel and Microsoft, which have opened research centers near Beijing where many of China's leading universities are clustered. Many companies are no longer using these centers only to adapt products to the Chinese market. P&G used its Chinese research center as a lead site for developing a new grease-fighting formula for the Tide detergent that the company markets in Asia, Eastern Europe and Latin America.[47]

Changes instituted by GM are indicative of actions taken by other MNCs. With the advent of world cars, GM realized that the company needed closer coordination between its domestic units and its overseas subsidiaries. Therefore, GM moved its international staff from New York to Detroit in order to speed up communication between domestic and international staffs, and it adopted the "project center" concept to manage its engineering effort. Each division or foreign subsidiary involved in a new car design lends engineers to a centrally organized project center, which designs, develops and introduces the new model. Upon introduction of the model, the project center is disbanded.

In the future, international companies will have to make better use of the talents of local subsidiaries in the development of new products. Increasingly, the role of the subsidiary as simply a selling or production arm of the company will have to be abandoned, and companies will have to find innovative ways to involve their foreign affiliates in the product development process. This involvement can be patterned after several role models. The strategic leader role, with responsibility for developing a new range of products to be used by the entire company, may be assigned to a highly competent subsidiary in a market of strategic importance. Another subsidiary with competence in a distinct area may be assigned the role of contributor, adapting some products in smaller but still important markets. Most subsidiaries, being smaller and located in less strategic markets, will be expected to be implementers of the overall strategy, without making a major contribution either technologically or strategically.[48]

Outsourcing Options for New Products

Instead of developing new products through its own R&D personnel, a company may acquire products from independent outside sources. This can be accomplished by licensing, purchasing products or acquiring other firms. Licensing products and technologies has been a traditional approach to gaining access to new developments from lead markets. Licensing can be a boon to entrepreneurs who have few funds for R&D. Alternatively, some corporations import finished products directly from another firm to supplement their product lines. For example, Dutch brewing giant Heineken NV formed an alliance with Mexico's Fomento Economico Mexicano SA (Femsa) to become the sole U.S. importer for three years of two popular Mexican beer brands. Such a strategy should be pursued with great care, because firms may establish or expand a market position for competitors who may choose to pursue the market on their own in the future. This strategy may best apply in areas that do not represent the core of the firm's business and technology.

Acquisitions as a Route to New Products

International acquisitions in order to gain new technology or unique products are increasingly common in global markets. Yahoo purchased BharatMatrimony in order to add a marriage site to its online business in India.[49] Conversely, Indian software companies have been acquiring software companies in the United States. These acquisitions are partially motivated by a desire to access more value-added products and services.

Acquisitions can be a way to move more quickly into a national market already dominated by competitors. The same holds true for adding a new product to a firm's product line. Madame Kin Wo Chong established the Wanchai Ferry brand in Hong Kong. The firm was later acquired by General Mills and used to introduce a line of frozen Chinese dinner kits into an already competitive U.S. market.[50]

Alliances for New Product Development

As noted in Chapter 9, many companies are finding alliances an effective way to share technology and R&D for competitive advantage. To share the huge cost of developing new products, some companies have established joint ventures or joined consortia to share in new product development.

The Consortium Approach

Under the consortium approach, member firms join in a working relationship without forming a new entity. On completion of the assigned task, member firms are free to seek other relationships with different firms. A shift toward such non-equity forms of R&D agreements has been encouraged by improved protection worldwide for contracts and intellectual property.[51]

Because the development of new aircraft is particularly expensive, the aircraft industry offers several examples of the consortium approach to product development. The high development costs require that large passenger aircraft be built and sold in series of 200 or 300 units to break even. Under these circumstances, several companies form a consortium to share the risk. One of the first highly successful efforts was the European Airbus, developed and produced by French, British and German manufacturers.

The consortium approach can be employed by global buyers as well as manufacturers. Several global airlines that have alliances to sell tickets and buy fuel together are considering joint purchases of jetliners. One such group comprises Air Canada, Austrian Airlines, Lufthansa and SAS. Joint purchases will require an alignment of normally diverse tastes for options such as cabin interiors, seating configurations and flight kitchens. In return for agreeing to standard features, manufacturers have agreed to pass some of the cost savings from standardization on to the customers.[52]

Introducing New Products to Global Markets

Once a product has been developed for commercial introduction, a number of complex decisions still need to be made. Aside from the question of whether to introduce the product abroad, the firm has to decide on a test-marketing procedure, select target countries for product introduction and determine the timing or sequence of the introduction. Given the large number of possible markets, decisions surrounding new product introduction often have strategic significance.

Determining which product to introduce abroad depends, of course, on sales potential. Following a careful analysis, a marketer develops a list of target countries. The company then can choose from among several paths leading to actual introduction in the target countries.

Concept Tests

Once a prototype or sample product has been developed, a company may decide to subject its new creation to a series of tests to determine its commercial feasibility. It is particularly important to subject a new product to actual use conditions. The concept-testing stage would be incomplete if the products were tested only in the company's domestic market. A full test in several major markets is essential so that any shortcomings can be addressed at an early stage before costly adaptations for individual countries are made. When Volkswagen tested its original Rabbit models, test vehicles were made available to all principal subsidiaries to ensure that each market's requirements were met by the otherwise standardized car.

Test Marketing

Just as there are good reasons to test market a product in a domestic market, an international test can give the firm valuable insights into the launch of global products. A common approach to international test marketing is to use a single country as a proving ground before other markets are entered. In Europe, smaller markets such as the Netherlands, Belgium, Austria and Switzerland may be used to launch a new product. Because of these countries' small size, a test would include national introduction, and the results would be assumed to be applicable in other countries.

Sometimes a test market takes place in a country other than the country of the initial launch. IBM tested a new branding campaign for its Global Services line in Canada but launched it in the United States, and Carewell Industries test marketed a toothbrush in Singapore before its U.S. launch.[53] Similarly, Microsoft and Motorola sometimes test market in South Korea before launching products in the U.S. market.[54] Of course, circumstances are never exactly the same from one national market to another, and extrapolating results from a test market in one country to other countries must be done with caution.

Timing of New Product Introductions

Eventually, a company must establish the sequence and the timing of its introduction of a new product in its home market and foreign markets. When should the product be introduced in each market? Should the firm use a staggered-entry or a simultaneous-entry approach?

As we have noted, firms usually introduce new products first in their domestic markets to gain experience in production, marketing and service. However, a foreign market may prove the better choice for a product launch. DaimlerChrysler of Germany, the largest truck company in the world, traditionally launches new innovations in its home market of Germany because of its large size and sophisticated buyers. However, German buyers are relatively slow to adopt service innovations. Analysis undertaken when the company was considering a launch of a remote diagnosis system (RDS) revealed that Japan would be a better market for an initial product launch.[55]

The Global Rollout

Choosing priority markets for product launches is an important decision with strategic consequences. Samsung designated India a priority smartphone market earlier than Apple did. As a result, Apple's iPhone market share lagged far behind Samsung's even as India rose to become the world's third largest smartphone market.[56]

Increasingly, companies have to invest ever larger amounts for developing new technologies or products. As these investments rise, the time required to bring new generations of products to the market has increased, leaving less time for the commercialization of products before patents expire or new competitors come out with similar products. Companies have been forced to introduce new products rapidly to virtually all markets, including those in major developing countries. As a result, today the average time lag between domestic introduction and foreign introductions has diminished considerably. One year after being introduced in the United States, Vanilla Coke was expanded to more than 30 countries.[57]

WATERFALL VERSUS SPRINKLER STRATEGY Global marketers must determine whether a waterfall strategy (staggering commercialization of new products across countries) is preferable to a sprinkler strategy (simultaneously introducing new products across countries). A waterfall strategy allows marketers to learn from their experiences in some countries before attempting to market their new products in other countries. A sprinkler strategy, which involves a global launch of a product or service in many different markets, is best to preempt competition that would steal new ideas.

When choosing between the two strategies, global marketers should consider whether consumers across the globe will be inclined to adopt the new product at the same rate. Deepa Chandrasekaran and Gerard Tellis studied the adoption of 16 new products across 31 countries and concluded that the adoption time of some products was similar across countries. These products include many "fun products" such as hand-held computers, video-game players and digital cameras. However, the time consumers took to adopt other products varied across countries, particularly when the product was associated with more culture-bound categories such as food. For example, rice cookers were adopted faster in Japan than in Germany.[58]

Global launches are not without their challenges. When DHL Worldwide Express rolled out a new supply-chain solution for its high-tech customers, 30 staff members from around the world engaged in what was described as a grueling process.[59] When Avon planned a worldwide launch of a new lipstick on a single day, the plan was later abandoned for fear that the product would not be available in all the markets by the appointed day.[60] Global launches are easier conceived than implemented.

Conclusion

To be successful in global markets, companies often need to be flexible in product and service offerings. Although a product may be very successful in a firm's home market, environmental differences between markets can often force a company to make unexpected or costly changes. A small group of products may be marketed worldwide without significant changes, but most companies will find that global success depends on a willingness to adapt to local market requirements.

Global marketers must seek the best balance between standardizing products and services and adapting them to specific markets. Understanding different national markets and planning early for the necessary adaptations these markets will require enables firms to develop new products that can be commercialized quickly in many markets. Well-planned international integration of product development results in the creation of more successful global products.

Managerial Takeaways

1. *There will always be tradeoffs between standardizing products and services worldwide and adapting them to local markets.*
2. *Whenever possible, global marketers should seek to achieve the best of both worlds—locally tailored products that capture many of the advantages of standardization. But this takes forethought.*
3. *Global marketers should think about how a new product will be adapted even as the product is being developed.*
4. *High R&D costs and savvy global competitors make speed to market—or more importantly, speed to many national markets—important to successful global rollouts.*
5. *Global launches allow less time for competitors to copy new products and services, but they are incredibly difficult to administer within a large MNC.*
6. *Increasingly, headquarters and subsidiaries must work together to develop products and services for the global market.*

Questions for Discussion

1. Compare probable product adaptations for consumer products versus high-tech industrial products. What differences exist? Why?
2. American fast food, music and movies have become popular around the world with little product adaptation, whereas U.S. retailers, banks and beer companies have had to adapt their products more to global markets. Why?
3. What, in your opinion, will be the future for global products?
4. What is the impact of a loss of lead-market position in several industries for U.S.-based corporations?
5. If you were to test market a new consumer product today for worldwide introduction, how would you select test countries for Europe, Asia and Latin America?

CASE 10.1   Making Products Ethical

As global competition increases, consumers demand quality products at cheap prices. To lower costs, many MNCs have moved production to developing countries. Much of this manufacturing is outsourced to local contractors. However, many consumers are increasingly factoring ethical, as well as economic, concerns into their buying decisions. To meet these new concerns, firms must now ensure that no products are produced in sweatshops where workers are underage, overworked or beaten.

Consumer concern over products made in sweatshops exploded when activists embarrassed famous brands with exposés of working conditions abroad. Key targets were Wal-Mart stores and Nike shoes. Student protests ensued, and consumer boycotts proved costly to the firms. In the United States, a White House task force was established, including consumer activists and industry representatives, to suggest codes of conduct for overseas production. The task force even considered allowing complying firms to label their products "not made in sweatshops."

Mattel and Disney are two companies that have adopted codes of conduct and attempt to enforce them. Mattel hired an independent panel to monitor its subcontractors and is considered by many to be a model for others. Social auditors visit factories where Mattel toys are made three times a year. Disney has completed over 10,000 overseas inspections and has cut off subcontractors that failed to make improvements.

Even high-tech firms are concerned about ethical suppliers after a major watchdog group alleged dire working conditions at overseas factories supplying the computer industry. After auditing its suppliers, Hewlett-Packard asked one supplier to decrease the noise in its factories. The supplier complied, spending tens of thousands of dollars to amend machinery and supplying workers with top-of-the-line ear protectors. Workers then complained that their ears got too hot.

In fact, a new industry of social auditing emerged practically overnight. Companies hurried to become certified under the new global standard in ethical production—Social Accountability (SA) 8000. Both nongovernmental agencies operating in developing countries and major international auditing firms became involved in overseeing firm compliance to the new standard. In a single year, PricewaterhouseCoopers conducted 15,000 inspections related to SA 8000 in the Chinese province of Guangdong alone.

Nike formed a labor practices department and supplied Global Alliance, a Baltimore-based activist group, with a $7.9 million grant to study social problems in its contracted factories. The company released a report identifying widespread problems among its Indonesian subcontractors. Major concerns dealt with limited medical care and forced overtime. Sexual molestation was widespread in a workplace environment where female workers accounted for over 84 percent of the workforce. Nearly 14 percent of interviewed workers reported witnessing physical abuse, especially when managers were under pressure to meet production goals. Nike, with six full-time staff in Indonesia for labor practices alone, was poised to respond to the findings. However, the company noted that it had far more leverage over its shoe subcontractors, who often worked exclusively for Nike. Its clothing subcontractors were a different story. Those local firms often worked for a dozen different companies.

Gap released a report admitting problems with working conditions in many of the 3,000 factories that produced Gap clothing. Ten to 25 percent of factories in China and Taiwan were found to use psychological coercion or verbal abuse. More than 50 percent of factories in sub-Saharan Africa violated safety procedures. Ninety percent of factories applying for contracts failed the retailer's initial evaluation. Gap also pulled 50 percent of its orders placed with one of its 200 Indian suppliers because the company determined that children were working in squalid conditions.

Labor-rights groups applaud this new openness on the part of the companies, but not everyone is happy. A trade minister of India insisted that reports of child labor in his country were overblown by activists determined to make India look bad. Managers of plants in developing countries that produce products for the global brands complain that the MNCs pay such low prices that it is virtually impossible to guarantee workers better conditions.

MNCs also set rigid deadlines. If a vendor company can't meet the deadline, it has no option but to re-outsource to yet another producer. This further complicates control within the system. Re-outsourcing was the reason why products made for Wal-Mart and Zara were found at the scene of a deadly fire at a textile factory in Bangladesh. The MNCs had no idea their products were being produced at that factory. Wal-Mart responded by declaring a "zero tolerance policy" that forbade re-outsourcing by any of their vendors.

A poll of Americans taken after that tragic fire revealed that 30 percent of Americans said that buying clothes made under safe working conditions was very important to them, but another 30 percent said it wasn't important to them. All Americans have become used to cheap clothing. In 1987, apparel accounted for 5.4 percent of all personal consumption in the United States. Twenty-five years later, the percentage had dropped to 3.2. Over the past 27 years, clothing prices have risen only 17 percent while the overall consumer price index rose 112 percent.

While most concern for ethical sourcing has focused on labor practices, there is also concern about environmental sustainability. Environmentalists have become concerned with the fact that palm-oil consumption is soaring worldwide and that palm-oil plantations have been responsible for mass deforestation in countries such as Malaysia and Indonesia. Unilever is the world's largest buyer of palm oil. The company uses the oil to produce a number of products such as Dove soap and Flora margarine. Unilever announced that it was establishing a system to trace the source of all the palm oil it buys, although the many sources will make this task difficult.

Discussion Questions

1. What can global firms do to make their products more socially acceptable?
2. What do you think they should do? Why?
3. What are the costs to global firms of keeping their products sweatshop-free?
4. What are the possible costs of not complying with SA 8000?
5. What ethical issue is more important to you—labor conditions or environmental sustainability? Why?

Sources: "Making Products Ethical," in Kate Gillespie and H. David Hennessey, *Global Marketing* (Mason, OH: Cengage, 2011), pp. 306–307; Syed Zain Al-Mahmood, Tripti Lahiri and Dana Mattioli, "Fire Warning Went Unheard," *Wall Street Journal*, December 11, 2012, p. B1; Shelly Banjo, "Wal-Mart Toughens Supplier Policies," Dow Jones Top North American Equity Stories, January 22, 2013; Shelly Banjo, "In a Bangladesh Factory," *Wall Street Journal*, October 4, 2013, p. B1; Tripti Lahiri and Christina Passariello, "Why Retailers Don't Know Who Sews Their Clothing," *Wall Street Journal Europe*, July 25, 2013, p. 10; Peter Evans, "Unilever to Verify Palm-Oil Suppliers," *Wall Street Journal*, November 13, 2013, p. B7; and Floyd Norris, "Era of Cheap Apparel May Be Ending in U.S.," *New York Times*, January 18, 2014, p. B3.

CASE 10.2   Launching Intuition

Estee Lauder is among the world's largest manufacturers and marketers of makeup, skincare and fragrance products. Its global reach is significant. Based in the United States, the company's overseas markets now account for the majority of its total sales. When Estee Lauder launched Intuition, its biggest new fragrance in five years, the new fragrance was allotted a record-breaking $30 million advertising budget. Lauder aimed for $100 million in sales in the first year, more than double the sales of most other new fragrances.

A typical launch of a Lauder fragrance began with its introduction in the United States. The product would then be introduced to overseas markets in six months to a year. In an unprecedented move, the launch of Intuition bypassed the United States. Instead, it was introduced in France and Britain in September, with a rollout to the rest of Europe, Asia and Latin America in October. Approximately 40 percent of sales of prestige fragrances take place in November and December. Only later would Intuition be introduced in the United States.

Estee Lauder owned five of the top ten women's fragrances sold at department stores across the United States. However, only one Lauder perfume, Pleasures, made the top ten in Europe. The U.S. fragrance market, especially for the premier lines sold in department stores, remained in a slump. For the past five years, sales had been flat or down each year. In Europe, the market had grown about 8 percent the previous year. Asia and Latin America were promising to be new growth markets that could further help balance a slowdown in the U.S. market.

Lauder had established creative divisions in Paris and Tokyo to develop products for local consumer needs. Intuition was the first collaborative effort between Lauder's U.S. and European development centers. Intuition's formula was lighter than the traditionally heavy European fragrances and was targeted at the younger woman (starting in her mid-twenties). It was marketed as Lauder's first fragrance with a European sensibility, although the company wanted Intuition eventually to be seen as a global fragrance. Some managers believed that future U.S. sales might even be improved if Intuition could be billed as previously "available only in Europe."

Discussion Questions

1.   What are possible reasons for the unconventional development and launch of Intuition?
2.   What difficulties might the company face with such a launch?

Sources: "Launching Intuition," in Kate Gillespie and H. David Hennessey, *Global Marketing* (Mason, OH: Cengage, 2011), p. 309; "Estee Lauder Trims Sales View as Growth Stalls," Dow Jones Global News Select, May 2, 2013; Elizabeth Paton, "Estee Lauder Sales Rise Despite Slowdown in Core Markets," *Financial Times*, October 31, 2013; and "Estee Lauder Results Top Expectation," Associate Press Newswires, May 2, 2014.

Notes

1   Lauren A.E. Schuker, "Plot Change," *Wall Street Journal Online*, August 2, 2010.
2   Sam Schechner, "C'est What? French TV in English," *Wall Street Journal Europe*, November 22, 2012.
3   Yasmine El-Rashidi, "D'oh! Arabized Simpsons Aren't Getting Many Laughs," *Wall Street Journal*, October 17, 2005, p. A42.

4   Amy Chozick, "Cold Stone Aims to Be Hip in Japan," *Wall Street Journal*, December 14, 2006, p. B10.

5   Carol Matlack, "Bordeaux Goes to the Lab," *Business Week*, April 9, 2007, p. 10.

6   Pierre Berthon, Leyland Pitt, Constantine S. Katsikeas and Jean Paul Berthon, "Virtual Services Go International: International Services in the Marketspace," *Journal of International Marketing*, vol. 7, no. 3 (1999), p. 96.

7   Peter Ford, "Need Software in, Say, Icelandic? Call the Irish," *Christian Science Monitor*, February 6, 2001, p. 1.

8   Sonya Misquitta, "Cadbury Redefines Cheap Luxury," *Wall Street Journal*, June 8, 2009, p. B4.

9   Erik German, "Morocco Loving the McArabia," *Global Post*, August 27, 2009.

10 Sarah Nassauer, "What's Selling Where, Pringle Chips," *Wall Street Journal*, April 24, 2013, p. D3.

11 Mike Esterl, "'King of Beers' Fizzling in U.S., Sets Goal of World Domination," *Wall Street Journal*, July 27, 2013, p. A1.

12 Geoffrey A. Fowler and Ramin Setoodeh, "Outsiders Get Smarter About China's Tastes," *Wall Street Journal*, August 5, 2004, p. B1.

13 Ford, "Need Software in, Say, Icelandic?"

14 Julie Jargon, "Kraft Reinvents Iconic Oreo to Win in China," *Wall Street Journal Asia*, May 1, 2008, p. 28

15 Arundhati Parmar, "Dependent Variable," *Marketing News*, September 16, 2002, p. 4.

16 Fowler and Setoodeh, "Outsiders Get Smarter About China's Tastes."

17 Deborah Ball, Sarah Ellison, Janet Adamy and Geoffrey A. Fowler, "Recipes Without Borders?" *Wall Street Journal*, August 19, 2004, p. A6.

18 Catherine Arnold, "Foreign Exchange," *Marketing News*, May 15, 2004, p. 13.

19 Antonio Regalado, "Marketers Pursue the Shallow-Pocketed," *Wall Street Journal*, January 26, 2007, p. B3.

20 Parmar, "Dependent Variable."

21 Deborah Ball, "Shelf Life," *Wall Street Journal*, March 22, 2007, p. A1.

22 Ellen Byron, "Emerging Ambitions," *Wall Street Journal*, July 16, 2007, p. A1.

23 Norihiko Shirouzu, "What Prosperity Has to Do with Price of Cars in China," *Wall Street Journal*, April 17, 2008, p. B1.

24 Cris Prystay, "Companies Market to India's Have-Littles," *Wall Street Journal*, June 5, 2003, p. B1.

25 Elisabeth Malkin, "Mexico Goes Top-Flight," *Business Week*, June 26, 2000.

26 Claudia Puig, "'Hannibal' Ignites Worldwide Controversy," *USA Today*, March 7, 2001, p. D06.

27 International Standards Organization website, www.iso.ch.

28 Trent Edison, "Heineken's New Design Sticks Its Neck Out," Brand Channel, December 7, 2010, www.brandchannel.com, accessed December 9, 2014.

29 John O'Neil, "Reducing Drug Overdoses, by Packaging," *New York Times*, May 29, 2001, p. 8.

30 Ford, "Need Software in, Say, Icelandic?"

31 Laurie Burkitt, "Wal-Mart Detentions Swept Up 37 People," *Wall Street Journal Online*, October 13, 2011.

32 Kathy Chen, "Cashmere Clothes to Undergo More FTC Monitoring," *Wall Street Journal*, May 4, 2001, p. B1.

33 J. Tsalikis and Walfried Lassar, "Measuring Consumer Perceptions of Business Ethical Behaviour in Two Muslim Countries," *Journal of Business Ethics*, vol. 89 no. 1 (2009), pp. 91–98.

34 Andria Cheng, "Costco Cracks Taiwan Market," *Wall Street Journal*, April 2, 2010, p. B5.

35 Paul Mozur, "Apple's Chief: We're Sorry," *Wall Street Journal*, April 2, 2013, p. B1.

36 Nadya Masidlover and Laurie Burkitt, "L'Oreal Pulls Its Garnier Brand from China," *Wall Street Journal*, January 9, 2014, p. B8.

37 David Twiddy, "Payless ShoeSource Opens in Middle East," Associated Press Newswires, March 31, 2009.

38 Dana Mattioli, "Tupperware's Beautiful Plan," *Wall Street Journal*, April 6, 2012, p. B2.

39 Laurie Burkitt, "L'Oreal Adds a Chinese Brand to Global Kit," *Wall Street Journal*, April 15, 2014, p. B3.

40 Cheng, "Costco Cracks Taiwan Market."

41 Lee Hawkins, Jr., "New Driver," *Wall Street Journal*, October 6, 2004, p. A1.

42 Bruce Orwall, "Can Grinch Steal Christmas Abroad?" *Wall Street Journal*, November 16, 2000, p. B1

43 Jason Bush, "Mouse Ears Over Moscow," *Business Week*, June 11, 2007, p. 42.

44 Julie Jargon, "Asia Delivers for McDonalds," *Wall Street Journal Asia*, December 14, 2011, p. 24.

45 Leslie Kwoh, "Boss Talk," *Wall Street Journal*, December 26, 2012, p. B5.

46 Lee Chyen Yee, "China Tops U.S., Japan to Become Top Patent Filer," Reuters, December 21, 2011.

47 Kathy Chen and Jason Dean, "Low Costs, Plentiful Talent Make China a Global Magnet for R&D," *Wall Street Journal*, March 13, 2006, p. A1.

48 Kasra Ferdows, "Making the Most of Foreign Factories," *Harvard Business Review*, 75 (March–April 1997), pp. 73–88.

49 Nandini Lakshman, "Here Come the Bride Sites," *Business Week*, November 6, 2006, p. 42.

50 Julie Jargon, "General Mills Tries to Convince Americans to Cook Chinese," *Wall Street Journal*, May 29, 2007, p. B1.

51 Rajneesh Narula and Geert Duysters, "Globalisation and Trends in International R&D Alliances," *Journal of International Management*, vol. 10 (2004), p. 213.

52 "Airlines Move Toward Buying Planes in Alliances," *Dow Jones Business News*, May 19, 2003.

53 Tim R.V. Davis and Robert B. Young, "International Marketing Research: A Management Briefing," *Business Horizons*, March–April 2002, pp. 31–38.

54 "Move Over, Myspace; Korean Social Site Targets U.S. Teenagers," *Marketing News*, September 15, 2006, pp. 52–53.

55 Marian Beise and Thomas Cleff, "Assessing the Lead Market Potential of Countries for Innovation Projects," *Journal of International Management*, vol. 10 (2004), pp. 453–477.

56 Amol Sharma and Jessica E. Lessin, "In India, iPhone Lags Far Behind," Dow Jones Top North American Equities Stories, February 28, 2013.

57 Chad Terhune, "Coca-Cola Posts 11% Increase in Profit," *Wall Street Journal*, July 18, 2003, p. B2.

58 Deepa Chandrasekaran and Gerard J. Tellis, "Global Takeoff of New Products: Culture, Wealth, or Vanishing Differences?" *Marketing Science*, vol. 27, no. 5 (September–October, 2008), pp. 844–860.

59 "DHL and EXE Begin Global Roll-Out," Business Wire, February 13, 2002.

60 Nanette Byrnes, "Panning for Gold in Local Markets," *Business Week*, September 18, 2000, p. 54.

Chapter 11

Global Strategies for Services, Brands and Social Marketing

MARKETING SERVICES GLOBALLY 342

BRANDING DECISIONS 347

TRADEMARKS AND BRAND PROTECTION 354

SOCIAL MARKETING IN THE GLOBAL CONTEXT 360

Hewlett-Packard corporation wins a US$3 billion contract to manage Procter & Gamble's global IT services.[1] The head of Microsoft's Russian operations lectures her employees on the value of intellectual property and exhorts them not to buy counterfeit products.[2] In Kenya, a local office of Care International promotes behavioral changes that will decrease diarrheal diseases.[3]

In Chapter 10, we discussed the global implications of products, product lines and product development. In this chapter we examine issues related specifically to services marketing, global brands and brand protection. In addition, we explore the role of social marketing in the international arena. Although many of the issues covered in Chapter 10 apply to services as well, we begin this chapter by discussing what makes services different from physical products. We then illustrate how culture can affect a number of issues associated with services marketing. We continue with a discussion of the various implications of selecting brand names for international markets and present the pros and cons associated with global branding. The following section focuses on brand protection. We conclude by examining how global marketing can be extended to many aspects of social marketing.

Learning Objectives

After studying this chapter, you should be able to:

➤ describe ways in which marketing services differs from the international marketing of physical products;
➤ explain how culture can affect key aspects of services marketing;
➤ compare the advantages and disadvantages of using global brand names and using single-country brand names;
➤ differentiate between a global brand name and a global brand strategy;
➤ identify the strengths and weaknesses of global brands versus local brands;
➤ define private branding and explain why it is used by some international firms;
➤ differentiate among trademark preemption, counterfeiting and product piracy, and suggest ways in which firms can seek to minimize each of these;
➤ explain how global social marketing is similar to—and different from—the international marketing of products and services.

Marketing Services Globally

More than half of Fortune 500 companies are primarily service providers. The value of services produced in the world today now exceeds that of manufactured physical products, and international trade in services represents about 20 percent of total world trade.

Business Services

One of the largest categories of service exports is business services. These services are provided to firms, governments or other organizations and include communication services, financial services, software development, database management, construction, computer support, accounting, advertising, consulting and legal services. Many services are now aimed at multinational corporations (MNCs) themselves. For example, IBM's Global Services supplies MNCs with a variety of IT services, from running a customer's IT department to consulting on system upgrades and building global supply-chain management applications.

Some of the services that have been most successfully marketed abroad are financial services. Commercial banks such as Citibank, Chase and Bank of America have built such extensive branch networks around the world that foreign deposits and profits make up nearly half of business volume. Advertising agencies have also expanded overseas either by building branch networks or by merging with local agencies. Similarly, many U.S.-based marketing research firms have expanded into foreign countries.

International accounting services have experienced tremendous growth as well. Overseas expansion is important to U.S.-based accounting firms for several reasons. Among the leading accounting firms, international revenue typically exceeds domestic revenue. Revenue is growing more rapidly abroad, and margins are also better for international operations. Many of the firms' accounting clients have internationalized and demand that their accountants have a global presence as well.

The legal profession is also finding numerous opportunities overseas. Many U.S. law firms have opened up overseas branch locations, primarily in London, to capture business from investment banks and other financial services firms that must have a presence in both New York and London, major capital market centers. U.S. and British law firms have targeted the Japanese market since 2005, when Japan first allowed foreign law firms to hire Japanese lawyers, merge with Japanese firms and practice Japanese law.[4]

Trade in business services has traditionally taken place primarily among developed economies such as the United States, the Netherlands, France, Japan, the United Kingdom, Germany and Italy. However, service providers from developing countries are increasingly visible on the global stage. Forty-three of the top 225 international construction companies are Chinese firms that operate projects in 180 countries.[5]

Consumer Services

Marketing services to consumers abroad—such as gyms, cleaning services, restaurant chains and insurance policies—has also expanded. U.S.-based Kelley Blue Book entered the Chinese market in order to supply Chinese consumers with used-car pricing data.[6] Even health care has internationalized. Johns Hopkins, a premier American health care research hospital and service provider, has opened medical facilities in Dubai and Singapore.

However, marketing services to consumers may turn out to be more difficult than selling to businesses. Because consumer behavior and usage patterns usually differ more between countries than business usage patterns do, many services have to be adapted even more to local conditions to make them successful.

Since services have often been considered more culture bound than physical products, they have usually been located close to the consumer. Technological advances, however, have allowed many services, such as customer-support call centers, to be outsourced. Still, culture matters. When a consultant investigated Monterrey, Mexico as a possible call center location for the U.S. market, he went to a local shopping mall to test the service culture. He discovered short lines and friendly sales clerks who approached customers. Both signified high expectations of service. English speakers, American movies showing at the mall and sales clerks who spent their spring vacations in Texas further suggested that local employees would understood U.S. culture and service expectations.[7]

Back-Stage versus Front-Stage Standardization

Services differ from physical products in four key ways. They are *intangible*. They cannot be stored or readily displayed or communicated. Production and consumption of services are *simultaneous*. Services cannot be inventoried, and production lines do not exist to deliver standardized products of consistent quality. Therefore, delivered services are *heterogeneous* in nature. Finally, because services cannot be stored, they assume a *perishable* nature.[8]

These unique qualities of services affect their global marketing. Guaranteeing service quality worldwide is more difficult, and there are fewer opportunities to realize economies of scale with services than with physical products. Back-stage elements of services (planning and implementation aspects of services invisible to the customer) are easier to standardize cross-culturally than front-stage elements of services (aspects of service encounters visible to the customer).[9] For example, a fast-food provider such as McDonald's might standardize purchasing and inventory procedures, but its counter personnel in Saudi Arabia would still need to speak Arabic, and its seating design would need to accommodate separate areas for men and women.

Culture and the Service Experience

Culture affects a number of aspects of the service experience, including customer expectations and customer satisfaction, the waiting experience and the recruitment and behavior of service personnel.

Customer Expectations

Customers may exhibit different expectations concerning service levels. Department stores in Japan still employ women in kimonos to bow and greet customers as they arrive at the store. Service personnel are available and solicitous. In the United States, consumers tend to be willing to forgo high levels of service in favor of low prices. They are more accustomed to self-service and may even feel nervous in the presence of hovering salespeople. Consumers in Switzerland are delighted when their local grocer chooses the best produce for them. As regular customers from the neighborhood, they deserve the best. Of course, this means that new customers may be given the poorer produce. This would seem discriminatory and unfair to American customers. If residing in

Switzerland, they would prefer to drive to a hypermarket where produce is prepackaged and the service encounter can be avoided altogether.

Asian cultures traditionally expect and deliver high levels of service. While an American saying purports that "the consumer is always right," a similar saying in Japan states that "the customer is God."[10] Despite higher expectations of service, Asian business customers complain less when they receive poor service than do customers in the West.[11] One possible explanation is that customers in more collectivist cultures may tend to self-sacrifice and maintain self-discipline in order not to harm the relationship with the service provider. Alternatively, lack of complaining may be attributed to an attempt not to embarrass the service provider or cause a loss of face. However, dissatisfied customers are likely to voice dissatisfaction to other members in their reference group.[12] Customers in collectivist cultures may exhibit more loyalty and stay with a poor service provider longer than customers in a more individualistic culture, but their loyalty is not absolute. Given a lack of complaints, service providers can be caught unaware when these dissatisfied customers eventually leave.

The Waiting Experience

Time is always an aspect of services, and attitudes toward the time it takes to be served vary across cultures. For example, waiters in European restaurants take care not to hurry patrons. Eating a meal is supposed to be an enjoyable experience most often shared with friends. Servers also wait to be asked to deliver the bill for the meal; diners may wish to sit for hours. Americans would wonder what had happened to their waiter. Americans expect fast service at restaurants and like the bill to be dropped promptly on the table. What would be a good service experience for a European diner would be a bad one for an American.

Attitudes toward waiting in line vary as well. The English are famous for their orderly and patient waits in lines, or queues. In the French-speaking part of Switzerland, members of this otherwise polite population are likely to become a jostling mob when caused to wait at an entrance. Americans introduced the idea of establishing a single line leading to multiple service points instead of having separate lines for each point. This invention addressed the common American complaint that one inevitably ended up standing in the slowest-moving line. Americans have difficulty understanding why the rest of the world hasn't adopted this idea.

World Beat 11.1

Higher Education Internationalizes

Harvard University announced that it would expand its executive education offerings in China to address growing demand in that country. The Harvard Business School has already expanded to Europe and India, but China is likely to be the fastest growing market. In Singapore, Yale has joint-ventured with the national University of Singapore to establish a liberal arts college in one of Asia's major financial centers. It will be the first new college to bear Yale's name in 300 years.

Elite universities are not the only institutes of higher education that are attempting to internationalize. Faced with declining U.S. applications, for-profit schools that provide specialized professional education have expanded abroad as well. DeVry entered Brazil where public college education is technically free but where many Brazilians cannot gain access to the best schools due to limited spaces and difficult entrance examinations.

But internationalizing higher education presents challenges. Many believe that setting up overseas branches is a way for U.S. educational institutions to make money by charging the same tuition that they do in the United States while containing costs abroad by offering limited courses and hiring most instructors locally at lower pay. In China, the demand for executive education—even at high prices—appears to be insatiable. In India, however, many companies remain skeptical of high prices charged by the Harvard Business School. And several institutions discovered that even slimmed down operations proved unsustainable in Singapore after government incentives expired. Apparently there were just not enough students willing to pay U.S. prices for an American education located in Asia.

Furthermore, academic freedom may mean different things in different cultures. In Singapore, protests are only allowed at a speaker's corner in a Singapore park. No organized political protests are allowed on Yale's Singapore campus. In Abu Dhabi, several foreign research institutions were shut down after the Arab Spring for fear of their spreading politically threatening foreign ideas. Limits on freedoms abroad have been controversial with faculty back home.

Sources: Joe Light, "Harvard Works at China, India," *Wall Street Journal*, November 4, 2010, p. B10; Paulo Trevisani, "Brazil Welcomes For-Profit Schools," *Wall Street Journal*, June 27, 2011, p. B7; Anna Kamenetz, "Should Top U.S. Colleges Expand Overseas?" *Newsweek*, March 19, 2013; and Paul Hockenos, "Academic Values Often Give Way as Universities Expand Overseas," *The Chronicle of Higher Education*, April 15, 2014.

In certain parts of the world, social norms may require that men and women stand in different lines. This can be observed at metro stops in Mexico City during rush hours. In Egypt, the imported design of having an "in" line leading to a service point and an exit leading away from it was reinterpreted as one line for men and one for women, with each line alternately taking its turn at the service point.

Service Personnel

When the local manager of a U.S.-based hotel chain was preparing to open a new hotel in Egypt, he was faced with a dilemma. American tourists would expect waitresses who could take their order in English. Egyptian women who spoke English almost invariably came from the upper classes. No young lady from those classes would be caught in public serving food to strangers. In a panic, the manager called friends and family and finally borrowed enough sisters, daughters and nieces to staff the restaurant in time for opening day. Within a week, one waitress met and married a Saudi multimillionaire who came to eat at the restaurant. Whether apocryphal or not, the story spread like wildfire, and the manager never again had trouble recruiting waitresses!

In many cultures, such as the Middle East, working in a service occupation is often considered akin to being a servant. This social stigma can make it hard to recruit qualified personnel for some positions, especially those that require higher levels of education as well as technical and interpersonal skills. Until relatively recently, stewardesses for many airlines from the Middle East had to be imported from Europe, and nursing has never achieved the same status in the Middle East as it has in the West. Men as well as women feel the stigma. It is not uncommon for well-paid technical repairmen, such as those who work in the air-conditioning industry, to dress in a suit and tie and carry their tools in a briefcase.

Therefore, companies can experience difficulties in hiring employees that share core organizational values when they leave their home country. Disney had no trouble re-creating the "Happiest Place on Earth" when transferring its Disneyland concept to Tokyo. Japanese cultural norms of safety, cleanliness and customer service are a natural fit with Disney's company ethos. But success at Disneyland Paris proved far more elusive. French citizens and potential employees highly value individuality and freedom of expression and have found Disney's human resource policies to be restrictive and invasive.[13]

Service personnel are critical for the delivery of services. Since properly trained professionals may be difficult to find in some countries, multinational service firms may need to exert greater effort to recruit and train employees. However, many MNCs gain a recruiting advantage by offering salaries in excess of local competition.

Branding Decisions

Whether marketing products or services, global firms must manage and defend the value of their brands. Brands provide a name or symbol that gives a product (or service) credibility and helps the consumer identify the product. A brand that consumers know and trust helps them make choices faster and more easily. A globally recognized brand name can be a huge asset even when a firm enters new markets. For example, when McDonald's opened its doors in Johannesburg, South Africa, thousands of people stood in line. When Coke entered Poland, its red and white delivery trucks drew applause at traffic lights.[14]

Interbrand Corporation ranks the top global brands annually. Their methodology estimates the net present value of future sales of the brand taking into consideration factors such as market leadership, stability and global reach—the brand's ability to cross geographical and cultural borders. Furthermore, all brands must be global in nature—at least a third of brand revenues must be derived outside the firm's domestic market. The top global brands are dominated by U.S. brands, followed by European brands, although a number of Asian companies such as Toyota, Honda, Sony and Samsung have built strong global brands.

Selecting Brand Names

Brand name and symbol selection is critical. Global marketers must carefully evaluate the meanings and word references in the languages of their target audiences. Can the name be pronounced easily, or will it be distorted in the local language? A good example of brand adaptation is the name choice for Coca-Cola, which means "tasty and happy" in Chinese. Mercedes-Benz's Chinese name means "striving forward fast," and Sharp's means "the treasure of sound." However, branding in Asia, and especially in China, may rely even more on the visual appeal of logos than on brand names.

Single-Country versus Global Brand Names

Global marketers are constantly confronted with the decision of whether the brand name needs to be universal. Brands such as Coca-Cola and Kodak, however, do not change names from one country to another. With worldwide travel so common, many companies believe they should only choose brand names that can be used in all markets.

However, using the same name worldwide is not always desirable. In such instances, different names have to be found. Procter & Gamble had successfully marketed its household cleaner, Mr. Clean, in the United States for some time. This name, however, had no meaning except in countries using the English language. This prompted the company to arrive at several adaptations abroad, such as *Monsieur Propre* in France and *Meister Proper* in Germany. In all cases, however, the brand's trademark, a symbol of the genie with gleaming eyes, was retained because it evoked similar responses across cultures. Google also opted for a local name for the Chinese market. Its new name, *Gu Ge*, means Harvest Song in Chinese. Before the change, some Chinese citizens had dubbed the company Gougou (doggy) or Gugou (old hound).[15]

Sometimes a change of name reflects a change of brand positioning abroad. In India where doughnuts are an unfamiliar food, Dunkin' Donuts chose to call their store Dunkin' Donuts & More to highlight a range of foods that included ciabatta sandwiches and savory croissants.[16] In other markets where the company positions itself not as a donut shop but as a competitor to Starbucks, the brand name is simply shortened to Dunkin'.

Selecting a Global Name

Selecting appropriate brand names on a global basis is substantially more complex than deciding on a brand name for just one country. Typically, a brand name is rooted in a given language and, if used elsewhere, may have either a different meaning or none at all. Ideally, marketers look for brand names that evoke similar emotions or images around the world.

In addition, a global brand name should not convey negative images in any market where it might be sold. There are dozens of stories about companies using a global name with negative or offensive meanings in another language. For example, a global construction equipment company marketed one piece of equipment as the Grab Bucket to describe its use in English. The company was surprised to discover that in Germany the name was interpreted to mean the sale of cemetery flowers since grab was interpreted as grave and bucket as bouquet.[17]

Given the almost unlimited possibilities for names and the restricted opportunities to find and register a desirable one, international companies now devote considerable effort to the selection process. Some consulting companies specialize in finding brand names with worldwide application. These companies bring citizens of many countries together and, under the guidance of a specialist, they are asked to state names in their particular language that would combine well with the product to be named. Speakers of other languages can immediately react if a name comes up that sounds unpleasant or has distasteful connotations in their language. After a few such sessions, the consultants may accumulate as many as 1,000 names that will later be reduced to 500 by a company linguist. The client company then is asked to select 50 to 100 names for further consideration. At this point, the names are subjected to a search procedure to determine which have not been registered in any of the countries under consideration. In the end, only about ten names may survive this process. From these, the company will have to make the final selection. Although this process may be expensive, the cost is generally considered negligible compared with the advertising expenditures invested in the brand name over many years.

Changing Brand Names

Because many MNCs internationalize via acquisitions, they often acquire local brands. At times, firms may choose to change the name of an acquired brand in the local market or even worldwide. This is not an easy choice. If a product has substantial market share in one or more markets, changing its name can confuse or even alienate consumers.

Colgate-Palmolive, the large U.S.-based toiletries manufacturer, purchased the leading toothpaste brand in Southeast Asia, "Darkie." With a minstrel in blackface as its logo, the product had been marketed by a local company since 1920. After the acquisition, however, Colgate-Palmolive came under pressure from many groups in the United States to use a less offensive brand name. The company sponsored a large amount of research to find both a brand name and a logo that were racially inoffensive and yet close enough to the original to be recognized quickly by consumers. The company changed the name to "Darlie" after an exhaustive search. Still, in some markets where the "Darkie" brand had as much as 50 percent market share, it was a substantial marketing challenge to keep brand loyalty intact through the change to the new name.[18]

China's Lenovo experienced a similar challenge. It saw its global market share shrink after it bought the PC division of IBM and proceeded to substitute the Lenovo brand for the IBM brand. The company had successfully negotiated for the rights to use the IBM name for five years after the acquisition. However, Lenovo's later decision to drop the IBM name prematurely hurt sales outside China.[19]

While many decisions to change a brand name are instigated by acquisitions, some name changes are undertaken to better reflect a company's growing international presence. Federal Express launched its courier business in the United States in the 1970s. The Federal Express name reflected the U.S. overnight delivery service. As Federal Express opened its international operations, however, the name was a problem. In Latin America *federal* connoted corrupt police, and in Europe the name was linked to the former Federal Republic of Germany. Therefore, Federal Express changed its name to FedEx, which in some cases is used as a verb meaning "to ship overnight."[20] Because FedEx dealt with many MNCs as clients, it wanted a single name to use globally.

Global Brand Strategies

McDonald's is the world's largest fast-food restaurant and operates in 119 countries. It is ranked among the top ten on Interbrand's list of best global brands. But the positioning of the brand (and how it is perceived) varies across the globe. In the United States, McDonald's represents convenience in a family-friendly environment. In India, where adaptations make McDonald's offerings affordable to even the lower classes, the brand connotes value for money. In other parts of Asia, the chain is viewed as a trendy rendezvous for teenagers and young adults.[21]

The concept of global branding goes beyond simply establishing a global brand name. Yet experts disagree on what exactly makes a global brand. Is it global presence or global name recognition? There are certainly brand names such as Coca-Cola that are well known in most countries of the world. Does the name connote similar attributes worldwide? Is the product the same? Is the brand a powerful player in all major markets? Heineken qualifies on the first two conditions, but not on the third. It has positioned itself as a quality imported beer in its many export markets. The beer and the bottle remain the same across markets. However, its lack of adaptation has kept it a well-known but minor player in the various national markets.

As we have noted, Interbrand defines a global brand as one with at least a third of sales outside the firm's domestic market. Other definitions are less encompassing, describing global brands as brands whose positioning, advertising strategy, personality, look and feel are in most respects the same in all countries.[22] Firms that develop global brands with these characteristics are said to follow a global brand strategy.

Several steps are involved in developing and administering a global brand strategy:

1. A firm must identify common customer needs worldwide and determine how the global brand can deliver both functional and emotional benefits to these customers.
2. A process must be established to communicate the brand's identity to consumers, channels and the firm's own employees.
3. There should be a way to track the success of the global identity of the brand, such as the customer opinion surveys.
4. The firm must determine whether it will follow a more centralized, top-down approach to global branding or a more gradual, bottom-up approach.

Top-Down and Bottom-Up Approaches

Sony and Mobil take top-down approaches wherein a global management team determines the global brand strategy and then country strategies are derived from it. In a bottom-up approach, country strategies are grouped by similarities in such variables as the level of economic development and the competitive situation (whether or not the brand is dominant in the market). Common elements are first identified within these groupings. Over time, a more global strategy emerges as subsidiaries share experiences and best practices.[23]

THE BRAND CHAMPION   In any case, a brand champion should be given the responsibility for building and managing a global brand. This should include monitoring the brand across markets, as well as authorizing the use of the brand on other products and businesses (brand extensions). The brand champion can be a senior manager at corporate headquarters, a product development group or the manager of a lead country or one with major market share for the brand. For example, Unilever at one time gave its French subsidiary custody over its Lipton brand.[24]

Hybrid Brand Strategies

For many MNCs, global branding offers a way to cut costs and present a consistent customer communication about the brand. Some of the original enthusiasm for global branding has abated, however, as consumers in different countries reject brands they judge as resulting from least-common-denominator thinking. MNCs have responded with more hybrid brand strategies, through which they attempt to combine the quality improvements and cost savings of backstage activities such as technology, production and organization with elements more tailored to local tastes such as adapting product features, distribution and promotion.[25]

Consumer Response to Global Brands

To better understand what consumers worldwide thought of global brands, Douglas Holt, John Quelch and Earl Taylor conducted the Global Brands Study. This study utilized both qualitative and quantitative research design and incorporated responses from 3,300 consumers in 41 countries.[26] The researchers concluded that consumers evaluate global brands on three key dimensions:

➤ **Quality signal** Consumers observe the fierce competitive battles among global brands over quality. Global brands become a cue for quality. Forty-four percent of brand preference was explained by this dimension.

➤ **Global myth** Global brands are symbols of cultural ideals relating to modernity and a cosmopolitan identity. A focus-group participant in the Global Brands Study opined, "Local brands show what we are; global brands show what we want to be." Another participant remarked, "Global brands make us feel like citizens of the world."[27] Twelve percent of brand preference was explained by this dimension.

➤ **Social responsibility** Because the firms behind global brands are perceived to have extraordinary power and influence, consumers expect these companies to address social problems—a demand that local firms can more easily dodge. For example, local companies would not be asked to address global warming, but multinational energy companies such as BP and Shell would be. Eight percent of brand preference was explained by this dimension.

The research team went on to identify four global segments based on these three dimensions of global brands:

➤ **Global citizens** These consumers rely on the success of a global brand to identify products of quality and innovation. However, they also expect MNCs to behave responsibly on issues such as workers' rights and the environment. This segment was the largest in the study and accounted for 55 percent of respondents. Global citizens were less common in Britain and the United States but more common in Brazil, China and Indonesia.

➤ **Global dreamers** This segment was the second largest in the study—23 percent of respondents. These consumers both equate global brands with quality and are attracted by the lifestyle they portray. However, these consumers are less concerned with social issues relating to MNCs. Another study confirmed the importance of the global dreamer segment. It reported that many young consumers in Romania, Russia, Ukraine and the United States viewed themselves as part of the global world and therefore preferred global brands across product categories.[28]

➤ **Antiglobals** This segment—about 13 percent of respondents—is skeptical of the quality of global brands as well as the MNCs who own them. They prefer to buy local and avoid global brands. This segment is relatively more common in Britain and China and relatively less common in Egypt and South Africa.

➤ **Global agnostics** This segment judges global brands and local brands by the same criteria and is neither impressed nor alienated by the fact that a brand is global. At about 8 percent of respondents, global agnostics' numbers are relatively high in the United States and South Africa but lower in Japan, Indonesia, China and Turkey.

Despite the existence of antiglobals and global agnostics, a later study found that global brands tend to evoke positive feelings overall. This positive halo effect was present among both pro-global and antiglobal respondents. The researchers concluded that despite the fact that some people voice negative attitudes toward global brands, there may still be something emotionally appealing about a brand that is widely recognized and available and is basically the same across markets.[29]

Pan-Regional Branding

Although there may be few genuinely global brands, pan-regional branding is increasing in importance. In Latin America, Brazil's Varig Airlines undertook a design and logo change to broaden its regional appeal. The revamped Varig logo was modern and warm-looking, which supported an advertising program that featured well-rested passengers getting off their flights.[30] Similarly, the Shangri-La Hotel chain has built a strong regional brand across Asia. Shangri-La offers all the amenities of a luxury hotel, along with Asian hospitality. The staff uniforms reflect the local costumes. Shangri-La uses its advertising to appeal to executives in Asia, who are often judged by the hotels they choose.[31]

To create Asian brands, managers suggest employing a mix of cultural symbols from different Asian countries, which is what the travel portal Zuji did. Zuji means "footprint" in Mandarin Chinese. However, market research revealed that the name was perceived to be Japanese, evoking feelings of quality and trust. The colors chosen for the site were bright blue and green, typically Thai colors.[32]

Furthermore, a study of Asian branding concluded that firms seeking to create successful regional brands should capitalize on a newfound Asian pride and confidence. For example, younger Asian women consider Japan and South Korea to be more fashionable than France or America in terms of fashion or music. The study also suggested that Asian consumers feel more affinity to brands. Still, utilizing a Western connection can help Asian brands overcome any negative country of origin associations which may persist. Such Western connections can range from a brand history of success overseas to shooting part of a brand commercial in New York City.[33]

Eurobrands

In Europe, regional brands are called Eurobrands. In a survey of more than 200 European brand managers in 13 countries, 81 percent indicated that they were aiming for standardization and homogenization of brands, whereas only 13 percent said they were leaving each country free to decide its own strategy.[34] The survey clearly indicates a strong preference for a Eurobrand strategy for most companies operating in Europe. Examples of Eurobrands—products marketed across Europe with the same brand name, formula and packaging, as well as the same positioning and advertising strategy—include Procter & Gamble's Pampers and Head & Shoulders shampoo, Michelin tires and Rolex watches.

Global Brands versus Local Brands

The findings from the Global Brands Study raise questions as to the intrinsic value of global or regional brands compared with local brands. Despite a significant trend toward multinational brands, local brands still survive. In Belgium, Procter & Gamble tried to replace its leading local detergent Dash with its European-wide brand Ariel—it discontinued advertising for Dash. However, P&G soon saw its sales in detergents plummet, and it was forced to renew its support for Dash.[35]

A study of consumers in France, Germany, Italy and the United Kingdom further highlights what might be the countervailing power of local brands. Consumers reported that local brands possessed the same quality as that of global brands. Furthermore, local brands were deemed more reliable and thought to deliver more value for money.[36] In fact, the global reach of a MNC's major brands will vary by brand. Some brands may be sold in only one or two countries, while others are sold in many more. Table 11.1 illustrates the global reach of selected brands owned by Mondelez International.

Table 11.1 Mondelez International Global Reach of Selected Brands

Chewing Gum

Dentyne: Canada, United States

Halls: Brazil, Canada, Mexico, Spain, Thailand, Ukraine, United States

Hollywood: France

Trident: Brazil, Canada, Mexico, Spain, United States

Chocolate

Alpen Gold: Poland, Russia, Ukraine

Cadbury Dairy Milk: Australia, Canada, India, Ireland, New Zealand, United Kingdom

Côte d'Or: Belgium, Canada, France, Germany, Italy, Middle East, Netherlands, United Kingdom, United States

Kent: Turkey

Toblerone: Australia, Denmark, France, Germany, Middle East, Netherlands, Philippines, Spain, Sweden, Switzerland, United Kingdom, United States

Coffee

Carte Noire: France, Ireland, Poland, Russia, Ukraine, United Kingdom

Grand Mere: France

Jacobs: Austria, Baltics, Czech Republic, Germany, Greece, Hungary, Poland, Romania, Russia, Slovakia, Switzerland, Turkey, Ukraine

Kenco: Ireland, United Kingdom

Cookies/Biscuits

Barni: Russia, Ukraine, Poland

Bis: Brazil

Chips Ahoy!: Brazil, Canada, China, Ecuador, Mexico, Philippines, Portugal, Puerto Rico, Spain, United States, Venezuela

Nilla: Canada, United States

Oreo: Argentina, Australia, Canada, China, Indonesia, Mexico, Peru, Poland, Puerto Rico, Netherlands, Romania, Russia, Spain, Taiwan, Thailand, Ukraine, United States, Venezuela

Trakinas: Argentina, Brazil, China

Source: Mondelez International; Brand Family at www.mondelezinternational.com (accessed March 28, 2014).

Although evidence indicates that local brands remain powerful in the United States and Europe, there is also evidence that local brands can be competitive in developing countries as well. Global brands were especially attractive to consumers in Russia and former Soviet satellite states during the late 1990s. More recently there appears to be a backlash against global brands, as many consumers possibly become disenchanted with their higher prices and the sometimes monopolization of markets by such brands. Nostalgia for local brands has motivated MNCs to resurrect local brands. Kraft bought the traditional Hungarian candy bar, Sport Szelet, and marketed it complete with its 50-year-old package design. Unilever followed suit with the traditional Baba personal-care brand.[37]

When asked whether they preferred a local or a global brand for products of identical price and quality, Chinese consumers preferred global brands for home electronics and were evenly split between local and global brands when it came to clothes. However, they overwhelmingly preferred local brands for food, toiletries and household items. Not surprisingly, when France's packaged-foods company Danone bought Chinese companies, it continued to sell products under their original Chinese brands. Today the majority of Danone's sales in China are credited to these Chinese brands.

Still, it is not all bad news for global brands. Surveys conducted in various developing countries suggest that across product categories, a well-known Western brand name increases perceived quality of the product or service. For specific product categories, global brands associated with a Western country of origin enjoy an additional benefit, as customers in developing countries relate their product with an enhanced social status.[38] Thus the controversy surrounding local and global brands continues.

Private Branding

The practice of private branding, or supplying products to another party for sale under that party's brand name, has become quite common in many markets. The Japanese company, Ricoh (now a global leader in small personal copiers and fax machines), once operated as a contract manufacturer for more established firms and used private branding to gain market access in Europe and the United States. Today many Chinese companies employ this strategy as a means to enter export markets.[39]

Private branding offers particular advantages to a company with strong manufacturing skills but little access to or experience with foreign markets. With control over marketing in the hands of another manufacturer or distributor, the firm remains dependent and can only indirectly influence marketing. For long-term profitability, companies often find that they need to spend the money to create brand equity, which requires promoting and selling products under their own brands. Changing from being a supplier to becoming a global brand power-house is not easy, however. In the 40 years since Asia emerged as a major manufacturing center, only a few companies have been successful in establishing world-class brands—among them Sony and Canon from Japan and Samsung from South Korea. Many Asian manufacturers still lack marketing departments and suffer from a lack of experience in direct selling to overseas retailers.[40]

Trademarks and Brand Protection

Violations of trademarks—the names, words and symbols that enable customers to distinguish among brands—have been an inescapable problem for global marketers.

Trademark Preemption

Britain's Imperial Tobacco Group PLC, the world's fourth largest cigarette maker, was planning to build a $70 million factory in Indonesia to produce its premier Davidoff cigarettes. But Sumatra Tobacco, a local company that specialized in claiming famous trademarks, already owned the Davidoff name in Indonesia. In total, this local company had registered 201 famous trademarks in Indonesia, including Chanel and Remy Martin. Sumatra Tobacco not only made products associated with the famous brands but applied the brands to product extensions as well—such as their Rolex cigarettes which Sumatra Tobacco sold in China.[41]

Incidents such as the one described above involve the legal hijacking or preemption of a brand name. For example, someone could register the Gucci brand name in a country where Gucci had yet to register its brands. If Gucci wanted to enter that market, it would have to buy back its brand name or sell under another. Trademark preemption is especially easy in countries that do not require that the brand be sold in the market after registration.

International Treaties to Prevent Preemption

International treaties to protect well-known international brands from being preempted in local markets go back to the Paris Convention of 1883. However, problems can arise even in signatory countries. Claiming its rights under the Paris Convention, Gucci fought two cases in Mexico against infringing firms. It won one case but lost the other. In the latter case, the Mexican judge was not convinced that the Mexican government had even ratified the Paris Convention more than 100 years before.

Today, the Paris Convention has been superseded by trademark protection rules under the WTO. Countries that join the WTO must establish national laws that protect global brands. Depending on a country's level of economic development, it may be allowed up to 11 years to bring its local laws into compliance.

Persistent Problems with Preemption

The norms established by the WTO are no doubt a step in the right direction, but problems still persist. Many newly industrialized countries, including Taiwan and South Korea, had already established local laws on a par with those of developed countries by the time they joined the WTO. However, a lack of resources undermined the ability of such countries to enforce these laws adequately.[42] Although the countries of the former Soviet bloc have adopted trademark protection laws in accordance with WTO guidelines, the enforcement of these laws also remains problematic. There have been concerns that Russian judges and prosecutors don't understand the nature of Russia's newly adopted trademark laws—although the laws look good on paper. The U.S.-based tobacco company Philip Morris lost a case it brought in an effort to stop a Russian company from producing cigarettes whose packaging closely resembled that of two of Philip Morris's best-selling brands. Grupo Modelo, the Mexican beer company that makes Corona, also lost a trademark dispute with a Russian brewery that Modelo accused of stealing its brand name.[43] Still, some headway is being made in Asia. Starbucks won a lawsuit in China against a coffee-shop chain whose Chinese name was nearly identical to Starbucks. Similarly, Honda won a case against a motorcycle manufacturer calling itself Hongda.[44]

Significant differences also persist in national trademark regimes despite moves to unify brand protection worldwide. In the United States, trademark rights usually extend to related goods and services. In China, this is not the case, and multiple registrations may be necessary to cover a firm's full product line.[45] Many, but not all, governments require that a trademark be used in their markets if it is to receive continued protection there. Starbucks registered its trademark in Russia but then let the trademark expire without using it in the Russian market. A local preemptor then registered the brand, since it was considered to be abandoned by its original owner. Starbucks retrieved the brand only after a prolonged legal battle.[46]

A final problem arises when two companies from different countries have legitimately used the same brand independently for years. Anheuser-Busch InBev was involved in trademark disputes in over 20 countries with Czech brewer Budejovicky Budvar. Each claimed the right to sell beer under the name *Budweiser*. AB InBev had already been forced to sell Budweiser under the name Bud in a number of major European markets such as France, Russia and Ukraine.[47] The problem was finally solved when the Czech company agreed to be acquired by AB InBev.

World Beat 11.2

McDonald's Versus McCurry

It was a blow to a global company whose strategy included targeting emerging markets in Asia. But in the eyes of many Malaysians, David just beat Goliath. Fast-food giant McDonald's tried to stop a family-owned restaurant in Malaysia from calling itself McCurry. An eight-year court battle ensued, but McCurry eventually won the right to keep its name.

McCurry serves traditional Indian and Malaysian dishes, and its owners argued that the different food served at their restaurant created no confusion between them and McDonald's. Furthermore, the McCurry name stood for Malaysian Chicken Curry, their signature dish. The company also noted that the prefix Mc was common in Scottish surnames, and it was unrealistic for McDonald's to lay claim to any brand name beginning with the prefix.

McDonald's consistently rates among the global top ten for most valuable global brand, best global brand and most respected company. No wonder McDonald's aggressively attempts to defend its brand. And despite its loss in Malaysia, an undaunted McDonald's fought another case of trademark infringement in nearby Indonesia. This time the global firm tried to stop a condiment maker from calling its curry McCurry. But McDonald's lost there as well. In the meantime, encouraged by its triumph in court, McCurry Malaysia was actively seeking partners to launch a chain of restaurants under the McCurry name.

Sources: "McDonald's to Chase Asia Growth," *Inside Retail Asia*, February 4, 2014; James Hookway, "McCurry Wins Big McAttack in Malaysia," *Wall Street Journal*, September 9, 2009, p. B5; Sarah Crawley-Boevey, "McDonald's Loses David and Goliath Battle Over Trademark," *Brand Republic*, September 14, 2009; "McDonald's Loses Second McCurry Case in Asia," ManagingIP.com, December 14, 2010; and McDonald's Awards & Recognition, www.aboutmcdonalds.com, accessed June 12, 2014.

Counterfeits and Piracy

Today, the biggest problem international marketers face in trying to protect their brands is counterfeiting. Counterfeiting is the illegal use of a registered trademark. A counterfeiter copies a branded product, cashing in on its brand equity. Thus counterfeiters injure legitimate businesses by stealing their brand equity. The World Customs Organization estimates that counterfeits account for nearly 10 percent of global merchandise trade.[48] It is estimated that many Fortune 500 firms spend from $2 to $10 million annually to combat counterfeit products.[49]

Consumers can be injured as well when they unwittingly buy counterfeits believing that they are buying the real product. This is particularly worrisome because counterfeits encompass far more than fashion items. For example, the U.S. government warned motorists that tens of thousands could have purchased counterfeit air bags. Since counterfeits usually do not mimic the quality or safety of the original product, they can fail to perform as expected. Counterfeit AC Delco brake pads last only half as long as the real thing. When Mitsubishi Elevator Company received a complaint from a customer concerning a new elevator that kept stopping between floors, the elevator turned out to be a counterfeit. One of the greatest consumer threats posed by global counterfeiting is the growth in counterfeit pharmaceuticals. The WHO notes that up to 10 percent of medicines worldwide are counterfeits.

The term piracy is often applied to the counterfeit production of copyrighted material such as books and computer software. Because illegal production—or more aptly, reproduction—of these products is relatively simple and inexpensive, they become easy targets. Recorded music has long suffered from piracy, and counterfeit music is believed to outsell legitimate music in many countries. In China, nearly all downloaded music is believed to be stolen. Chinese Internet search engines such as Baidu.com propagate this phenomenon by facilitating convenient downloads of pirated music.[50] Google China does not offer this service.[51] Some experts suggest that Google has paid dearly for this decision, controlling less than 3 percent of the search market, compared with 62 percent commanded by Baidu.[52]

DVDs are also a major target of pirates. Pirating DVDs once required a factory with disc-pressing equipment costing $1 million. As a result, the major players were Asian crime syndicates that could afford such an investment. Now the same technology that allows home-video buffs to "burn" their own DVDs is reshaping the competitive landscape of piracy—and threatening to make it even more costly to the motion picture industry. Piracy has now gone small and mobile, making counterfeiters harder for authorities to locate and crack down on. Hong Kong's authorities have shifted from looking for producers of counterfeits to shutting down the retailers that sell them. In a five-year period, such stores were cut from 1,000 to only 80.[53]

Counterfeiting of trademark-protected products flourishes in countries where legal protection of such trademarks is weak. China accounts for the production of about two-thirds of all counterfeits. Other problem countries include the Philippines, Russia, Ukraine, Brazil, Pakistan, Paraguay and Vietnam. In Vietnam, counterfeits thrive because the government has few resources to enforce existing laws effectively or control the borders. Some international consumer goods companies doing business in Vietnam claim their sales are reduced by as much as 50 percent by the ready availability of illegal, and cheaper, products. Procter & Gamble is believed to have lost sales of up to 25 percent as illegal operators collected its containers and refilled them with counterfeit products. The same happened to brand-name cognac and whiskies. Reused bottles were filled with sugar rum.[54]

The emergence of e-business has contributed to the further growth of counterfeit global trade. Total online counterfeit business volume is estimated at a tenth of the total counterfeit volume. Internet counterfeiters are scattered across an estimated 5,000 websites. They include both international operators and local teenagers operating out of a basement. Rolex, the Swiss-based producer of luxury watches, regularly checks eBay auctions where, on any given day, hundreds of counterfeit Rolex watches may be up for bids. The manufacturers of many other luxury items do the same. Louis Vuitton regularly checks eBay and acts on counterfeit products.[55]

Concerned that it could be held liable for frauds or other illegal sales, eBay began screening and removing from its site items that clearly infringed on copyrights.[56] Still, many luxury goods manufacturers believe the company has not done enough to curb the flow of counterfeit goods. Louis Vuitton and other luxury brands filed and won a $64 million lawsuit against the Internet retailer, which profits from each item sold through its site, authentic or not.[57]

Fighting Counterfeits

MNCs can try to stop the counterfeiting of their products in a number of ways:[58]

➤ *Do Nothing.* Firms may ignore counterfeits if they are not significantly threatening their brand. Stopping counterfeiters can become an expensive and time-consuming project for a firm. Unfortunately, most firms now realize that doing nothing is no longer an option.

➤ *Co-Opt the Offenders.* One manufacturer of hardware products discovered that a counterfeiter from Asia was producing an excellent copy of its product. The counterfeiter was asked to become the firm's legitimate contract manufacturer. Distributors of counterfeits may also be recruited to be legitimate distributors of the brand. However, this option has a downside: many legitimate contract manufacturers, licensees and distributors participate in the counterfeit market as well. Their legitimate status can help hide their more nefarious operations. Unilever discovered that one of its suppliers in Shanghai was making excess cases of soap and selling them directly to retailers. Procter & Gamble discovered that a Chinese supplier was selling empty P&G shampoo bottles to another company, which filled them with counterfeit shampoo.[59]

When New Balance discovered a licensee selling "unauthorized" shoes in international markets, they decided their best option was to buy the shoes back from the licensee at $10 per pair, rather than risk brand dilution by allowing the shoes to be sold at a discount in the market.[60]

➤ *Advertise.* MNCs can attempt to communicate the advantages of buying the authentic product rather than counterfeits. Additionally, campaigns may be devised to educate consumers about the ethical issues relating to counterfeits. When the Harry Potter series was launched in China, the publisher arranged for the books to be printed on a light green paper and planned a media blitz to explain to consumers how to tell the real thing from the counterfeit.[61] This option may become even more effective in the future as some counterfeit purchasers become more interested in buying authentic products. This trend has already been seen among some consumers in China. A survey by China Market Research revealed that 95 percent of Chinese women between the ages of 28 and 35 said they would be embarrassed to carry counterfeit handbags.[62]

➤ *Educate Governments.* Firms can take steps to educate governments about the social and political implications of counterfeits and solicit their assistance in shutting down counterfeiters. Some governments, particularly those in developing countries, have long been unsympathetic to multinational pleas to address counterfeits. Counterfeits often provide employment opportunities in developing countries, and some governments believe that the price consumers in poor countries pay for global brand equity is unnecessary and extreme. However, there are signs that even governments in developing countries are changing their minds about the value of counterfeits due to several factors:

➤ As already noted, counterfeits can sometimes hurt consumers. In Africa, counterfeit drugs account for as much as 40 percent of the market. Counterfeit, and ineffectual, pills have helped undermine Africa's attempt to treat malaria.[63]

➤ Many governments are increasingly concerned about the downside of their large informal economies (including counterfeiters and their distributors) because participants in the informal economy do not pay taxes or adhere to labor codes.[64] One exception to this rule is North Korea, whose government is purported to earn $100 million a year from counterfeits produced there.[65]

➤ Counterfeits increasingly harm firms from developing countries, not just foreign MNCs. Countries such as Brazil, South Korea and Taiwan now realize that their own domestic brands are being counterfeited. Chinese brands such as Tsingtao beer and Li-Ning shoes have become targets of counterfeiters, and a leading brand in the Pakistani clothing industry found itself plagued with counterfeits that sold for one-fourth the price of the real thing.[66] This phenomenon has motivated some local governments to become more serious about addressing the problem.

➤ Governments themselves can fall victim to counterfeits. A congressional probe identified 1,800 cases in which counterfeit electronics were discovered in U.S. weapons. Most of the counterfeits could be identified as originating in China.[67]

➤ Counterfeiting is increasing the domain of organized crime and even terrorists, the latter of which use proceeds from counterfeits to finance their terrorist activities. Both groups threaten the sovereignty of legitimate governments.

➤ *Push for Better Legislation Against Counterfeits.* The United States passed the Trademark Counterfeiting Act in 1984, which makes counterfeiting punishable by fines of up to $250,000 and prison terms of up to five years. China lowered its threshold for criminal prosecution of counterfeiters in 2004. Now an individual need only be caught with $6,000 worth of counterfeit goods to face prosecution versus $12,000 previously.[68] Many other countries are strengthening their laws and increasing penalties for counterfeiting. This is even true of many newly industrialized countries that were once major offenders. Still, new legislation is only the beginning. The enforcement of new legislation may remain weak in most developing countries for many years in the future.

➤ *Employ Coalitions.* Global firms may achieve better results if they work together to lobby governments for improvements in laws and enforcement. This can be true for home governments as well. The Chinese government appears to have begun to respond to complaints about counterfeiting more seriously since the United States, Europe and Japan have appeared to speak with a single voice.

➤ *Participate Directly in Investigation and Surveillance.* Governments cannot always be relied on to shut down counterfeiting. Increasingly, firms have begun to take over investigatory roles usually played by police. The Motion Picture Association hires its own private police to establish spy networks in Asia, track down pirates of DVDs and assist customs agents to raid illegal operations.[69] Many global marketers discover that counterfeits of their products are often sold online. Several software products have been developed to help these companies monitor websites and identify online sellers of counterfeits.

Louis Vuitton is reported to employ 20 full-time staff members to work with teams of investigators and lawyers to protect its brand from counterfeiters. However, such activities are not without peril. One executive of a major European alcoholic beverage company was shot at twice and wounded once while trying to help curtail counterfeiters in Thailand.[70]

➤ *Change Aspects of the Product.* Firms can continuously change aspects of their products and employ high-tech labeling and packaging. For instance, AstraZeneca's ulcer medication, Nexium, employs holograms, molecular tags and tamper-proof seals. Other approaches include invisible marking devices or inks, nanotracers, laser etchings and sophisticated bar codes which contain the date and location of production. However, many counterfeiters are very adept at countering these changes at their state-of-the-art manufacturing facilities.

➤ *Reconsider More Aggressive Pricing.* In some cases, brand owners may choose to forgo some brand equity and lower prices to address counterfeits. Yamaha decided to lower prices in order to fight counterfeits in China. Its cheapest bike was reduced to $725 from $1,800. Counterfeiters who previously charged $1,000 had to respond by charging only $500.[71] Similarly, Mexican film and video distributors Videomax and Quality Films, in cooperation with the Motion Picture Association of America, decided to drop prices in the Mexican market and sell legitimate movies through the same street vendors who traditionally sold pirated copies of films. The distributors slashed prices enough that they matched or fell below those of pirated copies.[72]

➤ *Exit or Avoid a Market.* When Microsoft entered the Russian market, it faced a piracy rate for its software of 99 percent. The firm decided that targeting the consumer market was futile. Instead it focused solely on the business market, offering after-sales technology support as an inducement to purchase software legally.[73]

Although international firms continue to devise methods to stop counterfeits, they will remain a problem that global marketers will have to deal with for the foreseeable future. And the longer governments fail to address the problem, the stronger organized crime becomes as a result of its participation in this lucrative industry.

Social Marketing in the Global Context

Social marketing is the adaptation of marketing practices to programs designed to influence the voluntary behavior of target groups in order to improve their personal welfare and that of the society to which they belong.[74] The targets of social marketing might not believe—at least in the beginning—that they suffer from or are contributing to a problem. Such might be the case with teenagers who abuse alcohol or drugs or fathers in Bangladesh who do not believe that their daughters should receive an education.[75]

Similar to marketing in the commercial sphere, social marketing has gone global. The global reach of NGOs undertaking philanthropic and educational projects has never been greater. And whether they are local or transnational, public or private, organizations involved in social marketing are increasingly interested in exploring best practices from other countries.

As is the case with global products, social marketing programs utilized across countries may exhibit standardized features as well as features adapted to various local conditions and cultures. For example, research demonstrates that high-risk behavior relating to the spread of AIDS can be reduced when popular opinion leaders (POLs) within a community are trained to introduce AIDS prevention endorsements into conversations with their peers. A team of social marketers from Wisconsin chose the POL model for international dissemination. The team identified leading AIDS prevention NGOs in 78 countries in Africa, Eastern Europe/Russia, Central Asia, Latin America and the Caribbean. Each NGO was paired with a behavioral science consultant who was very familiar with the culture of the region the NGO served. Consequently, the NGO received assistance in adapting the POL model to best fit local cultural demands. Fifty-five percent of the NGOs incorporated the POL model into their programs. In addition, these NGOs networked with other organizations in their countries to promote the model. In 26 percent of targeted countries, the government also adopted the model into its official AIDS prevention programs.[76]

As noted earlier, marketing practices developed for commercial enterprises are often readily applicable to social marketing. When the global consulting firm McKinsey developed a program to improve the welfare of coffee growers in developing countries, it first segmented its market. Some growers could reasonably switch to growing specialty coffees in order to realize greater profits. However, others would need to abandon coffee growing altogether in order to survive. Social marketing recommendations were then developed for two different segments.[77] Similarly, social marketers associated with international NGO Care targeted farming and fishing communities in rural Kenya in a campaign to improve water cleanliness and decrease diarrheal diseases. Careful attention was paid to market research that utilized both focus-group and survey methodologies.[78]

Social marketing has benefited from the growth of global networks like Facebook, Twitter and others. For example, a group of young people in Colombia started "One Million Voices Against FARC." FARC is a paramilitary group that has terrorized Colombians for over 40 years. Aided by social networks, the organization inspired 12 million people in 190 cities around the world to rally in the streets against FARC. Within weeks of the protest, FARC witnessed massive desertions from their forces.[79]

Still, certain aspects of social marketing differentiate it from commercial marketing:

➤ Social marketing is not concerned with the profitability of a project the way commercial marketing is. Nonetheless, when people buy into a behavioral change being promoted by a social marketer, they must pay some kind of price. That price may involve a monetary payment or it may involve extra effort or the forgoing of something pleasurable. In some cases it may require a difficult decision to abandon long-held cultural beliefs. For example, as developing countries become more affluent, they face an increase in alcohol abuse. To combat this, some governments are attempting to alter traditional consumption patterns. One social marketing intervention in Thailand successfully convinced villagers to forgo serving alcohol at funerals.[80]

To make the price of change more acceptable, social marketers may be called upon to offer incentives. The Care project in Kenya offered chemical tablets and water storage pots at subsidized prices to households willing to adopt new water quality procedures. The McKinsey report on coffee farming in developing countries suggested that NGOs and governments provide interim loans for farmers transitioning to new crops.

➤ Despite a lack of profit focus, social marketers must still seek monetary compensation to cover expenses and consequently stay in business. However, their funding comes from sources other than their target markets. These sources comprise governments as well as private donors.

Additional marketing aimed at these sources of funds is also necessary. Social marketers must understand the motivations and values of these donors, and they must often compete with other social marketers for funding.

➤ Although NGOs may compete for funding, they often work together—formally or informally—to accomplish a common goal. Such lateral partnerships help facilitate efficiency savings.[81] They can also assist in the development of better, more effective practices. In the international context they can be especially useful. Multinational social marketers can offer additional funding and experience to local social marketers who provide cultural understanding and community access.

➤ Social marketers, especially in the international context, must consider how governments—both host and home—view the product they are marketing. Sometimes social marketers undertake jobs that fall under the usual auspices of governments. Some governments welcome the help. Others may be embarrassed by it. Also, what constitutes the public good—and the actions needed to accomplish it—can be politically charged subjects.

Conclusion

In this chapter we see that social marketing and the marketing of services internationally have much in common with the global marketing of products. However, they each present unique challenges. Whether marketing products or services, additional efforts are required if a company wishes to develop global brands and to police counterfeits. For companies that successfully master these additional international difficulties while showing a commitment to foreign customers, global success can lead to increased profits and to more secure market positions both domestically and globally.

Managerial Takeaways

1. *Marketing services worldwide has much in common with marketing products. However, services can be more culture-bound. Differentiating between back-stage and front-stage aspects of services allows global marketers to customize for local cultures while capturing certain advantages of global reach.*

2. *Managing brands internationally involves deciding on single-country brand names versus global names. But increasingly, global marketers select global names for new products.*

3. *Global brands require special oversight. A MNC often assigns a brand champion to this difficult job.*

4. *Many consumers worldwide hold global brands to higher standards than local brands. This requires global brand strategies to incorporate elements of corporate social responsibility.*

5. *Global brand equity faces significant challenges from brand preemptors but especially from counterfeiters, many of whom are very sophisticated and tied to transnational organized crime.*

6. *Whether working as a professional or as a volunteer, global marketers can often put the skills they develop in the private sector to work toward social marketing and philanthropic endeavors.*

Questions for Discussion

1. Why is it more difficult to pursue product standardization when marketing services?
2. Why do you think Poles already recognized the Coke name and logo when the product was first introduced in Poland?
3. Why is it difficult to decide whether to change a local brand name to a global brand name?
4. What are the pros and cons of a top-down approach to global branding? What are the pros and cons of a bottom-up approach?
5. How might a global brand be valuable to a social marketer?
6. How can social networks like Facebook affect social marketing in different countries? Give specific examples.

CASE 11.1   Chasing Pirates

Pirated software is a major challenge to Microsoft which loses hundreds of millions of dollars a year to the practice. Piracy rates vary by country, the rates in developing countries being significantly higher than those in developed countries:

Argentina	69%
Brazil	53%
China	77%
Egypt	61%
Germany	26%
Indonesia	86%
Mexico	57%
Nigeria	82%
Russia	63%
Turkey	62%
United States	19%

Attempts to stop piracy overseas have taken many forms at Microsoft. The company has established a multi-million dollar Cybercrime Center to help collaborate with companies, legal authorities and police to stop software piracy. In Bulgaria, the company launched a campaign to eradicate pirated software by offering full packages discounted 60 percent off their previous price. Buyers were also entitled to the next version at no extra charge. In Pakistan, Microsoft offered to provide a training program for software instructors and to install laboratories in the top 50 universities and colleges in the country.

This $150 million package would be in exchange for better government enforcement of antipiracy laws. In Malaysia, Microsoft installed a toll-free phone number and offered substantial rewards for evidence against companies using pirated software.

In Singapore, a country of only four million people, Microsoft still loses millions of dollars a year to pirates. Microsoft began a campaign in the Singapore schools to educate students concerning the illegality of piracy. Despite Singapore's excellent reputation for law enforcement in general, U.S. officials had put it on their list of countries to watch for poor enforcement of copyrights. Under similar pressure from the United States, Taiwan has been cracking down more on piracy. A firm caught exporting pirated software was fined $7.9 million, and its owner was sentenced to two years in jail. Over a period of five years, the piracy rate dropped from 42 to 36 percent in Singapore and from 43 to 29 percent in Taiwan.

The Chinese market is also of concern. The CEO of Microsoft traveled to China to sign an agreement with the government there to promote the authentic use of software. Under the agreement, several key government entities pledged to buy Microsoft and to avoid pirated products. In exchange, Microsoft agreed to provide technical training and consulting. Later the same year, Microsoft brought its first piracy case to the Chinese courts. Engineers were found to be using pirated Microsoft products in the office building of the Yadu Group. The Yadu Group argued that they were innocent because the engineers worked not directly for them but for a sister company. The Chinese court found in favor of Yadu and ordered Microsoft to pay $60 in court costs.

Despite this setback, Microsoft appeared to be making some headway in its attempt to gain support from the Chinese government for piracy protection. The firm considerably expanded its R&D effort in China, raising it to world-class status and offering fellowships to doctoral students in China. Some industry observers believed that when the product was "Made-in-China" the government was more motivated to support protection.

However, Microsoft's rollout of an antipiracy program called Windows Genuine Advantage angered Chinese software users. The automatically installed system update turned desktops using pirated versions of Windows completely black every hour until the software was validated. This earned the product the nickname "Black Screen of Death" by critics. Within months of the product's introduction, a Chinese lawyer filed multiple complaints against Microsoft, claiming the program violated privacy and antimonopoly statutes in the country.

After pursuing various antipiracy policies, Microsoft decided to introduce a version of Windows software especially for consumers in developing countries. A multi-country launch included Malaysia, Indonesia, India and Russia. The new software offered fewer features for a lower price. It was installed in low-cost personal computers and not sold separately. The price Microsoft charged computer manufacturers for the product was not made public, but the low-end PCs are estimated to retail for about US$300. The company also decided to test market an aggressive pricing strategy in China, offering their Microsoft Office software for only $29.

Microsoft also pursues legal options to shut down pirates. In a single year, the company settled 3,265 lawsuits across 43 countries. Most of the cases were initiated when buyers of pirated software contacted Microsoft after their computers were infected by malware or viruses. Increasingly, cyber thieves are cooperating with pirates to access information on buyers' computers. A consumer survey undertaken by Microsoft revealed that 64 percent of the people respondents knew to have used pirated software had experienced security problems. Forty-five percent of respondents noted that their greatest concern with pirated software was data loss, and 29 percent noted their greatest concern was identity theft. According to Microsoft, 450,000 buyers of counterfeit software had already contacted the company about problems with pirated software.

Discussion Questions

1. What do you think accounts for the different piracy rates across countries?
2. Identify the different strategies Microsoft uses to combat counterfeits.
3. Why does Microsoft expect each of these efforts to be useful? What is your opinion?

Sources: "Chasing Pirates," in Kate Gillespie and H. David Hennessey, *Global Marketing* (Mason, OH: Cengage, 2011), pp. 335–336; "Shadow Market: Global Software Piracy Study," Business Software Alliance, May 2012; Britney Fitzgerald, "Software Piracy," *Huffington Post*, June 1, 2012; Melanie Lee, "Microsoft's Newest Weapon in China Piracy Fight," *Reuters*, October 23, 2012; Dara Kerr, "Microsoft Settles Thousands of Software Piracy Cases," *CNET*, July 9, 2013; "Software Piracy Costs Billions in Time, Money for Consumers and Businesses," *Microsoft News*, March 5, 2013; and James R. Hagerty and Shira Ovide, "Microsoft's New Tack on Piracy," *Wall Street Journal Europe*, March 18, 2014, p. 19.

CASE 11.2   Fighting AIDS in Asia

Mary Foster had just resigned from her job as a global product manager at a major multinational packaged foods company to head AIDS Prevention International (API), an NGO based in Washington, D.C., dedicated to slowing the spread of HIV/AIDS in developing countries. Mary had been an active volunteer as an MBA student, raising money for AIDS awareness programs in the United States. She welcomed the opportunity to return to this early interest.

API had been recently established by a very generous U.S. philanthropist. The investment return of API's current endowment would cover annual expenses for operating a headquarters located in the United States as well as small offices in up to four developing countries. In addition, funds would remain to support modest educational programs in these countries as well as further fundraising efforts.

Mary believed that the NGO's resources could best be deployed by focusing on a few countries in Asia. She was currently in the process of prioritizing target countries and deciding which population segments within those countries to target. Other key questions involved the extent to which API should ally with local NGOs and governments and whether API should apply for funding from the U.S. government.

The Global AIDS Epidemic

HIV was first identified in the 1970s. (HIV is the virus that triggers AIDS.) The disease spread first among homosexuals, intravenous drug users and workers in the sex industry but inevitably entered the general population. AIDS was now the world's fourth largest infectious killer. The disease first appeared in West

Table 11.2 Percent of Adult Population with HIV by Country

China	0.1
India	0.3
Indonesia	0.4
Russia	1.1
South Africa	18.1
Thailand	0.9
Ukraine	0.9

Source: Data derived from UNAIDS, 2012 Report on the Global AIDS Epidemic (www.unaids.org)

Africa. After remaining relatively contained in the Congo's sparsely populated jungles, it began to spread rapidly via rebel armies and truck drivers who frequented brothels. AIDS was already devastating the African continent when it first appeared in the United States in the early 1980s. Africa still remained the hardest hit area of the world.

There were substantial differences in HIV prevalence rates by region. Intraregional differences at the country level could be substantial as well (see Table 11.2). The highest estimates for new HIV/AIDS infections were in sub-Saharan Africa, Eastern Europe, Central Asia, South Asia and Southeast Asia. Who was most at risk also varied by region. In Eastern Europe and Russia, most HIV-positive people were under 30 years of age compared with only 30 percent in Western Europe and North America. In Ukraine, drug injection was the principal mode of transmission while it accounted for only 10 percent of the newly diagnosed HIV cases in Western Europe.

Besides the personal tragedy associated with the disease, the economic impact could be tremendous. For example, loss of productivity combined with increased expenditures to combat the disease contributed to a GNP decrease of 8 percent in Namibia. Kenya—where the government once hesitated in broadcasting the danger of AIDS in its sex industry for fear of scaring away tourists—saw its PCI drop 10 percent. In recognition of this economic impact on developing countries, the World Bank joined other transnational institutions such as the United Nations in supporting programs to halt the spread of the disease.

Prioritizing Markets

Mary had narrowed the potential countries to four: Thailand, China, India and Indonesia.

Thailand

HIV was first detected in Thailand in the mid-1980s among male homosexuals. The government immediately began to monitor high-risk groups, including drug users and prostitutes. Accurate information alerted the authorities to rapidly soaring infection rates. The government responded quickly with a survey of sexual behavior among Thais. This survey revealed that Thai men frequently indulged in unprotected commercial sex. These results were highly publicized and a campaign was launched to persuade prostitutes to insist on condom use. Safe sex was promoted via billboards, leaflets and television commercials. The results were impressive. In just a few years, adult men reporting nonmarital sex dropped from 28 percent to 15 percent. Men reporting seeing a prostitute fell from 22 percent to 10 percent. The proportion claiming to have used a condom during sex with a prostitute rose to 93 percent. The number of sexually transmitted diseases in government clinics fell from over 400,000 to 50,000. However, Virginia-based NGO International Social Justice (ISJ) claimed that many if not most of the women employed in Thailand's sex trade (estimated at 200,000) were sold or kidnapped into prostitution and asserted that these women needed liberation, not condoms. Influenced by organizations such as ISJ, the U.S. Leadership Against HIV/AIDS, Tuberculosis and Malaria Act forbade funding for any organization that advocated the legalization of prostitution or did not have a policy explicitly opposing prostitution.

Furthermore, in the wake of the Asian financial crisis, Thailand cut its expenditures for AIDS prevention. Years later, expenditures were still only about half of what they once were. New infection rates remained high among drug users and gay men. Some believed that Thailand's war on drugs, which resulted in the killing of 3,000 alleged drug dealers, had driven drug users underground and away from AIDS preventative services such as needle exchange programs. New HIV infection rates were also up from 11 percent to 17 percent among urban youth. Because earlier campaigns had associated condoms with commercial sex, safe sex may have become stigmatized. Condom usage by young men with steady girlfriends was low, and unprotected sex with multiple partners was on the rise among Thai teens. Local NGOs were calling for improved and expanded sex education in Thai schools.

China

HIV first entered China in the late 1980s via infected drug users. In the 1990s, a major epidemic arose in the province of Henan when villagers were recruited to donate blood. In order to donate up to four times a day, villagers were re-infused with their own blood after the plasma had been extracted. Activists estimate that one million became infected with HIV. In one village alone, one-third of the adult population contracted the disease. No one was ever held accountable. In fact, China's communist government was at first less than enthusiastic about raising AIDS awareness, and many AIDS prevention volunteers reported being harassed by government authorities. Statistics concerning the disease were treated as a state secret.

The government attributed most AIDS cases to intravenous drug use. However, international agencies estimated that only about 60 percent of Chinese infected with HIV/AIDS contracted the disease through the use of illicit drugs. Infection from unprotected sex was rising. China's younger generation was reaching puberty earlier and marrying later. Consequently, premarital sex was on the rise. Hundreds of millions of Chinese were on the move as well, as rural Chinese poured into urban areas in search of jobs. Many of these migrants were males who left wives behind in the country. However, many migrants were women in search of jobs that often failed to materialize. The result was a booming commercial sex industry in Chinese cities.

The government announced that it would redouble efforts to educate students regarding AIDS and launched AIDS prevention websites aimed at youth. Despite the new push by the central government, many believed provincial governments were ignoring—even covering up—the problem, and a surprising number of Chinese remained unaware of the disease. Only years later did the Chinese government announce that AIDS prevention would be added to the country's educational curriculum.

India

India, with an estimated 2.4 million infected with HIV, ranked third after South Africa and Nigeria for the highest number of infected persons. In recognition of this crisis, the government organized a Parliamentary Forum on HIV/AIDS, which brought together more than 1,200 elected political figures from across the country. As in many developing countries, controversy surrounded AIDS statistics collected by the government. To address this problem, the Indian government hired a prestigious (and independent) private company to estimate the level of HIV/AIDS in India.

Nonetheless, a government survey showed that prevention programs were only reaching about 30 percent of the population. Women who were infected by their husbands were often blamed by their in-laws. NGOs that operated homes for AIDS patients or AIDS orphans were often evicted if their landlords discovered the nature of their operations. Police were even known to harass health workers who were trying to disseminate the government's own AIDS prevention information.

Health workers in India believed that the disease was spreading fastest in rural areas where prevention programs were the weakest and record-keeping the worst. Hope Foundation was disseminating AIDS information and condoms at truck stops. India's five million truckers covered 5,000 miles of highways and reported three to five sexual partners a week. In six years, the HIV infection rate among truckers fell from 10 percent to 4 percent.

To address the threat of AIDS to young people, the government had established two national prizes to award colleges or youth groups who acted as agents of change by implementing their own AIDS awareness initiatives. Still AIDS carried a social stigma in India. When the disease first entered the country, many Indian officials declared that India's moral character and conservative sexual mores would prevent the spread of AIDS. Sex was rarely a subject of public discourse. It was largely absent from Indian films, and schools offered little or no sex education.

Nonetheless, numerous NGOs operated in India. Their programs included support for persons with HIV, general awareness and educational programs and care for orphans whose parents died from AIDS. Funding came from federal and state governments, international donors and local contributions.

One international donor, The Bill & Melinda Gates Foundation, pledged $100 million for a ten-year program for AIDS prevention in India. However, several years into the program, the Foundation decided to turn over its network of over 100 non-profit organizations to the Indian government to run. The government was unenthusiastic, noting that the costs of the network were astronomical. They pointed to air-conditioned clinics and glossy English posters and brochures that the clinics' illiterate clientele could not read. In addition, top managers were paid salaries commensurate with MBA salaries in the West. Results were disappointing as well. Despite an expensive campaign aimed at truckers, an internal report concluded that only 12 percent of truckers were even aware of the program's services and only 7 percent ever used them.

Indonesia

Indonesia historically enjoyed a low rate of HIV infection, but that was changing fast, particularly among drug users and throughout the nation's expanding commercial sex industry where only one man in ten used a condom. The WHO had given Indonesia an even higher priority for AIDS attention than China or Thailand, and international AIDS prevention groups stated that the Indonesian government vastly under-reported the cases in the country.

However, Indonesia was Islam's most populous country, and AIDS prevention endeavors were proving controversial with conservative Muslims. Islam forbade extramarital sex. One Muslim politician remarked that AIDS prevention should focus on improving people's morality and not urge them to protect themselves by using condoms. The Indonesian Ulemas' Council, the country's highest Islamic authority, proclaimed that Muslims should fight AIDS by being more religious and closer to family.

DKT Indonesia, a Washington-based NGO, produced a line of condoms that it sold at discount rates in Indonesia to truck drivers, sailors and prostitutes. The NGO also placed a few condom advertisements with Indonesia's MTV affiliate but used dancing strawberry cartoons rather than images of real people. Attempts to get other AIDS prevention advertisements aired met with less success. Another U.S.-based NGO, Family Health International, briefly aired a commercial that depicted men visiting prostitutes. But stations immediately pulled the ad when fundamentalist Muslim clerics complained.

The Indonesian government officially proposed new education programs in schools along with better training for health-care workers and voluntary HIV testing and counseling. However, some within the government questioned spending on AIDS prevention when the country needed basic education and health care. Also, much of the country's health-care budget fell under the auspices of provincial governments sympathetic to views of Islamic fundamentalist groups. As one local AIDS activist noted: many considered AIDS a punishment from God for wrongdoing. Others viewed it as a Western phenomenon and nothing to do with them.

As Mary contemplated the challenges of each of these four potential Asian markets, she wondered whether any of her experience as a global product manager could be put to use in this new context of international social marketing.

Discussion Questions

1. Given that there are many multinational and local "competitors" participating in the social marketing of AIDS prevention, what role should API play? What products/services could it deliver?
2. What elements of these services might be standardized across developing countries? What elements might need to be adapted? Why?
3. What suggestions would you give Mary for prioritizing the four Asian markets?
4. Should API partner with local governments? Local NGOs? Should it pursue funding from the U.S. government?
5. How might Mary's experience as a global product manager be useful in this new setting?

Sources: "Fighting AIDS in Asia," in Kate Gillespie and H. David Hennessey, *Global Marketing* (Mason, OH: Cengage, 2011), pp. 336–339; UNAIDS, World AIDS Day Report 2012; "HIV-AIDS Biggest Health Risk in Thailand," *Australia Network News*, August 21, 2013; Kate Kelland, "AIDS Proves Stubborn in Europe as New HIV Infections Rise," *Reuters*, November 27, 2013; "HIV/AIDS in India," *World Bank News*, July 10, 2012; Donald G. McNeil, Jr., "HIV Tests Urged for 800 Milliion in India," *New York Times*, June 17, 2013; Tan Ee Lyn and Fitri Wulandari, "With Head in Sand, Indonesia Struggles to Tackle AIDS," *Reuters*, April 12, 2011; and "China: In Need of More Protection," *The Economist*, January 30, 2014.

Notes

1   Pui-Wing Tam, "H-P Lands $3Billion Contract to Manage P&G Tech Services," *Wall Street Journal*, April 14, 2003, p. B4.

2   Cassell Bryan-Low, "Microsoft Battles Piracy in Developing Markets," *Wall Street Journal*, December 25, 2004, p. B4.

3   Philip Makutsa, Kilungu Nzaku, Paul Ogutu, Peter Barasa, Sam Ombeki, Alex Mwaki and Robert E. Quick, "Challenges in Implementing a Point-of-Use Water Quality Intervention in Rural Kenya," *American Journal of Public Health*, vol. 91, no. 10 (October 2001), pp. 1571–1573.

4   Martin Fackler and Ichiko Fuyuno, "Japan Lawyers See Seismic Shift," *Wall Street Journal*, September 16, 2004, p. A15.

5   David Murphy, "Chinese Builders Go Global," *Far Eastern Economic Review*, May 13, 2004, p. 30.

6   Colum Murphy, "Car-Price Bible Kelley is Heading to China," *Wall Street Journal*, November 8, 2013.

7   John Lyons, "Siting a Call Center? Check Out the Mall First," *Wall Street Journal*, July 3, 2006, p. B1.

8   Pierre Berthon, Leyland Pitt, Constantine S. Katsikeas and Jean-Paul Berthon, "Virtual Services Go International: Services in the Marketspace," *Journal of International Marketing*, vol. 7, no. 3 (1999), pp. 85–86.

9   Mary Anne Raymond and John D. Mittelstaedt, "Perceptions of Factors Driving Success for Multinational Professional Firms in Korea," *Journal of Consumer Marketing*, vol. 14, no 1 (2001), p. 26.

10 Michael Laroche, Linda C. Ueltschy, Shuzo Abe, Mark Cleveland and Peter P. Yannopoulos, "Service Quality Perceptions and Customer Satisfaction: Evaluating the Role of Culture," *Journal of International Marketing*, vol. 12, no. 3 (2004), pp. 58–85.

11 Ibid.; and Raymond and Mittelstaedt, "Perceptions of Factors," p. 39.

12 Laroche et al., "Service Quality Perceptions," p. 77.

13 Mary Yoko Brannen, "When Mickey Loses Face: Recontextualization, Semantic Fit and Semiotics of Foreignness," *Academy of Management Review*, vol. 29, no. 4 (2004), pp. 593–616.

14 Ibid.

15 "Google Becomes Gu Ge in China," *Financial Times*, April 13, 2006, p. 19.

16 Margherita Stancati, "Dunkin' Donuts Goes to India," *Wall Street Journal*, May 9, 2012.

17 Jean-Claude Usunier and Janer Shaner, "Using Linguistics for Creating Better International Brand Names," *Journal of Marketing Communications*, vol. 8, no. 4 (2002), pp. 211–229.

18 "Darkie No, Darlie Yes," *South China Morning Post*, May 16, 1999, p. 2.

19 Gary McWilliams and Evan Ramstad, "China's Aggressive Buyers Suffer Setbacks on Some Overseas Deals," *Wall Street Journal*, August 22, 2006, p. A1.

20 Alice Z. Cuneo, "Landor: Experts on Identity Crisis," *Ad Age International*, March 1997, p. I-44.

21 Michael Fielding, "Walk the Line," *Marketing News*, September 1, 2006, pp. 8, 10.

22 David A. Aaker and Erich Joachimsthaler, "The Lure of Global Branding," *Harvard Business Review*, vol. 77 (November–December 1999), pp. 137–144.

23 Ibid.

24 Susan P. Douglas, C. Samuel Craig and Edwin J. Nijssen, "Integrating Branding Strategy Across Markets: Building International Brand Architecture," *Journal of International Marketing*, vol. 9, no. 2 (2001), p. 110.

25 Douglas B. Holt, John A. Quelch and Earl L. Taylor, "How Global Brands Compete," *Harvard Business Review*, vol. 82 (September 2004), pp. 68–75.

26 Ibid., p. 69.

27 Ibid., p. 71.

28 Yuliya Strizhakova, Robin A. Coulter and Linda L. Price, "Branded Products as a Passport to Global Citizenship: Perspectives from Developed and Developing Countries," *Journal of International Marketing*, vol. 16, no. 4 (2008), pp. 57–85.

29 Claudiu V. Dimofte, Johny K. Johansson and Ilkka A. Ronkainen, "Cognitive and Affective Reactions of U.S. Consumers to Global Brands," *Journal of International Marketing*, vol. 16 no. 1 (2008), pp. 113–135.

30 Claudia Penteado, "Regional Brands: Varig Eyes the Skies Outside of Brazil," *Advertising Age International*, March 1997, p. I–19.

31 Jane Blennerhassett, "Shangri-La on Earth," *Advertising Age International*, March 1997, p. I-24.

32 Julien Cayla and Giana M. Eckhardt, "Asian Brands without Borders: Regional Opportunities and Challenges," *International Marketing Review*, vol. 24, no. 4 (2007), pp. 444–456.

33 Ibid.

34 "Who Favors Branding with Euro Approach?" *Advertising Age International*, May 25, 1992, p. I-16.

35 Isabelle Schuiling and Jean-Noel Kapferer, "Real Differences between Local and International Brands: Strategic Implications for International Marketers," *Journal of International Marketing*, vol. 12, no. 4 (2004), pp. 97–112.

36 Ibid.

37 Marta Karenova, "Nostalgia Revives Soviet-Era Brands," *Wall Street Journal*, November 19, 2004, p. A12.

38 Rajeev Batra, Venkatram Ramaswamy, Dana Alden, Jan-Benedict Steenkamp and S. Ramachander, "Effects of Brand Local and Nonlocal Origin on Consumer Attitudes in Developing Countries," *Journal of Consumer Psychology*, vol. 9, no. 2 (2000), pp. 83–95.

39 Paul Gao, Jonathan R. Woetzel and Yibing Wu, "Can Chinese Brands Make It Abroad?" in "Global Directions," special edition issue four, *McKinsey Quarterly* (2003), pp. 52–65.

40 Geoffrey A. Fowler, "A Starck Vision of Asia's Future as Elite Producer of Brands," *Wall Street Journal*, April 7, 2004, p. B1.

41 Timothy Mapes, "Big Cigarette Firm Fumes at Jakarta Over a Trademark," *Wall Street Journal*, May 22, 2003.

42 Kate Gillespie, Kishore Krishma and Susan Jarvis, "Protecting Global Brands: Toward a Global Norm," *Journal of International Marketing*, vol. 10, no. 2 (2002), pp. 99–112.

43 Guy Chazan, "Philip Morris Suffers a Setback in Russian Suit on Trademarks," *Wall Street Journal*, October 13, 1999, p. A26.

44 Gordon Fairclough, "From Hongda to Wumart, Brands in China Have Familiar, if Off-Key, Ring," *Wall Street Journal*, October 19, 2006, p. B1.

45 Bart A. Lazar, "Protect Trademarks when Marketing in China," *Marketing News*, June 15, 2006, p. 7.

46 "Starbucks Victory Opens Door to Russian Cafes," *Wall Street Journal*, November 18, 2005, p. A14.

47 Sean Carney and Mike Esterl, "Sadder Bud-Weiser in Italy," *Wall Street Journal Online*, October 8, 2013.

48 David Wright and Brandon Bauer, "LAPD, U.S. Customs Battle Counterfeit Goods," *ABC News*, October 21, 2013.

49 Barry Berman, "Strategies to Detect and Reduce Counterfeiting Activity," *Business Horizons*, vol. 51, no. 3 (2008), pp. 191–199.

50 Bruce Einhorn and Xiang Ji, "Deaf to Music Piracy," *Business Week*, September 10, 2007, pp. 42–44.

51 Geoffrey A. Fowler and Jason Dean, "In China, MySpace May Need to Be 'OurSpace'," *Wall Street Journal*, February 2, 2007, p. B1.

52 "Baidu Search Share Down," *China Internet Watch*, September 17, 2013.

53 Geoffrey A. Fowler, "Hollywood's Burning Issue," *Wall Street Journal*, September 18, 2003, p. B1.

54 "Vietnam's Prolific Counterfeiters Take a Walk on 'LaVile' Side," *Asian Wall Street Journal*, June 4, 1998, p. 1.

55 "Sleaze E-Commerce," *Wall Street Journal*, May 14, 1999, p. W1.

56 Glenn R. Simpson, "E-Bay to Police Site for Sales of Pirated Items," *Wall Street Journal*, February 28, 2000, p. A3.

57 Christina Passariello, "EBay Fined over Selling Counterfeits," *Wall Street Journal*, July 1, 2008, p. 1.

58 The first eight suggestions listed here are forwarded by Robert T. Green and Tasman Smith, "Countering Brand Counterfeiters," *Journal of International Marketing*, vol. 10, no. 4 (2002), pp. 89–106.

59 Gabriel Kahn, "Factory Fight," *Wall Street Journal*, December 19, 2002, p. A1.

60 Peggy Chaudhry, Victor Cordell and Alan Zimmerman, "Modeling Anti-Counterfeiting Strategies in Response to Protecting Intellectual Property Rights in the Global Environment," *Marketing Review*, vol. 5, no. 1 (2005), pp. 59–72.

61   Matt Forney, "Harry Potter, Meet 'Ha-li Bo-te'," *Wall Street Journal*, September 21, 2000, p. B1.

62   Laurie Burkitt, "Retailers Rush in As Chinese Lose Their Taste for Fakes," *Wall Street Journal*, February 14, 2012, p. B1.

63   Benoit Faucon, Colum Murphy and Jeanne Whalen, "Fake-Pill Pipeline Undercuts Africa's Battle with Malaria," *Wall Street Journal*, May 29, 2013, p. A1.

64   Diana Farrell, "The Hidden Dangers of the Informal Economy," *McKinsey Quarterly*, no. 3 (2004), pp. 26–38.

65   Ibid.

66   Mohammad, Bashir Ali, "Crusading Against Counterfeit Products," *Business Recorder*, March 27, 2011.

67   William Wan and Jason Ukman, "Chinese Counterfeit Parts Found in U.S. Weapons," *The Washington Post*, November 7, 2011.

68   Frederik Balfour, "Fakes," *Business Week*, February 7, 2005, pp. 54–64.

69   Geoffrey A. Fowler, "Hollywood's Burning Issue," *Wall Street Journal*, September 18, 2003, p. B1.

70   Green and Smith, "Countering Brand Counterfeiters," pp. 91, 101.

71   Ibid., p. 60.

72   Ken Bensinger, "Film Companies Take to Mexico's Streets to Fight Piracy," *Wall Street Journal*, December 17, 2003, p. B1.

73   Cassell Bryan-Low, "Microsoft Battles Piracy in Developing Markets," *Wall Street Journal*, December 23, 2004, p. B4.

74   Alan R. Andreasen, "Social Marketing: Its Definition and Domain," *Journal of Public Policy and Marketing*, vol. 13, no. 1 (Spring 1994), pp. 110–111.

75   George G. Brenkert, "Ethical Challenges of Social Marketing," *Journal of Public Policy and Marketing*, vol. 21, no. 1 (Spring 2002), pp. 14–25.

76   "AIDS Prevention Programs Can Be Transferred to Developing Countries," *Ascribe News*, September 23, 2004.

77   Steven G. Friedenberg, Charles Jordan and Vivek Mohindra, "Easing Coffee Farmers' Woes," *McKinsey Quarterly*, no. 2 (2004), pp. 8–11.

78   Makutsa et al., "Water Quality Intervention in Rural Kenya."

79   "Facebook, Google, YouTube, MTV, Howcast, Columbia Law School and U.S. Department of State Convene the Alliance of Youth Movements Summit," www.marketwatch.com, November 18, 2008.

80   Parveen Ahmed, "Affluence Leads to Alcohol Abuse in SE Asia, Report Says," *Marketing News*, September 15, 2006, p. 18.

81   Gerald Hastings, "Relational Paradigms in Social Marketing," *Journal of Macromarketing*, vol. 23, no. 1 (2003), pp. 6–15.

Chapter 12

Pricing for International and Global Markets

PROFIT AND COST FACTORS THAT AFFECT PRICING   375

MARKET FACTORS THAT AFFECT PRICING   379

ENVIRONMENTAL FACTORS THAT AFFECT PRICING   383

MANAGERIAL ISSUES IN GLOBAL PRICING   386

In recent years the U.S. Justice Department has brought some of America's largest criminal cases to trial. The defendants are global managers from Belgium, Britain, Canada, France, Germany, Italy, Japan, Mexico, the Netherlands, South Korea and Switzerland as well as from the United States. The charge is collusion with competitors to fix global prices. The penalty is a hefty fine for the company and a jail sentence for the manager. One price-fixing case involved vitamins. Multinational pharmaceutical firms reached production and price agreements that raised prices to packaged-foods companies such as General Mills, Kellogg's, Coca-Cola and Procter & Gamble. These higher prices were of course passed on to consumers who took vitamins, drank milk or ate cereal. Similarly, investigators uncovered a 17-year price-fixing conspiracy among American, German and Japanese producers of sorbates, a food preservative. This cartel is estimated to have affected over a billion dollars in sales in the United States alone.

Global cartels have raised prices on such diverse products as soft drinks, dynamite and offshore oil and gas drilling platforms. Increasingly, governments in Europe and emerging markets are joining the United States in investigating the pricing policies of global firms. French authorities fined Nestlé SA, Mars Inc. and Colgate-Palmolive €35.3 million for pressuring their distributors to keep pet food prices high.[1]

What would make a manager risk a jail sentence to fix a global price? The globalization of markets offers several possible explanations. Competition has intensified. Firms not only compete in foreign markets but also face foreign competition in their home markets. Consolidation in many industries has created fewer but bigger competitors. Demanding consumers want better products at lower prices. Pressures to lower prices abound. But pricing is the part of the marketing mix that delivers potential profits to the firm. For some companies, the temptation to bring order and certainty to a global market must seem overwhelming.

Managing global pricing is more complex than establishing national pricing strategies. This chapter provides an overview of the key factors that affect pricing policies in an international environment. First, we look at how cost considerations affect international pricing decisions. We next explore the impact of market and environmental factors. Then we examine managerial pricing issues such as transfer pricing, global pricing and countertrade.

Learning Objectives

After studying this chapter, you should be able to:

➤ differentiate between full-cost pricing and marginal-cost pricing and explain the implications of both to global marketers;

➤ note how international transportation costs, tariffs, taxes, local production costs and channel costs all affect pricing decisions;

➤ explain how different income levels, cultures, buyer power and competitive situations in national markets can require different pricing strategies across these markets;

> ➤ compare and contrast the ways in which exchange rate fluctuations and inflation rates complicate global pricing;
>
> ➤ list various examples of government price controls that global marketers might encounter;
>
> ➤ define dumping and describe how it can constrain pricing strategies;
>
> ➤ understand how the credit and collection infrastructure of a country can affect pricing decisions in that country;
>
> ➤ describe how global marketers can manage export price escalation, determine transfer prices and effectively quote prices in foreign currencies;
>
> ➤ define parallel imports, explain their causes and list ways in which they may be controlled;
>
> ➤ differentiate among various forms of countertrade and balance the risk and opportunities of dealing with noncash exchanges.

Profit and Cost Factors That Affect Pricing

Any effective pricing strategy starts with a clear understanding of these profit and cost variables. *What are the profit goals?* Danone determined that it wanted "satisfactory and durable profits" but not maximum profits for its bottled water business in emerging markets.[2] *What are the relevant costs?* American International Group introduced an insurance policy in rural India allowing farmers to insure a cow for only $10 a year.[3] Lower costs in India support this pricing strategy. Replacing a cow is cheaper in India than it is in the United States, and costs of employing service personnel in the insurance industry are lower in India as well.

Most companies begin pricing deliberations on the basis of their own internal cost structure. Therefore, understanding the various cost elements is a prerequisite for a successful international pricing strategy.

Fixed and Variable Costs

According to standard accounting practice, costs are divided into two categories: fixed costs and variable costs. Fixed costs do not change over a given range of output, whereas variable costs vary directly with output. The relationship of these variables is shown in Table 12.1 for a fictitious company, Western Machine Tool, Inc., a manufacturer of machine tools that sell for $60,000 per unit in the U.S. market.

The total cost of a machine tool is $54,000. Selling it at $60,000, the company will make a profit of $6,000 before taxes from the sale of each unit. However, if one additional unit is sold (or not sold), the marginal impact amounts to more than an additional profit (or loss) of $6,000, because the extra cost of an additional unit will be limited to its variable costs only, or $26,000, as shown in Table 12.2. For any additional units sold, the marginal profit is $34,000, the amount in excess of the variable costs.

Table 12.1 Profit and Cost Calculation for Western Machine Tool, Inc.

Selling price (per unit)		$60,000
Direct manufacturing costs		
Labor	$10,000	
Materials	$15,000	
Energy	$1,000	$26,000
Indirect manufacturing costs		
Supervision	$5,000	
Research and development	$3,000	
Factory overhead	$5,000	$13,000
General administrative costs		
Sales and marketing overhead	$10,000	
Full costs	$5,000	$54,000
Net profit before tax	$15,000	$6,000

Table 12.2 Marginal Profit Calculation for Western Machine Tool, Inc.

Selling price (per unit)		$60,000
Variable costs		
Direct manufacturing costs		
Labor	$10,000	
Materials	$15,000	
Energy	$1,000	$26,000
Total variable costs		$26,000
Contribution margin (selling price minus variable costs)		$34,000

Let's say Western Machine Tool has a chance to export a unit to a foreign country, but the maximum price the foreign buyer is willing to pay is $50,000. Machine Tool, using full-cost pricing, argues that the company will incur a loss of $4,000 if the deal is accepted. However, only $26,000 of additional variable cost will be incurred for a new machine, because all fixed costs are incurred anyway and are covered by all prior units sold. The company can in fact go ahead with the sale and claim a marginal profit of $24,000. In such a situation, a profitable sale may easily be turned down unless a company is fully informed about its cost composition.

Cost components are subject to change. For example, if growing export volume adds new output to a plant, a company may achieve economies of scale that result in overall reductions in unit cost. This consideration further supports the use of a marginal-pricing strategy. Marketers should beware, however, if marginal pricing significantly hurts domestic competition in the export markets. As we will see later in the chapter, this can lead to charges of dumping and consequent legal action against the exporters.

Transportation Costs

Spanish fashion chain Zara is one of the most important fashion chains in Europe, and is known for responding quickly to fashion trends and for delivering new stock quickly to its foreign operations. But with distribution centered in Spain, prices increase the further a store is from the home base. For example, Zara prices in the United States can be 65 percent higher than they are in Spain.[4]

International marketing often requires the shipment of products over long distances. The cost of shipping can become an important part of the pricing strategy of some firms. A study of how U.S. and Korean companies set overseas prices suggests that many companies that charge higher prices in foreign markets than in domestic markets do so because of transportation costs. In other words, these companies, both American and Korean, appear to use a cost-plus model for setting prices overseas, consciously adding in transportation costs to establish the price they eventually charge in foreign markets.[5]

For commodities in particular, low transportation costs can determine who gets an order. For more expensive and differentiated products, such as computers or sophisticated electronic instruments, transportation costs usually represent only a small fraction of total costs and have less influence on pricing decisions. For products between the two extremes, companies can substantially affect unit transportation costs by selecting appropriate transportation methods. For example, the introduction of container ocean vessels has made cost-effective shipment of many products possible. Roll-on, roll-off ships (ro-ro carriers) have reduced ocean freight costs for cars and trucks to very low levels, making exporters more competitive vis-à-vis local manufacturers. Still, because all modes of transportation, including rail, truck, air and ocean, depend on a considerable amount of energy, the total cost is of growing concern to multinational corporations (MNCs) and can be sensitive to the world price of oil.

Tariffs

When products are transported across national borders, tariffs may have to be paid. Tariffs are usually levied on the landed costs of a product, which include shipping costs to the importing country. Tariffs are normally assessed as a percentage of the landed value. The WTO, like its predecessor, the GATT, has gone a long way in reducing tariffs. However, they can still prove significant for certain products in certain markets. Tariff costs can have a ripple effect and increase prices considerably for the end user. Intermediaries, whether they are marketing subsidiaries or independent distributors, tend to include any tariff costs in their costs of goods sold and to calculate operating margins on the basis of this amount. As a result, the impact on the final end-user price can be substantial whenever tariff rates are high.

Sometimes international firms attempt to avoid or lessen the cost effects of tariffs by having their products reclassified. When the U.S. tariffs for trucks were temporarily increased from 2.5 to 25 percent in an effort to stem imports, Land Rover of the United Kingdom complained that its

$40,000 four-wheel-drive vehicle should not be classified as a truck, pointing out that the utility vehicle had four doors, not just two like the typical light truck. The vehicle was reclassified, and the higher duty was avoided.

Taxes

A variety of local taxes also affect the final cost of products, and different national taxes contribute to the different prices charged in different national markets. Fashion items in Brazil can cost 50 percent more than they do in the United States. In Brazil, apparel vendors pay about 35 percent in taxes on their products compared to only 8 percent in the United States. If the products are imported, the taxes can rise to 70 percent.[6] Similarly, when Sony launched Playstation 4 in Brazil its price was an incredible $1,800. When customers went online to complain the company immediately released in-house pricing information showing that the company only received 21.5 percent of the retail price. Local distributors took another 22 percent, but most of the retail price could be attributed to six different taxes.[7]

One of the most common taxes is the value-added tax (VAT) used by member countries of the EU. This tax is similar to the sales tax collected by state governments in the United States but involves more complicated assessment and collection procedures based on the value added to the product at any given stage.

Each EU country sets its own VAT structure. However, common to all is a zero tax rate (or exemption) on exported goods. A company exporting from the Netherlands to Belgium does not have to pay any tax on the value added in the Netherlands. However, Belgian authorities do collect a tax, at the Belgium rate, on products shipped from the Netherlands. Merchandise shipped to any EU member country from a nonmember country, such as the United States or Japan, is assessed the VAT rate on landed costs, in addition to any customs duties that may be applied to those products.

Different countries also assess different sin taxes. These are taxes assessed on products that are legal but are discouraged by the society. Cigarettes and alcoholic beverages commonly fall into this category. For example, Sweden countered a history of massive alcohol abuse by enacting Europe's highest taxes on alcoholic beverages. These taxes increased prices to consumers, who in turn reduced their consumption. Sweden's alcohol-related deaths and illnesses fell to among the lowest in the developed world. However, Sweden's membership in the EU threatened to undermine these gains. Swedes in the southern part of the country can now drive across a bridge to buy alcohol in Denmark at a far lower price and bring it back into Sweden.

Local Production Costs

Differences in local production cost affect pricing as well. KFC can charge lower prices on chicken in South Africa than it does in the United States because labor costs are cheaper. Also, South Africa is a major producer of corn to feed the birds, and this keeps costs down as well.[8] In Ghana, however, chicken feed is very expensive and most chicken must be imported. Consequently, costs are higher.[9]

Many MNCs manufacture products in several countries. In such cases, operating costs for raw materials, wages, energy and/or financing may differ widely from country to country, allowing a firm to ship from a particularly advantageous location in order to reduce prices by taking advantage of lower costs. MNCs increasingly choose production locations that give them advantages in production costs as well as freight, tariffs or other transfer costs. Judicious management of sourcing points may reduce product costs and result in added pricing flexibility.

Consumers themselves rarely cross borders in search of lower prices in lower cost countries. However, this is relatively common in Poland where prices are among the highest in Europe.[10] It is also increasingly common for patients seeking relief from costly medical procedures. One patient flew 22 hours to Madras in India to receive a hip replacement at the Apollo Hospital. The operation which cost $4,000 in Madras would have cost $30,000 in the United States or Europe.[11] Because of lower production costs, medical tourism is a growing industry in India.

Channel Costs

Channel costs are a function of channel length, distribution margins and logistics. Many countries operate with longer distribution channels than those in the United States, causing higher total costs and end-user prices because of additional layers of intermediaries. Also, gross margins at the retail level tend to be higher outside the United States. Because the logistics systems in many countries are less developed than that in the United States, logistics costs can be higher as well. All these factors add extra costs to a product that is marketed internationally.

Market Factors That Affect Pricing

Companies cannot establish pricing policies in a vacuum. Although cost information is essential, prices must also reflect the realities of the marketplace. International markets are particularly challenging because of the large number of local economic situations to be considered. Four factors in particular stand out and must be analyzed in greater detail: income level, buyer power, competition and culture.

Income Level

As we have previously discussed, the income level of a country's population determines the amount and type of goods and services bought, especially in consumer markets. We noted in Chapter 5 that converting GNP or GDP per capita into dollars on the basis of market exchange rates may understate the true purchasing power of a country's consumers. It may be more accurate to look at countries' purchasing-power parity when assessing markets, especially in developing countries.

Furthermore, discretionary income—the amount left after the basic necessities of food, shelter and clothing have been acquired—can vary from country to country. In much of Southeast Asia, children in their twenties still live with their parents. Virtually all the income they earn is discretionary, which makes them an attractive target market. In China, employees of state organizations often receive lucrative housing benefits, a practice that markedly increases their discretionary income.

Many MNCs can realistically target only a select segment of the population in poorer countries, even when they adjust their prices downward. To accommodate a lower income level in China, a Big Mac costs the equivalent of $1.83, which is significantly below the cost of $3.54 for a Big Mac in the United States. Still, a McDonald's meal remains expensive in the Chinese context. A Chinese family of three can pay about 10 percent of a typical monthly urban salary to eat one meal out.

Firms should regularly reassess their pricing policy in developing countries, especially if they are charging relatively high prices and targeting the elite. The growing middle classes in these countries can become a more attractive segment to target than a small upper class. For example, General Motors announced its development of a Farmers Car for China's 800 million rural inhabitants, whose incomes are even lower than those of city dwellers, in an attempt to tap a market segment hitherto ignored by multinational car manufacturers. The proposed price of the car was $7,000, down from the $40,000 charged for Buicks then sold to Chinese city dwellers.[12]

Keeping Prices Low in Developing Countries

In order to keep prices low in developing countries, global marketers often have to reconsider the costs of their products. They can adjust the size of the product, seek production-cost savings or even redesign the product.

DECREASING SIZES Perhaps the oldest strategy to keep costs down is to offer the consumers in developing countries less product. For example, Unilever developed Cubitos, small flavoring cubes that cost about two cents each, for markets in developing countries.[13] L'Oreal SA sells sample size sachets of shampoo and face cream in India, and Nestlé sells single-use sachets of its Nestea lemon tea.[14]

PRODUCT–COSTS SAVINGS When designing a new chocolate product for the lower end of the Indian market, Cadbury also produced a small sized package—just five ounces. But to keep its chocolate treats cheap, the company also had to decrease production costs. It has moved factories from high-cost locations like Mumbai and improved its supply chain. To avoid dependence on imported cocoa, the company actively supported increased cocoa production in India.[15] PepsiCo kept prices down in China by supporting agricultural projects as well. To provide reasonably priced potatoes for its potato chips, the company invested in improving potato yields and irrigation systems.[16] Similarly, SABMiller used locally produced sorghum instead of more expensive imported barley in order to keep prices low for a low-cost beer in Mozambique. It also convinced the government to lower the tax on its beer in exchange for creating new farming jobs.[17]

REDESIGNING PRODUCTS One way to keep prices low in developing countries is to take advantage of cost saving associated with global products as we discussed in Chapter 10. Ford Motor Co. considers India critical to its Asia strategy, but popular cars have low profit margins in that market. Ford leverages global designs to keep engineering and purchasing costs down.[18]

Another strategy is to redesign products for developing countries. Procter & Gamble utilizes what it calls "reverse engineering." The company begins with an assigned price for a new product in emerging markets and then proceeds to develop a product to fit the price, even if this means eliminating features available in developed countries. In creating a new razor for India, this entailed eliminating the lubrication strip and colorful handle as well as making the razor lighter weight.[19]

Redesigning products to keep prices low also applies to B2B markets. General Electric determined that one of the major problems facing Indian hospitals was a lack of funds and space for big, expensive equipment. It consequently developed the Lullaby baby warmer for Indian hospitals priced at $3,000 and then rolled it out to 62 other countries. The standard GE warmer in the United States was priced at $12,000.[20]

Culture and Consumer Behavior

Culture can also affect consumer behavior, which in turn affects pricing. Local traditions can play a role in surprising ways. In China, the number eight is associated with prosperity and good luck while the number four is associated with death. A research study confirmed that marketers in China avoided prices that ended in four, whereas prices ending in eight were advertised four times more often than prices ending in other numerals.[21]

One aspect that can vary by culture is the role that high prices play in the purchasing decision. For example, Japanese are observed to pay unusually high prices for status products, and status cars command higher prices in Japan than they do in the United States. Some observers refer to this phenomenon as the "special Japanese price." A BMW that lists for about $56,000 in the United States will sell for $84,000 in Japan. Similarly, a Mercedes that sells for $57,000 in the United States will cost over $85,000 in Japan.[22] High prices can also be a cue for quality, but this can vary by culture as well. A study of American and Thai consumers concluded that the Thai consumers perceived themselves to lack product knowledge compared to the perceptions of the U.S. consumers. This caused the Thais to more likely infer product quality from price.[23]

Bargaining for a better price is another aspect of consumer behavior that is more common in some cultures than others. In many emerging markets, such as Turkey, bargaining is acceptable— even expected—in the more traditional markets. Chinese consumers, who are also accustomed to bargaining, are using the Internet to increase their bargaining advantage. Websites encourage Chinese to get together and form buying teams to visit retail outlets and ask for quantity discounts. Hundreds of thousands of consumers registered on just one such site in a single year. In Shanghai such a buying team negotiated discount prices from a General Motors dealership. However, some international retailers have refused to bargain.[24]

Buyer Power

Just as discretionary income is an important consideration in consumer markets, buyer power is crucial in B2B markets. In the recent recession in Europe, a major grocery chain removed about 300 Unilever products from its Belgium stores, claiming the prices were too high.[25] Large buyers, whether they be in retailing, services or manufacturing, can become important to supplier firms, and in turn these buyers can demand lower prices from suppliers. If there are only a few buyers in a national industry, prices may be lower than in markets where there are many smaller buyers. In some global industries, such as aerospace, suppliers face the challenge of increasing buyer power at the international level.

Competition

The intensity and power of competition can also significantly affect price levels in any given market. A firm acting as the sole supplier of a product in a given market enjoys greater pricing flexibility. The opposite is true if that same company has to compete against several other local or international firms. Therefore, the number and type of competitors greatly influence pricing strategy in any market. China has become the world's second largest car market. It is also one of the most competitive. Price cuts by both domestic and global automobile companies cut profit margins for all competitors. It is not unusual to see as much as 27 percent discounted off a list price in China.[26]

Occasionally, price levels are manipulated by cartels, or pricing agreements among competitors. Cartels in the United States are forbidden by law. Furthermore, U.S. companies may find themselves in violation of U.S. laws if they actively participate in any foreign cartel. Although many other foreign governments allow cartels provided that they do not injure the consumer, the EU is becoming stricter toward cartels. Companies found guilty under EU antitrust laws can be fined 10 percent of their annual revenue.[27]

World Beat 12.1

Ordered to Cartel?

As China's manufacturing gains in global market share, China's ability to set world prices increases as well—especially as many Chinese firms apparently see no reason to avoid collaborating on pricing. The Chinese manufacturers call it "self-regulation." Of course, such collaboration has made them the targets of recent antitrust investigations in the United States.

Vitamin C is a case in point. After Vitamin C prices tripled, two U.S.-based companies, an animal feed company and a vitamin distributor, alleged that Chinese manufacturers of vitamin C had formed a cartel to establish high prices. The companies didn't dispute the charge. Instead they put forth two lines of defense: first, the companies asserted that they had raised prices to avoid accusations of dumping; second, the companies claimed they were acting as agents of the Chinese government and were therefore not subject to U.S. antitrust laws. The latter claim was based on the fact that the Chinese Ministry of Commerce had ordered the four companies to fix the higher price and an act of state is rarely prosecuted in a foreign court. For example, the member countries of the oil cartel OPEC are not prosecuted for price-fixing.

A U.S. district judge found the Chinese defense to be "unprecedented" and dismissed the claim to sovereign immunity. Many others were equally unsympathetic. One observer noted that Chinese companies priced their products low until they drove other competitors out of the market. Then they raised prices.

Several of the companies eventually settled out of court. The fourth was found guilty under U.S. antitrust laws and fined $162 million. China's Ministry of Commerce urged the court to reverse its ruling, pointing out that the judgment failed to defer to Chinese law. Perhaps in retaliation, the Chinese government also began its own sweeping investigation of possible price-fixing in China among foreign makers of baby formula.

Sources: Laurie Burkitt, Brent Kendall and Chad Bray, "Chinese Vitamin-C Suppliers Found Liable for Price-Fixing," *Wall Street Journal*, March 15, 2013, p. B1; Laurie Burkitt, "China Investigates Foreign Makers of Baby Formula," *Wall Street Journal*, July 2, 2013, p. B4; "Chinese to Appeal U.S. Price Fixing Fines," *China Daily*, December 6, 2013; and Jeff Sistrunk, "China Urges 2nd Circuit to Nix Vitamin C Price-fixing Ruling," *Law 360*, April 15, 2014.

Environmental Factors That Affect Pricing

We have thus far treated pricing as a matter of cost and market factors. A number of environmental factors also influence pricing at the international level. These external variables, which are not subject to control by any individual company, include foreign exchange rates, inflation and government price controls, dumping regulations and the credit and collection infrastructure of various markets. These factors restrict company decision-making authority and can become major concerns for country managers.

Exchange Rate Fluctuations

As discussed in Chapter 2, one of the most unpredictable factors affecting prices is the movement of foreign exchange rates. In a single year, currencies in at least 20 countries fell 6 to 37 percent against the U.S. dollar.[28]

As the exchange rate moves up and down, it particularly affects exporters. When a company's costs are in its domestic currency, as this currency weakens, the firm's costs appear lower in another currency. For example, when the euro was first launched, each euro was valued at $1.20. Six months later, the euro had dropped to $1.00. As a result, costs of products manufactured in Europe were cheaper in dollar terms and more attractive in the U.S. market, as well as in other national markets where governments pegged their currencies to the U.S. dollar.

Foreign exchange fluctuations can also present difficulties for companies that export from countries with appreciating currencies. These firms are forced to accept decreased margins on sales denominated in foreign currencies or else raise prices to maintain their prior margins. The latter option could, of course, cause a drop in export demand. This was clear when the Russian ruble fell 22 percent over a period of a few months. Exports to Russia fell 50 percent. Faced with the option of buying a tube of locally produced toothpaste for seven rubles or a tube of imported Colgate for 24 rubles, fewer Russian consumers chose the Colgate.[29]

Inflation Rates

The rate of inflation can affect product costs and may force a company to take specific action. Inflation rates have fluctuated over time and, more importantly, have differed from country to country. The United States and Europe have successfully managed inflation by raising interest rates whenever the economy starts to heat up, keeping inflation at 0 to 3 percent. Historically, inflation has been more of a problem in developing countries. In some cases, inflation rates have risen to several hundred percent. Argentina, Bolivia, Brazil and Nicaragua have all experienced four-digit hyperinflation in the past. A country can be particularly susceptible to inflation if its currency devalues. This causes most imported goods to rise in cost almost immediately, adding to inflationary pressures.

Host governments can be sensitive to high inflation rates because they can suggest mismanagement of the economy. The Chinese government fined Unilever for publicly speaking about price hikes in the wake of inflation, although other companies were not fined for actually raising prices.[30]

A company can usually protect itself from rapid inflation if it maintains constant operating margins by constantly adjusting prices. However, consumer incomes often lag inflation, and many consumers may decide that higher prices simply price products out of their reach. Also, this strategy can be undermined if governments decide to enact price controls. In any case, whether or not to raise prices in the face of inflation remains a managerial decision. McDonald's raised prices across its 1,200 stores in China as a result of inflation.[31] However, even when faced with skyrocketing inflation that affected its input costs for instant noodles in India, Nestlé determined that raising prices was not an option due to intense competition. Instead it decided to decrease the package size.[32]

Price Controls

Despite the official claim that nearly all prices are set by the market, the Chinese government has enforced price controls on such key products as fertilizers, fuel, medicines and transport services. Price controls are most common in developing countries and may be applied to an entire economy to combat inflation. Alternatively, regulations may be applied selectively to specific industries. As a result of market liberalization, across-the-board price controls are now rare. Industry-specific controls are more common. Pharmaceuticals are subject to price controls in many countries, including Canada, Japan and European states. In the Philippines, where one-third of the country lives on $2 a day, the government imposed price controls on five widely used medications.[33]

Strategic Responses to Price Controls

Governments may allow a firm to raise prices if the firm produces evidence that the cost of producing its product has increased, which is often the case. This procedure requires significant management time, and the outcome is uncertain. Even if the price increase is ultimately approved, profit margins are likely to have deteriorated in the meantime. Alternatively, or additionally, a firm might address price controls by seeking product modifications that result in lower input costs and thus maintain or increase margins. Companies can also decide to leave a market because of price controls. However, price controls are usually temporary. Firms often discover that exiting a market can hurt a brand should they ever decide to re-enter the market when price controls are retracted.

One of the best strategies to survive price controls is to have diversified markets. When corn prices shot up 67 percent during the ethanol craze, Mexico imposed price controls on tortillas and corn flour. Gruma, the country's largest flour manufacturer, supplied 75 percent of the corn flour used to make tortillas in Mexico. Luckily, the company had diversified internationally, and two-thirds of its sales were outside Mexico.[34]

Dumping Regulations

The practice of exporting a product at an "unfair" price and consequently damaging local competition is referred to as dumping. Because of potential injuries to domestic manufacturers, most governments have adopted regulations against dumping. Antidumping actions are allowed under provisions of the WTO as long as two criteria are met: prices are set at less than "normal value" and this results in "material injury" to a domestic industry. The first criterion is usually interpreted to mean selling abroad at prices below those in the country of origin, although there are some exceptions. Subsequently, a complainant government may be required to establish that prices in its country are indeed set below full costs of manufacture, transport and marketing. The WTO rules prohibit assessment of retroactive punitive duties and require all procedures to be open.

For many years most antidumping charges were brought by the United States, Canada, the EU and Australia—often against Asian countries. For example, Whirlpool asked the U.S. government to impose duties on refrigerators made by South Korean manufacturers LG and Samsung. Whirlpool alleged that the two South Korean companies were selling refrigerators at prices in the United States that were lower than the cost to produce them.[35]

However, many of the new antidumping cases have been brought to the WTO by developing countries such as South Africa, India, Brazil, Indonesia and Mexico. International marketers have to be aware of antidumping legislation that sets a floor under export prices, limiting pricing flexibility even in the event of overcapacity or an industry slowdown. On the other hand, antidumping legislation can work to a company's advantage, protecting it from foreign competition.

Credit and Collection Infrastructure

Pricing can also be affected by the availability of credit in a country and the ability to collect payment if credit is extended to consumers. In India, most rural cell phone customers use prepaid cards instead of signing up for a monthly payment plan.[36] One reason for this is the need for poorer consumers to buy service in affordable amounts. However, the simple act of billing for cell phone service is undermined if a bill cannot be sent because mail service is unreliable. Internet billing is equally untenable if consumers are unlikely to have access to the Internet to pay their bills online.

In China, credit cards have lagged Internet use, posing a problem for online marketing. Online marketers rely instead on expensive cash-on-delivery systems or online payment options similar to the U.S. service PayPal. Either of these options increases costs, which have to be paid by either the seller or the buyer.

Letters of Credit

Small manufacturers and wholesalers account for about 34 percent of U.S. exports. However, a survey by the Small Business Exporters Association revealed that 41 percent of respondents worried about getting paid, up from 26 percent just four years earlier.[37] Letters of credit exist to allay such fears. Letters of credit are documents issued by banks or similar financial institutions to assure that exporters are paid by their customers abroad.

The buyer, or applicant, arranges for the letter of credit and pays for its issuance. The applicant also arranges to pay the financial institution the amount due the exporter. When the exporter supplies the financial institution with the agreed paperwork, the financial institution releases payment to the exporter. The necessary documentation required for most letters of credit is governed by the International Chamber of Commerce and involves proper evidence of shipment. Because of some past problems with the delivery of inferior or damaged goods, some letters of credit may require that the shipments pass an agreed upon examination upon arrival at customs.

Managerial Issues in Global Pricing

Now that we have given you a general overview of the context of international pricing, we turn to managerial issues—matters that require constant management attention and are never really resolved. These issues include export price escalation, transfer pricing, quoting prices in foreign currencies, responding to parallel markets, setting global prices and managing countertrade.

Managing Export Price Escalation

As Table 12.3 illustrates, there are additional costs described earlier that can raise the price of an exported product substantially above its domestic price. This phenomenon is called export price escalation, and it raises both tactical and strategic questions. Tactically, an exporter must decide

Table 12.3 Export Price Escalation: An Example

Delivered Cost of Product	Domestic Market	Export Market
Factory Price	$10.00	$10.00
Domestic Transportation	$1.00	$0.75
Export Documentation		$0.75
Overseas Freight		$1.75
Insurance		$0.25
Tariff		$0.75
Final Price	$11.00	$14.25

who pays for the different costs involved in exporting, whether or not to re-engineer the product to keep costs down, and whether or not to explore a cheaper locale from which to export the product. The main strategic question is whether or not to reposition the product overseas.

If a firm employs a foreign distributor or sells directly to a customer abroad, it must clarify which of the various export costs are borne by the exporting firm and which are borne by the foreign distributor or customer. There are many terms utilized in export pricing that help clarify this issue. Lists of these terms are often available at national export portals including the U.S. export portal at www.export.gov. However among the more common terms are:

- **CIF (cost, insurance, freight)** is a term commonly used for ocean shipments and designates that the price quoted by the exporter includes the price for the goods and their transportation, including insurance, to a foreign port of debarkation.
- **CFR (cost and freight)** is similar to CIF in that it covers the cost of goods and transportation. However, the distributor or customer is responsible for paying to insure the goods in transit.
- **FOB (free on board)** designates that the exporter only pays for the cost of delivering the goods to the port of export. The buyer is responsible for the costs of loading, shipping and insuring the products.

No matter who pays these different costs, export price escalation is likely to make the product more expensive overseas unless the exporter, the distributor or both accept lower margins. Instead of accepting lower margins, a company may seek ways to decrease the costs of exported products such as re-engineering its products to be less costly. Also, export sales may generate greater economies of scale in production, eventually allowing for a lower export price. Global marketers should also be careful in export pricing not to attribute costs to exports that only apply to products sold domestically, such as the cost of advertising in the domestic market. Finally, an exporting firm may seek a cheaper production locale. If tariffs are high and the export market attractive, the firm might decide to produce, or assemble, in the foreign market itself. Ford was able to sell the cars it assembled in Russia at a much lower price than the imported cars of competitors, even though Ford imported 80 percent of the parts it used to make its Russian cars.[38]

Alternatively, a company may make the strategic decision to adjust the marketing mix to promote a more upscale status. This was a strategy adopted by California's My Dollarstore Inc. when the company entered India. The dollar stores offered middle-class Indians, many of whom had studied or worked in the United States, a sense of being back in America with offerings like Hershey's chocolate syrup and the latest flavor of Pringles potato chips. In the United States, dollar stores targeted bargain shoppers and were located in lower-rent strip malls. All products were priced at a dollar. In India, where transportation costs and tariffs had to be considered, products had to be priced at about two dollars. Consequently, dollar stores were opened in upscale malls and targeted the affluent.[39]

Determining Transfer Prices

A substantial amount of international market transactions take place between subsidiaries of the same company. It has been estimated that in-house trading between subsidiaries accounts for one-third of the volume among the world's 800 largest MNCs. An international transfer price is the price paid by the importing or buying unit of a firm to the exporting unit of the same firm. For example, the U.S. marketing subsidiary of a Taiwanese manufacturer of personal computers will pay a transfer price for the machines it receives from Taiwan. The actual transfer price may be negotiated by the units involved or may be set centrally by the MNC. How these prices are set continues to be a major issue for companies and governments alike.

Because negotiations of transfer prices do not represent arm's-length negotiations between independent participants, the resulting prices frequently differ from free-market prices. Companies may deviate from arm's-length prices to maximize profits or to minimize risk and uncertainty. To pursue a strategy of profit maximization, a company may lower transfer prices for products shipped from some subsidiaries, while increasing prices for products shipped to others, in order to accumulate profits in countries where it is advantageous, while keeping profits low elsewhere.

Different tax, tariff or subsidy structures among countries frequently invite such practices. By accumulating more profits in a low-tax country, a company lowers its overall tax bill and thus increases profit. Likewise, tariff duties can be reduced by quoting low transfer prices to countries with high tariffs. In cases where countries use a different exchange rate for the transfer of goods from that used for the transfer of capital or profits, a firm may attempt to use transfer prices to remove money from the country, rather than transferring profits at less advantageous rates. The same is true for countries with limits on profit repatriation. Finally, a company may want to accumulate profits in a wholly owned subsidiary rather than in one in which it has minority ownership. By using the transfer price mechanism, it can decrease the profits it shares with local partners.

Companies may also use transfer prices to minimize risk or uncertainty by moving profits or assets out of a country with chronic balance-of-payment problems and frequent devaluations. Because regular profit remittances may be strictly controlled in such countries, many firms see high transfer prices as the only way to repatriate funds and thereby reduce the amount of assets at risk. The same practice may be employed if a company anticipates political or social disturbances or a direct threat to profits through government intervention.

In actual practice, companies choose a number of approaches to transfer pricing. Market-based prices are equal to those negotiated with independent buyers. Of 30 U.S.-based firms, 46 percent were reported to use market-based systems.[40] Another 35 percent used cost-based systems to determine the transfer price. Costs were based on a predetermined formula that could include a standard markup for profits.

Internal Considerations

The use of the transfer prices mechanism to reduce a company's income taxes and duties or to maximize profits in strong currency areas can create difficulties for subsidiary managers whose profits are artificially reduced. It may be hard to motivate managers when the direct profit incentive is removed. Furthermore, company resource allocation may become inefficient, because funds are appropriated to units whose profits are artificially increased. Conversely, resources may be denied to subsidiaries whose income statements were subject to transfer-price-induced reductions. It is generally agreed that a transfer pricing mechanism should not be used for resource allocations; the gains incurred through tax savings may easily be lost through other inefficiencies.

External Problems

Governments do not look favorably on transfer pricing mechanisms aimed at reducing their tax revenues. U.S. government policy on transfer pricing is governed by tax law, particularly Section 482 of the Revenue Act of 1962. The act is designed to provide an accurate allocation of costs, income and capital among related enterprises to protect U.S. tax revenue.

Market prices are generally preferred by the U.S. Internal Revenue Service (IRS). The IRS will accept cost-plus markups if market prices are not available and economic circumstances warrant such use. Not acceptable, however, are transfer prices that attribute no profit to the U.S. unit. Other methods, such as negotiated prices, are acceptable as long as the transfer price is comparable to a price charged to an unrelated party. In addition, the IRS requires all companies to maintain detailed explanations of the rationale and analysis supporting their transfer pricing policy. The IRS developed the Advanced Pricing Agreement Program (APA), which became effective on December 31, 1993. Under this program, a company can obtain prior approval from the IRS for their transfer pricing procedures.

Australia, Japan and Korea all have formal transfer pricing arrangements, and China, India and New Zealand have informal programs.[41] However, the strengthening of government regulations all around the world makes it necessary for global businesses to document and defend their transfer pricing methods. According to a study of 280 MNCs operating in Europe, 85 percent had been audited on transfer pricing over a three-year period.[42] Audits of transfer pricing policies can result in billions of dollars of tax liability. The U.S. IRS issued GlaxoSmithKline a tax bill of $5 billion as a result of an IRS audit that began over 12 years earlier. The IRS argued that the company transferred costs to the United States from other countries at inflated prices to reduce their U.S. tax burden.[43]

For years the OECD established rules and best practices for transfer pricing to assure that companies didn't use transfer prices to manipulate the taxes they owed in different jurisdictions. More recently, emerging markets such as Brazil and India have challenged those rules, arguing that their own national laws that set appropriate margins for local subsidiaries are more appropriate. Critics argue, however, that the transfer pricing laws of these countries require companies to show disproportionally large profits in those countries.[44]

Quoting Prices in a Foreign Currency

For many international marketing transactions, it is not always feasible to quote in a company's domestic currency when selling or purchasing merchandise. Although the majority of U.S. exporters quote prices in dollars, there are situations in which customers may prefer quotes in their own national currency. In fact, a research study of 671 companies in the United States, Finland and Sweden found that companies that respond to customers' requests for prices quoted in their local currencies benefit from a larger volume of export business.[45]

Managing Transaction Risk

When two currencies are involved in a market transaction, there is the risk that a change in exchange rates may occur between the invoicing date and the settlement date for the sale. This transaction risk is an inherent factor in international marketing and clearly separates domestic from international business. Fortunately, alternatives are available to protect the seller from transaction risk.

For most major currencies, international foreign exchange dealers located at major banks quote a spot price and a forward price. The spot price determines the number of dollars to be paid for a particular foreign currency purchased or sold today. The forward price quotes the number of dollars to be paid for a foreign currency bought or sold 30, 90 or 180 days from today. The forward price, however, is not necessarily speculation about what the spot price will be in the future. Instead, the forward price reflects interest rate differentials between two currencies for maturities of 30, 90 or 180 days. Consequently, there are no firm indications of what the spot price will be for any given currency in the future.

A company quoting in foreign currency for purchase or sale can simply leave settlement until the due date and pay whatever spot price prevails at the time. Such an uncovered position may be chosen when exchange rates are not expected to shift or when any shift in the near future will result in a gain for the company. With exchange rates fluctuating widely on a daily basis, even among major trading nations such as the United States, Japan, Germany and the United Kingdom, a company can expose itself to substantial foreign exchange risks. Because many international firms are in business to make a profit from the sale of goods rather than from speculation in the foreign exchange markets, managers generally protect themselves from unexpected fluctuations.

HEDGING One such protection lies in hedging. Instead of accepting whatever spot market rate exists on the settlement in 30 or 90 days, a company can opt to contract through financial intermediaries for future delivery of foreign currency at a set price, regardless of the spot price at that time. This allows the seller to incorporate a firm exchange rate into the price determination. Of course, if a company wishes to predict the spot price in 90 days and is reasonably certain about the accuracy of its prediction, it may attempt to choose the more advantageous of the two: the expected spot or the present forward rate. However, such predictions should only be made under the guidance of experts familiar with foreign exchange rates.

To illustrate the selection of a hedging procedure, assume that a U.S. exporter of corporate jets sells a jet valued at $24 million to a client in Germany (see Table 12.4). The client will pay in euros quoted at the current (spot) rate on March 3 of $1.31. This amount will be paid in three months (90 days). As a result, the U.S. exporter will have to determine how to protect such an incoming amount against foreign exchange risk. Although uncertain about the outcome, the exporter's bank indicates that there is equal chance for the euro spot rate to remain at $1.31 (scenario C), to devalue to $1.20 (scenario A) or to appreciate to $1.45 (scenario B). As a result,

Table 12.4 Hedging Scenarios

	A	B	C
Spot rate as of March 3	$1.31	$1.31	$1.31
Spot rate as of June 3 (estimate)	1.20	1.45	1.31
U.S. dollar equivalent of H18,320,610 at spot rate on June 3	21,984,735	26,564,884	24,000,000
Exchange gain (loss)	(2,015,265)	2,564,884	0

the exporter has the option of selling the amount forward in the 90-days forward market, at $1.3213.[46]

One option available to the exporter is to sell forward the invoice amount to obtain a sure $23,947,980 at a cost of $52,020 on the transaction. In anticipation of a devaluation of the euro, such a hedging strategy would be advisable. Consequently, the $52,020 represents a premium to ensure against any larger loss such as the one predicted under scenario A. However, a company would also forgo any gain as indicated under scenario B.

Sometimes hedging is not an option when a firm is dealing with soft currencies or currencies undergoing upheaval. Prior to an expected devaluation of the ruble, nearly all exporters to Russia were seeking hedging contracts. Hedging contracts for rubles became increasingly hard to find and then disappeared from the market altogether. Once when the Turkish government allowed the pegged lira to float, the lira collapsed nearly 40 percent over a few days. In the immediate disarray that ensued, hedging opportunities for the lira were similarly difficult to locate.

COVERING THROUGH THE MONEY MARKET An alternative to hedging is covering through the money market. This involves borrowing funds in the currency at risk for the time until settlement. For example, a U.S. exporter that is holding accounts receivable in euros and is unwilling to absorb the related currency risk may borrow euros and exchange them for dollars for working-capital purposes. When the customer eventually pays in euros, the U.S. exporter uses these euros to pay off the euro-denominated loan. Any currency fluctuations will be canceled, resulting in neither loss nor gain.

Dealing with Parallel Imports or Gray Markets

Parallel imports, or gray markets, are imported products that enter a market outside the official distribution channels established by the trademark owner. Sometimes this occurs because of lack of supply. Apple Inc. launched its latest iPhone in nine countries in a single day. Russia, the tenth largest wireless market, wasn't among them. Instead the company waited three months to launch the new iPhone in the Russian market. As a result, a parallel market for the product in Russia appeared almost immediately.[47] In another case, Nevada Furniture, a parallel importer, decided to sell Ikea furniture in South Africa, a market where IKEA had yet to open stores.[48]

However, parallel imports often occur because global marketers choose to sell the same product at different prices in different national markets due to different market and competitive factors. When such price differences become large enough, entrepreneurs may step in and buy products in low-price countries to re-export to high-price countries, profiting from the price differential.

Gray markets have never been more robust. Parallel imports within the EU have been encouraged by the introduction of the euro, which allows easy price comparisons from country to country. Similarly, gray markets have soared in response to the Internet, which enables buyers to compare prices easily across markets. In some cases, intermediaries are not even necessary to fuel parallel imports. Many older Americans buy their prescription drugs through one of many online and mail order Canadian pharmacies where prices are considerably cheaper. Although it is technically illegal for individuals to import pharmaceuticals into the United States, the law is rarely enforced.

Companies deplore gray markets because they hurt relationships with authorized dealers and especially because they undermine a company's ability to charge different prices in different markets in order to maximize global profits. Parallel imports are even credited with adding to Coca-Cola's public relations difficulties subsequent to a product-harm crisis in Europe. The company began a product recall after hundreds of Coke drinkers in Belgium complained of getting sick. Unfortunately, tracking down the questionable Belgium-produced Coke was complicated; it began showing up in places it shouldn't have been, such as Spain, Germany and the United Kingdom. But this should have come as no surprise. The gray market for soft drinks is substantial in Europe.

Also worrisome is the fact that parallel imports of an authentic product and counterfeits of that product may become intermingled in the distribution system. Increasingly, companies discover that shipments of parallel imports, such as Davidoff Cool Waters cologne and Kia auto parts, are mixed in with counterfeits of their products.[49]

Seeking Legal Redress from the Country of Import

Global firms would like governments to forbid parallel imports from entering their countries. But legal attempts to stop parallel imports have been stymied by the fact that governments around the world have taken different stands on gray markets. At issue is the right of a trademark owner to manage the sale of a trademarked product versus the ability of consumers to enjoy the lower prices usually provided by parallel imports. Most countries adopt some variation of the exhaustion principle that establishes the conditions under which a trademark owner relinquishes its right to control the resale of its product.

World Beat 12.2

Cheaper Cars for Korea

Imported cars were once a luxury in South Korea, commanding high prices. Those days are over. Parallel importers of high-end foreign automobiles are discovering a new, more price conscious Korean consumer. Ironically, it isn't only foreign cars that enter Korea through parallel markets. When South Korean Hyundai Motors launched its premium sports sedan Genesis in the United States, the price was set at $33,000. In Korea, the Genesis sold for over $48,000. One of the reasons for such a large difference in price was a Korean tax of 24.3 percent levied on vehicles that are both made and sold in Korea.

Recent agreements with the United States and the EU have cut in half tariffs on automobiles imported from those regions, just as higher labor costs have driven up the price for many Korean-made cars. The result has been a surge in sales for imported cars, with some BMWs selling for cheaper than Hyundais. Overall, foreign brands saw their share of the Korean luxury vehicle market rise to 41 percent from 28 percent in only two years.

When the South Korea government reduced consumption taxes in an effort to spur the economy, this should have been good news for all car manufacturers. However a price war soon developed between local and imported cars as the local auto manufacturers attempted to abate the surge of imports.

Sources: "South Korean Carmakers Slash Prices," *Maeil Business Newspaper*, September 11, 2012; "Why is a Car That's Made in Korea Cheaper in the U.S.," Joins.com, September 2, 2008; "GM Korea Cuts Sticker Prices on Five Models," Joins.com, January 14, 2013; Rose Kim, "BMWs Cheaper Than Hyundais in Korea as Tariffs Crumble," *Bloomberg News*, May 15, 2013; and Norihiko Shirouzu Hyunjoo Kim, "GM Plans Gradual Pullout of S. Korea as Labor Costs Surge," *Reuters*, August 11, 2013.

NATIONAL EXHAUSTION PRINCIPLE National exhaustion provides that once a firm has sold its trademarked product in a specific country, it cannot restrict the further distribution of that product in that particular country. However, the firm retains the legal right to stop its products from entering another country as parallel imports. Unfortunately for global marketers, few countries adopt this principle, and when they do it often has limited application. For example, the United States recognizes national exhaustion for ethical pharmaceuticals. However, even this limited restriction of parallel imports is constantly under political attack by those who promote lower pharmaceutical prices in the U.S. market.

REGIONAL EXHAUSTION PRINCIPLE Regional exhaustion provides that once a firm has sold a trademarked product anywhere in a region it cannot restrict the resale of that product within that region. The EU follows the principle of regional exhaustion. Once a trademarked product is sold anywhere in the EU, the trademark owner cannot restrict its resale within the EU. However, the EU does allow trademark owners to stop parallel imports from coming into the EU from countries outside the EU. Nintendo, the Japanese video game firm, was found in violation of European antitrust laws for working with distributors to illegally prevent sales from one EU country to another in order to keep prices high.[50] But the European Court of Justice upheld the right of Levi Strauss to stop parallel imports of its jeans coming into the United Kingdom from the United States at lower prices.

INTERNATIONAL EXHAUSTION PRINCIPLE Many developed countries and most developing countries have adopted the principle of international exhaustion.[51] When a country adopts this principle it is virtually impossible to legally stop parallel imports from entering that national market. These countries welcome parallel imports into their country in order to encourage lower prices. In addition, developing countries are less concerned with the rights of trademark owners, since relatively few of their local firms hold valuable trademarks.

LEGAL COMPLEXITY AND LIMITS TO LEGAL REDRESS Whichever exhaustion principle is adopted by a country, national laws concerning parallel imports are in fact very complex. For example, Japan recognizes international exhaustion unless otherwise agreed by contract or if the original sale is subject to price controls. U.S. laws concerning parallel imports are among the most confusing, possibly because they have evolved within the case law system. Essentially, the United States asserts that a firm exhausts its rights to restrict the resale of a product into the United States once that product is sold anywhere in the world. However, similar to Japan, the United States recognizes certain exceptions, but most of these exceptions have had little effect on gray markets.

393

The one exception that companies have found useful in stopping parallel imports into the United States allows trademark owners to stop parallel imports from entering the U.S. market when those products are materially different from those being officially sold in the United States. For example, in the case of Perugina chocolate made in Venezuela under license from the Italian trademark owner, the court ruled that the parallel imported chocolate made in Venezuela was different from the chocolate produced in Italy. The quality level, fat content, ingredients and packaging varied and were likely to cause confusion to the American consumer.[52] Therefore, the Italian trademark owner could restrict the import of the Venezuelan product into the U.S. market.

However, simply being "materially different" in a minor way may not be enough. John Wiley & Sons, a U.S.-based textbook publisher, sued a Thai student for importing their cheaper Asian versions of textbooks sold in the United States and selling them for $1.2 million mostly on eBay. The textbooks in question contained a copyright notice stating, "This book is authorized for sale in Europe, Asia, Africa, and the Middle East only and may not be exported out of these territories." A lower court ruled that the U.S. first-sales doctrine that allowed buyers to resell purchased products did not apply to products first sold outside the United States and that the publisher could legally stop the parallel imports. However, the U.S. Supreme Court reversed that decision.[53]

Legal Redress from the Country of Export

While it remains difficult to convince governments from the countries of import to forbid parallel imports when such imports lower prices for their citizens, legal redress from the country of export may be possible in some cases. A recent U.S. court decision upheld the right of automakers to forbid the resale overseas of cars bought in the United States.

About 35,000 luxury automobiles sold in the United States enter the parallel market each year. One major market is China, where a car selling for $56,000 in the United States can sell for three times that price in the Chinese market. To try and control these sales, car manufacturers require buyers to sign contracts limited the exporting of cars for a stated amount of time. However, major gray marketers recruit individual buyers to buy the cars under false pretenses and to deliver the cars to them instead. Previously, the car manufacturers could try to sue the gray marketers for breach of contract only. However, they won a major victory when the U.S. government agreed to prosecute the gray marketers for fraud, a criminal offense. The gray marketers continue to argue that they should be able to do what they want with a car they purchase. But the manufacturers argue that they have a right to charge different prices in different countries and to garner the profits from such a pricing strategy.[54]

Other Corporate Responses to Gray Markets

Research involving U.S. exporters identified several factors that significantly discouraged parallel imports:[55]

CUSTOMIZE PRODUCTS BY MARKET First, firms that customize products more for local markets experience fewer problems with parallel imports. Even if the physical product stays the same, warranty customization may be employed. An authorized Porsche distributor in Singapore offered five years of free maintenance as a way to deter competition from parallel imports of the luxury automobile.[56]

MAINTAIN SYSTEM CONTROL Firms experience fewer problems with gray markets if they own or maintain greater control over their distribution systems. Parallel imports are also less likely to occur if a MNC maintains greater centralized control than if it allows national subsidiaries greater autonomy. One reason for this last observation is the fact that some local subsidiaries knowingly participate in parallel markets. For example, certain national managers at Bausch and Lomb cooperated with gray marketers in order to raise their own local sales figures, even though the parallel imports they helped fuel in other countries hurt the company overall.[57]

ALERT BUYERS Another option is to alert consumers to the benefits of purchasing products through legitimate channels. This can be effective when product warranties, only available through authorized dealers, are important to buyers. In fact, a law in South Africa requires parallel importers to alert consumers to the fact that the local authorized dealer is under no obligation to honor a manufacturer guaranty or warranty for products purchased on the gray market. This alert is required for all product displays and in-store promotions as well as for all advertisements and websites.[58]

CONTROL SUPPLY A somewhat controversial option to stop gray markets is to limit supplies to distributors in lower-priced markets. The Bayer Group attempted to stop the parallel imports into the United Kingdom of a Bayer cardiovascular medicine, Adalat, from France and Spain, where the price of the drug was 40 percent lower. Bayer limited the amount wholesalers in these two countries could receive to the estimated demand of their own markets. The wholesalers complained, and the European Commission fined Bayer for what it considered anticompetitive agreements to limit parallel imports. However, the European Court of Justice reversed the earlier ruling of the European Commission, therefore allowing pharmaceutical manufacturers to limit supply to countries that are involved in parallel trade.

CONSIDER STRATEGIC PRICING Finally, strategic pricing may be used to keep prices within a range of each other, thus destroying opportunities for arbitrage. Such a strategy usually requires cutting prices in higher-priced markets and thus forgoing prior profits. It may also require raising prices in lower-priced markets and consequently losing sales. However, given limited legal redress and increasingly sophisticated parallel importers, firms realize that this is perhaps a necessary strategy to effectively address gray markets.

Setting Global Prices

To maximize a company's revenues, it would appear logical to set prices on a market-by-market basis, seeking in each market the best combination of price and expected volume to yield the maximum profit. This strategy was common for many firms in the early part of their international development. For many consumer products there are still significant price differences across many countries.

With the advent of global branding, MNCs have become more concerned about issues of global pricing. They rarely dictate uniform prices in every country but do establish a particular pricing policy across countries—relatively higher prices for premium brands and relatively lower prices for value brands. In a study of global pricing policies among MNCs from developed countries, the likelihood that a subsidiary would follow a pricing policy similar to that of the parent company in the home market was found to be influenced by market similarity in economic conditions, legal environment, customer characteristics and stage in the product life cycle.[59]

Uniform Pricing Policy

However, for products that are similar in many markets and for which transportation costs are not significant, substantial price differences quickly result in the emergence of parallel imports. This has led some firms to consider a policy of more uniform pricing worldwide. Employing a uniform pricing strategy on a global scale requires that a company charge the same price everywhere when that price is translated into a base currency. For example, in India, LVMH sells the Tag Heuer sports watch at prices of Rs 18,000 to Rs 40,000 which is on a par with the international prices that would be paid for the same watch in Dubai.[60]

Furthermore, global firms need to be careful about presenting varying prices to business customers with international operations. Oracle Corporation began standardizing prices for its software in response to business customers who questioned why the price in their country was higher than the price in other countries. In fact, global customers usually pressure for lower prices as well as for uniform prices. In a research study done with more than 50 executives responsible for global account management in the Americas, Europe and Asia, global customers reported that they believed global procurement was a way to extract lower prices from their suppliers.[61]

Modified Uniform Pricing Policy

In reality, a uniform pricing strategy becomes very difficult to achieve whenever different taxes, trade margins and customs duties are involved. Furthermore, firms that start out with identical prices in various countries soon find that prices have to change to stay in line with often substantial currency fluctuations. Although it is becoming increasingly clear that market-by-market pricing strategies will cause difficulties, many firms have found that changing to a uniform pricing policy is rather like pursuing a moving target. However, a company can employ modified uniform pricing by carefully monitoring price levels in each country and avoiding large gaps that encourage gray marketers to move in and take advantage of large price differentials.

Noncash Pricing: Countertrade

Sometimes international marketers come across situations in which an interested customer in an emerging market will not be able to arrange hard-currency financing. In such circumstances, the customer might offer a product or commodity in return. Such transactions, known as countertrade, were once estimated at 15 to 25 percent of world trade, although with the collapse of the former Soviet Union the volume of countertrade has declined significantly. Still, many countries have some form of countertrade requirement as part of their public procurement program.

There are a number of different forms of countertrade, including compensation transactions, offset deals and cooperation agreements.

Compensation Transactions

One usually speaks of a compensation transaction when the value of an export delivery is at least partially offset by an import transaction, or vice versa. Compensation transactions are typical for large government purchases, such as for defense projects, when a country wants to obtain some additional exports in exchange for the awarding of a contract. For example, the government of Indonesia has required winners of major government contracts to take part of their payment in Indonesian commodities apart from oil and gas. Compensation transactions fall into two categories: full compensation and partial compensation. Under full compensation the exporter commits to purchasing products or services at an amount equal to that specified in the export contract. Under partial compensation, the exporter receives a portion of the purchase price in hard currency and the remainder in merchandise.

In either case, the exporter will not be able to convert such merchandise into cash until a buyer can be found, and even then must usually do so at a discount. An option exists to sell such a commitment to a third party who may take over the commitment from the exporter for a fee. Therefore, when deciding whether to accept products for compensation, global marketers should differentiate between hard goods (easily salable merchandise) or soft goods (heavily discounted merchandise that may prove more difficult to resell).

Offset Deals

One of the most rapidly growing types of countertrade is the offset transaction. In an offset transaction, the selling company guarantees to use some products or services from the buying country in the final product. These transactions are particularly common when large government purchases are involved, such as purchases of public utilities or defense-related equipment. Governments are motivated to require offset deals because they can assist local businesses. The South African government used offset deals very effectively to stimulate local industrial development.

Cooperation Agreements or Buybacks

Cooperation agreements, or buybacks, are special types of countertrade deals extending over longer periods of time. Cooperation agreements usually involve related goods, such as payment for new textile machinery by the output produced by these machines. Although the sale of large equipment or of a whole factory can sometimes be clinched only by a cooperation agreement involving buyback of plant output, long-term negative effects must be considered before any deal is concluded. In industries such as steel or chemicals, the effect of high-volume buyback arrangements between Western exporters of manufacturing technology and Eastern European importers has sometimes been devastating. Western countries, especially in Europe, have been flooded with surplus products, and the EU has established a general policy on cooperation arrangements to avoid further disruption of its domestic industries.

Managing Countertrade

The participants in a survey of 196 firms in Australia agreed that countertrade was of great importance (71 percent) and that it increased sales potential (67 percent), strengthened the firms' competitive position (61 percent) and fulfilled their buyers' requirements (53 percent).[62] Nonetheless, countertrade agreements can be complex and time-consuming. Thus they can be surprisingly demanding of corporate resources. Many larger firms have established specialized units whose single purpose is to engage in countertrade. Smaller companies can also take advantage of counter-trade by utilizing independent trading companies or a specialist broker.

Another challenge of countertrade arrangements is the difficulty in finding a buyer for the merchandise accepted as part of the transaction. Sometimes such transactions are concluded with organizations in countries where industry is protected. The merchandise, not easily salable on its own merits, may be of low quality. As a result, the exporter may have to sell the merchandise at a discount. The size of these discounts can vary considerably and can even run as high as a third of product value.

At the conclusion of the sales agreement, the exporter should obtain a very clear understanding of the merchandise offered for countertrade. The origin, quality, quantity and delivery schedules for the merchandise should all be spelled out. Given such a detailed description, a specialized trader can provide an estimate of the appropriate discount. The astute exporter will raise the price of the export contract to cover such potential discounts. Therefore, it is paramount that the exporter does not agree on any price before this other information is in hand. Maintaining flexibility in negotiation requires skill and patience but can spell the difference between making a profit and incurring a loss on a countertrade transaction.

Conclusion

Managing pricing policies for an international firm is an especially daunting task. The global marketer is confronted with a number of uncontrollable factors deriving from the economic, cultural and regulatory environment, all of which have an impact on how prices are established in various countries. In addition, coordinating pricing across countries is increasingly critical. Managing price differences across countries and keeping them within tolerable limits are major tasks in global pricing.

Because the factors that affect price levels on an international scale are always fluctuating, the global pricing task is a never-ending process in which each day may bring new problems to be resolved. Competitors and arbiters are quick to exploit any weaknesses whenever a company is slow to adapt or makes a wrong judgment. Therefore, the pricing strategies of any firm selling abroad, whether a new exporter or an established MNC, should remain under constant review.

Managerial Takeaways

1. *Pricing is critical for success in global marketing.*
2. *Costs to deliver a product or service can vary widely across markets.*
3. *Differences in market conditions—income levels, culture and competition—argue for different prices in different countries.*
4. *Differences in environment conditions—inflation rates, price controls and exchange rate fluctuations—also support national pricing strategies.*
5. *Due to savvy customers and the phenomenon of parallel imports, however, global marketers may discover that their options to differentiate prices across markets may be limited. In these cases, a modified uniform pricing policy may prove the most advantageous.*
6. *Managers in MNCs must also determine transfer prices between their firm's units, adhering to various national regulations while maintaining morale across units.*
7. *Pricing is becoming more and more competitive. It may be tempting to break antitrust laws concerning price-fixing. However, national governments are increasingly strict in their enforcement of these laws.*

Questions for Discussion

1. Discuss the difficulties involved in having a standardized price for a company's products across all countries. What advantages does charging a standardized price offer?
2. You are an exporter of industrial installations and have received a $100,000 order from a Japanese customer. The job will take six months to complete and will be paid in full at that time. Now your Japanese customer has called you to request a price quote in yen. What will you quote in yen? Why?
3. What factors may influence McDonald's to price their Big Mac differently throughout Latin America?
4. What should be the government's position on the issue of parallel imports? Should the government take any particular actions?

CASE 12.1   The Price of Coffee in China

When Starbucks, the Seattle-based coffee shop chain, first entered China, it faced a country of tea drinkers. Still, Japan too had been a country of tea drinkers but had evolved into a major coffee market. Starbucks itself had recently entered Japan and was already the top-ranked restaurant chain, according to a prestigious industry study. Top management at Starbucks was astounded at the firm's brand recognition across Asia, an awareness that had come about with virtually no investment in advertising. The company soon promoted China to a priority market.

In considering China, Starbucks noted that coffee consumption in a country is directly related to income. The firm sought to take advantage of growing disposable income in China, where PCI had reached $750 a year. In particular, Starbucks believed there would be substantial demand among younger urbanites in China. Confident in their decision, the firm entered the Chinese market with plans to open ten shops in Beijing in 18 months. The first Starbucks in Beijing was located in a shopping center across the street from a five-star hotel. Still, some were skeptical about the Starbucks move. Coffee sales had been growing between 5 and 8 percent a year in China. However, in the wake of the Asian financial crisis, many foreign expatriates left the country. Consequently, coffee sales growth had tapered off.

When Starbucks opened in Beijing, the store offered the same coffee products and other merchandise as was available in its U.S. shops. Starbucks' stated strategy was to set prices lower than those of comparable coffee shops already open in China. These other coffee shops targeted expatriates, tourists and elite Chinese. China's luxury market was among the fastest growing in the world. Luxury shoppers were largely young professionals, many of whom enjoyed trying new foreign brands. Starbucks hoped to target a larger segment of Chinese society. Therefore, prices were set similar to those charged in New York City, with a grande latte priced at $4.50. A local coffee shop in the same complex that charged prices even higher than those at Starbucks announced that it would lower prices to below those of the new U.S. competitor.

Fifteen years after Starbucks entered the Chinese market, prices in China were higher than in the United States, with a latte costing a full dollar more in China. China's major television channel, CCTV, ran a special news report on Starbucks' prices, professing outrage and noting that a tall latte in Beijing cost twice as much as it did in Bombay. Starbucks responded by explaining that theirs was a luxury brand in China and noting that several costs were higher in China such as staff training and supply-chain management. Also, stores had to be bigger due to the fact that Chinese didn't buy coffee to go but stayed and lingered over their drinks, socializing or doing their work.

Many Chinese bloggers ridiculed the CCTV segment: of course Starbucks was expensive. Why didn't the government focus on more important things? Others pointed out that the Starbucks report was but one among many exposés against foreign companies in the state-owned media. Apparently Beijing wants its citizens to begin buying Chinese. Nonetheless high prices were increasingly sensitive in China due to rising inflation. With increased travel and e-commerce, Chinese consumers are beginning to become aware of and consequently disturbed by price discrepancies between China and other markets. For Starbucks the pricing controversy came at a particularly bad time. A drought in Brazil had sent prices for Arabica beans from $1 a pound to $1.77 a pound.

Discussion Questions

1. What are the possible arguments for pricing a grande latte at $4.50 in Beijing?
2. What are the possible arguments for pricing lower? For pricing higher?
3. What might explain why the price of a Starbucks coffee in China increased in relation to its price in the United States over the years?
4. Evaluate Starbucks' response to the CCTV exposé. What response would you suggest?

Sources: "The Price of Coffee in China," in Kate Gillespie and H. David Hennessey, *Global Marketing* (Mason, OH: Cengage, 2011), pp. 365–366; "Hating Starbucks in Bejiing," *Wall Street Journal*, October 26, 2013, p. A12; Laurie Burkitt, "Starbucks Feels Heat Over Prices in China," *Wall Street Journal*, October 22, 2013, p. B8; Laurie Burkitt, "In China, the Veil Begins to Lift on High Consumer Prices," *Wall Street Journal*, September 4, 2013, p. B1; Katie Holliday and Wendy Min, "Why a Grande Latte Costs $1 More in China: Starbucks," CNBC, February 24, 2014; and Trefis Team, "Starbucks Delivers Strong Figures Again," *Forbes*, April 29, 2014.

CASE 12.2   The Price of Life

In a surprising announcement, the world's second largest pharmaceutical company, GlaxoSmithKline (GSK), announced that it would slash prices on the pharmaceuticals it sold in the world's poorest countries. The company challenged other pharmaceutical firms to do the same. Specifically, GSK declared that it would cut prices for all drugs in the 50 least developed countries to a level no higher than 25 percent of the price charged in the United States. The company also pledged to re-direct 20 percent of its profits from poor countries to hospitals, clinics and medical staff in those countries. In addition to slashing prices in the very poor markets, GSK also noted that it was determined to make drug prices more affordable in what it termed to be middle-income countries such as Brazil and Mexico.

This was not the first time a global pharmaceutical company had taken such action. Eight years earlier, Merck declared that it would cut prices by 40 to 55 percent in African markets on two of its recent AIDS-fighting drugs. Merck's powerful three-drug cocktail would be available in Africa for $1,330 a year, compared to approximately $11,000 in the United States. The company noted that it would be realizing no profits at this new price. Merck also pledged to extend these discounts to poor countries elsewhere in the world. Bristol-Myers followed suit, promising to slice the price of its AIDS drug Zerit to only $54 a year in Africa. At this price, Bristol-Myers claimed to be selling below costs. The company called on donor governments in Europe, Japan and the United States to join in a vigorous international response to the AIDS crisis in Africa, where over 26 million people were estimated to be infected with the HIV virus that eventually causes AIDS.

Shortly before, however, 39 major pharmaceutical companies had begun litigation to stop Indian pharmaceutical firms from selling generic versions of their patented drugs, including AIDS drugs, in the South African market. India had long refused to recognize pharmaceutical patents in order to supply its vast poor population with recent pharmaceutical products at much cheaper prices. Indian firms had become adept at reverse-engineering drugs and had become efficient producers and exporters of high-quality generics. When two Indian generic drug firms, Cipla and Hetero, entered a price war in Africa, prices on some key AIDS drugs fell precipitously. India had joined the WTO, and the country consequently agreed to bring its pharmaceutical protection laws more in line with world norms. However, change was not immediate. Patent protection cases were slowly working their way through the Indian legal system, and some global pharmaceutical companies doubted that the Indian government was truly supportive of patent protection.

In the meantime, the fight to keep the prices of AIDS drugs high in Africa eventually failed, resulting in an embarrassing public relations misstep for many global pharmaceutical companies. Consumer boycotts had even been threatened in developed markets. Many companies that held patents on AIDS pharmaceuticals lowered their prices to below that of the Indian generics. In some cases, donor organizations such as the United Nations helped supplement the low prices, bolstering the margins the pharmaceutical companies made off the sales. But primarily, the global pharmaceutical companies simply agreed to lower their prices. In the years that followed, access to life-saving AIDS treatments increased significantly in Africa, and the growth of Indian generics was somewhat abated.

Nonetheless, the fact that pharmaceutical companies continued to charge different prices in different countries for the same drug fueled controversy. For example, as markets matured in developed countries, many firms were counting on substantial growth among the middle classes in the developing world, especially in middle-income countries such as Mexico. However, they faced pressure to keep prices low in these countries as well. When Abbott Laboratories was told by the Thai government to lower its price on its latest version of the AIDS drug Kaletra, the company had threatened to remove it from the Thai market. A consumer boycott of the company ensued, and Abbott agreed to lower the price to $1,000 a year. In another lower middle-income country, Guatemala, the drug sold for $2,200. The average salary in Guatemala was $2,400.

Similarly, Bristol-Myers Squibb charged four times as much for two of its AIDS drugs in Mexico as it did in sub-Saharan Africa. An AIDS treatment in middle-income Mexico could cost $6,000 in a country where the PCI was only about $7,300. An AIDS organization launched an ad campaign in the United States, specifically in Los Angeles, against Bristol-Myers demanding that the company lower its prices in Mexico.

Of course consumers in developing countries rarely pay the full price of a drug, since governments often purchase and dispense critical drugs. As major buyers, governments too were concerned with costs. However, Indian generic giant, Aurobindo, sued the South African government when it chose a local producer's bid over Aurobindo's to supply an AIDS drug. Aurobindo claimed that their bid was priced about 30 percent lower than the winner's bid. However, the South African government produced a study showing that the local producer's tax contribution, linkages with local suppliers and job creation supported the government decision to procure locally. In fact, emerging markets enforced some of the world's highest tariffs on pharmaceuticals. Iran had tariffs of 50 percent, India of 36 percent and Brazil and Mexico of over 35 percent.

Controversy was not limited to emerging markets. Even in developed countries, pharmaceutical prices could differ substantially. For example, drug prices were higher in the United States than in Europe, where governments paid for most prescription drugs. Consequently, European governments negotiated prices with pharmaceutical firms. For example, the antipsychotic drug Clozaril could cost $51.94 in Spain, $89.55 in Germany, $271.08 in Canada and $317.03 in the United States. Ironically, over-the-counter drugs and generic versions of prescription drugs whose patents had expired could be cheaper in the United States than in Europe because of greater competition in the U.S. market.

Discussion Questions

1. What factors might contribute to GlaxoSmithKline's announcement to discount prices in emerging markets? Do you think these reasons are altruistic or self-serving?
2. Should U.S. consumers pay higher prices for pharmaceuticals than Africans? Why or why not?
3. Should Mexican consumers pay higher prices for pharmaceuticals than Africans? Why or why not?
4. Should U.S. consumers pay higher prices than Europeans for pharmaceuticals? Why or why not?
5. Should national governments pay more for locally produced pharmaceuticals?
6. What challenges might pharmaceutical companies face from widely disparate prices?

Sources: "The Price of Life," in Kate Gillespie and H. David Hennessey, *Global Marketing* (Mason, OH: Cengage, 2011), pp. 366–367; Josh Ruxin, "AIDS Drugs—for Profit or Not?" *Forbes*, November 11, 2010; Gardiner Harris, "India's Efforts to Aid Poor Worry Drug Makers," *New York Times*, December 29, 2013; and "The New Drug Wars," *The Economist*, January 4, 2014.

CASE 12.3   Gamali Air

Jennifer Beaudreau, an account manager at Ameridere, was very excited to learn that Gamali Air was seriously considering purchasing two of her company's L700 Turboprop planes. Ameridere had been invited to bid on the contract and had subsequently offered to deliver the two planes for US$46 million. Gamali Air was to pay $12 million in cash upon delivery, $12 million one year later and $22 million three years after delivery. Interest charges were already included in the $46 million bid.

Gamali, once a part of French West Africa, was now a multiparty democracy with a population of 10 million, 85 percent of whom were Muslim. The GDP per capita in Gamali was only US$1,600, and the illiteracy rate remained at about 60 percent. The main industries of Gamali were tourism, agriculture, fish processing, phosphate mining, fertilizer production and petroleum refining. The latter required the importation of oil since Gamali had no crude oil reserves itself. The country's exports of $1.1 billion included fish, peanuts, refined petroleum products, phosphates and cotton. Tourism was another substantial source of foreign exchange.

For the past year, however, rising world oil prices had caused Gamali to run a significant balance-of-trade deficit, and inflation had risen to 15 percent from a prior low of 8 percent. Inflation was also fueled by government spending to try and offset unemployment, which was currently estimated at 48 percent. High unemployment in the cities contributed to a number of social problems, including juvenile delinquency and drug addiction. Although rebel groups recently signed a peace treaty with the government, the south of Gamali was still plagued with intermittent armed conflict by separatist groups and bandits.

Gamali Air originated in 1965 when it was established as a SOE. As a result of privatization, 30 percent of the company had been sold to a Gamali business group whose other group companies included several hotels, a trading company and investments in construction and textiles. The Gamali government retained the remaining 70 percent of the airline. With flights to Paris, Lyons, Marseilles, London and New York, the stated goal of Gamali Air was to become the leading carrier in Africa. The two additional planes would add to the airline's current fleet of four planes. Gamali Air had purchased Boeing and Airbus aircraft in the past, but it was now in the market for planes appropriate for medium hauls. The airline was expanding its regional service within Gamali primarily to service increased demand from tourists visiting its wildlife parks.

Jennifer had supervised the original bid for the sale. Now the vice president of Gamali Air had formally notified her that Ameridere was one of two finalists for the contract. Their remaining competitor was a Brazilian firm that Ameridere had never before bid against. However, Jennifer knew that the Brazilian firm, which was about half the size of Ameridere, was strong in Latin America and Asian markets and had recently won a substantial contract in Europe. Both firms specialized in making smaller planes for regional markets. For example, Ameridere's L700 Turboprop was designed for flights shorter than 500 miles and carried 86 passengers. Ameridere was especially well known for the comfort and quietness of its planes as well as its after-sales service. The Brazilian firm was well known for the creative financing packages it offered customers.

Although the recent communication from Gamali Air was exciting, Jennifer realized that Ameridere would have to respond quickly to three requests forwarded by its potential customer:

- Ameridere was now asked to present a bid for after-sales service and training for flight and maintenance crews.
- Management at Gamali Air also suggested that payment for the planes be made by countertrade. The airline would arrange through the Gamali government to deliver fertilizer or phosphate valued at $46 million over a period of three years. These products would be valued at their world market price less 5 percent on the day it was received by Ameridere. The 5 percent was supposed to cover the cost of shipping the products to possible markets in France or Spain.
- Finally, Ameridere was asked to agree to quote the price in Gamali dinars instead of U.S. dollars. The vice president of Gamali Air reminded Jennifer that the dinar had been pegged 1:1 to the euro three years earlier and the euro had increased 30 percent against the dollar in the past year. He noted that if the sale had been concluded a year ago, Ameridere would have realized 30 percent more dollars on its second payment had it quoted the price in dinars rather than in dollars.

Jennifer knew that her company wanted to expand out of its current markets in North America and Europe where sales growth had slowed, and management at Gamali Air had intimated that, all things being equal, they would prefer to work with an American rather than a Brazilian supplier. However, Ameridere had never become involved in countertrade or pricing in foreign currencies. As she sat down to develop answers to the requests made by Gamali Air, Jennifer remembered what her boss had said that morning: "Let's make them a counteroffer both sides can live with."

Discussion Questions

1. Evaluate Gamali Air's countertrade proposal.
2. Evaluate the proposal to quote the price in dinars rather than in U.S. dollars.
3. How would you address each of Gamali Air's requests? Develop a counterproposal that "both sides can live with." Explain why your proposal would be reasonably attractive to both Ameridere and Gamali Air.

Notes

1   Noemie Bisserbe, "France Fines Pet-Food Makers over Pricing," *Wall Street Journal*, March 21, 2012, p. B3.
2   Christina Passariello, "Danone Expands Its Pantry to Woo the World's Poor," *Wall Street Journal*, June 29, 2010, p. A1.
3   Ian McDonald, Liam Pleven and Eric Bellman, "Agents of Change," *Wall Street Journal*, February 12, 2007, p. A1.
4   Kerry Capell, "Fashion Conquistador," *Business Week*, September 4, 2006, p. 38.
5   Mary Anne Raymond, John F. Tanner Jr. and Jonghoo Kim, "Cost Complexity in Pricing Decisions for Exporters in Developed and Emerging Markets," *Journal of International Marketing*, vol. 9, no. 3 (2001), pp. 19–40.
6   Loretta Chao, "In Brazil, 7-Hour Waits for $20 Clothes," *Wall Street Journal*, March 18, 2014, p. B1.
7   Dave Thier, "Sony: High PS$ Price in Brazil is Bad for Gamers," *Forbes*, October 22, 2013.
8   Julie Jargon, "KFC Savors Potential in Africa," *Wall Street Journal*, December 10, 2010, p. B1.
9   Drew Hinshaw, "KFC Leads Fast-Food Race to Africa," *Wall Street Journal*, February 9, 2013, p. B1.
10 "Poland Consents to High Prices," Polish News Bulletin, September 8, 2008.
11 Jay Solomon, "From Its Base in India, Private-Hospital Chain Enjoys Global Reach," *Wall Street Journal* (Europe), April 26, 2004, p. A1
12 Karby Leggett, "In Rural China, GM Sees a Frugal But Huge Market," *Wall Street Journal*, January 16, 2001, p. A19.
13 Passariello, "Danone Expands Its Pantry to Woo the World's Poor."
14 John Revill, "Food Makers Rethink Europe," *Wall Street Journal*, May 29, 2012, p. B8.
15 Sonya Misquitta, "Cadbury Redefines Cheap Luxury," *Wall Street Journal*, June 8, 2009, p. B4.
16 Laurie Burkitt, "PepsiCo Chips Away at China," *Wall Street Journal Online*, July 10, 2012.
17 Paul Sonne, Devon Maylie and Drew Hinshaw, "With West Flat, Big Brewers Peddle Cheap Beer in Africa," *Wall Street Journal Online*, March 19, 2013.
18 Megha Bahree, "GE Remodels Businesses in India," *Wall Street Journal Asia*, April 27, 2011, p. 16.
19 Ellen Byron, "Gillette's Latest Innovation in Razors," *Wall Street Journal*, October 1, 2010, p. B1.
20 Mike Ramsey, "Ford to Unveil SUV in India," *Wall Street Journal*, January 4, 2012, p. B4.
21 Lee C. Simmons and Robert M. Schindler, "Cultural Superstitions and the Price Endings Used in Chinese Advertising," *Journal of International Marketing*, vol. 11, no. 2 (2003), pp. 101–111.
22 Jathon Sapsford, "Toyota Introduces a New Luxury Brand in Japan: Lexus," *Wall Street Journal*, August 3, 2005, p. B1.
23 Rujirutana Mandhachitara, Randall M. Shannon and Costas Hadjicharalambous, "Why Private Label Grocery Brands Have Not Succeeded in Asia," *Journal of Global Marketing*, vol. 20, no. 2/3 (2007), pp. 71–87.

24 James T. Areddy, "Chinese Consumers Overwhelm Retailers with Team Tactics," *Wall Street Journal*, February 28, 2006, p. A1.

25 Cecilie Rohwedder, Aaron O. Patrick and Timothy W. Martin, "Grocer Battles Unilever on Pricing," *Wall Street Journal*, February 11, 2009, p. B1.

26 Gordon Fairclough, "China's Car-Price Wars Dent Profits," *Wall Street Journal*, September 18, 2007, p. A11.

27 Eva Perez and Corey Boles, "US Fines British, Korean Airlines for Price Fixing," Dow Jones Financial Wire, August 1, 2007.

28 Maxwell Murphy, "When Hedging Isn't Enough," *Wall Street Journal*, May 6, 2014, p. B5.

29 Betsy McKay, "Ruble's Decline Energizes Firms Who Manage to Win Back Consumers," *Wall Street Journal*, April 23, 1999, p. B7.

30 Annie Gasparro, "McDonald's Raises Some of Its Prices in China," *Wall Street Journal*, July 16, 2011, p. B3.

31 Leo Lewis, "China Beijing Chokes on Rising Cost of a Big Mac," *The Times*, November 18, 2010.

32 Girija Shivakumar, "Pricing Goods in Inflationary India," *Financial Times*, September 22, 2010, p. 12.

33 "Philippine Price Controls Hamper Rise of Generics," *Manila Bulletin*, June 19, 2010.

34 Geri Smith and Michael Arndt, "Wrapping the Globe in Tortillas," *Business Week*, February 26, 2007, p. 54.

35 James Hagerty and Bob Tita, "Whirlpool Calls for Duties," *Wall Street Journal*, March 31, 2011, p. B3.

36 Eric Bellman, "Rural India Snaps Up Mobile Phones," *Wall Street Journal*, February 9, 2009, p. B1.

37 Rhonda Colvin, "Small Business: The Cost of Expanding Overseas," *Wall Street Journal*, February 27, 2014.

38 Anna Smolchenko, "They've Driven a Ford Lately," *Business Week*, February 26, 2007, p. 52.

39 Eric Bellman, "A Dollar Store's Rich Allure in India," *Wall Street Journal*, January 23, 2007, p. B1.

40 For a conceptual treatment, see *Transfer Pricing* (Washington, DC: Tax Management, Inc., 1995).

41 Michael Happell, "Asia: An Overview," *International Tax Review*, 10 (February 1999), pp. 7–9.

42 Foo Eu Jin, "Transfer Pricing Poses Threat to Firms," *Business Times* (Malaysia), March 10, 1999, p. 3.

43 Jeanne Whalen, "GlaxoSmithKline Gets New Tax Bill from U.S. Agency," *Wall Street Journal* (Europe), January 27, 2005, p. A4.

44 Maxwell Murphy, "Hot Markets, Tax Headaches," Dow Jones Top Global Market Stories, February 12, 2013.

45 Saeed Samiee, Patrick Anckar and Abo Akademi, "Currency Choice in Industrial Pricing: A Cross-National Evaluation," *Journal of Marketing*, vol. 62, no. 3 (July 1998), pp. 25–27.

46 "Market Data: Currency Futures," *Financial Times*, March 3, 2005, p. 27.

47 Thomas Gryta and Alexander Kolyandr, "Gray Market for iPhone Undermines Apples's Growth in Russia," *Wall Street Journal Online*, September 24, 2013.

48 Nevada Furniture, www.nevadafurniture.co.za, accessed May 26, 2014.

49 Mark Schonfeld, "Fight Grey Goods with Trade Mark Law," *Managing Intellectual Property*, June 2010.

50 Philip Shishkin, "Europe Decides to Fine Nintendo," *Wall Street Journal*, October 25, 2002, p. B5.

51 Keith E. Maskus and Yongmin Chen, "Parallel Imports in a Model of Vertical Distribution: Theory, Evidence and Policy," *Pacific Economic Review*, vol. 7, no. 2 (2002), pp. 319–334.

52 Mary L. Kevlin, "United States: Parallel Imports," *Mondaq Business Briefing*, June 22, 2001.

53 Sarah Jeong and Alex Shank, "Holds the First Sale Doctrine Applicable to Parallel Importation," *Jolt Journal: Harvard Journal of Law & Technology*, March 30, 2013.

54 Andrew Grossman, "A Profitable Trade," Dow Jones Top North American Equities Stories, December 3, 2013.

55 Mathew B. Myers, "Incidents of Gray Market Activity Among U.S. Exporters: Occurrences, Characteristics, and Consequences," *Journal of International Business Studies*, vol. 30, no. 1 (1999), pp. 105–126.

56 Samuel Ee, "Porsche Offers Benchmark Warranty to Beat Grey Imports," *Business Times*, October 29, 2008.

57 Mark Maremont, "Blind Ambition," *Business Week*, October 23, 1995, pp. 78–92.

58 Lyse Comins, "Consumer Groups Welcome New 'Grey Goods' Legislation," *The Mercury*, February 15, 2007, p. 6.

59 Marios Theodosiou and Constantine S. Katsikeas, "Factors Influencing the Degree of International Pricing Strategy Standardization of Multinational Corporations," *Journal of International Marketing*, vol. 9, no. 3 (2001), pp. 1–18.

60 "Christian Dior Watches Now in India," *Businessline* (Chennai), November 22, 2002, p. 1.

61 Das Narayandas, John Quelch and Gordon Swartz, "Prepare Your Company for Global Pricing," *Sloan Management Review*, vol. 42 (Fall 2000), pp. 61–70.

62 Aspy P. Palia and Peter W. Liesch, "Survey of Counter-trade Practices in Australia," www.netspeed.com.au/jholmes/default.htm, accessed March 4, 2005.

Chapter 13

Managing Global Distribution Channels

THE STRUCTURE OF THE GLOBAL DISTRIBUTION SYSTEM	411
FOREIGN-MARKET CHANNEL MEMBERS	411
ANALYZING NATIONAL CHANNELS	413
FACTORS INFLUENCING THE SELECTION OF CHANNEL MEMBERS	417
LOCATING AND SELECTING CHANNEL PARTNERS	419
MANAGING GLOBAL DISTRIBUTION	420
GAINING ACCESS TO DISTRIBUTION CHANNELS	422
GLOBAL LOGISTICS	424
GLOBAL TRENDS IN RETAILING	427
SMUGGLING	434

When India relaxed its foreign-investment rules concerning retailing, Wal-Mart sought to enter a new $490 billion market. But soon the company came face-to-face with distribution challenges that threatened its business model of utilizing an efficient logistics system to deliver low prices to consumers. India is the world's second largest producer of fruits and vegetables. But a lack of refrigerated trucks and proper roads causes the country to lose one-third of its produce to spoilage on the way to market. A system of government-imposed middlemen creates numerous agents each taking a fee along the way. Those fees alone can increase farm-to-store costs six-fold. And Wal-Mart stores themselves could prove costly, with most real estate in India's large cities selling at a premium.[1] Global marketers face similar problems with distribution infrastructure in Indonesia. But poor roads and a lack of retail space across Indonesia's 17,000 islands didn't prove as great a challenge to Tupperware, a producer of plastic containers for leftovers. The company circumvented traditional channels and used a salesforce primarily consisting of housewives to store and deliver their products. Soon Indonesia became Tupperware's largest national market.[2]

Distribution systems have traditionally been shaped by a variety of factors—level of economic development, disposable income of consumers, the quality of infrastructure such as roads and telecommunications, as well as culture, physical environment and the legal/political system. Global marketers need to understand how environmental influences may affect distribution strategies and options. Using this knowledge, they must establish efficient channels for products on a country-by-country basis. They must also consider how the emergence of regional and global distributors and changes in global logistics can affect their operations at the transnational level.

In this chapter, we discuss the structure of global distribution systems and methods for selecting, locating and managing channel members. We explore how the multinational corporation (MNC) gains access to local channels and manages international logistics. We conclude with a look at global trends in retailing and the managerial implications of international smuggling.

Learning Objectives

After studying this chapter, you should be able to:

- ➤ list and describe the key players within foreign-market channels;
- ➤ explain the impact on national channel strategy of distribution density, channel length and channel alignment;
- ➤ describe how costs, product line, control, coverage and synergy all influence the proper choice of channel members;
- ➤ suggest ways to locate foreign distributors;
- ➤ list ways to motivate and control foreign distributors;
- ➤ suggest alternative entry strategies for markets where competitors already control distribution channels;
- ➤ identify the differences between global logistics management and global supply chain management;
- ➤ list and explain the five key areas of global logistics management;
- ➤ explain the growing global importance of large-scale retailers, international retailing, direct marketing, online retailing, and smuggling.

The Structure of the Global Distribution System

Marketers who develop distribution strategies must decide how to transport products from manufacturing locations to the consumer. Although distribution can be handled completely by the manufacturer, often products are moved through intermediaries, such as agents, wholesalers, distributors and retailers. An understanding of the structure of available distribution systems is extremely important in the development of a marketing strategy. The various channels available to a manufacturer are shown in Figure 13.1. Home-country channel members were discussed in Chapter 9. Host-country channel members are discussed below.

Foreign-Market Channel Members

As shown in Figure 13.1, once products have left the home market, there are a variety of channel alternatives in the global marketplace: import intermediaries, local wholesalers or agents, and retailers. Even with local manufacturing, the company will still need to get its products from the factory to the consumers.

Import Intermediaries

Import intermediaries identify consumer needs in their local market and search the world to satisfy those needs. They normally purchase goods in their own name and act independently of manufacturers. As independents, these channel members use their own marketing strategies and keep in

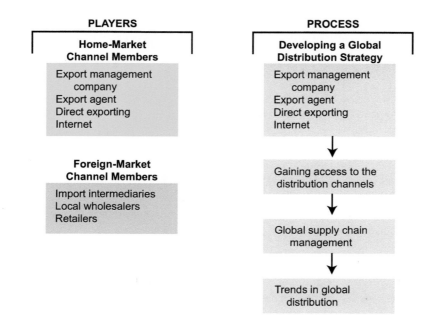

Figure 13.1 International Marketing Channel Alternatives

close contact with the markets they serve. A manufacturer that wants to distribute in an independent intermediary's market area should investigate this channel partner as one way to reach wholesalers and retailers in that area.

Local Wholesalers or Agents

In each country, there will be a series of possible channel members who move manufacturers' products to retailers, to industrial firms or in some cases to other wholesalers. Local wholesalers will take title to the products, whereas local agents will not take title. Local wholesalers are also called distributors or dealers. In some cases, a local wholesaler receives exclusive distribution rights for a specific geographic area or country.

The functions of wholesalers can also vary by country. In some countries, wholesalers provide a warehousing function, taking orders from retailers and shipping them appropriate quantities of merchandise. Wholesalers in Japan perform basic wholesale functions but also share risk with retailers by providing them with financing, product development and even occasional managerial and marketing skills.

Retailers

Retailers, the final members of the consumer distribution channel, purchase products for resale to consumers. The size and accessibility of retail channels vary greatly by country. The population per retailer in Europe varies from lows of only 74 people in Hungary, 103 in Portugal and 109 in Spain to highs of 182 people in Russia, 228 in Austria and 267 in Germany.[3]

World Beat 13.1

Asia Disasters Ripple Round the World

An earthquake and tsunami in Japan forced auto and auto parts plants to shut down across the country. The result: General Motors, Toyota Motor Corp. and PSA Peugeot-Citroën were forced to cut back production in the United States and Europe. Japan also makes about 60 percent of the world's silicon wafers. The closing of two silicon wafer plants in the country reduced global supply by 25 percent. The disasters in Japan were credited for depressing second-quarter growth rates in countries around the world as manufacturing decreased across many industries that relied on Japanese inputs, especially electronic components and specialty chemicals.

Later that same year, catastrophic flooding in Thailand, another major source for auto parts, disrupted the global supply chain of automakers once again. Thailand is also the world's second largest exporter of hard-disk drives, accounting for about 40 percent of drives produced worldwide. Consequently the floods shut down PC production in the United States. Apple's chief executive remarked that the hard-drive shortage could last for months. Then a dispute between China and Vietnam over islands in the South China Sea sent Vietnamese protesters into the streets, ransacking or otherwise shutting down factories in the country. These disruptions affected the supply chains of products as diverse as Adidas sports shoes and Apple iPhones.

These various Asian events left many managers re-thinking their global supply chains. Keeping costs low was a driving force. But too lean a supply chain could be devastating in the face of natural disasters and political risk.

Sources: Mike Ramsey and Sebastian Moffett, "Japan Parts Shortage Hits Auto Makers," *Wall Street Journal Online*, March 24, 2011; Andrew Dowell, "Japan: The Business Aftershocks," *Wall Street Journal Asia*, March 28, 2011; Shara Tibken, "Thai Floods Jolt PC Supply Chain," *Wall Street Journal*, October 18, 2011, p. B5; James Hookway, "Flood's Global Ripples," *Wall Street Journal*, October 27, 2011, p. B1; and Demetri Sevastopulo, "Vietnam Riots Land Another Blow on the Global Supply Chain," *Financial Times*, May 20, 2014.

Retailing is exploding in many parts of Asia, where a large portion of the population is crossing the income threshold at which they start to buy entirely new categories of goods, such as packaged foods, televisions or mopeds. This phenomenon, called magic moments, has hit Taiwan, Indonesia, Thailand, Malaysia and China. When a country crosses the magic-moments threshold, distribution systems start to improve with the emergence of modern stores.[4] Furthermore, China has seen a significant shift from state-owned to private distribution. There has been a significant decline in state-owned retail and wholesale enterprises and a surge in privately owned retail and wholesale enterprises. The global marketer must evaluate the available retailers in a country and develop a strategy around the existing—and sometimes evolving—retail structure.

Global marketers must also be aware of the different retail regulations in foreign markets. Regulatory barriers include land-use zoning, codes restricting building size, environment impact requirements and laws concerning hours of operation. European countries have long restricted the hours retailers can be open, although some of these laws are changing. In 2012, Italy deregulated operating hours for shops, bars and restaurants in an attempt to invigorate a sluggish economy.[5] However, new restrictions can arise as well. Sri Lanka recently introduced rules requiring local stores and restaurants of foreign franchisors to carry 80 percent local content.[6]

Business-to-Business Channels

When the firm is selling to businesses instead of consumers, channels may still resemble those we have described. Small businesses in particular may purchase supplies from retail outlets that have been supplied by wholesalers. Many B2B sales go through shorter channels, however. Export agents, import intermediaries or the manufacturer itself often contact business customers directly without the use of further intermediaries.

Analyzing National Channels

A distribution strategy is one part of the marketing mix, and it needs to be consistent with other aspects of the marketing strategy: product policies, pricing strategy and communication strategy. Figure 13.2 depicts important factors to consider when developing a distribution strategy. Before

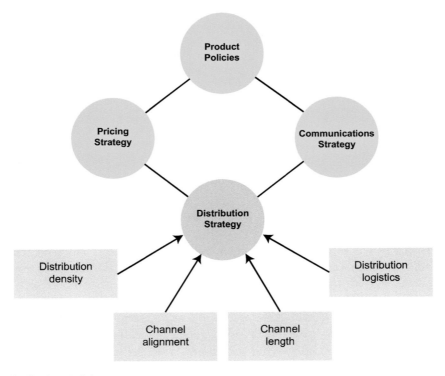

Figure 13.2 Distribution Policies

deciding on distribution strategies, global marketers must understand the nature of channels in their various markets. Of particular interest are the following variables:

1. *Distribution density.* Density is the amount of exposure or coverage desired for a product, particularly the number of sales outlets necessary to provide for adequate coverage of the entire market.
2. *Channel length.* The concept of channel length involves the number of intermediaries involved in bringing a given product from the firm to the consumer.
3. *Channel alignment and leadership.* Alignment is the structure of the chosen channel members to achieve a unified strategy.
4. *Distribution logistics.* Logistics involves the physical flow of products as they move through the channel.

The decisions involved in the first three of these areas cannot be approached independently. The decisions are interrelated, and they need to be consistent with other aspects of the marketing strategy. Although it is important to evaluate the distribution strategy logically, marketing managers often must work with an international distribution structure established under previous managers. That existing system may limit a company's flexibility to change and grow. Nevertheless, a creative marketer can usually find opportunities for circumventing the current arrangement. For example, Nordica of Italy had been selling in Japan for 25 years when the company decided it wanted more

414

direct control over distribution. Nordica reached a financial agreement with its exclusive distributor, Daiwa Sports, and hired the 85 employees who had been handling its line. This allowed Nordica, which was later acquired by Tecnica, to take control without losing the experience and contacts developed by its distributor.[7] The following sections illustrate how company policies must adapt to distribution density, channel length and channel alignment.

Distribution Density

The number of sales outlets or distribution points required for the efficient marketing of a firm's products is referred to as the density of distribution. The density is dependent on the shopping or buying habits of the average customer. Choosing the optimum distribution network requires the marketer to examine how customers select dealers and retail outlets by product category. For many consumer goods, an extensive, or wide, distribution is required if the consumer is not likely to exert much shopping effort. Such products, which are called convenience goods, are bought frequently and in nearby outlets. For other products, such as appliances or clothing, consumers may visit two or more stores. These products require a more limited, or selective, distribution, with fewer outlets per market area. For specialty goods, products that inspire consumer loyalty to specific brands, a very limited, or exclusive, distribution may be adopted. It is assumed that the customer will search for the desired product and will not accept substitutes.

The key to distribution density, then, is the consumer's shopping behavior, in particular the effort expended to locate a desired item. This behavior, however, may vary greatly from country to country. In the United States, for example, where PCI is high, consumers shop for many regular-use items in supermarkets and other widely accessible outlets, such as drugstores. In other countries, particularly some with a much lower PCI, the purchase of such items is likely to be a less routine affair, and consumers may be willing to exert more effort to locate such items. This makes possible a less extensive distribution of products.

Where consumers buy certain products also varies a great deal from country to country. Whereas most magazines are sold in grocery stores in the United States, in the United Kingdom many are sold through newsagents. It is important to find out, early in your distribution analysis, where consumers buy the types of products you plan to market.

In the B2B sector as well, differences in buyer behavior or in the use of a particular product may require changes in distribution outlets and density. In the United States, for instance, radiology supply products are sold directly to hospitals and radiology departments through hospital supply distributors. In France, however, patients must pick up radiology supplies by prescription from a pharmacy before visiting the radiology department at the hospital. In this latter case, radiology supplies have to be promoted to physicians and then stocked at pharmacies to be successful. The distribution necessary in France is much more extensive than in the United States, where only hospitals are channel members.[8]

Channel Length

The number of intermediaries directly involved in the physical or ownership path of a product from the manufacturer to the customer is indicative of the channel length. Long channels have several intermediaries. Short or direct channels have few or no intermediaries. Channel length is usually influenced by three factors: (1) a product's distribution density, (2) the average order quantity and (3) the availability of channel members. Products with extensive distribution, or large numbers of final sales points, tend to have longer channels of distribution. Similarly, as the average order quantity decreases, products move through longer channels to enhance the efficiency of distribution.

Because distribution density affects channel length, it is clear that the same factors that influence distribution density influence channel length; foremost among these is the shopping behavior of consumers. The average order quantity often depends on the purchasing power or income level of a given customer group. In countries with lower income levels, people often buy food on a daily basis at nearby small stores. This contrasts sharply with more affluent consumers who can afford to buy enough food or staples for a week or even a month and who don't mind traveling some distance to do more infrequent shopping.

Wholesale channels in Japan are the longest in the developed world, with most products moving through as many as six intermediaries. This lengthy distribution channel is more reminiscent of distribution systems in developing countries than of those in developed countries. However, the Japanese distribution system is responding to consumer demands for change. Following the lead of Dell Computer, Japan's Seiko Epson bypassed traditional Japanese channel members and began a direct sales effort to sell its personal computers. In doing so, the company was able to attract consumers by offering significant savings through its direct-marketing effort.[9]

Channel Alignment

Channel alignment can be one of the most difficult tasks of marketing. The longer the channel, the more difficult it becomes to ensure that various channel members coordinate their actions so that a unified approach to the marketing of a product or service can be achieved. On an international level, the coordinating task is made all the more difficult because the company organizing the channel may be far away from the distribution system, with little influence over the local scene. The international company will find it much easier to control the distribution channel if a local subsidiary with a strong sales force exists. In countries where the company has no local presence and depends on independent distributors, control is likely to slip to the independent distributor. This loss of control may be further aggravated if the international company's sales volume represents only a small fraction of the local distributor's business. Of course, the opposite will be true when a high percentage of the volume consists of the international firm's products.

The Channel Captain

Often one participant emerges as the channel captain or dominant member. The channel captain frequently dictates terms of pricing, delivery and sometimes even product design that affect other channel members. As a general rule, wholesalers are relatively powerful in developing countries. When countries develop, power shifts from wholesalers to either retailers or manufacturers. This can be seen in the United States where once-strong wholesalers have become less influential, and manufacturers or large retailers (such as Home Depot and Wal-Mart) have become channel captains.

416

Global marketers must be aware of national differences that can significantly affect a firm's bargaining power in channel negotiations, and they must be prepared to respond to changes that affect bargaining power within national channels. In China, wholesalers capture about 80 percent of the revenues from distributing consumer products while retailers only realize 20 percent. (In the United States, these numbers are nearly reversed. Wholesaler get about 30 percent with the rest going to retailers.) The Chinese government has traditionally protected its local wholesalers, many of whom are government owned. However, joining the WTO is forcing change in China and encouraging the country to slowly open its distribution system to increased competition.

Distribution Logistics

Distribution logistics focuses on the physical movement of goods through the channels. An extremely important part of the distribution system, logistics is discussed in detail later in the chapter.

Factors Influencing the Selection of Channel Members

A marketer needs to identify and select appropriate distribution partners in various national markets. This selection of distribution partners is an extremely important decision, because the partner will often assume a portion of the marketing responsibility, or even all of it. Also, the distribution partner is usually involved in the physical movement (logistics) of products to the customers. A poor decision can lead to lackluster performance. Changing a distribution partner can be expensive or sometimes impossible because of local laws. Vulcan Chemical was fined $23 million for unfairly terminating the rights of Phillip J. Barker, which had a contract to market and distribute sodium chlorine and chlorine dioxide in Japan, China, South Korea and Taiwan. Vulcan reported that its sales had fallen to less than $2 million per year, therefore warranting termination of the distribution contract.[10] The very success of a firm's international efforts depends on the partners it selects. Several factors influence the selection of distribution partners. These include costs, the nature of the product and product line, the desired level of control and coverage and the potential synergy between the international firm and its channels.

Costs

Channel costs fall into three categories: initial costs, maintenance costs and logistics costs. Predicting all of these various costs when selecting different channel members is often difficult, but it is necessary in order to estimate the cost of various alternatives. High distribution costs usually result in higher prices at the consumer level, which may hamper entry into a new market.

Initial Costs

The initial costs include all the costs of locating and setting up the channel, such as executive time and travel to locate and select channel members, the costs of negotiating an agreement with channel members and the capital costs of setting up the channel. Capital costs include the costs for inventories, goods in transit, accounts receivable and inventories on consignment. The establishment of a direct-sales channel often requires the maximum investment, whereas use of distributors generally reduces the investment required. Firms can expect these costs to be higher in certain countries due to the necessity of selecting the proper channel members. Japan is one example of a country where it makes sense to spend more time and money upfront, as the social and economic costs of dissolving a relationship can be unacceptably high.[11]

Maintenance and Logistics Costs

The maintenance costs of the channel include the costs of the company's salespeople, sales managers and travel expenses. They also include the costs of auditing and controlling channel operations and the profit margin given to channel intermediaries. The logistics costs comprise the transportation expenses, storage costs, the cost of breaking bulk shipments into smaller lot sizes and the cost for customs paperwork.

Product and Product Line

The nature of a product can affect channel selection. If the product is perishable or has a short shelf life, then the manufacturer is forced to use shorter channels to get the product to the consumer more rapidly. ProFlowers.com, an online flower portal, developed a distribution network that gets flowers from farmer to consumer in half the time of traditional florists. The delivery system's success has led to its adoption in selling meats, fruit and other perishables online. Through its affiliate company, Flowerfarm, delivery became available in nearly 80 countries.[12]

A technical product often requires direct sales or highly technical channel partners. For example, Index Technology of Cambridge, Massachusetts, sold a sophisticated software product to automate the development of software systems called computer-aided systems engineering. The company entered the United Kingdom and Australia with a direct-sales effort, but to limit initial costs it decided on distributors for France, Germany and Scandinavia. However, insufficient revenues from these distributors led the company to set up its own sales efforts in France and Germany and to purchase its distributor in Scandinavia. The highly technical nature of the product required Index to invest more time and money in distribution than would be necessary if the firm sold a generic or unsophisticated product.

The size of the product line also affects the selection of channel members. A broader product line is more desirable for channel members. A distributor or dealer is more likely to stock a broad product line than a single item. Similarly, if a manufacturer has a very broad, complete line, it is easier to justify the cost of a more direct channel. With more products to sell, it is easier to generate a high average order on each sales call. With a limited product line, an agent or distributor will group a firm's product together with products from other companies to increase the average order size.

Control and Coverage

Selection of channel members is also determined by the amount of control and market coverage that a global marketer seeks in any national market.

Each type of channel arrangement offers the manufacturer a different level of control. With direct sales, a manufacturer can control price, promotion, amount of effort and type of retail outlet used. If these are important, then the increased level of control may offset the increased cost of a direct-sales force. Longer channels, particularly with distributors who take title to goods, often result in little or no control. In many cases, a company may not know who is ultimately buying the product.

Coverage is the geographic reach that a manufacturer wishes to attain. Although coverage is usually easy to get in major metropolitan areas, gaining adequate coverage of smaller cities or sparsely populated areas can be difficult. Selection of one channel member over another may be influenced by the market coverage that the respective agents or distributors offer.

Locating and Selecting Channel Partners

Building an international distribution system normally takes one to three years. The process involves the series of steps shown in Table 13.1. The critical aspect of developing a successful system is locating and selecting channel partners.

The development of an international distribution strategy in terms of distribution density, channel length and channel alignment will establish a framework for the "ideal" distribution partners. Selection criteria include geographic coverage, managerial ability, financial stability, annual volume and reputation. Several sources are useful in locating possible distribution partners. They include:

➤ *National export portals.* For example, the U.S. export portal, www.export.gov, assists U.S. exporters in locating distributors and agents overseas.
➤ *Banks.* If the firm's bank has foreign branches, they may be happy to help locate distributors.
➤ *Directories.* Country directories of distributors or specialized directories, such as those listing computer distributors, can be helpful.

Table 13.1 Process of Establishing an International Distribution System

1. Develop a distribution strategy.
2. Establish criteria for selecting distribution partners.
3. Locate potential distribution partners.
4. Solicit the interest of distributors.
5. Screen and select distribution partners.
6. Negotiate agreements.

➤ *Trade shows.* Exhibiting at an international trade show, or just attending one, exposes managers to a large number of distributors and their salespeople.

➤ *Competitors' distribution partners.* Sometimes a competitor's distributor may be interested in switching product lines.

➤ *Consultants.* Some international marketing consultants specialize in locating distributors.

➤ *Associations.* There are associations of international intermediaries or country associations of intermediaries; for example, a firm looking for a representative or agent in the United States could contact the following: Manufacturer's Agents National Association or www.mana online.org.

➤ *Foreign consulates.* Most countries post commercial attachés at their embassies or at separate consulates. These individuals can be helpful in locating agents or distributors in their country.

After compiling a list of possible distribution partners, the firm may contact each, providing product literature and distribution requirements. Prospective distributors with an interest in the firm's product line can be asked to supply such information as lines currently carried, annual volume, number of salespeople, geographic territory covered, credit and bank references, physical facilities, relationship with local government and knowledge of English or other relevant languages. Firms that respond should be checked against the selection criteria.

Managing Global Distribution

Selecting the most suitable channel participants and gaining access to the market are extremely important steps in achieving an integrated and responsive distribution channel. However, without proper motivation of and control over that channel, sales may remain unsatisfactory. This section discusses the steps that must be taken to ensure the flow of the firm's products through the channel by gaining the full cooperation of all channel members.

Motivating Channel Participants

Keeping channel participants motivated is an important aspect of international distribution policies. Financial incentives in the form of higher-than-average gross margins can be a very powerful inducement, particularly for the management of independent distributors, wholesalers and retailers. The expected gross margins are influenced by the cultural history of that channel. For example, if a certain type of retailer usually gets a 50 percent margin and the firm offers 40 percent, the effort the retailer makes may be less than desired. Inviting channel members to annual conferences and introductions of new products is also effective. By extending help to the management of distributorships in areas such as inventory control, accounts collection and advertising, the international firm can cultivate goodwill that will later stand it in good stead. Special programs may also be instituted to train or motivate the channel members' sales forces.

More intense contact between the export manufacturer and the distributor will usually result in better performance by the distributor. The amount of effort an international firm needs to expend depends on the marketing strategy for that market. For example, if the firm is using extensive advertising to pull products through a channel, the intermediary may be expected only to take orders and deliver the product; there is no need for it to contribute to the sales effort. If, on the other hand, the marketing strategy depends on the channel members developing the market or pushing the product through the channel, then a significant sales effort will be required.

Periodic visits to distribution partners can have a positive effect on their motivation and control. Often it is helpful to travel with a channel member salesperson to gain knowledge of the marketplace and to evaluate the skills of the salesperson. The most important benefit of a visit to the channel member is that it gives a clear message that the member's performance is important to the firm. Visits strengthen the personal relationship between the manufacturer and the channel member. A research study on the performance of international distribution partners found that using output controls such as how much volume the partner sold is actually less effective than social controls. Social controls refer to the patterns of interpersonal interactions between the partners, which highlights the need for in-depth relationships with mutual respect and trust.[13]

Changing channel strategies can be costly but necessary, especially as national markets evolve. However, until a global marketer decides to eliminate a channel member, it should beware of strategies that cause conflict within the channel. Channel conflict between a manufacturer and independent distributor most often arises due to competition for sales between the distributor and a manufacturer's own direct sales force or competition between multiple distributors in the same channel and market.[14] Opening new discount channels that offer the same goods at lower prices is also problematic.

Controlling Channel Participants

An international firm will want to exert enough control over channel members to help guarantee that they accurately interpret and appropriately execute the company's marketing strategies. The firm wants to be sure that the local intermediaries price the products according to the company's policies. The same could be said for sales, advertising and service policies. Because the company's reputation in a local market can be tarnished when independent intermediaries handle local distribution ineffectively or inefficiently, international firms closely monitor the performance of local channel members. One way to exert influence over the international channel members is to spell out the specific responsibilities of each, such as minimum annual sales, in the distribution agreement. Attainment of the sales goal can be required for renewal of the contract.

Many companies grant distribution rights only for short time periods, with regular renewal reviews. Caution is advised, however, because cancellation of distribution rights is frequently subject to both social norms and local laws that prohibit sudden termination. Although termination of a distributor or agent for nonperformance is a relatively simple action in the United States, termination of international channel members can be very costly in many parts of the world. In Japan, foreign firms must be especially careful in their selection of a local distributor, because firms are expected to commit themselves to a long-term relationship. When a firm terminates a distributor, it reflects poorly on that firm.[15] Finding another distributor could prove difficult under those circumstances.

In some countries, the international firm may have to pay a multiple of its local agent's annual gross profits in order to terminate the agent. In other countries, termination compensation for agents and distributors can include the value of any goodwill that the agent or distributor has built up for the brand, in addition to expenses incurred in developing the business. A global marketer may also be liable for any compensation claimed by discharged employees who worked on the product line. As a result, termination of a channel member can be a costly, painful process governed in nearly all cases by local laws that may tend to protect and compensate the local channel member.

Nonetheless, research suggests that MNCs operating in developing countries commonly buy or fire their local distributors or develop their own marketing and sales subsidiaries. These firms complain that distributors in emerging markets often fail to invest in business growth and aren't ambitious enough.[16]

Gaining Access to Distribution Channels

Entry into a market can be accomplished through a variety of channel members. However, the channel member whom it seems most logical to approach may already have a relationship with one of the firm's competitors. This poses some special challenges to international marketers. This section is aimed at illustrating alternatives that companies may employ when they encounter difficulties in convincing channel members to carry their products.

The "Locked-Up" Channel

A channel is considered locked up when a newcomer cannot easily convince any channel member to participate, despite the fact that both market and economic considerations suggest otherwise. Channel members customarily decide on a case-by-case basis what products they should add to or drop from their lines. Retailers typically select products that they expect to sell easily and in volume, and they can be expected to switch sources when better opportunities arise. Similarly, wholesalers and distributors compete for retail accounts or industrial users on economic terms. They can entice a prospective client to switch by buying from a new source that can offer a better deal. Likewise, manufacturers compete for wholesale accounts with the expectation that channel members can be convinced to purchase from any given manufacturer if the offer improves on the offers made by competitors.

Yet there are barriers that limit a wholesaler's flexibility to add or drop a particular line. The distributor may have an agreement not to sell competitive products, or its business may include a significant volume from one manufacturer that it does not want to risk upsetting. In Japan, relationships among manufacturers, wholesalers and retailers are long-standing in nature and do not allow channel participants to shift their allegiance quickly to another source even when offered a superior product or price. Japanese channel members develop strong personal ties that make it very difficult for any participant to break a long-standing relationship. When Kodak entered the Japanese market, it had difficulty gaining access to the smaller retail outlets because Japan's Fuji Film dominated the four major wholesalers. Kodak worked for years to gain access to these large wholesalers, but it had little success. So when Kodak entered the digital camera market, it decided to acquire Chinon, a Japanese precision instrument company, to ensure better access to the market.[17]

Cultural forces may not be the only impediments blocking access to a channel of distribution. The members of a channel may not be willing to take any risks by pioneering unknown products. Competitors, domestic or foreign, may try to obstruct the entry of a new company. To respond to these challenges, global marketers should think creatively. When American Standard, the world's largest supplier of plumbing fixtures, tried to enter the Korean market, it found itself locked out of the normal plumbing distributors, which were controlled by local manufacturers. American Standard looked for an alternative distribution channel that served the building trade. It found Home Center, one of the largest suppliers of homebuilding materials and appliances, and thus successfully circumvented the locked channels.[18]

Alternative Entry Approaches

Global marketers have developed several approaches to the difficult task of gaining access to locked-up distribution channels. These include piggybacking, joint ventures and acquisitions.

Piggybacking

When a company does not find any channel partners interested in pioneering new products, the practice of piggybacking may offer a way out of the situation. Piggybacking is an arrangement whereby another manufacturer that sells to the same customer segment takes on the new products. The products retain the brand of the true manufacturer, and both partners normally sign a multi-year contract to provide for continuity. The new company is, in essence, "piggybacking" its products on the shoulders of the established company's sales force.

Under a piggyback arrangement, the brand owner retains control over marketing strategy, particularly pricing, positioning and advertising. The partner acts as a rented sales force only. Of course, this is quite different from the private-label strategy, whereby the manufacturer supplies a marketer, which then places its own brand name on the product. The piggybacking approach has become quite common in the pharmaceutical industry, where companies involve competitor firms in the launch of a particular new drug. Warner-Lambert, a major pharmaceutical company, launched its leading cholesterol-lowering drug Lipitor in the United States with the help of Pfizer. The drug was one of the most successful introductions ever.

Coca-Cola initiated a new twist on the piggyback arrangement when it offered its extensive distribution system across Africa to assist UNAIDS, a United Nations agency fighting AIDS. Coke's distribution reaches almost every country in Africa, and its products find their way even to the poorest villages. The company contributed warehouse and truck space, as well as logistics assistance, to help AIDS charities find the best routes for their literature and testing kits. However, Coca-Cola couldn't help distribute AIDS drugs that have to be kept cool, because its trucks are not refrigerated.[19]

Joint Ventures

As we noted in Chapter 9, when two companies agree to form a new legal entity, it is called a joint venture. Such operations have been quite common in the area of joint production. Our interest here is restricted to joint ventures in which distribution is the primary objective. Normally, such companies are formed between a local firm with existing market access and a foreign firm that would like to market its products in a country where it has no existing market access. For example, two domestic beer producers had tied up retail outlets in Mexico with exclusivity contracts. As a result, Anheuser-Busch decided to enter Mexico through a joint venture with Mexican beer giant Modelo rather than trying to build a distribution system from scratch.

Acquisitions

Acquiring an existing company can give a foreign entrant immediate access to a distribution system. To gain access to pharmaceutical distribution channels in Japan, Merck purchased Japan's Banyu pharmaceutical company. Similarly, Roche Pharmaceutical of Switzerland purchased a controlling stake in Chugai Pharmaceutical. Although it requires a substantial amount of capital, operating results tend to be better than those of new ventures, which usually entail initial losses. It is often less important to find an acquisition candidate with a healthy financial outlook or top products than to find one that has good relationships with wholesale and retail outlets.

Global Logistics

The logistics system, including the physical distribution of manufactured products, is also an important part of international distribution. It involves planning, implementing and controlling the physical flow of materials and finished products from points of origin to points of use. A capital- and labor-intensive function outside of the core business of most companies, logistics has become increasingly complicated to manage. It is also costly, representing 15 to 35 percent of total revenues for most firms.

On a global scale, the task becomes more complex because so many external variables have an impact on the flow of materials or products. As geographic distances to foreign markets grow, competitive advantages are often derived from a more effective structuring of the logistics system either to save time or costs or to increase a firm's reliability. The emergence of logistics as a means of achieving competitive advantage is leading companies to focus increased attention on this vital area. Many manufacturers and retailers are restructuring their logistics efforts and divesting themselves of their in-house distribution divisions in favor of outside logistics specialists.

Logistics Decision Areas

In this section we describe the objectives of an international logistics system and the various operations that have to be managed and integrated into an efficient system. The total task of logistics management consists of five separate though interrelated jobs: (1) traffic or transportation management, (2) inventory control, (3) order processing, (4) materials handling and warehousing and (5) fixed-facilities location management. In what follows, we examine each of these decision areas in more detail.

Traffic or Transportation Management

Traffic management deals primarily with the modes of transportation for delivering products. Principal choices are air, sea, rail and truck, or some combination thereof. Transportation expenses contribute substantially to the costs of marketing products internationally, so special attention must be paid to selecting the transportation mode. Such choices are made by considering three principal factors: lead time, transit time and cost. Companies operating with long lead times tend to use slower and therefore lower-cost transportation modes such as sea and freight. When a short lead time is called for, faster modes of transportation such as air and truck are used. Long transit times require higher financial costs, because payments arrive later and because higher average inventories are stocked at either the point of origin or the destination. Here again, the modes of transportation appropriate for long transit times are sea and rail, whereas air and truck transportation can result in much shorter transit times. Transportation costs are the third factor to consider when selecting a mode of transport. Typically, air or truck transportation is more expensive than either sea or rail for any given distance.

Local laws and restrictions can have a significant impact on transport costs. For example, conflicting regulations at the national and local level make transport in Indonesia notoriously expensive and inefficient. In addition, illicit payments to corrupt police officials and criminal organizations make moving goods to and from Indonesia even more burdensome.[20] Similarly, managing logistics in China continues to be difficult because of corruption and provincial protectionism that often allows only local companies to deliver within many cities. The American Chamber of Commerce in Shanghai estimates that logistics costs are four times higher in China than in many developed economies.[21]

Inventory Control

The level of inventory on hand significantly affects the service level of a firm's logistics system. To avoid the substantial costs of tied-up capital, inventory is ideally reduced to the minimum needed. To reduce inventory levels, a number of companies have adopted the Japanese system of just-in-time (JIT) deliveries of parts and components. For example, many firms kept 30–40 days of buffer stocks of parts and components before instituting JIT. After JIT was implemented, buffer stocks could be lowered to one or two days.

However, cost containment is not the only concern. Adequate inventories are needed as insurance against unexpected breakdowns in the logistics system. Shipments from China to the United States take 22–24 days and can sometimes be delayed due to power outages or floods; therefore, instituting JIT with components or parts from China can be problematic.[22] A major earthquake and tsunami in Japan led to parts shortages especially for many manufacturers in Europe and the United States and highlighted the fragility of their global supply chains. Consequently, many global manufacturers invested more time and money in contingency planning.[23]

Order Processing

Because rapid processing of orders shortens the order cycle and allows for lower safety stocks on the part of the client, this area becomes a central concern for logistics management. The available communications technology greatly influences the time it takes to process an order, and the Internet has vastly improved our ability in this regard. It is still true, however, that to offer an efficient order-processing system worldwide represents a considerable challenge to any company today. Doing this can be turned to competitive advantage; customers reap added benefits from such a system and satisfied customers mean repeat business.

Swisscom, Switzerland's largest telecommunications provider, had been plagued with an opaque and inefficient ordering process which could take as long as 40 days to complete. The company installed new order processing software, enabling it to cut that figure to less than ten days. This not only improved satisfaction ratings by employees and customers alike, it also increased the speed of customer payments.[24]

Materials Handling and Warehousing

Throughout the logistics cycle, materials and products will have to be stored and prepared for moving or transportation. How products are stored or moved is the principal concern of materials handling management. For international shipments, the shipping technology or quantities may be different, requiring firms to adjust domestic policies to these new circumstances. Warehousing in foreign countries involves dealing with different climatic conditions, and longer average storage periods may make it necessary to change warehousing practices.

Fixed-Facilities Location Management

The facilities crucial to the logistics flow are production facilities and warehouses. To serve customers worldwide and to maximize the efficiency of the total logistics system, production facilities may have to be placed in several countries. This often entails a tradeoff between economies of scale and savings in logistics costs.

The location of warehousing facilities can greatly affect the company's ability to respond to orders once they are received or processed. It can also support the company's warranty policy, particularly its ability to deliver replacement products and parts on a timely basis. A company with warehouses in every country where it does business would have a natural advantage in delivery, but such a system increases the costs of warehousing and, most likely, the required level of inventory system-wide.

Therefore, the international firm should seek a balance that satisfies the customer's requirements for timely delivery and also reduces overall logistics costs. Microsoft opened a single warehouse and distribution center in Dublin, Ireland, to serve Europe. The new distribution center allowed the company to serve all European markets effectively and made it unnecessary for Microsoft to keep a warehouse and inventory in each country.

Global Supply Chain Management

Global supply chain management is a term increasingly used to encompass the many interrelated jobs involved in global logistics. Global supply chain management is the collective managerial behavior and decisions essential to the development of a functioning global supply chain. Its areas of responsibility include system integration, business process management and supplier/customer relationship management. While often used interchangeably with global logistics, global supply chain management covers several items often not considered part of logistics, including marketing relationships, product development and rollout, and the management of returns or goods flowing backwards in the supply chain. Its goal is to seamlessly integrate supply and demand management across companies and across borders.[25]

Managing Supplier/Customer Relationships

MNCs depend on a variety of suppliers across the globe. Sophisticated suppliers may be found in many industries and countries. When this is the case, global marketers need only identify appropriate suppliers, negotiate contracts, integrate suppliers into their systems and monitor the performance of their suppliers. In some cases, however, global marketers may need to become more involved in developing their suppliers' capabilities. Global chocolate companies such as Mars Inc. and Mondelez International Inc. work with cocoa growers in developing countries to help improve crop yields in order to provide growers a better income and consequently assure the companies a future supply of cocoa.[26] For hamburger chains, establishing meat supplies can be difficult in Africa. Burger King invested $5 million in a cattle ranch in order to assure its beef supply.[27] Supplier relations can also be subject to local regulations. In order to encourage the creation of larger and more efficient farms, the Chinese government mandated the country's top producers of dairy products purchase a substantial portion of their milk from large farms.[28]

Management of supplier and customer relationships will no doubt need tailoring to company and country-specific needs. A study of supply chain relationships between the U.S. and Brazil revealed that the high-context Brazilians preferred more personal forms of contact such as visits and phone calls rather than e-mails.[29] However, a survey of firms operating in North America, Europe and the Pacific Basin confirmed several commonalities crucial to supply chain success. Delivery reliability and customer service were ranked as most important, followed by cost containment, delivery flexibility and speed of delivery.[30]

Global Trends in Retailing

Retail systems throughout the world are continually evolving in response to economic and social changes. A manager developing a worldwide distribution strategy must consider not only the state of retail today but also the expected state of retail systems in the future.

Larger-Scale Retailers

Shoppers in Caracas habitually patronize the small corner store. Venezuela's retail sector essentially consists of family-owned shops, modest-sized supermarkets and a few specialty chains. Even the modern malls are amalgams of boutiques. When hypermarket Tiendas Exito opened in an eastern suburb of Caracas, the new joint venture of French, Colombian and Venezuelan partners met with some skepticism in the press. Would Venezuelans really abandon the social ritual of shopping at the small local store? The new hypermarket promised low prices, the result of volume purchasing, centralized warehousing and computerized inventory control—all revolutionary in the local context. One month after Tiendas Exito opened its doors, sales were running 35 percent above expectations.[31]

There is a trend toward fewer but larger-scale retailers worldwide. As countries become more economically developed, the retail scene comes to be dominated by fewer, larger stores. This is particularly apparent in grocery retail, where the number of smaller retailers throughout the world has decreased or remained constant while larger discount outlets and hypermarkets have increased in number. Three factors contribute to this trend: an increase in car ownership, an increase in the number of households with refrigerators and freezers and an increase in the number of working wives. Whereas the European housewife of 30 years ago may have shopped two or three times a day in local stores, the increase in transportation capacity, refrigerator capacity and family cash flow, along with the reduction in available shopping time, has increased the practice of one-stop shopping in supermarkets. As retailers become bigger and more sophisticated, they often become more powerful relative to both producers and wholesalers.

Renewed Interest in Smaller-Scale Retailers

While larger-sized retail outlets are increasing in number, independent stores are the dominant players in many markets and will be for some time to come. In Latin America, for example, small mom-and-pop stores continue to contribute 60 percent of total in-store sales.[32] This reality has not escaped many global players who have recently refocused attention specifically on how to work with these smaller concerns.

Procter & Gamble is one such company. Disappointed with its percentage of sales coming from developing countries (26 percent compared to 40 percent for Colgate-Palmolive), the company aimed to add one billion additional customers in the next few years, specifically targeting women in developing countries. P&G's plan focused on placing its products in so-called "high-frequency stores" or tiny shops often run inside of someone's house. The company estimated that there were 20 million such stores worldwide, only 2.5 million of which carried P&G products.[33] P&G has even entered an agreement with the Chinese government to improve existing retail outlets, to build new ones and to provide retailing training to locals from 10,000 villages. The Chinese government supported the idea because of its potential to increase rural consumption and spur economic growth.[34]

International Retailers

The number of international retailers is rising. Most originate in advanced industrial countries and spread to both the developed and the developing countries of the world. The trend was started by a number of large retailers in mature domestic markets that saw limited growth opportunities at home compared to the potential opportunities overseas. Among the most successful international retailers have been franchises such as McDonald's and KFC and discount retailers such as Wal-Mart.

Similar to other MNCs, retailers that seek markets abroad face many cultural factors that affect their marketing strategies and business operations. For example, in the Middle East, shopping is a major pastime of many Arab women, most of whom do not work outside the home. Some visit the same store several times a week to look for new merchandise. Dressing rooms are large, and family and friends often shop together. Service demands are high, and Arab women like to be pampered.[35] Understanding these cultural demands often gives local retailers an edge over foreign competition.

Despite the challenges of entering foreign markets, the internationalization of retailing has been facilitated by a number of factors, such as enhanced data communications, new forms of international financing and lower governmental barriers to entry. The single European market has also motivated European retailers to expand abroad as they see a number of new international retailers entering their domestic markets. Retailers are attracted to international markets such as China and India, which often offer higher growth rates than their home markets. As retail growth slows in more mature markets, many retailers search for future growth in emerging markets. Table 13.2 presents the rankings of 30 emerging markets considered most attractive to international marketers.

Overall, American retailers have entered foreign markets later than European and Japanese retailers. However, Wal-Mart's entry into its first foreign market, Mexico, met with phenomenal success. Ten years after first entering the Mexican market, Wal-Mart dominated the country's retail sector. The U.S. retailer joint-ventured with Cifra, the leading Mexican retailer and pioneer of

Table 13.2 Retail Potential of Emerging Markets

Country	2013 Potential Rank	Market Attractiveness	Time Pressure for Entry
Brazil	1	100.0	48.3
Chile	2	95.6	54.3
Uruguay	3	92.0	36.5
China	4	62.1	100.0
United Arab Emirates	5	95.8	60.8
Turkey	6	86.8	50.9
Mongolia	7	17.1	96.5
Georgia	8	36.6	61.9
Kuwait	9	87.8	22.2
Armenia	10	32.3	43.6
Kazakhstan	11	44.1	57.8
Peru	12	52.9	49.3
Malaysia	13	63.4	39.8
India	14	36.8	60.6
Sri Lanka	15	16.6	58.6
Saudi Arabia	16	71.4	30.7
Oman	17	77.5	29.1
Colombia	18	59.2	32.4
Indonesia	19	47.4	61.4
Jordan	20	53.1	19.6

(Continued)

Table 13.2 (Continued)

Country	2013 Potential Rank	Market Attractiveness	Time Pressure for Entry
Mexico	21	79.0	30.6
Panama	22	49.7	37.2
Russia	23	92.4	37.4
Lebanon	24	74.1	38.4
Botswana	25	38.7	38.5
Namibia	26	20.8	73.2
Morocco	27	30.1	44.0
Macedonia	28	40.7	43.9
Azerbaijan	29	28.5	37.3
Albania	30	30.6	40.9

Source: Selected data from 2013 Global Retail Development Index, A.T. Kearney and Economist Intelligence Unit, LTD, Euromoney, IMF, World Bank, Planet Retail.

discount stores in Mexico. In its early years, the venture faced several problems. Tariffs inflated the prices of products imported from the United States, and Wal-Mart faced considerable red tape in obtaining import permits. Delivery schedules were unreliable because of poor road systems. With the inauguration of NAFTA, tariffs tumbled, paperwork diminished and road construction and improvement soared. Wal-Mart buys directly from U.S. suppliers and consolidates orders in its own distribution center in Laredo, Texas. Trucks hired from Wal-Mart deliver products to its Mexican stores the next day. As a large-volume buyer, Wal-Mart can require suppliers to label in Spanish. Most important, it can demand lower prices. The company passes these cost savings on to the Mexican consumer, offering prices that the traditional small retailers can't match.

Despite its success in Mexico, other markets proved more difficult. When first entering the Brazilian market, Wal-Mart failed to note that most target families owned only one car and did all their shopping on weekends. Car parks and store aisles at their superstores were unable to accommodate the weekend rush. Relationships with suppliers were strained as meetings in this Portuguese-speaking nation were always held in English. Wal-Mart has since adapted its practices to the local market by making small but significant operating changes, such as increasing the space devoted to selling food and building just one entrance to the store to reduce confusion.[36]

World Beat 13.2

Faking the Retail Experience

Why counterfeit a product when you can counterfeit a whole store? An American blogger posted a picture of a supposed Apple store in China. It set off a media storm. The store was a fake. A follow-up investigation revealed that there were other fake Apple stores operating in China. Apple authorizes about

1,000 resellers in China to sell its products. The company requires these outlets to meet a number of standards pertaining to proper store layout and the creation of a positive consumer experience. A counterfeit store could undermine Apple's global brand image even if the products in the store were the real thing.

Then there are the copiers. Jambo Juice in Beijing sells smoothies with energy boosters and tropical colors which appear to mimic U.S.-based Jamba Juice. A Chinese furniture seller, 11 Furniture, set up shops in the far west of China where IKEA has yet to enter. The stores look very much like those of IKEA, sporting the company's iconic blue and yellow colors, miniature pencils, in-store displays and crinkling plastic bags. Perhaps the only variation in marketing strategy is the store's menu. Chinese braised pork replaced IKEA's Swedish meatballs.

Commentators point out that this is another indication that China falls short of protecting intellectual property. But the phenomenon may not be limited to China. After the posting of the counterfeit Chinese store, Apple executives received word of questionable Apple stores in Burma, Croatia, Colombia, Spain, Slovenia and Venezuela.

Sources: "Fake Apple Store Cuts to Core of China Risk to Brands," Reuters News, July 22, 2011; "Made in China: Fake Stores," Dow Jones Chinese Financial Wire, August 2, 2011; "Chinese Retailers Hijack the Ikea Experience in Fast-Growing West," Reuters News, August 1, 2011; Charles Arthur, "Fake Apple Stores Not Limited to China," *Guardian & Observer*, July 26, 2011; and Fan Yang, "China's 'Fake' Apple Store: Branded Space, Intellectual Property and the Global Culture Industry," *Theory, Culture & Society*, March 17, 2014.

Sometimes international retailers have decided to abandon difficult markets. Wal-Mart retreated from the German and South Korean markets, and Home Depot pulled out of Chile. Despite the many obstacles abroad, successful international retailers tend to fall into three distinct categories: replicators, performance managers and reinventors.[37]

Replicators

Replicators such as Benetton, Zara and Starbucks develop a simple retail model, identify markets where that model will work, then export the model virtually unchanged. This strategy allows for fast international expansion, and economies of scale can be reaped from standardization even if local variations are accommodated by making minor adaptations to retail format or product offerings. Home and overseas businesses can be globally (or at last regionally) centralized, leading to easier coordination of markets and management of global brands.

Performance Managers

Performance managers such as Ahold and Kingfisher expand globally by acquiring existing retail businesses that they then develop as independent entities. These international retailers add value to these acquisitions in the form of their expertise in corporate finance, post-merger management and especially sophisticated management systems. For example, one study revealed that competence in retail logistics was a major determinant of success for large retailers that moved abroad. This competence allowed these retailers to contain costs, shorten procurement times and respond more quickly to customer needs.[38] Acquisitions can be a fast way to enter foreign markets, but transferring expertise and upgrading acquisitions can be time-consuming. Once expertise is transferred, however, performance managers tend to relinquish autonomy to local management.

Reinventors

Reinventors such as Carrefour and Tesco employ standardized back-end systems and processes while creating a largely tailored retail format for each overseas market. For example, a Tesco supermarket in London will appear vastly different from one in Bangkok or Warsaw.

Every national market is a potential market for reinventors. But understanding the different markets and adapting to them takes time and can slow the process of internationalization. Finding the proper balance between centralized and local control can also prove challenging.

Direct Marketing

Although the United States is the global leader in direct marketing, the market is also growing elsewhere. Direct-sales firms such as Amway, Avon and Mary Kay have proven highly successful in many emerging markets. For Avon, Brazil is second only to the United States in volume sales. The success of these companies was due in large part to their ability to recruit independent salespersons to promote their products. Many people in developing countries saw this as an opportunity to supplement meager incomes. In addition, direct sales appeals to collectivist cultures where people often mix business and personal relationships. Many Brazilian customers admit they will pay more to buy from someone they know rather than purchase the product cheaper at a store.[39] As a result, many local clones have emerged and flourished. Brazil's own Natura Cosmeticos is a formidable rival to Avon and has experienced phenomenal growth. The company is credited with causing the world's largest cosmetics company L'Oreal SA to falter in the lucrative Brazilian cosmetic market.[40]

However, direct marketing in emerging markets has faced a number of challenges. The infrastructure in most developing countries in terms of delivery and telecommunications lags behind markets in the developed world. Telemarketing is hampered by a lack of phones. For example, only one in ten Brazilians has a phone. Still, Brazil is a large market and tends to be ahead of the rest of Latin America in direct marketing. Urban consumers in Brazil receive an average of ten direct-mail pieces a month.

In certain countries, including Russia, direct marketing tends to be viewed negatively. The Chinese government has also been wary of direct marketers that recruit independent sales associates. Potential saleswomen for Avon in China must take a written test and listen to a lecture on China's latest sales regulations. Although China lifted a prior ban on direct sales, the industry is tightly regulated. The government caps sales commissions at 30 percent and sales representatives can only make money selling the product, not recruiting other sales representatives.[41]

Online Retailing

The Internet has opened an entirely new channel for retailers and manufacturers to sell their products. U.S.-based online retailers, such as Amazon.com, have expanded abroad with specific "stores" in the United Kingdom and Germany. Some online retailing, however, crosses borders; consumers can reach any store anywhere with a legitimate Internet address.

Online retailing requires a large connected population. Some parts of the world have reached near 100 percent adoption rates of e-commerce. The most active online purchasers come from South Korea, where 99 percent of Internet users shop online.[42] Online marketing surged in South Korea with the advent of smartphones. In one Seoul subway station a local warehouse chain posted photos of household goods that customers could purchase by simply taking pictures with their smartphones of bar codes on posters.[43]

China's Alibaba Group Holding Ltd. announced that sales on its shopping sites exceeded $3.1 billion on a single day during its annual Shopping Festival Sale held on November 11.[44] The growth in e-commerce in China is partially attributable to the growing use of mobile devices but also to improved methods of online payment.[45] However, payment issues remain a key concern in some developing countries. Nigeria is a country that has become synonymous with online fraud, and potential consumers refuse to enter their credit numbers online. Instead online retailers send delivery vans to meet their online buyers and collect payment in cash.[46]

Online retailing also depends on a solid fulfillment cycle that delivers the ordered merchandise quickly into the hands of the consumer and a return policy that assures customer satisfaction. In Brazil, online retailers are offering better return policies, and one online retailer offers four-hour delivery in the Sao Paulo area. However, distribution remains a problem in many markets.[47] The major challenge for online retailers in China is establishing a distribution system to deliver the product beyond the country's major cities.[48] Of course, when products are shipped across borders, issues of taxation and tariffs may still remain, further slowing delivery time.

Companies must also consider where their product is located in the product life cycle when trying to sell electronically in a foreign country. When Dell learned that over 90 million people in China had access to the Internet, it hurriedly implemented its famous American e-tailing strategy in the country with few modifications.[49] The strategy was unpopular with Chinese customers, who were often buying their first personal computer, and simply unwilling to make a significant purchase, sight-unseen.[50] Acknowledging its miscalculation, Dell signed a deal with Gome, China's largest electronics retailer, to sell its computers through the brick-and-mortar channel.[51]

In some cases, the ancient and modern worlds are meeting via the Internet. New websites are selling home furnishings, accessories and toys made by traditional craftspeople in developing countries. By giving artisans direct access to a global marketplace, the Internet has the potential to improve the lot of poor families from Asia to the Americas. Specific success stories include Himalayan artists selling handmade copper jugs and pots, originally thought to be a dying art, on a site called Worldtomarket.com.[52] Elsewhere, Ugandan women are earning four times their country average by making sparkling jewelry to be sold by Bead for Life, a Colorado company.[53]

Smuggling

Smuggling has recently emerged as a serious challenge to many international marketers.[54] Indian customs has credited the smuggling of gold, silver and consumer durables into India with supporting a black-market economy equivalent to 20 percent of the national GDP. In a single year, about half of all computer sales in Brazil involved smuggled computers. Today, smuggling accounts for an estimated 10 percent of all cigarettes sold worldwide.

Smuggling is the illegal transport of products across national borders and may involve the distribution of illicit products such as illegal drugs and arms. It also encompasses the illegal distribution of products that are legal to sell and use, such as computers, cosmetics and VCRs. Prior to trade liberalization, the products most commonly smuggled into Mexico were consumer electronics, food and alcohol, clothing, automobiles and auto parts, and toys and games. It is the smuggling of legal products that concerns us here.

Smuggling is most prevalent in developing countries and in the transitional economies of the former Soviet bloc. It arose in response to traditionally high tariffs and low quotas placed on imported goods. For example, a smuggled VCR in Mexico could sell for US$200, whereas its legally imported equivalent would sell for US$600. With the move toward trade liberalization in the emerging world, we would expect smuggling to fade as tariffs and quotas decline.

Although smuggling has decreased in some countries, it hasn't been eradicated. There are several reasons for this. To begin with, trade liberalization is not universal or complete. The tariff levels on many products in many countries still promote smuggling. Governments may also restrict the inflow of products for reasons other than protecting local industries. For example, the Malaysian government banned beef byproducts from Australia and New Zealand when 40 cattle ranches in those countries were accused of failing to meet Islamic halal standards. This resulted in a surge of smuggled beef byproducts entering Malaysia.[55] Furthermore, tariffs are not the only taxes that smugglers can avoid. They can also avoid sales taxes and value-added taxes. If smugglers are to become legitimate importers, they must declare themselves to customs. This enables governments to identify them and demand income taxes from them. Therefore, the lowering of tariffs decreases the cost advantage that smugglers previously enjoyed but doesn't completely remove it. Finally, as many countries heighten surveillance at customs in order to stop and seize counterfeits entering their markets, counterfeiters are increasingly turning to smuggling. In a single incident, the U.S. government broke up a smuggling ring of counterfeit Nike shoes and seized $16 million of merchandise.[56]

For many years, international marketers viewed smuggling as a benign and even positive phenomenon. In some cases, smugglers distributed products to otherwise inaccessible markets. In other cases, smugglers delivered products to consumers at a considerably lower price, supporting greater sales and market growth. In either case, the international firm stood to gain by realizing greater sales revenue as the result of the smuggling of its products.

An analysis of the records of major multinational cigarette companies revealed that many executives in these firms knew that certain international distributors were involved in large-scale smuggling operations and cooperated in some ways to assist them. Three managers of British American Tobacco (BAT) pleaded guilty or were convicted of smuggling.[57] Several countries in Europe and the developing world have initiated lawsuits against cigarette companies to recover taxes lost as a result of smuggling, although many of these suits have largely been dismissed on jurisdictional grounds. Still, the behavior of the international cigarette industry is likely to make governments all the more skeptical of other international firms that claim ignorance of smuggling operations.[58]

Nevertheless, governments have sometimes exhibited ambivalent attitudes toward smuggling. Prior to Poland's joining the EU, 25 percent of liquor and 15 percent of cigarettes consumed in Poland were smuggled in from Russia, Belarus or Ukraine. But patrolling the Polish border was stymied by a lack of money and agents, and customs inspectors often turned a blind eye to contraband. Officials who caught Russian smugglers just sent them back home. The Polish government also recognized that smuggling provided a livelihood to many in Poland's depressed eastern border economy where unemployment reached 35 percent.[59] Once Poland joined the EU, however, Brussels insisted that fines be levied on smugglers and their cars impounded. In addition, the EU assigned funds to ensure that Poland's customs department had the latest in detection equipment, such as state-of-the-art X-ray scanners.[60]

The darker side of smuggling is becoming ever more apparent. In the past 20 years, smuggling has evolved along lines of traditional organized crime. It has become more centralized and violent. As margins are squeezed by trade liberalization, smugglers have sought ways to protect their cost advantage, such as counterfeiting the products they previously bought. Some smugglers who transport consumer goods into developing countries have allied themselves with drug cartels to launder drug money. This phenomenon has caused firms such as Hewlett-Packard, Ford, General Motors, Sony, Westinghouse, Whirlpool and General Electric to be invited by the U.S. Attorney General to answer questions about how the distribution of their products may have become involved in the laundering of drug money.[61] In the future, both host and home governments may require international marketers to take more precautions to ensure that their products are not distributed through these illegal channels.

Conclusion

To be successful in the global marketplace, a company needs market acceptance among buyers. Except for direct marketers, companies also need market access via distribution channels. To achieve access, the firm must select the most suitable channel members, keeping in mind that substantial differences exist among countries on both the wholesale and the retail levels. Local habits and cultures, legal restrictions and infrastructure can all affect the success of distribution in a new country. Whether a company sells directly or through channels, it must establish an efficient supply chain in order to deliver products at lower costs. Technological advances have revolutionized many aspects of global distribution and have far-reaching implications for all global marketers.

Managerial Takeaways

1. *Global marketers not only sell to buyers but usually sell through channels as well. Understanding the needs of channel members can be nearly as important as understanding the needs of buyers.*
2. *The choice of channel members is complex and incorporates issues of costs, product line, control and coverage.*
3. *Choosing, motivating and controlling channel members are all important aspects of a distribution strategy. Changing channels can be difficult and costly.*
4. *Gaining access to channels may be impossible for a late entrant to a market. If channels are locked-up, global marketers can consider piggybacking, joint ventures or acquisitions.*
5. *Global supply chain management is increasingly important to a successful global strategy. In addition to establishing efficient logistics, global marketers must manage supplier and customer relationships to assure low costs and reliable delivery.*
6. *Firms that sell through retailers should be aware that retailers are growing in size worldwide but small retailers remain important especially in emerging markets.*
7. *Online commerce is increasing rapidly. Early problems with payment and delivery are being addressed, although these issues remain challenging in some developing countries.*
8. *Smuggling of legitimate and counterfeit products by transnational criminal organizations will threaten more and more global marketers in the years to come.*

Questions for Discussion

1. You have been assigned the task of selecting distributors in Malaysia to handle your firm's line of car batteries. What criteria will you use to select among the 12 possible distributors?
2. The performance of your agents and distributors in South America has been poor over the past three years. List possible ways in which to improve the management of these agents and distributors.
3. Given the trends in global retailing, what distribution strategies should a worldwide manufacturer of women's clothing consider?
4. Your firm has just entered the Polish market for bottled water. The major distributor is owned by a competitive producer of bottled water. What strategies can you use to gain access to this market?
5. Compare and contrast, from the manufacturer's point of view, the problems that parallel imports cause (Chapter 12) with those caused by smuggling. If governments increasingly restrict international marketers from stopping parallel imports, can these same marketers be held responsible for products being smuggled? Explain your reasoning.

CASE 13.1   Giants in Asia

The world's two largest retailers have targeted Asia with varying results. U.S.-based Wal-Mart and France's Carrefour both offer large stores stocked with groceries and general merchandise. Their entry into new national markets is invariably a shock to local retailers, who suddenly see the status quo of decades upset by these international competitors.

Government officials in China have credited Wal-Mart with revitalizing the retail sector. For years, government-owned retailers offered the same limited products, while employees took naps on the counters. When Wal-Mart opened its new store underneath the soccer stadium in the city of Dalian, the store was soon packed to capacity. Still, Wal-Mart chose to enter China slowly in order to learn as it went along. When it opened its first stores, customers arrived on bicycles and made only small purchases. Wal-Mart also discovered that it couldn't sell a year's supply of soy sauce to customers who lived in small apartments, and many potential customers preferred to shop for bargains in small shops or online. Furthermore, the firm faced a variety of government restrictions. Foreign retailers needed government-backed partners, and cities often restricted the size of stores. In response to these challenges, Wal-Mart invited government officials to visit its headquarters in the United States, donated to local charities and even built a school. Wal-Mart sourced nearly all its products locally, and nearly all employees were Chinese. To understand Chinese consumption patterns better, Wal-Mart's American manager walked the streets to see what the Chinese were buying.

The company's decision to enter Japan presented its own set of problems. Wal-Mart studied the Japanese market for four years and decided it needed a local partner. It agreed to buy 6 percent of Japan's fifth largest supermarket chain, Seiyu, with the option to increase its share to 67 percent. Still, Wal-Mart faced challenges: Japanese consumers associated low prices with poor quality. If the price of fish was low, it must be old. And employees balked at the idea of approaching customers and asking them if they needed assistance. Traditionally employees waited for the customer to ask them for assistance. Perhaps the biggest challenge was the speed at which competition responded by slashing prices, building single-story supercenters, providing acres of parking, launching "Made in Japan" campaigns and streamlining their logistics systems. Wal-Mart operated in Japan for seven years before showing a profit.

Carrefour, which has stores in 34 countries, began its Asian operations in Taiwan and then moved into China and South Korea. Carrefour entered Indonesia at the height of the Asian financial crisis, opening six stores in the capital city of Jakarta in just two years. The new stores competed on selection and low prices and challenged both open-air markets and the city's small, Chinese-owned neighborhood grocers. The 280-member Indonesian Retail Merchant Association urged Jakarta to impose zoning restrictions on hypermarkets. Carrefour also proved a threat to the larger, locally established grocery chains. One such chain, Hero supermarkets, admitted it couldn't compete with Carrefour on overall prices and chose instead to discount high-visibility products such as rice and to offer a variety of promotional specials. Hero also competes on freshness and has an excellent reputation among consumers for its produce.

Carrefour entered the Japanese market about the same time as Wal-Mart, investing $150 million to set up its first three stores. Carrefour had avoided Japan previously because of its high land prices. Although a depressed Japanese economy had lowered land prices, it meant the stores were opening in a climate of slow retail sales. Like Wal-Mart, Carrefour found itself making adaptations to local culture.

437

Within days of opening in Japan, the stores began selling more vegetables in packages of two or three, as other Japanese grocers do, instead of by weight. To provide competitive prices, Carrefour announced plans to buy 54 percent of its products directly from Japanese suppliers. This would circumvent the cumbersome wholesaling system of Japan, but it would require convincing Japanese producers to abandon long-standing relationships with their distributors—something that other foreign retailers previously had difficulty doing. In the meantime, Japanese grocery chains were restructuring and moving more to direct sourcing themselves.

Indonesian and Japanese competitors could take some hope from the fact that Carrefour had to retreat from the Hong Kong and Thai markets. The company cited stiff competition and restrictive development laws. Analysts suggested that the hypermarkets were unable to attract enough customers, most of whom were unwilling to go out of their way to do their daily shopping.

Both Carrefour and Wal-Mart had also exited South Korea, despite the fact that South Koreans were very accepting of hypermarkets and had the highest penetration per capita of hypermarkets in Asia. Local competitor E-Mart bought Wal-Mart's stores in South Korea. Wal-Mart was credited with inspiring E-Mart's cost-cutting efficiency. However, the South Korean retailer had its own unique spirit. The atmosphere in their stores was bright, loud and frenetic, as if E-Mart was attempting to capture the feel of a traditional outdoors market.

Discussion Questions

1. Why do you think hypermarkets are more common in some countries than others?
2. What competitive advantages do foreign retailers such as Wal-Mart and Carrefour enjoy when they enter Asian markets?
3. What are some possible competitive advantages of local retailers? Are those advantages transferable to other Asian countries?
4. Why do you think governments regulate retailing practices?

Sources: "Giants in Asia," in Kate Gillespie and H. David Hennessey, *Global Marketing* (Mason, OH: Cengage, 2011), pp. 400–401; Mariko Sanchanta, "Wal-Mart Bargain Shops for Japanese Stores to Buy," *Wall Street Journal*, November 15, 2010, p. B1; Mimosa Spencer, "Carrefour Sells 42 Thai Stores to French Rival," *Wall Street Journal*, November 16, 2010, p. B4; Kathy Chu and Laurie Burkitt, "Retail's New Pace in China," *Wall Street Journal*, November 7, 2012, p. B6; Ulrike Dauer, "Europe's Metro to Exit Retail Market in China," *Wall Street Journal*, January 17, 2013; and "Wal-Mart Plans More Stores and E-Commerce in China," Reuters, October 24, 2013.

CASE 13.2   Who's to Blame?

Several European countries, including Germany, Italy, France, Belgium and Finland, filed lawsuits against U.S. tobacco giants Philip Morris and R.J. Reynolds alleging that the two firms had cooperated with smugglers of cigarettes. The countries sought compensation for unpaid customs duties as well as unpaid value-added taxes. The EU estimated that these losses came to billions of dollars. European governments weren't the only losers. An estimated third of all cigarettes sold in the world are smuggled. Malaysia has estimated that its losses in taxes due to smuggled cigarettes amounted to US$1.3 billion in one year alone. These cigarettes arrived mainly from Indonesia and Thailand and were brought in under the aegis of crime syndicates. Malaysia, like most other countries, taxed cigarettes heavily not only as a source of revenue but also as a proven method for discouraging smoking.

At the same time in India, British American Tobacco (BAT) was facing an exposé resulting from the public examination of its internal communiqués. For example, BAT products were legally restricted in India to duty-free shops and hotels but were in fact smuggled into India on an extensive scale from the UAE. A memorandum issued by a top BAT executive discussed how the firm could advertise its brands without calling attention to the fact that most of the cigarettes were smuggled into the country. The memorandum went on to discuss contingency plans if any of the normal smuggling channels were shut down. When the *Business Standard* called BAT for comment, the company sent the following reply:

> Where governments are not prepared to address the underlying causes of the smuggling problem (excessive tax on tobacco), businesses such as ours are faced with a dilemma. If the demand for our products [is] not met, consumers will either switch to our competitor brands or there will be the kind of dramatic growth in counterfeit products that we have seen in Asian markets. . . . Where any government is unwilling to act or their efforts are unsuccessful, we act, completely within the law, on the basis that our brands will be available alongside those of our competitors in the smuggled as well as the legitimate market.

Despite the attempts by government to stem smuggling, it continued to grow. Nearly 300 million contraband cigarettes, most from China, were seized at British ports in a single year. Factories in Eastern Europe and Russia were also the source of many cigarettes smuggled into Western Europe. The lost tax revenues to governments from contraband cigarettes worldwide were estimated at over $50 billion annually. But for criminals, smuggled cigarettes are a bonanza. Japan Tobacco estimates the markup for smugglers to be 900 percent, and cigarettes can be easily transported.

The Chinese government had introduced severe penalties for smuggling consumer goods into China, including life sentences and even the death penalty. China's smuggling law not only targets smugglers but also encompasses anyone who buys from smugglers. They, too, can be charged with smuggling. Vietnam is another country that has taken serious steps against smugglers. The head of a private company and the chief of the smuggling investigation bureau of Ho Chi Minh City's customs department were sentenced to death for smuggling. The case involved 74 people who were charged with smuggling $71.3 million worth of electrical goods and home appliances into Vietnam.

Some politicians contend that cigarette companies over-supply low-tax jurisdictions such as Dubai and Poland knowing that smugglers will buy the product there to smuggle elsewhere. The companies deny this and point to their in-house anti-illicit teams whose task it is to shut down smuggling. Imperial Tobacco has a staff of 30 on its anti-illicit team. Philip Morris, the world's largest cigarette manufacturer by revenues, contends that extreme taxes on cigarettes in some jurisdictions are the major contributor to the problem. In Europe, prices for a pack of Marlboros can vary from €1 ($1.50) in Belarus to €13.80 ($20.70) in Norway. In the wake of the financial crisis, consumers appear even more ready to buy smuggled cigarettes that can cost them half as much as the legal alternative.

Discussion Questions

1. Why would BAT, or any other MNC, cooperate with smugglers?
2. How could smuggling hurt a MNC?
3. Why do you think some countries are introducing stiff penalties for smuggling?
4. Who do you think should be held responsible for smuggling—the manufacturer, the smugglers themselves, the retailers or the final consumer?

Sources: "Who's to Blame," in Kate Gillespie and H. David Hennessey, *Global Marketing* (Mason, OH: Cengage, 2011), pp. 402–403; Jennifer Booton, "Underground Cigarette Market Flourishes in Europe," *Fox Business News*, April 18, 2013; Peter Evans, "Tobacco Firms Track Down Smugglers," *Wall Street Journal*, March 25, 2013, p. B8; Larry Neumeister, "U.S. Court Revives European Suit vs. R.J. Reynolds," *Associate Press Newswires*, April 23, 2014; "Tobacco Smuggling, Terrorism and the Economy," *All Africa*, May 12, 2014; and Keith Humphreys "Why the Massive Black Market Trade in Cigarettes Affects You Even If You Don't Smoke," *Washington Post Online*, June 25, 2014.

Notes

1 Amol Sharma and Biman Mukherji, "Bad Roads, Red Tape, Burly Thugs Slow Wal-Mart's Passage in India," *Wall Street Journal*, January 12, 2013, p. A1.
2 Eric Bellman, "Indonesia Serves Tasty Dish for Tupperware," *Wall Street Journal Europe*, April 26, 2013, p. 24.
3 Passport Euromonitor, Retailing in: Austria, Germany, Russia, Spain, Hungary, and Portugal and The World Factbook, CIA. Accessed July 31, 2014.
4 "Overview of the Current State and Potential of China's Cosmetics and Toiletries Market," *Household and Personal Products Industry*, vol. 39, no. 2 (February 2002), p. 1.
5 Elisabeta Povoledo, "More Time to Buy in Italy," *New York Times*, January 6, 2012.
6 2013 Global Retail Development Index Report, A.T. Kearney, p. 5.
7 "Tecnica Acquires Nordica," *Powder Magazine*, January 14, 2002, www.powdermag.com, accessed March 9, 2005.
8 Warren Keegan, *Global Marketing Management*, 7th ed. (Englewood Cliffs, NJ: Prentice-Hall, 2001), p. 183.
9 "Seiko Epson Clones Strategy of U.S. Rival," *Nikkei Weekly*, January 17, 1994, p. 8.
10 "Arbitrator Fines Vulcan $23 Million," *Chemical Week*, March 14, 2001, p. 13.
11 Keysuk Kim and Changho Oh, "On Distributor Commitment in Marketing Channels for Industrial Products," *Journal of International Marketing*, vol. 10, no. 1 (2002), pp. 72–97.
12 Bridget Finn, "A More Profitable Harvest," *Business 2.0 Magazine*, May 1, 2005.
13 Preet S. Aulakh and Esra F. Gencturk, "International Principal-Agent Relationships," *Industrial Marketing Management*, vol. 29 (2000), pp. 521–538.
14 Karl Edmunds, "How to Tell When Channel Conflict is Destructive," *Frank Lynn & Associates*, March 2008.
15 Keysuk Kim and Changho Oh, "On Distributor Commitment in Marketing Channels for Industrial Products: Contrast Between the United States and Japan," *Journal of International Marketing*, vol. 10, no. 1 (2002), p. 89.

16   David Arnold, "Seven Rules of International Distribution," *Harvard Business Review*, vol. 78 (November–December 2000), pp. 132–133.

17   "Kodak Japan to Make Chinon Fully Owned Subsidiary," Knight-Ridder Tribune Business News, January 22, 2004, p. 1.

18   "American Standard Succeeds in Korea by Outflanking Local Firms' Lockout," *Financial Times*, August 26, 1993, p. A6.

19   Donald G. McNeil Jr., "Coca-Cola Joins AIDS Fight in Africa," *New York Times*, June 21, 2001, p. 8.

20   "The Cost of Moving Goods: Road Transportation, Regulations and Charges in Indonesia," *The Asia Foundation*, April 2008, pp. 47–50.

21   Ben Dolven, "The Perils of Delivering the Goods," *Far Eastern Economic Review*, July 25, 2002, p. 29.

22   "Importing with a Little Help from Friends," *Modern Plastics*, February 1, 2005, p. 50.

23   Maxwell Murphy, "Reinforcing the Supply Chain," *Wall Street Journal*, January 11, 2012, p. B6.

24   "Swisscom Slashes Order Processing Time Through Process Monitoring with ARIS PPM from IDS Scheer," IDS Scheer Press Release, 29 April 2008, www.ids-scheer.com/en/News/Swisscom_slashes_order_processing_time_through_process_monitoring_with_ARIS_PPM_from_IDS_Scheer/113211.html?referer=3673, accessed March 26, 2009.

25   Dale Rogers, "Supply Chain Management: Retrospective and Prospective," *Journal of Marketing Theory and Practice*, vol. 2, no. 4 (2004), pp. 60–65.

26   Neena Rai, "Chocolate Makers Fight for Farmers' Loyalty," *Wall Street Journal*, May 30, 2013, p. B6.

27   Drew Hinshaw, "Hamburgers Come to Africa," *Wall Street Journal*, December 11, 2013, p. B1.

28   Alex Frangos, "China Grows Its Dairy Farms with a Global Cattle Drive," *Wall Street Journal Online*, April 23, 2012.

29   Linda C. Ueltschy, Monique L. Ueltschy and Ana Christina Fachinelli, "The Impact of Culture on the Generation of Trust in Global Supply Chain Relationships," *Marketing Management Journal*, vol. 17, no. 1 (2007), pp. 15–26.

30   Edward Morash and Daniel Lynch, "Public Policy and Global Supply Chain Capabilities and Performance: A Resource-Based View," *Journal of International Marketing*, vol. 10, no. 1 (2002), pp. 25–51.

31   Marc Lifsher, "Will Venezuelans Shun Mom and Pop for the Hypermarket?" *Wall Street Journal*, June 28, 2001, p. A13.

32   Evette Treewater and John Price, "Navigating Latin American Distribution Channels," *Logistics Today*, vol. 48, no. 9 (2007), pp. 1–43.

33   Ellen Byron, "Emerging Ambitions—P&G's Global Target: Shelves of Tiny Stores," *Wall Street Journal*, July 16, 2007, p. A1.

34   Dexter Roberts, "Scrambling to Bring Crest to the Masses," *Business Week*, June 25, 2007.

35   Cecilie Rohwedder, "Style and Substance, The Chic of Arabia," *Wall Street Journal*, January 23, 2004, p. A11.

36   Kerry A. Dolan, "Latin America: Bumps in Brazil," *Forbes*, April 12, 2004.

37   The section on replicators, performance managers and reinventors is taken from Luciano Catoni, Nora F. Larssen, James Naylor and Andrea Zocchi, "Travel Tips for Retailers," *McKinsey Quarterly*, no. 3 (2002).

38   Irena Vida, James Reardon and Ann Fairhurst, "Determinants of International Retail Involvement: The Case of Large U.S. Retail Chains," *Journal of International Marketing*, vol. 8, no. 4 (2000), pp. 37–60.

39   Miriam Jordan, "Knock Knock," *Wall Street Journal*, February 19, 2003, p. A1.

40   Christina Passariello, "For L'Oreal, Brazil's Women Need a New Way to Shop," *Wall Street Journal Europe*, January 24, 2011 p. 20.

41   Mei Fong, "Chinese Rules May Tie Up Foreign Retailers," *Wall Street Journal*, July 17, 2006, p. A6.

42   Chandra Devi and Siti Syameen Md Khalili, "Is E-Shopping Safe?" *The New Straits Times*, October 3, 2008.

43   Evan Ramstad, "A New Look for South Korean Retail," *Wall Street Journal*, April 16, 2013, p. B8.

44   Paul Mozur and Juro Osawa, "Web Spree Takes China," *Wall Street Journal*, November 12, 2013, p. B3.

45   Shirley Zhang, Yao Lu and Eunice Ku, "China's E-Commerce Legislative and Regulatory Framework," *China Briefing*, August 9, 2013.

46 Drew Hinshaw, "In Nigeria, Rising Dreams of Web Commerce," *Wall Street Journal*, June 4, 2012, p. B1.

47 "Retailing in Brazil," Euromonitor International, April 2013.

48 Paul Mozur, "Scooters Rule as China Shops Online," *Wall Street Journal*, March 5, 2013, p. B8.

49 Evan Ramstad and Gary McWilliams, "Computer Savvy: For Dell, Success in China Tells Tale of Maturing Market," *Wall Street Journal*, July 5, 2005, p. A1.

50 Louise Lee, "Dell May Have to Reboot in China," *BusinessWeek*, November 7, 2005, p. 26.

51 Christopher Lawton and Mei Fong, "Dell to Sell PCs through China Retail Titan," *Wall Street Journal*, September 24, 2007, p. A4.

52 Miriam Jordan, "Web Sites Revive Fading Handicrafts," *Wall Street Journal*, June 12, 2000, p. B1.

53 Jenny Deam, "Beads for Life," *Denver Post*, January 25, 2005, p. F1.

54 This section is largely taken from Kate Gillespie and J. Brad McBride, "Smuggling in Emerging Markets: Global Implications," *Columbia Journal of World Business*, vol. 31 (Winter 1996), pp. 40–54.

55 "Beef Importers: Banned Offal Smuggled into Malaysia," Dow Jones Newswire, January 22, 2006.

56 Meredith Derby and Liza Casabona, "Counterfeiting Wars Heat Up for Shoe Players," *Footwear News*, October 3, 2006, p. 1.

57 Maud S. Beelman, Duncan Campbell, Maria Teresa Ronderos and Erik J. Schelzig, "Major Tobacco Multinational Implicated in Cigarette Smuggling, Tax Evasion, Documents Show," Investigative Report, The Center for Public Integrity, www.public-i.org/story_01 _013100.htm, accessed December 9, 2014.

58 For more on smuggling, see Kate Gillespie, "Smuggling and the Global Firm," *Journal of International Management*, vol. 9, no. 3 (2003), pp. 317–333.

59 Marek Strzelecki, "'Ants' Carry Contraband into Poland," *Wall Street Journal*, October 9, 2002, p. B31.

60 Guy Chazan, "Suddenly Boxed In, Russian Smugglers Plot Their Next Move," *Wall Street Journal*, May 4, 2004, p. A1.

61 Lowell Bergman, "U.S. Companies Tangled in Web of Drug Dollars," *New York Times*, October 10, 2000, p. 1.

Chapter 14

Global Promotion Strategies

GLOBAL PROMOTION STRATEGIES   445

PERSONAL SELLING   447

GLOBAL ACCOUNT MANAGEMENT   454

SELLING TO BUSINESSES AND GOVERNMENTS   456

OTHER FORMS OF PROMOTION   458

PUBLIC RELATIONS   465

CORPORATE SOCIAL RESPONSIBILITY   466

Each year the goliaths of the civil aircraft industry face off at the Paris Air Show. America's Boeing Company and Europe's Airbus Industrie attempt not only to make sales but also to capture the imaginations of potential clients. Company representatives meet with major customers to discuss current products and establish the leads that will eventually result in sales of these big-ticket items. But promoting current products is not enough. The Paris Air Show is a time to unveil new ideas and present the company's vision of the future of flight. This vision, as well as actual products, will help establish the image of each company. In this global industry, corporate image is very important. Can the firm deliver on its promises of speed, economy in-cabin amenities and innovative ideas?[1] International marketers in civil aircraft must communicate to potential customers that the answer is yes.

Global promotion strategies encompass a firm's marketing communications and include personal selling, sales promotion, public relations and advertising. Managing the communications process for a single market is no easy task. And the task is even more difficult for global marketers who must communicate to prospective customers in many national markets. In the process, they struggle with different cultures, habits and languages.

We begin this chapter by examining the cross-cultural implications of push strategies and pull strategies. We proceed to the challenge of developing a personal-selling effort on both the international and the local level, discussing differing sales practices as well as issues of recruitment and compensation of sales forces. Other promotion issues involving B2B and government sales are then discussed. We continue by exploring other aspects of global promotion such as sales promotions, sports sponsorships, spam, product placements, buzz and public relations. Advertising, another key element of the promotion mix, will be covered in detail in Chapter 15.

Learning Objectives

After studying this chapter, you should be able to:

➤ list the major factors that determine a firm's ability to use a push or a pull promotion strategy in different national markets;

➤ contrast the benefits to the international marketer of using an international sales force with those of using local sales forces;

➤ describe the impact that different purchasing behaviors, buying criteria, languages and negotiation styles can have on international selling;

➤ explain the importance of global account management;

➤ describe how global marketers can successfully utilize international trade fairs and consortia as well as manage the international bidding process;

➤ cite examples of how sales promotions vary across cultures, and suggest reasons for these differences;

➤ note recent international trends in sales promotions, sports sponsorships, telemarketing, product placement and managing word of mouth;

➤ give examples of international public relations disasters, and suggest ways in which global marketers can promote the goodwill of their firms;

➤ explain the role of corporate social responsibility in global marketing.

Global Promotion Strategies

How to manage the promotion mix globally is a critical question for many companies. Some firms do business in a certain way and do not rethink their promotion decisions when they internationalize. However, many companies find themselves in countries or situations that require an adjustment or a substantial change in their promotion mix.

Global marketers have many options for promotion. What they choose depends first on their basic promotional strategy. A multinational corporation (MNC) can employ a pull strategy, a push strategy or sometimes a combination of the two.

Pull Strategies

A pull strategy is characterized by a relatively greater dependence on promotion, including sales promotions and advertising, directed at the final buyer or end user for a product or service. Pull campaigns are typical for consumer-goods firms that target a large number of consumers. Pull campaigns are usually advisable when the product is widely used by consumers, when the channel is long, when the product is not very complex and when self-service is the predominant shopping behavior. Increased or decreased reliance on pull campaigns for global markets depends on a number of factors. Most important are access to advertising media, channel length and the leverage the company has with the distribution channel.

Marketers accustomed to having a large number of media available may find the choices limited in overseas markets. For many products, pull campaigns that rely heavily on advertising work only if access to electronic media, particularly television, is available. In some other countries, access to those media is restricted through time limits imposed by governments. Consequently, companies find it difficult to duplicate their promotional strategies when moving from an unregulated environment to more restricted environments.

Channel length is another major determinant of the feasibility of a pull campaign. Companies in consumer markets often face long channels. As a result, they try to overcome channel inertia by aiming their promotion directly at end users. When a company markets overseas, it may face an even longer channel because local distribution arrangements are different. Such is the case in Japan, where channels tend to be much longer than those in the United States. As a result, a greater reliance on a pull strategy may be advisable or necessary.

Distribution leverage is also different for each company from market to market. Gaining cooperation from local selling points, particularly in the retail sector, may be more difficult than in the domestic market. The fight for shelf space can be very intensive; shelf space in most markets is limited. Under these more competitive situations, reliance on a pull campaign becomes more important. If consumers are demanding the company's product, retailers will make every effort to carry it.

Push Strategies

In contrast to a pull strategy, a push strategy focuses on the distributors of a product rather than on the end user or ultimate buyer. Incentives are offered to wholesalers or retailers to carry and promote a product. A company may have to resort to a push strategy when lack of access to

445

advertising media makes a pull strategy less effective. Limited ability to transfer a pull strategy from a company's home market has other effects on the company's performance in foreign markets. Reduced advertising tends to slow the product adoption process in new markets, forcing the firm to accept slower growth. In markets crowded with existing competitors, newcomers may find it difficult to establish themselves when avenues for pull campaigns are blocked.

World Beat 14.1

Hindu Festivals Attract Marketers

The Hindu festival of Diwali is associated with sweets. In India, companies like Cadbury, PepsiCo and Pantaloon develop special promotions for the festival which include special gift packs and festival-specific advertising campaigns. In the United Kingdom, Indian companies such as Patak's sponsor parades and musical events targeted at the country's ethnic Indian population. It is a season when Indians spend the most and borrow the most. Marketers experience a surge in big-ticket items from household appliances to houses themselves.

India has many annual festivals offering promotion opportunities to global and local marketers. However, the Kumbh Mela festival occurs only once every 12 years. This Hindu festival draws 30 million participants to a ritual cleansing at the confluence of the Ganges and Yamuna rivers. Many participants come from rural villages and small towns where 80 percent of India's one billion people live. Many of these potential consumers are beyond the reach of most modern media. Getting them to try a product while at the festival could be the start of potentially extensive word-of-mouth advertising. Unlike television commercials, mass marketers can use the Kumbh Mela to get potential consumers to touch and taste their products.

The Kumbh Mela has traditionally attracted vendors from across India. More recently the festival set off a promotion war between Coca-Cola and Pepsi in the increasingly important Indian market. PepsiCo's Indian unit teamed up with the state tourism department to sell Pepsi at stalls and restaurants at the festival. Rival Coca-Cola sold their product at 115 stalls. Coke also had 15,000 posters, as well as billboards, banners and police assistance booths painted red with the famous logo.

Some Indians criticize the commercialization of ancient religious traditions and particularly abhor the role of global marketers. Many nationalist Indians object to foreign products as symbols of economic imperialism. Still, the festival promotions appear to be successful. Car sales rise in India during many religious festivals. It is considered auspicious to purchase expensive items at those times, and car dealers offer attractive purchase plans to further promote this belief.

Sources: Priyanka Pani, "Kumbh is Maha Sales Opportunity," The Hindu Business Line, February 12, 2013; Rajiv Mani, "Vendors of Exotic Stuff Roam the Kumbh Mela," *The Times of India*, February 27, 2013; Rasul Bailay, "A Hindu Festival Attracts the Faithful and U.S. Marketers," *Wall Street Journal*, February 12, 2001; Rasul Bailay, "Pantaloon to Launch its Own Chocolate Brand," Mint, Delhi, June 10, 2008; Bindu D. Menon, "No Festival Cheer for Realty Developers," The Hindu Business Line, November 2, 2013; and "Banks Ready to Lower Rates for Diwali," Dow Jones Global Equities News, October 8, 2013.

Consequently, a company entering a new market may want to consider such situations in its planning and adjust its expected results accordingly. A company accustomed to a given type of communications mix usually develops an expertise or a distinctive competence in the methods commonly used. When the firm is suddenly faced with a situation in which that competence cannot be fully applied, the risk of failure or underachievement multiplies. Such constraints can even affect entry strategies and the market selection process.

Personal Selling

Personal selling takes place whenever a customer is met in person by a representative of the marketing company. When doing business globally, companies must meet customers from different countries. These individuals may be used to different business customs and will often speak a different language. That is why personal selling is extremely complex and demands some very special skills on the part of the salesperson.

The complexity of a product usually influences how extensively personal selling is used. The level of complexity has to be compared with the product knowledge of the clients. A company selling the same products abroad as those sold domestically may find that more personal selling is necessary abroad if foreign clients are less sophisticated than domestic clients. A U.S. company may use the same amount of personal selling in Europe as it does in the United States but may need to put forth a greater personal-selling effort in developing countries if the product is new to those markets.

Although very effective as a promotion tool, personal selling requires the intensive use of a sales force and can be costly. Costs vary across countries. In the United States, a typical sales call is estimated to cost in excess of $300. This has motivated some companies to investigate other forms of promotion. Dell Computer considered sales calls too expensive in Brazil and instead mailed brochures to potential small-business clients. It took the company over a year to put together a list of names and addresses, because these were not readily available in Brazil. However, the mail campaign was a success in the end.

International versus Local Selling

When a company sends its sales force abroad to meet directly with clients, it is practicing international selling. This type of selling requires the special skill of being able to manage within several cultures. Much more often, however, MNCs engage in local selling. They organize and staff a local sales force made up of local nationals to do the selling in only one country. Different problems arise in managing and operating a local sales force than in managing multicountry salespersons.

International Selling (Multicountry Sales Force)

The job of the international salesperson seems glamorous. One imagines a professional who frequently travels abroad, visiting a large number of countries and meeting with businesspeople of various backgrounds. However, this type of work is quite demanding and requires a special set of skills.

447

International salespersons are needed only when companies deal directly with their clients abroad. This is usually the case for industrial equipment or business services but is rarely required for consumer products or services. One recent exception is the recruitment of foreign students to U.S. MBA programs.

Overseas students are an attractive target market for many MBA programs at U.S. business schools because they pay a higher out-of-state tuition. In addition, a significant percentage of international students lend programs an aura of sophistication that can boost the school's prestige and attract corporate recruiters. However, in the early 2010s the poor economic climate in the United States made job placement more difficult for foreign students convincing many that an MBA program at home was the better decision. To offset a decline in this important market segment, many U.S. business programs sent admissions professionals overseas to countries as diverse as Japan and Turkey in order to promote their programs.[2]

UNDERSTANDING PURCHASING BEHAVIOR One of the most important tasks of international selling consists of identifying the buying unit in the client company. The buying unit consists of all persons who have input into the buying decision. The seller must locate and access the actual decision-makers, who may hold different positions from company to company or from country to country. In different countries, the purchasing manager may have different responsibilities, and engineers may play a greater or a lesser role. Buying decisions are more centralized in many Asian and Latin American firms, and often the owner of the firm will make the final buying decision. Gaining access to top management may not be easy and may cause delays. Even in Europe, the time between a first sales call and a purchase can be 50 percent longer than in the United States. Sales times in Japan can also be longer because of the Japanese emphasis on consensus in the buying unit. The members of the buying unit will want to explore and debate alternatives, while striving for a sense of unity and collegiality among themselves.

UNDERSTANDING BUYING CRITERIA In addition to different purchasing patterns, the international salesperson may have to deal with different decision criteria or objectives on the part of the purchaser. Buyers or users of industrial products in different countries may expect to maximize different goals. For example, Sealed Air had difficulty convincing businesses in Taiwan to purchase more expensive packaging systems to protect their products during shipping, even though these systems had proved cost-effective in avoiding breakage. Unlike buyers in other markets, Taiwanese manufacturers focused almost exclusively on the purchase price of the packaging.[3]

LANGUAGE CHALLENGES Overcoming the language barrier is an especially difficult task for the international salesperson. In Chapter 3, we discussed several issues related to culture and language that can affect international marketing in general and personal selling in particular. Different societies apply different forms of address, use or avoid certain body language, and feel differently about the appropriateness of showing emotion. Certain societies are low-context cultures wherein the meanings of words are explicit. Other societies are high-context cultures wherein the meanings of words are implicit and change according to who speaks them as well as when and where they are spoken. It is very difficult for a non-native speaker to become fluent in the language of a high-context culture.

Of course, the personal-selling effort is markedly enhanced if the salesperson speaks the language of the customer, but for many industries, dependence on the local language is not so strong today as it was just one or two decades ago. For many new and highly sophisticated products, such as electronics and aerospace, English is the language spoken by most customers. Consequently, with more and more executives speaking English in many countries, many firms can market their products directly without local intermediaries.

English is widely spoken in Europe and is the leading second language in Asia and Latin America. Consequently, the ability to speak a number of foreign languages is less of a necessity. Still, learning a foreign language can be an excellent way to understand a foreign culture, and language proficiency continues to have a very favorable impact on the sales process. Local customers often appreciate a sales representative who speaks their language; it indicates the company's commitment to their market as well as its appreciation of their people and culture.

In industries where knowledge of the local language is important, companies tend to assign sales territories to salespersons on the basis of language skills. A European multinational manufacturer of textile equipment assigns countries to its sales staff according to the languages they speak. This is more important in traditional industries such as textile manufacturing, where businesses are more local in orientation and where managers may not speak English well.

Even executives who speak fairly good English may not understand all the details of product descriptions or specifications. As a result, a company can make an excellent impression by having its sales brochures translated into some of the key languages. European companies routinely produce company publications in several languages. Translations from English may not be needed for Scandinavia, where English proficiency is common. However, they may be valuable for other parts of the world, where the level of English-language skills is not high.

BUSINESS ETIQUETTE Global marketers selling to many markets are likely to encounter a diverse set of business practices as they move from one country to another. Because interpersonal behavior is intensely culture-bound, this part of the salesperson's job will vary by country. Many differences exist in how an appointment is made, how (and whether) an introduction is made and how much lead time is needed for making appointments. Whereas it is acceptable for visitors to arrive late in China, India or Indonesia, arriving late in Hong Kong is not acceptable. Lateness causes the visitor to "lose face," which is an extremely serious matter among Hong Kong businesspeople. In Switzerland, where punctuality is also highly valued, clients may be favorably impressed if the salesperson arrives 10 or 15 minutes early for an appointment.

The salesperson must also know whether or not gifts are expected or desired. In most Chinese cultures, gift-giving is viewed as a sign that the vendor is committed to establishing or sustaining a relationship with the client.[4] Exchanging business gifts is popular in Taiwan but less common in Saudi Arabia. In Switzerland, it is better to wait until the sale is finalized before offering a gift to a client. Even then the gift should not be too expensive, or it may be construed as a bribe and thus give offense. In short, what is expected or tolerated in some markets may be taboo in others.

No manager can be expected to know the business customs of every country, so important information must be obtained from special sources. A company's own foreign market representatives or sales subsidiary can provide key information or suggestions. Also, governments tend to collect data on business practices through their commercial officers posted abroad. Some business service companies, such as global accounting firms or global banks, also provide customers with profiles of business practices in foreign countries.

Foreign businesspersons receiving visitors from the United States or any other foreign country rarely expect the foreign visitor to be familiar with all local customs. However, it is always appreciated when the visitor can exhibit familiarity with the most common practices and some willingness to try to conform. Learning some foreign customs helps to generate goodwill toward the company and can increase the chances of making a sale.

International Sales Negotiations

It is the ultimate job of most sales forces to make a sale. As we mentioned in Chapter 5, negotiations can play an important role in selling, especially to businesses and governments. The terms of a sale—price, delivery terms and financing options—can all be negotiable. Negotiations in the global arena are complicated because the negotiating partners frequently come from different cultural backgrounds. As a result, misunderstandings or misjudgments can occur among them. To maximize their effectiveness in these often difficult and protracted negotiations, international sales personnel must be attuned to cultural differences. Careful background preparation on the cultural norms prevalent in the foreign country is the starting point in successful negotiations and selling.

For example, the time it takes to negotiate sales can vary between countries. In some countries, such as China, negotiations tend to take much more time than in the United States or some other Western countries. One European company that operated a joint venture in China observed that during one negotiation, two weeks were spent in a discussion that elsewhere might have taken only a few hours. In this situation, much of the time was used for interdepartmental negotiations among the Chinese themselves rather than for face-to-face negotiations with the European company. However, in Pakistan many international sales negotiations occur between the seller and the client's CEO, or a team including the CEO. Authority is centralized and decisions are relatively quick.[5]

Another difference between cultures is their attitude toward the final negotiated contract. Managers from the United States like to "get it all in writing." Contracts often spell out many contingencies and establish the position of both sides in light of these contingencies. Americans believe that the business relationship will proceed more smoothly if this is all worked out ahead of time. Other cultures consider this insistence on elaborate written contracts a sign of inflexibility or even lack of trust on the part of Americans. In Brazil, even a written contract may not be regarded as binding but, rather, as open for continued renegotiation. In any case, an understanding of the prevailing cultural attitudes is necessary to successfully negotiate the final sale.

A recent study suggests, however, that these cultural differences toward contracts should not be overemphasized. The study found that businesspeople from relationship-oriented countries such as Mexico and Turkey did in fact appreciate written contracts, and Americans approved of broad contracts that allowed for good working relationships to develop. This apparent cultural convergence may be the result of increased global marketing.[6]

Local Selling (Single-Country Sales Force)

When a company is able to maintain a local sales force in the countries where it does business, many of the difficulties of bridging the cultural gap with clients are minimized. The local sales force can be expected to understand local customs, and the global company typically gains additional acceptance in the market. This is primarily because local sales forces are usually staffed with local nationals.

However, many challenges remain. A firm must determine the scope and size of its sales force. It must understand local sales practices, and it must effectively manage its sales team.

Missionary Sales Force

For firms that still use distributor sales forces to a large extent, a missionary sales force with limited responsibilities may suffice. A missionary sales force concentrates on visiting clients together with the local distributor's sales force. Its focus is on promoting the product rather than distributing the product or even finalizing the sale. Missionary sales forces can also be used to introduce new products to new markets. For example, Procter & Gamble sent marketers in vans to nearly 40,000 rural villages in India and used DVD players to show villagers how to use P&G products such as shampoo and disposable diapers.[7]

Company-Owned Local Sales Force

If the global company's sales force needs to do the entire job of selling, a much larger sales force will be necessary. The size of the local sales force depends to a large extent on the number of clients and the desired frequency of visits. This frequency may differ from country to country, which means that the size of the sales force will differ accordingly.

Control over a firm's sales activities is a frequently cited advantage of operating a company-owned local sales force. With its own sales force, the company can emphasize the products it wants to market at any time and can maintain better control over the way it is represented. Price negotiations, in the form of discounts or rebates, are handled in-house rather than leaving these decisions to an independent distributor. Having a company sales force helps ensure that the personnel have the necessary training and qualifications. Control over all of these parameters usually means higher sales than those achieved with a distributor sales force.

Also, the local sales force can represent an important bridge to the local business community. For industries in which the buying process is local rather than global, the sales force speaks the language of the local customer. It can be expected to understand the local business customs and to bring the international firm closer to its end users. In many instances, local customers, although they may not object to buying from a foreign firm, may prefer to deal with local representatives of that firm.

The role of the local sales force needs to be coordinated with the promotion mix selected for each market. As many companies have learned, advertising and other forms of promotion can be used to make the function of the sales force more efficient. In many consumer-goods industries, companies prefer a pull strategy, concentrating their promotion budget on the final consumer. In such cases, the role of the sales force is restricted to gaining distribution access. However, as we have noted before, there are countries in which access to communications media is severely restricted. As a result, companies may place greater emphasis on a push strategy, relying heavily on the local sales force. This will affect both the role and the size of the firm's sales force.

Furthermore, cultural differences can affect how much time a local sales force must allot to attracting new customers versus retaining current ones. A study comparing buyer-seller relationships in Latin America and the United States concluded that Latin American buyers felt a stronger sense of loyalty to their current suppliers and were more willing to tolerate problems.[8] In such markets, a sales force would need to spend more time and exert more effort to attract new customers away from their current suppliers.

Foreign Sales Practices

Although sales forces are employed virtually everywhere, the nature of their interaction with the local customer is unique to each market and may affect local sales operations. For most Westerners, Japanese practices seem substantially different. Here is an example reported by Masaaki Imai, president of Cambridge Corporation, a Tokyo management consulting and recruiting firm.

When Bausch & Lomb first introduced its new soft-lens line into Japan, the company targeted influential eye doctors in each sales territory for its introductory launch. The firm assumed that once these leading practitioners signed up for the new product, marketing to the majority of eye doctors would be easier. However, a key customer quickly dismissed one salesperson. The doctor said that he thought very highly of Bausch & Lomb equipment but preferred regular lenses for his patients. The salesperson did not even have a chance to respond. He decided, because it was his first visit to this clinic, to wait around for a while. He talked to several assistants at the clinic and to the doctor's wife, who was handling the administration of the practice.

The next morning, the salesperson returned to the clinic and observed that the doctor was very busy. He talked again with the assistants and joined the doctor's wife when she was cooking and talked with her about food. When the couple's young son returned from kindergarten, the salesperson played with him and even went out to buy him a toy. The wife was very pleased with the well-intentioned babysitter. She later explained to the salesperson that her husband had very little time to listen to any sales presentations during the day, so she invited him to come to their home in the evening. The doctor, obviously primed by his wife, received the man very warmly, and they enjoyed *sake* together. The doctor listened patiently to the sales presentation and responded that he did not want to use the soft lenses on his patients right away. However, he suggested that the salesperson try them on his assistants the next day. Therefore, on the third day, the salesperson returned to the clinic and fitted several of the clinic's assistants with soft lenses. The reaction was very favorable, and the doctor placed an order on the third day of the sales call.

Japanese customers often judge whether a company really wants to do business by the frequency of the sales calls they receive. Salespeople who make more frequent calls to a potential customer than the competition may be regarded as more sincere. This means that companies doing business in Japan have to make frequent sales calls to their top customers, even if only for courtesy reasons. Although this contact may occasionally be just a telephone call, the need to make frequent visits significantly affects the staffing levels of the company-owned sales force.

Best Buy experienced a similar phenomenon in China. Many consumers in China's inland cities are buying major appliances for the first time, and sales personnel must take extra time to explain all the product features. Sales staff at Best Buy's Five Star Stores give customers their phone numbers to call at any time. This has created loyal shoppers who recommend Five Star to their friends and family. One salesman has even attended a half-dozen customer weddings.[9]

Recruiting a Sales Force

Companies have often found recruiting sales professionals quite challenging in many global markets. Although the availability of qualified sales personnel is a problem even in developed countries, the scarcity of skilled personnel is even more acute in developing countries. Global companies, accustomed to having sales staff with certain standard qualifications, may not find it easy to locate the necessary salespeople in a short period of time. One factor that limits their availability in many countries is the local economic situation. A good economic climate will limit the number of people a company can expect to hire away from existing firms unless a substantial increase over their present compensation is offered.

Furthermore, sales positions don't enjoy uniformly high esteem from country to country. Typically, sales as an occupation or career has generally positive associations in the United States. This allows companies to recruit excellent talent, usually fresh from universities, for sales careers. These university recruits often regard sales as a relatively high-paying career or as a path to middle management. Such an image of selling is rare elsewhere in the world. In Europe, many companies continue to find it difficult to recruit university graduates into their sales forces, except in such highly technical fields as computers, where the recruits are typically engineers. When selling is a less desirable occupation, the quality of the sales force may suffer. The time it takes to fill sales positions can be expected to increase dramatically if the company wants to insist on top-quality recruits.

Compensation

In their home markets where they usually employ large sales forces, global companies become accustomed to handling and motivating their sales forces in a given way. In the United States, typical motivation programs include some form of commission or bonus for meeting volume or budget projections, as well as vacation prizes for top performers. When a global company manages local sales forces in various countries, the company must determine the best way to motivate them. Salespersons from different cultures may not all respond the same way. Motivating practices may need to differ from country to country.

Jorge Vergara joined U.S.-based Herbalife when it first entered the Mexican market, and he soon became a star salesman. He then left to start his own nutritional supplements company, Omnilife. Breaking with Herbalife's sales practices, Mr. Vergara modified his compensation system. Instead of rewarding on the basis of sales volume, he rewarded salespersons who sold consistently. He also paid them every two weeks, which is customary in Latin America, instead of monthly. After only eight years, Omnilife became one of Latin America's largest sellers of nutritional supplements, ahead of both Herbalife and Amway Corporation.[10]

One of the frequently discussed topics in the area of motivating salespeople is the value of the commission or bonus structure. In countries that rate high on uncertainty avoidance, sales representatives may prefer to receive guaranteed salaries. U.S. companies, on the other hand, have tended to use some form of commission structure for their sales forces. Although this may fluctuate from industry to industry, U.S. firms tend to use a more flexible and volume-dependent compensation structure than European firms do. Japanese firms more often use a straight-salary type of compensation. To motivate the sales force to achieve superior performance, the global company may be faced with using different compensation practices depending on local customs.

Global Account Management

Traditionally, account management has been performed on a country-by-country basis. This practice invariably leads, even in large global firms, to a country-specific sales force. However, as we noted in Chapter 5, some companies have created global account teams. The global account team services an entire customer globally, or in all countries where a customer relationship exists. Global account teams may comprise members in different parts of the world, all serving segments of a global account and coordinated through a global account management structure.

Global accounts arose in response to more centralized purchasing within global firms. Companies that purchased similar components, raw materials or services in many parts of the world realized that by combining the purchasing function and managing it centrally they could demand better prices and service from suppliers. Today, many companies search the globe for the best buy.

Siemens's Automotive Systems Division has tailored its sales structure to these new realities. The company maintains global account teams for key customers such as Volkswagen and Ford. The teams are in charge of the firm's entire business, regardless of where the components are sourced or used. From the customer's perspective, the advantage stems from the clear designation of a counterpart who will handle all aspects of their business relationship.[11] The system of global account management is also practiced widely in the professional-service sectors. Globally active banks such as Citibank have maintained global account structures for years. Likewise, advertising agencies offer global clients global account management with seamless coordination across many countries. The world's leading accounting firms, such as Deloitte Touche Tohmatsu International, have long-standing traditions of managing international clients from a single unit.[12]

Global account management is greatly enhanced by sophisticated IT. With members of the team dispersed around the globe, it becomes essential to coordinate all actions meticulously. The development and rapid spread of such tools as videoconferencing and e-mail have greatly extended the reach of a management team beyond the typical one-location office.

Identifying Worthwhile Global Accounts

Nonetheless, global account management can present challenges to global marketers. A study of 16 large MNCs revealed that prices quoted to global accounts were more likely to fall than to rise. In 27 percent of cases, prices were assessed as becoming much lower within three years.

Although global account management has been shown to be very effective in certain situations, it is a difficult and expensive structure to implement. Because of these concerns, many vendors set clear criteria as to which customers qualify as worthwhile global accounts. Potential global accounts may need to meet minimum revenue levels that will support the additional overhead required by global account management. Marriott International requires that potential global accounts purchase over $25 million annually in hotel services. While customers often desire to become a global account to obtain volume price discounts, vendors should expect a global account client to differentiate them as a vendor, resulting in increased sales volume.[13] Marriott International once halted a global account with a client worth $100 million in annual sales when the hotel company determined that the client was only interested in receiving a global discount.[14]

Implementing Successful Global Account Programs

To implement a successful global account program, vendor companies should be as global and as coordinated as their customers—or problems can arise.[15] One firm was surprised to receive a call from a global customer demanding service for a plant in Indonesia. The vendor had no sales or service operation in Indonesia but felt obliged to respond. Someone was flown out from a neighboring country at considerable expense.[16] Senior management commitment is essential as well. Global customers will expect to meet with senior managers from their key vendors on a regular basis. Top management must also authorize the allocation of essential people and resources to global account teams. This may require moving personnel and resources from countries and regions to a unit located at central headquarters.

Global account management requires a robust IT system. Global IT systems can track the progress of a global account in such areas as orders, back orders, shipments, accounts payable, complaints and returns. They can also create value for the customer as well as for the vendor. For example, at Marriott International, the global account manager for IBM was able to track IBM's conference cancellations globally. These were costing IBM over $1 million annually. Marriott International's account managers created an internal electronic bulletin board for IBM employees to purchase cancelled space, thereby reducing IBM cancellation fees and substantially reducing IBM's cost.

The customer must also have the organizational structure, processes and information systems that will support centrally coordinated global purchasing. If not, the supplier will find itself still selling country by country, reaping no efficiency gains but still having to give the customer a cheaper price.[17]

Finally, global account managers must possess special skills. Many national account managers may not have sufficient cross-cultural skills or the broader business acumen required for the job. Required skills of global account managers are more aligned with those of a general manager than a senior salesperson. Global account managers may be called upon to analyze an industry, understand competitive strategies and identify new ways in which their firm can contribute to a customer's strategy. Many companies with global account management programs will find that additional training may be necessary to managers assigned this task.

Selling to Businesses and Governments

Promotion methods that are oriented largely toward business or government markets can be important to international firms operating in those markets. In particular, the use of international trade fairs, bidding procedures for international projects and consortium selling all need to be understood in their international context.

International Trade Fairs

Participation in international trade fairs has become an important aspect of B2B marketing abroad. The Pet Vet Russia Expo held in Moscow allows global marketers to exhibit products and services for pets. The trade fair is attended by manufacturers and distributors from Europe, Asia, Russia and the United States, as well as their potential customers—pet stores, veterinary clinics, local distributors and pet salons.[18]

Trade fairs are ideal for exposing new customers and potential distributors to a company's product range and have been used extensively by both newcomers and established firms. In the United States, business customers can be reached through a wide range of media, such as specialized magazines with a particular industry focus. In many overseas countries, the markets are too small to allow for the publication of such trade magazines for only one country. As a result, prospective customers usually attend these trade fairs on a regular basis. Trade fairs also offer companies a chance to meet with prospective customers in a less formal atmosphere. For a company that is new to a certain market and does not yet have any established contacts, participating in a trade fair may be the only way to reach potential customers.

There are an estimated 600 trade shows in 70 countries every year. Germany's Hannover Fair is considered the largest industrial fair in the world, attracting approximately 6,000 exhibitors in engineering and technology from over 60 countries. Other large general fairs include the Canton Fair in China and the Milan Fair in Italy. Germany hosts the most trade fairs, drawing a total of about ten million visitors a year.[19] In addition to general trade fairs, specialized trade fairs concentrate on a certain segment of an industry or user group. Such fairs usually attract limited participation in terms of both exhibitors and visitors. Typically, they are more technical in nature. Some of the specialized trade fairs do not take place every year. One of the leading specialized fairs for the chemical industry is the Achema, which is held in Frankfurt, Germany, every three years. Other specialized fairs that enjoy an international reputation include the air shows of Paris and of Farnborough, England, where aerospace products are displayed.

Participation in trade fairs can save both time and effort for a company that wants to break into a new market and does not yet have any contacts. For new product announcements or demonstrations, the trade fair offers an ideal showcase. Trade fairs are also used by competitors to check out one another's most recent developments. They can give a newcomer an idea of the potential competition in some foreign markets. Consequently, trade fairs are a means of both selling products and gathering important and useful market intelligence. Therefore, marketers with global aspirations will do well to seek out the trade fairs directed at their industry or customer segment and to schedule regular attendance.

International exhibiting may require more planning than is necessary for domestic shows. First, begin planning 12 to 18 months in advance, taking into account the fact that international shipping may involve delays. Second, check show attendance. Many shows allow the general public to attend, in which case you may want to arrange for a private area for meeting with viable prospects. Third, in the United States, a show may be staffed by salespeople and middle managers. At many international shows, however, customers expect to see the CEO and senior management. Finally, use a local distributor, consultant or sales representative to help with the local logistics and acquaint you with the local culture.[20]

Selling Through a Bidding Process

Global marketers of industrial products may become involved in a bidding process, particularly when major capital equipment is involved. Companies competing for such major projects must take a number of steps before negotiations for a specific purchase can begin. Typically, companies actively seek new projects and then move on to prequalify for the particular project(s) they locate before a formal project bid or tender is submitted. Each phase requires careful management and the appropriate allocation of resources.

Search Phase

During the search phase, companies want to make sure that they are informed of any project meriting their interest that is related to their product lines. For particularly large projects that are government sponsored, full-page advertisements may appear in leading international newspapers or may be posted on government websites. Companies can also utilize their networks of agents, contacts or former customers to inform them of any project being considered.

Prequalifying Phase

In the prequalifying phase, the purchaser frequently asks for documentation from interested companies that wish to make a formal tender. No formal bidding or tender documents are submitted. Instead, the buyer is more interested in general company background and is likely to ask the firm to describe similar projects it has completed in the past. At this stage, the company will have to sell itself and its capabilities. A large number of companies may be expected to pursue prequalification.

Formal Bid

In the next phase, the customer selects the companies—usually only three or four—to be invited to submit a formal bid. Formal bids consist of a written proposal of how to solve the specific client problem and the price the firm would charge for the project. For industrial equipment, this usually requires personal visits on location, special design of some components and the preparation of full documentation, including engineering drawings, for the client. The bid preparation costs can be enormous, running as high as several million dollars for some very large projects. The customer will select the winner from among those submitting formal proposals. Rarely is it simply the lowest bidder who obtains the order. Technology, the type of solution proposed, the financing arrangements and the reputation and experience of the firm all play a role.

Performance Bond

Once an order is obtained, the supplier company may be expected to insure its own performance. For that purpose, the company may be asked to post a performance bond, which is a guarantee that the company will pay certain specified damages to the customer if the job is not completed in accordance with the agreed-upon specifications. Performance bonds are usually issued by banks on behalf of the supplier. The entire process, from finding out about a new prospect until the order is actually in hand, may take from several months to several years, depending on the project size or industry.

Consortium Selling

Because of the high stakes involved in marketing equipment or large projects, companies frequently band together to form a consortium. A consortium is a group of firms that share in a certain contract or project on a preagreed basis but act as one company toward the customer. Joining together in a consortium can help companies share the risk in some very large projects. A consortium can also enhance the competitiveness of the members if they are involved in turnkey projects. A turnkey project is one in which the supplier offers the buyer a complete solution so that the entire operation can commence "at the turn of a key."

Most consortia are formed on an ad hoc basis. For the job of creating a major steel mill, for example, companies supplying individual components might combine into a group and offer a single tender to the customer. The consortium members have agreed to share all marketing costs and can help one another with design and engineering questions. Similarly, a consortium could form to deliver a turnkey hospital to the Saudi Arabian government. This would involve building the physical facilities, installing medical equipment, recruiting doctors and training staff—among other things. In either case, the customer gets a chance to deal with one supplier only, which substantially simplifies the process. Ad hoc consortia can be formed for very large projects that require unique skills from their members. In situations where the same set of skills or products is in frequent demand, companies may form a permanent consortium. Whenever an appropriate opportunity arises, the consortium members will immediately prepare to qualify for the bidding.

Consortium members frequently come from the same country. However, telecommunications consortia often combine a local firm, whose local connections are of great value, with one or two international telephone operating companies, which offer expertise in running a network. On occasion, these consortia include equipment suppliers that join to ensure that their equipment will be included in any eventual contract.

Other Forms of Promotion

So far, our discussion has focused on personal and industrial selling as key elements of a promotion mix. However, forms of promotion other than selling and advertising can play a key role in marketing. As we discussed in Chapter 13, direct sales is not only a distribution strategy but a promotion strategy as well, because it involves communicating directly with the consumer. Another form of global promotion is sales promotion, which can include such elements as in-store retail promotions and coupons. Many of these tools are consumer-goods-oriented and are used less often in the marketing of industrial goods. In this section, we look at sales promotions, sports sponsorships, promotional aspects of direct sales, product placements and management of word of mouth.

Sales Promotion

Sales promotion encompasses marketing activities that generate sales by adding value to products in order to stimulate consumer purchasing and/or channel cooperation. Sales promotions such as coupons, gifts and various types of reduced-price labels are used in most countries. In some countries, free goods, double-pack promotions and in-store displays are also important. Government regulations and different retailing practices, however, tend to limit the options for global firms.

The area of sales promotion is largely local in focus. For example, in Mexico, 85 percent of cement sales are to individuals. Millions of do-it-yourselfers buy bags of cement to build their own homes. Cemex, the market leader in cement sales, sometimes buys food for a block party when a house is finished. And the company's 5,000 distributors can earn points toward vacations by increasing sales.[21]

Couponing

Couponing—where consumers bring product coupons to a retail store and obtain a reduced price for a product—varies significantly from country to country. In the United States, coupons are the leading form of sales promotion. Coupon distribution is popular and growing in Italy, while in the United Kingdom and Spain, couponing is declining. Couponing is relatively new in Japan, where restrictions on newspaper coupons were once outlawed.

Slotting Allowance

An example of a sales promotion aimed at distributors is the slotting allowance. This is a payment made to retailers in return for their agreeing to take a new product. A slotting allowance helps compensate them for the time and effort expended in finding a space for the new product on their shelves. As products proliferate, finding shelf space is increasingly difficult, and firms must compete for access to that space. Slotting allowances in Europe's increasingly concentrated supermarket industry have become quite costly. Similarly, slotting allowances are expensive in Saudi Arabia where shelf space in supermarkets is limited.

Loyalty Programs

Although most sales promotions are relatively short-term, some may continue indefinitely. Promotions that encourage customer loyalty and repeat purchases are being used increasingly worldwide. Not all loyalty programs have been well managed. Polish Airlines once established three levels of awards and service for frequent flyers (blue, silver and gold) but actually treated all customers the same. This resulted in customer dissatisfaction with the program and a large defection of frequent flyers to competitor British Airways.[22]

Government Regulation of Sales Promotions

Most countries impose restrictions on some forms of sales promotions. Games of chance are frequently regulated. Japan, for instance, limits the value of a promotional gift attached to a product to a maximum of 10 percent of the product's price. Japan also restricts the value of prizes awarded through lotteries. In the United States, American Express offered free trips from New York to London as prizes to qualifying customers. The company was unable to offer similar promotions to its Japanese customers, however, since Japan further restricted the values of such awards.

Historically, Germany has been among the most restrictive countries as far as most sales promotions are concerned. Laws enacted in the 1930s drastically restricted the use of discounts, rebates and free offers that the Nazi government regarded as products of Marxist consumer cooperatives. Only a few years ago, a German court stopped a drugstore from giving away free shopping bags to celebrate the store's birthday. A large retailer was blocked from donating a small sum to AIDS research for each customer transaction using a Visa card. A court declared that this promotion unfairly exploited the emotions of customers.

A European directive on e-commerce finally necessitated the repeal of Germany's decades-old laws against promotions. The directive required that the rules of the country in which a vendor was based be applied to promotions throughout the EU. At the time, fewer than one in ten Germans had ever made a purchase over the Internet. Still, the German government feared that this directive would eventually put German competitors at a disadvantage by preventing them from offering promotions similar to those allowed in neighboring countries. Despite the repeal of the anti-promotion laws, a broad law against unfair competition remains on the books in Germany. Some fear that certain competitors could still attempt to use it to block the promotions of others.[23]

Sales Promotions within the MNC

Because global firms will encounter a series of regulations and restrictions on promotions that differ among countries, there is little opportunity to standardize sales promotion techniques across many markets. Sales promotion can also be influenced by local culture, as well as by the competitiveness of the marketplace. A study of consumer attitudes regarding sales promotions found significant differences even among Taiwan, Thailand and Malaysia. The Taiwanese consumer preferred coupons to sweepstakes. The Malaysians and Thais both preferred sweepstakes to coupons.[24] In Europe, McDonald's discovered that children were content with a simple word puzzle on a menu tray or a small stuffed animal and did not require the more expensive Happy Meal promotions that the company used in the United States.[25] This variation among markets has caused most companies to make sales promotions the responsibility of local managers, who are expected to understand the local preferences and restrictions.

Nonetheless, a firm should make certain that there is adequate communication among its subsidiaries to ensure that the best practices and new promotion ideas are disseminated throughout the firm. Sometimes it is even critical to communicate problems associated with promotions so that they will not be repeated in other national markets. A Pepsi promotion in the Philippines that was intended to award $37,000 to one lucky winner fell victim to a computer error that produced thousands of winners. When Pepsi refused to honor the claims of all these winners, 30 Pepsi delivery trucks were burned, and company officials were threatened. Tragically, a woman and child were killed when a grenade tossed at a Pepsi truck rolled into a nearby store.[26]

Sports Promotions and Sponsorships

Major sports events are increasingly being covered by the mass media worldwide. The commercial value of these events has soared over the last decade. Today, large sports events, such as the Olympics and world championships in specific sports, cannot exist in their present form without funding by companies.

World Beat 14.2

The Olympics versus the World Cup

During the Olympic Games, teams from over 200 countries compete in almost every imaginable sport, hoping to bring home the gold, silver or bronze medal. Global brands compete as well. The Seoul Games are credited with transforming Samsung from a regional to a global brand, and Chinese computer giant, Lenovo, was among the top 12 global firms that spent at least $60 million each to be a sponsor of the Beijing Olympics. The International Olympic Committee garnered about $1 billion from the four-year cycle ending with the London Olympics. Top Olympic sponsors paid more than $100 million for the right to participate. Among the top sponsors of the Sochi Olympics were Coca-Cola, McDonald's, Procter & Gamble, Acer, Visa and Samsung.

The World Cup of football (referred to as soccer in the United States) is one sports event that challenges the Olympics as a promotion platform for global brands. In the United States, soccer does not have the viewership of other major league sports such as baseball, American football, basketball and hockey, but the United States is not representative of the rest of the world. Football (soccer) reigns as the favorite sport in most countries, and the World Cup is a major media event around the world. The 2012 Euro Cup final alone generated 16.5 million tweets from a viewing audience of nearly 300 million.

Unlike the Olympics, television advertising is limited during the World Cup, because football (soccer) is played in 45-minute continuous halves. Instead sponsors depend on dynamic digital billboards surrounding the football field that are caught by cameras for broadcast to both television and smartphone viewers. Increasingly, sponsors promote through social media. A campaign for Marriott International featuring Omar Gonzalez and Alexis Lalas was designed to be viewed mostly online. Listerine's first foray into marketing through the World Cup was directed to a digital ad agency. Nonetheless, the World Cup sponsor list includes many of the same names as the Olympic sponsors including Coca-Cola, McDonald's and Visa.

Sources: Tara Clarke, "The Companies Spending the Most on 2014 Sochi Olympics," *Money Morning*, February 14, 2014; Mike Mikho, "Brazil's World Cup Is a Marketer's Dream," *Ad Week*, October 7, 2013; Stuart Elliott, "With 2014 World Cup, Soccer Ascends to Role as Premier Ad Platform," *New York Times*, June 4, 2014; and Duane Stanfor, "Will World Cup Sponsors Get Kicked, Too?" *Bloomberg Business Week*, June 5, 2014.

For some events, companies can purchase space for signs along the stadiums or arenas where sports events take place. When the event is covered on television, the cameras automatically take in the signs as part of the regular coverage. Aside from purchasing advertising spots or signage space in broadcast programs, individual companies can also engage in sponsorship. Sports sponsorship is common in Europe and the United States, and its popularity is growing fast in certain parts of East Asia, the Middle East, Brazil and India.[27]

To take advantage of global sports events, a company should have a logo or brand name that is worth exposing to a global audience. It is not surprising to find that the most common sponsors are companies that produce consumer goods with global appeal, such as soft-drink manufacturers, makers of consumer electronics products and film companies. More recent global players, such as Samsung and Hyundai from South Korea, often make extensive use of sports sponsorship abroad, especially in the emerging markets of Africa, East Europe and Latin America.

A firm must consider the popularity of certain sports. Few sports have global appeal. Baseball and American football have little appeal in Europe or parts of Asia and Africa. However, football (soccer) is the number one spectator sport in much of the world. Nike spends an estimated 40 percent of its global sports advertising budget on soccer and has sponsored the national football teams of six countries, including Brazil and the United States.

Through the intensive coverage of sports in the news media all over the world, many companies continue to use the sponsorship of sporting events as an important element in their global communications programs. Successful companies must exhibit both flexibility and ingenuity in the selection of available events or participants. In some parts of the world, sports sponsorship may continue to be the only available way to reach large numbers of prospective customers. However, in some cultures, global marketers must beware of the backlash associated with a losing team. For example, fans called for a boycott of products such as Pepsi that were endorsed by the Indian cricket team following a humiliating loss against Australia.[28] Chinese fans are also fickle. When their teams lose, they stay at home—to the dismay of sponsors. Consequently, MNCs in China are increasingly focusing on grass-roots programs. Pepsi sponsors teen soccer, Adidas funds soccer camps and Nike has started a high school basketball league.[29]

Attempts by competition to hijack sports sponsorships also occur on a regular basis. In addition to its own legitimate sponsorships, Nike has been known to hijack promotion at major global sports events—such as buying up massive billboard space in Olympic cities when the company doesn't partake in official sponsorship. Both the Olympics and World Cup are plagued by ambush marketers, non-sponsoring brands that pirate an association with the games. There have been around 400 cases of ambush marketing since the technique first emerged at the Los Angeles Olympics in 1984. When Budweiser was an official sponsor for one World Cup, Dutch fans came to the stadium wearing outfits with the name of rival beer brand Bavaria. Officials asked them to remove the outfits, and the fans were forced to watch the match in their underwear. The incident generated widespread buzz for Bavaria.[30]

Telemarketing, Direct Mail and Spam

Telemarketing

Telemarketing can be used both to solicit sales and to offer enhanced customer service to current and potential customers. To make telemarketing effective, however, an efficient telephone system is required. Telephone sales for individual households may become practical when many subscribers exist and when their telephone numbers can be easily obtained. Because of the language problems involved, companies must make sure their telemarketing sales forces not only speak the language of the local customer but also do so fluently and with the correct local or regional accent.

However, not all countries accept the practice of soliciting business directly at home. A telemarketing directive in the EU allows consumers to place their names on a telephone preference list to eliminate telemarketing calls to their homes. Any firm that continues to call potential customers can be fined. Even so, telemarketing is already big business in Europe; total full-time employment in the field is estimated at above 1.5 million.

Telemarketing has been intensifying elsewhere as well. In Latin America, growth has been substantial, and call centers have expanded rapidly throughout Brazil. Still, many Brazilians can be more effectively reached by loudspeaker than by telephone. Wal-Mart successfully sent out green vans to roam modest neighborhoods in São Paulo inviting people, via loudspeaker, to apply for credit cards at the company's Todo Dia stores.[31]

Direct Mail

Similar to phone campaigns, direct-mail campaigns are largely dependent on good infrastructure. However, creativity and perseverance can sometimes overcome the obstacle of a poor mail delivery system. When the Carsa Group launched its first direct-mail campaign for financial services in Peru, it faced a postal system that was essentially nonexistent. Even using private courier firms was problematic: such firms were known to broker clients' mailing lists to their competitors. Provincial couriers delivered mail as a sideline to their main business focus, such as fertilizer sales. Nonetheless, the Carsa Group went forward with the campaign, designing its own catalogues and establishing a call center to support the campaign. Response rates topped 26 percent—more than ten times what many U.S. campaigns would consider to be outstanding results. What was the reason for such a high response? In Peru, 69 percent of families received fewer than two pieces of mail monthly, so the impact of the campaign's personalized letters was amazing![32]

Spam

With the advent of the Internet, many marketers saw an opportunity to reach many potential customers cheaply and efficiently via e-mail. However, their would-be targets rebelled against unsolicited commercial bulk e-mail, or spam. Although some emerging markets, such as those in Asia, have less strict regulations on spam, laws in developed countries discourage it—as do new technologies to block incoming spam. On October 31, 2003, an EU directive went into effect requiring its member states to implement legislation banning unsolicited commercial e-mail without consumer consent or, in some cases, without a prior business relationship. The EU rule covers e-mail, faxes, automated calling systems and mobile messaging. National governments are allowed to determine enforcement, but consumers must be allowed to claim damages.[33] Europe now has stronger privacy laws than the United States.

Product Placement

Marketers increasingly seek to have their products appear in television shows and motion pictures. Some even pay to have discussions of their products written into scripts that air. However, global marketers are discovering that different cultures and regulatory environments may restrict the international expansion of this practice. For example, a study has shown that Chinese consumers are less accepting of product placements than are Americans.[34] And placement faces tough regulations in the United Kingdom, a society that worries about the blurring between advertising and entertainment. A brand name can be mentioned, but only if it is "editorially justified" in the opinion of the United Kingdom's Independent Television Commission, the agency that licenses and regulates commercial television. For example, when Heinz sponsored a cooking series entitled "Dinner Doctors," its name appeared only in the sponsorship credits. No Heinz product could be mentioned or shown anywhere in the content of the show.[35]

Buzz Marketing: Managing Word of Mouth

When importer Piaggio USA wanted to revive stagnant sales of Vespa scooters, it hired extremely attractive young women to pose as motorbike riders in front of trendy cafés in Los Angeles. The scooter-riding models would then strike up conversations with other patrons at the cafés. When anyone complimented their bikes, they would pull out a notepad and write down the name and phone number of the local Vespa dealer. In Kenya, where 70 percent of the Christian population doesn't drink alcohol, East African Breweries introduced Alvaro as an alcohol-free alternative for young cosmopolitans who enjoyed the country's vibrant pub culture. With a limited advertising budget, the company successfully relied on creating buzz by hiring limousines to drive around the capital city towing skateboarders who handed out samples.[36] In both these cases, marketers were attempting to catch the attention of potential customers not only to promote a sale but also to get people talking about their product to their friends. This managed word of mouth is called buzz marketing.

Buzz can be cheap; there are no national media to buy and no costly price promotions. Instead, product recommendations appear to come from a customer's coolest friends. Still, experts suggest that buzz marketing can backfire if consumers feel it is subversive or if too many companies are trying to do it. Then buzz can become merely annoying.[37]

In an individualistic culture such as that which prevails in the United States and Canada, one's "coolest friend" can conceivably be a person one has just met. In more collectivist cultures, where people are more wary of outsiders, marketers may need to recruit members from each target in-group very carefully to play this role. In Kaler, a town of 300 families in rural India, Hyundai reached out to the village headman whose advice is sought on marriage, crops and, more recently, which TV or car to buy. Says the headman, "If I tell them I like a particular brand, they'll go out and get it."[38]

Word of mouth is especially crucial to marketing in many Asian cultures. In Japan, the average high-school girl sends around 200 cell phone text messages a day. Word of mouth is seen as a key way to reach this market.[39] In fact, six of the top ten markets where consumers rely most on word of mouth are Asian countries. These include Hong Kong, Taiwan, Indonesia, India, South Korea and the Philippines. The other four countries among the top ten are surprisingly disparate—New Zealand, Ireland, Mexico and the UAE.[40]

In China, Mars Inc. used buzz marketing to effectively promote its Snickers candy bar. Since older Chinese considered the candy bar to be too sweet, the company decided to target teenage boys. Mars became a sponsor of the Beijing Olympics and hosted its own outreach events. Among these were the Snickers Street Olympics and Snickers Jump Satisfaction. In the latter event, participants attempted to jump over as many Snickers bars as possible in order to win them. To promote these events to its target market, Mars created buzz on the Internet. For example, online games were linked to the Street Olympics but required four to play. This inspired one participant to reach out to three more. The company was pleased with the results. One manager remarked that teenage boys "flocked to the events like seagulls."[41]

Word of mouth can also be important in B2B marketing, where referrals are often crucial. However, there appear to be cultural differences in how managers seek advice concerning potential purchases. A study of U.S. and Japanese corporate buyers of financial services revealed that the Japanese used referral sources—both business and personal—almost twice as often as did U.S. corporate buyers. This supported prior research that suggested that Japanese corporate buyers use a greater variety of referral sources than their American counterparts.[42]

Public Relations

When Pepsi employees noticed critical Twitter posts concerning a Pepsi ad in a German trade magazine, they notified their company. The ad for diet cola depicted a calorie killing itself. A popular commentator, whose sister had committed suicide, objected to the ad. Pepsi's global director of digital and social media quickly posted an apology.[43]

Public relations is a strategic communication process undertaken to maintain a favorable public image of an organization. A company's public relations function consists of marketing activities that enhance brand equity by promoting (or protecting) goodwill toward the organization. In turn, this goodwill can encourage consumers to trust a company and predispose them to buy its products. In Texas, a market loyal to U.S. vehicles, Japanese automaker Toyota undertook to change consumer attitudes by becoming a major patron of the arts in the city of San Antonio.

Sometimes international marketers find that public relations activities are necessary to defend the reputation of a brand against bad publicity. With millions of Europeans afraid of contracting mad-cow disease by eating beef, McDonald's Corporation began an unusual public relations campaign. Customers were invited to visit the McDonald's meatpacking plant in France, which supplies its 860 restaurants in that country. Touring visitors learned that ground meat was made of 100 percent muscle, not of the nerve tissue that caused the risk of disease.[44]

Public relations campaigns themselves can go wrong. Instead of neutralizing bad publicity, such campaigns can sometimes increase it. In our global society, such gaffes can be heard around the world. Philip Morris's subsidiary in the Czech Republic—in an attempt to bolster goodwill with the Czech government—commissioned a study to show that cigarettes have positive financial benefits to the state. In addition to benefiting from the taxes assessed on cigarette sales, the Philip

Morris subsidiary maintained that the state saves a great deal of pension money when a citizen dies prematurely from diseases attributed to smoking. When the press heard of this study, outraged editorials appeared in newspapers around the world.

One of the best-known public relations crises arose from the promotion strategy for baby formula that Nestlé employed in developing countries in the 1970s. Over 40 years later, the crisis still haunts the firm and its industry. In the 1970s, Nestlé and other producers of baby formula flooded maternity wards in less developed countries with free samples of their products. When new mothers ran out of the samples, they often discovered that their own breast-milk had dried up. Few could afford the expensive formula. Some diluted it in an effort to make it last longer, and this sometimes resulted in the death of the baby. Activists organized a global boycott of Nestlé products, and UNICEF, the United Nations agency charged with protecting children, refused to accept cash contributions from the company.

Major formula producers agreed to comply with a voluntary marketing code devised by UNI-CEF and the WHO that practically forbids any distribution of free formula. But the controversy hasn't stopped there. The companies have always understood this code to apply to less developed countries only, whereas UNICEF has stated that it understands the code to apply to developed countries as well. The controversy has also heated up in the shadow of the AIDS epidemic in Africa. Studies show that about 15 percent of women with HIV in Africa will transmit it to their children through breast-feeding. Nestlé claimed it had received desperate pleas from African hospitals for free formula but was afraid to violate the code. Both Nestlé and Wyeth-Ayerst Laboratories Inc. offered to donate tons of free formula to HIV-infected women in Africa. However, UNICEF refused to lend its approval because it didn't want to appear to endorse an industry it had long accused of abusive practices.[45]

Global marketers are often accused of promoting products that change consumption patterns to the detriment of local cultures. Proactive public relations campaigns can often help to offset this xenophobia. After the United States began bombing raids into Afghanistan, Muslim radicals in Indonesia bombed a KFC store. But no ill feeling was expressed at a McDonald's franchise in Indonesia that had established goodwill over the years by donating food and dining facilities to Islamic institutions.[46]

Corporate Social Responsibility

Many companies go beyond the mere attempt to establish a favorable image with the public. They attempt to deserve that good image. Corporate social responsibility is an initiative to assess and take responsibility for a company's effect on the environment and the quality of life of society. Some corporate responsibility initiatives, however, face cross-cultural challenges. IKEA retreated from its early attempts to establish environmentally friendly policies in China. Price-sensitive consumers complained about paying extra for plastic bags and didn't want to bring their own bags. Furthermore, the company decided that the investment needed to help its Chinese suppliers' produce green products would be too expensive to support sufficiently low prices in the country.[47]

In addition to monitoring and improving their impact on society, many firms become involved in charitable donations involving both money and employees' time. Others offer corporate-sponsored scholarships. Increasingly, many within MNCs have embraced the idea that corporate giving should be more than simply the donation of money to charitable or educational organizations. They argue that a MNC can do more good if it taps into its core competencies or management capabilities when attempting to help others. A number of companies such as Dow Corning, PepsiCo, FedEx, Intel and Pfizer send small teams of employees to developing countries such as Brazil, Ghana, India and Nigeria to provide free consulting services to non-profits and other organizations. IBM has sent teams to develop plans to improve Kenya's postal service and develop an eco-tourism industry in Tanzania.[48] In addition to addressing social responsibility, companies can garner good publicity and can gain name recognition from these initiatives.

Conclusion

Promotion in an international context is particularly challenging because managers are constantly faced with communicating to customers with different cultural backgrounds. This tends to add to the complexity of the communications task, which demands a particular sensitivity to culture, habits, manners and ethics.

Aside from the cultural differences and regulatory constraints that affect the content and form of communications, international firms also encounter a different set of cost constraints for the principal elements of the promotion mix, such as selling and advertising. Given such diversity from country to country, international firms have to design their communications carefully to fit each individual market. Furthermore, fostering goodwill for the corporation in local communities, via publicity or corporate social responsibility, will likely play an increasing role in global promotion strategies in the years to come.

Managerial Takeaways

1. *Most promotion strategies involve speaking to potential buyers in order to convince them to adopt products and services. As a result, promotion tends to be culture-bound.*
2. *There are many promotion options to choose from, but these options can be constrained by culture and the regulatory environment.*
3. *Negotiating styles vary across cultures, but there is evidence of some convergence possibly as a result of increased international trade.*
4. *A firm's sales force is its front line, but managing sales forces across cultures is complex.*
5. *Global account management is a growing phenomenon, but global marketers should take care to differentiate between worthwhile global accounts and buyers who are simply seeking lower prices.*
6. *Trade fairs remain an important tool in global marketing—not only for finding buyers but for identifying potential distributors and for researching competition.*
7. *Some sales involve complicated bidding processes and their complexity often argues for a consortium approach.*

8. *Word of mouth remains one of the most trusted sources of information worldwide, increasing the importance of buzz marketing.*
9. *Public relations is critical for protecting global brands. Corporate social responsibility takes public relations a step further: global marketers should attempt to earn the respect of buyers and not simply manage the brand's reputation.*

Questions for Discussion

1. What difficulties could arise if a U.S. salesperson expected to make a sale of industrial equipment during a two-week visit in China?
2. Why do you think many countries restrict the promotional use of sweepstakes and other games of chance?
3. What types of companies would you suggest sponsor the next Olympic Games? How would such firms profit from their association with the Olympic Games?
4. Do you support UNICEF's decision to oppose the donation of baby formula to African hospitals? Why or why not?

CASE 14.1 The South American Sales Dilemma

Shortly after his 34th birthday, Jay Bishop was promoted from director of North American sales to director of global sales at Intelicon, a worldwide provider of digital marketing services. Among the services Intelicon provided were customized e-mail campaigns, online surveys and online customer loyalty and incentive programs. Jay moved into his new position in January. One of his first tasks was to review all global sales numbers in order to identify areas for growth and improvement. During this exercise, he noticed a number of discrepancies between the Latin American sales numbers and numbers for the rest of the world. In particular, he noted that 420 sales calls in the United States had resulted in 180 actual sales, whereas in Latin America, only 40 sales had resulted from 200 such sales calls. Eager to make a good start in his new job (and under pressure from his superiors to fix the situation), Jay immediately scheduled a trip to visit offices in Brazil and Argentina in February. He was surprised, however, to receive calls from the country managers in both São Paulo and Buenos Aires telling him to put the trip off until after the Mardi Gras season. Recognizing that he knew little about Latin American culture and not wanting to ignore the advice of his new subordinates early on, Jay followed their advice and rescheduled his trip for mid-March.

As often happens when one is busy, Jay's Latin American trip arrived quickly. Stepping off the plane in São Paulo after the ten-hour trip, he was exhausted but ready to work. Passing through customs and into the passenger arrival area, he looked furtively for Rivaldo Pessoa, the Brazilian country manager. Mr. Pessoa, however, was nowhere in sight and did not arrive for 30 minutes. Jay was quite frustrated, not to mention jet-lagged. Moreover, Mr. Pessoa did not seem very apologetic when he blamed his tardiness on traffic and rain.

Rather than stopping at the hotel so he could drop off his luggage, Jay insisted that they go straight to the office and start analyzing why sales were down in Brazil. He kept trying to bring the topic up on the long drive into the city, but Mr. Pessoa insisted on asking him questions about his family and pointing out landmarks in the city, this being Jay's first visit to Brazil. "Why does this guy want to know my life story? Doesn't he know his job is at stake?" thought Jay. Eventually resigning himself to the fact that nothing would get done until they got to the office, Jay tried to sit back and enjoy the ride.

When they arrived at the office, Mr. Pessoa ushered Jay into the small conference room and then left for ten minutes before returning with coffee and his two salespeople, Renata Pinheiro and Joao Prestes. Both spoke English well and seemed eager to make a good impression. Jay felt that neither had any idea why he was in Brazil, other than that it might be a goodwill tour. He wanted to get to the point, so he came out and said, "The reason I'm here is that we are not meeting our sales numbers for Latin America, and we need to change that." Mr. Pessoa looked a bit surprised, as did Renata and Joao. Jay pressed on, "I need to run through a few analytical questions to determine the root causes of the challenges in the Brazilian market so that we can fix them and take some of the pressure off of you guys." All three seemed to relax at that.

"Okay, let's begin," said Jay. "First, I want to learn more about your backgrounds, what brought you to Intelicon." Mr. Pessoa began: "Well, before I joined Intelicon three years ago, I worked over 20 years in the banking sector, most recently in investment banking at BNP Paribas. I helped take a number of Brazilian companies public and worked on numerous bond issues." Impressed, Jay turned to Joao, who said, "I started in professional services at IBM and worked there for six years. As the Internet took off, I wanted to get involved in a smaller, more web-based business, which is when I came to Intelicon." Renata finished: "I graduated from the Fundacao Getulio Vargas a year ago," she said, "and took a degree in marketing. My parents pressed me to go into the family business, but I wanted to make a name for myself and felt that consultative sales would be a great place to start. My parents, however, were shocked that I wanted to sell things rather than doing something they considered more respectable, like marketing or finance. I'm out to prove myself."

Needless to say, Jay was very impressed with his new staff and was even more confused about why they were having so much trouble selling Intelicon's services. He decided to move on to more probing questions. Looking to Mr. Pessoa, he asked, "How do you get your sales prospects? Do you cold-call? Is that successful?" Mr. Pessoa looked a bit perplexed. "I suppose," he said, "that we could probably cold-call more. Mostly we rely on personal contacts within the different organizations." Jay was puzzled. He had heard that this was a common practice in Latin America, but felt that it could be contributing to the long sales cycles that were causing the closing rates in Latin America to be so much lower than in the rest of the world.

Jay believed he was starting to fill in the picture. However, to understand thoroughly the challenges he was facing in Latin America, he knew he would have to attend some sales calls. Mr. Pessoa mentioned that he had two meetings scheduled later in the afternoon, one with Abril, a large media conglomerate in São Paulo, and the other with CVRD, a powerful mining company. Jay said he would like to attend, and although Mr. Pessoa looked wary for an instant, he readily agreed.

The meeting with Abril started well. Mr. Pessoa clearly had a lot of experience presenting to an audience, and he seemed to know two of the four executives in the room as they caught up on family and friends for the first few minutes of the meeting. At the end of the presentation, Mr. Pessoa and Jay asked a number of probing questions and generally felt the meeting was going well. However, the executives kept raising objections. Eventually Mr. Pessoa folded, thanking them for their time and leaving. Once again, Jay was puzzled. He made a point of mentioning to Mr. Pessoa that sometimes getting a "no" was part of sales and that to be successful he needed to find ways to turn a "no" into a "yes." Mr. Pessoa looked a bit embarrassed but said that he did need to do more of this.

The traffic on the way to the meeting with CVRD was horrible, and much to Jay's chagrin, they arrived nearly an hour late. This did not seem to be a problem, however, because the vice president they were slated to meet was also running late. Once again, Mr. Pessoa did an excellent job in the presentation of products and services, and there was clear interest on the part of the vice president. Jay thought for sure they would close him on the spot and was getting that tingly feeling. Both sides went through the motions, discussing timelines and pricing structures, but just when Jay was ready to go in for the kill, Mr. Pessoa thanked the gentleman for his time, said he would send him a proposal and scheduled lunch together the following week. Jay did not know what to say. He guessed that the sale would eventually happen, but he also knew he needed to get revenue as soon as possible.

Exhausted, Jay headed back to his hotel and fell fast asleep. He had learned a lot in one day but realized that he still had a long way to go if he wanted to succeed. Tomorrow, he would fly to Argentina and do it all over again.

Discussion Questions

1. What might explain the lower ratio of sales to sales calls in Latin America compared with the United States?
2. In what ways might cultural differences explain differences in personal selling between Brazil and the United States?
3. What advice would you give Jay?

Source: Case prepared by Michael Magers. Used by permission.

CASE 14.2 Flying to Armenia

British Airways (BA) is one of the world's largest international airlines, flying passengers to 143 destinations in 69 countries. One such destination was the Republic of Armenia, a small country at the crossroads of Europe and Asia. The whole territory of Armenia is only 11,506 square miles with a population of three million. However, an additional seven million ethnic Armenians live outside Armenia. This Armenian diaspora remains intimately tied to its homeland across generations. Armenian communities around the world attend Armenian churches, teach their children the Armenian language and celebrate Armenian national and cultural days with great passion. Many Armenians live in various countries of the Middle East and Europe, and one of the largest Armenian communities resides in the United States.

During the past 20 years, Armenia has been undergoing a rapid but difficult transition from a Soviet, centrally planned economy to a democratic society with a market economy. The 1990s were particularly difficult for the country. Armenia shared all the economic problems that resulted from the breakup of established economic relations among what had been the Soviet republics. In addition, it faced an electricity crisis combined with a military territorial conflict with neighboring Azerbaijan. These problems led to a marked lowering of the standard of living of the population in the country and to overall economic difficulties.

However, with foreign aid from the IMF, the World Bank, the EU and the U.S. government, as well as substantial assistance from the diaspora, the economy began to stabilize. By the end of the decade, a legal and regulatory framework for the private sector was being created, and an increasing number of MNCs, including Coca-Cola, Adidas, Samsung Electronics, Mercedes-Benz and Kodak, had established a presence in the country.

Armenia had attracted several international airlines that competed alongside its national carrier, Armenian Airlines. These carriers included BA, Swiss Air, Austrian Air, Russian Aeroflot and Syrian Air. Although traveling was not something many Armenians could afford, it remained the only viable way to travel in and out of the country. Armenia was landlocked, and traveling through neighboring countries was not practical because of poor transportation infrastructure and intermittent political tensions. Most air travelers were employees of international aid organizations operating in Armenia, business travelers or diaspora Armenians visiting their homeland.

BA first entered the Armenian market with a twice-weekly service from London to Yerevan, the capital of Armenia. Along with Swiss Air and Austrian Air, BA charged higher prices than Armenian Airlines, Aeroflot or Syrian Air. BA embarked on several successful promotions to attract customers, to establish brand recognition in the market and to enhance its international reputation as a caring company. To mark the second anniversary of its instituting flights between London and Yerevan, BA put together a program of events designed to support cultural and humanitarian programs in Armenia. For example, it supported the Third International Chamber Music Festival, which took place in Yerevan, by bringing two leading Armenian musicians—cellist Alexander Chaoshian and pianist Seda Danyel—from London to Yerevan to participate in the event.

The company also announced a special discount rate to about a dozen destinations, substantially increasing the number of tickets sold. During this campaign, BA contributed $10 from the price of each economy-class ticket and $50 from the price of each business-class ticket to one of Armenia's largest orphanages. (For comparison, per-capita spending for a child in such institutions was around $700 per year.) A special ceremony was held to bestow the funds on the orphanage. For that ceremony, the BA hot-air balloon, a familiar ambassador around the world, was brought to Armenia for the first time. The balloon was set to spend a day in Opera Square, the foremost center for cultural activities in Yerevan. Prior to that, BA ran a competition in which questions about BA were posed in the local media. People who phoned in with the right answers could meet the crew of the balloon and go for a short ride. This event was widely covered in the Armenian press and on the television news.

BA also introduced the Executive Club, BA's frequent-flyer program, to the Armenian market. As with other frequent-flyer programs, members of the Executive Club could earn free flight miles by traveling via BA as well as using certain hotels and car rentals. Club membership also offered a variety of other benefits, such as priority on flight waiting lists and a special agent to handle inquiries. BA ran a special promotion of the Executive Club at the elite Wheel Club, a favorite dining place of expatriates working in Armenia, especially English speakers. Any member of the Executive Club who ate at the Wheel received an entry into a prize draw. Anyone who was not a member of the Executive Club could join at the Wheel. The top prize was a pair of tickets to any destination.

BA also ran a "Where in the World?" competition. People were invited to write in and say where in the world they dreamed of spending Valentine's Day with the person they loved and why they wanted to go there. The three most creative, funny or touching entries won a pair of tickets to the dream destination. The event was announced on Hay FM, one of Armenia's most popular radio channels among young people. The event enjoyed a high response rate and engendered considerable word of mouth among Hay FM listeners, as well as publicity in the local press.

Discussion Questions

1. For each of the five promotions discussed in the case, identify the target market, explain the motivation behind the promotion and suggest ways in which to measure the success of the promotion.
2. Why do you think each of these promotions worked well in the Armenian market?
3. Would these promotions be as successful in your country? Why or why not?

Source: Case prepared by Anna V. Andriasova. Used by permission.

Notes

1 J. Lynn Lunsford, Daniel Michaels and Andy Pasztor, "At the Paris Air Show, Boeing–Airbus Duel Has New Twist," *Wall Street Journal*, June 15, 2001, p. B4.
2 Diana Middleton, "B-Schools Redouble Efforts Overseas," *Wall Street Journal*, November 9, 2010, p. B11.
3 "Sealed Air Taiwan (A)." Harvard Business School, Case No. 9-399-058.
4 Michael Ewing, Albert Caruana and Henry Wong, "Some Consequences of Guanxi: A Sino-Singaporian Perspective," *Journal of International Consumer Marketing*, vol. 12, no. 4 (2000), pp. 75–89.
5 Hussain G. Rammal, "International Business Negotiations: The Case of Pakistan," *International Journal of Consumer Marketing*, vol. 15, no. 2 (2005), pp. 129–140.
6 Lynn E. Metcalf, Allan Bird, Mark F. Peterson, Mahesh Shankarmahesh and Terri. R. Lituchy, "Cultural Influences in Negotiations: A Four Country Comparative Analysis," *International Journal of Cross-Cultural Management*, vol. 7, no. 2 (2007), pp. 147–168.
7 Anjali Cordeiro, "P&G Targets India for Expansion Push," *Wall Street Journal*, June 23, 2010.
8 Kelly Hewitt, R. Bruce Money and Subhash Sharma, "National Culture and Industrial Buyer-Seller Relationships in the United States and Latin America," *Journal of the Academy of Marketing Science*, vol. 34, no. 3 (2006), pp. 386–402.
9 Laurie Burkitt and Bob Davis, "Chasing China's Shoppers," *Wall Street Journal*, June 15, 2012, p. B1.
10 Jonathan Friedland, "Sweet Solution," *Wall Street Journal*, March 2, 1999, p. A1.
11 Jean-Pierre Jeannet, "Siemens Automotive Systems: Brazil Strategy" (Lausanne: IMD Institute, European Case Clearinghouse).

12 Jean-Pierre Jeannet and Robert Collins, "Deloitte Touche Tohmatsu International Europe" (Lausanne: IMD Institute, European Case Clearinghouse).

13 H. David Hennessey, "Discovering the Hidden Value in Global Account Management," unpublished working paper, Babson College, 2004.

14 George S. Yip and Audrey J.M. Bink, "Managing Global Accounts," *Harvard Business Review*, September 2007.

15 Except where otherwise noted, ideas from this section are taken from H. David Hennessey, "Discovering the Hidden Value in Global Account Management," and H. David Hennessey and Jean-Pierre Jeannet, *Global Account Management* (Chichester, United Kingdom: John Wiley & Sons, 2003).

16 David Arnold, Julian Birkinshaw and Omar Toulan, "Can Selling Be Globalized?: The Pitfalls of Global Account Management," *California Management Review*, vol. 44, no. 1 (Fall 2001), pp. 8–20.

17 Yip and Bink, "Managing Global Accounts."

18 Pet Vet Russia Expo, www.zoorussia.ru, accessed May 30, 2014.

19 Roger Daniels, "MT Survey of Surveys: Trade Fairs," *Management Today*, February 7, 2005, p. 62.

20 Iris Kapustein, "Selling and Exhibiting Across the Globe," *Doors and Hardware*, September 1, 1998, p. 34.

21 Peter Fritsch, "Hard Profits," *Wall Street Journal*, April 22, 2002, p. A1.

22 R. Bruce Money and Deborah Colton, "The Response of the 'New Consumer' to Promotion in the Transition Economies of the Former Soviet Bloc," *Journal of World Business*, vol. 35, no. 2 (2000), pp. 189–205.

23 David Wessel, "Capital: German Shoppers Get Coupons," *Wall Street Journal*, April 5, 2001, p. A1.

24 Lenard C. Huff and Dana L. Alden, "An Investigation of Consumer Response to Sales Promotion in Developing Markets," *Journal of Advertising Research*, vol. 38 (May/June 1998), pp. 47–57.

25 Lisa Bertagnoli, "Continental Spendthrifts," *Marketing News*, October 22, 2001, p. 15.

26 David A. Griffith and John K. Ryans, Jr., "Organizing Global Communications to Minimize Private Spill-Over Damage to Brand Equity," *Journal of World Business*, vol. 32, no. 3 (1997), pp. 189–202.

27 William Fenton, "The Global Sponsorship Market," *Journal of Sponsorship*, vol. 2, no. 2 (2009), pp. 120–130.

28 Arundhati Parmar, "Jiminy, Cricket!" *Marketing News*, March 17, 2003, pp. 4–5.

29 Frederik Balfour, "It's Time for a New Playbook," *Business Week*, September 15, 2003, p. 56.

30 Roger Blitz, "'Ambush Marketing' Threat to 2012 Olympics," *Financial Times*, July 3, 2009, p. 4.

31 Miriam Jordan, "Wal-Mart Gets Aggressive About Brazil," *Wall Street Journal*, May 25, 2001, p. A8.

32 William A. Kotas, "Starting From Scratch," *Marketing News*, September 30, 2002, p. 16.

33 Catherine Arnold, "The Spam Update," *Marketing News*, December 8, 2003, p. 9.

34 Sally A. McKechnie and Jia Zhou, "Product Placement in Movies: A Comparison of Chinese and American Consumer Attitudes," *International Journal of Advertising*, vol. 22 (2003), pp. 349–374.

35 Erin White, "U.K. TV Can Pose Tricky Hurdles," *Wall Street Journal*, June 27, 2003, p. B7.

36 Sarah Childress, "Soft-Drink War Rages in Kenya," *Wall Street Journal*, June 4, 2009, p. B4.

37 White, "U.K. TV Can Pose Tricky Hurdles."

38 Cris Prystay, "Companies Market to India's Have-Littles," *Wall Street Journal*, June 5, 2003, p. B1.

39 Amy Chozick, "Cold Stone Aims to be Hip in Japan," *Wall Street Journal*, December 14, 2006, p. B10.

40 *Word-of-Mouth the Most Powerful Selling Tool: Nielsen Global Survey*, October 1, 2007.

41 Hiroko Tabuchi, "Mars's Snickers Gets Olympic Lift," *Wall Street Journal*, August 22, 2008, p. B6.

42 R. Bruce Money, "Word-of-Mouth Referral Sources for Buyers of International Corporate Financial Services," *Journal of World Business*, vol. 35, no. 3 (Fall 2000), pp. 314–329.

43 Sarah E. Needleman, "For Companies, a Tweet in Time Can Avert PR Mess," *Wall Street Journal*, August 3, 2009, p. B6.

44 John Carreyrou and Geoff Winestock, "In France, McDonald's Takes Mad-Cow Fears by the Horns," *Wall Street Journal*, April 5, 2001, p. A17.

45 Ibid.

46 Jay Solomon, "How Mr. Bambang Markets Big Macs in Muslim Indonesia," *Wall Street Journal*, October 26, 2001, p. A1.

47 Valerie Chu, Alka Girdhar and Rajal Sood, "How IKEA Adapted Strategies to Expand and Become Profitable in China," *Business Today*, July 6, 2013.

48 Anne Tergesen, "Doing Good to Do Well," *Wall Street Journal Online*, January 9, 2012.

Chapter 15

Managing Global Advertising

GLOBAL VERSUS LOCAL ADVERTISING   477

DEVELOPING GLOBAL CAMPAIGNS   477

THE GLOBAL–LOCAL DECISION   479

OVERCOMING LANGUAGE BARRIERS   483

GLOBAL MEDIA STRATEGY   484

ORGANIZING THE GLOBAL ADVERTISING EFFORT   491

Shortly after the Exxon Mobil merger, the new company based in Irving, Texas, announced plans to promote its four key brands—Exxon, Mobil, Esso and General—with a global television advertising campaign.[1] Global campaigns were not new to the company. Exxon's 1965 Esso tiger campaign, "Put a tiger in your tank," was launched in the United States, Europe and the Far East.[2] However, the new campaign was aimed at 100 countries at a cost of $150 million. Five hours of film footage were developed centrally to be accessed by the company's various national subsidiaries. Up to six different casts stood by to act out essentially the same story line—with a few variations. The same scene could be shot with a Japanese man, a sub-Saharan African, a Northern European or a Southern European. Actors varied the hand they used in a scene depicting eating. (In some cultures, food is customarily eaten only with the right hand.) A voice-over told the same story in 25 different languages. Centralized production saved considerable production costs for Exxon Mobil and helped ensure that television spots would be consistent and of similar quality around the world. It also meant substantial business for the agency—in this case, Omnicon Group's DDB Worldwide—that landed the job. Not everyone agreed that centralization of advertising was a good idea. The CEO of a rival agency, Bcom3 Group's Leo Burnett Worldwide, noted that brands at different stages around the world require different messages and advertising campaigns.[3]

International marketers face an important question: Should advertising campaigns be local or global? The first part of this chapter is organized around key factors that impact this decision. The chapter continues with a discussion of the major issues relating to media choices and campaign implementation.

Learning Objectives

After studying this chapter, you should be able to:

➤ list both the advantages and the special requirements of standardized campaigns;

➤ define the global theme approach to advertising, and explain how it differs from a totally standardized campaign;

➤ explain the market and cultural limitations on the advertising message and on its execution;

➤ identify key issues related to advertising that tend to be regulated by national governments;

➤ cite ways to avoid faulty translations and ways to minimize the need to translate;

➤ explain how media availability, media habits and scheduling international advertising all affect the advertising campaign;

➤ differentiate among the three options of utilizing domestic advertising agencies, using local advertising agencies and using international advertising networks;

➤ list the external and internal factors that influence a firm's decision over whether to centralize or localize its advertising efforts.

Global versus Local Advertising

Global marketers are among the major advertisers worldwide. An important question facing these international firms is whether to standardize or localize advertising across national markets. Standardizing advertising across all markets has received considerable attention and is considered the most controversial topic in international advertising. Advertising campaigns must first establish the message they wish to convey to their target market. In order to standardize advertising, the message to the target audience must resonate across countries and cultures.

One of the best—and earliest—examples of a successful standardized campaign was Philip Morris's Marlboro campaign in Europe. Marlboro's success as a leading brand began in the 1950s when the brand was repositioned to ensure smokers that the flavor would be unchanged by the effect of the filter. The theme "Come to where the flavor is. Come to Marlboro country" became an immediate success in the United States and abroad. Similarly, Monster Worldwide, the operator of the employment website *Monster*, developed a series of humorous advertisements that featured very little speaking but ended with a six-second graphic that promoted its website in the local language of the country in which the ad was aired.[4]

Standardized campaigns have increased over the years. Most studies of international advertising standardization in the 1970s and 1980s concluded that very little standardization was being used. However, a later study of 38 multinational corporations (MNCs) revealed that about half of these companies employed extensive or total standardization when developing and executing their global advertising. Only a quarter stated that standardization was very limited or nonexistent.[5] Still, many marketing executives remain skeptical of the value of global advertising campaigns, and trends can reverse themselves. For example, Coca-Cola abandoned a more standardized approach to advertising in India and now creates ads for the market that are made in India and tailor-made for Indian consumers.[6]

Developing Global Campaigns

Of course, firms do not need to choose solely between totally standardized worldwide campaigns and totally localized ones. Similar to developing global products, many firms adopt a modularized approach to global advertising: A company may select some features as standard for all its ads while localizing other features.

Global Theme Approach

Most common is the global theme approach, wherein the same advertising theme is used around the world but is varied slightly with each local execution. Coke's global campaign featuring "Coke Moments" was developed and shot in a number of the brand's top markets, including Brazil, Germany, Italy, France and South Africa as well as the United States. In "Spanish Wedding," a demure young woman enjoys a Coke while dressing for the big day.[7] Furthermore, if a global campaign is not appropriate, a regional one might be.

When developing global (or regional) campaigns, a company should follow procedures that are similar to those utilized in developing global products. In other words, local adaptation should not be an afterthought. Input should be sought early from markets where the campaign will ultimately air and should be incorporated into the design of the campaign. This ensures that a message will indeed be appropriate for each market and that the media necessary for the campaign will be available. It also identifies what adaptations need to be made and usually shortens the time of making such adaptations.

For example, standardized campaigns launched by automaker Fiat were originally developed in Italy and adapted with minor changes (such as translation) by local agencies in different national markets. Subsequently, the company allied with Publicis Groupe to establish a Fiat-specific advertising agency for all of Europe that would create pan-European campaigns. A key mandate for the new agency was to seek input early in the development of campaigns to determine if a marketing message could use a single campaign across Europe or whether it required different campaigns for different markets.[8]

World Beat 15.1

Advertising Egypt

The tourism industry in Egypt once accounted for one-tenth of the nation's economic output. But three years of political unrest made foreigners wary to visit the country. When Islamist radicals bombed a bus killing three South Korean tourists and their driver, the industry was hit with another flurry of cancellations.

In order to restart interest in Egypt's historical sites and beach resorts, the government embarked on a global advertising campaign. The campaign strategy included ads placed on international television channels and outdoor advertising on public transport systems in Europe. But before reaching out to consumers, the government invested in a round of public relations efforts to try to convince countries in Europe and elsewhere to relax their official travel advisories warning their citizens to avoid going to Egypt.

Nonetheless, attracting more tourists from Europe and the United States proved difficult. So the strategy shifted to Arab tourists instead. Arab tourists had traditionally accounted for 20 percent of all tourists to Egypt. Addressing potential summer visitors from the wealthy Arab countries of the Persian Gulf, the Egyptian Ministry of Tourism ran ads with the tag line "We've missed you." Perhaps the Ministry was betting on regional goodwill and memories of prior good times in Egypt. Still, an adviser to Egypt's tourism minister opined that nobody would come to visit unless they could convey the feeling that the country was safe.

Sources: "Hope Glimmers for Demoralised Egyptian Tourist Industry," Reuters, October 14, 2013; "Egypt Mounts Drive to Lure 13.5 Million Visitors Next Year," Reuters, October 29, 2013; Peter Aspden, "Fit for a King," *Financial Times*, April 19, 2014; and Kareem Fahim, "Egypt's Tourism Industry Grows Desperate Amid Sustained Turmoil," *New York Times Online*, May 9, 2014.

The Global–Local Decision

A number of cost, market and regulatory factors influence the extent to which advertising can be standardized.

Cost Savings

One advantage of a more standardized approach to advertising involves the economics of a global campaign. To develop individual campaigns in many countries is to incur duplicate costs, such as those for photographs, layouts and the production of television commercials. In a standardized approach, these production costs can be reduced, and more funds can be spent on purchasing media space.

Branding

In Chapter 11 we discussed the increased interest in global branding by MNCs. Many companies market products under a single brand name globally or regionally. With the substantial amount of international travel occurring today and the considerable overlap in media across national borders, companies are increasingly interested in creating a single brand image. This image can become confused if local campaigns are in conflict with each other. The following list shows some examples of companies' efforts to create a single brand image:

➤ H.J. Heinz developed a global campaign for Heinz ketchup to develop consistency in the brand image and advertising across its various national markets.[9]

➤ Jaguar found that its new model appealed to similar customers around the world, so it launched the same campaign from "Chicago to Riyadh, Tokyo and Berlin." This allowed Jaguar to enjoy a consistent image worldwide and save money by not having to develop a different theme for each market.[10]

➤ Disney embarked on its first global advertising campaign for its theme parks. Previously, the company advertised each park regionally. Now, Disney wants to address travelers worldwide and pull them into any Disney theme park anywhere.[11]

Target Market

Global campaigns may be more successful if the target market is relatively narrowly defined. For example, Procter & Gamble doubled the sales of Pringles potato chips in four years to $1 billion. Now one of P&G's top three global brands, Pringles is sold in over 40 countries. P&G attributes the global success of Pringles to a uniform advertising message aimed at young children and teens. The message used around the world is "Once you pop you can't stop." Although P&G allows some local differences in product market-to-market, such as flavor variations, the bulk of the advertising is standardized.[12]

479

Market Conditions

While cost savings, global branding and focused target markets argue for more standardized advertising, varying market conditions may limit the utility of standardization.

Stage in Life Cycle

Because products may be at different stages of their product life cycles in different countries, different types of advertising may be necessary to take into account various levels of customer awareness. Typically, a campaign during the earlier stages of the product life cycle concentrates on familiarizing people with the product category, because many prospective customers may not have heard about it. In later stages, with more intensive competition, campaigns tend to shift toward emphasizing the product's advantages over competitors' products. Sometimes Frito-Lay's products are so unfamiliar in certain overseas markets that advertising campaigns focus on educating consumers with the goal of changing their consumption habits. For example, the company's Chinese ads once showed potatoes actually being sliced so people knew where potato chips came from. In Turkey, Frito-Lay distributed pamphlets suggesting new recipes and eating habits: "Try a tuna sandwich for lunch, and join it with a bag of chips."[13]

Similarly, when Procter & Gamble entered the Chinese market it employed utilitarian ads such as ones that showed consumers the right way to wash their hair. However, as consumers became more sophisticated and needed less instruction, P&G changed the focus of their advertisments from instruction to evoking positive emotions toward their products.[14]

Perception of Product

Products may also face unique challenges in certain markets requiring nationally tailored advertising campaigns. In China, where consumers worry about food quality and safety, McDonald's aired a campaign emphasizing the fresh quality of its food.[15]

Regulatory Environment

In many instances, the particular regulations of a country prevent firms from using standardized approaches to advertising even when these would appear desirable. Malaysia, a country with a large Muslim population, has prohibited ads showing women in sleeveless dresses and pictures showing underarms. Russian law forbids ads that advocate violence and cruelty. One Pepsi ad portrayed boisterous young people drinking Pepsi and playing music in the courtyard of an apartment building. After tenants complained, the Pepsi drinkers responded by cranking up the music. Russia's watchdog agency that oversees advertising ordered the ad off the air.[16]

In China, advertising is subjected to substantial scrutiny and regulation. All outdoor ads have to be approved by multiple government organizations.[17] Children portrayed in commercials are required to show respect for their elders, and children's advertisements must not attempt to instill a sense of superiority for owning a certain product. Television ads for "offensive products" such as hemorrhoid medications and athlete's-foot ointments cannot be aired during the three daily meal times.[18] China also prohibits marketing claims using superlatives such as "the best" or "No. 1." AB InBev markets its Budweiser beer as the "King of Beer" everywhere but in China where the slogan was considered superlative and was therefore changed to "Style of the King".[19] Furthermore, Chinese regulations can change practically overnight. In preparation for the Beijing Olympics, authorites began removing or covering up billboards across the city including those along the road leading to Beijing's international airport. Officials declared that the ubiquitous billboards were an eyesore, but advertisers and their advertsiing agencies were shocked by the unanticipated move.[20]

Certain industries face more regulation than others. In some European countries, candy ads must show a toothbrush symbol. Differing national rules often govern the advertising of pharmaceuticals, alcohol and financial services. Advertising for cigarettes and tobacco products is strictly regulated in many countries. The EU banned all advertising of tobacco on billboards and in print advertising. One of the few areas where cigarette and tobacco advertising is still relatively restriction free is Central Asia and the Caucasus, formerly part of the Soviet Union. Most of these countries permit cigarette advertising on radio and television, although some relegate it to late-night slots. Such freedoms, however, are rare and global marketers are well advised to check the local regulations carefully before launching any type of advertising campaign. A stunt pilot was arrested in Lithuania for illegally advertising cigarettes during his maneuvers. The national parliament had just recently banned tobacco ads.[21]

Currently, the EU is cracking down on health benefit claims in the ads for various food products. After examining the first 43 health claims out of an estimated 4,000, the European Food and Safety Authority determined that only nine were valid. Not surprisingly, industry experts consider the EU's rules to be the most stringent in the world.[22]

Cultural Differences

Cultural differences can also restrict the use of standardized advertising. Taco Bell, a U.S.-based chain with 7,000 restaurants, found that Gidget, the talking Chihuahua dog used in ads in the United States, could not be used in Asia where many consider dogs a food delicacy, or in Muslim countries where many consider it taboo to even touch a dog. When Coty Inc. ran an ad aimed at the Middle East market for its Jennifer Lopez perfume, it placed the ad in the newly launched Middle East edition of *Elle*. But the ad, adapted for regional sensitvities, only showed the singer's face instead of her signature curvy silhouette which ran in the original ad.[23]

Cultural differences also stymied Western advertisers when they first entered Eastern Europe. One Western food company wanted to introduce bouillon cubes to Romania via ads featuring a happy family gathered around the dinner table. The campaign had to be changed because Romanian consumers were not familiar with the family dinner concept.[24]

Even if nudity in advertising is not prohibited by law, it can be controversial in many cultures. Sara Lee, the U.S.-based firm that owns such lingerie brands as Playtex, Cacharel and Wonderbra, faced intense opposition to a series of billboards in Mexico. The company launched its global Wonderbra campaign, which, as part of its outdoor advertising, featured a Czech model posing in the bra. In several Mexican cities, citizens protested the ads as offensive. The company redesigned its billboards for Mexico, clothing the model in a suit.

Land of the Soft Sell: Advertising in the Japanese Market

Japan is the world's second largest advertising market, after the United States. However, many Western firms face special challenges when developing advertising themes for this important market. The dominant style of advertising in Japan is an image-oriented approach, or "soft sell." This contrasts sharply with the more factual approach, or "hard sell," typical in the United States and with the use of humor prevalent in the United Kingdom.

In Japan, as in many other Asian cultures, consumers tend to be moved more by emotion than by logic in ads, in contrast to North Americans or Europeans. Consequently, consumers need to be emotionally convinced about a product. This leads to advertising that rarely mentions price, shies away from comparative advertising aimed at discrediting the products of competing firms, and occasionally even omits the distinctive features or qualities of a product. According to some experts, Western advertising is designed to make the product look superior, whereas Japanese advertising is designed to make it look desirable. The Japanese language even has a separate verb to describe the process of being convinced to buy a product contrary to one's own rational judgment.

Nonetheless, the Japanese are interested in foreign countries and words, particularly those of the English language. Research conducted for the Nikkei Advertising Research Institute in Japan compared the number of foreign words appearing in advertising headlines. Japan, with 39.2 percent, used the highest number of foreign words, followed by Taiwan with 32.1 percent, Korea with 15.7 percent and France with 9.1 percent. The United States used foreign words in only 1.8 percent of the headlines investigated.[25]

Japanese television commercials are full of U.S. themes. They frequently incorporate U.S. landscapes or backgrounds and often employ U.S. celebrities. By using American actors in their commercials, Japanese companies give the impression that these products are very popular in the United States. Thanks to the Japanese interest in and positive attitudes toward many U.S. cultural themes, such strategies have worked out well for advertisers.

Credibility of Advertising

In addition to other cultural differences among markets, there are national differences as to the credibility of advertising. British secondary schools teach students how to be "responsible consumers." Among other things, the required curriculum encourages students to criticize corporate advertising.[26]

A comparative survey conducted by a marketing research company investigated advertising credibility in 40 countries.[27] In the United States, 86 percent of consumers were eager to criticize advertising practices, particularly those aimed at children, whereas 75 percent of consumers praised advertising's creativity. In Asia, consumers were more positive. Forty-seven percent indicated that ads provided good product information, and 40 percent said that advertisers respected consumers' intelligence. Globally, the results were 38 percent and 30 percent, respectively.

Consumers in the former Soviet Union were among the most skeptical. Only 9 percent of consumers there believed that advertising provided good information, and only 10 percent said it respected consumers' intelligence. Globally, 61 percent of consumers appreciated advertising for both its creativity and its entertainment value, but only 23 percent of consumers living in the former Soviet Union agreed. Another study that examined attitudes toward online advertising in Romania revealed similar results. Romanian consumers found online advertising to be fun and interesting, but they had doubts about its credibility.[28]

Differences in the credibility of advertising should be taken into consideration by global marketers. While credibility remains a concern, a recent Nielsen study of consumers worldwide suggests that advertising credibility may be increasing overall. Sixty-two percent of global respondents trusted television advertising up from 56 percent six years earlier. Trust in magazine advertising and display ads on mobile phones also increased to 60 percent and 45 percent respectively.[29]

Addressing Cultural Differences

Global firms can take a proactive approach to cultural differences when employing the global theme approach. In a major rebranding campaign for the Mars candy bar, outdoor billboards ran phrases aimed to trigger feelings of pleasure in local audiences. In Britain, the slogan ran "Saturday 3 p.m.," referring to the much-anticipated soccer kickoff time. In France, the word *August* evoked the month when the whole country traditionally goes on vacation. In Germany, the words *the last parking space* were chosen for their particular national appeal.[30]

Another way to address the cultural challenges facing multinational advertising campaigns is to consider limiting such campaigns to countries within a single region of the world that share a single culture. A study of ads in Egypt, Lebanon and the UAE suggests that this might be possible. However, marketers should remember that countries that share many cultural attributes can differ on others. For example, literacy rates vary considerably within the Middle East, and this in turn can impact how products and services are advertised.[31]

To ensure that a message is in line with the existing cultural beliefs of the target market, companies can turn to a variety of resources. Local subsidiary personnel or local distributors can judge the cultural content and acceptability of the message. Advertising agencies with local offices can be helpful as well. Whether considering a local, regional or global approach, it is the responsibility of the international marketer to make sure that knowledgeable local nationals have enough input so that the mistake of using an inappropriate appeal in any given market can be avoided.

Overcoming Language Barriers

Even when employing global campaigns, the proper translation of ads remains a major cultural challenge to global marketers. Even among English-speaking peoples, common words can vary, as Table 15.1 illustrates. Most translation blunders that plagued global advertising in the past were the result of literal translations performed outside the target country. Today, faulty translations can be avoided by enlisting local nationals or language experts. Global marketers typically have translations checked by a local advertising agency, by their own local subsidiary or by an independent distributor located in the target country.

These same rules apply when translations are needed within a single country or regional market to reach consumers who speak different languages. When the California Milk Processor Board decided to translate its popular "Got milk?" campaign into Spanish, an adwoman who had moved to Los Angeles from Caracas, Venezuela, warned the board members that the slogan took on the meaning "Are you lactating?" in Spanish. The board wisely decided to adapt the campaign to ask, "And you, have you given them milk today?"[32]

Table 15.1 English versus English

American Dialect	British Dialect
Apartment	Flat
Appetizer	Starter
Attic	Loft
Baby carriage	Pram
Car trunk	Boot
College	University
Commercial	Advert
Cookie	Biscuit
Doctor's office	Surgery
Pantyhose	Tights
Paper towel	Kitchen towel
To rent	To let
Realtor	Estate agent
Stove	Cooker
Sweater	Jumper
Washcloth	Flannel
Yard	Garden

In the EU, many advertisers emphasize visual communication rather than attempting to communicate their message through the region's various languages. Visual ads that incorporate pictures rather than words can be more universally understood. Visuals have the advantage of being less culture-specific. For example, Cartier, the French luxury-products firm, launched a campaign in 123 countries. The campaign used magazines only and featured minimal copy (words). It emphasized dramatic photography so that the same message could be conveyed in Brazil, Japan, Russia and dozens of other countries.

Still, some managers of global brands are rethinking the power of local language. The Welsh Language Board encourages the use of the traditional language of Wales in ads. Although in decline through most of the twentieth century, Welsh is enjoying a renaissance, and today it is spoken by half a million people in Britain. Consequently, Coca-Cola agreed to use Welsh in bilingual posters.[33]

Global Media Strategy

As noted earlier, global marketers today account for major purchases of media space. A variety of media are available across the world. Still, difficulties arise because not all media are available in all countries. And if they are available, their technical capability to deliver a message to the required audience may be limited. Therefore, global marketers must consider the availability of various media for advertisers as well as the media habits of the target country.

Global Media

Marketers sometimes have the option of employing global media. Global television includes news networks, such as BBC World and CNN, and consumer channels, such as Animal Planet, Discovery, ESPN and MTV. However, the global print media consist largely of magazines targeted at business executives, such as Bloomberg *Business Week* and *The Economist* along with only a few consumer magazines such as *Cosmopolitan* and *Elle*. Nonetheless, these magazines can be particularly attractive for promoting global brands. A study of ads in national editions of *Cosmopolitan* appearing in Brazil, China, France, India, South Korea, Thailand and the United States revealed that there were more multinational product ads than domestic ones in every country except India.[34]

Satellite television channels, which are not subject to government regulations, have revolutionized television in many parts of the world. English is the common language of the majority of satellite channels. However, there is a trend toward local-language satellite broadcasts. Satellite channels are now available in several languages, such as Arabic, German, French and Swedish.

One of the most successful global satellite ventures is MTV. This music channel, which was launched in the United States 35 years ago, now reaches about one billion people in 18 different languages and in more than 164 countries, with 80 percent of viewers living outside the United States. McDonald's strategy of engaging MTV globally in some 160 countries was aimed at taking advantage of its global reach and the young audience attracted everywhere. As a result, McDonald's became the sole sponsor of MTV Advance Warning, a program focused on new musical talent and MTV's first truly global program.[35]

Local Media Availability

Advertisers' spending on media (or adspend) varies by country as shown in Table 15.2. Advertisers in the United States and many European countries have become accustomed to the availability of a full range of local media for advertising purposes. Aside from the traditional print media, consisting of newspapers and magazines, the U.S. advertiser has access to radio, television, billboards, cinemas and the Internet. In addition, direct mail can be used with most prospective client groups.

This wide choice among media may not be available in every country, particularly in rural regions. Therefore, a company marketing its products in several countries may find itself unable to apply the same media mix in all markets. Global managers must remain flexible in crafting their media plans. When international insurers entered India's life insurance market, they estimated that only a quarter of the market had been tapped. Soon ads explaining the benefits of life insurance proliferated. But instead of appearing on television, the ubiquitous ads appeared on billboards, in newspapers, on colorful websites and on posters decorating kiosks.[36]

Even when certain media options are available, access may be restricted by law. Global marketers of liquor in Turkey faced a market of inexperienced drinkers who knew little about how to use and mix different spirits, but they were forbidden to advertise on radio or television. As a result, they depended heavily on instructional campaigns in print media.[37]

Table 15.2 Total Ad Spend in Selected Countries

Countries	2013 Ad Spend in Millions	2013 Ad Spend Per Capita
Argentina	3,506.1	84.5
Australia	13,107.5	567.5
Brazil	15,892.3	79.3
Canada	11,387.1	323.6
Chile	1,617.7	92.0
China	44,584.3	32.9
Colombia	1,509.8	31.2
Czech Republic	1,289.7	122.6
Egypt	379.7	4.5
France	12,940.1	202.8
Germany	24,143.0	295.0
Hungary	737.7	74.3
India	5,342.4	4.3
Indonesia	5,868.5	23.7
Israel	1,149.7	143.2
Italy	9,728.1	159.3
Japan	41,966.5	329.6
Malaysia	2,476.6	83.3
Mexico	6,544.2	55.7
Norway	2,960.7	585.7
Pakistan	408.7	1.9
Philippines	2,133.9	21.7
Poland	2,301.0	59.7
Russia	8,700.1	60.7
Saudi Arabia	618.1	21.1
Singapore	2,091.9	383.6
South Africa	3,775.3	71.5
South Korea	11,183.6	222.7
Spain	6,599.7	141.3
Sweden	3,839.7	401.8
Taiwan	2,199.2	94.3
Thailand	3,912.0	57.4
Turkey	2,668.6	35.3
Ukraine	922.5	20.3
United Arab Emirates	578.8	68.8
United Kingdom	19,049.6	298.2
USA	165,302.0	522.5
Venezuela	1,060.6	35.0
Vietnam	816.9	9.0

Source: Selected Data from Euromonitor Passport Data Base, 2014

Media Habits

Adspend by media category varies by country as shown in Table 15.3. The choice between using one medium or another is affected not only by availability and market penetration of various media but also by the media habits of the national population or more importantly the media habits of the target market in particular. When Heineken NV decided to target South Africa's middle class, it advertised its Amstel-brand lager on a popular soap opera about a successful middle-class black family in Johannesburg.[38] In South Korea, advertisers targeting women can take advantage of four cable-TV shopping networks that attract an unusually large audience of middle-income and upper-income females.[39]

Table 15.3 Percentage of Advertising Spending on Major Media for Selected Countries

Geographies	% TV	% Radio	% Print	% Cinema	% Outdoor	% Online	TOTAL Million U.S. $
Argentina	43	3	41	1	5	7	3
Australia	32	8	30	0	4	25	13,108.2
Brazil	70	4	18	0	3	6	15,893.2
Canada	32	14	21	0	4	29	11,387.8
Chile	49	6	28	0	8	8	1,618.6
China	44	4	24	0	13	15	44,585.1
Colombia	45	16	23	0	10	5	1,510.7
Czech Republic	44	3	24	0	6	21	1,290.5
Egypt	13	7	80	0	0	0	380.8
France	35	8	23	1	12	21	12,940.9
Germany	22	4	49	0	4	20	24,143.9
Hungary	33	5	29	1	11	20	738.5
India	40	3	48	1	5	3	5,343.3
Indonesia	54	2	39	0	4	0	5,869.5
Israel	38	5	31	1	5	20	1,150.5
Italy	59	8	23	1	3	6	9,728.9
Japan	44	3	20	0	12	21	41,967.3
Malaysia	35	5	54	0	3	3	2,477.6
Mexico	72	9	19	0	0	0	6,545.1
Norway	23	4	40	1	4	29	2,961.4
Pakistan	62	3	21	4	8	1	409.7
Philippines	66	10	12	0	9	3	2,134.9
Poland	52	7	14	2	7	18	2,301.8
Russia	50	4	9	2	13	22	8,700.8

(Continued)

487

Table 15.3 (Continued)

Geographies	% TV	% Radio	% Print	% Cinema	% Outdoor	% Online	TOTAL Million U.S. $
Saudi Arabia	4	10	72	0	15	0	619.1
Singapore	32	8	41	0	9	10	2,092.8
South Africa	44	15	32	2	4	3	3,776.4
South Korea	34	2	27	1	3	33	11,184.4
Spain	40	10	22	1	8	20	6,600.6
Sweden	25	3	39	1	4	28	3,840.4
Taiwan	44	6	24	0	6	19	2,200.0
Thailand	53	5	24	7	9	1	3,913.0
Turkey	58	3	22	1	7	9	2,669.4
Ukraine	56	5	17	0	16	5	923.5
United Arab Emirates	7	19	55	2	17	0	579.8
United Kingdom	28	4	25	1	6	36	19,050.1
USA	38	10	27	0	5	20	165,302.9
Venezuela	38	10	30	3	10	8	1,061.5
Vietnam	80	0	16	0	4	1	818.0

Sources: Cinema Adspend: Euromonitor International from World Association of Newspapers; Online Adspend: Euromonitor International from World Association of Newspapers; Outdoor Adspend: Euromonitor International from World Association of Newspapers; Print Adspend: Euromonitor International from World Association of Newspapers; Radio Adspend: Euromonitor International from World Association of Newspapers; Total Adspend: Euromonitor International from World Association of Newspapers; TV Adspend: Euromonitor International from World Association of Newspapers.

The ownership or usage of television and radio can vary considerably from one country to another. The readership of print media (newspapers and magazines) varies as well and is influenced by the literacy of a country's population. Although national literacy levels are less of a concern for companies in the industrial-products market, they can be a crucial factor in consumer-goods advertising. In countries where large portions of the population are illiterate, the use of print media is of limited value. Both radio and television have been used by companies to circumvent the literacy problem. However, these media cannot be used in areas where the penetration of receivers is limited. Media availability is, however, becoming increasingly similar across regions. For example, the number of Internet users in North America and South America has significantly converged.

Urbanization in emerging countries has created opportunities for using media in creative ways. In Beijing, Communication Radio serves the needs of China's new commuters. In addition to offering traffic updates, the station plays light pop music to calm the nerves of motorists stuck in traffic. Eighty percent of Beijing drivers tune in. As private car ownership surges in China, Communication

Radio has become one of the country's highest-ranked stations for advertising revenues.[40] To take advantage of Shanghai's busy subway system, which carries 2.2 million commuters a day, Starbucks created a "subopera" to run on high-tech flat screen monitors on the subway cars and station platforms. The subopera combined advertisement and soap opera.[41] In Dubai, the government opened negotiations with businesses in order to sell naming rights for two dozen stations being built as part of the emirate's new mass-transit system.[42] This could provide marketers with a unique and highly viewed medium.

In fact, modernization in developing countries has created a number of new media opportunities. Across Asia—where cell phones have proliferated and there is little regulation of spam—advertisers increasingly reach consumers via text messages to their phones. In India, where cell-phone penetration is high compared to other media such as television and the Internet, cell-phone ads have proven effective in reaching the country's large and diverse population. Although cellular adspend is still low in countries such as India, it is expected to grow in the future.[43] Furthermore, the soft-sell cultures of Asia may be particularly well-suited to the brevity necessary for cellular ads.[44] As we noted earlier concerning Japan, soft-sell cultures tend to want and expect less product information delivered in their ads.

Old versus New Media

Internet accessibility worldwide has spurred the use of banner advertising and brand-sponsored online games as a way to try to reach literate, online consumers in many different countries. In some countries such as South Korea, many young consumers now spend considerable time online and little time watching television.[45] This phenomenon has been observed in China as well. China has experienced a decline in traditional media such as print and radio ads while Internet advertising, especially mobile Internet advertising, has surged.[46] As a result, adspend in these countries is shifting from the older media to the newer. In Brazil, online advertising increased by 40 percent in a single year.[47] Advergaming, the use of online video games designed to promote a brand, has proven especially successful on social media across cultures, partly because such games more easily overcome the language barrier.[48]

The Middle East, where 50 percent of the population is under the age of 25, is another growing market for online advertising.[49] Social media exploded in the region after the Arab Spring. Ninety percent of Internet users are on social media. Arab users of Facebook tripled in only two years. Social media marketers are quickly moving into smartphones due to a high penetration of the phones in some Arab countries. In Saudi Arabia, there are on average nearly two smartphones per person![50] The cosmetic industry particularly utilizes social media to reach female consumers. Due to gender separation in the Middle East, women spend most of their spare time with other women, and young girls are introduced to beauty regimes at a young age. Information about beauty products is traditionally spread by word of mouth, and over 71 percent of Arab women participate in social networking online. To tap into this phenomenon, Olay launched a regional site dedicated to beauty and featuring an interactive forum that allows women to build online networks.[51]

World Beat 15.2

China's Internet Ads

China is the world's third largest market for advertising—and the fastest growing one. Television has long dominated as the medium of choice. However, even China's booming economy was hit hard by the global recession. This inspired marketing managers and ad-agency executives to seek cheaper media outlets for advertising to the Chinese market. As a result, Nielsen Company estimates that online advertising in China grew an astounding 42 percent in a single year. Brands are also exploring unique ways to collaborate with Chinese web platforms. Although Coca-Cola still buys expensive air time on China's national television, the company increasingly turns to Internet ads. In one four-minute documentary, the company focused on the millions of children in rural China who are left behind when their parents seek jobs in the city and Coke's program for reuniting some of these families during the Chinese New Year.

In only a few years, digital advertising is expected to attain a 55 percent market share of advertising spending in China. The new media is especially important for reaching China's young consumers who spend a lot of time on the Internet and little time watching television. To this end, Estee Lauder's Clinique brand developed a 40-episode digital sitcom about a Shanghai college student to promote its cosmetics. Viewers could blog posts or send text messages stating what they thought about the challenges faced by the heroine. In three months the series attracted more than 20 million views.

With car sales down in many major markets, automobile companies look to the growing Chinese market to support global sales. When buying a car, word of mouth is important in China, but many car buyers are the first among their family and friends to buy a car. Therefore, they look to the Internet as a key source of information. Shanghai GM increased its Internet advertising to 10 percent of total ad spending and expects to further increase its presence on social-networking sites.

Sources: Johnson Yeh and Ming Zhang, "Taking the Pulse of China's Ad Spending," *McKinsey Quarterly*, June 2013; Loretta Chao, "Online Advertising Gets Boost in China," *Wall Street Journal*, December 11, 2008, p. B6; Juliet Ye, "Auto Makers, Flock to the Web to Woo Chinese Buyers," *Wall Street Journal*, April 9, 2009, p. B9; "Coke Reunites Families for Chinese New Year," *Advertising Age*, January 27, 2014; and Sophie Yu, "Digital Adverts in China Tipped to Soar," *South China Morning Post*, June 5, 2014.

Scheduling International Advertising

Media expenditures tend to peak before sales peak. How long before depends on the complexity of the consumers' buying decision and the length of their deliberation. This principle, though somewhat generalized here, applies to international markets as well as to domestic ones. Differences exist, however, because of varying sales peaks, national vacations and religious holidays, and because of differences in the deliberation time with regard to purchases. As noted in Chapter 3, religious holidays may also affect consumer purchases and consequently the placement or timing of advertising. Sales peaks can also be influenced by climatic seasons. Winter months in North America and Europe are summer months in countries of the Southern Hemisphere, such as Australia, New Zealand, South Africa, Argentina and Brazil. The season influences the purchase and consumption of many consumer goods, such as clothing, vacation services, travel and ice cream and soft drinks.

For industrial products, the timing of advertising in support of sales efforts may be affected by the budgetary cycles that prevail in a given country. Companies tend to be heavily influenced by their own budgetary cycles, which usually coincide with their fiscal years. In Japan, for example, many companies begin their fiscal year in June rather than in January. To the extent that capital budgets are completed before the new fiscal year commences, products that require budgetary approval will need advertising support in advance of budget completion.

The time needed to think about a purchase has been cited as a primary consideration in deciding how long it is appropriate for the advertising peak to precede the sales peak. In its domestic market, a company may be accustomed to a given deliberation time on the part of its customers. But because deliberation times may be determined by income level or other environmental factors, other markets may exhibit different patterns. The purchase or replacement of a small electrical household appliance may be a routine decision for a North American household, and the purchase may occur whenever the need arises. In a country with lower income levels, such a purchase may be planned several weeks or even months ahead. Consequently, a company engaged in international advertising needs to evaluate carefully the underlying assumptions of its domestic advertising policies and not automatically assume that they apply elsewhere.

Organizing the Global Advertising Effort

A major concern for global marketing executives revolves around the organization of the company's global advertising effort. Key concerns include the role of the head office versus the roles that subsidiaries and the advertising agency should play. Marketers are aware that a more harmonious approach to the international advertising effort may enhance both the quality and the efficiency of the total effort. Organizing the effort deserves as much time as individual advertising decisions about individual products or campaigns. In this section, we look in greater detail at the selection of an advertising agency and at the managerial issues that arise in running a global advertising effort in a MNC.

Selection of an Advertising Agency

Global companies have a number of options with respect to working with advertising agencies. Many companies develop an agency relationship domestically and must decide whether they expect their domestic agency to handle their global advertising business as well. In some foreign markets, companies need to select foreign agencies to work with them—a decision that may be made by the head office alone or left to the local subsidiaries. Alternatively, MNCs can employ advertising with global reach or agencies that have banded together to form international networks.

Working with Domestic Agencies

When a company starts to grow internationally, it is not unusual for the domestic advertising agency to handle the international business as well. However, this is possible only when the domestic agency has global experience and capability. Many smaller domestic agencies do not have international experience. Companies are then forced to make other arrangements. Frequently, the global company begins by appointing individual agencies in each of the various foreign markets where it is operating. This may be done with the help of the local subsidiaries or through the staff at the company's head office. Before long, however, the company will end up with a series of agency relationships that may make global coordination very difficult.

Working with Local Agencies Abroad

The local advertising agency is expected to understand the local environment fully and is in a position to create ads targeted to the local market. Although it markets one of the world's best-known brands, Mercedes-Benz is one of many firms that have chosen at times to utilize a variety of local agencies. Prior to 1980, the company did engage heavily in global advertising, using the Ogilvy & Mather Worldwide agency. When Ogilvy & Mather pursued the business of competitor Ford Motor Company, Mercedes fired the agency. Mercedes then adopted a policy of varying its brand image from country to country and employing the most creative agency in each country.

Working with International Advertising Networks

Many companies with extensive international operations find it too difficult and cumbersome to deal simultaneously with a large number of agencies, both domestic and international. For this reason, MNCs have tended to concentrate their accounts with some large advertising agencies that operate their own global networks. The first generation of international networks was created by U.S.-based advertising agencies in the 1950s and 1960s when clients encouraged their U.S. agencies to move into local markets where the advertising agencies were weak. Leaders in this process were J. Walter Thompson, Ogilvy & Mather, BBDO and Young & Rubicam. British entrepreneurs Saatchi & Saatchi and WPP dominated the second wave of international networks. Other networks were developed by French and Japanese agencies. The 1980s saw many mergers of medium-sized agencies around the world. In the 1990s, mergers and acquisitions occurred among even the largest global agencies. Some of these mergers utilized the umbrella of a holding company that allowed each agency to retain its brand identity while enjoying the advantages of greater size and the ability to access the full global reach of all alliance partners.[52]

Utilizing global advertising agencies or networks can be desirable in countries where advertising is not as developed as in the major markets of North America and Europe. For example, global agencies are favored in Eastern Europe, where up to 90 percent of the advertising in some markets is handled by affiliates of global agencies. They can leverage a vast knowledge within the agency network and transfer much-needed skills in order to attract business from such leading firms as Coca-Cola, Nestlé and Unilever. When Vietnam opened to foreign advertising agencies—albeit those operating with a local, Vietnamese partner—nearly two dozen international agencies flooded into Vietnam, the world's thirteenth most populous country.[53]

International advertising networks are especially sought after because of their ability to execute global campaigns. Usually, one set of ads will be created and then circulated among the local affiliates. Working within the same agency or network guarantees consistency and a certain willingness among affiliate offices to accept direction from a central location. Therefore, as companies develop their global business and coordinate their global campaigns, they are likely to consolidate agencies.

Coordinating Global Advertising

The role the international marketing executive plays in a company's international advertising effort may differ from firm to firm and depends on several factors. Outside factors, such as the nature of the market or of the competition, as well as internal factors, such as company culture or philosophy, may lead some firms to adopt a more centralized approach in international advertising. Other firms may prefer to delegate more authority to local subsidiaries and local agencies. Key factors that can cause a firm to either centralize or decentralize decision-making for international advertising are reviewed in the sections that follow.

External Factors Affecting Advertising Coordination

One of the most important factors influencing how companies allocate decision-making for international advertising is market diversity. For products or services where customer needs and interests are homogeneous across many countries, greater opportunities for standardization exist, and companies are more likely to centralize decision-making. Companies operating in markets with very different customer needs or market systems are more likely to decentralize their international-advertising decision-making. Local knowledge is more important to the success of these firms.

The nature of the competition can also affect the way an international firm plans for decision-making related to advertising. Firms that essentially face local competition or different sets of competitors from country to country may find it more logical to delegate international advertising to local subsidiaries. On the other hand, if a company is competing everywhere against a small set of international firms, the company is more apt to centralize key marketing decisions in an attempt to coordinate its actions against its global competitors. In such cases, advertising decision-making may be centralized as well.

Internal Factors Affecting Advertising Coordination

A company's own internal structure and organization can also greatly influence its options in terms of centralizing or decentralizing decision-making about international advertising. Opportunities for centralizing are few when a company's approach is to customize advertising for each local market. However, when a company adheres to a standardized advertising format, a more centralized approach will be possible and probably even desirable.

Skill levels and efficiency concerns can also affect the level of centralization. Decentralization is possible only when the advertising skills of local subsidiaries and local agencies are sufficient for them to perform successfully. Decentralization is often believed to result in inefficiencies or decreased quality because a firm's budget may be spread over too many individual agencies. Instead of having a large budget in one agency, the firm has created mini-budgets that may not be adequate to attract the best creative talent to work on its products. Centralization often gives the firm access to better talent, though knowledge of the local markets may be sacrificed. On the other hand, international advertising cannot be centralized successfully in companies where the head-office staff does not possess a full appreciation of the international dimension of the firm's business.

The managerial style of the international company may also affect the centralization decision on advertising. Some companies pride themselves on giving considerable freedom to managers at their local subsidiaries. Under such circumstances, centralizing advertising decisions may be counterproductive. The general approach taken by the company's top management toward international markets is closely related to its desire to centralize or decentralize international advertising.

However, because the internal and external factors that characterize the company are subject to change over time, the decision to centralize or decentralize will never be a permanent one. For example, Coca-Cola shifted more advertising decision-making to its subsidiaries. Then two years later, advertising oversight shifted back to headquarters in Atlanta. Lackluster sales and some embarrassing ads—an angry grandmother streaking down a beach in Italy—proved fatal to Coke's "think local" strategy.[54]

Conclusion

The complexity of dealing simultaneously with a large number of different customers in many countries, all speaking their own languages and subject to their own cultural heritage, presents a real challenge to the international marketer. Proponents of global advertising point to the convergence of customer needs and the emergence of "world consumers," customers who are becoming ever more homogeneous whether they live in Paris, London, New York or Tokyo. However, many aspects of the advertising environment remain considerably diverse.

Many marketers, however, realize that total customization is not desirable because it would require that each market creates and implements its own advertising strategies. Top creative talent is scarce everywhere, and better creative solutions tend to be costlier ones. As a result, companies appear to be moving toward modularization, in which some elements of the advertising message are common to all ads whereas other elements are tailored to local requirements. Successful modularization requires that companies plan such an integration of responsibilities from the very outset, considering the full range of possibilities and the requirements that will need to be satisfied across their major markets. This is a considerable challenge to global marketing executives and their advertising partners.

Managerial Takeaways

1. *Some products and services still profit from local advertising campaigns, especially when the product or service is at different stages in its life cycle across markets.*

2. *However, global campaigns are increasingly relevant to multinational brands, and they allow global marketers to capture benefits of both localization and standardization.*

3. *Cultural constraints still pose challenges for global campaigns. These include national regulation of advertising, and national differences in social norms, media availability and media habits, and the perception of advertising credibility.*

4. *New media is gaining on old media worldwide, although at present old media commands more credibility.*

5. *A global campaign requires more centralized decision-making. More power gravitates to headquarters and to international advertising agencies and away from local subsidiaries and local agencies.*

6. *Nonetheless, the insights from local managers are key to avoiding advertising missteps in national markets. To execute successful global campaigns, global marketers must receive constant input from their subsidiaries beginning with the planning stage.*

Questions for Discussion

1. What has motivated the apparent increase in the use of more standardized advertising across national markets?

2. What do you think are the reasons that attitudes about the credibility of advertising vary among countries and across media?

3. What advice would you give to a U.S. firm interested in advertising in Japan?

4. How should the advertising industry react to evolving conditions in developing countries?

5. How will increased Internet access affect international advertising?

CASE 15.1   Advertising to Children

Children in the United States see an estimated 20,000 commercials a year. Marketers spend $5 billion a year directly targeting children. And much more advertising reaches children when they are not even the target audience.

An investigation by the U.S. Federal Trade Commission (FTC) discovered internal memos detailing how companies commonly target their marketing of violent games, music and movies to children. This prompted lawmakers to reconsider tightening laws on advertising to children. In a follow-up study the next year, the FTC discovered that the movie and video-game industries had improved their practices but that the recording industry continued to show total disdain for public concerns about marketing violent and sexually explicit products to underage children. This encouraged the call for laws that would restrict ads—whether targeted directly to children or not—that reached large audiences under the age of 17. A number of industries already set their own standards for advertising to children. The beer industry discourages placing ads on programs where half or more of the audience is under the age of 18. Many global brands police themselves by agreeing not to advertise to children. But they consider television shows with audiences of less than 35 percent children to be fair game. Several movie studios set their cutoff standard at 35 percent as well.

Still, the Association of National Advertisers continues to lobby against any legislation that would restrict advertising for violent movies, video games or music; it contends that such restrictions would curtail free speech, a fundamental American freedom enshrined in the American Bill of Rights. Ironically, a study conducted by the National Institute on Media and the Family discovered that 99 percent of students in grades 7 through 12 could identify Budweiser as a brand of beer—significantly more students than those who could identify the purpose of the Bill of Rights. Nonetheless, advertisers won a legal victory when the Supreme Court struck down the state of Massachusetts' restrictions on billboard advertising of cigars and smokeless tobacco products. The law, aimed at protecting children, was deemed to violate the advertisers' freedom of speech.

The controversy over advertising to children is not restricted to the United States. Russia has outlawed cartoon characters in alcohol ads. Russian law also forbids advertisers to criticize parents or grandparents

495

or cast parents or tutors in a bad light. In addition, ads cannot induce children to convince their parents to buy a product. In short, advertising for products consumed by children should be aimed at parents not children. In Britain, ads that provoke children to behave improperly are also taboo. Regulators have no direct authority to ban ads, but they enjoy powerful influence with the nation's media. A television ad created by the Publicus Group for Hewlett-Packard featured children throwing snowballs at a passing train. Regulators considered this an incitement to antisocial behavior, and the ad was removed.

Sweden's top advertising watchdog is promoting gender neutrality for advertising toys. In the catalog for Top-Toy, a licensee of Toys R Us, boys now replace girls in ads for dolls and stuffed dogs. Any television advertising aimed at children has been illegal in Sweden since the 1990s. Critics of the Swedish advertising ban are quick to point out that Swedish children have access to international channels that allow them to see ads from other countries. TV3, a Swedish channel that broadcasts from the United Kingdom, is free to advertise to children because of its British location. A number of European countries are debating tightening their restrictions, but advertisers argue that increased regulation across Europe could greatly curtail children's programming on the many private channels not subsidized by governments.

Across the world in Indonesia, a cigarette-advertising campaign came under attack by educators and politicians. The campaign featured animated characters, including ants, roosters and snails, dancing to music. Critics believed that the ad encouraged children, who make up the majority of cartoon lovers, to think that smoking was a good thing. The company quickly removed the offending ad. In Indonesia, the penalty for marketers who target children is a hefty fine and a jail sentence of up to five years.

Many countries now restrict advertising to children by firms in the food, beverage and fast-food industries because their products don't promote a healthy diet. A number of food companies in South Africa have voluntarily agreed not to advertise to children under 12 unless the products being promoted represent healthy dietary choices. After determining that Mexican children saw 12,000 junk-food ads per year, the Mexican government drafted plans to ban ads in the afternoons, evenings and weekends. In Malaysia, the country's health ministry, the Malaysian Advertisers Association and the Federation of Malaysian Manufacturers' Food Manufacturing group developed a pledge by which signatory companies agreed not to advertise food products to children 12 years of age or under unless the products adhered to international dietary guidelines. Among the signatory companies were Coca-Cola, Mars, McDonald's, Mondelez, Nestlé, PepsiCo and Unilever. In fact, Coca-Cola announced that it would not advertise to children younger than 12 anywhere in the world.

In the United States, a group of Democratic Senators requested that energy-drink companies such as Red Bull and Monster stop advertising to children who might not understand the health risks involved with the heavy consumption of caffeine. Energy-drink companies denied they advertised to children, but opponents pointed out that these companies engage in social media and distribute free samples where teens hang out. In fact, digital marketing expands the horizon for reaching children and teens via advergames. Consumer groups also filed a complaint against PepsiCo's Frito-Lay brand, arguing that the company disguised their marketing efforts by utilizing video games and social media that teens would not clearly identify as advertising.

New online promotional options can also increase the chance for reaching children even when companies don't particularly target them. For example, Coca-Cola launched a campaign on Facebook that allowed users to create a "Sprite Sips" character and share it with their friends. However, the company could not control the age of the recipients when the ad went viral. Similarly, Mondelez's NabiscoWorld.com, one of the world's most popular food websites, created a game around the concept of rapidly twisting, licking and dunking an oversized Oreo cookie in a glass of milk. The site is designed for children over the age of 12 but its games appeal to children much younger.

Discussion Questions

1. Why is advertising directed at children and teens regulated in so many cultures? Why is there so much variation in these regulations?
2. Should the EU develop a common policy toward advertising that targets children? Why or why not? What barriers to such a policy might exist?
3. What restrictions on advertising directed at children would you favor? Why?

Sources: "Advertising to Kids," in Kate Gillespie and H. David Hennessey, *Global Marketing* (Mason, OH: Cengage, 2011), pp. 455–456; Irina Anyukhina and Yulla Gurieva, "Youth Advertising in Russia," *Young Consumers*, vol. 11, no. 3 (1999); "Consumer Groups File Complaint Against PepsiCo Over Teen Marketing," *The Hill*, October 19, 2011; Anna Molin, "In Sweden, Playtime Goes Gender-Neutral for Holidays," *Wall Street Journal*, November 22, 2012, p. D1; Tom Risen, "Democratic Senators Ask Red Bull, Monster to Stop Marketing to Kids," *U.S. News and World Report*, September 23, 2013; S.M. Mohamed Idris, "Protecting Children from Unhealthy Food Advertising," *The Malaysian Insider*, August 26, 2013; "Cookie Monster Crumbles," *The Economist*, November 23, 2013; and "Changes in Russian Alcohol Advertising Regulations, Amendments of 2012," Ad Consul, www.adconsul.org, accessed March 17, 2014.

CASE 15.2   ShanghaiCosmopolitan.com

Andy Chen was a young and successful journalist in Shanghai, the financial capital of China. It was Andy's job to interview young professionals and feature their lifestyles in the newspaper where he worked. His large and well-connected social circle was full of well-educated and high-income individuals. Similar to Andy, most of these young professionals were single and lived with their parents. Their salaries were relatively high by local standards. When they were not working, they often banded together and frequented expensive restaurants, night clubs, coffee shops and unique boutiques for clothes.

A year ago, Andy met his friend, Ma Li, to have a coffee together at Starbucks. Li was an electrical engineer who worked for a large Chinese telecommunication company. Li had extensive computer and Internet skills and always wanted to start up his own online business instead of working for a company. After a few sips of coffee, Andy asked Li:

> Do you think creating a social networking website for our friends would be a good idea? It's inconvenient to contact everyone by phone to get together somewhere. If we are able to create a website solely for young professionals in Shanghai, it would make it easier for everyone

to get together. In foreign countries, user-generated social networking websites are gaining in popularity. This will surely influence the Chinese market in the future. It will be popular, at least among our circle of friends. And they have incredible buying power and like to spend money. Advertisers will be interested in such a site, too. We can make some money out of it.

Li's eyes lit up when he heard the idea. As an electrical engineer, he had been concerned about the development of Web 2.0 (user-generated online media) in China. There were already quite a few major players such as sina.com.cn that provided blog services, and social networking websites were beginning to become popular. Currently, only one holding company, Xiang Shu, created multiple social networking websites to target college students, similar to Facebook in the United States. However, there appeared to be no special social networking website that targeted high-income young professionals.

With about $1,000 investment in hardware, Andy and Li established their social networking website, ShanghaiCosmopolitan.com. In order to minimize the startup investment, Andy and Li served as both the owners and employees of the site, although both kept their prior jobs. Li designed the site and Andy promoted the site to his large circle of friends. As predicted, the site became extremely popular in Shanghai among moderate- to high-income young professionals in a short time.

In China, young professionals, in particular, were well-connected offline since they relied on relationships, or *guanxi*, to develop their own careers. *Guanxi* describes a tightly integrated social network. Members within this network of trusted friends depend on each other and respect each other's opinions. Friends within a network not only develop deep feelings for each other, they also have a moral obligation to maintain the relationship, even if it requires personal sacrifice. Frequent socialization and hanging out with friends helps to nurture and strengthen *guanxi*.

Once Andy sent out news of ShanghaiCosmopolitan.com to his friends, they relayed the message to their own well-connected social circles by word of mouth. The site became popular practically overnight. Young professionals felt proud to have a social networking website designed specifically with their needs in mind.

The Advertising Challenge

With the exponential growth of its online community, ShanghaiCosmopolitan.com was recently forced to hire three full-time employees to manage the site. In contrast with the popularity of the site, however, the advertising revenues had not run as well as expected. Andy and Li needed to increase advertising revenue soon to support their growing business. They determined early on that they could not charge a membership fee for signing up for the site, since most other social networking websites in China are free of charge to their members.

Other social networking websites invited marketers to advertise in the form of banners and pop-ups on users' personal web pages. They also set up profile pages for brands in order for a brand to come to life as a "person" and socialize with users in a more friendly and personalized way. This marketing communication strategy had been successful on Facebook as well as on the social networking sites in China, which mainly targeted college students. However, many of Andy's friends told him that they regarded such promotion strategies as naïve. Only college students or childish people would fall for this type of advertising or perceive a brand to be a friend.

Andy's friends had also voiced objections to traditional banners and pop-up ads. They were quick to emphasize that ShanghaiCosmopolitan.com should be used to connect with friends and share lifestyles and hobbies. They did not want to be interrupted by a deluge of ads on the site unless the information being communicated was exactly the type they wanted to hear. They also complained that a site full of banners and pop-ups made them feel as if they were being watched and used by advertisers. Despite these objections, Andy ran a trial during which he allowed certain marketers to exhibit banners on the site for free. The outcome of the trial was somewhat disappointing since the click-through rate to those banners was relatively low, about one-fifth of the click-through rate on websites such as Yahoo.com.cn.

Group Bargaining Zone

ShanghaiCosmopolitan.com currently received most of its advertising revenues from a single site feature, Group Bargaining Zone (GBZ). There were two ways that marketers could participate in the site's group bargaining option. First, site users could post their wants and needs for a group discount on the GBZ. A list of marketers was then allowed to browse those needs every day. These marketers signed contracts with ShanghaiCosmopolitan.com and were regarded as credible by Andy. If a firm saw that there was demand from site members for their goods, the firm paid ShanghaiCosmopolitan.com a fee to be connected to those consumers. However, marketers were not allowed to directly contact site members. Members' personal information, including contact information, was not made available to marketers. However, ShanghaiCosmopolitan.com allowed participating marketers to use its instant chatting software to make counter offers to consumer groups. A second way in which firms could participate on the site was to regularly post quantity discount offers on the GBZ. These firms paid ShanghaiCosmopolitan.com for advertising space on a monthly basis. Consumers could then browse those offers. If interested, they would seek out their friends to see if they could reach the required number of buyers to qualify for the discounted price.

Andy believed that young Shanghai professionals liked the GBZ for several reasons. They could save money and have fun with friends at the same time. It also allowed them to feel like super-achievers by overpowering marketers. The major advertisers on the GBZ were taxi companies and upscale restaurants. Most of ShanghaiCosmopolitan.com's young clientele worked close to each other in fashionable business districts with jammed subways and favored commuting by taxi. However, most young professionals could not afford to take taxis by themselves to work and back on a daily basis because the fees were too high. Restaurants supported the GBZ because it helped them to maximize profits. Some restaurants in Shanghai were mainly set up with four-person table settings. If an individual customer, or even a couple, visited the restaurant they most likely would be seated at a four-person table. If four people would agree to come in and sit together, the restaurants could offer a group discount.

Furthermore, in Shanghai the number of consumers eating in a restaurant was considered a good indicator of the restaurant's quality. Restaurants especially welcomed the patronage of large groups of diners. Following the success that restaurants and taxi companies experienced on the site, gyms and travel agencies also exhibited interest in advertising on the GBZ.

Although ShanghaiCosmopolitan.com enjoyed steady advertising revenues from local restaurants as well as transportation, gym and tourism companies, Andy wanted to expand the advertising revenue and attract more MNCs as advertisers. One idea was to approach brands that targeted women. Andy observed that women were more active than men on his social networking website. Young female professionals liked to purchase luxury goods such as LV handbags and Christian Dior make-up. However, on average, a classic LV handbag was priced more than $1,000 in the Chinese market while high-income young professionals in Shanghai only earned $1,500 to $2,000 per month. Andy realized that many marketers of luxury goods disparaged group bargaining. However, he did note that some of those same marketers would hold an end-of-the-year clearance sale. At these sales, items could sell for 20 to 40 percent off list price.

Andy also needed to reply to a request from a friend, Wang Hong. Hong now worked for a Chinese contract manufacturer that produced products for a MNC operating in China. The local company routinely manufactured 20 percent more products than were ordered by its multinational client. This practice was not uncommon in China, since contract manufacturers were uncertain whether or not all the products they produced would meet their clients' standards. However, contract manufacturers rarely destroyed the surplus inventory that they produced. Hong was inquiring whether he could sell his company's surplus on the GBZ.

Discussion Questions

1. Why do you think young Chinese professionals frequent expensive restaurants and purchase luxury goods? What are the implications for MNCs that wish to communicate to this market segment?
2. Evaluate Andy's option of promoting banners and pop-up ads for increasing advertising revenue.
3. Why do you think the GBZ appears to work in a social networking site in China? Would the GBZ work in social networking websites in your country? Why or why not?
4. Why would a MNC be interested in participating in the GBZ? Why might they be disinterested?
5. Should Andy allow Wang Hong to sell surplus products on the GBZ? Why or why not?

Source: Case prepared by Jie Zhang for the purpose of class discussion. Used by permission.

Notes

1. PR Newswire, "ExxonMobil Launches Advertising Campaign to Announce New Company," December 3, 1999.
2. Bill Chase, "Letters to the Editor," *Wall Street Journal* (Europe), July 24, 2001, p. 9.
3. Vanessa O'Connell, "Exxon 'Centralizes' New Global Campaign," *Wall Street Journal*, July 7, 2001, p. B6.
4. Stephanie Clifford, "Monster.com Tries Gallows Humor," *International Herald Tribune*, January 14, 2009.
5. Greg Harris, "International Advertising Standardization: What Do Multinationals Actually Standardize?" *Journal of International Marketing*, vol. 12, no. 4 (1994), pp. 13–30.
6. Stephanie Kang, "Indian Ads Come into Their Own," *Wall Street Journal*, December 19, 2007, p. B4.
7. Hillary Chura and Richard Linnett, "Coca-Cola Readies Global Assault," *Advertising Age*, April 2, 2001, p. 1.
8. Erin White, "Publicis Groupe Creates Agency Dedicated Just to Serve Fiat," *Wall Street Journal*, July 11, 2003, p. B4.
9. Patricia Sabatini, "Heinz Re-Enlists Leo Burnett for Global Campaign," *Pittsburgh Post-Gazette*, March 27, 1999, p. C1.
10. Bradford Wernie, "Jaguar Goes Global," *Automotive News Europe*, April 12, 1999, p. v.
11. Suzanne Vranica and Bruce Orwall, "Disney Will Launch Global Campaign to Boost Ailing Parks," *Asian Wall Street Journal*, December 30, 2004, p. A6.

12 Judann Pollack, "Pringles Wins Worldwide with One Message," *Ad Age International*, January 11, 1999, p. 14.

13 "Using Potato Chips to Spread the Spirit of Free Enterprise," ABCNEWS.com, accessed September 9, 2002.

14 Geoffrey A. Fowler, "For P&G in China, It's Wash, Rinse, and Don't Repeat," *Wall Street Journal*, April 7, 2006, p. B3.

15 Laurie Burkitt, "McDonalds Pushes for More Gains in China," *Wall Street Journal*, February 12, 2012, p. B7.

16 Jason Bush, "Wooing the Next Pepski Generation," *Business Week*, October 29, 2007, pp. 74–75.

17 Philip J. Kitchen and Tao Li, "Perceptions of Integrated Marketing Communications: A Chinese Ad and PR Perspective," *International Journal of Advertising*, vol. 21, no. 1 (2005), p. 68.

18 Geoffrey A. Fowler, "Advertising: China Cracks Down on Commercials," *Wall Street Journal*, February 19, 2004, p. B7.

19 Mike Esterl, "'King of Beers' Fizzling in U.S., Sets Goal of World Domination," *Wall Street Journal*, July 27, 2013, p. A1.

20 Jason Leow, "Beijing Mystery: What's Happening to the Billboards?" *Wall Street Journal*, June 25, 2007, p. A1.

21 "Cigarette Stunt Pilot Fined for Airborne Cigarette Advertising," Associated Press, September 20, 2000.

22 Matthew Dalton, "In EU, Food Claims Aren't Taken Lightly," *Wall Street Journal*, February 4, 2009, p. B5A.

23 Christina Passariello, "Chic Under Wraps," *Wall Street Journal*, June 20, 2006, p. B1.

24 Normandy Madden and Andrew Hornery, "As Taco Bell Enters Singapore, Gidget Avoids the Ad Limelight," *Ad Age International*, January 11, 1999, p. 13.

25 Jae W. Hong, Aydin Muderrisoglu and George M. Zinkhan, "Cultural Differences and Advertising Expression: A Comparative Content Analysis of Japanese and U.S. Magazine Advertising," *Journal of Advertising*, vol. 16, no. 1 (1987), pp. 55–62.

26 Erin White, "U.K. Gives Lessons on Ad Messages," *Wall Street Journal*, December 2, 2002, p. B6.

27 Leah Rickard, "Ex-Soviet States Lead World in Ad Cynicism," *Advertising Age*, June 5, 1995, p. 3.

28 Ying Wang, Timothy J. Wilkinson, Nicolae Al. Pop and Sebastian A. Vaduva, "Romanian Consumers' Perceptions and Attitudes Toward Online Advertising," *Marketing Management Journal*, vol. 19 no. 1 (2009), pp. 73–83.

29 "Earned Advertising Remains Most Credible Among Consumers; Trust in Owned Advertising on the Rise," Nielsen, September 17, 2013.

30 Dagmar Mussey, "Mars Goes Local," *Ad Age Global*, May 10, 2002.

31 Kiran Karande, Khalid A. Almurshidee and Fahad Al-Olayan, "Advertising Standardization in Culturally Similar Markets," *International Journal of Advertising*, vol. 25, no. 4 (2006), pp. 489–512.

32 Christopher Woodward, "Got Spanish? Anita Santiago Helps Advertisers Bridge the Gap Between Anglo and Latino Cultures," *Business Week*, August 14, 2000, p. F12.

33 Jim Pickard, "Coca-Cola to Use Welsh in Adverts," *Financial Times*, July 6, 2000.

34 Michelle R. Nelson and Hye-Jin Paek, "A Content Analysis of Advertising in a Global Magazine Across Seven Countries," *International Marketing Review*, vol. 24, no. 1 (2007), pp. 64–86.

35 "McDonald's Strikes Sweeping International Music Deal," *Ad Age Online*, February 15, 2005.

36 Beverly Matthews, "Foreign Life Insurers Eye India," Reuters English News Service, April 3, 2001.

37 Dana Mattioli, "Liquor Makers Eye Turkey," *Wall Street Journal*, November 29, 2012, p. B8.

38 Robb M. Stewart, "Heineken Moves Step Up Beer Challenge in South Africa," *Wall Street Journal*, March 26, 2010, p. B5.

39 Evan Ramstad, "A New Look for South Korean Retail," *Wall Street Journal*, April 16, 2013, p. B8.

40 Kathy Chen, "Beyond the Traffic Report," *Wall Street Journal*, January 2, 2003, p. A9.

41 James T. Areddy, "Starbucks, Pepsico Bring 'Subopera' to Shanghai," *Wall Street Journal*, November 1, 2007, p. B1.

42 Margaret Cocker, "Dubai Pulls Out the Stops," *Wall Street Journal*, August 8, 2008, p. B8.

43 Eric Bellman and Tariq Engineer, "India Appears Ripe for Cellphone Ads," *Wall Street Journal*, March 10, 2008, p. B3.

44   Yung Kyun Choi, Jang-Sun Hwang and Sally J. McMillan, "Gearing Up for Mobile Advertising: A Cross-Cultural Examination of Key Factors that Drive Mobile Messages Home to Consumers," *Psychology & Marketing*, vol. 25, no. 8 (2008), pp. 756–768.

45   Dae Ryun Chang, "The 'We-Me' Culture: Marketing to Korean Consumers," *Advances in International Marketing*, vol. 18 (2007), pp. 145–161.

46   "Ad Industry Prepares for Big Transformation," *Industry Updates*, May 6, 2014.

47   Tatiana Koike, "The Seven Hottest Trends in Brazil's Online Market," *Latin Link*, January 16, 2012.

48   Shintaro Okazaki and Charles R. Taylor, "Social Media and International Advertising: Theoretical Challenges and Future Directions," *International Marketing Review*, vol. 30, no. 1 (2013), pp. 56–71.

49   "Middle East Online Advertising Report," *Middle East North Africa Financial Network*, February 19, 2014.

50   Sara Hamdan, "After Arab Spring, A Shift in Ads," *International Herald Tribune*, February 8, 2013, p. 14.

51   Global Cosmetics Industry, Gale Group, November 1, 2010.

52   Marye Tharp and Jaeseok Jeong, "The Global Network Communications Agency," *Journal of International Marketing*, vol. 9, no. 4 (2001), p. 113.

53   Michael Flagg, "Vietnam Opens Industry to Foreigners," *Wall Street Journal*, August 28, 2000, p. B8.

54   Betsy McKay, "Coke Hunts for Talent to Re-Establish Its Marketing Might," *Wall Street Journal*, March 6, 2002, p. B4.

Part 5

Managing the Global Marketing Effort

16 ORGANIZING FOR GLOBAL MARKETING   505

Chapter 16

Organizing for Global Marketing

ELEMENTS THAT AFFECT A GLOBAL MARKETING ORGANIZATION 507

TYPES OF ORGANIZATIONAL STRUCTURES 511

CONTROLLING THE GLOBAL ORGANIZATION 523

CONFLICT BETWEEN HEADQUARTERS AND SUBSIDIARIES 525

CONSIDERING A GLOBAL MARKETING CAREER 527

3M created its international operations group in 1951, launching subsidiaries in Australia, Canada, France, Germany, Mexico and the United Kingdom. Forty years later it became the first foreign firm to have a wholly owned subsidiary in China. Today, two-thirds of the company's sales are outside the United States, and many of its managers have worked in a foreign country. Yet despite its long history as an international firm, 3M still grapples with the question of how best to organize itself.

Over the years, 3M developed an organizational matrix—several structures superimposed on one another. Managers of country subsidiaries shared responsibility with division managers located at headquarters in St. Paul, Minnesota. Disagreements over strategy sometimes arose. Subsidiary managers sought to maximize total sales and profits in their countries. Division managers sought to maximize the global sales and profits of their product lines. However, most conceded that the country managers often exercised the greater power. In this respect, some were concerned that 3M had been left behind. Most other global firms had centralized power over the past 20 years.[1] Despite the company's dedication to its unique organization, a survey of 3M managers revealed that many believed the matrix structure had the potential to dilute accountability, hamper collaboration and create duplication of effort.[2]

An important aspect of global marketing is the establishment of an appropriate organization. The organization must be able to formulate and implement strategies for each local market and for the global market as well. The objective is to develop a structure and control system that will enable the firm to respond to distinct variations in each market while applying the relevant experience that the company has gained in other markets and with other products. To be successful, companies need to find a proper balance between these two needs. A number of organizational structures are suitable for different internal and external environments. No one structure is best for all situations.

Learning Objectives

After studying this chapter, you should be able to:

- ➤ list and explain the internal and external factors that affect how global organizations are structured and managed;
- ➤ note the advantages and disadvantages of the different ways of structuring a firm with international sales;
- ➤ discuss global mandates, and note how global mandates can affect a firm's organization;
- ➤ explain why organizational issues for born-global firms differ from those for traditional multinational corporations (MNCs);
- ➤ give examples of how technology can be utilized to support internal global communications systems;
- ➤ list and explain the elements of an effective global control strategy;
- ➤ discuss the conflicts that can arise between international headquarters and national subsidiaries;
- ➤ consider a career in global marketing.

Elements That Affect a Global Marketing Organization

The success of a global strategy will be acutely influenced by the selection of an appropriate organization to implement that strategy. The structure of an international organization should be congruent with the tasks to be performed, the need for product knowledge and the need for market knowledge. The ideal structure of such an organization should be a function of the products or services to be sold in the marketplace, as well as of the external and internal environments. Theoretically, the way to develop a global marketing organization is to analyze the specific tasks to be accomplished within an environment and then to design a structure that will support these tasks most effectively. A number of other factors complicate the selection of an appropriate organization, however. In most cases, a company already has an existing organizational structure. As the internal and external environments change, companies will need to reevaluate that structure. The search for an appropriate organizational structure must balance local responsiveness against global integration. It is important that global managers understand the strengths and weaknesses of different organizational structures as well as the factors that usually lead to change in the structure.

Corporate Goals

Every company needs a mission. The mission is the business's framework—the values that drive the company and the vision it has for itself. The mission statement is the glue that holds the company together. Yahoo asserts that its mission is "to connect people to their passions, their communities, and the world's knowledge."[3] Starbucks' mission is "to inspire and nurture the human spirit—one person, one cup, and one neighborhood at a time."[4] Reconsidering a firm's mission can result in organizational change. When Bayer introduced a new mission statement emphasizing innovation and sustained growth, the company also announced a structural realignment to better attain these goals. Three global product divisions—health care, nutrition and high-tech materials—were established.[5]

After declaring its mission, no company should begin establishing an international organization until it has reviewed and established its strategies and objectives. Some global firms even include strategy statements in their missions. Corporate leaders have at times developed strategic visions with slogans such as "Encircle Caterpillar" for Komatsu and "Beat Xerox" for Canon. If the head of a company can instill this sense of winning throughout the firm, it will inspire the organization to excel and achieve far greater goals.

Corporate Worldview

Corporate management can adopt one of several worldviews concerning global markets. These worldviews, or orientations, will significantly affect the choice of organizational structure. Some firms adopt an ethnocentric orientation. Management is centered on the home market. Ideas that emanate from there are considered superior to those that arise from the foreign subsidiaries.

Headquarters tells its subsidiaries what to do and solicits little or no input from the subsidiaries themselves. Top managers in the foreign subsidiaries are most often managers sent from headquarters on relatively short-term assignments.

Alternatively, corporate management can take a polycentric orientation, wherein each market is considered unique. This is at the heart of the multidomestic strategies discussed in Chapter 1. Local subsidiaries are given great leeway to develop and implement their own strategies. Little or no interdependencies arise among subsidiaries. Management positions in local subsidiaries are usually filled by local nationals. Some polycentric firms evolve a focus that is regional rather than national. Geographic regions such as Europe and Latin America, rather than single national markets, are seen as possessing unique features that require separate marketing strategies. Decision-making becomes centralized at the regional level, but regions still remain relatively independent of headquarters and of one another. A geocentric orientation returns power to global headquarters, but this orientation is very distinct from an ethnocentric orientation.

World Beat 16.1

Where's Headquarters?

Lenovo used to be a Chinese computer company headquartered in China. That changed after it acquired IBM's personal computer business. The company is incorporated in Hong Kong but sales headquarters are divided among Paris, Beijing, Singapore and Morrisville, North Carolina. The company claims to have forgone a traditional headquarters model and focuses instead on centers of excellence around the world. Similarly, Procter & Gamble decided to move its global headquarters for skincare, cosmetics and personal care from its home country location in Cincinnati, Ohio, to Singapore in response to growing demand in Asia and decelerating demand in the United States.

Why do global firms move their headquarters out of their home countries? The motives are varied, but the top reasons appear to be markets, mergers and acquisitions and, of course, tax evasion. After Tyco International moved to tax-haven Bermuda, the United States passed a law making it harder to move abroad to avoid taxes. There was a public outcry of tax evasion when oil services company Halliburton split its CEO and headquarters between Houston and Dubai. Management rejected these claims, noting that the company was still incorporated in the United States. Management further asserted that the shift of headquarters overseas was motivated by the company's new emphasis on developing international markets.

But when it comes to value for money, it is hard to beat New York City as a site for global headquarters. NYC is rated number one among top global cities for business activity and human capital. It only ranks 26th for cost of living.

Sources: "P&G Moves Person Care Hub to Asia," *Financial Times*, May 10, 2012; Jason Chow, "The World's Most Expensive City Is . . . ," *Wall Street Journal*, March 4, 2014; Halliburton Corporate Profile, www.halliburton.com, accessed March 14, 2014; and Lenovo-Locations, www.lenovo.com, accessed March 14, 2014.

A geocentric firm focuses on global markets as a whole rather than on its domestic market. Good ideas can come from any country, and the firm strives to keep communication lines open among its various units. Even top management at corporate headquarters is likely to come from many nations. Most important, all national units, including the domestic one, must consider what is best for the whole organization and act accordingly.

Other Internal Forces

Other internal factors can also affect the international marketing organization. These factors include the volume and diversity of the firm's international business, its economic commitment to international business, the available human resources, flexibility within the company and home-country culture.

Importance of International Sales

The size and importance of a firm's international business affect its organizational structure. If only a small percentage of sales (1 to 10 percent) is international, a company will tend to have a simple organization such as an export department. As the proportion of international sales increases relative to total sales, a company is likely to evolve from having an export department to having an international division and then to having a worldwide organization. Companies may even consider moving global headquarters out of the home country as overseas sales become increasingly important. Oil services company, Halliburton, moved part of its global headquarters from Houston to Dubai to be closer to its growing business in the Middle East and Asia.[6]

Diversity of International Markets Served

As the number and diversity of international markets increase, it becomes necessary to have a more complex organization to manage the marketing effort, and it requires a larger number of people to understand the markets and implement the strategies.

Level of Economic Commitment

A company that is unwilling or unable to allocate adequate financial resources to its international efforts will not be able to sustain a complex or costly international structure. The less expensive organizational approaches to international marketing usually result in less control by the company at the local level. It is extremely important to build an organization that will provide the flexibility and resources to achieve the corporation's long-term goals for international markets.

Human Resources

Available and capable personnel are just as vital to a firm as financial resources. Some companies send top domestic executives to foreign operations only to find that these expatriates do not understand the nation's culture. The hiring of local executives is also difficult, because competition for such people can be extremely intense. Motorola puts hundreds of executives through workplace simulation exercises to try to identify the best candidates with the necessary international management skills to run a global business.[7] Because people are such an important resource in international organizations, a lack of appropriate personnel can constrain a firm's organizational growth.

Flexibility

When a company devises an organizational structure, it must build in some flexibility, especially to be prepared in case reorganization becomes necessary in the future. A study of the implementation of a global strategy for 17 products found that organizational flexibility was one of the keys to success.[8] The structure must be flexible enough to respond to the needs of consumers and the challenges of global competitors. Even companies that establish a perfect design for the present find themselves in trouble later on when the firm grows or declines.

Home-Country Culture

The home country of a MNC may also affect its organization. For example, appointing foreign managers to the position of chief executive is relatively rare in continental Europe. It is more common in Great Britain and the United States. McDonald's appointed an Australian as CEO, and Coca-Cola appointed an Irishman as CEO. The foreign CEO may be more common in the United States for several reasons. As we saw in Chapter 3, U.S. culture is more individualistic and, consequently, open to foreigners. Furthermore, foreign-born managers began seeking jobs in U.S. MNCs years ago as U.S. MNCs hired many foreigners to manage their many overseas subsidiaries. These managers often had to develop good English skills to advance, and many were willing to relocate overseas—including to the United States—in order to advance their careers.[9]

External Forces

A number of external factors can affect how global organizations are structured and managed. The most important of these are geographic distance, time zone differences, types of customers and government regulations. In the international environment, each issue should be examined to determine its effect on the organization.

Geographic Distance

Technological innovations have somewhat eased the problems associated with physical distance. Companies, primarily in the United States and other developed countries, enjoy such conveniences as next-day mail and e-mail, facsimile machines, videoconferencing, mobile phones, mobile data transmissions, rapid transportation and, of course, the Internet. However, these benefits cannot be taken for granted in international operations. Distance becomes a distinct barrier when operations are established in less developed countries, where the telecommunications infrastructure may be more primitive. Moreover, companies invariably find it necessary to have key personnel make trips to engage in face-to-face conversations. Organizations in the same region are often grouped together to help minimize travel costs and the travel time of senior executives. Technology has shortened, but not eliminated, the distance gap.

Time Zones

One problem even high technology cannot solve is time differences. Managers in New York who reach an agreement over lunch will have a hard time finalizing the deal with their headquarters in London until the following day, because by that time, most executives in England will be on their way home for the evening. The five-hour time difference results in lost communication time and impedes rapid results. E-mail has contributed substantially to the interaction among far-flung units, but adaptations still need to be made. Brady Corporation of Milwaukee produces industrial sign and printing equipment. About 45 percent of its sales are outside the United States. Managers in Milwaukee commonly take conference calls at 6 a.m. and place calls late at night to catch the company's Asian managers during their workdays.[10]

Types of Customers

Companies may need to take their "customer profiles" into account in structuring their global marketing organizations. Companies that serve a very few, geographically concentrated global customers will organize their global marketing efforts differently from firms that serve a large number of small customers in country after country. For example, if a firm has key global customers, it may adjust its organization and select its office locations according to where its customers are located. Many companies that sell equipment or parts to automotive firms maintain marketing units near major concentrations of automotive activity, such as Detroit and Stuttgart, Germany. Supplier parks sit adjacent to Ford manufacturing sites in Spain, Germany and Brazil.[11] On the other hand, companies that sell to large numbers of customers tend to maintain more regional, or even country-specific, organizations, with relatively less centralization. Similarly, if customer needs or competition varies greatly from country to country, there is less impetus to centralize.

Government Regulations

How various countries attract or discourage foreign operations can affect the structure of the global organization. Laws involving imports, exports, taxes and hiring differ from country to country. Local taxes, statutory holidays and political risk can deter a company from establishing a subsidiary or management center in a country. Some countries require a firm that establishes plants on their territory to hire, train and develop local employees and to share ownership with the government or local citizens. These requirements for local investment and ownership may dictate an organization that allows greater local decision-making.

Types of Organizational Structures

The global marketplace offers many opportunities. To take advantage of these opportunities, a company must evaluate its options, develop a strategy and establish an organization to implement the strategy. The organization should take into account all the factors affecting organizational design in determining which structure is best suited to its current strategic needs. In this section, we review the various options for international and global organizational structures.

Companies Without International Specialists

Many companies, when they begin selling products to foreign markets, operate without an international organization or even an international specialist. A domestically oriented company may receive inquiries from foreign buyers who saw an advertisement in a trade magazine or attended a domestic trade show. The domestic staff will respond to the inquiry in the same way they respond to any other. Product brochures will be sent to the potential buyer for review. If sufficient interest exists on the part of both buyer and seller, then more communication (e-mails, telephone calls, personal visits) may transpire. With no specific individual designated to handle international business, it may be directed to a sales manager, an inside salesperson, a product manager or an outside salesperson.

Companies without an international organization incur limited costs, but on the other hand, with no one responsible for international business, that business will probably provide little sales and profit. When the firm attempts to respond to the occasional inquiry, no one will understand the difficulties of translation into another language, the particular needs of the foreign customer, the transfer of funds, fluctuating exchange rates, shipping, legal liabilities or the other many differences between domestic and international business. As the number of international inquiries grows or management recognizes the potential in international markets, international specialists will have to be added to the domestic organization.

International Specialists and Export Departments

The complexities of selling a product to a variety of different countries prompt most domestically oriented firms to establish some international expertise. This can vary from retaining a part-time international specialist to having a full complement of specialists organized into an export department. Figure 16.1 is a sample organization chart for an organization operating with an international specialist.

International specialists and export departments primarily perform a sales function. They respond to inquiries, manage exhibits at international trade shows and handle export documentation, shipping, insurance and financial matters. International specialists may also maintain contact with embassies, export financing agencies and various departments of commerce. The international specialist or export department may use an export agent, an export management company or import intermediaries to assist in the process.

Hiring international specialists gives firms the ability to respond to and process foreign business. The size of this type of organization will be directly related to the amount of international business handled. The costs should be minor when compared to the potential.

However, international specialists and export departments are often reactive rather than proactive in nature. They usually respond to inquiries. Few evaluate the worldwide demand for a product or service, identify opportunities or develop a global strategy. Also, because international sales are so small, the international specialist may have little opportunity to modify current products or services to meet international market needs. In most cases, products are sold as is, with no modification.

512

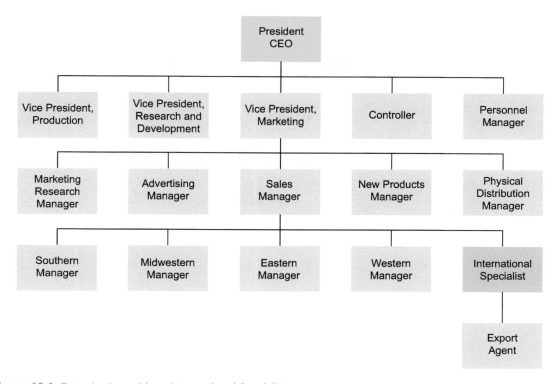

Figure 16.1 Organization with an International Specialist

International Divisions

As sales to foreign markets become more important to the company, and the complexity of coordinating the international effort extends beyond the capacity of a specialist or an export department, the firm may establish an international division. The international division normally reports to the president. This gives it equal status with other functions such as marketing, finance and production. Figure 16.2 illustrates the organizational design of a firm using an international division.

International divisions are directly involved in the development and implementation of global strategy. Heads of international divisions have marketing managers, sales managers and perhaps even production managers reporting to them. These divisions focus all their efforts on international markets. As a result, they are often successful at increasing international sales.

The international division actively seeks out market opportunities in foreign countries. The sales and marketing efforts in each country are supported through regional or local offices. These offices understand the local environments, including legal requirements, customer needs and competition. This close contact with the market improves the organization's ability to perform successfully. The use of an international division may be particularly appropriate for a firm with many different product lines or businesses. When none of these divisions has extensive experience outside the domestic market, all foreign business may be combined into the international division.

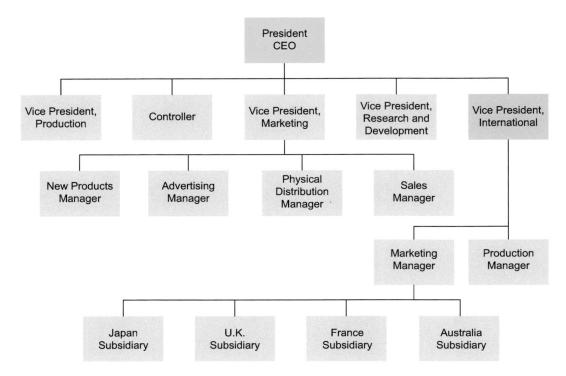

Figure 16.2 Organization with an International Division

When Robert Iger (later CEO of Disney) became head of the company's new international division, Disney's international operations represented only 20 percent of corporate sales and even less of profits. Mr. Iger soon discovered that the company's disorganized forays into foreign markets had resulted in a lack of synergy between different divisions resulting in overlap and lack of coordination. In Japan, the manager in charge of Disney's studio division didn't even know who ran the television division. In addition, local managers complained that product decisions were being made at headquarters in Burbank, California with little regard to local tastes. Over the next decade, the international division allowed local managers to make more decisions and recruit partners to help develop more culturally attuned products.[12]

Worldwide or Global Organizations

As a firm recognizes the potential size of the global market, it begins to change from a domestic company with some business overseas to a worldwide company pursuing a global strategy. At this point, international divisions are superseded by new global structures. A company can choose to organize in terms of one of three dimensions: geography, function or product. The matrix organization, another possible type of worldwide organization, combines two or more of these dimensions.

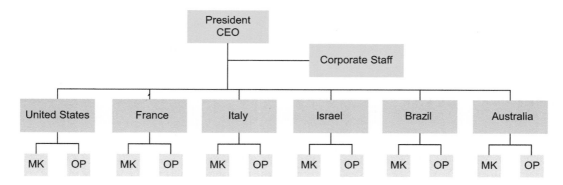

Figure 16.3 Country-Based Geographic Organization

MK = Marketing
OP = Operation

Geographic Organizational Structures

The geographic organizational design is appropriate when the company needs an intimate knowledge of its customers and their environments. Such a design gives the company an opportunity to understand the local culture, economy, politics, laws and competitive situation. Geographic organizational structures can be either regionally focused or country-based structures.

COUNTRY-BASED ORGANIZATIONS   The second type of geographic organization is the country-based organization, which utilizes a separate unit for each country. Figure 16.3 illustrates a simple country-based geographic organization.

A country-based organization resembles a regional structure, except that the focus is on single countries rather than on a group of countries. For example, instead of having a regional management center in Brussels overseeing all European sales and operations, the company has an organizational unit in each country. The country-based organization can be extremely sensitive to local customs, laws and needs, all of which may differ considerably even though the countries participate in a regional organization such as the EU or NAFTA.

One difficulty that plagues a country-based organization is its higher costs. Therefore, it is important to ensure that the benefits of a local organization offset its cost. Coordination with headquarters can also prove difficult. If a company is involved in 40 countries, it can be cumbersome to have all 40 country-based organizational units reporting to one or a few people in the company's headquarters. Furthermore, country managers too often duplicate efforts. Before Unilever abandoned its emphasis on national market autonomy, its Chinese and Hong Kong subsidiaries each developed their own formulations for shampoo despite the fact that hair and hair-washing habits were nearly identical in the two markets.[13]

Country organizations are being phased out or reduced as regional organizations emerge. For example, in response to the signing of NAFTA, many firms began to integrate their separate organizations for Canada, the United States and Mexico. Among these was Lego, the Danish toy-maker. Lego reduced the responsibility of its Canadian operation and combined some executive positions at its Enfield, Connecticut, operation. At the same time, it decided to develop its Mexican market from the U.S. location as well. Other firms have chosen the same path, integrating their Canadian subsidiaries with their U.S. companies and developing their Mexican markets from the U.S. base.

REGIONAL MANAGEMENT CENTERS Regional management centers enable an organization to focus on particular regions of the world, such as Europe, the Middle East, Latin America, North America, the Caribbean or the Far East. Figure 16.4 illustrates the regional structure of a worldwide geographic organization.

The reasons for using a regional geographic approach to organizational design are related to market similarity and size. A group of countries that are located close together and have similar social and cultural histories, climates, resources and (sometimes) languages may have many similar needs for products. Sometimes these regional country groups have unified themselves for political and economic reasons. The EU and Mercosur are such regional groupings. Also, once a market

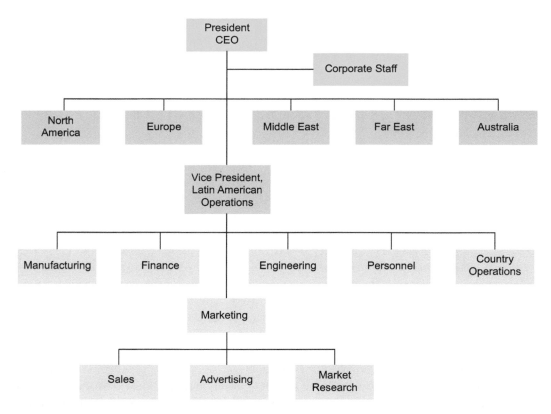

Figure 16.4 Geographic Organization by Region

reaches a certain size, the firm must employ a staff dedicated to maximizing revenues from that area of the world and to protecting the firm's assets there.

Regional management can respond to local conditions and react faster than a totally centralized organization where all decisions are made at global headquarters. At the same time, a regional organization captures some of the benefits associated with greater centralization. In Europe, many large international companies were originally organized on a national basis. The national organizations, including those in France, Germany, Italy and the United Kingdom, often were coordinated loosely through European headquarters. The development of a single European market caused companies to rethink their European organizations often to reduce the role of the national organization in favor of a stronger pan-European management. A major benefit of a regional or pan-European structure is reduced operational costs. In addition, a study of Western European and U.S.-based firms with significant operations in Central and Eastern Europe revealed that regional management centers are an attractive organizational device to exploit market similarities and supply local offices with additional support and expertise.[14]

Regional organizations have their disadvantages, however. First, regional organization implies that many functions are duplicated at the different regional head offices. Such duplication tends to add significantly to costs. This may be one reason why Avon reorganized six business units into only two—the Developed Market Group (including North America, Western Europe, Africa and the Middle East) and the Developing Market Group (including Latin America, Central and Eastern Europe and Asia Pacific).[15]

A second serious disadvantage is that regional organizations inherently divide global authority. In a purely regionally organized company, only the CEO has true global responsibility. Developing global marketing strategies for products or services is difficult, because regional managers tend to focus on a limited regional perspective.

OTHER GEOGRAPHIC ORGANIZATIONAL OPTIONS Many firms combine the concepts of regional and country-based organizations, as shown in Figure 16.5. And increasingly, MNCs set up sub-regional headquarters such as a Greater China sub-regional headquarters under an Asian regional headquarters.[16]

Combining regional and country-based or sub-regional approaches minimizes many of the limitations of both designs, but it also adds an additional layer of management. Some executives think that superimposing a regional headquarters makes the country-level implementation of strategy more cumbersome rather than improving it. In order for the company to benefit from a regional center in such a combined approach, there must be some value in a regional strategy. Each company must reach its own decision regarding the proper geographic organization design, its cost and its benefits.

Functional Organizational Structures

A second way of organizing a global firm is by function. In such an organization, the top executives in marketing, finance, production, accounting and research and development (R&D) all have worldwide responsibilities. For international companies, this type of organization is best for narrow or homogeneous product lines, with little variation between products or geographic markets. As

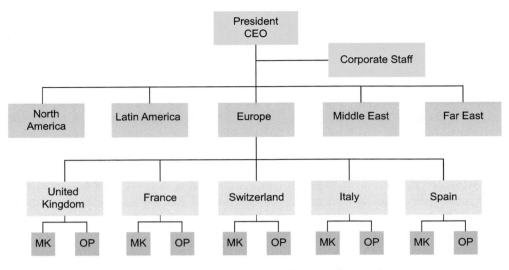

Figure 16.5 Organization Using Both Country-Based Units and Regionally Based Structure

MK = Marketing
OP = Operations

Note: Country organizations similar to those shown for the European center would be under each regional office.

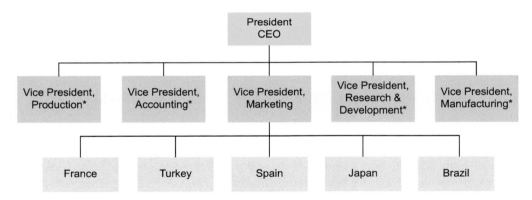

Figure 16.6 Functional Global Organization

*Each functional vice president has managers of that function in the countries served reporting to him or her, as illustrated with the Vice President, Marketing.

shown in Figure 16.6, the functional organization has a simple structure. Each functional manager has worldwide responsibility for that function. Usually, the manager supervises people responsible for the function in regions or countries around the world.

Ford Motor Company abandoned its regional structure for a functional one. Previously, Ford had major operating units in North America, Europe, Latin America, Africa and Asia. Each regional unit was responsible for its own operations, developing and producing cars for its regional markets. Faced with strong competition from the more efficient Japanese companies such as Toyota, Ford realized that under its regional setup it incurred a massive penalty for unnecessary duplication of key functions and efforts. Even though Ford served almost identical customer needs in many countries, the company was developing separate power trains and engines and was purchasing different component parts.

The new organization of Ford Automotive called for four major functions—marketing and sales, manufacturing, purchasing, and product development. The most important function was vehicle development, structured around five development centers in the United States and in Europe. The development center for small cars was located in Europe with locations in both Germany and the United Kingdom. The United States received the development centers for rear-wheel-drive cars and commercial trucks, all with global development responsibility. Some 25,000 Ford managers either moved from one location to another or were reassigned to report to new supervisors. The company expected to cut development costs by using fewer components, fewer engines and fewer power trains, as well as by speeding up development cycles. As a result of this reorganization, Ford projected savings of $2–$3 billion per year.

Still, the reorganization was soon undergoing modifications. Ford's then chairman, Jacques Nasser, decided to return some power to Ford's regional business units. The move was made to enable Ford to respond more quickly to consumer trends. It would allow managers on the ground to respond quickly without waiting for direction from headquarters.

Product Organizational Structures

A third type of worldwide marketing organization is based on product line rather than on function or geographic area (see Figure 16.7). Under this structure, each product group is responsible for marketing, sales, planning and (in some cases) production and R&D. Other functions, such as legal, accounting and finance, can be included in the product group or performed by the corporate staff. Both Procter & Gamble, a leading global U.S. consumer products company, and Kraft Foods, a leading U.S. food company, have adopted the global product organization.

A firm may choose to organize by product line for several reasons. Structuring by product line is common for companies with several unrelated product lines. A product focus is also appropriate when the differences involved with marketing the various product lines are greater than the perceived differences between the geographic markets. Typically, the end users for a product organization vary by product line, so there is no advantage in having the same group handle marketing for the different product lines.

A product organization concentrates management attention on the product line, which is an advantage when the product line constantly changes with advancements in technology. Headquarters can develop global products and arrange global rollouts. A product organization is effective in monitoring competition that is globalized rather than localized. Also, the firm can add new product groups as it adds new, unrelated products through acquisition.

The product organization has limitations as well. Knowledge of specific geographic areas can be limited, because each product group may not be able to afford to maintain a large local

519

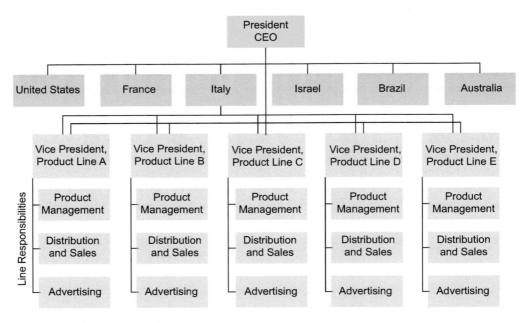

Figure 16.7 Global Product Organization

Note: Product-line managers in national subsidiaries report directly to their product-line managers at headquarters.

presence in each market. Because decision-making becomes more centrally located under a product structure, sensitivity to local market conditions can be diminished. This lack of knowledge and sensitivity may cause the company to miss local market opportunities. The top managers of international product divisions can themselves present a problem, particularly if they are promoted from the domestic side of the business. They can be ethnocentric and relatively uninterested in or uneasy with international markets.

Also, if each product group goes its own way, the company's international development may result in inefficiencies. For example, two product divisions may be purchasing advertising space independently in the same magazine. This will prove more expensive than combining the purchases. To offset such inefficiencies, some companies supplement their worldwide product organizations with global units that provide for coordination of activities such as advertising and customer service across countries.

Matrix Organizational Structures

As the Ford example suggests, some companies have grown frustrated with the limitations of a one-dimensional geographic, functional or product organization structure. To overcome these drawbacks, the matrix organization was developed. As shown in Figure 16.8, the matrix organization allows for two or more dimensions of theoretically equal weight (here, geographic and product dimensions) in the organizational structure and in decision-making responsibility. A matrix organization often includes both product and geographic management components. Product

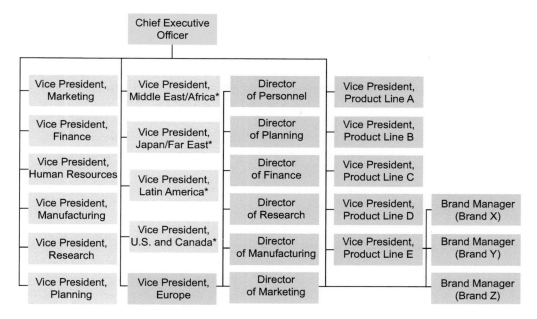

Figure 16.8 Matrix Organization

*Each regional vice president has functional managers reporting to him or her, as illustrated for the Vice President, Europe.

Note: Product-line vice presidents report to both Vice President, Marketing and their respective regional presidents.

management has worldwide responsibility for a specific product line, whereas geographic management is responsible for all product lines in a specific geographic area. These management structures overlap at the national product/market level. A matrix organization structure has a dual rather than a single chain of command, which means that many individuals will have two superiors. Under this organizational structure, the brand managers for brands X, Y and Z in any European country would report directly to two different bosses—vice president product line E and the director of marketing for Europe.

Firms tend to adopt matrix organizations when they need to be highly responsive to two dimensions (such as product and geography). But matrix organizations are not without their challenges. Some critics of Unilever's matrix structure complained that its complexity—with some managers in charge of product categories, others in charge of brands and still others in charge of geographic areas—resulted in duplication of authority and confusion of responsibility.[17] Power struggles are a common problem, especially when a matrix organization is first established. Relationships are tested as each side of the matrix attempts to "find its place" in the organization. In fact, the key to successful matrix management is the degree to which managers in an organization can resolve conflict and achieve the successful implementation of plans and programs. The matrix organization requires a change in management behavior from traditional authority to an influence system based on technical competence, interpersonal sensitivity and leadership.

The matrix organization also requires a substantial investment in dual budgeting, accounting, transfer pricing and personnel evaluation systems. Matrix structures may become even harder to manage as a result of corporate downsizing. Shrinking staffs add to the difficulties surrounding the multiplicity of bosses. Most companies have cut the assistants or liaison personnel who used to smooth things out and made sure everyone could get together on a certain day. As a result, some managers with more than one boss are now saddled with more work coordinating meetings and assignments, increasing their already heavy workloads.[18] Nonetheless, the additional complexity and cost of a matrix organization can sometimes be offset by the benefits of the dual focus. Overall, the matrix structure can permit an organization to function better in an uncertain and changing environment.

Global Mandates

Whichever structure a firm employs, the question of who should administer global mandates remains an important concern. A global mandate is the expressed assignment to carry out a task on a global scale. As such, they often fit poorly into established organizations and lines of communication. Global mandates may be assigned to individual managers or to newly created global teams. In either case, responsibility can extend across functions and across all geographic locations, and the teams or marketing managers often make decisions that can affect all national subsidiaries. We have already discussed two types of global mandates—global brand management (Chapter 11) and global account management (Chapter 14). Global mandates can also be of a temporary nature, such as a team to determine how to respond to a major change in product technology.

Organization of the Born-Global Firm

In Chapter 8 we introduced the concept of born-global firms. From their inception, or very shortly thereafter, these new firms target global markets. Almost immediately, international sales account for a large proportion of their total sales. There are several explanations for this phenomenon. Entrepreneurs are increasingly exposed to global opportunities as a result of the communications revolution. Many global entrepreneurs have themselves worked or studied in foreign countries. Many realize that their customers and competition are global. A large number of global startups can be found in Silicon Valley, where rapidly changing technologies encounter worldwide demand.

Born globals can benefit from the fact that they have no organizational history. Other firms have traditionally passed through several structural reorganizations as they evolved into global firms. Born-global firms can adopt global organizations from the start. This is enviable in that structural change can entail heavy costs and business disruptions. However, there is something to be said for the more traditional, gradual evolution of a global organization. Firms that move into international markets more slowly can build up market and cultural knowledge over time. They cultivate and support ever more extensive worldwide organizations by recruiting and training knowledgeable and experienced managers and staff. Born globals attempt to do this practically overnight and can find their managerial resources stretched to the limit. As is the case with other entrepreneurial ventures, they can find themselves with fewer assets than opportunities.

Controlling the Global Organization

As an international company becomes larger and more globally focused, maintaining control of international operations becomes increasingly important. Establishing a system to control marketing activities in numerous markets is not an easy job. However, if companies expect to implement their global strategies, they must establish a control system to regulate the many activities within their organizations.

Elements of a Control Strategy

Control is a cornerstone of organization. Control provides the means to direct, regulate and manage business operations. The implementation of a global marketing program requires a significant amount of interaction not only among various national subsidiaries but also among the individual areas of marketing, such as product development and advertising, and among the other functional areas, such as production and R&D. The control system is used to measure these business activities along with competitive and market reactions. Deviations from the planned activities and results are analyzed and reported so that corrective action can be taken.

A control system has three basic elements: (1) the establishment of standards, (2) the measurement of performance against those standards and (3) the analysis and correction of any deviations from the standards. Although control is a conceptually simple aspect of the organization process, a wide variety of problems arise in international situations, resulting in inefficiencies and intracompany conflict.

Developing Standards

Corporate goals are achieved through the effective implementation of a marketing strategy in the international firm's many national markets. Standard setting is driven by these corporate goals. Standards must be clearly defined, universally accepted and understood by managers throughout the global organization. The standards should be set through joint deliberations involving corporate headquarters' personnel and each local marketing organization. Normally, the standard setting is done annually when the operational business plan is established.

Firms can employ both performance and behavioral standards. Performance standards refer to market outcomes. They extend beyond financial data and might include sales by product line, market shares, product trial rates by customers, innovation and customer satisfaction. Behavioral standards refer to actions taken within the firm. They can include the type and amount of advertising to be developed and utilized, the market research to be performed and the prices to be charged for a product. Behavioral standards also apply to ethical conduct within the firm. After Wal-Mart revealed that it was conducting an internal investigation of possible violations of the U.S. Foreign Corrupt Practices Act in India, the global retailer sought to establish clearer behavioral standards concerning questionable payments to government officials. Wal-Mart hired a U.S. law firm and global auditing firm KPMG to develop compliance procedures in accordance with U.S. law and provide training to nearly 1,700 employees in India.[19]

Measuring and Evaluating Performance

After standards are set, performance must be monitored. In order to monitor performance against standards, management must be able to observe current performance. Much of the numerical information, such as sales and expenses, will be reported through the accounting system. Other items, such as the implementation of an advertising program, will be communicated through a report. At times, personal visits and meetings may be advisable when management is attempting to evaluate more complex issues, such as the success or failure of coordinated national actions against a global competitor.

Correcting Deviations from the Standards

The purpose of establishing standards and reporting performance is to ensure achievement of corporate goals. To achieve these goals, management must evaluate how well performance is living up to the standards the company has set and must initiate corrective action when performance is below those standards. However, control systems within MNCs must also take into account the different attitudes toward rules across cultures. Rule-centered societies such as the United States and Great Britain believe that rules have global application. Relationship-centered countries like China, Russia and India value bonds with family and friends above abstract rules. In such cultures, headquarters' attempt to correct performance or modify behavior may conflict with the local subsidiary's desire to preserve valued relationships with its employees.[20] As a consequence of distance, communication issues and cultural differences, the control process can be difficult in the international setting.

Control strategy can be related to the principle of the carrot and the stick: using both positive and negative incentives. On the positive side, outstanding performance can be rewarded with increased independence, more marketing dollars and salary increases or bonuses for the managers. On the negative side, unsatisfactory performance can mean reduction in all those items, as well as the threat that the managers responsible will lose their jobs. The key to correcting deviations is to get managers to understand and agree with the standards and then ensure that they have the means to correct the deficiencies. Therefore the managers are often given some flexibility with resources. For example, if sales are down 10 percent, managers may need the authority to increase advertising or reduce prices to offset the sales decline.

Communication Systems

Effective communication systems facilitate control. Global strategies that require standardization and coordination across borders will need an effective communication system to support them. Headquarters' staff will need to receive timely and accurate local input from national subsidiaries. Then decisions can be made quickly and transmitted back to the local management for rapid implementation.

Global information networks are now available that allow improved communication around the world. The Internet links millions of computer users and reduces many of the constraints imposed by geography. For example, Siemens operates in 190 countries and has instituted an internal system, or "sharenet," for posting knowledge throughout the global company. The sharenet came in handy when Siemens Malaysia wanted to bid on a high-speed data network linking Kuala Lumpur and its new airport. Lacking the know-how necessary for such a project, the subsidiary turned to the sharenet and discovered that Siemens was already working on a similar project in Denmark.[21]

Corporate Culture as Control

In addition to the processes we have described, many international firms attempt to establish cultural control. If an international firm can establish a strong corporate culture across its subsidiaries, then managers from its various units share a single vision and values. Some believe that this corporate socialization enables global firms to operate with less burdensome hierarchical structures and fewer time-consuming procedures.

Matsushita (Panasonic) provides managers with six months of cultural training, and Unilever's new hires go through corporate socialization as well. Such initiation programs help to build the vision and shared values of a strong corporate culture. Managers also receive ongoing training. For example, Unilever brings 400 to 500 international managers from around the world to its international management-training center. Unilever spends as much on training as it does on R&D, not only to upgrade skills but also to indoctrinate managers into the Unilever family. This helps build personal relationships and informal contacts that can be more powerful than any formal systems or structures.

We must remember that the corporate culture of a firm mirrors to a large extent the national culture of its homeland. When a U.S. MNC socializes its local managers to "think and act American," this can make communication and control within the MNC easier. Nonetheless, local managers must still operate within many national cultures that are different from the American culture. It is equally important that they maintain their local culture and remain capable of relating to local customers, competitors and governments. One way to encourage cultural sensitivity at the highest levels within a MNC is to include board members who are not from the home country of the firm. One study revealed that 90 percent of Europe's largest businesses have at least one director from outside their home countries. In the United States, however, this number was only 35 percent.[22]

Conflict Between Headquarters and Subsidiaries

Despite attempts to build a transnational corporate culture within MNCs, a universal problem facing international marketing managers is the internal conflict that arises between headquarters and subsidiaries. Table 16.1 summarizes several significant differences in perceptions of marketing issues between subsidiaries and home offices that emerged from a study of U.S. companies with operations in Hong Kong. The study also identified three areas in which subsidiaries perceived their autonomy as significantly less than did headquarters—pricing, logo and name, and the choice of an advertising agency.[23] This is probably not surprising given our prior discussion of the impact of global branding, increased price coordination worldwide and the trend among MNCs to consolidate advertising within one or a few agency networks.

Table 16.1 Perceptions of Issues Related to Marketing in Home Office and Subsidiaries

MARKETING ISSUE	HOME OFFICE	SUBSIDIARY
1. Visits from home office managers to subsidiaries are usually productive.	Agrees more	Agrees less
2. Problems come up frequently because the home office doesn't understand the variety of opinions that can exist at a subsidiary as a consequence of the more widely differing backgrounds there than at the home office.	Agrees less	Agrees more
3. Problems come up frequently because the home office doesn't understand that a subsidiary's culture can be different from that of the home office.	Agrees less	Agrees more
4. There is not enough emphasis at the subsidiaries on strategic thinking and long-term planning.	Agrees more	Agrees less
5. Subsidiaries are encouraged to suggest innovations to the home office.	Agrees more	Agrees less
6. The home office generally tries to change subsidiaries, rather than trying to understand and perhaps adapt to them.	Agrees less	Agrees more
7. Subsidiaries have enough flexibility to cope effectively with changing local conditions.	Agrees more	Agrees less
8. Knowledge is transmitted freely from the home office to subsidiaries.	Agrees more	Agrees less
9. There is a lack of carryover of marketing knowledge from one subsidiary to another.	Agrees more	Agrees less
10. The home office tries to involve subsidiaries' marketing managers meaningfully in decision making.	Agrees more	Agrees less

Source: Reprinted from *Journal of World Business* 36, no. 2, Chi-Fai Chan and Neil Bruce Holbert, "Marketing Home and Away," p. 207. Copyright © 2001, with permission from Elsevier.

Conflicts between headquarters and subsidiaries are inevitable because of the natural differences in orientation and perception between the two groups. The subsidiary manager usually wants more authority and more local differentiation, whereas headquarters wants more detailed reporting and greater unification of geographically dispersed operations. The parent is usually the more powerful in the relationship, but sometimes a subsidiary can take over a parent company. U.S. retailer Esprit watched its sales in the United States decline while sales in Asia and Europe soared to over $1 billion a year. Its Hong Kong office later bought full rights to the Esprit brand around the world for $150 million. Its first goal: revamp strategy in the U.S. market.[24]

Conflict is not all bad. Conflict generates constant dialogue between different organizational levels during the planning and implementation of strategies. This dialogue can result in a balance between headquarters and subsidiary authority, global and local perspective, and standardization and differentiation of the global marketing mix. And it can allow new and better ideas to surface from any part of the global organization.

Nigel Hollis, Chief Global Analyst at marketing research company Millward Brown, offers this advice:

At the end of the day, the key ingredient is trust. The local marketing team has to trust that the global team isn't going to overrule them unnecessarily, and global teams have to trust that the local team is looking out for the best interest of the brand.[25]

Considering a Global Marketing Career

A viable organizational structure, a unifying corporate culture and effective control systems all enable a firm to compete in the global arena. Equally important are the individuals who manage the firm. Throughout this book, we have presented the argument that virtually all firms are affected by increased global competition. In turn, most firms not only will deal with competitors from other countries but also will depend on sales that are increasingly multinational. Many will need to adapt to buyers who are becoming global themselves. Because of this, firms will need managers who understand the issues we have discussed here: the impact of the global environment on marketing, global strategic planning, managing a marketing mix across cultures and effectively managing relations between headquarters and subsidiaries to ensure that global strategy is well implemented. Any marketer who eventually reaches the upper echelons of management will need an understanding of the concepts we have covered in this book.

World Beat 16.2

Recruiting in Asia

As MNCs seek more local talent in China, local talent is increasingly looking toward careers with domestic firms. Previously top Chinese students sought jobs with MNCs because of relatively high pay and flexible working hours. Today Chinese companies are recognized as having advantages over their foreign rivals. Local companies are raising salaries and are seen as less likely to fire someone unless a big problem arises. In addition, Chinese companies are recruiting more aggressively and have even been known to woo the parents of students they try to recruit.

A survey of Chinese workers revealed that 47 percent preferred to work for a Chinese firm compared to only 24 percent who preferred a foreign firm. Five years earlier these numbers looked quite different: 9 percent preferred to work for a domestic firm and 42 percent preferred the foreign firm. This turnaround has led some foreign firms to reassess their position and offer more perks such as increased benefits and travel opportunities.

Despite the increased competition for managerial talent across Asia, there are relatively few Asians in the upper ranks of management at MNCs operating in the region. One reason may be a cultural preference to hire and promote managers from the home countries. However, local input into marketing strategies is increasingly important as companies expand beyond luxury segments and into smaller cities across Asia. In addition, expatriate hires are expensive. To address their growing need to groom Asians for top management, Wal-Mart launched a Global Leadership Institute to help Asian managers build the skills necessary to move into senior leadership roles.

Sources: Dana Mattioli, "China Recruiting Gets Harder," *Wall Street Journal Online*, May 23, 2011; Mariko Sanchanta and Riva Gold, "In Asia, Locals Rise Only So Far at Western Firms," *Wall Street Journal*, August 14, 2013, p. B6; and Lilian Lin and Paul Mozur, "Chinese Firms to Woo Coveted Workers," Dow Jones Top Global Market Stories, December 16, 2013.

MNCs recruit managers from both home and host countries. Most business schools in the United States now offer some global component in their curriculum and are increasing their offerings abroad often through alliances with foreign universities. However, recruiters note that an opportunity to go overseas while in school is rarely enough to qualify for a global position. Consulting firm Bain & Company looks for proficiency in another language and previous experience with international companies. Other recruiters seek cultural understanding and a willingness to relocate abroad.[26]

Recruiting local management talent is increasingly important to managing global marketing operations, and competition for this talent has pushed up local salaries. For example, salaries for mid-level Chinese executives working in high-tech MNCs in China doubled in just six years to an average of $300,000 annually.[27]

In many companies, global marketing is not always an entry-level job, especially for recent university graduates. Firms often choose to fill globally oriented positions with marketers who have first had domestic experience. A good career strategy is to join a company that has global operations and whose culture you admire. After proving yourself in the home market, you should be eligible for a global position in only a few years. This is especially true if you are assigned to the firm's headquarters. Informal networking with international executives can be a good way to broadcast your interest in international markets and global strategy—and companies are always in need of such motivated managers.

Besides this traditional route to a career in global marketing, there are other ways to go international—even at an entry level. Consider smaller companies that need help with international markets immediately. Born-global companies are increasingly common. Export management companies are another option. For these types of firms, skills in the local language of a key target market can make you stand out. If you are an American citizen, you might join the Peace Corps. The Peace Corps offers positions that are business oriented, and you receive language and cultural training. You can also look for a job with a foreign MNC that operates in your country. Even if you don't work with foreign markets right away, you will gain the experience of working with different cultures within your organization. Or consider positions in purchasing with a company that deals extensively with foreign suppliers. Knowing about global marketing can make you a more sophisticated buyer. Many U.S. managers in entry-level positions in purchasing or supply chain management find themselves flying to Mexico or the Far East to help manage the buyer–supplier relationship. Finally, government positions such as those with local or national commerce departments can provide excellent experience and can put you in touch with many corporate executives working in international markets.

Whether you choose a more traditional route to a career in global marketing or find a particular niche that is right for you, the need for a global mindset and the numbers of challenging and exciting positions for global marketers will only increase in the future.

Conclusion

Organizing the marketing efforts of a company across a number of countries is a difficult process. As the scope of a company's international business changes, its organizational structure must be modified in accordance with the internal and external environments. In this chapter, we have reviewed the various types of organizations commonly used, showing the benefits of each. The dynamic nature of business requires that a company constantly reevaluates its organizational structure and processes and makes any modifications necessary to meet the objectives of the firm.

The task of molding an organization to respond to the needs of a global marketplace also involves building a shared vision and developing human resources. A clear vision of the purpose of the company that is shared by everyone gives focus and direction to each manager. Managers can be a company's scarcest resource. A commitment to recruiting and developing managers who understand the complexities of global markets and the importance of cross-cultural sensitivity should help the international firm build a common vision and values, which in turn facilitates the implementation of a global strategy.

Managerial Takeaways

1. *People are responsible for any global marketing strategy. How a company organizes for global marketing will be critical to its success.*
2. *Structure should follow strategy. If a company needs to centralize authority, its structure should reflect this. If a company needs to decentralize authority, its structure should reflect this. This is true of a company's control system as well.*
3. *Increasingly the global nature of most industries suggests a shift toward centralization of authority. However, a company's local subsidiaries are its frontline. Subsidiary managers often have greater insights into both customers and competition.*
4. *Conflict between headquarters and subsidiaries has always existed and always will. It doesn't have to be a bad thing.*
5. *No organization is perfect. Flexibility should always be part of the culture of a MNC.*
6. *In the end, people make global marketing work. The right person in the right job can make all the difference.*

Questions for Discussion

1. How does a domestic organization evolve into an international organization? What type of international organization is likely to develop first? What type is likely to develop second? Why?
2. To achieve better international sales, which accounted for about 30 percent of total revenues, the U.S.-based toy manufacturer Mattel decided to put U.S. division heads in charge of international sales. Discuss the pros and cons of such a move in general and for a firm in the toy industry in particular.
3. Apart from its formal organizational structure, in what ways can the global company ensure that it is responding to the market and achieving efficiency, local responsiveness and global learning?
4. What are the advantages and limitations of using the Internet as a means of internal communication within a global organization?
5. What suggestions would you propose to bridge the gaps between headquarters and subsidiaries that are noted in Table 16.1?

CASE 16.1   How Local Should Coke Be?

For 20 years, Coke had expanded its soft-drinks business rapidly overseas. It had consolidated its bottling networks to cover increasingly large territories in response to an increasingly centralized retail trade. Many decisions about advertising and packaging were dictated from Atlanta. With the purchase of Minute Maid orange juice, Coke was hoping to gain economies of scale for global dominance in the juice business in addition to its presence in soft drinks.

Now Coke was rethinking its U.S.-based centralized approach to running its global business. For the first time in its history, Coke's top executives met together outside Atlanta headquarters. It was a harbinger of things to come. From now on, the Coke board would meet outside the United States once a year. This change was one of many instigated by Coke's CEO, Douglas Daft, who was attempting to turn the company around after two years of poor profits. Daft himself was an Australian who had attracted attention with his successful management of Coke's Japanese subsidiary, where his localization approach had built a successful tea and coffee business. Under Daft, Atlanta was envisioned as a support to Coke's national subsidiaries, rather than as the traditional central headquarters that would mandate and direct the company's worldwide operations. Coke would cease to be big, slow and out of touch and would instead be light on its feet and sensitive to local markets. One immediate effect of Daft's more localized strategy was the cutting of 2,500 jobs at Atlanta headquarters. Asian and Middle Eastern operations, previously managed out of Atlanta, would be transferred to Hong Kong and London, respectively.

The backlash against Coke's centralized approach first emerged in Europe, where the company sold 17 percent of its case volume of soft drinks. Europe's contribution to corporate profits was even higher. Two incidents caused Coke's new management to reconsider its European policy. As a result of various court rulings across Europe, Coke had to scale back significantly its attempt to buy Cadbury Schweppes's beverage brands. A contamination scare also forced Coke to destroy 17 million cases of Coke at a cost of $200 million. Amid the bad publicity arising from this incident, Coke was accused of being evasive and arrogant and of delaying too long in its response while waiting for direction from Atlanta.

Daft decided to break up responsibility for Europe, which had long been handled by a single division that oversaw 49 markets. Ten new geographic groups were formed on the basis of culturally and economically clustered markets. After all, what did Finland and Italy have in common? Furthermore, per-capita consumption of Coca-Cola beverage products varied greatly across European countries. France's per-capita consumption stood at 130 glasses a year. In Germany this number rose to 179 and in Spain to 303. Growth rates varied as well. In Italy, consumption doubled in ten years. Growth during the same period in Turkey was even greater. Consumption was up from 12 glasses per capita to 140.

In another break with the past, nine of the new European groups were to be run by non-Americans. Previously, half of the top executives in Europe had been sent over from the United States. Europe would be the test case to see whether Coke could get closer to its consumers by altering its organization. The new European groups were still under orders to push Coke's four core brands—Coca-Cola, Fanta, Sprite and Diet Coke—but they were encouraged to explore new products and develop flavors with local appeal. Germany responded with a berry-flavored Fanta, and Turkey developed a pear-flavored beverage.

Soon other changes were evident. The formal suits seen at headquarters in Atlanta were replaced by more informal attire. Local lawyers were employed instead of lawyers sent from the United States.

Reporters seeking a Coke spokesperson could contact expanded communications offices in European countries instead of having to contact Atlanta. Previously, only a single global website had been allowed; now, local subsidiaries could run their own websites. Coke's Belgian site—in Dutch, French and English—received three million hits in its first month. One manager noted that developing the website took only a few weeks, whereas it would have taken eight months under the old centralized system. Belgium was also the site for a new localized promotion idea. Coke hostesses were sent to discos at night to hand out bottles of Coke and promote the idea of a "Coke pause" in a night of otherwise hard drinking. A local spokesman supported the new promotional idea, noting that Belgians were party animals—something Atlanta headquarters might have been slow to appreciate.

Although a euphoric freedom appeared to spread across Europe, the success of the new organizational structure was less clear when it came to the bottom line. Sales slipped slightly in Europe just as localization was being put in place. Some believed that Coke's restructuring of Europe was an overreaction to some bad publicity. They argued that Coke would always be a foreign target. McDonald's had tried to assuage French farmers with a local purchasing campaign, only to meet with indifference. Was Coke doomed to face similar indifference as it attempted to localize? As for the contaminated-bottles crisis, a year later in Belgium, sales had returned to normal levels, and schools where students had reported getting sick had renewed their contracts with Coke. And Atlanta was sending further messages that there would be limits to localization. One top executive at the German operations was fired for running television advertisements aimed at the radical youth movement.

Another early challenge to localization would likely be Coke's launch of its sports drink Powerade in Europe. The sports-drink market in Europe was only $1 billion, compared to $61 billion in the United States, but it was growing fast. Competition in Europe was fragmented but included Powerade's archrival Gatorade, owned by Coke's archrival PepsiCo. Gatorade held 78 percent of the U.S. market and was strong in Europe as well. Powerade would essentially retain its American formula but would taste slightly different because of ingredient regulations of the EU. The new launch might possibly cannibalize Aquarius, Coke's other recent launch into the sports-drink market in Europe. However, a company spokesperson noted that Aquarius was meant to be drunk after exercising, whereas Powerade was to be drunk while exercising as well. At headquarters, managers envisioned the target market for their new introduction as European males age 13 to 29. Powerade was scheduled to debut in Europe in nine national markets—France, Germany, Greece, Hungary, Italy, Poland, Spain, Sweden and Turkey.

Discussion Questions

1. What are the pros and cons of changing Coke's single European structure into ten different regional groups?
2. Do you agree with Coke's firing of the executive in Germany? Why or why not? How should Coke avoid incidents like this in the future?
3. If you were the manager of Coke in Germany or Turkey, where would you invest your greatest effort: behind the launch of Powerade or behind the launch of your locally developed fruit-flavored drinks? What factors would guide your decision?
4. What suggestions would you offer to Coke about its global organizational structure and control?

5. Search Coca-Cola's corporate website to better understand the company's current organization within Europe. What does the current organization structure suggest about Coca-Cola's decision to localize control in Europe?

Sources: "How Local Should Coke Be?" in Kate Gillespie and H. David Hennessey, *Global Marketing* (Mason, OH: Cengage, 2011), pp. 487–489; William J. Holstein, "How Coca-Cola Manages 90 Emerging Markets," Strategy-business.com, November 7, 2011; "Coca-Cola International President Discusses Global Business, Growth Prospects," Coca-Cola Corporate Website, September 6, 2013; and Coca-Cola Corporate Website-European Careers, www.europeancareers.coca-cola.com, accessed March 14, 2014.

CASE 16.2   The Globalization of Indian IT

Wipro Ltd. originated as an Indian firm operating in the vegetable oils trade about half a century ago. In the twenty-first century, it had evolved into one of India's largest software services companies. Located in India's high-tech city of Bangalore, Wipro began in the software business by writing code on contract and handling multimillion-dollar contracts with international companies such as General Electric, Nokia and Home Depot. However, its president aspired to bring the company up the value-added chain to become one of the top ten IT companies in the world. Instead of simply writing code, Wipro would expand into the more lucrative area of business process consulting, offering supply chain management and deciphering customer trends from sales data—and competing with the likes of IBM Global Services and Electronic Data Services. But was this vision viable? Could Wipro go from an Indian firm with overseas clients to a truly global corporation virtually overnight? One estimate suggested that Wipro would need to hire an additional 30,000 employees worldwide in order to accomplish this goal.

Key Indian software development companies such as Wipro Ltd. and Infosys Technologies Ltd. had already captured a lucrative market by handling code-writing jobs from larger international companies. Tata Consultancy Services had become India's largest software exporter and the Tata Group's most important business, surpassing traditional group businesses such as Tata Steel and Tata Motors.

Working from sites such as a high-tech industrial park in India's high-tech showcase Bangalore, Indian software companies could take advantage of both lower-paid Indian talent and the telecommunications revolution in order to service overseas markets quickly and effectively. In addition, these companies had invested heavily in training their workforces, which resulted in dramatic improvements in productivity and quality.

Indian IT firms faced several challenges, however. Infrastructure problems such as electricity shortages and poor roads still plagued Bangalore. Although programmers in Bangalore were cheap by Western standards, their salaries had been rising at a rate of 15 percent a year, at least until the global recession hit. Indian IT now faced competition from such other low-cost countries as China, the Philippines and Vietnam, and Western consulting companies were challenging the competitive advantage of Indian firms by opening Asian software centers. In addition, some U.S. clients had decided to move their IT outsourcing to Latin American locations such as Costa Rica, because they found the time zone differences between India and the United States too difficult to handle. Despite their successes, Indian IT increasingly competed with IBM and Accenture for multinational contracts, and, unlike these global rivals, Indian firms remained far more dependent on short-term contracts.

Therefore, moving into more sophisticated and higher-margin IT products was attractive to Indian firms, but it meant both converting current clients and attracting new ones. Infosys won a contract from EveryD.com, a Japanese online shopping and banking service for housewives. Its job encompassed developing the business plan, designing the portal and writing the operational software. The Japanese customer noted that Infosys wasn't the cheapest of alternatives but that it had the necessary expertise and delivered the product on time.

Wipro convinced Thomas Cook Financial Services not only to use them for designing a system for automating Thomas Cook's foreign currency transactions but also to hire them to install the system within the British MNC. But new, smaller accounts would also be necessary if Indian firms were to carve out a significant global market share. VideosDotCom sent some work to Wipro when its Texas-based staff was too busy. Subsequently, it switched most of its development work to Bangalore, citing Wipro's extensive e-commerce experience, development skills, pricing and overall quality. Wipro later won a large technology outsourcing contract from Citibank with an estimated worth of $500 million.

In addition to these more established companies, Indian startup software companies were developing their own products and taking them directly to the U.S. market. Some executives of these Indian startup companies found themselves moving overseas almost immediately. The chairman of Bombay-based I-Flex Solutions, a financial services software developer, moved to New Jersey in order to be able to call on potential clients personally. Over a period of just a few years, the company had posted 25 percent of its 1,425 employees to four continents.

Soon the U.S. market accounted for about half of all revenues of the Indian IT industry. Large Indian companies such as Wipro, Infosys and Tata Consultancy Services sponsored about half of the 65,000 skilled-worker permits or H1-B visas issued each year to foreign workers with at least a bachelor's degree. Some accused these companies of exploiting the visa system to underbid U.S. competitors. Federal prosecutors accused Infosys of gaining a competitive advantage by importing workers using H1-B visas but then paying them Indian wages. Infosys denied any criminal wrongdoing but agreed to pay a $34 million settlement and to bring its employment procedures into compliance with U.S. law.

In addition to the large Indian IT companies, IT startups contributed to the fact that India had become one of Asia's major destinations for venture capital. Still, Indian capital markets were generally noted for their conservatism. Firms were expected to post profits consistently. A loss of money, even in the short term, was considered unacceptable. Laying out large sums of money, such as those needed for the acquisition of other firms, was often judged to be very risky.

Some of the venture capital flowing into India came from expatriate Indians. Many Indian IT engineers worked or had worked in the United States. Silicon Valley's Indian high-tech population numbered around 200,000 and was considered to be the area's most successful immigrant community. Many Indians working in the IT industry in the United States believed that despite their technical expertise—or possibly because of it—they were being overlooked for management positions. Ironically, American companies considered their technical skills too valuable to lose by transferring them to management. Partially as a

533

reaction to this, many Indians working in the United States considered starting their own businesses either in India or in the United States. Indians living in the United States often invested in each other's startup companies, sat on each other's boards and hired each other for key jobs. In fact, companies with Indian founders could often hire teams of developers more rapidly than the average U.S. company without the benefit of ethnic ties to the Indian community. IndUS Entrepreneurs (TIE) of Santa Clara emerged as one of the preeminent networking groups for Indian entrepreneurs. It hosted monthly Angel Forums at which entrepreneurs could pitch plans to potential investors. The IndUS Entrepreneurs website states as the group's goal the duplication of the Silicon Valley success story in India.

Discussion Questions

1. Why will Indian IT firms have to transform themselves into more global corporations in the future?
2. How will their internationalization experience differ from the experience of U.S.-based firms in the latter half of the twentieth century?
3. What unique advantages and disadvantages do these firms possess?
4. Which organizational structure do you think would be appropriate for a more global Wipro? Why?

Sources: "The Globalization of Indian IT," in Kate Gillespie and H. David Hennessey, *Global Marketing* (Mason, OH: Cengage, 2011); Dhanya Ann Thoppil, Dean McLain and Danny Yadron, "New Bill Targets Indian IT Firms," *Wall Street Journal*, April 24, 2013, p. B1; Nomaan Merchant, "Indian Outsourcing Giant Infosys to Settle U.S. Visa Fraud Case for $34 Million," Associated Press Newswires, October 30, 2013; N. Shivapriya, "Wipro Wins Large Technology Outsourcing Contract," *The Economic Times*, June 21, 2013; and "Tata Consultancy Services: How It Became the Jewel in Tata Group's Crown," *The Economic Times*, February 14, 2014.

Notes

1 Kevin Maler, "3M Looks to Expand Global Sales," Knight-Ridder Tribune Business News, June 17, 2001.
2 Leadership Survey 2009, 3M Human Resources Measurement, 3M Corporation, p. 9.
3 Adam Lashinksy, "Yahoo's Mission Quest," *Fortune*, February 2, 2007.
4 "Mission Statement, Starbucks Coffee Company," www.starbucks.com, accessed August 5, 2009.
5 "Science for a Better Life: Mission Statement for the Bayer Group," www.bayer.com, accessed August 5, 2009.
6 Jim Krane, "Halliburton CEO Moves from Houston to Dubai to Focus on Mideast, Asian Ventures," Associated Press Newswires, March 11, 2007.
7 David Woodruff, "Your Career Matters," *Wall Street Journal*, November 11, 2000, p. B1.
8 Kamran Kashani, "Why Does Global Marketing Work—or Not Work?" *European Journal of Management*, vol. 8, no. 2 (1990), pp. 150–155.
9 Carol Hymowitz, "Foreign-Born CEOs are Increasing in U.S., Rarer Overseas," *Wall Street Journal*, May 25, 2004, p. B1.
10 Jason Gertzen, "Milwaukee-Based Manufacturer Seeks Overseas Expansion," Knight-Ridder Tribune Business News, June 11, 2001.
11 Will Pinkston, "Ford Mulls Suppliers Park Near Atlanta," *Wall Street Journal*, July 12, 2000, p. S1.
12 Merissa Marr, "Small World," *Wall Street Journal*, June 11, 2007, p. A1.
13 "The Legacy that Got Left on the Shelf: Unilever and Emerging Markets," Economist Intelligence Unit Executive Briefing, February 12, 2008.

14 Arnold Schuh, "Global Standardization as a Success Formula for Marketing in Central Eastern Europe?" *Journal of World Business*, vol. 35, no. 2 (Summer 2000), pp. 133–148.

15 "Avon Announces Management Realignments," PR Newswire, February 24, 2011.

16 Guey-Huey Li, Chwo-Ming Yu and Dah-Hsian Seetoo, "Toward a Theory of Regional Organization," *Management International Review*, February 3, 2010.

17 Ernest Beck, "Familiar Cry to Unilever: Split It Up!" *Wall Street Journal*, August 4, 2000, p. A7.

18 Carol Hymowitz, "In the Lead: Managers Suddenly Have to Answer to a Crowd of Bosses," *Wall Street Journal*, August 12, 2003, p. B1.

19 Megha Bahree, "A Bumpy Road in India," *Wall Street Journal*, April 2, 2013, p. B1.

20 Fons Trompenaars and Peter Woolliams, "Lost in Translation," *Harvard Business Review*, April 2011.

21 "Electric Glue," *The Economist*, June 2, 2001.

22 Joann S. Lublin, "Globalizing the Boardroom," *Wall Street Journal*, October 31, 2005, p. B1.

23 Chi-fai Chan and Neil Bruce Holbert, "Marketing Home and Away: Perceptions of Managers in Headquarters and Subsidiaries," *Journal of World Business*, vol. 36, no. 2 (Summer 2001), pp. 205–221.

24 Sarah McBride, "Can Esprit Be Hip Again?" *Wall Street Journal*, June 17, 2002, p. B1.

25 Piet Levy, "The International Exchange," *Marketing News*, September 30, 2011, p. 18.

26 Diana Middleton, "Schools Set Global Track, For Students and Programs," *Wall Street Journal Online*, April 7, 2011.

27 Joann S. Lublin, "Hunt is On for Fresh Executive Talent – Cultural Flexibility in Demand," *Wall Street Journal*, April 11, 2011, p. B1.

Country Market Report

The outline below guides you through a market assessment and market-entry plan for a particular business and country such as Dick's Sporting Goods to Japan, IKEA to Brazil or Sea World to Dubai. Source suggestions are presented and include Internet sources and sources commonly available through online university library sites. Your instructor may suggest alternative or additional options based on sources available at your particular university.

Executive Summary

- Briefly describe your product/service and the state of your business.
- Briefly state the international experience of your business. Check out your firm's corporate website to see when and where the firm internationalized.

  - PLEASE NOTE: This experience might provide very useful insights for your own project such as product adaptations abroad or pricing policies. If your firm has already entered a country with a similar culture to your target country, investigate its experience in that earlier market. See if there have been any cultural or strategic missteps that should be avoided in the future. Do an Internet search and look for appropriate business news articles via the *Business Source Complete* or *Factiva* found on most university online library sites.

- Provide a very short summary of your report:

  - How attractive or unattractive is the proposed market and why?
  - What mode of entry do you propose?
  - What key product or service and product-line adaptations do you propose?
  - What distribution, pricing and promotion strategies do you suggest?

Economic Environment

- What is the general economic outlook for your market? What implications could this have for your business model? A good and timely source for this is *Business Monitor* found on most university online library sites. *Business Monitor* may even provide a specific report pertaining to your industry. And their *Retail Reports* can be useful overviews for any consumer-product market.
- Review issues in Chapter 2 to identify pertinent issues for assessing the economic environment. Address:

  - trade restrictions;
  - membership in economic integration organizations;
  - foreign exchange issues.

- For your section on implications of exchange regime and rates, specifically address the following:

  - What is the nature of the local currency regime—freely floating, pegged to dollar, pegged to the euro, etc.? For a description of different currency regimes see the IMF website: www.imf.org/external/np/mfd/er/2006/eng/0706.htm.
  - What has been the recent history of the local currency versus the home currency? Examine the past three years (at least) for developed countries and ten years for developing countries. If you have a major global competitor from a third country, also look at the recent history of the local currency versus the currency of their home country.

    - Wikipedia often provides a good summary of national currencies. For example look under Russian ruble or Mexican peso.
    - A good source for current and historical exchange rates is Oanda: www.oanda.com/.

  - Do experts propose that the local currency will devalue/revalue against the local currency/third-country currency? What are the pressures to do so? PLEASE NOTE: If you have a pegged currency, recent stability is no indicator of future trends. The currency could be stable or it could be heading for a steep devaluation.

    - *Business Monitor* is one possible source for expert insight.
    - An Internet search using the name of your currency (e.g. Egyptian pound), the current year and "prediction" often results in several authoritative articles.

  - What are the implications of your analysis above for your business plan? For example, how might a relative change in currency values affect:

    - Value of profits when translated to the home currency?
    - Value of licensing or franchising fees when translated to the home currency?
    - Choice of target markets?
    - Pricing strategies?
    - Decision to import products or not—and from where?
    - Competitive positioning against local and international competitors?

538

Political Environment

- Review Chapter 4.
- What are the short-term and longer-term *macro* political risks associated with your country? What are the *micro* political risks associated with your particular industry or home country? *Business Monitor* is a good source for this as well.
- Go to the IFC/World Bank site www.doingbusiness.org. What is the general regulatory environment like in your country? Which specific regulatory areas are salient to your proposed business venture? How does your country rank on those particular areas of regulations? For example, if you plan to export through independent distributors you will not be interested in how difficult it is to get electricity. You will be more interested in trading across borders and enforcing contracts.
- Research more about specific regulations concerning your industry in your country. This can be done on the Internet and *Factiva*.
- Also address government corruption in this section (see Chapter 5) and, if appropriate, explain how corruption could affect your business operations in the targeted country. Be sure to look at *Transparency International*'s website at www.transparency.org, but go beyond just listing a number or ranking for your country. Particularly address the types of corruption that apply to your proposed business model.

Cultural Environment

- Address the different cultural issues discussed in Chapter 3 that could apply to buyers of your product or service.
- In addition to the topics raised in this textbook, think how other more specific aspects of culture might affect your specific business model and research accordingly. Food culture? Furniture aesthetics? Dating and marriage habits? These specific aspects of culture will vary by business. An Internet search can be useful not only for articles but for visuals as well.
- Look for articles or websites that discuss the cultural aspects of doing business in your particular target country. Use search terms such as "business culture" and "business etiquette." How might these insights affect how you market in the country and how you relate to local stakeholders such as employees, partners and regulators? Specifically note how any of these cultural insights relate to concepts covered in Chapter 3, such as attitudes toward time, context of language or expression of emotions.
- Do any of these cultural insights appear to support the Hofstede scores for your target country? Can you find any cultural paradoxes related to the Hofstede scores or other generalizations concerning national culture?

Competition

- Review Chapter 6.
- Identify local competitors and discuss their strengths and weaknesses vis-à-vis your own.

- Identify global competitors operating in the market (or considering entering it) and discuss their strengths and weaknesses vis-à-vis your own.
- Can your business expect a country-of-origin advantage? Disadvantage? Explain.
- Check your university online library site. *Business Monitor*, *Business Source Complete*, *Euromonitor* and *Marketline Advantage* may have industry reports that can be helpful in identifying and evaluating competitors.
- Also Wikipedia may list competitors under your industry in your targeted country. Once you have names you can do further research on these competitors. Remember to look at corporate websites and check business news via library sites such as *Factiva*.
- A general Internet search can be useful too and even take you to competitors' corporate websites. It can also be useful for identifying smaller local competitors.

Mode of Entry

- Review Chapter 9.
- What are the *realistic* entry options given your product/service and the target country? For example, if your business model consists of establishing restaurants or retail outlets, you will not choose exporting as a mode of entry. You could however be interested in franchising, joint-venturing, establishing a new wholly owned subsidiary or acquiring an existing company.
- Does your firm have a history of using a particular mode of entry? Is there any reason that the firm must keep to this historical mode of entry—or can you suggest a change?
- Briefly identify the pros and cons of each realistic entry option.
- What is your choice and why?
- How will you attempt to mitigate the cons of your choice?
- If your plan includes partners such as distributors, franchisees or joint venture partners, identify the qualities you want from these partners. How might you locate such partners? Try to identify an *actual target* firm or individual. Why might they be interested in partnering with you? If you can't identify a potential partner, do you need to reconsider your mode of entry?
- Similarly, if you plan to enter via acquisition, you should identify an actual acquisition target and present a reasonable argument of why the target would be interested in being acquired by you. You should also check the business news and determine if your firm is likely to be able to afford the acquisition. Is it in good financial shape?

Target Market(s)

- Review the section on target markets in Chapter 5.
- Identify your target market or markets. On which specific segments of the population will you focus your marketing efforts? This is an important question to answer. Think about demographics, lifestyles and even geography. When you later design a marketing strategy, you must meet the needs of these segments. You will need to communicate with these segments through media that will reach them and with a message that resonates with them.

- After identifying the target market(s), determine the various steps you would take to put a number (customers and sales) on your target market. Try to find numbers as you work through these steps. Don't worry if you can't find all the necessary numbers. This is to be expected. This missing information can later be added to your *Unanswered Questions* section of the report. However, attempt to establish that your target market is large enough to be viable and specific enough to address with the marketing strategy you will later propose.

- For many projects, it is reasonable to think of more than one target market—each of which will need a distinct marketing strategy. For example, dating services seek male clients and female clients. In some countries the needs and availability of single males and single females will be more similar than in others where they would need to be treated as distinct segments. For other businesses (such as fast-food franchises or theme parks) locals and foreign tourists could be distinct segments. This might sound like a lot of extra work. However, dealing with this issue is actually much easier than it sounds. Alternatively, ignoring multiple segments when they in fact exist can result in confusion, frustration and wasted time.

Marketing Strategy

For the marketing strategy section, see if your library has any country-industry reports appropriate for your project. Again, these reports may be found via *Business Monitor*, *Business Source Complete*, *Euromonitor* or *Marketline Advantage* on your university online library site. The U.S. Export Portal at www.export.gov provides *Country Commercial Guides* that often have good information and can be accessed for free. It also has some specific country-industry reports. These special reports are free but require registration.

- *Product/Service Adaptations*

  - Review Chapters 10 and 11.
  - What will your product line consist of and how will it differ from that in the home market? Why?
  - How and why might the proportions of different lines vary from your home country?
  - What product/service adaptations do you propose? Why?
  - Do warranties or after-sales service apply to your business? If so, does either need adaptation?
  - What will be your branding policy? Why?

- *Pricing Strategy*

  - Review Chapter 12.
  - How might cost factors affect your pricing strategy?
  - How might market factors affect your pricing strategy?
  - How might competitive factors affect your pricing strategy?
  - Do government policies or laws restrict your pricing in any way?
  - In general, how do buyers respond to pricing strategies? Your *Country Commercial Guide* can be useful in answering this question.

- Revisit the *Economic Environment* section of your report: How could exchange-rate issues between the currency of the home country of your business and the currency of your potential host country possibly affect your pricing strategy—now or in the near future?
- Based on the discussion above, what is your proposed pricing strategy? For example, will you price the same as in the home market, a bit lower, a lot higher, etc.? Explain.

Distribution Strategy

- Review Chapter 13.
- What do you suggest as your distribution strategy? Why?

  - If appropriate to your product, describe the wholesale/retail environment of your target country. How would you identify potential channel partners in your country?
  - If you plan to utilize channel partners, how will you motivate these partners?
  - If your service or product/service does not market (ever!) via wholesalers or retailers (e.g. Joe's Crab Shack or Disney theme park) then you should focus on the number and location of your own stores, and it might be useful to look at Case 7.2 in this textbook. On the other hand, if you are investigating Ben & Jerry's, your ice cream could sell through these channels, and you should consider them—even if you later decide only to sell via Ben & Jerry stores.
  - Will you consider selling via the Internet? If so, discuss the e-commerce environment in your country.

- What impact does your country's infrastructure (e.g. ports, railroads, roads) have on your distribution strategy? How might this affect your logistics?
- If appropriate to your product, discuss any problems with parallel markets (Chapter 12) or smuggling (Chapter 13) that you have uncovered.

Promotion Strategy

- Review Chapters 14 and 15.
- What is the message you wish to convey to your target market(s)? Remember to tie your promotion strategy clearly to your target market.
- Which promotion options—personal selling, sales promotions, telemarketing, advertising, buzz, etc.—are best suited for your business model in your target country? Why?
- What insights can you find concerning your proposed promotion choices in your target country?
- Are there any regulations pertaining to promotion that might affect your strategy?
- If you will pursue advertising, address issues concerning media strategy and agency choice. The *Country Commercial Guides* of the U.S. Export Portal at www.export.gov can be useful for this.
- Do you think your product/service is better served by a local or a global campaign? Explain your choice.
- Does your business participate in any corporate social responsibility projects? If so, will they be extended to your country—or do you suggest other projects? Why?

Unanswered Questions

- Did you identify important questions that proved difficult to research? If so, how did you attempt to address these questions? Why were your attempts unsuccessful?
- If you were given a research budget, what are some sources of for-pay information that could enrich your report?

Glossary

Adspend money spent on advertising in a particular medium

Advergaming the use of online video games designed to promote a brand

Aesthetics a cultural concept pertaining to what a society considers to be beautiful or pleasing

Affective culture a culture in which speakers are allowed—even expected—to express emotions

Antiglobals consumers who are skeptical of the quality of global brands and of the transnational companies who own them

Antitrust of or relating to legislation preventing or controlling monopolies with the intention of promoting competition

Appreciation an increase in value or price of a currency compared to another currency

B2B business to business

Back translation a technique in which a questionnaire is translated from one language into a second language, translated back from the second language into the first language, and then compared with the original text

Back-stage elements of services the planning and implementation aspects of services invisible to the customer

Balance of payments (BOP) an accounting record of the transactions between the residents of one country and the residents of the rest of the world over a given period of time

Behavioral standards standards relating to actions taken within the firm

Benchmarking the act of identifying best practices in an industry in order to adopt those practices and achieve greater efficiency

Big data the technologies used to collect, store, process and analyze massive volumes of data including text, documents, pictures and videos

Body language nonverbal communications, including touching, making arm and hand gestures and keeping a proper distance between speakers

Born global a firm that establishes marketing and other business operations abroad upon formation of the firm or immediately thereafter

Bottom of the pyramid (BOP) consumers in developing countries who earn less than $2 a day

Bottom-up approach an approach to global branding in which brand strategy emerges from shared experiences and best practices among the firm's subsidiaries

Brand champion a manager or group within a firm charged with the responsibility for building and managing a global brand

Bribery giving something of value to an individual in a position of trust to influence his or her judgment or behavior

BRIC Brazil, Russia, India and China

BRICK Brazil, Russia, India, China and South Korea

BRICS Brazil, Russia, India, China and South Africa

Bundling the act in which a firm combines all its operations in a certain country or region into a single legal unit

Business groups large business organizations consisting of firms in diverse industries interlinked by both formal and informal ties

Buy-backs/cooperation agreements countertrade arrangements extending over years and usually involving capital equipment in exchange for output of that equipment

Buzz marketing managed word of mouth in which a firm attempts both to promote a sale and to encourage people to talk about the firm's product or service

Capital account principal BOP account that records a country's international financial assets and liabilities over the BOP period

Cartel a group of companies acting together to control the price of certain goods or services

Channel alignment the coordination of various channel members to the end of providing a unified approach to the marketing of a product or service

Channel captain the dominant channel participant; dictates terms of pricing, delivery and sometimes product design

Channel length the number of intermediaries directly involved in the physical or ownership path of a product from the manufacturer to the buyer

Channel maintenance costs the costs of managing and auditing channel operations

Common market a form of economic integration with all the characteristics of a customs union and in which the free flow of resources, such as labor and capital, is encouraged among member nations

Competitive screen a requirement that firms bidding on government contracts in developing countries be competitive in experience, reputation and cultural sensitivity as well as in price

Compounding the last stages of manufacturing in the chemical and pharmaceutical industries

Confiscation expropriation without compensation

Consortium a group of firms that participate in a project on a pre-agreed basis but act as one company toward the buyer

Consortium approach an approach involving firms united in a working relationship without the formation of a new legal entity

Consumer animosity political objection to purchasing products from a specific foreign country

Consumer ethnocentrism the belief that purchasing imported products results in job loss and consequently hardship for a buyer's home country

Consumer ethnographies carefully crafted observational studies designed to capture nuances in consumer behavior

Contributor a subsidiary responsible for adapting some products for smaller markets

Cooperation agreements/buy-backs countertrade arrangements extending over years and usually involving capital equipment in exchange for output of that equipment

Corporate social responsibility an initiative to assess and take responsibility for a company's effect on the environment and the quality of life of society

Cosmopolitans consumers who purchase global brands to enhance their self-image of being sophisticated and modern

Cost-performance criterion the expected performance of industrial products or capital equipment relative to the costs to purchase and use such products or equipment

Counterfeiting the illegal use of a registered trademark

Counterparry a counterattack against a competitor in one country in response to a prior attack by that competitor in another country

Countertrade a transaction in which goods are exchanged for other goods

Country of manufacture the country in which a product is manufactured or assembled

Country of origin the country with which a firm is associated—typically its home country

Country of parts the country in which an input to a final product is produced

Courtesy bias a phenomenon in which respondents fail to reply honestly but instead supply the answer they believe an interviewer wishes to hear

Critical mass the minimal effort and investment needed to compete effectively in a market

547

Cross-country subsidization the utilization of profits from one country in which a business operates to subsidize competitive actions in another country

Cultural paradox a common behavioral norm in a culture that appears to contradict a prior conceptual model of that culture

Culture all human knowledge, beliefs, behavior and institutions transmitted from one generation to another

Culture shock stress and tension resulting from coping with new cultural cues and expectations

Current account a principal part of the balance of payments statement that includes the key sub-accounts of goods, services and unilateral transfers

Customs union two or more countries that formally sign an agreement to drop trade barriers among themselves and to establish common external barriers between member and nonmember countries

Density of distribution the number of sales outlets or distribution points utilized for a given geographic market

Depreciation a decrease in value or price of a currency compared to another currency

Diaspora a group of people who live outside their ancestral homeland but who retain a psychological tie to that homeland

Direct exporting exporting through an intermediary located in a foreign market

Discretionary adaptation a product adaptation that is optional but possibly desirable for a certain market

Discretionary income income remaining after the basic necessities of food, shelter and clothing have been acquired

Domestic marketing marketing activities aimed at a firm's domestic market

Domestication the limitation of certain economic activities to local citizens

Dumping the practice of exporting a product at an "unfair" price and consequently damaging competition in the export market

Economies of scale profitability gained through the increasing levels of production

Eligibility screen the initial requirement placed by governments on firms seeking to bid on government contracts in developing countries. Firms must be judged to be serious in their intent and large enough to handle the contracts.

Emerging market a market outside of the triad

Emic approach research studies developed to capture the uniqueness of each cultural context

Entry strategy configuration the process by which a firm determines the best possible entry strategy for a country or region

Ethnocentric orientation a corporate worldview in which management is focused on the home market and considers ideas from the home market to be superior to those from foreign subsidiaries

Etic approach concepts and measures of concepts developed in one cultural context that are translated and used in other cultural contexts

Eurobrands regional brands in Europe

Exchange rate the ratio that measures the value of one currency in terms of another currency

Exclusive distribution a distribution strategy in which a product is available through only one outlet in a relatively large geographic area

Exhaustion principle a legal principle that establishes the conditions under which a trademark owner relinquishes its right to control the resale of its product

Expediting payments small bribes paid to civil servants to perform their duties in a timely manner

Export consortium a group of companies that agrees to share the logistical and promotional costs of exporting to foreign markets

Export marketing marketing activities undertaken when a firm sells its products abroad and when those products are shipped from one country to another

Export price escalation the phenomenon in which the costs of export documentation, overseas transportation, insurance and tariffs raise the price of products abroad to a level above that of the price in the domestic market

Expropriation the formal seizure of a business operation, with or without the payment of compensation

Extensive distribution a distribution strategy that employs many sales outlets per market area

Facilitating payments see expediting payments

First-mover advantage a market advantage relating to brand awareness, sales and profits that accrues to the first significant competitor to enter a new market

Fixed costs costs that do not vary with changes in production levels

Foreign direct investments foreign investments over which investors assume some if not all direct management control

Formal bid a phase in the bidding process in which a potential supplier states the price it will charge a client for a project and details the terms of the project

Forward price/forward rate the price agreed upon by two parties for one to deliver to the other a set amount of currency at a fixed future date

Free-trade area two or more countries that formally sign an agreement to drop trade barriers among themselves but to allow each member country to maintain independent trade relations with nonmember countries

Freely floating currency a currency whose exchange rate is determined by the market forces of supply and demand

Front-stage elements of services the aspects of service encounters that are visible to the customer

Generic management system standard an international standard covering a particular set of corporate behaviors to which companies can choose to comply and consequently become certified as to their compliance

Geocentric orientation a corporate worldview in which management pursues a global marketing strategy and decision-making is shared by headquarters and subsidiaries

Global account management the assignment of special account executives and service teams to handle the needs of valuable but demanding global buyers

Global account team a team dedicated to servicing a multinational global buyer

Global agnostics consumers who judge global brands and local brands by the same criteria and are neither impressed nor alienated by the fact that a brand is global

Global brand strategy a strategy in which the positioning, advertising, look and personality of a brand remain constant across markets

Global citizens consumers who associate global brands with quality and innovation and expect transnational firms to behave responsibly regarding workers' rights and the environment

Global competence the ability to balance local market needs with the demands of global efficiency and the opportunities of global synergies

Global dreamers consumers who equate global brands with quality and are attracted by the lifestyle they portray

Global launch the introduction of a product or service in many markets at the same time

Global mandate a responsibility assigned to a manager or team within a firm to carry out a task on a global scale

Global marketing strategy a single transnational strategy for a product, service or business that nonetheless incorporates flexibility for local adaptation

Global product a product for which a portion of the final design is standardized and a portion can be adapted to individual markets

Global segments transnational consumer segments based on lifestyle or demographics such as age and social class rather than on nationality

Global supply chain management the collective managerial behavior and decisions essential to the development of a functioning global supply chain

Global team a task force established to address at the global level a particular issue facing a firm

Global theme approach the use of an advertising campaign in which a single advertising theme is utilized in all markets but is varied slightly with each local execution

Globally coordinated move the employing of simultaneous actions across countries to gain competitive advantage over global or local rivals

Goods (or merchandise) account balance-of-payments account stating the monetary value of a country's international transactions in physical goods

Gray market/parallel imports imports that enter a market outside the official distribution channels established by the trademark owner

Gross domestic product (GDP) the total market value of all goods and services produced within the borders of a country during a specific period

Guanxi a system of social networks and influential relationships in Chinese culture that facilitate business and other dealings

Hadith an authoritative collection of the sayings and reported practices of Mohammed

Halal permitted under Islamic law

Hard goods countertraded merchandise that is easy to resell

Hedging the act of contracting through financial intermediaries for the future exchange of one currency for another at a set rate

High-context culture a culture in which communication is more implicit and the meanings of words change depending on who is speaking to whom, where that person is speaking and under what circumstances he or she is speaking

High-trust society a society in which trust is extended to persons beyond the immediate family, encouraging the emergence of various voluntary organizations such as civic groups and modern corporations

HNO (human nature orientation)-negative societies societies that assume people cannot be trusted to obey the rules

HNO (human nature orientation)-positive societies societies that assume people can be trusted to obey the rules

Horizontal keiretsus large and diverse industrial groups in Japan

Host country a country that contains an operational unit (marketing, sales, manufacturing, finance or research and development) of an international company

Hybrid a firm in which a government holds a partial, though usually significant, equity position

Hybrid brand strategy a strategy that captures the quality improvements and cost savings of standardized backstage activities but adapts key elements of the marketing mix, such as product features, distribution and promotion, to local tastes

Implementer a subsidiary, the primary role of which is to implement a firm's global strategy

Indirect exporting exporting through an intermediary located in the exporter's home country

Individualism-collectivism a Hofstede measure of culture capturing the extent to which a society evaluates a person as an individual rather than as a member of a group

Influence screen a requirement that firms bidding on government contracts in developing countries identify key decision-makers and assure their proposals meet the needs of all parties

Informal economy the totality of economic activity of individuals and businesses that operate without licenses, permits or reporting procedures required by law

Initial channel costs the costs of locating or establishing a channel

International brand a brand that follows a global strategy but does not maintain a strict standardized marketing strategy and mix across all national markets

International exhaustion an exhaustion principle that states that once a firm has sold a product anywhere in the world, it cannot restrict its resale into a particular country

International marketing marketing activities undertaken when a company becomes significantly involved in local marketing environments in foreign countries

International selling selling that crosses national boundaries and utilizes salespersons who travel to different countries

International transfer price the price paid by one unit of a firm to import a product or service supplied by another unit of the same firm

Internationalization the expansion of a firm beyond its domestic market into foreign markets

Invisible exports a country's earnings abroad from intangibles such as services, remittances and income earned on overseas investments

Just-like-us segments market segments in foreign countries that closely resemble marketers' domestic buyers

Keiretsu a network of Japanese companies operating in many industries that own stakes in each other and are organized around a bank

Koran the sacred text of Islam

Kosher conforming to Jewish dietary laws

Lateral partnerships formal or informal agreements between nongovernmental organizations to work toward a common goal and to facilitate efficiency

Lead markets countries or regions possessing major research and development sites for an industry or recognized for being trendsetters

Letter of credit document issued by a bank or similar financial institution to assure an exporter is paid by its customer abroad

Linkage screen a common requirement that international firms bidding on government contracts in developing countries identify ways in which specific local businesses will participate in or otherwise benefit by the proposed contracts

Local selling selling that targets a single country

Logistics costs the costs of transporting and storing products and processing those products through customs

Loose cultures societies with few rules, norms or standards for correct behavior

Low-context culture a culture in which communication is explicit and words tend to retain their meaning in all situations

Low-trust society a society in which trust is extended only to immediate family members

Macroindicators data useful in estimating the total market size of a country or region

Magic moments the point at which modern retailing emerges within a country

Mandatory adaptation a product adaptation that a firm must make to sell a product in a certain country or region

Marginal profit the change in total profit resulting from the sale of one additional unit of a product

Market liberalization the encouragement of competition where monopolies or strict entry controls previously existed

Market segmentation the aggregation of prospective buyers into groups (segments) that have common needs and will respond similarly to a particular marketing strategy

Masculinity-femininity a measure of culture relating to assertiveness/modesty and competitiveness/nurturance

Maslow's hierarchy of needs a theory stating that human needs are divided into five levels and that humans satisfy lower-level needs before seeking to satisfy higher-level needs

Master franchise franchise that includes exclusive rights to market within a whole city or country

Material culture the aggregate of physical objects and technologies used by a society

Merchandise (or goods) account balance-of-payments account stating the monetary value of a country's international transactions in physical goods

Microindicators data useful in estimating the consumption of a certain product in a country or region

Missionary sales force salespeople who promote a firm and its products or services but do not close a sale

Mobile consumers consumers who are aware of and purchase foreign products because of exposure to foreign markets due to overseas work, study or travel

Modified uniform pricing a pricing strategy in which a firm monitors price levels in different countries to close large price differentials and discourage gray markets

Modularity a process involving the development of standard components that can easily be connected with other standard components to increase the variety of final products

Monetary union a common market in which member countries no longer regulate their own currencies

Monochronic culture a culture in which activities are undertaken one at a time and people respect schedules and agendas

Most favored nation (MFN) status a guarantee in a trade agreement between countries binding signatories to extend trade benefits to each other equal to those accorded any third state

Multidomestic strategy a strategy pursued by a multinational corporation in which various marketing strategies are developed, each tailored to a particular local market

Multinational corporation (MNC) a company that possesses extensive investments in assets abroad and operates in a number of foreign countries as though it were a local company

Multinational global buyers firms that search the world for products to be used throughout their global operations

Must-win markets markets crucial to a firm's global market leadership

National champion a large company in a strategy industry chosen by its home government to receive special treatment and support in exchange for advancing the interests of the nation

National exhaustion an exhaustion principle that states that once a firm has sold a trademarked product in a specific country, it cannot restrict the further distribution of that product in that country

National global buyers firms that search the world for products that are used in a single country or market

Neutral culture a culture that discourages a show of emotion

Nontariff barriers nonmonetary restrictions on trade

Orderly marketing arrangement (or voluntary export restriction) an agreement between countries in which one country agrees to limit its exports to the other

Parallel firm A firm established by local partners or managers of a joint venture to illegally compete with the joint venture by using the joint venture's technology, market knowledge and brand

Parallel imports/gray market imports that enter a market outside the official distribution channels established by the trademark owner

Parallel translation a technique in which two or more translators translate a questionnaire, compare their translations and resolve any differences between the translations

Pegged currency a currency whose price is fixed by its government to another currency or basket of currencies

Per-capita income (PCI) a country's average income per person for a specific period

Performance bond money supplied by a supplier and held in escrow to guarantee that a buyer will be reimbursed if a project is not completed in accordance with agreed-upon specifications

Performance standards evaluation standards relating to market outcomes

Personal selling communication between a potential buyer and a salesperson to the end of understanding buyer needs, matching those needs to the supplier's products or services and ultimately achieving a sale

Piggyback arrangement an arrangement in which one company agrees to distribute through its established channels the products of another company

Piracy the counterfeit production of copyrighted material

Political mapping the process of identifying all individuals involved in a regulatory decision—politicians, bureaucrats, key members of pressure groups—and understanding their various points of view

Political risk the possibility that an unexpected and drastic change due to political forces will result in adverse circumstances for business operations

Polycentric orientation a corporate worldview in which each market is considered unique and local subsidiaries are given power to develop and implement independent strategies

Polychronic culture a culture in which multitasking is common, schedules and agendas bend to the needs of people and interruptions are common

Portfolio investments investments, such as the purchase of stocks and bonds, over which investors assume no direct management control

Power distance a Hofstede measure of culture capturing the extent to which the less powerful members within a society accept that power is distributed unevenly

Preemption the legal hijacking or registration of a brand name when the brand is not yet registered

Prequalifying phase a phase in the bidding process in which prospective buyers ask for documentation from interested suppliers to verify that bidders are trustworthy and capable of handling the proposed project

Primary data data collected for a specific research purpose and obtained by direct observation or by direct contact with sources of information

Privatization the practice of selling state-owned enterprises or their assets to private firms or individuals

Procedural screen a requirement that firms bidding on government contracts in developing countries follow numerous bureaucratic procedures

Product life cycle the market stages a product experiences over time: introduction, growth maturity, decline and withdrawal

Proxy a product the demand for which varies in relationship with the demand for another product being investigated

Psychic distance the perceived degree of similarity between markets

Psychic-distance paradox a phenomenon in which a market thought to be similar to another market turns out to be dissimilar

Psychographics the classification of people according to their attitudes, aspirations, worldviews or other psychological criteria

Public relations a strategic communication process undertaken to maintain a favorable public image of an organization

Pull strategy a promotional strategy directed at the final buyer or end user of a product or service

Purchasing-power parity a theory that prices of internationally traded commodities should be the same in every country and therefore the true exchange rate is the ratio of these prices in any two countries

Push strategy a promotional strategy directed at the distributors of a product

Quota a physical limit on the amount of goods that can be imported into or, less commonly, exported from a country

R&D research and development

Regional exhaustion an exhaustion principle that states that once a firm has sold a trademarked product anywhere in a region (such as the EU), it cannot restrict the resale of that product within that region

Regulatory change moderate and relatively predictable change in laws and regulations

Royalties payments by a licensee to a licensor in exchange for the right to produce and market the licensor's product or service within a certain region

Scalar equivalence the similarity among respondents in their interpretation of calibrations along a continuum

Search phase a phase in the bidding process in which potential suppliers identify projects of interest to them

Secondary data data already in existence that was collected for some purpose other than the current study

Selective distribution a distribution strategy that employs few sales outlets per market area

Services account balance-of-payments account stating a country's international transactions in intangibles such as transportation services, consulting, royalties on intellectual property and dividends on foreign investment

Sin taxes taxes assessed on products that are legal but discouraged by society

Situational animosity consumer animosity as a response to a current economic or political event

Smuggling the illegal transport of products across national borders

Soft currency a currency that attracts little global demand

Soft goods countertraded merchandise that is difficult to resell

Sovereignty supremacy of authority or rule free from external control

Spam unsolicited commercial bulk e-mail

Spot price/spot rate the rate of exchange between two currencies for delivery, one for the other, within one or two business days

Stable animosity consumer animosity arising from difficult historical relations between two countries

Strategic alliance an alliance involving two or more firms in which each partner contributes a particular skill or resource—usually complementary—to a venture

Strategic leader the home base or major subsidiary of a multinational corporation, responsible for developing products used by the entire company

Sunna a way of life prescribed for Muslims based on the practices of Mohammed and scholarly interpretations of the Koran

Takeover a host-government-initiated action that results in a loss of ownership or direct control by a foreign company

Targeting of global competitors the process of identifying actual and potential global competitors, planning how to compete against each of them, and implementing those plans

Tariff a tax on goods or services moving across an economic or political boundary

Temporal orientation a society's predominant time focus—either on the past, the present or the future

Tight cultures societies with many rules, norms and standards for correct behavior

Top-down approach an approach to global branding in which a global team determines the global brand strategy and country strategies that are derived from this strategy

Trademarks the names, words and symbols that enable customers to distinguish among brands

Transaction risk the risk that a change in exchange rate that will prove unfavorable to either the seller or the buyer will occur between invoicing and settlement dates

Triad the traditional developed markets, primarily consisting of the United States, Western Europe and Japan

Turnkey project a project in which the supplier provides the buyer with a complete solution for immediate use, occupation or operation

Unbundling the act in which a firm divides its operations in a certain country or region into different legal units

Uncertainty avoidance a Hofstede measure of culture relating to general worry about the future

Uncovered position a strategy in which a firm chooses not to take any action that would alleviate transaction risk

Uniform pricing strategy a pricing strategy in which a firm charges the same price everywhere when that price is translated into a base currency

Unilateral transfers all the transactions for which there is no quid pro quo, such as private remittances, personal gifts, philanthropic donations and aid

Value-added tax (VAT) a tax that is levied at each stage in the production and distribution of a product or service based on the value added by that stage; the tax is ultimately passed on to the buyer

Variable costs costs that vary with changes in production levels

Voluntary export restriction (or orderly marketing arrangement) an agreement between countries in which one country agrees to limit its exports to the other

Worthwhile global account an account that meets minimum revenue levels that support the additional overhead required by global account management

Index

Note: page numbers in *italic* type refer to Figures; those in **bold** type refer to Tables.

11 Furniture 431
11 September 2011 attacks 49, 175
3G Capital 297
3M 506

AB InBev (Anheuser-Busch InBev NV) 244, 265, 316, 356, 481; joint venture case study 301–2
Abbott Laboratories 402
ABC brand 173
Abril 469–70
absolute advantage 21, **22**
Abu Dhabi 153, 190, 346
AC Delco 357
accede strategic option 114, *115*, 116
account management, global 454–5
accounting services 343
Acer 182, 461
Achema 456
acquisitions 296–8, **299**, 424, 432; and branding 349; and new product development 331
Adidas 412, 462, 471
adspend 485, **486**, **487–8**
Advanced Pricing Agreement Program (APA) 389
advergaming 489
advertising 476; to children, case study 495–7; developing global campaigns 477–8; global media strategy 484–5, **486**, 487, **487–8**, 488–91; global *vs.* local 477; global-local decision 479–83; language barriers 483–4, **484**; organising for 491–4; ShanghaiCosmopolitan.com case study 497–500
advertising agencies 4, 343, 476; selection of 491–2
Aeroflot 471
aesthetics 72–3
Afghanistan 245

Africa 78; and AIDS 366; as an emerging market 251; counterfeiting and piracy 359; marketing research 215; pharmaceutical prices 401, 402 *see also* individually named African countries
AFTA (ASEAN Free Trade Area) **42**
after-sales service 324
agents, local 412
aging populations 272
AGT, Inc. case study 226–35
Ahold 171, 264, 431
AIDS 466; pharmaceutical pricing 401–2; social marketing case study 361, 365–9, **366**
Aids Prevention International (API) 365
Air Canada 332
Air France 260–1
air shows 444, 456
Airbus 153, 169, 182–3, 332, 444
aircraft industry 332, 444
airlines 332; British Airways flights to Armenia case study 470
Ajegroup 193–4
Ajinmoto 64
Al-Manar Television 122
Alcantara 248
alcohol abuse 361
alcoholic beverages, and taxes 378
AlertDriving 216
Alfa SA 289, 318
Algeria, population trends **271**, 272
AlibabaGroup Holdings Ltd. 433
All-Africa Games 100
ally strategic option 114, *115*, 116
Alshaya Group 287
alter strategic option 114, *115*, 115–16
Alvaro 464
Amazon.com 433
ambush marketing 462
American Express 460

American International Group 375
American National Standards Institute (ANSI) 319
American Standard 423
American Textile Manufacturing Institute 102
Americana Foods 186
Ameridere 403–5
AmLife Insurance Bhd. 298
AMMB Holdings Bhd. 298
Amway 432, 453
Anadolu 292
analysis by inference 207–8
analytic competence, of global marketing managers 10, **11**
Andean Community (CAN) **42**
Anglo cluster 262
Anheuser-Busch InBev NV *see* AB InBev
Animal Planet 485
ANSI (American National Standards Institute) 319
anthropology 58
antiglobals (global segmentation category) 351
antitrust laws 174, 177, 193, 374, 382
APA (Advanced Pricing Agreement Program) 389
API (Aids Prevention International) 365
Apple 207, 257, 323–4, 333, 391, 412, 430–1
Aquarius 531
Arab Contractors 181
Arab Dairy 285
Arab League, boycott of Israel 104, 106
Arab Spring 489
Arçelik 173, 181, 182, 183
Argentina 171; color preferences 73; currency controls 40; expediting payments 158; inflation 205–6, 384; international trade **19**, 46–8; marketing research 205–6; nontariff

trade barriers 40; operating restrictions 104; tariffs 38
Ariel 353
Arla Foods 187
Armenia 262, 470–1
Armenian Airlines 471
arms sales, Middle East case study 190–1
arts, the 278
ASEAN Free Trade Area (AFTA) **42**
Asia 7, 218; and advertising 482, 489; cola market 194; consumer needs 139; counterfeiting and piracy 359; customer expectations of service 344, 345; distribution 412; language 82–3; life insurance 298; marketing research 216; pan-regional branding 352; as polychronic cultures 71; religions **60**, 64–5; retail giants in 437–8; retailing 413; word-of-mouth advertising 464–5; and working hours 90 *see also* Central Asia, marketing research; individually named Asian countries; Southeast Asia
Asian financial crisis, 1997 46
assembly 288–9
Association of National Advertisers 495
AstraZeneca 360
AT&T 295
Attaturk 79
Auchon 252
Aurobindo 402
Austin, James 114–15
Australia 32–3, 34, 44, 49, 50, 64, 127, 216, 262; countertrade 398; dumping 385; psychic distance 259, **260**; transfer pricing 389
Austrian Airlines 332, 471
Automatic Feed Company of Ohio 33
automobile industry, product development 327
Automotive Parts Manufacturers Association 186
avoid strategic option 114, *115*, 116
Avon 28, 104, 154, 264, 334, 432, 517
Azerbaijan 208, 262, 471
Azko Nobel 204

B2B *see* business markets
BA (British Airways) 460, 470
back translation 211–12
Baidu.com 357
Bain & Company 528
balance of payments (BOP) 25–7, **26**
Bangladesh 50–1, 337
Bango 173
Bank for Investment and Development of Vietnam (BIDV) 298
BankAmerica 343
bankruptcy 111
banks: Islamic 63; US 4
Banyu 217, 424
Barbarino, Ken 224–6
Barbie doll case study 88–9
Barclays International 105
bargaining 381
Barkema, Harry 263
Baskin-Robbins 186
BAT (British American Tobacco) 435, 439

Bausch and Lomb 395
Bavaria 462
Bayer group 395, 507
BBC World 485
BBDO 492
Bcom3 Group 476
Bead for Life 433
Beaudreau, Jennifer 403–5
Bechtel 153
behavioural standards 523
Beijing Olympics 170, 461, 465, 481
Beko 185
Belgium 264, 378, 381
Belgium Beer Cafe 286
benchmarking 217
Benneton 431
Best Buy 453
BharatMatrimony 331
Bharti Airtel 142, 251
Bic 169–70
bidding processes 457–8
BIDV (Bank for Investment and Development of Vietnam) 298
Big Apple Bagels 287
Big Boy 86
Big Burger 224
Big C 264
Big Cola 193–4
big data 214–15
Bill and Melinda Gates Foundation 368
Bimbo 4, 173, 297
Bioplastic Feedstock Alliance 171
Bishop, Jay 468–71
blogging, as a form of protest 102
BMW 289, 318, 381, 392
body armor 329–30
body language 83
Boeing 3, 153, 169, 182–3, 190, 444
Bolivia 81, 206, 384
Bolshoi Ballet 278
BOP (balance of payments) 25–7, **26**
BOP (bottom of the pyramid) 144–5
born globals 245–6, 259; organizational structures 522
Bosch 72
bottom of the pyramid (BOP) 144–5
bottom-up approaches to branding 350
boycotts **98**, 104, 107–8, 115, 185
BP Amoco 157
Brady Corporation 511
brand champions 350
branding 347; brand names 85, 101, 347–9; of countries 184–5; and export pricing 34; global brand strategies 349–52; global *vs.* local 353–4, **354**; local 168, 349, 353–4, **354**; pan-regional 352; private 354; and standardized advertising 479 *see also* trademarks
Brasil Telecom 294
Brazil 7, 250, 252, 290, 352, 389, 467; and advertising 489; attitudes toward time 71; cola market 4, 193; counterfeiting and piracy 357, 359; direct marketing 432; distribution 427; dumping 385; education 346; exchange rates 32; facilitating payments 157; global segmentation categories 351; government contracts

153; IMF assistance for 36; inflation 384; international trade statistics **19**; language 81; marketing research 210, 212, 213; online retailing 433; personal selling 447; price controls 116; retailing 430; sales negotiations 450, 468–70; smuggling 434; tariffs 38; taxes 378; telemarketing 463; trade with Argentina 46, 47, 48 *see also* BRIC (Brazil, Russia, India, China)
Bretton Woods conference, 1944 20, 36
bribery 148, 154, 449; and government markets 155, **155–6**, 157–60, **159**
Bribery Act, 2010 (UK) 159
BRIC (Brazil, Russia, India, China) 253–4 *see also* Brazil; China; India; Russia
Brink's Company 263–4
Bristol-Myers Squibbs 168, 401, 402
Britain *see* United Kingdom
British Airways (BA) 460, 470
British American Tobacco (BAT) 435, 439
British Standards Institution (BSI) 319
British Telecom 295
BRL Hardy 262
Brunei 189
BSE (mad-cow disease) 465
BSI (British Standards Institution) 319
Buddhism **60**, 64–5
Budejovicky Budvar 356
Budweiser 216, 244, 302, 356, 462, 481, 495
Bulgaria 144, 363
Burger King 265, 286, 297, 427
business etiquette 449–50
business groups **178**, 181–2
business markets (B2B markets) 137, 148–51, 248; buyer power 381; distribution channels 413, 415; and pricing 381; selling to 456–8; word-of-mouth advertising 465
Business Monitor International 118
business services 343 *see also* service industries
Business Week 485
buybacks 397–8
buyer power 381–2
buying criteria 447
buying decisions 447
buzz marketing 464–5

Caballero 329–30
CACM (Central American Common Market) **42**
Cadbury 185, 252, 315, 380, 446
Cadbury Schweppes 126, 127, 530
Cadillac 7
California Milk Processing Board 483
Cambodia, textile industry 50
Cambridge Corporation 452
Cameroon 261
CAN (Andean Community) **42**
Canada 261, 262; bankruptcy 111; consumer animosity 186; dumping 385; and exchange rates 33; G7/G8 membership 37; international trade statistics **19**; test marketing

in 333; textile industry 49 see also
NAFTA (North American Free Trade
Association)
Canadian Standards Association 319
candy advertising 481
Canon 354, 507
Canton Fair, China 456
capital account (balance of payments)
26, 26–7
car roofs, standards for 320–1
Care International 342, 361
careers in global marketing 527–8
Carewell Industries 333
Carlsberg 252
Carrefour 171–2, 262, 264, 432, 437–8
Carsa Group 463
cartels 374, 382–3; Europe 174 see also
price-fixing
Carter, Jimmy 117
Cartier 484
Casino 252
Casino Guichard-Perrachon SA 264
Castro, Fidel 125, 126
Caterpillar 217, 248
Cell Alliance 295
cell-phones, and advertising 489
Cemex 96, 182, 183, 264, 318, 459
Cencosud 171
Central American Common Market
(CACM) **42**
Central Asia, marketing research
205, 210
central banks 28–9, **29**
Cereal Partners Worldwide 296
CFR (cost and freight) 387
Chad 73, 205, 261
Chandrasekaran, Deepa 334
channel alignment 414, *414*, 416–17
channel captains 416–17
channel costs 378
channel length 379, *414*, *415–16*, 445
channel members 411–13; factors
influencing selection of 417–19;
location and selection of **419**, 419–20
channel participants: controlling 421–2;
motivation of 420–1
Chaoshian, Alexander 471
Chase 343
Chavez, Hugo 96, 250
Cheesecake Factory 287
Chen, Andy 497–500
Chevron Texaco 106
children, advertising to 495–7
Chile 85, 171, 172, 389
China 7, 35, 102, 183, 189, 262, 381,
466; advertising 480–1, 488–9, 490;
AIDS 367; arms purchases 153,
191; bankruptcy 111; bargaining
381; beauty market 325; blogging
102; branding 354; car market 382,
394, 490; careers in marketing 527,
528; cartels 382–3; coffee price case
study 399–401; cola market 170;
color preferences 72, 73; competitive
advantage 24; consumer animosity
186; corruption 425; counterfeiting
and piracy 357, 358, 359, 360, 364,
430–1; country-of-origin perceptions
184; credit cards 385–6; and

demographic segmentation 142, **142**,
144; diaspora markets 147–8; direct
marketing 432; discretionary income
380; distribution 417, 425; elite
markets 144, 147; emerging markets
case study 268–9; exchange rates
31; family life 65, 67; first-mover
advantage 246; food preferences 316;
franchising 287; garlic production 21;
global segmentation categories 351,
352; as a globally strategic market
252; halal food 63–4; ideology 101;
income distribution 138; infant
formula marketing 108; international
trade statistics **19**; Internet market
293; and Iraq 115; labeling 323;
labor practices 336; legal environment
109; local firms 120, 172; magic
moments 413; market segmentation
141, 144, 146–7; marketing
research 205, 206, 208, 214, 215,
219; melamine contamination of
infant products 285; mergers and
acquisitions 297; as a must-win
market 247–8; online retailing 433;
operating restrictions 104, 292;
parallel imports 394; population
trends **271**, 272; price controls 384;
re-entry strategies 265; regulatory
environment 110; religion **60**, 62,
65; research and development 330;
retailing 428, 437; sales negotiations
450; sales practices 453; service
industries 343; shampoo market 168;
ShanghaiCosmopolitan.com case
study 497–500; smuggling 439; SOEs
(state-owned enterprises) 101, 178,
179–80, 183; sports sponsorship 462;
strategic pork reserve 113–14; textile
industry 49–50, 51; trade fairs 456;
trade restrictions 40, 41; trademark
protection 356; universities 345–6;
urban and rural populations 141,
142; VERs (voluntary export
restrictions) 39; word-of-mouth
advertising 465 see also BRIC (Brazil,
Russia, India, China)
China Post 180
Chinon 422
Christianity **60–1**, 61–2
Christmas 61–2
Chugai Pharmaceuticals 285, 424
CIF (cost, insurance and freight) 387
cigarettes 378; advertising 481, 496;
smuggling 434–5, 438–40
Cinnabon Inc. 329
Cipla 401
CIS (Commonwealth of Independent
States) **42**
Citibank 252, 343, 454, 533
CIVETS (Colombia, Indonesia, Vietnam,
Egypt, Turkey, South Africa) 254 see
also Colombia; Egypt; Indonesia;
South Africa; Turkey; Vietnam
civil law 108–9
Clearasil 116
climate 315
Clorox 28
CNN 485

Coca-Cola 4, 7, 32, 62, 64, 100, 103,
104, 107, 122, 168, 170, 171, 177,
185, 189, 243, 251, 252, 262, 347,
348, 350, 374, 392, 423, 446, 461,
471, 477, 490, 494, 496–7, 510; cola
wars case study 192–4; organizational
structure case study 530–1; political
climate case study 126–7
Cold Stone Creamery 248, 314
Colgate 28, 384
Colgate-Palmolive 168, 349, 374, 428
collection infrastructure 385–6
Colombia 145, 251, 329–30, 361 see
also CIVETS (Colombia, Indonesia,
Vietnam, Egypt, Turkey, South Africa)
color preferences 72–3, 316
commission, sales forces 454
common law 108
common markets **42**, 43
Commonwealth of Independent States
(CIS) **42**
Communication Radio 488–9
communication systems 524–5
comparability, of marketing research data
206, 216
comparative advantage 21–3, **22**
compensation: for expropriation 96, 105;
sales forces 453–4
compensation transactions 397
competition 168–9, 248; and advertising
493; business groups 181–2; Cola
wars case study 192–4; competition
research 201, 216–18, **218**;
country-of-origin 183–7; cultural
attitudes towards 174–7; from
emerging markets 177–8; and exit
strategies 264; between global firms
169–71; globalization of 169–73;
home country actions 182–3; and
joint ventures 292; Jollibee case
study 188–9; as a microindicator
of market size and growth 257;
Middle East arms sales case study
190–1; new global players 182; and
pricing 382–3; SOEs (state-owned
enterprises) 178–80
competitive advantage 23–4
competitive screen 153–4
competitiveness, and exchange rates 32–3
complaints 345
concept testing 332
Concert 295
Conforama 185
Confucianism 64, 65
consortium selling 458
consumer animosity 186–7
consumer behavior 139–40, **140**, 209,
381, 415 see also purchasing behavior
consumer ethnocentrism 185–6
consumer ethnographics 209
consumer markets 137–9, **138**; consumer
behavior 139–40, **140**, 209, 381,
415; consumer needs 139; pull
strategies 445
consumer safety 320–1, 322
consumer services 343–4 see also service
industries
consumers: country-of-origin perceptions
183–7; expectations of service 344–5;

harm from counterfeits 357, 359; physical size of 317; response to brands 351
contract manufacturing 288, 354
contracts, written 450
Control Component Inc. 158
control, of global organizations 523–5
convenience goods 415
convenience sampling 213
cooperation agreements 397–8
Coptic Orphans 162
Cornell, School of Hotel Administration 247
Corona 301, 302, 355
corporate culture 525
corporate goals 507
corporate security 122, 123
corporate social responsibility 466–7
corporate socialization 525
corporate worldview 507–9
corruption 148, 154, 449; and distribution 425; and government markets 155, **155–6**, 157–60, *159*
Corruption Perception Index (CPI) 155, **155–6**
Cosmopolitan 485
cosmopolitans, as a market segment 145–6
cost savings: and overseas production 289–90; and standardized advertising 479
cost-based pricing 388
Costa Rica 41
CostCo Wholesale Corp. 326
costs: of personal selling 447; and pricing 375–9, **376**; transportation 425
Coty Inc. 7, 481
counterfeits 357–8, 392, 430–1, 434; strategies for fighting 358–60
counterparry strategy 170, 248
countertrade 396–8
countries, branding of 184–5
country market report 537–43
country selection 254; grouping international markets 261–2; psychic distance 259–61, **260**; screening process 254–5, **255**; selection criteria 255–9, **256**, *257*, *258*
country-based organizational structures *515*, 515–16, *518*
country-of-origin perceptions 183–5; consumer animosity 186–7; consumer ethnocentrism 185–6
couponing 459
courtesy bias 216
CPI (Corruption Perception Index) 155, **155–6**
credibility, of advertising 482–3
credit cards 318–19
credit infrastructure 385–6
Cristal 294
critical mass 261
cross-country subsidization 169–70
cross-cultural negotiations 150
Cuba 106, 209; political climate case study 125–6
cultural identity 98, **98**, 101
culture 56–7, *57*; adapting to cultural difference 86–7; and advertising

481–3; and attitudes towards time 71–2, 89–90; Barbie doll case study 88–9; cultural change 79; definition of 58; and education 69–71, **70**; and the family 65, **66**, 67–9; Hofstede measures of culture 73, **74–5**, 76–80; influences on marketing *58*, 58–9; language and communication 81–6, **82**; material culture and aesthetics 72–3; and organizational structure 510; and pricing 381; and religion 59, **60–1**, 61–4; and service industries 344–7; tight/loose 112
culture shock 261
currencies: foreign exchange restrictions 40 *see also* exchange rates
current account (balance of payments) 26, **26**
Curves 286–7
customer profiles 511
customization 394–5
customs unions **42**, 43
CVRD 470
Cyworld 76
Czech Republic 252, **253**, 465–6

D&S 171–2
Daft, Douglas 530
DaimlerChrysler 123, 333
Daiwa Sports 415
Dangdang 172
Danone 171, 294, 354, 375
Danyel, Seda 471
Dasani 171
Dash 353
Dassault Aviation S.A. 190
data collection: government regulation of 210, 215–16; in marketing research 213–14
Dawar, Niraj 172
DDB Worldwide 476
defender strategy 172
defensive strategies 245
Dell 215, 416, 433, 447
Deloitte Touche Tohmatsu International 454
demand, analysis of demand patterns 208
demographic dividend 272
demographic segmentation 142, **143**, 144–5
Denmark 73, 77, 184, 187
Deutsche Telekom 296
devaluation: Russia 32; Venezuela 27–8
developed countries, market attractiveness of **249**, 249–50
developing countries: competition in 176–7; government markets in 152–4; low price strategies 380–1; market attractiveness of **249**, 250–2; urban and rural populations 141–2, **142**
DeVry 346
DHL 180, 245, 334
dialects 84, **484**
diaspora markets 147–8, 161–2
Dior 144
direct exporting 281–4, **283**, *299*, 300
direct mail 463
direct marketing 432
direct subsidies 103

Discovery 485
discretionary income 379–80
Disney 7, 56, 81, 329, 347, 479, 514; Hong Kong Disneyland 56, 114, 168, 202
disposable diaper market 137
distribution 410–11, **411**; access to channels 422–4; analyzing national channels 413–17, *414*; channel member selection 417–19; channel partner location and selection **419**, 419–20; cigarette smuggling case study 438–40; foreign-market channel members 411–13; logistics 424–7; management of 420–2; and parallel markets 395; retail giants in Asia case study 437–8; retailing 427–33, **429**; smuggling 434–5
distribution density 414, *414*, 415
distribution logistics *see* logistics
distribution margins 379
Diwali 446
DKT Indonesia 369
dodger strategy 173
domestic marketing 5, *5*
domestication 96, 105
Dominican Republic 251
Dow Chemical 107
Dow Corning 123, 467
drug overdoses 322
Dubai 122–3, 153, 189, 216, 489
Dubai Ports World 99
dumping 377, 385
Dunkin' Donuts 2, 170, 265, 348
DuPont 102, 289
DVDs 357, 359

e-commerce 433; counterfeiting and piracy 358; payment issues 385–6; regulation of 111
E-Mart 438
Eachnet 297
East African Breweries 464
Eastern Europe 67, 72, 252, 439, 481 *see also* individually-named countries
eBay 4, 293, 297, 358
economic integration 41–4, **42**
economies of scale 261, 262, 313, 376
Economist Intelligence Unit (EIU) 118
Ecowash 287
Ecuador 100, 193
education 69–71, **70**, 345–6, 448
EFTA (European Free Trade Area) **42**
Egypt 153, 176; and advertising 483; arms purchases 191; attitudes toward time 71; attitudes towards rules 112; banking industry 297; business groups 181; consumer animosity 187; exports 100; expropriation 105; franchising 287; and global segmentation categories 351; marketing research 210; political risk 121, 264–5; SOEs (state-owned enterprises) 178, *179*; tourism advertising 478 *see also* CIVETS (Colombia, Indonesia, Vietnam, Egypt, Turkey, South Africa)
eHarmony 202
EIU (Economist Intelligence Unit) 118

El Salvador 251
Eli Lilley 96
eligibility screen 152–3
Elite 62
elites, as target markets 144
Elle 485
EMC (export management companies) 280
emerging markets 242; attractiveness of 242–54, **249, 253**; competition from 177–8; competition in 176–7; retail potential of **429–30**
emic approach to marketing research 203–4, 209, 211
emotion: and advertising 482; and language 83–4
employees, and cultural adaptation 86
English language 81, 85–6, 449, 482, 483–4, **484**, 485
entry strategies 278, 298–300, **299**; AB InBev case study 301–2; exporting 279, 279–84, **280, 283**; foreign production 279, 284–90; mergers and acquisitions 296–8, **299**; ownership strategies 279, 290–6, **293**; Volkswagen/Suzuki case study 303–5
environmental competence, of global marketing managers 10, **11**
environmental laws, China 102
environmental studies 201
environmental sustainability 337
espionage, commercial 217
ESPN 485
Esprit 526
Esso 476
Estee Lauder 338, 490
Estonia 184
ethical products case study 335–7
Ethiopia 120, 205, 251
ethnocentric orientation 507–8
etic approach to marketing research 203, 211
etiquette 449–50
EU (European Union) **42**, 43–4, 183, 261; and advertising 481, 484; competition policy 174–5, 382–3; dumping 385; government regulation of sales promotion 460; marketing research 215–16; parallel imports 391, 393, 395; privacy laws 215–16, 463; product liability law 110–11; standards certification 319, 320, 321; taxes 378; telemarketing 463; and translation 84; and VERs (voluntary export restrictions) 39 *see also* Europe; individually-named countries
euro 43–4, 383, 391
Eurobrands 352
EuroDisney 18, 56, 347
Euromonitor 204
Europe: attitude toward time 71; cola market 192–3; color preferences 73; competition in 174–5; market attractiveness of 249, 250; marketing research 209; pharmaceutical prices 402; retail regulation 413; road safety standards 320–1; sales force recruitment 453; sales promotions 460; tariffs 44; vacation time 72

see also EU (European Union); individually-named countries
European Central Bank 43
European Digital Library 101
European Food and Safety Authority 481
European Free Trade Area (EFTA) **42**
European Monetary System 43
Eurostat 225
EveryD.com 533
Evian 171
exchange rates 27–8; causes of movements in 29–30; foreign exchange market 28–9, **29**; implications for global marketing 32–5; managed currencies 30–1; and pricing 383–4, 389–91
exhaustion principle 392–3
exit strategies 263–5
expectations, of customers 344–5
expediting payments 157–8 *see also* bribery
export agents 280–1
export consortiums 282
export departments, organizational structures 512
export management companies (EMC) 280
export marketing **5**, 6
export markets, and exchange rates 32–4
export prices, and exchange rates 32–4
export tariffs 38
exporting, as an entry strategy 279, 279–84, **280, 283, 299**, 300
exports: export price calculation **386**, 386–7; and national prosperity 100; VERs (voluntary export restrictions) 39 *see also* protectionism
expropriation 96, 105, **121**
extender strategy 172–3
Exxon 105, 250
Exxon Mobil 106, 476

facilitating payments 157–8 *see also* bribery
Factiva 204
families: and consumer behavior 140, **140**; and cultural differences 65, **66**, 67–9
Family Health International 369
family-owned businesses 181; Europe 174
FARC 361
Farnborough Air Show 456
FCPA (Foreign Corrupt Practices Act) (US) 154, 157–8, 523
Federal Trade Commission (FTC) 495
FedEx/Federal Express 180, 349, 467
Ferrero SpA 320
Fiat 303, 478
financial difficulties, and exit strategies 264
financial services 343
Finland 7, 184
Firestone tires 111, 116
First Gulf War 83
first-mover advantage 246
fixed costs 375–7
Fleet Bank 106
flexibility 510
FOB (free on board) 387

focus groups 209–10
Fomento Economico Mexicano SA 331
Fonterra Co-Operative Group 285
food: advertising 481, 496–7; and cultural differences 56, 58, 59, 62, 63–4, 114, 315, 316
football sponsorship 461, 462
Ford 3, 104, 107, 111, 116, 243, 387, 435, 454, 492, 518–19
foreign currencies, and pricing 389–91
foreign direct investment 20
foreign exchange market 28–9, **29**
Foreign Exchange Regulation Act, 1973 (India) 103
foreign exchange, restrictions on 40
foreign production, as an entry strategy 279, 284–90
forward prices 390
Foster, Mary 365
Fox, Vicente 43, 193
France 7; and advertising 483; attitudes toward rules 112; bankruptcy 111; cola market 192; consumer animosity 186; cultural identity 101; EuroDisney 18, 56, 347; exports 100; franchising 286; G7/G8 membership 37; international trade statistics **19**; Iraq War 115; language 81; marketing research 206, 216; power distance 73; trade fairs 456; wine industry 314; and working hours 72, 89–90
France Telecom 296
franchising 286–7, 428
franchising fees, and exchange rates 35
free trade 37; free-trade areas **42**, 42–3 *see also* protectionism
Friedman, George 76
Frito-Lay 316, 480, 496
Frost, Tony 172
FTC (Federal Trade Commission) 495
Fuji 151, 170, 217, 422
Fujitsu 175, 324
Fukuyama, Francis 58, 68, 69
full-cost pricing 376
full compensation 397
Fulla doll 89
functional competence, of global marketing managers 10, **11**
functional organizational structures 517–19, *518*

G7 (Group of Seven) 37
G8 (Group of Eight) 37
Gabon 261
Gallup Organization 206
Gamali Air case study 403–5
games of chance 460
Gap 336
garlic production 21
Garnier 264, 325
Garret, Geoffrey 44
Gatorade 531
GATT (General Agreement on Tariffs and Trade) 20, 40.49, 370
GCC (Gulf Cooperation Council) **42**
GDP (gross domestic product) 29, 206, 379
gender: and consumer behavior 140, **140**; and cultural differences 65, **66**,

67–8; and demographic segmentation 142, **142**; and marketing research 210; masculinity-femininity (Hofstede measures of culture) **74–5**, 77; and waiting in line 346
General Agreement on Tariffs and Trade (GATT) 20, 40.49, 370
General Electric 96, 106, 122, 175, 295, 381, 435, 532
General Mills 296, 374
General Motors 38, 101, 107, 120, 151, 174, 243, 246, 288, 291, 292, 303, 320, 327, 330, 380, 381, 412, 435
Geni index (income inequality) 139
geocentric orientation 508–9
geographic distance 510
geographic organizational structures *515*, 515–17, *516, 518*
Georgia 262
Germany 22–4, **23**; and advertising 483; attitudes toward rules 112; bankruptcy 111; and bribery 158; color preferences 73; consumer animosity 186; country-of-origin perceptions 184; education 69; exports 100; family life 67; family-owned businesses 174; G7/ G8 membership 37; government regulation of sales promotion 460; as a high-trust society 69; international trade statistics **19**; marketing research 205, 206, 214, 215; nontariff trade barriers 39; outsourcing 24–5, **25**; population trends **271**, 272; trade fairs 456; working hours 72, 90
Ghana 251, 378, 467
gifts 449
Gillette 116, 269
GlaxoSmithKline 389, 401
global account management 454–5
global agnostics (global segmentation category) 352
Global Alliance 336
global baby bust case study 270, **271**, 272–3
Global Brands Study 351, 353
global buyers 150–1
global citizens (global segmentation category) 351
global dreamers (global segmentation category) 351
global economy 18, 45; Argentina case study 46–8; and the balance of payments 25–7, **26**; basic theories of world trade 20–4, **22**, **23**; and economic integration 41–4, **42**; and exchange rates 27–35, 29; and global outsourcing 24–5, **25**; and globalization 44–5; and international agencies 36–7; and international trade 18–20, **19**; protectionism and trade restrictions 37–41; textile industry case study 49–52
global information systems 220–1
global mandates, and organizational structures 522
global marketing: development of *5*, 5–9, **9**; importance of studying 9–10, **11** *see also* marketing

global marketing managers 9–10, **11**
global markets *see* markets
global media 485
Global One 296
global organizations: organizational structures 514–22, *515, 516, 518, 520, 521 see also* MNCs (multinational corporations)
global segments 146–7
global theme approach to advertising 477–8
globalization 44–5, 72
globally strategic markets **247**, 247–8, 252
glossary 545–58
GNP (gross national product) 137–8, **138**, 206, 258, 379; GNP per capita 99, 206
Gome 433
Gonzalez, Omar 461
Google 99, 101, 251, 348, 357
government markets 151; and bribery 155, **155–6**, 157–60, **159**; buying process in 151–2; in developing countries 152–4; selling to 456–8
government policies, and exchange rate movements 30
government regulation: of data collection 210, 215–16; of sales promotion 460
government statistics 205–6
government subsidies/incentives 98, 102–3, 247
governments, and counterfeiting and piracy 358–9
Grab Bucket 348
Grand Hyatt Hotel, Cairo 287
Grand Metropolitan 175
gray markets 391–5
Greece, population trends **271**, 272
Grey Poupon 186
gross domestic product *see* GDP (gross domestic product)
gross national product *see* GNP (gross national product)
Group of Eight (G8) 37
Group of Seven (G7) 37
Groupo Mondelo 301–2
Groupon 168
Gruma 245, 385
Grupo Mondelo 355
guanxi 498
Guatemala 78, 117, 402
Gucci 355
Guggenheim Museum 278
Guinea 261
Guinness 175
Gulf Cooperation Council *see* GCC (Gulf Cooperation Council)
Gulf Oil 179

Hague Conference on International Private Law 111
Haier 297
halal food 63–4
Halliburton 508, 509
Hannover Fair, Germany 456
Hardee's 186
Harris, Jennifer 122
Harry Potter 358

Harvard Business School 345, 346
HCL Industries 80
headquarters: conflict with subsidiaries 525–6, **526**; location of 508
hedging **390**, 390–1
Heineken 321, 331, 350, 487
Heinz 173, 254, 464, 479
Herbalife 453
Hero supermarkets 437
Hertz 286
Hetero 401
Hewlett-Packard 142, 336, 342, 435, 496
Hezbollah 122
hierarchy of needs 139
Hikma Pharmaceuticals 182
Hilton Worldwide 244
Hinduism 59, **60**, 64, 65, 139, 446
Hindustan Lever Ltd 317
Hitachi 175
HNO (human nature orientation) 112
Hofstede measures of culture 73; individualism-collectivism **74–5**, 76–7; masculinity-femininity **74–5**, 77; power distance 73, **74–5**, 76; uncertainty avoidance **74–5**, 77–8; uses and limitations of 78–9
Holcim Ltd. 264
Holderbank 245
Holiday Inn 286
Hollis, Nigel 526
Hollywood movies 312
Holt, Douglas 351
Home Center 423
home country: government actions 105–7, 182–3, 282; political climate 105–8; pressure groups 107–8
Home Depot 171, 416, 431, 532
Honda 96, 347, 355
Honeywell International 175
Hong Kong: business etiquette 449; counterfeiting and piracy 357; Hong Kong Disneyland 56, 114, 168, 202; marketing research 213
hookahs 286
Hoover 218
Hope Foundation 368
host country: government actions 98, 102–3, 384; political climate 97–105, **98**; pressure groups 102
Huawei 179–80
human resources 509–10
Hungary 23
Huntington, Samuel 58
Hyatt 107, 287
hybrid brand strategies 350–1
Hyundai 65, 206, 252, 392, 462, 464

I-Flex Solutions 533
IBM 103, 175, 245, 249, 295, 333, 343, 455, 467, 508
Icelandic language 314
ideology 98, **98**, 101
IDS (Integrated Defense Systems) 190
iEconomist 485
Iger, Robert 514
IKEA 9, 317, 391, 431, 466
Ilkone Mobile Telecommunications 63
Imai, Masaaki 452

IMF (International Monetary Fund) 36, 138, 206
immigration 273
Imperial Tobacco Group PLC 355
import intermediaries 411–12
import tariffs 38
imports 208; import pricing 34; parallel imports 391–5. see also protectionism
incentives 445–6
income distribution 138–9
income level, and pricing 379–81
income statistics 205
independent distributors 281
Independent Television Commission 464
India 4, 7, 252, 262, 292, 378, 467; advertising 489; and AIDS 368; arms purchases 191; business groups 181, 182; cell phone use 385; cola market 170, 193; color preferences 72, 73; consumer animosity 187; and demographic segmentation 142; diaspora markets 148; distribution 410; dumping 385; English language use 85; exchange rates 33; foreign exchange regulations 116; foreign retailers policy 100; franchising 287; as a globally strategic market 252; higher education 346; income distribution 138; informal economy 144; insurance market 375; international trade statistics **19**; IT sector 531–4; labor practices 337; language 81; local firms 172; management styles 79–80; market liberalization 176; marketing research 208, 209; mergers and acquisitions 297; outsourcing 24–5, **25**, 80, 85; ownership conditions 103, 116; pharmaceutical prices 401; regulatory environment 110; religion 59, **60**, 64, 65, 446; smuggling 434, 439; textile industry 49; transfer pricing 389; urban and rural population 142, **142** see also BRIC (Brazil, Russia, India, China)
indirect exporting 279–81, **299**
indirect subsidies 103
individualism-collectivism (Hofstede measures of culture) **74–5**, 76–7
Indonesia 254, 289, 355, 356, 466; advertising 496; and AIDS 368–9; cola market 193; compensation transactions 397; corruption 425; distribution 410, 425; dumping 385; and global segmentation categories 351, 352; halal food 64; IMF assistance for 36; labor practices 336; local firms 173; magic moments 413; marketing research 210, 213; palm oil production 337; poorer consumers 145; quotas 38; retailing 437 see also CIVETS (Colombia, Indonesia, Vietnam, Egypt, Turkey, South Africa); MINT (Mexico, Indonesia, Nigeria, Turkey)
IndUS Entrepreneurs (TIE) 534
INFACT (Infant Formula Action Coalition) 108
infant formula marketing 107–8, 466

inflation: and exchange rate movements 29; and pricing 384
influence screen 154
informal economy 144–5, 205
Informatics Holdings Inc. 286
infrastructure 315; and terrorism 123
Ingersoll-Rand PLC 106
Inland Revenue Service (IRS) 389
Innocent 192–3
INSEAD 247
Institute of Public and Environmental Affairs, China 102
insurance: life insurance 298; political risk **121**, 121–2
Integrated Defense Systems (IDS) 190
Intel 330, 467
Intelicon 468–70
Interbrand Corporation 347, 349, 350
Interbrew 86, 286
interest rates 30
intermediaries: import intermediaries 411–12; indirect exporting 29–281
International Bank for Reconstruction and Development see World Bank (International Bank for Reconstruction and Development)
International Chamber of Commerce 386
international divisions, and organizational structures 513–14, 514
international education 122–3
international exhaustion principle 393
international marketing 5, 5, 6, 7, 8
International Monetary Fund (IMF) 36, 138, 206
International Social Justice (ISJ) 367
International Standards Organization (ISO) 319–20
international trade 3; basic theories of 20–4, **22**, **23**; overview of 18–20, **19**
international trade fairs 456–7
internationalization 243–6, **244**
Internet 391; and advertising 489, 496–7; and communication systems 524–5; and exporting 282–4, **283**; online retailing 433; and order processing 426; product adaptation 314; and spam 463
Intuition, case study 338
inventory control 425
inventory, spare parts 324
Iran 176, 262; 1979 revolution 117; Barbie doll case study 88; cola market 192; cultural identity 101; language 81; local partnerships 120; political risk 121; religion 62; terrorism 122; trade embargoes 106
Iraq 103, 106, 115, 121; Iraq War 117, 186
Ireland 262
IRS (Inland Revenue Service) 389
ISJ (International Social Justice) 367
Islam 59, **60**, **61**, 62, **63**, 63–4, 114, 139–40; Barbie doll case study 88–9; and consumer animosity 187
Islamic law 109
ISO (International Standards Organization) 319–20

Israel: Arab League boycott 104, 106; attitude toward time 71; attitudes toward rules 112; and exchange rates 33; religion 59, **61**, 62; and terrorism 122
Isuzu Motors 151
IT sector, India 531–4
IT systems, and global account management 455
Italy **19**, 68, 112, 184, 456, 459
Ivory Coast 261

J. Crew Group Inc. 259, 294
J. Walter Thompson 492
J.C. Penney 171
Jaguar 182, 479
Jambo Juice 431
Japan 7, 78; and advertising 482; automobile manufacturers 4; bankruptcy 111; color preferences 72, 73, 316; competition in 175–6; competition information 257; competitive advantage 24; consumer animosity 186; consumer behavior 139; country-of-origin perceptions 184; couponing 459; customer expectations of service 344, 345; defensive strategies 245; disposable diaper market 137; distribution 416, 421, 422, 424; earthquake and tsunami 412–13, 425; English language usage 85–6; exchange rates 30–1, 34; franchising 287; G7/G8 membership 37; gender roles **66**, 67–8; global segmentation categories 352; government regulation of sales promotion 460; as a high-trust society 69; international trade statistics **19**; language 81; and language 84; laundry products 315; as a lead market 248; legal firms 343; market attractiveness of 249, 250; marketing research 210, 213, 215; parallel imports 393; population trends **271**, 272, 273; and pricing 381; product regulations 115–16; quality expectations 318; re-entry strategies 265; regulatory environment 110; religion 59, **60**, 65; retailing 437–8; sales forces 454; sales practices 452; service personnel 347; tariffs 44; transfer pricing 389; vacation time 72; word-of-mouth advertising 464, 465; and working hours 90
Japan Institute of Product Maintenance 173
JIT (just-in-time) inventory control 425
John Wiley & Sons 394
Johns Hopkins Medicine International 292, 343
joint ventures 291–5, **293**, **299**, 300, 423–4
Jollibee 161, 188–9
Jordan 182
JST (Jeff Sons Trading Company) 226
Judaism 59, **61**, 62
judgment sampling 213
Jung, Andrea 154
just-in-time (JIT) inventory control 425
just-like-us segmentation 147–8

Kadokawa, Yoshihiko 84
Kao 168, 245
Kazakhstan 208, 210, 287
keiretsus 175, 176
Kelley Blue Book 343
Kellogg 7, 296, 374
Kellogg, Brown & Root 157
Kenya 215, 251, 361, 366, 464, 467
KFC 64, 186, 187, 245, 286, 378, 428, 466
Kia 185
kidney dialysis equipment example **258**, 258–9
Kin Wo Chong 331
Kinder eggs 320
Kingfisher 431
Koç group 181
Kodak 170, 217, 348, 422, 471
Kola Real 193
Komatsu 217, 507
Korea *see* North Korea; South Korea
Kraft 242, 354, 519
Krishnan, R. 267–8
Krispy Kreme Doughnuts 2
Kumb Mela 446
Kuwait 117, 179

L'Oreal 145, 168, 264, 325, 380, 432
labeling 322–3
labor practices 335–7
Lalas, Alexis 461
Land Rover 182, 377–8
language 81, **82**, 84, 85–6, 152; and advertising 483–4, **484**; body language 83; context of 82–3; and emotion 83–4; forms of address 81; and personal selling 448–9 *see also* translation
lateness 449
Latin America: buyer-seller relationships 452; cola market 193; language 81; marketing research 216, 219; pan-regional branding 352; remittances from migrants 251; retailing 428; telemarketing 463
lead markets 248, 329–30
lead time 425
Leadership Against HIV/AIDS, Tuberculosis and Malaria Act (US) 367
Lebanon 483
Leclerc 252
legal environments 108–9
legal firms 343
Lego 516
leisure time 72, 89–90
Lenevo 180, 297, 349, 508
Lenovo 141, 461
Leo Burnett Worldwide 476
Let's Bonus SL 297
letters of credit 386
Levi Strauss 393
Lexus 144
LG 385
Liberia 214
licensing 35, 284–6, **299**, 300; and new product development 331
life insurance 298
lingerie advertising 481
linkage screen 153

LivingSocial 297
Lloyds Banking group 264
local agents 412
local firms 169; competition with MNCs (multinational corporations) 171–2; strategies for 172–3
local manufacturing 288–90
local media 485, **486**, **487–8**
local partnerships 120
local production costs 378–9
local wholesalers 412
locked-up channels 422–3
Lockheed Martin 190–1
logistics 379, 414, *414*, 417, 424; fixed-facilities location management 426; inventory control 425; materials handling/warehousing 426; order processing 425–6; traffic or transportation management 425
Logitech 246
London Olympics 461
Longman, Philip 270
loose cultures 112
Lopez, Jennifer 481
Los Angeles Olympics 462
Louis Vuitton 358, 360
Lowenstein Corporation 316
loyalty programmes 459–60
Lubineau, Valerie 185
Lufthansa 332
LVMH 396

Ma Li 497–500
macroindicators, of market size and growth 254–5, **255**, 255–6, **256**
mad-cow disease 465
magic moments 413
Malaysia 289, 356; and advertising 480, 496; color preferences 316; counterfeiting and piracy 364; halal food 63; life insurance 298; magic moments 413; marketing research 210; palm oil production 337; sales promotions 460; smuggling 434, 439; textile industry 49
Mali 261
managed currencies 30–1
managerial competence, of global marketing managers 10, **11**
Manpower 286
manufacturing: contract 288, 354; local 288–90
marginal pricing 376–7
market conditions, and advertising 480
market growth rates 244, **244**
market liberalization 176, 250, 252
market participation 242; country selection 254–62, **255**, **256**, **257**, **258**, **260**; emerging markets case study 268–70; evaluating national markets 246–8, **247**; exit strategies 263–5; geographic market choice 248–54, **249**, **253**; global baby bust case study 270, **271**, 272–3; in-country expansion 262; internationalization 243–6, **244**; limits to expansion 262–3; re-entry 265; SIFL case study 267–8
market segmentation 141; demographic segmentation 142, **143**, 144–5; global

brands 351–2; global segments 146–7; just-like-us segmentation 147–8; psychographic segmentation 145–6; regional segmentation 141–2, **142**; and social marketing 361
market similarity 259 *see also* psychic distance
market studies 201
market-based pricing 388, 389
marketing: careers in 527–8; cultural influences on *58*, 58–9
marketing information system (MIS) 220–1
marketing organization 506; Coca-Cola case study 530–1; and control 523–5; factors affecting 507–11; headquarters/subsidiary conflict 525–6, **526**; Indian IT case study 531–4; and organizational structure 511–22, *513*, *514*, *515*, *516*, *518*, *520*, *521*
marketing research 200; AGT, Inc. case study 226–35; challenges in planning 203; competition research 216–18, **218**; global information systems 220–1; outsourcing of 219, **219–20**; primary data 208–16; research process 203–4; scope of 200–2, **203**; secondary data 203, 204–8; Selector case study 224–6, **225**; Turkish clothing industry case study 222–3
marketing research firms 219, **219–20**, 343
marketing subsidiaries 281–2, **299**
markets 136–7; diaspora markets 161–2; evaluating national markets 246–8, **247**; geographic market choices 248–54, **249**, *253*; government markets 151–5, **155–6**, 157–60, **159**; importance of 3–4; market segmentation 141–2, **142**, **143**, 144–8; relative market size 207 *see also* business markets (B2B); consumer markets
Marriott 123, 244, 455, 461
Mars Inc 2, 374, 427, 465, 483, 496
Mary Kay 136, 432
masculinity-femininity (Hofstede measures of culture) **74–5**, 77
Maserati 144
Maslow, Abraham 139
Massachusetts 108
master franchisees 286–7
Matador AS 288
material culture 72–3, 317
materials handling 426
matrix organizational structures 520–2, *521*
Matsushita 525
Mattel 217
Mauritius 50, 51
Max Factor 263
Maytag Corporation 297
Mazda 175
MBA programs 69–70, 448
McCormick & Company 245
McCurry 356
McDonald's 2, 59, 64, 86, 187, 188, 208, 245, 262, 265, 286, 329, 344, 347,

349, 356, 380, 384, 428, 460, 461, 465, 466, 485, 496, 510, 531
McDonnell Douglas 190
Mecca Cola 192
media strategy 484–5; global media 485; local media 485, **486**, **487–8**; media habits **487–8**, 487–9
Mercedes-Benz 289, 347, 381, 471, 492
Merck 217, 401, 424
MERCOSUR (Southern Common Market) **42**
mergers and acquisitions 175, 296–8, **299**
MetLife Inc. 298
metric standard 317
Metro 2
Mexico 4, **7**, 136, 254, 355; and advertising 481, 496; antitrust laws 177; attitudes toward time 71; cement market 459; cola market 193; counterfeiting and piracy 360; country-of-origin perceptions 185; diaspora markets 148; distribution 424; dumping 385; expediting payments 158; exports 100; franchising 286; government contracts 153; IMF assistance for 36; international trade statistics 19, **19**; local firms 173; marketing research 212, 214, 216; operating restrictions 104; pet food market 2; political risk 116, 118, **119**; population trends **271**, 272; price controls 385; production in the US 289, 293, **293**; quality expectations 318; remittances from migrants 251; retailing 429–30; smuggling 434; soft drinks market 100, 127, 177; textile industry 49; vacation time 72 see also MINT (Mexico, Indonesia, Nigeria, Turkey); NAFTA (North American Free Trade Association)
MFA (Multifibre Arrangement) 49, 50
MFN (most favored nation) status 40, 41
Michelin 352
microindicators of market size and growth 255, 256–7, **257**
Microsoft 174, 216, 314, 330, 333, 342, 360, 426; software piracy case study 363–5
middle classes 144, 250, 251, 380
Middle East **7**; and advertising 481, 483, 489; arms sales case study 190–1; attitudes toward time 71; cola market 192–3; franchising 287; informal economy 144; language 81; marketing research 210–11; retailing 428–9; service personnel 346
Middle East and North Africa (MENA) Franchise Association 287
migrants: and diaspora marketing 161–2; and remittances 250–1
Milan Fair, Italy 456
Millward Brown 526
MINT (Mexico, Indonesia, Nigeria, Turkey) 254 see also Indonesia; Mexico; Nigeria; Turkey
MIS (marketing information system) 220–1
mission statements 507

missionary sales force 451
Mitsubishi Elevator Company 357
Mitsubishi Motors 263
MNCs (multinational corporations): competition with local firms 171–2, **178**; global competition between 169–71, **178**; and international marketing 6, 8; location of headquarters 35; sales promotions within 460–1
Mobil 350
modified uniform pricing policy 396
modularity 327
Molecular Simulations (MSI) 294
Mondelez 242, 353, **353**, 427, 496, 497
monetary unions **42**, 43–4
money market 391
Monster 496
Mont Royal General Trading LLC 287
Morinaga 290
Morocco 286
most favored nation (MFN) status 40, 41
Motion Picture Association 359, 360
motivation: of channel participants 420–1; political 97–8
motor vehicles, assembly operations 288–9
Motorola 115–16, 217, 333, 509–10
Mozambique 380
Mrs. Baird's Bakeries 297
MTV 2, 485
Mubadal Development Company 190
Multifibre Arrangement (MFA) 49, 50
multinational corporations see MNCs (multinational corporations)
music, and piracy 357
must-win markets 247–8
mutually advantageous trading ratios 23, **23**
My Dollarstore Inc. 387
Myanmar 108, 298
MyS Consultores 206

NabiscoWorld.com 497
NAFTA (North American Free Trade Association) 4, 8, **42**, 42–3, 136, 301, 430, 515–16 see also Canada; Mexico; United States
Namibia 366
Nasser, Jacques 519
National Beverage Company (NBC) 192
national differences, adaptations to 6, **7**
national exhaustion principle 393
National Highway Traffic Safety Administration (NHTSA) 320
national prosperity 98, **98**, 99–100
national security 97, **98**, 99, 152
national sovereignty 98–9
natural disasters, and supply chains 412–13, 425
Naturo Cosmeticos 432
NBC (National Beverage Company) 192
NEC 175
negative HNO (human nature orientation) 112
Nepal 161–2
Nestlé 2, 114, 189, 296, 316, 317, 374, 380, 384, 466, 496
Netherlands **60**, 61–2, 214, 378

Nevada Furniture 391
New Balance 358
new product development see product development
New York City 508
New York Yankees 106
New Zealand 262, 389
Newboy Studios 89
Next Linx 284
NGOs (non-governmental organizations): and diasporas 162; and social marketing 360–1, 362
NHTSA (National Highway Traffic Safety Administration) 320
Nicaragua 121, 384
niches 173
Nigeria 251, 467; color preferences 73; marketing research 205, 215; national prestige 100; online retailing 433 see also MINT (Mexico, Indonesia, Nigeria, Turkey)
Nike 336, 434, 462
Nikkei Advertising Research Institute 482
Nintendo 393
Nissan Motors 31
Nokia 532
Nokian Tyres 288
Nomenclature of Territorial Units for Statistics (NUTS) 225
non-verbal communication 83
noncash pricing 396–8
nondiscrimination (GATT principle) 40
nonmetric standard 317
nonprobablistic sampling 212–13
nontariff trade barriers 39–40
Nordica 414–15
Norinco 104
North Africa 144
North Korea 101, 106, 359
nudity, and advertising 481
NUTS (Nomenclature of Territorial Units for Statistics) 225

O.R.T. Technologies 33
O'Neill, Jim 254
Obasabjo, Olesegun 100
observation 208–9
OECD 389
official transactions account (balance of payments) 26, **26**
offset transactions 397
Ogilvy & Mather Worldwide 492
Ohmae, Kenichi 249
oil industry 178, 179
Olay 489
Olive 168
Olivetti 217
Olympic Games 170, 461, 462, 465, 481
Omnicom Group 476
One Million Voices Against FARC 361
online retailing see e-commerce
Onmnilife 453
operating restrictions **98**, 103–4
OPIC (Overseas Private Investment Corporation) **121**, 121–2
opportunistic expansion 243
Opportunity 294
Oracle 123, 396
orange juice production 290

orchestras 3
order processing 425–6
orderly marketing arrangements 39
organizational structures 511; born-global firms 522; companies without international specialists 512; global mandates 522; international divisions 513–14, *514*; international specialists/export departments 512, *513*; and regulatory environments 511; worldwide/global organizations 514–22, *515, 516, 518, 520, 521*
organized crime 359, 435
Oriental Brewery 265
Ottoman Empire 79
outsourcing 24–5, **25**, 80, 85, 188; of marketing research 219, **219–20**; and new product development 331
Overseas Private Investment Corporation (OPIC) **121**, 121–2
Overseas Security Advisory Council 122
ownership conditions **98**, 103, 282
ownership strategies *279*, 290–6, **293**

P&G (Proctor & Gamble) 122, 137, 157, 168, 169, 189, 209, 219, 245, 263, 294, 315, 318, 322, 330, 342, 348, 352, 353, 357, 358, 374, 381, 428, 451, 461, 479, 480, 508, 519; emerging markets case study 268–70
packaging 321–2
Pakistan 102; arms purchases 191; counterfeiting and piracy 357, 359, 363–4; remittances from migrants 251; sales negotiations 450; war on terror 49
palm oil 337
pan-regional branding 352
pan-regional marketing 8
Panasonic 525
Pantaloon 446
Paraguay 357
parallel firms 292
parallel imports 391–5
parallel translation 211
Paris Air Show 444, 456
Paris Convention, 1883 355
partial compensation 397
partnerships, local 120
Patak's 446
Payless 287, 325
PayPal 386
PCI (per capita income) 138, **138**
Peace Corps 528
pegged currencies 30–1
Pepsi 116, 127, 177, 296, 446, 461, 462, 465, 467, 480, 496, 531; cola wars case study 192–4
PepsiCo 102, 123, 170, 380
per capita income (PCI) 138, **138**
performance expectations 318
performance managers 431–2
performance standards 523, 524
personal selling 447; international 447–50; local 450–4
Peru 193, 463
Perugina chocolate 394
Pessoa, Rivaldo 469–70
Pet Vet Russia Expo 456

Pfizer 155, 217, 423, 467
pharmaceuticals 391, 424; and counterfeiting 357, 359, 360; parallel imports 391, 393, 395; piggybacking 423; price controls 384; price-fixing 374; pricing case study 401–3
Pharmacopeia 294
Philip Morris 179, 297, 355, 438, 439, 465–6, 477
Philippines 188–9, 254, 289; counterfeiting and piracy 357; diaspora markets 161; price controls 384; remittances from migrants 251; sales promotions 461; vacation time 72; World Bank assistance for 37
Philips 86, 318
Piaggio USA 464
piggybacking 423
Pinheiro, Renata 469
Pioneer 120
piracy 357, 359, 360, 363–5
Pizza Hut 186
Poland 184, *252*, **253**, 254, 378, 435
Polish Airlines 459–60
political climate 96, 153; Coca-Cola case study 126–7; Cuba case study 125–6; and exit strategies 264–5; home country 105–8; host country 97–105, **98**; legal environments 108–9; as macroindicator of market size and growth 256, **256**; and political risk 116–22, **119**, **121**; regulatory environments 110–16, *115*; and terrorism 122–3
political mapping 115
political risk 116–17; and exchange rate movements 30; political risk assessment (PRA) 117–19, **119**; risk reduction strategies 119–22, **121**
POLs (popular opinion leaders) 361
polycentric orientation 508
poor, the, as target markets 144–5
popular opinion leaders (POLs) 361
Porsche 394–5
Porter, Michael 23–4
Portugal 184, **271**, 272
positive HNO (human nature orientation) 112
power distance (Hofstede measures of culture) 73, **74–5**, 76, 112
Powerade 531
Prahalad, C.K. 144–5
pressure groups 102, 107–8
Prestes, Joao 469
prestige 98, **98**, 100
prestige products, and export pricing 34
price controls 384–5
price-fixing 374 *see also* cartels
PriceWaterhouseCooper 218, 336
pricing 317–18, 374–5; coffee pricing in China case study 399–401; and counterfeiting and piracy 360, 363, 364; environmental factors 383–6; Gamali Air case study 403–5; managerial issues **386**, 386–98; market factors 379–83; pharmaceutical pricing case studies 401–3; and pressure groups 107;

profit and cost factors 375–9, **376**; setting global prices 395–6
primary data 203, 208; big data 214–15; focus groups 209–10; government regulation 210, 215–16; observation 208–9; social media 214–15; surveys 211–14
Princess Polly 200
Pringles 315, 479
privacy 215–16, 463
private branding 354
privatization 179
probability samples 212
problem definition, in marketing research 203–4
procedural screen 153
product adaptation 394–5; benefits of 313, **313**, 314–15; and climate 315; cost and price factors 317–18; and cultural preferences 316; and global standards 319–21; and infrastructure 315; performance and quality factors 318; and pricing 380–1; product size and dimensions 317; and use conditions 315–16
product design 313–21
product development 327–8; alliances for 331–2; and research and development 328–32
product introduction 332–4
product liability law 110–11
product life-cycles *326*, 326–7, 480
product lines 325; additions 325–6; deletions 325
product organizational structures 519–20, *520*
product placement 464
product quality, and licensing 285
product simplification 318
product size 317, 380
product standardization **313**, 313–14, 327, 328
product strategies 312; ethical products case study 335–7; Intuition case study 338; new product introductions 332–4; packaging and labeling 321–3; and pressure groups 107; and product design 313–21; product development 327–8; product line management 325–7; research and development 328–32; warranty and service policies 323–4
products: new product development 209; related products 207
profit, and pricing 375–9, **376**
promotion 444–7; account management 454–5; buzz marketing 464–5; corporate social responsibility 466–7; direct mail 463; flying to Armenia case study 470–2; personal selling 447–54; and pressure groups 107; product placement 464; public relations 465–6; sales promotion 249–461; selling to business and government 456–8; South American sale case study 468–70; sports promotion and sponsorship 461–2; telemarketing 462–3
Pronto Cafes 325

prosperity, national 98, **98**, 99–100
protectionism 37–41, 181 *see also* free trade
proxies 207, 257
PSA Peugeot-Citroën 412
psychic distance 259–62, **260**
psychographic segmentation 145–6
public relations 465–6
Publicis Groupe 478
Publicus Group 496
Puerto Rica 273
pull strategies 445
purchasing behavior 448 *see also* consumer behavior
purchasing-power parity 138, **138**, 206, 379
push strategies 445–6

Qibla Cola 192
quality expectations 318; and brands 351
Quality Films 360
quality standards 319–20
Quelch, John 351
quota sampling 213
quotas 38, 40, 41, 50, 176, 182

R.J. Reynolds 117, 120, 438
Rakuten Inc. 85–6
Ralph Lauren Corporation 158
Ramadan 64, 211, 260
Ramamurti, Ravi 115
Ray Ban **7**
RCA 297
re-entry strategies 265
reciprocity (GATT principle) 40
RecycleBank 84
Red Bull 496
regional exhaustion principle 393
regional management centers *516, 516–17, 518*
regional segmentation 141–2, **142**
regulatory environments 110–16, *115*; and advertising 480–1, 495–6; attitudes toward rules 112; legal evolution 110–11; and logistics 425; and organizational structures 511; regulatory change 113–16, *115*; and retailing 413
reinventors 432
Reliance 142
Reliance MediaWorks 148
Reliance Retail Limited 287
religion 59, **60–1**, 80, 316; Eastern **60**, 64–5; Islam 59, **60**, **61**, 62, **63**, 63–4; Western 59, **60–1**, 61–2
remittances, from migrants 250–1
Renner, Gretchen 222–3
replicators 431
research and development 326, 328–32
research objectives 203–4
retailing 427; international 428–32, **429–30**; large-scale 427–8; online retailing 433; retailers, as channel members 412–13; slotting allowances 459; smaller-scale 428
Revenue Act 1962 (US) 389
reverse engineering 381
Ricardo, David 21
Ricoh 354

risk: political risk assessment (PRA) 117–19, **119**; risk reduction strategies 119–22, **121**
risk aversion 77
Roche 285, 424
Rolex 352, 358
Romania 351, 481, 482
royalties 284, 285
rural populations 141–2, **142**
Russia 387; and advertising 480, 495–6; as an emerging market 252, 253, **253**; arms exports 153, 191; branding 354; cola market 170; consumer ethnocentricity 185; counterfeiting and piracy 357, 360; country-of-origin perceptions 184; cross-cultural negotiations 150; direct marketing 432; elite markets 144; emerging markets case study 269; exchange rates 32, 383–4, 391; G8 membership 37; global segmentation categories 351; legal environment 109; marketing research 205; parallel imports 391; political risk 118, **119**; population trends **271**, 273; re-entry strategies 265; smuggling 439; SOEs (state-owned enterprises) 179; trade restrictions 39, 41; trademark preemption 355, 356 *see also* BRIC (Brazil, Russia, India, China); Soviet Union
Russian Federation, international trade statistics **19**

SA (Social Accountability) 336
Saab 320
SABMiller PLC 103, 172–3, 182, 251, 297, 380
Sacred Seat Collection 65
SAIC 291
Sainsbury 264–5
sales negotiations, international 450
sales promotion 459–61
sampling, marketing research 212–13
Samsung 333, 347, 354, 385, 461, 462, 471
sanctions 106
Sara Lee 481
SAS 332
Saudi Arabia 78, 322; and advertising 489; business etiquette 449; collectivism 76; consumer animosity 187; and consumer behavior 140; country-of-origin perceptions 184; expropriation 105; marketing research 210, 212; ownership restrictions 282; product liability law 111, 116; religion 59, **60**
scheduling, of advertising 490–1
screening process, government contracts 152–4
Scripto 169–70
Sears 171
secondary data 203, 204; analysis by inference 207–8; export opportunities 279, **280**; problems with 205–6; sources of 204
security industry 117
Seiko Epson 416

Seiyu 437
Selector Inc. case study 224–6, **225**
self-preservation 97, **98**, 98–9
Senegal 251, 261
Seoul Olympics 461
service industries 3, 342–7
service personnel 346
service policies 324
shampoo market, China 168
Shanghai Automotive Industry Corporation 120, 292
ShanghaiCosmopolitan.com case study 497–500
Shangri-La Hotel 352
sharenet 524–5
Sharp 347
Shinto-ism 59, 64, 65
Siar Research International 208
Siemens 106, 155, 183, 454, 524–5
SIFL (South Indian Foods Ltd.) 267–8
Simpsons, The 314
sin taxes 378
Singapore: counterfeiting and piracy 364; government subsidies/incentives 247; halal food 63–4; higher education 345, 346; international education 122–3; marketing research 216; test marketing in 333
Singapore Airlines 189
situational animosity 186–7
Slim, Carlos 177
slotting allowances 459
SMEs (small and medium-sized enterprises) 282
Smith, Adam 21
Smithfield 114
smuggling 434–5; cigarette smuggling case study 438–40
Snickers 465
snowball sampling 213
Snowden, Edward J. 180
soccer sponsorship 461, 462
Sochi Olympics 461
Social Accountability (SA) 336
social marketing 360–2
social media 361, 489; and consumer animosity 186; and marketing research 200, 214–15; ShanghaiCosmopolitan.com case study 497–500
social responsibility: and brands 351; ethical products case study 335–7
socialist law 109
SOEs (state-owned enterprises) 292; China 101, 178, 179–80, 183; and competition **178**, 178–80; Vietnam 182
soft sell advertising 482
software piracy 363–5
Sony 295, 347, 350, 354, 378, 435
South Africa 251, 253, 262, 378, 2 402; and advertising 496; dumping 385; and global segmentation categories 351, 352; international trade statistics **19**; language 81; local firms 172–3; marketing research 213; ownership conditions 103; parallel imports 391, 395; political risk 118, **119**; trade embargoes 107; US investment in

107 *see also* CIVETS (Colombia, Indonesia, Vietnam, Egypt, Turkey, South Africa)
South Indian Foods Ltd. (SIFL) 267–8
South Korea 78, 86, 101, 177, 180, 253, 254, 355; and advertising 487, 489; car imports 392; collectivism 76; color preferences 72, 73; competitive advantage 24; counterfeiting and piracy 359; country-of-origin perceptions 184, 185; dumping 385; and exchange rates 31; family life 67; and globalization 44–5; government subsidies/incentives 247; IMF assistance for 36; marketing research 213; online retailing 433; parallel imports 392–3; political risk 121; re-entry strategies 265; retailing 438; test marketing in 333; transfer pricing 389; and working hours 90; World Bank assistance for 37
Southeast Asia **7**, 379–80
Southern Common Market (MERCOSUR) **42**
sovereignty, national 98–9
Soviet Union 101, 125, 482 *see also* Russia
Spain **271**, 272, 459
spam 463
spare parts 324
sponsorships 461–2
sports promotions 461–2
spot prices 390
sprinkler strategy of product introduction 334
Sprint 296
Sri Lanka 179, 413
stable animosity 186
standalone attractive markets 246–7, **247**, 252
standardization 431; of advertising 477, 478–83, 493; of products **313**, 313–14, 327, 328; of services 344
standards: company 523, 524; global 318–21
Starbucks 2, 6, 65, 101, 102, 122, 136, 138, 145, 170, 181, 244, 246, 250, 261, 265, 286, 294, 296, 325, 348, 355, 356, 431, 489, 507; China coffee pricing case study 399–401
state-owned enterprises *see* SOEs (state-owned enterprises)
Stella Artois 141
strategic alliances 295–6
strategic competence, of global marketing managers 10, **11**
strategic decisions 201
strategic pricing 395
Strauss group 290
subsidiaries 290–1, **299**, 300; conflict with headquarters 525–6, **526**; and research and development 329–31; transfer prices 387–9
subsidiary earnings, and exchange rates 35–6
subsidies **98**, 102–3, 182; cross-country subsidization 169–70
Subway 186
Sudan 106
Sumatra Tobacco 355

Sumitomo Bank 175
Super 8 Worldwide 215
supply and demand, and exchange rate movements 29
supply chain: management of 426–7; and natural disasters 412–13, 425
surveys 211–14
Suzuki 102, 142, 151, 263; case study 303–5
Suzuki, Osamu 303, 304
sweatshops 335–7
Sweden 23, 73, 209, 250, 378, 496
Swiss Air 471
Swisscom 425
Switzerland: attitudes toward rules 112; bankruptcy 111; business etiquette 449; customer expectations of service 344–5; and exchange rates 35; international trade statistics 19, **19**
Syrian Air 471

Tabak 179
Taco Bell 245, 265, 481
tactical decisions 201, **202**
Tag Heuer 396
TAI (Textile Association of Istanbul) 222
Taiwan 41, 355; business etiquette 449; counterfeiting and piracy 359, 364; and exchange rates 31; labor practices 336; magic moments 413; sales promotions 460
Tan, Tony 188, 189
Tanzania 467
Tapulous International 207
target markets, and advertising 479
tariffs 38, 40, 41, 49, 102, 182; and pricing 377–8; and smuggling 434; and transfer pricing 388
Tata business group 181, 182
Tata Coffee 181
Tata Consultancy Services 3, 24, 246, 532, 533
Tata Teleservices 142
Tatlises, Ibrahim 172
taxes 389; and pricing 378
Taylor, Earl 351
TCL Corporation 297
Tecate 148
Tecnica 415
Teijin 294
Telecom Italia 294
Telefonica 27
telemarketing 462–3
Televisa 173
Tellis, Gerard 334
tenders 457
terrorism 122–3, 359
Tesco PLC 262, 263, 432
test marketing 333
Tetley Tea 182
Textile Association of Istanbul (TAI) 222
textile industry: international trade case study 49–52; labor practices 335–7; Pakistan 102
TGI Friday's 186
Thailand 86, 264, 289, 412; and AIDS 366–7; cola market 193; and exchange rates 31; IMF assistance for 36; magic moments 413; marketing

research 209, 210; pharmaceutical prices 402; population trends **271**, 272; and pricing 381; sales promotions 460; World Bank assistance for 37
Thamel.com 161–2
Thomas Cook Financial Services 533
Thomson 297
Tide 322, 330
TIE (IndUS Entrepreneurs) 534
Tiendas Exito 427–8
tight cultures 112
time zones 511
time, cultural attitudes toward 71–2
timing, of advertising 490–1
Titan corporation 157
tobacco advertising 481, 496
top-down approaches to branding 350
Top-Toy 496
Toray Industries 248
Toshiba 31, 295
tourism, and terrorism 122
Toyota 31, 100, 106, 116, 186, 189, 250, 347, 412, 465
Toys R Us 496
trade embargoes 106, 125–6
trade fairs 217, 456–7
trade restrictions 37–41
Trademark Counterfeiting Act, 1984 (US) 359
trademarks 354; counterfeiting and piracy 357–60; and parallel imports 392–4; trademark preemption 355–6
traffic deaths 320
traffic management 425
transaction risk 389–90
transfer prices 387–9
transit time 425
transitional economies, market attractiveness of **249**, 252
translation 84–5; and market research surveys 211–12; and product development 328; sales brochures 449
transparency (GATT principle) 40
transportation costs 377
transportation management 425
Travel Act (US) 158
Travelers Group 252
Triandis, Harry 112
TRW 324
Tulumba 161
Tupperware 325
Turkey 259–60, 262, 292; and advertising 485; and bargaining 381; business groups 181; country-of-origin perceptions 183, 185; and cultural change 79; diaspora markets 161; exchange rates 35, 391; and global segmentation categories 352; IMF assistance for 36; language 81; local firms 172, 173; marketing research 222–3; religion 62; remittances from migrants 251; textile industry 49, 51, 222–3 *see also* CIVETS (Colombia, Indonesia, Vietnam, Egypt, Turkey, South Africa); MINT (Mexico, Indonesia, Nigeria, Turkey)
Turkmenistan 210

TV3 496
Tyco International 508

UAE (United Arab Emirates) 64, 103, 177, 190–1, 247, 483
Uganda 251
Ukraine 38, 351, 357
UNAIDS 423
uncertainty avoidance (Hofstede measures of culture) **74–5**, 77–8
UNICEF 466
uniform pricing policy 396
unilateral restrictions 107
Unilever 157, 168, 169, 173, 317–18, 337, 350, 358, 380, 381, 384, 496, 515, 521, 525; emerging markets case study 269–70
United Kingdom 78–9, 262; and advertising 483, 496; bankruptcy 111; cola market 192–3; consumer animosity 186; couponing 459; drug overdoses 322; G7/G8 membership 37; and global segmentation categories 351; international trade statistics **19**; product placement 464; re-entry strategies 265; trade fairs 456
United Nations 97, 106, 107; Convention against Corruption 158
United States 78–9, 262; and advertising 482, 485, 495, 496; antitrust laws 174, 374, 382; arms sales 191; attitudes toward rules 112; attitudes toward time 71; bankruptcy 111; boycotts 104; buyer-seller relationships 452; cartels 374, 382–3; Census Bureau statistics 224–5, **225**; color preferences 73; consumer animosity 186; consumer behavior 139; counterfeiting and piracy 359; country-of-origin perceptions 184; couponing 459; credit cards 318–19; cross-cultural negotiations 150; customer expectations of service 344; distribution 421; dumping 385; education 69–71; exiting from market 263; family life 65, 67; franchising 286; G7/G8 membership 37; and global segmentation categories 351, 352; government regulation of sales promotion 460; as a high-trust society 69; income distribution 44; individualism 76; international trade statistics 19, **19**, 20; investment in South Africa 107; Iraq War 115; language 81; marketing research 209, 215, 216; as a masculine society 77; Mexican firms' production in 289, 293, **293**; as a must-win market 247; outsourcing 24–5, **25**; parallel imports 391, 393–4; population trends **271**, 272, 273; pork industry 114; price-fixing 374; privacy laws 215; religion 59, **61**, 61–2, 80; road

safety standards 320–1; sales forces 452, 453–4; soccer sponsorship 461; tariffs 38, 44; taxes 389; and terrorism 122, 123; textile industry 49, 102; trade embargoes 106; trade fairs 456; and trademark protection 356; vacation time 72; and VERs (voluntary export restrictions) 39; word-of-mouth advertising 465; and working hours 72, 89 *see also* NAFTA (North American Free Trade Association)
universities 247, 345–6
University of Chicago 247
University of Singapore 345
Univision 173
Uno Chicago Grill 287
Uppal, Rajiv 284
UPS 141, 180
urban populations 141–2, **142**
US Export Portal 279, **280**
use conditions 315–16
Usunier, Jean-Claude 112
Uzbekistan 38, 210

vacation time 72
Valentine's Day 62
variable costs 375–7, **376**
Varig Airlines 352
VAT (value-added tax) 378
Vatican, the 278
Venezuela 394; Chavez presidency 96; cola market 193; cultural identity 101; and exchange rates 27–8, 31; expropriation 96, 250; product liability law 427–8; retailing 427–8; SOEs (state-owned enterprises) 179
Vergera, Jorge 453
Vermeulen, Freek 263
VERs (voluntary export restrictions) 39
Vespa scooters 464
Victoria Secret 259
Videomax 360
VideosDotCom 533
Vietnam 22–4, **23**, 289, 292; and advertising 492; cola market 193; counterfeiting and piracy 357; life insurance 298; marketing research 209–10, 212; political risk 118, **119**; smuggling 439; SOEs (state-owned enterprises) 182; trade embargoes 106; urban and rural populations 141, **142** *see also* CIVETS (Colombia, Indonesia, Vietnam, Egypt, Turkey, South Africa)
Visa 461
visas 104
visual advertising 484
Vitamin C 382–3
Vodaphone 251
Volkswagen 246, 332, 454; case study 303–5
voluntary export restrictions (VERs) 39

Wahaha 294
waiting experience 345, 346
Wal-Mart 3, 50, 56, 100, 106, 136, 145, 158, 172, 186, 208, 221, 262, 323, 336, 337, 410, 416, 428, 429–30, 431, 437, 438, 463, 523, 527
Walsh, Katrina 224–6
Wanchai Ferry 331
war on terror 49
warehousing 426
Warner-Lambert 423
warranties 323–4
waterfall strategy of product introduction 334
Welsh language 484
Westinghouse 435
Whirlpool 250, 297, 385, 435
WHO 368
wholesalers, local 412
wholly owned subsidiaries 290–1, **299**, 300
Wipro Ltd. 532, 533
Wonderbra 481
Wool Products Labeling Act 323
word-of-mouth promotion 446, 464–5
work permits 104
working hours 72, 89–90
World Bank (International Bank for Reconstruction and Development) 36–7, 42, 155
World Cup 461, 462
World Customs Organization 357
World Trade Organization *see* WTO (World Trade Organization)
World Wildlife Fund (WWF) 171
Worldtomarket.com 433
worldwide organizations, organizational structures 514–22, *515, 516, 518, 520, 521*
WTO (World Trade Organization) 20, 103, 109, 111, 151, 176, 182, 262, 355, 377, 385, 417; Agreement on Textiles and Clothing 49; and trade restrictions 39, 40, 41, 44, 99
WWF (World Wildlife Fund) 171
Wyeth-Ayerst Laboratories 466

Xerox 104, 245

Yadu Group 364
Yahoo 4, 293, 314, 331, 507
Yale 345
Yamaha 360
Yip, George 169–70, 246
Yohinoy D&C 286
Yoplait 186
Young & Rubicam 492

Zam Zam cola 192
Zara 200, 337, 377, 431
Zuji 352